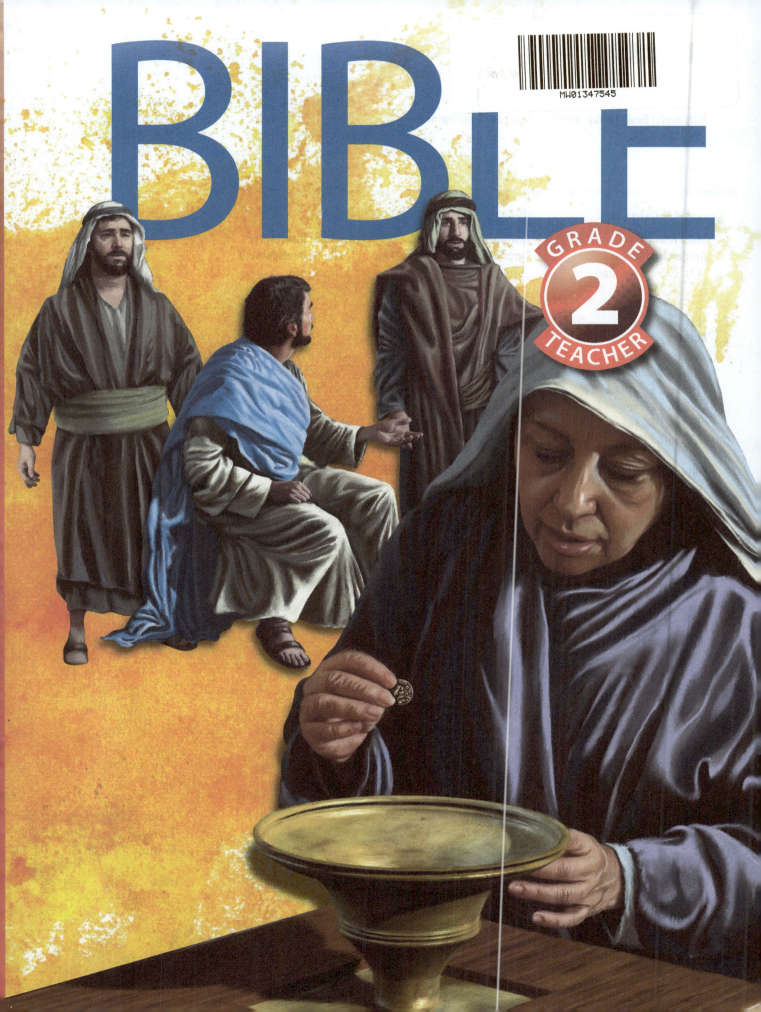

Development Team

Third Edition

Vice President for Purposeful Design Publications
Steven Babbitt

Director for Textbook Development
Lisa Wood

Editorial Team
Merrilee Berndt
Sheryl Harrigan
Jessica Reid
Ian Work

Design Team
Jeff Barnes
Patrick Flowers

Second Edition

Vice President for Academic Affairs
Dr. Derek Keenan

Assistant Vice President, Purposeful Design Publications
Steven Babbitt

Assistant Director for Textbook Development
Don Hulin

Authors

Gary Brohmer	Macki Jones	Denise Morris	Julia Taves
Cheryl Chiapperino	JoAnn Keenan	Vance Nichols	Lorraine Wadman
Rockie Fordham	Tammy Kennington	Jean Paulsen	Melissa Hardy Wetzel
Rachel Geyer	Jennifer Kleiner	Maria Phillips	Lisa Wood
Judy Gillispie	Anna Long	Rebecca Stone	
Connie Gunther	Susan Martins Miller	Nancy Sutton	

Editorial Team

Gary Brohmer	Ellen Johnson	Jennifer Lonas	Cindi Shipman
Barbara Carpenter	Macki Jones	Susan Martins Miller	Nancy Sutton
Cheryl Chiapperino	JoAnn Keenan	Maria Phillips	Lorraine Wadman
John Conaway	Jennifer Kleiner	Christina Reidl	Lisa Wood

Early Education Consultants
Dr. Deborah Carter
Sara Jo Dillard
Leanne Leak
D'Arcy Maher

Design Team
Claire Dunham
Susanna Garmany
Ana Murray

First Edition

President, ACSI
Dr. Paul A. Kienel

ACSI Director of Curriculum/Managing Editor
Dr. Sharon R. Berry

Editors
Mary Jo Kynerd
Renee Pate
Dr. Bette Talley

Authors

Barbara Alexander	Jan Gillette	Marilyn Phillips	Karen Stimer
Mary Lou Carney	Kersten Hamilton	Elizabeth Renicks	Darlene Troxel
Linda Causey	Laure Herlinger	Cheri Schoenrock	Connie Williams

Production Staff
Sherry Berry
Donna Harden
Alice Parker
Linda Terry

Designers
Chuck Haas
Bill Thielker

Production Artists
Craig Clear
Tim Jaycox
Pat Reinheimer

Artist
Barbara Crowe

BIBLE

Teacher Edition • Grade 2
Third Edition

Colorado Springs, Colorado

© 1995, 2011, 2020 by Purposeful Design Publications
All rights reserved. First edition 1995.
Second edition 2011
Third edition 2020

No portion of this book may be reproduced, stored in a retrieval system, or transmitted, in any form or by any means—mechanical, photocopying, recording, or otherwise—without prior written permission of Purposeful Design Publications.

Purposeful Design Publications is the publishing division of the Association of Christian Schools International (ACSI) and is committed to the ministry of Christian school education, to enable Christian educators and schools worldwide to effectively prepare students for life. As the publisher of textbooks, trade books, and other educational resources within ACSI, Purposeful Design Publications strives to produce biblically sound materials that reflect Christian scholarship and stewardship and that address the identified needs of Christian schools around the world.

References to books, computer software, and other ancillary resources in this series are not endorsements by ACSI. These materials were selected to provide teachers with additional resources appropriate to the concepts being taught and to promote student understanding and enjoyment.

Unless otherwise identified, all Scripture quotations are taken from the Holy Bible, New King James Version® (NKJV®), © 1982 by Thomas Nelson, Inc. Used by permission. All rights reserved.

Printed in the United States of America
26 25 24 23 22 21 20   1 2 3 4 5 6 7

Elementary Bible, Grade 2 – Teacher Edition
Purposeful Design Elementary Bible Series
ISBN 978-1-58331-630-6   Catalog #103022

Purposeful Design Publications
A Division of ACSI
731 Chapel Hills Drive • Colorado Springs, CO 80920
Customer Service: 800-367-0798 • www.purposefuldesign.com

Table of Contents

Foreword ix
Understanding Purposeful Design Bible xi
Preparing a Lesson xvi

Lesson 1 Abraham Listens
Lesson Preparation.................................1
Abraham Listens to God.............................2
Blessings 4
God Leads Abraham to Shechem 6
Remembering God's Provision.....................8
Review and Assessment............................10

Lesson 2 Abraham Prays
Lesson Preparation................................11
Abraham Prays for Lot............................12
How to Pray......................................14
Interceding for Others...........................16
God Responds to Prayer...........................18
Review and Assessment............................20

Lesson 3 Moses Is Humble
Lesson Preparation................................21
God Speaks to Moses..............................22
Moses Humbly Leads 24
God Sends 10 Plagues.............................26
God Delivers the Hebrews 28
Review and Assessment............................30

Lesson 4 Moses and Miriam Praise God
Lesson Preparation................................31
The Israelites Leave Egypt 32
The Israelites Cross the Red Sea.................34
Acts of Worship..................................36
Praise God.......................................38
Review and Assessment............................40

Lesson 5 Moses Is Diligent
Lesson Preparation................................41
Israelites Journey into the Desert 42
The Ten Commandments.............................44
The Bronze Serpent...............................46
Courage to Do What Is Right 48
Review and Assessment............................50

Lesson 6 Miriam and Aaron Learn Respect
Lesson Preparation................................51

Miriam and Aaron Challenge Moses 52
Respecting Authority 54
Disrespecting Authority 56
Consequences 58
Review and Assessment............................60

Lesson 7 Joshua Leads Israel
Lesson Preparation................................61
Godly Leaders Are Prepared 62
Godly Leaders Trust God's Promises 64
Godly Leaders Know God's Word 66
Godly Leaders Share God's Word................68
Review and Assessment............................70

Lesson 8 Joshua Obeys God
Lesson Preparation................................71
Joshua Obeys and Conquers Jericho.............72
God's Plan for His Children 74
Listening to and Obeying God 76
Nothing Is Impossible with God..................78
Review and Assessment............................80

Lesson 9 Joshua Follows God
Lesson Preparation................................81
Joshua Follows God Wholeheartedly...........82
Memorial to God 84
God's Faithfulness 86
Overcoming Temptation 88
Review and Assessment............................90

Lesson 10 Ruth Is Loyal
Lesson Preparation................................91
Ruth Is a Loyal Friend 92
Being a Loyal Friend 94
Finding Good Friends.............................96
Loyalty from God and to God 98
Review and Assessment............................100

Lesson 11 Ruth Serves with Love
Lesson Preparation................................101
Ruth and Naomi..................................102
Ruth Serves Naomi 104
Boaz Is a Kinsman-Redeemer 106
Boaz Loves Ruth.................................108
Review and Assessment............................110

Bible Grade 2

Table of Contents

Lesson 12 David Faces the Giant
Lesson Preparation 111
David Faces Goliath 112
God Uses the Small 114
Fear Versus Courage 116
Giant Problems 118
Review and Assessment 120

Lesson 13 Thanksgiving
Lesson Preparation 121
David Leads in Thanksgiving 122
David's Song of Thanksgiving 124
Giving Thanks to God 126
Giving Thanks for Others 128
Review and Assessment 130

Lesson 14 Elijah Trusts God
Lesson Preparation 131
Elijah Is Encouraged 132
Trusting God 134
God's Ways 136
Miracles Occur 138
Review and Assessment 140

Lesson 15 Elijah Is Bold
Lesson Preparation 141
Elijah Continues in Courage 142
Hearing God 144
Boldness 146
Disciples 148
Review and Assessment 150

Lesson 16 Nehemiah Leads
Lesson Preparation 151
Nehemiah Leads as God Directs 152
Cooperation 154
Resistance from Mockers 156
Nehemiah Perseveres 158
Review and Assessment 160

Lesson 17 Christmas
Lesson Preparation 161
Jesus' Birth Announced 162
Jesus' Birth 164
The Shepherds Worship 166
The Wise Men Worship 168
Review and Assessment 170

Lesson 18 Nehemiah Stands Firm
Lesson Preparation 171
Nehemiah Does Not Fear Opposition 172
Nehemiah Shows Integrity 174
Nehemiah Deals with Adversaries 176
Nehemiah Finishes Despite Pressure 178
Review and Assessment 180

Lesson 19 Esther Listens to Wise Advice
Lesson Preparation 181
Esther Listens and Obeys 182
Choosing Wise Advice 184
Wisdom's Rewards 186
Giving Wise Advice 188
Review and Assessment 190

Lesson 20 Esther Is Unselfish
Lesson Preparation 191
Esther Shows Unselfishness and Resolve 192
Mordecai Is Rewarded............................ 194
Honor God and Others First 196
Prepared by God 198
Review and Assessment 200

Lesson 21 Job Is Patient
Lesson Preparation 201
Patience Defined 202
Patience Shown 204
Patiently Control Your Words 206
Eagerly Waiting 208
Review and Assessment 210

Lesson 22 Daniel Is Faithful
Lesson Preparation 211
Daniel Shows Faithfulness 212
The King's Dream................................... 214
Faithfulness in Prayer 216
Pressure to Choose 218
Review and Assessment 220

Lesson 23 Daniel's Friends Are Faithful
Lesson Preparation 221
Faithfulness to God 222
Resolve to Obey God 224
Courage and Deliverance 226
Others Praise God 228
Review and Assessment 230

Table of Contents

Lesson 24 Daniel Is Confident
Lesson Preparation......................231
God Reveals the Answer 232
God Delivers Daniel......................234
Daniel Prays 236
God's Faithfulness to Daniel 238
Review and Assessment................240

Lesson 25 Mary and Joseph Obey God
Lesson Preparation......................241
God Sends an Angel......................242
God Knows Everything...................244
Prophecies About the Messiah 246
Humility and Submission...............248
Review and Assessment................250

Lesson 26 Jesus Is Merciful
Lesson Preparation......................251
Jesus Heals the Blind....................252
Jesus Heals the Sick......................254
God Shows You Mercy....................256
Showing Mercy to Others 258
Review and Assessment................260

Lesson 27 Jesus Is Compassionate
Lesson Preparation......................261
A Shepherd Shows Compassion 262
Jesus, the Good Shepherd..............264
A Gracious Father 266
God Shows Compassion 268
Review and Assessment................270

Lesson 28 Martha Grows in Faith
Lesson Preparation......................271
Martha's Faith Grows 272
Believing in Jesus.........................274
Telling Others About Jesus 276
Jesus Is All-Powerful 278
Review and Assessment................280

Lesson 29 Easter
Lesson Preparation......................281
Jesus' Triumphal Entry 282
Jesus' Last Supper........................284
Jesus' Arrest, Crucifixion, and Burial...........286
Jesus Is Risen..............................288
Review and Assessment................290

Lesson 30 Peter Acts Boldly
Lesson Preparation......................291
Peter's Fearful Reactions...............292
The Holy Spirit............................294
Amazing Deliverance 296
Power in Peter's Life 298
Review and Assessment................300

Lesson 31 Peter Accepts Others
Lesson Preparation......................301
Peter Accepts Cornelius 302
Accepting Others 304
The Body of Christ 306
Go and Tell.................................308
Review and Assessment................310

Lesson 32 Paul and Barnabas Encourage
Lesson Preparation......................311
Barnabas Encourages Saul.............312
A Journey of Exhortation 314
Encouragement Encounters 316
Encouragement to Missionaries 318
Review and Assessment................320

Lesson 33 Paul and Silas Witness
Lesson Preparation......................321
Paul and Silas Share Their Faith.................322
Reactions to Persecution...............324
Prayer as a Lifestyle 326
Ways to Praise God 328
Review and Assessment................330

Lesson 34 Review
Lesson Preparation......................331
Who God Is 332
Responses to God.........................334
Relationship to God 336
Relationship to Others 338
Review and Assessment................340

Glossary.....................................341

Song Titles on the Grade 2 URL

1. All Things Work Together
2. *Instrumental*
3. Armor of God
4. *Instrumental*
5. Away in a Manger / Silent Night
6. *Instrumental*
7. Books of the Bible
8. *Instrumental*
9. Create In Me
10. *Instrumental*
11. Easter Rise Up
12. *Instrumental*
13. First Christmas Day
14. *Instrumental*
15. For I Am Not Ashamed
16. *Instrumental*
17. Glory
18. *Instrumental*
19. I Am Not Ashamed
20. *Instrumental*
21. I Can Obey
22. *Instrumental*
23. It Is Good
24. *Instrumental*

25. Jesus Can
26. *Instrumental*
27. Little Is Much
28. *Instrumental*
29. Love with the Love of Jesus
30. *Instrumental*
31. Only God Can Do
32. *Instrumental*
33. Plagues
34. *Instrumental*
35. Praying
36. *Instrumental*
37. Promised Land
38. *Instrumental*
39. Ten Commandments
40. *Instrumental*
41. Walk Like Jesus
42. *Instrumental*
43. What Seems Impossible
44. *Instrumental*
45. You Are My God
46. *Instrumental*

Foreword

Welcome to the most effective, stimulating, and wonderfully engaging Bible series for Christian schools. The Bible should be taught with the utmost care, enthusiasm, and passion, as well as a deep sense of responsibility for its eternal impact on the life of every student. Scriptures remind us just how important this responsibility is:

> The fear of the Lord is the beginning of wisdom, and the knowledge of the Holy One is understanding. Proverbs 9:10

> How can a young man cleanse his way? By taking heed according to Your word. Psalm 119:9

> All Scripture is given by inspiration of God, and is profitable for doctrine, for reproof, for correction, for instruction in righteousness. 2 Timothy 3:16

Essential to the mission of Christian schools—which is preparing children and young people for living the Christian life—is guiding students to become grounded in and shaped by God's Word. In his book *Educating for Life*, Nicholas Wolterstorff notes, "A careful, loving, devotional study of Scripture is an indispensible component of the curriculum of the Christian school—for the reason that Scripture is the basis and nourishment of that Christian way of being in the world, which, as I have argued, is the ultimate goal of our enterprise." The Bible is the foundation of the Christian schooling enterprise!

The thematic strands that flow through the Purposeful Design Elementary Bible Series are as follows:
- God tells us His great story (meta-narrative) in the Bible.
- God's Word is truth.
- The great story is the gospel of Jesus Christ and our need of saving faith through Him.
- Knowledge, wisdom, and understanding come from a life grounded in the Scriptures.
- Becoming a spiritually formed disciple of Jesus is impossible without knowing God's Word.
- Developing a vital and authentic Christian worldview requires study, worship, and disciplined practice.

Included in the series are these key features:
- The program consists of 34 lessons spanning a week in length, with a specific lesson focus for each day.
- Scripture memory is embedded in each week's lesson.
- Vivid, inspiring illustrations bring the Bible truths to life.
- Primary grades incorporate custom music that relates to the lesson.
- Various Bible translations may be used throughout the series.
- Computer presentations, digital masters, and interactive-whiteboard materials are included.
- Thanksgiving, Christmas, and Easter lessons are stand-alone optional lessons.
- Chapel programs are included for teacher convenience.

Each grade level in this series, Early Education/Preschool through Grade 6, focuses on the foundational teachings from the Bible about the nature and character of God, the qualities of His people, and His church. During these school years, students are given an overview of the entire Bible, with an emphasis on God's attributes, biblical characters, the early Church, and what it means to know Jesus Christ and live for him.

We pray that this series will support your efforts to develop vibrant followers of Christ who will impact the world around them.

Derek J. Keenan, EdD
former Vice President, Academic Affairs

Acknowledgments

The Peer Review process is an important step in the development of this textbook series. ACSI and the Purposeful Design staff greatly appreciate the feedback we receive from the schools and teachers who participate. We highly value the efforts and input of these faculty members; their recommendations and suggestions are extremely helpful. The institutions listed below have assisted us in this way.

Black Forest Academy, Kandern, Germany
Calvary Baptist Day School, Winston-Salem, NC
Calvary Christian Academy, Philadelphia, PA
Chinese Christian Schools, San Leandro, CA
Christian Academy of San Antonio, San Antonio, TX
Davidson Academy, Nashville, TN
Faith Academy, Victoria, TX
Fellowship Christian School, Roswell, GA
Grove City Christian School, Grove City, OH
Hebron Christian Academy, Dacula, GA
Lenawee Christian School, Adrian, MI
Linfield Christian School, Temecula, CA
Manhattan Christian Academy, New York, NY
McKinney Christian Academy, McKinney, TX
Morrison Academy, Taichung, Taiwan
New Jerusalem Christian School, Jackson, MS
Northside Christian School, Saint Petersburg, FL
Pan American Christian Academy, São Paulo, Brazil
Peoria Christian School, Peoria, IL
Providence Christian School, Dothan, AL
Redwood Christian Schools, Castro Valley, CA
Scottsdale Christian Academy, Scottsdale, AZ
Seattle Christian Schools, Seattle, WA
Valley Christian Academy, Aurora, OH
Wheaton Christian Grammar School, Winfield, IL

Art Illustrations
Ron Adair
Aline Heiser
Steve Miller

Understanding Purposeful Design Bible

Background

ACSI developed its Elementary Bible Series in the early 1990s with the goal of producing a quality elementary Bible program that reflected the needs and desires of Christian school teachers, administrators, and students at that time. The Bible is timeless, but society has changed over the years, necessitating a fresh, new approach to teaching the Bible. Purposeful Design has now revised the series based upon surveys completed by Christian school educators who had regularly taught from the original series. The results of the questionnaires were then tabulated and carefully analyzed. Keeping the results in mind, a team of talented and experienced teachers from a variety of geographic areas wrote new lessons that were then suffused with updated graphics, songs, terminology, and technology.

Overview of the Purposeful Design Elementary Bible Series

Christian Worldview

The goal of the Purposeful Design Elementary Bible Series is for every student to develop a Christian worldview. A worldview is that framework from which each person views reality, makes sense of life, and interacts with the world. The Christian worldview holds that the primary reason for each person's existence is to love and serve God. People develop a Christian worldview through both the knowledge and application of Scripture. For this reason, it is essential for students to have an in-depth knowledge of Bible truths, as well as the ability to apply Scripture to their daily lives.

Themes and Concepts

Key to the development of a Christian worldview is the presentation of overarching themes that permeate all the Elementary Bible materials, regardless of the lesson topic or grade level. These themes, as follows, are woven throughout the series both directly and indirectly:

- **God tells His great story in the Bible.** God's Word displays His nature, His works, and His plan of redemption. The teaching of sound doctrine from the Bible is central to every lesson. It is this knowledge of God that establishes a solid foundation for life.

- **God's Word is truth.** Because God's Word is true, the series presents students with Bible truths, not Bible stories. Students learn that the Bible is the best source for guidance and direction in life.

- **God loves everyone.** God loves and cares for people. His desire is for all people to have a right relationship with Him. His intentions toward every person are always gracious and good.

- **Everyone needs to come to a saving faith in Jesus.** All people must experience salvation to have a right relationship with God, so the series often presents the message of repentance, personal faith, and acceptance of Jesus Christ as Savior and Lord. A personal relationship with Jesus Christ is dynamic and life-changing as each Christian faithfully grows in knowledge and in obedience to the Lord.

- **Christlike behavior, evangelism, ministry, stewardship, and apologetics are all applications of spiritual growth in Christ.** Personal faith is demonstrated by behavior. Students learn to serve others in response to God's love for them and to share the good news of salvation in their homes and neighborhoods and throughout the world.

- **Bible study, prayer, and worship are disciplines for spiritual growth.** The series emphasizes spiritual disciplines as a way to establish and reinforce a biblical worldview as students grow in their faith by consistently using these methods for growth. God's desire is that Christians be conformed to the character of Jesus Christ. This involves a transformation of the mind and heart through the work of the Holy Spirit, who gives Christians the desire to change and enables them to do the will of God.

© Bible Grade 2

• **Students need to know and understand spiritual concepts.** In addition to overarching themes, each weekly Bible lesson teaches and develops spiritual concepts. These concepts include salvation, grace, mercy, repentance, perseverance, faith, forgiveness, worship, thanksgiving, praise, aspects of God's divine nature, and a personal relationship to God.

Expected Student Outcomes

A strong Bible program requires that students not only acquire skills and knowledge but also grow in faith and demonstrate that faith by their behavior. For this reason, each lesson has a unique set of expected student outcomes—statements of desired student outcomes in the areas of knowledge, skills, and life application through studying the lesson. Because growth in faith is an individual matter, students will come to apply Scripture over the course of time as they grow in their relationship with God.

Translations

The Purposeful Design Elementary Bible Series can be used in conjunction with any translation of the Bible. Teachers are encouraged to use the Bible translation endorsed by their school. The New International Version (NIV), the New King James Version (NKJV), the New American Standard (NASB), and the King James Version (KJV) are all compatible with Purposeful Design Elementary Bible. In an effort to maintain a nontranslation-specific Bible series, verses or passages of Scripture are frequently referenced but seldom quoted. Unless otherwise noted, any direct quotes from Scripture that appear in the teacher or student editions have been taken from the New King James Version (NKJV).

Doctrinal Differences

The Purposeful Design Elementary Bible Series adheres firmly to the doctrinal statement that all ACSI schools sign as a condition of membership. Beyond these fundamentals of the faith, a diversity of traditions, practices, and beliefs exist within the evangelical Christian community. Purposeful Design recognizes that conscientious Christians have differing views on many theological issues. The Elementary Bible Series focuses primarily on those beliefs Christians hold in common. When doctrinal differences are known to exist, teachers are given some background information on these differences and encouraged to use the opportunity to reflect the doctrinal statement of their individual school or supporting church(es).

The Purposeful Design Elementary Bible Series is organized by grade level, from Early Education (EE)/Preschool through Grade 6. Lessons for each grade level emphasize a key biblical concept in an age-appropriate and engaging way. The Bible truths presented in each grade level build on the foundational truths students have learned in previous grades. The following table provides an overview of each grade level and subject focus in the series:

Structure of the Series

Level	Subject
EE/Preschool	Familiar Bible truths that emphasize God's love
Kindergarten	Familiar Bible truths that emphasize God's loving care
First Grade	Familiar Bible truths that emphasize God's relationship to people
Second Grade	Studies on character traits of various people in the Bible with application to students' life

Level	Subject
Third Grade	Studies in the life of Christ, the early Church, and missions from the time of Paul until now
Fourth Grade	Studies in the basic doctrines of the Church
Fifth Grade	Studies in the Old Testament that emphasize choices and their consequences
Sixth Grade	Studies in the New Testament that emphasize application of Scripture

Schedule

Each grade level includes 34 weekly lessons. The series easily accommodates a four- or five-day instructional program and provides a weekly test for Grades 1 through 6. Thanksgiving (Lesson 13), Christmas (Lesson 17), and Easter (Lesson 29) are stand-alone lessons and should be scheduled at the appropriate times in the school year.

xii

Components of the Series

Purposeful Design Elementary Bible Series instructional materials are designed to help students appropriate and apply both knowledge of the Scriptures and skills in using the Bible. These materials include:
• Teacher edition
• Student edition
• Grade-level URL, which includes blackline masters, chapel programs, and visual aids in all grades, songs and lyrics in Early Education/Preschool through Grade 2, and digital masters and computer presentations in Grades 1 through 6
• Visual aids in all grades (Early Education/Preschool through Grade 2 include corresponding narratives)
• Time lines in Kindergarten through Grade 6

Features of the Teacher Edition

The teacher edition includes all the information necessary to plan and teach each weekly lesson.

Table of Contents

The table of contents lists the lesson numbers, titles, and page numbers for each lesson. The stand-alone lessons of Thanksgiving, Christmas, and Easter, listed in the table of contents, are positioned near the time of year when these lessons might fall. These lessons can be presented at the appropriate time and do not need to be taught in sequence with the other lessons.

Lesson Preparation Page(s)

Teachers can see at a glance what materials are needed for the weekly lesson by looking at the lesson Foci (Early Education/Preschool and Kindergarten), Memory Verse, Glossary terms (Grades 2 through 6), song list (Early Education/Preschool through Grade 2), Expected Student Outcomes, an outline of the lesson content (Grades 1 through 6), Teacher and Student Resources, and a devotional called *Teacher's Heart*. Teacher and student resources are suggested as optional materials to explore the lesson topic. Items listed in Teacher and Student Resources do not constitute an endorsement by Purposeful Design Publications but may be used to extend the lesson.

Lesson Pages

Each teacher edition lesson page contains the title and focus of the lesson in addition to helpful sidebars and a main body of instructional information that is laid out in a step-by-step format. In Early Education/Preschool and Kindergarten, each lesson page is divided into *Worship Time*, *Listening Time*, and *Activity Time* sections. Lesson pages for Grades 1 through 6 include *Introduction*, *Directed Instruction*, and *Review* sections. All grade levels contain questions in the *Review* section to test the students' comprehension and help them recall facts from the Bible truth.

The sidebars are *Memory Verse*, *Memory Work*, *Preparation*, *Application*, and *Reinforcement*. Grades 1 through 6 have an *Extension* sidebar as well.

Memory Verse suggests a Bible verse or passage for students to memorize.

Memory Work provides creative ideas for helping students memorize the weekly memory verse. *Memory Work* is included on the first day of each lesson, but these suggested activities are designed to be used throughout the week.

Preparation gives teachers an advance notice of supply needs to allow for ample time to acquire and assemble any materials necessary for the lesson. This sidebar lists supplemental materials provided on the grade-level URL.

Reinforcement is for teacher use. This sidebar contains information related to each lesson's topic and may be read to students, but it is primarily designed to provide background information or instructional strategies.

Application contains questions that are vital to helping students internalize Bible truths. Questions in this sidebar call for students to relate concepts from the Bible truth to their own life and should be asked after the

© Bible Grade 2

xiii

review questions. Teachers should allow questions and answers during this class time to help students develop a Bible-based, Christian worldview.

Extension provides a variety of optional activities, such as games, songs, map work, computer presentations, and art projects, to reinforce and review the lesson. Extension activities can be done at any time during the school day. Many songs, sermons, videos, and other resources are available free or for a fee on the internet. When one of these is suggested as an extension activity, teachers need to download or present them in accordance with school policy.

Bible costumes are frequently suggested in the lower grades. Simple costumes are easily made by cutting neck openings and armholes into king-size pillowcases. Headpieces may be cut from old bed sheets or hand towels.

Recipes and foods are also frequently suggested in the lower grades. Food allergies should always be taken into account when using anything edible in a lesson. Baking temperatures given are in Fahrenheit.

The teacher edition includes a formal assessment at the end of each lesson. Reduced student edition pages with the answers to each exercise appear on instructional days.

Icons

The teacher edition includes two types of icons that alert the teacher to specific information or activities. The *Preparation* icon ★ points out the need for the teacher to prepare a material in advance. The materials needed and directions for preparation are noted in the sidebar that bears the same icon. The *Extension* icon ⌐ prompts the teacher to note the availability of an extension activity to reinforce the Bible truth.

Features of the Student Edition

The student edition is a consumable workbook designed with colorful, realistic illustrations and photographs to capture the students' interest in the Bible and subject matter. Four student edition pages are provided for each lesson. The pages are perforated for easy removal. They are labeled at the top with the lesson number and the day of the lesson. For example, student edition page 2.4 refers to Lesson 2, Day 4. Each page is also paginated. Odd-numbered pages have name lines.

Supplemental Materials

The Purposeful Design Elementary Bible series includes the following types of supplemental materials found on https://www.acsi.org/textbooks/mu9/2:

GRADE	Blackline Masters (BLMs)	Digital Masters (DMs)	Time Line	Computer Presentations (PPs)	Chapels	Visual Aids (VAs)	Music with Lyrics
EE/Preschool	Y	N	N	N	Y	Y*	Y
Kindergarten	Y	N	Y	N	Y	Y*	Y
1st	Y	Y	Y	Y	Y	Y*	Y
2nd	Y	Y	Y	Y	Y	Y*	Y
3rd	Y	Y	Y	Y	Y	Y	N
4th	Y	Y	Y	Y	Y	Y	N
5th	Y	Y	Y	Y	Y	Y	N
6th	Y	Y	Y	Y	Y	Y	N

*includes a grade-appropriate narrative with each illustration

- Time lines are only available in printed form.
- The music includes one track of vocals and music and another of only instrumental music for each song suggested in Early Education/Preschool through Grade 2. All songs are performed by Mary Rice Hopkins.
- Visual aids and preprinted time lines are provided for classroom use.

Visual Aids are original, full-color illustrations of Bible truths provided for all grades. On the back of each visual aid for Early Education/Preschool through Grade 2 is a paraphrased version of the Bible truth. Before reading the paraphrased text, teachers are encouraged to hold up the Bible and remind students that the Bible truth comes from God's Word.

The following abbreviations have been used to facilitate identifying the supplemental materials needed for each lesson. **VAs** are visual aids, **BLMs** are blackline masters, **DMs** are digital masters, and **PPs** are computer presentations. Each Supplemental Material has a title and a label containing a lesson number and a letter, indicating the order in which the material is used. For example, **VA 12A The Psalms** is the first (A) visual aid in Lesson 12. *The Psalms* is the title of the visual aid. **VA 7C The Red Sea Crossing** is the third (C) visual aid in Lesson 7.

Blackline masters serve a variety of purposes and may include craft projects, weekly tests, teaching aids, recipes, and supplemental activities. Weekly review tests for Grades 1 through 6 are included on blackline masters, along with answer keys. To enhance student comprehension, it is suggested that teachers review the answers to the tests in class after all students have finished. Tests may be graded if desired. Because blackline masters are in electronic format, they may be projected for classroom use. **Digital masters** are also provided for teacher use.

Computer presentations are optional and can be used to reinforce lesson content.

Chapel programs centered on biblical themes are provided and may be used if desired.

Additional Information

A chart of abbreviations used for books of the Bible is listed below:

OLD TESTAMENT						
Genesis	Gen		2 Chronicles	2 Chron	Daniel	Dan
Exodus	Ex		Ezra	Ezra	Hosea	Hos
Leviticus	Lev		Nehemiah	Neh	Joel	Joel
Numbers	Num		Esther	Esth	Amos	Amos
Deuteronomy	Deut		Job	Job	Obadiah	Obad
Joshua	Josh		Psalms	Ps	Jonah	Jonah
Judges	Judg		Proverbs	Prov	Micah	Micah
Ruth	Ruth		Ecclesiastes	Eccl	Nahum	Nahum
1 Samuel	1 Sam		Song of Solomon	Song	Habakkuk	Hab
2 Samuel	2 Sam		Isaiah	Isa	Zephaniah	Zeph
1 Kings	1 Kings		Jeremiah	Jer	Haggai	Hag
2 Kings	2 Kings		Lamentations	Lam	Zechariah	Zech
1 Chronicles	1 Chron		Ezekiel	Ezek	Malachi	Mal

NEW TESTAMENT						
Matthew	Mt		Ephesians	Eph	Hebrews	Heb
Mark	Mk		Philippians	Phil	James	James
Luke	Lk		Colossians	Col	1 Peter	1 Pet
John	Jn		1 Thessalonians	1 Thess	2 Peter	2 Pet
Acts	Acts		2 Thessalonians	2 Thess	1 John	1 Jn
Romans	Rom		1 Timothy	1 Tim	2 John	2 Jn
1 Corinthians	1 Cor		2 Timothy	2 Tim	3 John	3 Jn
2 Corinthians	2 Cor		Titus	Titus	Jude	Jude
Galatians	Gal		Philemon	Philem	Revelation	Rev

© *Bible Grade 2*

Preparing a Lesson

① MEMORY VERSE

The **Memory Verse** sidebar contains the verse students are to memorize during the week of the lesson. Teachers can choose which Bible version to use based on the reference given.

② MEMORY WORK

Memory Work offers suggestions to help teach the memory verse in fun and meaningful ways that encourage active participation from students.

③ PREPARATION

The **Preparation** sidebar gives an advance notice to acquire and assemble any materials needed to teach the lesson. Materials not assumed to be in the classroom are listed in BLUE BOLDFACE TYPE. Visual aids and supplemental materials provided on the Grade 2 URL are listed as well. The star icon is a quick visual reminder to alert teachers to sections needing prepared materials.

④ EXTENSION

The **Extension** sidebar appears in most lessons to offer optional enrichment activities. Extension materials are listed in BLUE BOLDFACE TYPE. These materials are also listed on the Lesson Preparation page. The arrow icon is a reminder that an extension activity is available and can be done at any time.

⑤ Glossary

Glossary words may occur throughout the lesson. The Glossary appears in the back of the teacher and student editions.

16.1 Nehemiah Leads
Focus: Nehemiah Leads as God Directs

📖 MEMORY VERSE ①
Nehemiah 4:6

MEMORY WORK ②
- Practice saying the Memory Verse several times together. Divide the class into four groups. Distribute a set of prepared INDEX CARDS to each group. Instruct students to shuffle the cards on the floor or desk in front of their group. Challenge each group to cooperate quickly to place the cards in correct order to show the verse.

★ PREPARATION ③
Write each of the words from the Memory Verse on an INDEX CARD. Do this to make four sets of cards. (Memory Work)

Have on hand a PICTURE OF THE GREAT WALL OF CHINA. (Introduction)

Select VA 16A Nehemiah Leads and DM-1 Character Traits. (Directed Instruction)

↪ EXTENSION ④
1A Display **DM-9 Map of Persia** to show how far the Israelites were taken away from the Promised Land during their captivity, from Jerusalem to Babylonia.

1B Instruct students to write a journal entry on how they would approach cooperating with others to complete a difficult task.

Introduction ★ ⑥
Show a PICTURE OF THE GREAT WALL OF CHINA. Explain to students that this wall was originally about 5,500 miles long. It took over 2,000 years to build the wall. Ask students why a country would build a wall such as this. (for protection from invasion by people from other countries or areas) Walls around countries and cities are used as a defense, which is *a means of protection.* Ask students how countries today usually protect their land. (**Possible answers: army, police**) Explain that the ancient Israelites rebuilt a wall that was used as a defense to protect their city, Jerusalem.

Directed Instruction ★ ↪ ⑦
Instruct students to listen as you read VA 16A Nehemiah Leads. Explain that cities in Nehemiah's time usually had a wall built around them for protection. A wall made it difficult for robbers to get in at night and also made it hard for armies to quickly capture a city. When Nehemiah heard that the city of Jerusalem had no protection, God led him to rebuild the walls around the city.

Nehemiah was a good leader, and the people liked his idea to make the city strong again. The people listened to Nehemiah because Nehemiah cared deeply for them, and he looked to God as he planned ahead what to do.

It would have been difficult for Nehemiah to rebuild this wall by himself. He knew it would take a lot of people and would be very hard work. Nehemiah had courage to go before King Artaxerxes and ask for his help. Nehemiah did not give up. He encouraged others, planned, and helped do anything he was able to do in order to complete what God had led him to do. Nehemiah showed good *leadership*, which means *the ability to guide and influence others.* Refer to **DM-1 Character Traits.**

Nehemiah showed good leadership because he:
- fasted, prayed, repented, and trusted God's direction (Nehemiah 1:4–11)
- helped to protect and take care of others (Nehemiah 1:11–2:1)
- received assistance from others (Nehemiah 2:1–9)
- encouraged others (Nehemiah 2:17–18)
- answered God's way when others insulted him (Nehemiah 2:19–20)
- worked hard, cooperated, and delegated work (Nehemiah 3)
- was faithful to see the work done (Nehemiah 7:1–2)

Teach students the following acronym to help them remember attributes of Nehemiah being a good leader:
- **N** ever doubted what God wanted him to do
- **E** ncouraged others
- **H** elped protect others
- **E** xpected others to offer assistance
- **M** ade prayer a priority
- **I** nitiated cooperation
- **A** nswered God's way when insulted
- **H** ad a hardworking and faithful character

152

---

⑥ Introduction

Introduction contains a variety of ideas ranging from music selections, group discussion topics and questions, to prayer topic suggestions and object lessons that will prepare students and invite them to fully engage in learning the concepts presented in the lesson.

⑦ Directed Instruction

Directed Instruction gives step-by-step instructions for the lesson. The Bible truth is presented in this section. Also, fictional stories set in various locations around the world introduce students to other perspectives and applications of Bible concepts.

xvi

Discuss ways students can show good leadership as Nehemiah did. (**Possible answers: help others, cooperate, make godly decisions**)

Student Page 16.1
Have students complete the page. Upon completion, pray with students for God to help them be good leaders.

Review 8
- Why did Nehemiah want to rebuild a wall around Jerusalem? (**Possible answers: God led him to do so; he wanted to help provide protection.**)
- To whom did Nehemiah go to ask for help? (**King Artaxerxes**)
- Name one way Nehemiah was a good leader. (**Possible answers: Nehemiah made good decisions; he initiated cooperation; he was hardworking and never doubted God.**)

Time Line 9
Identify the biblical characters students have studied so far in the Old Testament, ending with Nehemiah. Encourage students to recall one fact about each character.

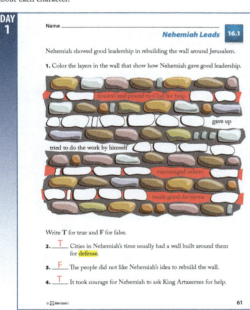

APPLICATION 10
- What kind of person was Nehemiah? (**Possible answers: faithful to God, caring, helpful, cooperative, hardworking**)
- Would you want Nehemiah to lead a project you were working on? Why or why not? (**Answers will vary.**)
- What do you think is the most important thing about being a good leader? (**Answers will vary but should include being a good example to show others a good way to behave.**)
- How could you be a good leader to others? (**Possible answers: pray, speak the truth, do what is right**)

REINFORCEMENT 11
Nehemiah, a Jew living in exile in Persia, had the trust and ear of Artaxerxes, the king of Persia. As a cupbearer, Nehemiah had the privileged position of taste testing the king's wine before he drank it, which could have been a fatal role. God placed Nehemiah in this important role for a reason. During Old Testament times in Israel and surrounding nations, this job was an honored position in the royal courts. The Persians called the cupbearer or king's butler *Saky*. The Hebrew name is *Mashkeh*, and is written about in Genesis 40:9–13, where Joseph interpreted the dream of Pharaoh's cupbearer. The term is also included in 1 Kings 10:3–7, where the queen of Sheba is talking about King Solomon's prosperity and wisdom, and Solomon's cupbearers are listed as part of his royal household.

---

8 **Review**
Review questions focus on comprehension of key concepts from the Bible truths and/or daily lessons. Answers and suggestions help teachers guide class discussions.

9 **Time Line**
Use of the **Time Line** appears in various lessons to help students review biblical characters and understand when each character lived within the scope of biblical history.

10 **APPLICATION**
Application questions provide an opportunity to evaluate both students' understanding of the concepts presented and their ability to apply those concepts in daily life.

11 **REINFORCEMENT**
The **Reinforcement** sidebar provides additional Bible background for the lesson or supplemental information related to each lesson's theme. The information is designed for teachers, but can be shared with students.

Supplemental materials are available to download at **https://www.acsi.org/textbooks/mu9/2**.

Lesson Preparation
Abraham Listens

Expected Student Outcomes

KNOW
Abraham listens to God. God promises to bless Abraham.

DO
Students will:
- apply the reading of a devotion to God's working in their life
- create a flowchart of Abraham's descendants
- fill in an acrostic portraying blessings God has given
- order the events of Abraham's journey and recall how God cared for him
- compare and contrast Abraham's provisions from God to how He provides for us

APPLY
Students will conclude that listening to and obeying God's Word lead to wisdom and contentment.

Lesson Outline

I. Abraham listens to God (Gen 12:1–8)
   A. Abraham obeys and I can obey
II. Blessings
   A. God's promises to Abraham (Gen 12:2–4)
   B. Descendants
III. God leads Abraham to Shechem (Gen 12:4–8)
   A. Obeying and worshipping
IV. Remembering God's provision (Gen 12:7)

♥ TEACHER'S HEART

Many people are retired and settled in a comfortable place by age 75. Think about Abraham. He had already moved from Ur to Haran. Then beginning at age 75, God asked him to leave his new country, change his name and identity, and trust Him to start over (again). Abraham was a tried man who left all that was familiar. Yet he trusted God and believed the blessing God promised would be fulfilled.

How many times does God ask you to do the uncomfortable or seemingly impossible? Yet when you listen and obey as Abraham did, He takes you from a place of insecurity and fear to a place of blessing and peace. James 1:5 prompts you to ask God for wisdom. When you are lacking, He will give generously. As God directs and gives wisdom, your obedience is tried and you are set apart, as Abraham was, to come into a place of contentment and communication with a living, faithful God. Determine in your heart to step out from the familiar to a place where the hidden things of God are disclosed and discovered.

Supplemental Materials are available to download. See Understanding Purposeful Design Bible at the front of this book for the Grade 2 URL.

📖 MEMORY VERSE
Psalm 78:1

GLOSSARY WORDS
- descendant

★ MATERIALS

Day 1:
- Flip chart or poster board, index cards
- DM-1 Character Traits
- VA 1A Abraham Listens and Obeys God, Time Line

Day 2:
- DM-2 Descendants, index cards
- Shoe box or container, wrapping paper (*Extension*)

Day 3:
- BLM 1A Map of Abraham's Journey, highlighters
- Small object, compass (*Extension*)

Day 4:
- No additional materials are needed.

Day 5:
- VA 1A Abraham Listens and Obeys God
- BLM 1B Lesson 1 Test

♪ SONGS
Only God Can Do (*Extension*)

TEACHER RESOURCES
Book by Book. CD. Walk Thru the Bible, 2008.

STUDENT RESOURCES
Busch, Melinda Kay. *God Calls Abraham … God Calls You*. Concordia Publishing House, 2003.
Davis, Mary J. *My Prayer Journal*. Legacy Press, 2013.

Abraham Listens
Focus: Abraham Listens to God

📖 MEMORY VERSE
Psalm 78:1

MEMORY WORK
Have students practice the Memory Verse throughout the week using the following directions:
- Lead students to read the Memory Verse together several times. Explain that this verse is telling Christians to listen and obey God. Tell students that they need to purposefully be ready to hear God and do what God says. Count the number of words in this week's Memory Verse. Invite the same number of students to come to the front of the class. Give each student an INDEX CARD with one word on it from the verse. Instruct students to stand in the correct order to show the Memory Verse. When students are in the correct order holding their card, have the class read the verse in unison.

★ PREPARATION
Display the Memory Verse on a FLIP CHART, piece of POSTER BOARD, large piece of construction paper, or the board so that students will have visual access to the verse all week. Prepare INDEX CARDS by printing one word from the Memory Verse on each card. (*Memory Work*)

Select **DM-1 Character Traits**. (*Introduction*)

Select **VA 1A Abraham Listens and Obeys God.** (*Directed Instruction*)

Display the **Time Line** so that all students can easily see it. Keep the Time Line on display for the entire school year. (*Directed Instruction*)

Introduction ★
Display **DM-1 Character Traits** and read about *obedience*. Ask a compliant student to gather personal items and move to another location in the room. Instruct the student to follow directions as you guide where to go. After the student is placed, give a blessing by allowing the student to have a special privilege. Inform students that they will be learning about someone in the Bible who had to gather what he had, leave a comfortable place, and move to a new location. This resulted in blessing.

Directed Instruction ★
Direct students to locate the Glossary in the back of the Student Edition. Inform them there is a word they will want to know for today's lesson. Practice looking for the word together. Find and read the definition for the word *descendant*. A **descendant** is *a person who comes from a certain family line of parents, grandparents, and great-grandparents.*

Display **VA 1A Abraham Listens and Obeys God**. Instruct students that whenever you read Bible "stories" you will call them *Bible truths* because God's Word is always true. Enlighten students that reading out of God's Word will make a difference in their lives. Just as they see God working in the lives of people in the Bible, God can be working through them in similar ways!

Read the Bible truth for today from the back of VA 1A. Remind students that God called Abraham to go to a new land. God spoke to Abraham directly. The Lord promised to make Abraham's name great and to form a new nation with Abraham's descendants. Abraham and his wife had not been able to have children, so all this seemed impossible. Yet, Abraham gave up all he knew and left home to follow God. Abraham trusted God to take care of him.

As Abraham listened and obeyed, God spoke words of comfort and gave direction. Abraham stopped at the place called *Shechem* and built an altar, or place of worship. God kept His promise of making Abraham a great nation. Through Abraham's descendants, many years later, Jesus was born. Jesus would die for the sins of all people. Those who believe in Jesus as Savior are saved by God's grace, become members of God's family, and have eternal life.

Student Page 1.1
Direct students to locate the student page for today's lesson. Read the introductory paragraph. Be sure to emphasize that God's Word is truth and shows how to live. Inform students that they will be reading a devotion written by another student. The devotion shows how God's Word can be useful to help a person obey, just like they learned Abraham obeyed. Assist students in locating **John 14:23** in their Bible. Read the Scripture together, and then tell students to complete the page.

Review
- What made Abraham a good listener? (**Possible answers: He knew God's voice; he knew what God was telling him when God told him to stop at Shechem; he didn't just listen, he obeyed.**)
- How do you think Abraham felt when God told Abraham what He wanted him to do? (**Possible answers: He was worried about leaving his home; he was surprised at what God told him.**)
- What did it mean when God told Abraham he would make him a great nation? (**He would give him many descendants.**)
- Why did Abraham build an altar when he got to the place near Shechem? (**He wanted to worship and show thankfulness to God.**)
- Since Abraham listened to and obeyed God, how did God bless all people through Abraham? (**Jesus was one of Abraham's descendants.**)

Time Line
Explain that there is no beginning or end of God. Point out the Creation, Noah and the Flood, and Abraham for students to understand the order of events.

DAY 1

Name _____

Abraham Listens 1.1

Welcome to Second Grade Bible!

Genesis 12:1–8 shows the Bible truth about how Abraham listened to and obeyed God and was rewarded with many descendants. This year, you will hear about many more people in the Bible who followed God's voice. The stories in the Bible are not pretend, they are truths that help you know how to obey, love, and honor God, and how to live your life well. As you serve God together with others and study His Word, you will see God make a difference in the world around you.

Read John 14:23. Grace, age 9, wrote a devotion showing how God's Word helped her obey. Answer the question at the end of the devotion.

To Obey or Disobey

Have you ever disobeyed? I have disobeyed a lot! Once my sister and I were fighting and I was calling her mean names because she wouldn't practice basketball with me. My mom came out and asked me to go to my room. I did not want to go. I said, "No!" She made me go anyway. I opened my Bible and read John 14:23. God helped me tell my sister I was sorry for calling her mean names. She forgave me! It felt good to obey. When is it hard for you to obey?

Answers will vary.

EXTENSION
1A Have students close their eyes and listen to an instruction from a classmate. Secretly ask a student to give an instruction, such as "raise your hands and clap three times." After students have followed the instruction, ask them to open their eyes and guess who said it. Discuss how it is easy to know someone's voice if you spend time with that person. Lead to the conclusion that Abraham must have been very familiar with God to know His voice and obey what He said.

APPLICATION
- How did Abraham respond when God asked him to go? (**Possible answers: He listened and obeyed; he gathered his things and went; he obeyed even though it was hard.**)
- What do you think was hard about leaving for Abraham? (**He was older and left all his relatives and what was familiar.**)
- When is it hard for you to listen to God? (**Possible answers: It is hard to listen when I want my own way; it is hard to listen when I am afraid.**)
- What did you learn about God from this Bible truth? (**Possible answers: God blesses us and others when we obey; God takes care of us and guides us; God has a plan for us.**)

REINFORCEMENT
Abraham was honored for his obedience and faith, not only in Genesis, but in Acts 7, Romans 4, Galatians 3, Hebrews 11, and James 2. Abraham, a humble man, would not have given honor to himself, yet God and many others chose to do so, even after Abraham had died.

1.2 Abraham Listens
Focus: Blessings

★ PREPARATION

Prepare **DM-2 Descendants** to display. (*Directed Instruction*)

Write the following on separate INDEX CARDS. For cards that will contain more than one word, write each word or phrase on a separate line. 1) husband > dad > grandfather, 2) wife > mom > grandmother, 3) son, 4) daughter, 5) wife to the son > aunt, 6) husband to the daughter > uncle, 7) child > grandchild > cousin, 8) child > grandchild > cousin (*Directed Instruction*)

⟲ EXTENSION

2A Convert a SHOE BOX or CONTAINER into a box for blessings. Cover the box with WRAPPING PAPER and label it *Blessing Box*. Cut a slit in the top of the box. Show students the Blessing Box. Invite them to think about a special way to bless others, and encourage them to observe ways that students in the class show kindness or love to others. Throughout the week, have students write what they observe and place the paper in the box. (Examples: Mario shared his markers when I had none. Melissa was obeying the teacher.) Inform students that the Blessing Box will be placed somewhere in the class with paper beside it for them to write about the ways others showed love or kindness. At the end of the week, read some of the blessings. Remind students that they are not only seeing someone bless others, but they are blessing that person by writing about it!

Introduction

Inform students that the Bible is divided into two major parts—the Old and the New Testaments. The Old Testament records God's work prior to when Jesus was born on the earth; the New Testament tells about Jesus' birth and work on the earth, and also God's work in His Church and future events. Have students locate the table of contents in their Bible and practice finding different books of the Bible. Ask for the page number those books begin on. (**Page numbers will vary depending on the Bible used.**) Look up **Psalm 100:5** and read it together.

Directed Instruction ★ ⟲

Display **DM-2 Descendants**. Review the definition of *descendant* at the top. Explain to students that eight of them will be acting out a pretend family line. To avoid an uncomfortable situation, remind students that this is a pretend activity and that it is not a true scenario. Using the INDEX CARDS and **DM-2 Descendants** as a guide, follow the directions for this activity:

- Have a boy volunteer come to the front of the class. Hand him the card that reads *husband* in the top heading. Inform him that he will be the pretend husband in this scenario.
- Have a girl volunteer receive the card that says *wife*. She is the pretend wife of the husband. Explain that the pretend husband and wife have a son and daughter. This makes the husband and wife become the *dad* and *mom*. Ask the *dad* and *mom* to step back.
- Ask two students to receive cards that say *son* and *daughter*. Have them stand in front of the *dad* and *mom*. Explain that the son and daughter get married to two others. Hand out the *wife to the son* and *husband to the daughter* cards to two more students. Have them stand beside their spouses and then all four step back, in front of the first two volunteers.
- Inform the class that now two children are born. They are *children* to their parents, *grandchildren* to their grandparents, and *cousins* to one another. The spouses of the son and daughter are now the *aunt* and *uncle* of these children. Hand out the two cards that read *child* in the top heading. Have these two students stand in front of the first two rows of this family tree.
- Direct the volunteers to return to their seat.

As promised in Psalm 100:5, God's blessing came through Abraham's descendants—throughout the generations of his family line. God used Abraham to begin a new nation. Abraham was 75 years old when he left the city of Ur. His wife Sarah had not been able to have children. God had made a promise to begin a new nation through Abraham. But, Abraham had to wait a long time! Explain that the promise was fulfilled when Abraham and Sarah had a son named *Isaac*. Isaac had a son named *Jacob* who had 12 sons. Jacob's name was changed to *Israel* and he was the father of 12 tribes through his 12 sons. These descendants became what is called *the nation of Israel*. It is still known by the same name today.

Remind students of the following: *descendant* means *a person who comes from a certain family line of parents, grandparents, and great-grandparents.*

4

Use Genesis 21:1–5 to review God's promises and discuss how they were fulfilled. Many years later, Jesus was born into Abraham's family line. Jesus was the King they were waiting for. He died for the sins of every person to offer everyone eternal life. Read **John 5:24** together.

Student Page 1.2
Complete the page together as a class. Conclude the lesson by sharing acrostic responses.

Review
- What are descendants? (**A descendant is a person who comes from a certain family line of parents, grandparents, and great-grandparents.**)
- How did God's promises bless Abraham? (**God gave Abraham many descendants. He made Abraham's name great by starting a new nation.**)
- Even to this day, what is this new nation called? (**Israel**)
- Why were the blessings Abraham received so special? (**At the time he received the promise, Abraham was old and his wife couldn't have children. God blessed them with Isaac, their promised son. Eventually through Abraham's descendants, Jesus was born.**)

APPLICATION
- What do you notice about people who obey God? (**Possible answers: They are blessed; they are satisfied; they are at peace.**)
- What blessings did God promise Abraham? (**Answers will vary but should include that Abraham would have many descendants and a great name, and be the father of a great nation.**)
- How has God blessed you? (**Possible answers: family, food, a place to live, friends**)
- Because God has blessed you, how can you bless others? (**Possible answers: Encourage others; give others something they need; guide others to God's Word.**)

DAY 2

1.2 Abraham Listens

1. God blessed Abraham by promising him many descendants and a new nation. Fill in the boxes of Abraham's descendants through the generations. The list of descendants is in the correct order. Use the following words: **Abraham, Isaac, Jacob, 12 tribes**.

Abraham → Isaac → Jacob → 12 tribes

2. As God blessed Abraham, He also blesses us. Fill in the acrostic with blessings God has given you with each letter in the word blessing. The first one is an example for you.

B eautiful family
L _____ Answers will vary. _____
E _____
S _____
S _____
I _____
N _____
G _____

3. As God has blessed you, name one way you can bless others.
Answers will vary.

1.3 Abraham Listens
Focus: God Leads Abraham to Shechem

★ PREPARATION
Duplicate copies of **BLM 1A Map of Abraham's Journey** for each student. Make sure each student has a HIGHLIGHTER available. (*Directed Instruction*)

EXTENSION
3A Hide a SMALL OBJECT on the playground and measure in footsteps how far away the object is from something stationary. Take the class and use a COMPASS to find the object. For example, tell students that the object is 10 paces north of the swings, and then find the object. Discuss how the compass is used as a guide and can remind students that God is like a compass to guide them through their life. He shows them where to go and how to live.

Introduction
Instruct students to stand. Show them which way is north, east, south, and west. (An option would be to write the words on paper and put the titles of *north, east, south,* and *west* around the room.) Remind students of the following sentence: **N**ever **E**at **S**oggy **W**orms. Inform students that this sentence will help them to remember the location of something in a certain place. Call out a direction and have students point which way you are referring to. Invite a volunteer to come to the front of the room and repeat the same procedure.

Directed Instruction ★ ↪
Provide each student a copy of **BLM 1A Map of Abraham's Journey**. Have students use a HIGHLIGHTER to highlight north, east, south, and west on the map. Inform students that the map shows the areas where Abraham journeyed. Scholars do not know the exact route that Abraham traveled, but do have evidence of where he began, visited, and stopped.

Instruct students to find the city of Ur on the eastern part of the map. Explain that this city is where Abraham and his family lived when God first spoke to Abraham. Then, Abraham, his wife, Sarah, his nephew, Lot, and his father, Terah, left Ur to go live in the land of Canaan. Direct students to use the highlighter to circle the city of Ur.

After leaving Ur, Abraham and his family settled in the city of Haran. Haran is located on the northern part of the map. Direct students to circle the city of Haran with their highlighter.

After living there for some time, Abraham's father died. Abraham was now 75 years old, yet he remembered all that God had spoken to him. Abraham left Haran and traveled southwest toward Canaan. He took his wife, Sarah, his nephew, Lot, and the people who worked for him toward Shechem, which is located near the eastern shore of the Mediterranean Sea. Direct students to use the highlighter to circle Shechem. It was at Shechem that God told Abraham to end his journey. Inform students that Shechem is in the land of Canaan, the place Abraham's family had first started to go to.

Take some time to read the map and understand where places are that Abraham would have traveled. Have students find the light gray area that indicates the desert. Explain that it would have been very difficult to travel through the desert because of the lack of water and food. Remind students that Abraham had to trust God to show him which way to go and follow God's leading each step of the way.

Point out to students that scholars assume that Abraham's family traveled a little north from Ur and then west along the Euphrates River toward Haran. Encourage students to highlight the most direct route possible from Ur to Haran to Shechem. After highlighting the journey, remind students that it was at Shechem that Abraham made an altar to worship and thank God for guiding him and blessing him.

Student Page 1.3

As a class, complete Exercise 1 together. Assign the rest of the page to be completed independently. If time permits, conclude by allowing students to share ideas of ways they are thankful to God, as Abraham was when he built the altar at Shechem.

Review

- What three places does the Bible mention to be on Abraham's journey? **(Ur, Haran, and Shechem)**
- In which city did God speak to Abraham about the future? **(Ur)**
- What part of Abraham's travels do you think was the most difficult? **(Possible answers: leaving Ur and what was familiar, finding food between cities, not knowing where he was going to stop)**
- What did Abraham do at the end of his journey? **(Possible answers: He remembered to worship God; he built an altar; he thanked God for God's guidance and blessing.)**

Notes:

DAY 3

Name _____

Abraham Listens **1.3**

1. Read Genesis 12:1–8. Number the events in the order they happened.

3 Abraham left Ur with his father and other family members.

6 Abraham built an altar and worshipped God.

4 Abraham obeyed and left Haran.

2 God spoke to Abraham and told him to move.

5 Abraham went to Shechem.

1 God gave Abraham promises.

2. Write about how God cared for Abraham and his family while traveling.

Possible answers: He provided places with food available; He directed which way to go; He gave them peace and assurance.

3. Abraham built an altar, and worshipped and thanked God in Shechem. Draw a picture of something you are thankful for. Remember to worship and thank God for it.

Drawings will vary.

© *Bible Grade 2*   3

APPLICATION

- How would it feel to travel without knowing exactly where you are going? (**Possible answers: It would be scary; we would have to trust God to guide us.**)
- How did God guide and care for Abraham on his journey? (**Possible answers: God spoke to Abraham and provided for him; God told Abraham exactly where to stop.**)
- How does God guide and care for you today? (**Possible answers: He helps me do what is right; He shows me who to be friends with; He gives me food and shelter.**)

REINFORCEMENT

Terah, Abraham's father, left Ur with Abraham, Lot, and Sarah, and traveled with them as far as Haran (Genesis 11:31–32). It must have been difficult for Terah to travel and leave Ur as he was over 70 years old. Terah was 205 years old when he died in Haran. Abraham showed respect to his father as a descendant, as he waited to leave Haran after his father died there. After Terah's death, Abraham obeyed God's call and journeyed with Lot and Sarah to Shechem.

© *Bible* Grade 2

1.4 *Abraham Listens*
Focus: Remembering God's Provision

EXTENSION

4A As a class, sing the song "Only God Can Do" from the Grade 2 URL. The lyrics are also on the URL.

4B Encourage students to help provide for someone in need. Explain that God has blessed and provided for them, so they can help provide for others. Discuss ideas to sponsor a needy child, rake an elderly neighbor's yard, or collect canned food for a local homeless shelter. Give students an opportunity to help others in their community by asking parents for ideas and assistance.

4C Help students design a personal plan for listening and obeying God. The plan should include time for reading God's Word and writing in a journal or prayer book about some of the promises God gives, things to be thankful for, and questions for and about God. Encouraging quiet time to listen to God will reinforce a heart of obedience and thankfulness for the provision, love, and guidance God gives.

Introduction

Read the following realistic story to your class:

> You wake up in the morning and your parents tell you to pack up your favorite things because they are taking you on a surprise trip. You don't know where you're going, but you're excited. Your parents say that you're going somewhere you've never been and will be gone for two weeks! Even though it sounds exciting, you are a little nervous about leaving your dog, not seeing your friends, and figuring out what things you need to pack. You listen to your parents and trust they will lead you on a great adventure. As you travel, your parents teach you about all the places you are visiting. Trying new foods, hiking new areas, and enjoying their company are great memories you'll keep for a long, long time. Finally, you reach your destination. It is a beautiful place and you're thankful you are there. You thank your parents for doing all these special things for you.

Ask students to brainstorm ways the parents might have provided for the child on the trip. (**Possible answers: food, clothing, shelter, guidance, safety**) Just as the parents guided the child, God provides for and guides those who trust Him. Encourage students who have moved or gone on a trip to share memories of fun or difficult things along the way. Prompt them to share ways God provided when they moved or traveled.

Directed Instruction

Discuss how God was faithful in providing for Abraham and all his descendants. Write the following list on the board to name some of the ways God provided for Abraham as he traveled:

- health (traveling from Haran at age 75)
- family to travel with (Sarah and Lot)
- a place to stay
- promise of a great nation
- guidance
- belongings to take
- protection from harm
- food

Inform students that just as God provided for Abraham, they can trust that God will provide for them, too. Some people think God should provide large houses, many toys, all the food they want, lots of friends, and fun times every day. God never promised Abraham or anybody that they would have everything they wanted or that life would be easy. Read **Jeremiah 29:11** and remind students how God promises to be with them, take care of them, and give them hope and a future.

Make another list on the board of ways God has provided for you and your family. (**Possible answers: a place to live, a loving family, food, protection, all your belongings**) Prompt students to understand how God provides for them in the same way he provided for Abraham. Remind students to think about and remember what God has provided each day.

Student Page 1.4
Use the lists on the board to assist students in completing the page.

Review

- How did God provide for Abraham? (**Possible answers: He gave Abraham direction; He blessed Abraham's family; He gave Abraham a new land; He fulfilled His promises to Abraham.**)
- Who did God provide to travel with Abraham? (**Sarah and Lot**)
- According to Jeremiah 29:11, what does God promise to provide you with? (**God promises to be with us, take care of us, and give us hope and a future.**)

Notes:

APPLICATION

- What did you learn about Abraham? (**Possible answers: I learned that Abraham followed God; Abraham obeyed even when it was hard; God chose to bless Abraham; Abraham had many people in his family.**)
- Can you remember a time when God provided and blessed you when you obeyed? (**Answers will vary.**)
- What are some different ways you can worship and thank God like Abraham did in Shechem? (**Possible answers: I can sing praises to Him; I can pray to Him; I can serve others; I can honor Him in all I think, do, and say.**)
- In our journey of life, how does God provide along the way? (**Possible answers: God gives us shelter and food; God gives us guidance and peace.**)

DAY 4

1.4 *Abraham Listens*

The list on the left shows how God provided for Abraham. Read the list and think about ways God takes care of you. Write a list with different ways that God provides for you.

Ways God provided for Abraham:

1. family (Sarah and Lot)

2. food during his journey

3. protection from harm

4. guidance to Shechem

5. promise of a great nation

Ways that God provides for me:

Answers will vary but should be similar in nature except for Exercise 5.

6. Using the above information, fill in the Venn diagram comparing ways God provided for Abraham to ways God provides for you.

Abraham — family (Sarah and Lot), food during his journey, protection from harm, guidance to Shechem, promise of a great nation

Both — Answers will vary.

Me — Answers will vary.

4

© *Bible Grade 2*

1.5 Abraham Listens
Focus: Review and Assessment

★ PREPARATION

Select **VA 1A Abraham Listens and Obeys God**. (*Lesson Review*)

Make one copy of **BLM 1B Lesson 1 Test** for each student. (*Directed Instruction*)

Lesson Review ★

Use **VA 1A Abraham Listens and Obeys God** to review the Bible truths from this lesson. Cover the following concepts:
- God's Word is always true.
- God blesses those who listen and obey.
- Descendants are people who come from the same family line.
- God promised Abraham to make Abraham a great nation and give him many descendants.
- Abraham obeyed when God spoke to him and told him to leave the city of Haran.
- God guided and provided for Abraham on his journey and showed him where to go.
- Abraham built an altar and worshipped God in Shechem, his stopping place at the end of his long journey.
- God blessed Abraham and all people through Jesus, who is a descendant of Abraham.

Directed Instruction ★

Distribute a copy of **BLM 1B Lesson 1 Test** to each student. Verify that your students understand the test format. Read the directions and pronounce any difficult words. Have students complete the test. Review the answers in class. Collect for assessment.

Notes:

Lesson Preparation
Abraham Prays

2.0

Expected Student Outcomes

KNOW
Abraham prays for Lot's deliverance from Sodom.

DO
Students will:
- recount the events of Abraham praying for Lot's deliverance
- contrast positive and negative characteristics to have in prayer
- discover two characteristics, humility and persistence, needed for prayer
- identify people and requests they can pray for
- differentiate between needs and wants to ask for in prayer

APPLY
Students will recognize that God responds to prayer, and they will intercede for others.

Lesson Outline
I. Abraham prays for Lot (Gen 18:17–33)
II. How to pray (James 4:6–10)
  A. Humility
  B. Persistence
III. Interceding for others (James 5:16)
IV. God responds to prayer (Gen 18:33, 19:29; Mt 7:7–11)
  A. God gives good gifts
  B. God does not always answer the way we expect

♥ TEACHER'S HEART

When a fisherman looks at the wind, the waves, and the clouds and knows that a storm is brewing, he takes measures to prepare for the hard blow that will surely come to his boat. In life, sometimes you can also look at the circumstances and see storms brewing around you or the ones that are close to you. Your most natural preparation is to worry or try to control as much as possible, but worry and a pursuit of control often lead to desperation and hopelessness. These stand in direct opposition to the hope God longs to bring in your life storms.

Abraham shows you what your first response should be when you face storms: draw near to God. His nephew, Lot, was in trouble; Abraham's reaction was to not worry, but to pray. Prayer gives freedom to release the situation into God's large, capable hands. Jeremiah 33:3 promises that when you call to Him, He will answer. He will remember your petition, and He will act on your behalf. In your life right now, you might be looking at circumstances and seeing storms brewing. Come near to God. Pour out your heart to Him. Humbly and persistently bring your requests to Him. You will find Him a compassionate listener, a capable healer, and a very certain deliverer.

Supplemental Materials are available to download. See Understanding Purposeful Design Bible at the front of this book for the Grade 2 URL.

© *Bible* Grade 2

11

📖 MEMORY VERSE
James 5:16

GLOSSARY WORDS
- prayer
- sin
- righteous

★ MATERIALS
Day 1:
- VA 2A Abraham Prays
- Rope *(Extension)*

Day 2:
- DM-3 Books of the Bible

Day 3:
- String or ribbon *(Extension)*

Day 4:
- Wrapped gift
- Time Line
- PP-1 The Patriarchs
- Christian magazines *(Extension)*

Day 5:
- VA 2A Abraham Prays
- BLM 2A Lesson 2 Test

♪ SONGS
Books of the Bible
Praying

TEACHER RESOURCES
Sacks, Cheryl, and Arlyn Lawrence. *Prayer-Saturated Kids: Equipping and Empowering Children in Prayer*. NavPress, 2007.

Spraggett, Daphne, and Jill Johnstone. *Window on the World*. Authentic, 2007.

STUDENT RESOURCES
Arthur, Kay, and Janna Arndt. *Lord, Teach Me to Pray for Kids*. Harvest House Publishers, 2002.

2.1 Abraham Prays
Focus: Abraham Prays for Lot

MEMORY VERSE
James 5:16

MEMORY WORK
Have students practice the Memory Verse throughout the week by using the following directions:
- Tell students to stand in a circle and hold the hand of the classmates beside them. Select one student to begin reciting the Memory Verse by saying the first word and then lightly squeezing the hand of the person to his or her left, indicating it is that student's turn. The second student then says the second word of the verse and gently squeezes the hand of the student to his or her left. Continue in this way until the verse has been said a few times.

★ PREPARATION
Display the Memory Verse so that students will have visual access to the verse throughout the week. (*Memory Work*)

Select **VA 2A Abraham Prays**. (*Directed Instruction*)

EXTENSION
1A Have a student stand close to the board. Write *God* on the board, above the student's head. Tie a long ROPE around the student's waist. Tell the student to take a big step away from the board for each sin you mention from a list of five or more. Pick up the rope. Have a few students pray for the volunteer. After each prayer, tug the rope gently, causing the student to take a step closer to the board. Explain that intercession draws people back to God.

Introduction
This week's lesson is about prayer. Begin the lesson by asking students the following questions and record each answer on a chart on the board:
- What is prayer? (**talking to God**)
- When can you pray? (**Possible answers: before meals, at bedtime, anytime**)
- Why do you pray? (**Possible answers: to ask God to help us, to thank God for what He has done, to give Him praise, to tell Him about what is going on in our lives**)

Directed Instruction ★ ↪
Display **VA 2A Abraham Prays**. Direct students to open their Bibles to **Genesis 18:17–33** and put their index finger on the beginning verse when they locate it. Explain that this is where today's Bible truth is taken from. Abraham's conversation—which was face-to-face with the Lord in this case—is a good example of what prayer is. **Prayer** means *talking to God*.

Encourage students to listen for the reason Abraham prayed as you read the paraphrase from VA 2A. Explain that the people of Sodom and Gomorrah were sinning greatly. **Sin** means *anything thought, said, or done that goes against what God requires*. God has to punish sin. Sin brings judgment. Explain that to be **righteous** means *following God wholeheartedly*. People who are righteous try not to sin, but when they do, they quickly ask for forgiveness.

Inform students that *persistence* means *not giving up*. Tell them that you are going to guide them in a responsive reading of God's answers to Abraham's requests. Explain that this reading will show them Abraham's persistence in prayer. Write *I will not destroy the town* on the board and tell students that this was the Lord's response to Abraham. Read the phrases from Abraham's prayer and invite students to answer with the Lord's response at the end of each phrase.

Responsive Reading
If 50 righteous are found there …
If 45 righteous are found there …
If 40 righteous are found there …
If 30 righteous are found there …
If 20 righteous are found there …
If only 10 righteous are found there …

Abraham was very worried for Lot, so he talked to God on behalf of his nephew. Explain to students that when they pray out of concern for other people, God hears their prayers. Note that when the Lord looked over the town, there were not even 10 people who were righteous, but the Lord remembered Abraham's prayer and did not destroy the righteous with the wicked. Lot and his family were spared. God allowed them to leave before destroying the town and all the unrighteous people in it.

Have students look up the words *prayer*, *sin*, and *righteous* in the Glossary. Chorally read the definitions.

Review
- Why did Abraham pray? (**He was concerned for Lot.**)
- How many times did Abraham ask the Lord to spare the town? (**He asked Him six times.**) Explain to students that this is persistence.
- Why did Abraham ask so many times? (**He was very concerned, or worried.**)
- How did the Lord respond to Abraham's requests? (**God said he would spare the town each time.**)
- Why did the Lord respond this way to Abraham? (**God loved Abraham.**)
- How many towns were destroyed? (**two**)

Student Page 2.1
Read the instructions aloud to the students, and have them complete the page.

APPLICATION
- Think of a time when you have been afraid or concerned about something. Use Abraham as an example to state what you should do when you are afraid or concerned. (**talk to God, bring my requests to Him**)

REINFORCEMENT
The exact location of the ancient towns of Sodom and Gomorrah has been difficult to pinpoint. Traditionally, archaeologists have positioned them at the southern tip of the Dead Sea, now covered over by water. However, some modern archaeologists have discovered remains of cities buried in ash on the northeastern side of the Dead Sea. These scientists believe that the cities include the remains of Sodom and Gomorrah. Some geologists believe that an earthquake caused balls of burning sulfur to come out of the ground, eject into the sky, and rain down over the plain cities.

DAY 1

Name _____

Abraham Prays 2.1

In Genesis 18:17–33, Abraham talks to the Lord. Draw lines to match each sentence on the left to the word on the right that best completes the sentence.

1. People of Sodom and Gomorrah were _____ and sinned greatly. • — worried
2. The Lord was _____ with the sin. • — Lot
3. The Lord told Abraham He was going to bring _____ on the towns for their sin. • — displeased
4. Abraham's nephew, _____, lived in Sodom. • — wicked
5. Abraham was very _____ because of what might happen to Lot. • — judgment
6. Abraham asked the Lord through prayer to spare _____ if there were righteous people in it. • — Sodom

7. Fill in the blank with the number representing Abraham's repeated requests to the Lord.

    50, __45__, 40, __30__, __20__, 10

8. On the following lines, tell how the story ended. What happened after Abraham prayed?

    God remembered Abraham. Lot and his family escaped the city before it was destroyed.

© Bible Grade 2   5

© Bible Grade 2

2.2 Abraham Prays

Focus: How To Pray

★ PREPARATION

Select the song "Books of the Bible" from the Grade 2 URL and **DM-3 Books of the Bible**. *(Directed Instruction)*

REINFORCEMENT

Persistence is a trait that can be taught and learned. Watching others try then fail, try then fail, then try and succeed helps elementary-age children learn that initially failing at something is not the final result. Attempting something new is easier with the attitude of "I won't quit," "I can do it," or "It's always hardest the first time, but it'll get easier." Persistence flourishes in an environment of encouragement, but not in repeated or early rescue efforts. The trial-and-error method of learning along with an optimistic attitude establish good problem-solving skills that bring understanding to the life lesson that sometimes succeeding comes after several times of failing.

Introduction

Begin the lesson by praying with your students. Ask students what they should do when they pray. (**Possible answers: close our eyes, bow our heads, focus our thoughts, kneel**) Explain that God cares more about heart attitudes in prayer than He does about the motions of their bodies. Abraham provided a great example of what a right attitude in prayer should be; he was humble and persistent.

Directed Instruction ★

Inform students that the Bible tells them that when they pray, God sees their heart attitude (1 Samuel 16:7). He knows what they think and how they feel, not just what they say. Invite a volunteer to look up and read **James 4:6–10**. Explain that God promises that if they are humble and not proud, He will come near to them, and He will hear their prayers. Explain the following: *humility* means *thinking and caring about God and others first*. (To enable better understanding, start with defining the word *proud* and then work with opposite definitions.) Explain that God wants those who love Him to be humble when they ask him for things in prayer. Ask students what it looks like to be humble. (**Possible answers: not demanding things, asking nicely, giving thanks**)

Review how many times Abraham brought his request to the Lord. (**six times**) What behavior was Abraham expressing? (**persistence**) Read **Genesis 18:27** and **18:30–32**. Ask students to share the wording that indicates Abraham's humility. (**I have taken it upon myself or I have been so bold; I am nothing but dust and ashes; please do not be angry.**)

Student Page 2.2
Direct students to complete the page.

Remind students that Abraham prayed because he was concerned about his nephew, Lot. Explain that God welcomes your students' prayers when they are worried, concerned, or afraid. God also is pleased when they pray for other people. Ask students if there is anything they are worried or concerned about, and if there is someone in their family or circle of friends for whom they would like to pray. Spend the last few minutes of the lesson leading students in prayer. Ask if any of them would like to pray for those concerns, and finish by modeling a prayer for them and the requests they mentioned.

Practice reciting books of the Bible by singing the song "Books of the Bible" from the Grade 2 URL. The lyrics are also on the URL. Display **DM-3 Books of the Bible** for students to reference while singing.

Review

- What attitude did Abraham have when he prayed? (**He was humble.**)
- When you pray, what is more important, the words that you say or the attitude you have? Why? (**My attitude is more important because God sees my heart.**)

- What quality did Abraham show when he made his request six different times? (**persistence**)

Notes:

APPLICATION
- What is a good way to express humility to God? (**Possible answers: I can ask nicely for my requests; I can thank God for what He has given; I should not demand my own way.**)
- Why should we be persistent when we pray? (**It shows God that I really care about what I am asking for.**)
- Think of some things you want to ask from God. What two qualities should you have when you pray for those things? (**humility and persistence**)

DAY 2

2.2 Abraham Prays

Match each negative behavior to the positive behavior you are supposed to have. Write the letter of the correct answer on the line.

1. demanding I get what I want __b__
2. praying for my needs only __d__
3. giving up after asking one time __a__
4. not caring for what I ask __c__

a. asking persistently
b. asking nicely for what I need
c. caring about what I am asking
d. praying for the needs of others

Use the clues in the box to find out the two behaviors that Abraham displayed when he prayed to the Lord.

| 1 = c | 2 = e | 3 = h | 4 = i | 5 = l | 6 = m | 7 = n |
| 8 = p | 9 = r | 10 = s | 11 = t | 12 = u | 13 = y | |

5.   3   12   6   4   5   4   11   13
      h   u   m   i   l   i   t   y

6.   8   2   9   10   4   10   11   2   7   1   2
      p   e   r   s   i   s   t   e   n   c   e

6

2.3 Abraham Prays

Focus: Interceding for Others

★ PREPARATION
Select the song "Praying" from the Grade 2 URL. (*Introduction*)

⟳ EXTENSION

3A Have students braid STRING or RIBBON to make wristbands as a reminder to pray for friends that are hurt, sick, or are not part of God's family.

3B Work together with an upper-grade class to correlate praying for the world with discovering new facts about a country. Assign a country of the world to each student or group of students. Students should look up basic demographic or cultural information about their country. Help them research the name of a missionary in each country. Show students how the new information can be used to pray for that country and the missionary there. For example, a student might find out that more than 60% of the population in a particular country is living in dire poverty; this, then, could lead into a prayer that God would provide through the missionary's work for those who are in need.

Introduction ★

Sing the song "Praying" from the Grade 2 URL. The lyrics are also on the URL. Ask students how the song defines praying. (**Praying is talking to Jesus [God].**)

Directed Instruction ⟱

Begin today's lesson by reading the following story:

Josh and Taylor were best friends. One day, Josh and Taylor were riding bikes in the park. As they raced down a steep hill, Taylor lost control of his bicycle and fell. Josh ran to get his parents, and both families rushed to the hospital.

Taylor had broken his leg and was going to need surgery. Josh was worried. His parents reminded him that God could help Taylor, and Josh should pray for him, which he did right then.

As Josh was praying for Taylor's leg, he had a sudden thought—Taylor was not a follower of God. This made Josh even more concerned. Starting right then, Josh prayed every day that God would make Taylor's leg better and that Taylor would soon believe in Jesus as his Savior.

Later on that year, Taylor's leg did get better, and Josh knew that God had answered his prayer. Taylor still didn't believe in Jesus, though. During Easter, Josh invited Taylor to come with him to his church. Taylor came, and he understood about and believed in Jesus for the first time. Josh realized that God had heard and answered his prayers not only for Taylor's leg, but also for Taylor to have a relationship with God.

Explain to students that God instructs them to pray in all situations (Philippians 4:6), and He also welcomes their prayers for their friends and family to know Jesus as Savior.

Student Page 2.3

Have students complete the page. Explain that because today's lesson is focused on praying for others, they will spend time in prayer using what they have learned from Abraham. Place students in pairs. Encourage them to pray for friends that are hurt, sick, or are not part of God's family. Tell students that they can pray silently or in soft voices for each other and their friends. Guide students to think about requests for their families, their country, and the world.

Review

- What is prayer? (**talking to God**)
- Why did Josh pray for his friend Taylor? (**because Taylor had hurt his leg and was not a follower of God**)

- What things should you pray about for your friends and family? (**Possible answers: their relationship with God, their health, their relationship with others**)

Notes:

APPLICATION
- Think of someone who is hurt, sick, or not part of God's family. Commit to pray for them every day this week.

REINFORCEMENT
The word *intercede* comes from two Latin words: *inter* which means *between* and *cedere* which means *go*. When believers intercede, or pray for people, they go between the people and God and bring their requests to God.

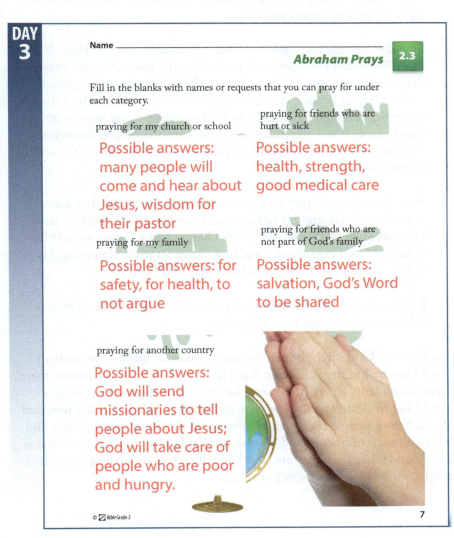

DAY 3

Name _____

Abraham Prays 2.3

Fill in the blanks with names or requests that you can pray for under each category.

praying for my church or school

Possible answers: many people will come and hear about Jesus, wisdom for their pastor

praying for friends who are hurt or sick

Possible answers: health, strength, good medical care

praying for my family

Possible answers: for safety, for health, to not argue

praying for friends who are not part of God's family

Possible answers: salvation, God's Word to be shared

praying for another country

Possible answers: God will send missionaries to tell people about Jesus; God will take care of people who are poor and hungry.

2.4 Abraham Prays
Focus: God Responds to Prayer

★ PREPARATION

Have a WRAPPED GIFT ready to show the class. *(Introduction)*

Select **PP-1 The Patriarchs**. *(Directed Instruction)*

↪ EXTENSION

4A Direct students to design a poster about prayer on construction paper. Have them draw their own illustrations or cut pictures depicting prayer from CHRISTIAN MAGAZINES, and then glue them on construction paper. Use Philippians 4:6 and 1 Thessalonians 5:17 as captions for the posters.

4B Have students write the word *PRAY* vertically on a piece of paper. Direct them to write words or sentences that they have learned about prayer by beginning with each letter from the word *PRAY*. For example, P is for Persistence.

Introduction ★

Show students a WRAPPED GIFT. Tell a story of a good gift you have received. Discuss some good gifts they have received. Explain to students that God wants them to ask Him for things they need. God loves them and answers them when they pray. Have students open their Bibles to **Matthew 7:7–11** and put their finger on the passage. Invite a volunteer to read it aloud. Ask students to share what this passage is talking about. (**God answers us when we ask, and like our parents, He likes to give us good gifts.**)

Directed Instruction ★ ↪

Tell students the following story of a man who asked much of God, and God answered:

> In the 1800s, there was a man named George Mueller, who loved God. He started an orphanage in Bristol, England, to help children who were poor, hungry, and had no one to care for them. He soon found out that helping children required a lot of money. George did what he had always done when he needed something—he prayed. He saw so many of his prayers answered, sometimes just when he needed them, sometimes many years later.

> One day, George had gathered all of the children for breakfast. It was soon discovered that there was no food in the house. George prayed that God would provide breakfast for them. As soon as the prayer ended, they all heard a knock at the door; he opened it to find the baker with enough fresh bread to feed everyone. Soon after another knock came; it was the milkman whose cart had broken down just outside the orphanage, and he wanted to give his bottles of fresh milk to the children.

> Not all of George's prayers were answered as quickly as that. George prayed every day that his father would one day put his faith in Jesus. Well, when his father was very old, George had a chance to visit his father and told him about Jesus' love. After 50 years of praying, his father finally accepted Jesus as his Savior and Lord.

> Because George Mueller faithfully prayed and trusted God, he was able to see God work in mighty ways.

Explain that God might not always answer how or when your students want Him to, but they can trust that He loves them and will answer them. Remind students about Abraham—he asked that the town of Sodom would not be destroyed if there were righteous people in it. God removed the righteous people first, then He destroyed the unrighteous people and the two towns of Sodom and Gomorrah. Explain to students that God is bigger and wiser than they are, and He will answer in the best way, which might not be how they expect or want.

Review

- Why does God answer prayer? (**because He loves me and loves to give me good gifts**)
- What was Abraham's exact prayer? (**that God would spare the town of Sodom if there were righteous people in it**)
- What was God's answer to Abraham? (**God spared the righteous.**)
- How did God answer Abraham's prayer? (**God removed Lot and his family before destroying the towns of Sodom and Gomorrah.**)

Student Page 2.4

Assist students as they complete the page.

Time Line

Guide students through the life events of Abraham by drawing their attention to the **Time Line**. Note Abraham's place on the time line, and use **PP-1 The Patriarchs** to explain Abraham's role and the importance of the promise God gave him. Use PP-1 as an informative bridge to link Abraham and Moses.

APPLICATION

- Why does God give you good gifts? (**because He loves us**)
- Does God always answer prayer how you want? Why or why not? (**No, He doesn't. He gives us what is best for us.**)
- Think of a time when you asked your parents for something, and they didn't give it to you in the way you asked for it or when you asked for it. How did that make you feel? Did something good come later? (**Answers will vary.**)
- Think of a time God answered a prayer in your life. How should you respond when you know that God answered a prayer? (**We should respond with gratitude and worship.**)

DAY 4

2.4 *Abraham Prays*

1. Draw a picture or make a list to show that God loves to give you good gifts.

Drawings will vary.

2. Draw a picture or make a list of how you can pray for yourself.

Drawings will vary.

3. Draw a picture or make a list of how you can pray for someone else.

Drawings will vary.

God promises to take care of all your needs. He wants you to ask Him for your wants too, but He might not answer those the way that you want or expect Him to.

4. Mark each of the following words with an **N** if it is a need and a **W** if it is a want.

W a new game system		**W** a lot of money
N food		**W** tickets to a baseball game
W a brand new house		**W** candy
W a new toy		**N** air
N water		**W** going to a water park

8

2.5 Abraham Prays

Focus: Review and Assessment

★ PREPARATION

Select **VA 2A Abraham Prays**.
(Lesson Review)

Make one copy of **BLM 2A Lesson 2 Test** for each student.
(Directed Instruction)

Lesson Review ★

Use **VA 2A Abraham Prays** to review the Bible truths from this lesson. Cover the following concepts:

- God was going to judge Sodom and Gomorrah because most people in those towns sinned greatly.
- Abraham prayed to the Lord because he was concerned about his nephew, Lot, who lived in Sodom.
- Prayer is talking to God.
- Sin is anything thought, said, or done that goes against what God requires.
- *Righteous* means *following God wholeheartedly*.
- Abraham showed great humility when he prayed.
- Abraham showed great persistence because he asked the Lord six different ways to spare the town of Sodom.
- God remembered Abraham and saved Lot from the destruction of Sodom.
- God answers prayer but not always in the way people expect or want.

Directed Instruction ★

Distribute a copy of **BLM 2A Lesson 2 Test** to each student. Review the instructions and format with students. Have students complete the test. When finished, read over the test and provide the answers for immediate feedback.

Notes:

Lesson Preparation
Moses Is Humble

3.0

Expected Student Outcomes

KNOW
God calls Moses to lead His people out of Egypt.

DO
Students will:
- identify the speaker in the conversation between God and Moses and explain how they speak to God
- recognize humility and pride
- acknowledge God's power through the Ten Plagues
- select true statements about the first Passover

APPLY
Students will identify that humility is an essential quality of leadership and demonstrate humility in their behavior.

Lesson Outline

I. God speaks to Moses (Ex 2:1–4:28, Num 12:3)
  A. Conversations with God
II. Moses humbly leads (Ex 2:1–4:28, Num 12:3, Eph 6:6–8, Rom 12:8)
  A. Compare and contrast humility and pride
III. God sends 10 plagues (Ex 4:29–12:31)
  A. God shows His power
IV. God delivers the Hebrews (Ex 12:1–31)

♥ TEACHER'S HEART

Moses, a bold, educated member of Pharaoh's court had the world at his fingertips. Yet, his concern for his poor, enslaved brothers was inspiring. He could have easily been prideful and avoided them. Moses witnessed the beating of a Hebrew slave by an Egyptian, and it marked Moses.

Moses' flight to the land of Midian prepared him for humble service. He became a shepherd. Shepherds in Bible times lived in lonely places caring for smelly sheep. They were considered insignificant people. Oftentimes, when a person is alone and humble, he or she can hear God more readily. Moses may have spent more time with God out in the desert with sheep than he did all his time growing up in Pharaoh's court.

As a teacher in education and an authority in what you do, at times it is hard to remember humility. When you humble yourself, willingly say, "Here I am," and trust God, He draws you near and guides you in teaching and serving your students. Just as God appeared to Moses in his humble state, God comes to you. As a humble servant of God ready to listen and do God's work, the world is at your fingertips.

MEMORY VERSE
Exodus 4:12

GLOSSARY WORDS
- humility
- plague
- Passover

MATERIALS

Day 1:
- VA 3A The Burning Bush

Day 2:
- DM-1 Character Traits

Day 3:
- BLM 3A Readers Theater: Ten Plagues (*Extension*)
- PP-2 Those Pesky Plagues (*Extension*)

Day 4:
- Crackers (unleavened, if possible)

Day 5:
- VA 3A The Burning Bush
- BLM 3B Lesson 3 Test

♪ SONGS
Little Is Much
Plagues (*Extension*)

TEACHER RESOURCES
Kimmel, Eric A. *Wonders and Miracles: A Passover Companion.* Scholastic Press, 2004.
Rubin, Barry and Steffi Rubin. *The Passover Haggadah,* rev. ed. Lederer Books, 2005.

STUDENT RESOURCES
Koralek, Jenny. *The Moses Basket*. Wm. B. Eerdmans Publishing Co., 2003.
Mackenzie, Carine. *Moses the Leader: Used by God*. Christian Focus Publications, 2008.

Supplemental Materials are available to download. See Understanding Purposeful Design Bible at the front of this book for the Grade 2 URL.

© *Bible* Grade 2

3.1 Moses Is Humble
Focus: God Speaks to Moses

MEMORY VERSE
Exodus 4:12

MEMORY WORK
- Display the Memory Verse in the classroom. Have students stand and read the verse several times together. Then, prompt students to watch as you point to each student. Tell students that the first person you point to is to say the first word of the verse and be seated, the second person should say the second word of the verse, be seated, and so on, until all the words of the verse have been spoken in order. Repeat the verse until all students have had a turn.

★ PREPARATION
Select **VA 3A The Burning Bush**. (*Directed Instruction*)

EXTENSION
1A Instruct students to find the word *holy* in a dictionary. Ask them to put the definition in their own words and discuss the meaning. *Holy* means *pure, or set apart for service to God*. Walk students outside to a patch of grass, bush, or place where there is dirt. Ask students if there is anything special about this place. (**No.**) Tell them that the ground Moses was on when he talked to God at the burning bush was special because it was holy. It was set apart since God was there. God's heart longs for a relationship with everyone as with Moses, but He is a holy God, set apart from any type of sin. God allows people to worship and have a relationship with Him through acceptance of Jesus' redemptive death on the cross. Through His salvation, people can forever worship Holy God.

Introduction
Write the following words on the board: *donkey, gentle voice, people, angel, burning bush*. Select volunteers to read the words. Teach that God used all these things to speak to people in the Bible! He spoke to a man named *Balaam* by talking through his donkey (Numbers 22:28). Elijah heard God in a gentle voice (I Kings 19:10–13). God told his servant Jonah what to say to the people of Ninevah (2 Kings 14:25). Through the angel Gabriel, God told Mary the good news of Jesus (Luke 1:26–33). Inform students that today they will learn about God speaking through the flames within a burning bush to a man named *Moses*.

Directed Instruction ★ ↻
Display **VA 3A The Burning Bush** and read the back for today's Bible truth. Instruct students there are times when their parents may ask them to complete a task that is difficult. Discuss how sometimes students may be fearful that the job is too big for them to handle. At times, they may give excuses why they cannot do a particular task. Maybe they think someone else would be better at doing the job. Expound on how Moses must have felt this way, because he responded to God with the same excuses.

Inform students that when God first spoke to Moses, he replied, "Here I am." This response showed that Moses was willing to listen. Explain that at times students, too, may be willing to listen to their parents or teacher, yet still be a little nervous or fearful about doing what is asked of them.

Remind students that God talked to Moses through the flames within the burning bush and told Moses to go to Pharaoh and lead the people out of Egypt. Moses told God what he was concerned about. He asked God, "What if the people don't believe me?" God told Moses He would do miracles that they would believe (Exodus 4:8). Next, he asked God, "What if I don't speak well?" God told Moses He would help him speak and teach Moses what to say (Exodus 4:12). Moses also asked God, "Can you send someone else?" God told Moses He would give him Aaron, Moses' brother, to speak for Moses (Exodus 4:14–16).

God and Moses had a conversation with each other. God answered each of Moses' questions and concerns. God helped Moses and gave him all he needed to complete the job. God also speaks to people today. He speaks through His Word, the Bible, and when people pray. God tells people everything they need to know. God also speaks to children through their parents, pastors, teachers, and other people. God shows Himself to people in nature and all that He has made. The God of the universe loves everyone enough to let them talk to Him, too. They need to be ready to say, "Here I am," and listen as God speaks. As people have a conversation with God, they can be assured God will help them.

Student Page 3.1
Read the directions and text on the page. Have students complete the page.

Review

- How did Moses respond when God spoke to him? (**Possible answers: Moses listened to God; Moses said, "Here I am."**)
- How did God speak to Moses? (**He spoke to him from the flames within the burning bush.**)
- What did God say to Moses' arguments when God called him? (**Possible answers: God promised to be with Moses and perform mighty miracles; God told Moses he would teach him what to say; God said He would give Moses a helper—Aaron—to help speak for him.**)
- Why did God pick Moses to lead the Hebrew people? (**Possible answers: Moses was willing to listen to God; Moses showed humility.**)

Notes:

APPLICATION

- How do you know Moses cared about the Hebrew slaves? (**He killed an Egyptian who had been hitting a Hebrew.**)
- What was Moses worried about when God called him? (**Possible answers: He didn't feel able to do it; he thought other people would be better doing it; he didn't know how to tell them who God is.**)
- How does God speak to you? (**Possible answers: He tells me things through His Word; He talks to me through my parents.**)
- When God asks you to do something, how do you know you will be able to do it? (**Possible answers: God will give me the strength and help me do it; I can trust God to help me.**)

DAY 1

Name _____

Moses Is Humble | 3.1

In Exodus 3, God spoke to Moses from the flames within the burning bush. Moses spoke to God about what God asked him to do. Fill in the circle to show who said the following. Answer the question at the bottom of the page.

1. "People won't believe me."
   ● Moses   ○ God

2. "I can't speak well."
   ● Moses   ○ God

3. "I will help you speak and teach you what to say."
   ○ Moses   ● God

4. "Can you send someone else?"
   ● Moses   ○ God

5. "I will do miracles that they may believe."
   ○ Moses   ● God

6. "I will give you Aaron as a helper to speak for you."
   ○ Moses   ● God

7. How or when do you speak to God?

Possible answers: I talk to God through prayer;
I talk to God when I am alone; I talk to God about my
troubles; I talk to God all the time.

© Bible Grade 2

3.2 Moses Is Humble

Focus: Moses Humbly Leads

★ PREPARATION

Have available **DM-1 Character Traits**. (*Introduction*)

Select the song "Little Is Much" from the Grade 2 URL. (*Directed Instruction*)

↶ EXTENSION

2A Brainstorm with the class what it looks like to be humble. Give ideas to help students by mentioning the following: pick up other people's trash, wipe the lunch tables for another class, or open a door for someone else. Choose one act of service to do together. After the class has completed the act of service, ask them if they felt like a leader or a follower. Encourage students to think about how leading with humility helps others.

Introduction ★

Display **DM-1 Character Traits** and explain that **humility** means *thinking and caring about God and others first*. Guide a discussion on ways God works in and through His people when they are humble.

Directed Instruction ★ ↶

Read the following statements and ask students to decide which one stands out from the rest:
- The teacher ate a snack.
- The principal watched the game.
- The king served the preschoolers lunch. (**This statement stands out.**)
- The athlete ran around the track.

The teacher, principal, and athlete were all doing something for themselves and their own benefit. Discuss how the king was serving and thinking of others more than himself, so he modeled humility as a leader.

Remind students that Moses was raised in Pharaoh's palace. Being raised in Pharaoh's palace made Moses very important compared to being raised as a Hebrew slave. Yet, Moses cared about his Hebrew friends and family. Moses could have easily avoided the Hebrews, as he was thought of as an important Egyptian.

Review with students that after protecting the Hebrew slave, Moses fled for his life to the land of Midian and became a shepherd. Inform students that shepherds in the Bible lived in lonely places with smelly sheep. Their job was not considered as important as other jobs. Even though Moses had lived in the pharaoh's court, he was humble and did not consider himself better than others (Numbers 12:3). It was when Moses was taking care of sheep that God appeared to him, spoke to him, and instructed Moses to be a leader for the Hebrews in captivity. When God first spoke to Moses, Moses' response was, "Here I am." God had a plan to use Moses as a leader. Moses had been set apart for a job as a leader to go to Egypt and deliver the Hebrew people out of slavery.

Inform students that humble people are not proud and that they do not boast about what they can do. Humble people trust God to help achieve what God has asked them to do. Teach the following acrostic to help students remember what it is to be humble:

H elping to
U plift
M any others
B efore myself by
L oving God and
E veryone else

24

Student Page 3.2
Read the directions and text on the page. Have students complete the page. Conclude the lesson by singing together the song "Little Is Much" from the Grade 2 URL.

Review
- What would it have been like for Moses to have been raised in Pharaoh's court? (**Possible answers: Moses would have been very important; Moses would have been given many of the best things in life; Moses would have had many servants.**)
- Why was it strange that Moses helped the Hebrew slave? (**Possible answers: He was raised in the Pharaoh's palace and was seen as more important than the slaves; He didn't have to help the slave.**)
- How was Moses' life different when he went to the land of Midian? (**Possible answers: He now lived in a lonely place and took care of sheep; he had to trust God to supply his needs; he went from a very important position to an ordinary one.**)

APPLICATION
- Why do you think God called Moses *humble* (Numbers 12:3)? (**Possible answers: Moses was a great man but thought of and cared about God and others first.**)
- How would you describe a person showing humility? (**Possible answers: A humble person looks to God for help; a humble person thinks of and cares about God and others first; a person showing humility does not brag about himself.**)
- Why is it important for leaders to be humble? (**Leaders need to be humble so they can trust God for answers to help others and not rely on themselves.**)
- How can you be a humble leader? (**Possible answers: I can think of and care about God and others first; I can ask God to help me to lead; I can serve others before myself.**)

REINFORCEMENT
The Hebrew slaves made bricks, which was a dirty, rigorous job (Exodus 1:14). Back then, many structures were made of brick, so thousands of bricks were needed all the time. The slaves worked long and hard in the hot sun. Hebrews had to gather straw, carry mud and water, shape bricks by hand, let the bricks dry, and then carry them to the job site.

DAY 2

3.2 Moses Is Humble

Moses knew he needed God's help. Moses showed humility and that is why God used him as a leader. Read James 4:6, and answer the questions below.

1. To whom does God give grace?
   God gives grace to the humble.

2. What do you think it means to be filled with pride, or to be proud?
   Possible answers: to not trust God, to do things my own way, to think I am better than others, to be bossy

Look at each picture. Beside each picture, write **humble** if humility is being shown or **proud** if pride is being shown.

3.  humble

5. humble

4.  proud

6. humble

| 3.3 | # Moses Is Humble
Focus: God Sends 10 Plagues |

⤻ EXTENSION

3A Give each student a copy of **BLM 3A Readers Theater: Ten Plagues**. Assign reading parts to students to assist in review of the Bible truth.

3B Select **PP-2 Those Pesky Plagues** to use for a discussion about the Ten Plagues.

Introduction

Instruct students to locate the word *plague* in their Glossary. A **plague** is *a sudden disaster or sickness that spreads quickly and causes harm*. Inform students that in today's Bible truth they will learn how God used plagues to help deliver the Hebrews, who were also known as *Israelites*.

Directed Instruction ⤻

Share this story based on Exodus 4:29–12:31. When Moses and Aaron arrived in Egypt, they told the Hebrew leaders that God had promised to free them from slavery. The pharaoh of Egypt would not let the Hebrews leave, so God began showing His power through 10 different plagues.

1. God told Moses to have Aaron raise his walking stick and strike the river's water. It turned to blood, and all the fish died! The Egyptians and their animals could not drink from the river now.

2. God sent frogs up out of the water. They covered the land of Egypt. Frogs were everywhere—in the houses, in the bedrooms, on the beds, on the people, in their ovens, and even in their food bowls!

3. Aaron used his walking stick to strike the dust of the ground. God sent little tiny bugs called *lice* (*gnats*). They bit the people and their animals.

4. God sent swarms of biting flies that filled the Egyptians' homes and covered the ground. Thick swarms of flies came and bothered the Egyptians, but not the Hebrews. No swarms of flies were in the land of Goshen where the Hebrews lived.

5. A terrible disease made all the animals sick. The Egyptians' horses, donkeys, oxen, and sheep began to die, but not those of the Hebrews.

6. God told Moses to toss ashes into the sky. When the ashes settled back down and became dust, the dust caused the Egyptians and their remaining animals to break out with painful sores called *boils*.

7. God sent very large, heavy hail. He told Moses to warn the pharaoh that it was coming and to bring animals and people inside. Any animal or person left outside would die because of this hail. Egypt had never seen hail like this before. However, there was no hail in the land of Goshen.

8. After the hail had beaten down the crops, God caused a wind to blow all day and night from the east. The next day, millions of locusts, insects similar to grasshoppers, were there and ate what was left of the crops.

9. God caused heavy darkness for three days. The Egyptians could not see one another; however, all the Hebrews had light in their homes.

10. God sent the tenth plague, and it was worse than all the rest! At midnight, all the firstborn sons of the Egyptians and the firstborn of

their animals died. God had given the Hebrews special instructions so death would pass over their homes. Right before the Hebrews left Egypt, they ate a meal known as *the Feast of the Passover*. The Hebrews followed God's directions and then waited. After this happened, Pharaoh told the Hebrews to leave Egypt. The Hebrews traveled toward Canaan. This was the land that God had promised to them.

Student Page 3.3
Assist students in reading the instructions and completing the page.

Review
- How did God show His power and deliver the Hebrews? (**Possible answers: God sent 10 plagues to convince Pharaoh to let the people go; God used Moses to lead.**)
- In what ways did God protect the Hebrews? (**Possible answers: The Hebrews' animals did not die from disease; the lives of the firstborn sons of the Hebrews were spared.**)
- Which plague convinced Pharaoh to let the Hebrews go? (**the tenth plague—the death of the firstborn son**)

APPLICATION
- Pharaoh said no to Moses 10 times. How do you think Moses felt? (**Possible answers: He was discouraged; he was frustrated; Moses wondered what God was doing; he felt like a failure.**)
- Why do you think Pharaoh was so stubborn? (**Possible answers: He liked having many slaves; he liked having power over people; he didn't believe God could do any of those miracles; he was full of pride.**)
- God asked Moses to do a very hard job. What do you learn from this? (**Possible answers: God may ask me to do something that is hard; I can trust in God to help me do hard things; God can help me to bring about change.**)
- What hard job has God asked you to do? (**Possible answers: to obey my parents, to help someone who was sick, to tell someone else about Jesus**)

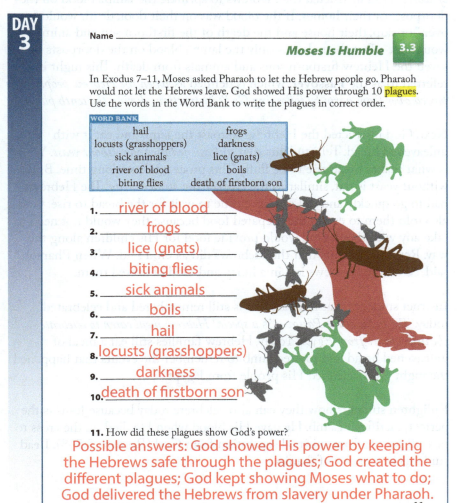

3.4 Moses Is Humble

Focus: God Delivers the Hebrews

★ PREPARATION

Have an unleavened CRACKER on hand for each student. (*Introduction*)

↪ EXTENSION

4A Write the following prompts from today's lesson on the board:
- Moses told the Hebrew people to get ready to go.
- God told Moses to tell the Hebrew people to sacrifice a lamb.
- Moses told the Hebrew people how God would keep them safe.

Direct volunteers to retell the Bible truth in their own words using the prompts.

4B Listen to and sing the song "Plagues" from the Grade 2 URL.

Introduction ★

Simulate the night in which the Hebrews had to leave Egypt quickly. Ask students to pretend to put on any clothing that they might need to go outside. Direct them to come quickly and sit on the floor of the classroom. If possible, turn off the lights. Tell students to be very still, quiet, and to wait. Give them a CRACKER to eat. Explain to students that the night the Hebrews had to leave Egypt may have been a little like this. They had to be still and ready to do what God instructed them to do to quickly get out of Egypt. The Hebrews also needed to eat what God told them to eat. Tell students that the cracker they ate is similar to what the Hebrews had to eat as they waited.

Directed Instruction ↩

Remind students that God sent 10 plagues to afflict Egypt. Before the tenth plague, Moses and Aaron went to Pharaoh one more time and asked Pharaoh to let the Hebrew people go. God gave directions to the Hebrews to prepare to leave quickly. They had to be ready. The night they were to go, God told them to sacrifice a lamb. *Sacrifice* means *to give up something of worth*. God instructed the Hebrews to sprinkle the lamb's blood on the doorposts of their homes. If the blood was on their door, death would "pass over," or skip, their house and the death of the firstborn son and animals would not affect them. It was only the lamb's blood on the doorposts that saved the Hebrew firstborn sons and animals from death. This night is referred to as the **Passover**, which is defined as *when the Hebrew people were passed over from harm by following God's instructions during the tenth plague*.

Next, God instructed the Hebrews to roast the lamb and eat it with unleavened bread. Tell students that *unleavened* means *without yeast*. Yeast is what makes bread rise to be fluffy. This process takes a long time. Bread without yeast is flat, similar to the cracker the students ate. The Hebrews had to go quickly and did not have time to wait for the bread to rise. God also told them to eat all the prepared food because they would not need to take any with them. God would provide food for His children along the way. Remind students that the Hebrews did as God said. When Pharaoh said, "Go!" the Hebrews left in a hurry and God delivered them.

Instruct students that the Passover is still remembered and celebrated today. *The Feast of the Passover* is *a special Hebrew meal eaten to celebrate the deliverance from Egypt*. Today, Hebrew families still eat a meal of unleavened bread and roasted lamb to remember the events that happened the night God delivered His people from Egypt.

Enlighten students how they can also celebrate today because Jesus is the perfect, sacrificial Lamb. He gave His blood when He died on the cross to save all people from spiritual separation from God (Romans 5:5–8). Lead students in a prayer of thanks.

Student Page 3.4

Read the directions and the text on the page. Have students independently complete the page.

Review

- What did the Hebrews have to do to be ready to leave quickly? (**Possible answers: eat unleavened bread, get their houses in order**)
- What does *sacrifice* mean? (*To sacrifice* means *to give up something of worth*.)
- What did God ask the Hebrews to sacrifice? (**a lamb**)
- How were the Hebrews spared from the death of their firstborn son and their firstborn animals? (**They put the blood of the sacrificed lamb on the doorpost.**)

Notes:

DAY 4

3.4 Moses Is Humble

Moses humbly followed God so that he could lead the Hebrews out of Egypt. God gave the Hebrews clear directions about the Passover. Read the sentences about the Passover from Exodus 12. Write **T** for true and **F** for false before each sentence.

1. **F** Abraham told the Hebrews to leave.
2. **T** The Hebrews had to leave quickly.
3. **F** God told the Hebrews to sacrifice a cow.
4. **F** The tenth plague was biting flies.
5. **T** Lamb's blood on the doorposts saved the Hebrews' firstborn sons and animals.
6. **T** Unleavened bread is bread that does not have yeast.
7. **F** When Pharaoh told the Hebrews to go, they stayed.
8. **T** The Passover is still celebrated today.
9. **T** Aaron spoke to Pharaoh for Moses.
10. A Hebrew celebration to remember God freeing the Hebrews from slavery in Egypt is called the Feast of the **Passover**.

APPLICATION

- Why do Hebrew people today still celebrate the Passover? (**They celebrate the Passover to remember that God delivered His people from slavery in Egypt.**)
- What part of the Passover was most important to save the Hebrews? (**The lamb's blood on the doorpost was most important to save the Hebrews.**)
- Do you still have to sacrifice a lamb today to be saved? Why or why not? (**No, Jesus was the sacrifice for us as He died on the cross to save us.**) Explain that just as the Hebrews had to trust that the lamb's blood would save them, so people today must trust that Jesus' blood will save them.
- God delivered the Hebrews and protected them in a special way. What does God deliver you from today? (**Possible answers: sin, harm, fear**)

REINFORCEMENT

The Passover is still celebrated in many Jewish households today. To prepare for the Passover celebration, the mother of the family clears the house of all yeast (leaven) products. She leaves a few yeast-bearing crumbs around the house for all to see. The father searches throughout the house and collects the crumbs with a wooden spoon and feather. This act parallels the Passover custom of a Jewish father searching for leaven with an oil lamp as his guide. The custom is from Zephaniah 1:12, where God promised to search the Jerusalem households for sin. In Scripture, leaven is a symbol for sin.

3.5 Moses Is Humble

Focus: Review and Assessment

★ PREPARATION

Select **VA 3A The Burning Bush**.
(*Lesson Review*)

Make one copy of **BLM 3B Lesson 3 Test** for each student.
(*Directed Instruction*)

Lesson Review ★

Use **VA 3A The Burning Bush** and the information on the Ten Plagues from Lesson 3.3 to review the Bible truths from this lesson. Cover the following concepts:

• Pharaoh's daughter rescued Moses and raised him as her son.
• Moses went to the land of Midian after he killed an Egyptian for hitting a Hebrew slave.
• God spoke to Moses through the flames within a burning bush while Moses was tending sheep in the desert.
• God promised to be with Moses to help Moses lead the Hebrews, or Israelites, out of Egypt.
• God told Moses that He would tell him what to say.
• Moses was a humble leader because he looked to God for help and served others.
• God allowed Aaron, Moses' brother, to help Moses speak with others.
• God sent ten plagues to convince Pharaoh to let the Hebrew people go.
• Pharaoh let the Hebrews go when the firstborn sons and firstborn animals of the Egyptians were killed.
• God gave the Hebrews a way to escape the tenth plague—they were passed over when they had the blood of the lamb on their doorposts.
• Hebrew people continue to celebrate the Passover today.

Directed Instruction ★

Distribute a copy of **BLM 3B Lesson 3 Test** to each student. Read the directions and pronounce any difficult words. Have students complete the test.

Notes:

30

Lesson Preparation
Moses and Miriam Praise God

4.0

Expected Student Outcomes

KNOW
Moses and Miriam praise God after the Red Sea Crossing.

DO
Students will:
- explain how God provided for and protected the Israelites with the pillar of cloud and fire
- illustrate the events of the crossing of the Red Sea
- write their own praise to God
- highlight the words of praise that describe God in a traditional hymn
- write a poem or song of praise to God

APPLY
Students will praise and worship God in a variety of ways.

Lesson Outline

I. The Israelites leave Egypt (Ex 12:31–14:20)
   A. God provided for them
   B. God protected them
II. The Israelites cross the Red Sea (Ex 14:21–31)
III. Acts of worship (Ex 15:1–21)
   A. With attitudes
   B. With words
   C. With actions
IV. Praise God (Ps 145)
   A. For who He is

♥ TEACHER'S HEART

Have you ever stopped to consider that the God who knit the heavens together is the same God who forms children in the womb? He is the one who paints the sky every night with rays of color. He is the one who forms the beetles, butterflies, flowers of all colors, trees, oceans, and mountains. This God is the Creator and Sustainer of the entire universe. He is majestic and wonderful, the Author of Life. He is God, whose finger can part a sea, whose words can deliver a nation, whose gaze can change a heart.

Laura Story, who wrote the praise song "Indescribable," once said, "What words could mere humans give to express His grandeur? Any praises we lift to Him are our feeble attempts at capturing a small glimpse of the magnitude of who God is." Though your praise might be merely feeble attempts, God delights in hearing it nonetheless. He loves to hear you praise who He is and thank Him for what He has done. So the next time you hear a young child laugh, you feel a gentle touch, you see a wonder of beauty, and your breath is caught in your throat, take a moment to praise and thank the Wonderful Creator behind the moment.

Supplemental Materials are available to download. See Understanding Purposeful Design Bible at the front of this book for the Grade 2 URL.

📖 MEMORY VERSE
Exodus 15:2

GLOSSARY WORDS
- chariot
- miracle

★ MATERIALS

Day 1:
- VA 4A The Red Sea Crossing, poster board, candle, lighter
- BLM 4A Pillar in the Desert, cotton balls, red and orange tissue paper (Extension)

Day 2:
- VA 4A The Red Sea Crossing, walking stick
- Pan, index cards, balls, drinking glass (Extension)

Day 3:
- Potpourri; bowl; DM-1 Character Traits; dried beans; paper plates; cylindrical containers; yarn; aluminum pie plates; empty, aluminum, soft drink cans

Day 4:
- DM-4 God's Attributes, BLM 4B God's Attributes
- DM-4 God's Attributes, BLM 4B God's Attributes, BLM 4C Banner (Extension)

Day 5:
- VA 4A The Red Sea Crossing
- BLM 4D Lesson 4 Test

♪ SONGS
You Are My God

TEACHER RESOURCES
Giglio, Louie. *Indescribable*. DVD. EMI CMG Distribution, 2012.

STUDENT RESOURCES
Hillsong Kids. *Supernatural*. CD. Integrity Music, 2013.

4.1 Moses and Miriam Praise God
Focus: The Israelites Leave Egypt

MEMORY VERSE
Exodus 15:2

MEMORY WORK
- Encourage students to create, in groups, their own tune to the Memory Verse and present to the class.
- Tell students to say the Memory Verse out loud as they put the puzzle of the verse together.

★ PREPARATION
Write the Memory Verse on construction paper, and cut the paper into unique shapes to form puzzle pieces. (*Memory Work*)

Select **VA 4A The Red Sea Crossing**, and cut out a POSTER BOARD to look like a big cloud. Have a CANDLE and a LIGHTER on hand. (*Directed Instruction*)

EXTENSION
1A Duplicate enough copies of **BLM 4A Pillar in the Desert** for each student. Provide students with COTTON BALLS, RED AND ORANGE TISSUE PAPER, scissors, and glue. Use BLM 4A as a visual reminder of how God provided for and protected the Israelites.

1B Instruct students to write a journal entry on how they would have felt and responded if they were on the shores of the Red Sea with the Egyptians chasing after them in chariots.

Introduction
Ask students why they might need a suitcase. (**Possible answers: to go on a trip, to store precious items**) Brainstorm with students what they might bring to different destinations. Examples of destinations could be the mountains, the beach, an amusement park, or Grandma and Grandpa's house. (**Possible answers: favorite toy, stuffed animal, jacket, swimsuit**) Ask students how they would pack differently if they knew they were not returning. (**Possible answers: They would only pack things of importance; they would pack needed provisions for the long trip.**)

Directed Instruction ★
Today's lesson begins as the *Israelites*, also known as *Hebrews*, are all packed and on their way out of Egypt. Remind students that God had spared the Israelites from the last plague through the Passover, but the Egyptians had lost all their firstborn sons and the firstborn of their animals. After that, Pharaoh had commanded the Israelites to go. Encourage students to listen attentively to the Bible truth to discover how God provided for the Hebrews as they were leaving Egypt. Read **VA 4A The Red Sea Crossing**.

Ask students how God provided for the Israelites as they left Egypt. (**God provided them with a pillar of cloud by day and fire by night.**) Explain that the word *pillar* means *a long, upright column*. Illustrate a pillar of cloud by displaying the cloud cut from the POSTER BOARD. Hold the cloud vertically to show a column. To represent the pillar of fire, turn out the lights and light a CANDLE with the LIGHTER. Explain that the pillar would have been large enough for all of the Hebrew people to see it. God used the pillar to show His people the direction they should go. The cloud also gave them shade during the day; it gave them light at night.

God also used the pillar to protect the Israelites. Direct students to close their eyes and picture the situation the Israelites were in. There were a lot of Israelites. They were all packed and probably moving very slowly. God had directed them with the pillar of cloud straight to the shore of the Red Sea. The water was in front of them and there were rocky areas on both sides. The Egyptians had changed their minds, and were now chasing after the Hebrews in chariots. Invite a student to look up the definition of *chariot* in the Glossary. A **chariot** is *a two-wheeled vehicle, without seats, that is pulled by a horse*. Point out the Egyptian chariots on VA 4A. Remind students that there were at least 600 Egyptian chariots chasing after God's people.

Invite a volunteer to find and read **Exodus 14:19–20**. Ask how God used the pillar of cloud to protect the Israelites. (**God moved the pillar of cloud between the Israelites and the Egyptians so that the Israelites had light, and the Egyptians had darkness and could not move.**) Instruct students to think of a scary situation they have been in, and share about how God protected them.

Student Page 4.1
Read the instructions and have students complete the page.

Review
- How did God provide direction, light, and shade for the Israelites? **(He sent a pillar of cloud by day and fire by night.)**
- How did God protect the Israelites from the Egyptians? **(He moved the pillar of cloud between them, giving light to one and darkness to the other.)**
- How were the Egyptians chasing after the Hebrew people? **(The Egyptians—Pharaoh's horsemen and his army—were in chariots as they chased after the Hebrews.)**

Notes:

APPLICATION
- How has God provided for you? **(Answers will vary.)**
- How has God protected you and your family? **(Answers will vary.)**
- How does God want you to respond to His provision and the ways He has protected you? **(Possible answers: thank Him, praise Him, worship Him)**

DAY 1

Name _____

Moses and Miriam Praise God 4.1

Answer the questions according to the Bible truth from Exodus 13:17–14:3.

1. How did the pillar of cloud and fire <u>provide</u> for the Israelites after they left Egypt?

   The pillar of cloud directed the Israelites where to go. It also gave shade during the day and light during the night.

2. How did the pillar of cloud and fire <u>protect</u> the Israelites from the chariots of the Egyptians?

   The pillar moved between the Israelites and Egyptians giving light to one and darkness to the other.

3. How has God provided for you?

   Answers will vary.

4. How has God protected you?

   Answers will vary.

4.2 Moses and Miriam Praise God
Focus: The Israelites Cross the Red Sea

PREPARATION
Select **VA 4A The Red Sea Crossing**. Bring a **WALKING STICK**. (*Introduction*)

EXTENSION
2A Fill a **PAN** with water. Direct students to try to part and hold back the water in the pan by using pencils, **INDEX CARDS**, **BALLS**, and a **DRINKING GLASS**. Ask students if they were successful in holding back the water. They might be somewhat successful by forming some sort of wall. Man-made structures, such as dams, are successful at holding back water, but they take years to build. Remind students that God was able to hold back the waters of the Red Sea instantly with His mighty power alone.

Introduction ★
Show students **VA 4A The Red Sea Crossing**. Remind students that the Israelites were in a very scary situation with the Egyptians close behind. Instruct students to act out the parting of the Red Sea. Choose several students to act as *the water*, one to be *Moses*, several to be *Israelites*, and several to be *Egyptians*. Position the students acting as *the water* together in front of *Moses*; position the *Israelites* behind *Moses*, and the *Egyptians* farther back. Give *Moses* a **WALKING STICK**. As *Moses* does this, the students representing *the water* should separate, and the *Israelites* should pass through. Once the last *Israelite* has gone through, direct the *Egyptians* to enter *the water*. Direct *Moses* to lower his staff, and *the water* to come together surrounding the *Egyptians*.

Directed Instruction
Explain that, at some point, all people get into situations that are impossible for them to get out of on their own, and they need someone to rescue them. Likewise, the Israelites were in a position where they needed God to rescue them. God had protected the Israelites from the Egyptians with the pillar of cloud between them, but the Israelites still had to move. Invite a volunteer to read **Exodus 14:10–14**. Ask students how the Israelites felt and responded to the situation they were in. (**They were terrified and said it would have been better to serve the Egyptians than to die in the desert.**) What did Moses tell the Israelites to do? (**He told them to not be afraid, to be still, and to watch God fight for them.**)

Explain that God was about to perform a huge **miracle**. Define for students that a *miracle* is *an act of God that is impossible by human or natural causes*. In the Old Testament, it says that no one was able to perform as many miracles through God's mighty power as Moses (Deuteronomy 34:10–12). Remind students that the 10 plagues and the pillar of cloud and fire were already really big miracles, but God was not done! Moses and the Israelites were standing at the shore of the Red Sea, and God was going to show His power in a huge way. Read **Exodus 14:18**. Explain that there are two reasons God performs miracles—so that He will get glory (honor), and people will know that He is God.

Invite a student to read **Exodus 14:29–31**. Ask students how the response of the Israelites was different after they walked across on dry ground and the Egyptians did not. (**They were in awe of God and trusted God.**)

Student Page 4.2
Direct students to complete the page.

Review
- What is a miracle? (**an act of God that is impossible by human or natural causes**)
- What miracle did God perform at the Red Sea? (**He parted the waters, allowing the Israelites to cross on dry ground. The Egyptian army chased the Israelites into the Red Sea and drowned.**)

- What are two reasons that God performs miracles? (**to get glory and honor for Himself and to show people that He is God**)
- How did the Israelites respond when they crossed on dry ground? (**They were in awe of God and put their trust in God.**)

Notes:

APPLICATION

- Can you recall a time you have seen or heard of a miracle? (**Answers will vary.**)
- How do those miracles make you feel about God? (**Possible answers: that He is really big, that He is powerful, that He is worthy of praise**)
- How should we respond when we see God do miracles? (**Possible answers: praise Him, show reverence to Him, trust Him**)

REINFORCEMENT

Egyptian chariots were made with two wooden wheels and a center axle made out of metal. There were no springs, so when the chariots hit rocky terrain, they would often tip over, the axle would break, or the wheels would fall off. Exodus 14:24–25 says that God threw the Egyptians into confusion and the wheels of their chariots came off. The wheels coming off would have been normal for rocky terrain, but it was not normal for them to come off all at once.

DAY 2

4.2 *Moses and Miriam Praise God*

1. Draw a picture of the Israelites being chased by the Egyptians at the edge of the Red Sea. Make sure to include the Egyptian chariots behind them.

Drawings will vary.

2. Draw a picture of the miracle of the Israelites crossing the Red Sea on dry ground.

Drawings will vary.

3. Draw a picture of the Israelites after they crossed the Red Sea, saved from the Egyptians.

Drawings will vary.

14 © *Bible* Grade 2

4.3 Moses and Miriam Praise God
Focus: Acts of Worship

★ PREPARATION

Obtain some POTPOURRI and place it into a BOWL. (*Introduction*)

Select **DM-1 Character Traits**. (*Directed Instruction*)

Have DRIED BEANS, PAPER PLATES, CYLINDRICAL CONTAINERS (such as oatmeal containers, coffee cans, or plastic cartons), YARN, ALUMINUM PIE PLATES, and EMPTY, ALUMINUM, SOFT DRINK CANS on hand. Select the song "You Are My God" from the Grade 2 URL. (*Directed Instruction*)

↪ EXTENSION

3A Cut several strips of colored construction paper and hand one or two strips to each student. Direct students to write on the middle section of the paper the things for which the Israelites praised God, and reasons they themselves can praise God. Attach the strips together to form a paper chain. Use the chain to decorate the classroom to remind students of reasons to praise God.

Introduction ★

Carry the BOWL of POTPOURRI around the room so that each student can smell it. Ask students to describe the fragrance. Explain to students that praise is a sweet-smelling fragrance to God (Numbers 29:6, 2 Corinthians 2:15). Explain that *praising God* means *describing God by His many qualities*. Mention that *praise* and *worship* are two words often used together or in place of the other. There are many ways to praise God.

Directed Instruction ★ ↪

Review the Bible truths from Lessons 4.1 and 4.2—how God made the way possible for the Israelites to leave Egypt and cross the Red Sea. Ask students to listen for ways that Moses and Miriam praised God as you read **Exodus 15:1–21** aloud.

Make a two-column chart on the board with the headings shown below. Brainstorm a list of reasons why Moses, Miriam, and the Israelites praised God. Write them on the board. Have students describe some ways that Moses, Miriam, and the Israelites praised God. Write these on the board.

Reasons why Moses, Miriam, and the Israelites praised God	Ways that Moses, Miriam, and the Israelites praised God
Possible answers: God is mighty; God rescued the Israelites from the Egyptians; He parted the Red Sea; God provided guidance through the pillar of cloud and fire.	Possible answers: They sang; they danced; they played instruments; they obeyed.

Explain that the ways of praise pertinent in Moses' day are ways that all believers can praise God. This praise is a sweet aroma to Him. Christians can praise God with their attitudes, words, and actions. Reiterate that obedience is as much an act of worship as singing or dancing, and if people praise God with their words but not their actions, their words are nullified.

Display **DM-1 Character Traits** and review *joyfulness*. Moses, Miriam, and the Israelites were joyful as they celebrated God's goodness, after He rescued them from the Egyptians.

Distribute the materials to make musical instruments. Construct and use the instruments with students as follows:
- *Tambourine*: Place DRIED BEANS inside TWO PAPER PLATES. Staple the plates together at the rims. Show students how to shake the tambourine by moving their wrists.
- *Drums*: Allow students to tap their hands or pencils against the CYLINDRICAL CONTAINERS to create rhythms.
- *Cymbals*: Loop YARN through holes in the center of TWO ALUMINUM PIE PLATES. Tell students to hold the yarn as they clash the plates together.
- *Maracas*: Fill EMPTY, ALUMINUM, SOFT DRINK CANS with a few dried beans. Tape the openings shut. Shake the cans in a rhythmic motion.

Praise God with the instruments while singing the song "You Are My God" from the Grade 2 URL.

Student Page 4.3

Encourage students to make this lesson on praise personal by thinking of reasons to praise God. Have students independently complete the page.

Review

• What does it mean to praise God? (**It means to describe God by His many qualities.**)
• What did God do for His people that motivated Moses, Miriam, and the Israelites to praise God? (**God parted the Red Sea and saved the Israelites from the Egyptians.**)
• In what ways did Moses, Miriam, and the Israelites praise God? (**They sang, played instruments, danced, and obeyed.**)
• What things did Moses, Miriam, and the Israelites sing about? (**how mighty God is and how He defeated the Egyptians**)

DAY 3

Name _____

Moses and Miriam Praise God `4.3`

Complete the sentence with some words of praise about God. Write more sentences of praise to Him.

I will praise You with my whole heart because You are

Answer will vary but should include that God is good, loving, near, my Father, and my friend.

© Bible Grade 2   15

APPLICATION

• What are some of the most wonderful things you know about God? (**Possible answers: God is love; God is near; God is kind.**)
• What are some ways that you can praise God? (**Possible answers: sing, pray, dance, play instruments**)
• Obeying is a wonderful way to praise God. What are some ways you can praise God by obeying? (**Possible answers: by obeying my parents, by obeying my teachers**)

REINFORCEMENT

The word *aroma* is used many times in the Bible. In the Old Testament, *aroma* is used to describe sacrifices and offerings. These grain offerings and burnt offerings were pleasing to God. In the New Testament, *aroma* is mentioned in 2 Corinthians 2:15, where believers are said to be a fragrance of Christ—He was the ultimate sacrifice. When believers, then, give themselves as "living sacrifices" (Romans 12:1), they are the fragrance of Christ, an aroma pleasing to the Lord. Ephesians 5:2 also tells how Christ's sacrifice is a sweet-smelling aroma to the Lord.

© Bible Grade 2   37

4.4 Moses and Miriam Praise God
Focus: Praise God

★ PREPARATION
Select **DM-4 God's Attributes**. Make copies of **BLM 4B God's Attributes** for each student. (*Introduction*)

↻ EXTENSION
4A Duplicate and cut out 13 copies of **BLM 4C Banner** for a total of 26 banners. Distribute the banners. While you display **DM-4 God's Attributes** and students have their copies of **BLM 4B God's Attributes**, direct students to write one attribute of God on their banner. (Depending on the size of the class, some students might need to have multiple banners.) Encourage students to stand and say "I praise God because He is … " and complete the statement with the attribute written on their banners. Use the banners to decorate notebooks, folders, or the classroom.

4B Obtain the song "Praise Him, Praise Him" by Fanny Crosby and play it for the class.

Introduction ★
Explain to students that they can praise and thank God for two big reasons—for who He is and for what He does. Brainstorm with students some things for which to praise and thank God. (**Possible answers: He is mighty; He knows everything; He is always present; He created us; He saved us; He provides for us.**) Display **DM-4 God's Attributes** and hand out **BLM 4B God's Attributes** to each student. Define *God's attributes* as *qualities that are true about God*. Spend time praising God together using some of the attributes listed. Take time to also thank God for what He has done.

Directed Instruction ↻
There are poems or songs in the book of Psalms that were written in order to praise God. Instruct students to turn to **Psalm 145** and invite them to take turns reading a verse from the psalm one at a time. Explain to students that this psalm was written as a verbal song of praise to God.

Tell students the following true story about a woman who spent her whole life praising God:

> If there was ever a person who had reason not to praise God, it was Fanny Crosby. When Fanny was six weeks old, she got very sick. Her parents took her to a man who pretended to be a doctor; he gave them medicine to put on Fanny's eyes. She eventually recovered from the sickness, but the medication left her completely blind.
>
> Not long after they discovered she was blind, Fanny's father died, and her mother had to find work as a maid just to feed the family. Though Fanny grew up blind and poor, she did not let that affect her spirit. In fact, when she was eight years old, she wrote her first verses of poetry in which she declared she would be content for all the blessings she had received.
>
> When Fanny was fifteen years old, she was allowed to go to the New York Institute for the Blind, where her ability to write poetry was eventually greatly encouraged. Throughout her life, Fanny was described as a cheerful and praising servant. God used Fanny to write thousands of hymns in her lifetime, many of which are still sung in churches today.

Student Page 4.4
Direct students to the student page, where they will find some of the words to a traditional hymn entitled "Praise Him! Praise Him!" by Fanny Crosby. Explain to students that they will be completing the hymn and underlining words that describe who God is (His attributes) and what He has done. If you are familiar with the tune, sing the hymn to students, asking them if they recognize it. If you are not familiar with the tune, read through the song lines. Assist students, as needed, to complete Exercise 1 before allowing them to complete Exercise 2 independently.

Review

- What are two main reasons you should praise and thank God? (**for who He is and for what He does**)
- What does *God's attributes* mean? (**qualities that are true about God**)
- How did Fanny Crosby praise God with her attitude? (**She was cheerful and praised God even though she was blind and poor.**)

Notes:

APPLICATION

- What is one attribute of God that you think is wonderful? Why? (Refer to the list on **LM-4 God's Attributes** or **BLM 4B God's Attributes**.) (**Answers will vary.**)
- Think of a hard situation you or your friends might go through. How could you praise God through some of those hard times? (**Possible answers: by asking for God's help, by having a good attitude, by obeying**)
- How can you, like Fanny Crosby, praise God with your attitude? (**Possible answers: by being content and happy with what I have, by not complaining, by not being greedy**)

DAY 4

4.4 *Moses and Miriam Praise God*

1. Write the words **Praise Him** on each empty writing line. Read this hymn of praise. Underline all the words that describe who God is or what He does.

> **Praise Him! Praise Him!**
> by Fanny Crosby
>
> First Verse:
>
> _____Praise Him_____! _____Praise Him_____!
> Jesus, our blessed Redeemer!
> Sing, O Earth, His wonderful love proclaim!
> Hail Him! Hail Him! Highest archangels in glory;
> Strength and honor give to His holy name!
> Like a shepherd, Jesus will guard His children,
> In His arms He carries them all day long.
>
> Chorus:
>
> _____Praise Him_____! _____Praise Him_____!
> Tell of His excellent greatness;
> _____Praise Him_____! _____Praise Him_____!
> Ever in joyful song!

2. Write a poem or song of praise to God.

Answers will vary.
_____
_____
_____
_____

4.5 Moses and Miriam Praise God

Focus: Review and Assessment

★ PREPARATION

Select **VA 4A The Red Sea Crossing**. (*Lesson Review*)

Make one copy of **BLM 4D Lesson 4 Test** for each student. (*Directed Instruction*)

Lesson Review ★

Use **VA 4A The Red Sea Crossing** to review the following Bible truths:

- Pharaoh told the Israelites, or Hebrews, to leave Egypt after the death of the firstborn sons and of the firstborn animals of Egypt. This was the tenth and final plague.
- Pharaoh and the Egyptians sent clothing, gold, and silver to the Israelites before they left.
- Pharaoh changed his mind and went after the Israelites.
- Pharaoh and his Egyptian army chased the Israelites in chariots.
- Chariots are two-wheeled vehicles, without seats, that are pulled by horses.
- God sent a pillar of cloud and fire to lead the Israelites to the edge of the Red Sea.
- The pillar of cloud and fire provided direction and light during the long journey.
- God moved the pillar in between the Israelites and Egyptians so the Israelites would have time to cross the Red Sea.
- God parted the waters of the Red Sea to allow the Israelites to go through on dry ground. The Egyptian army chased the Israelites into the Red Sea and drowned.
- A miracle is an act of God that is impossible by human or natural causes.
- Moses, Miriam, and the Israelites praised God for who He is and thanked Him for what He had done.
- Moses, Miriam, and the Israelites praised God by singing, dancing, playing instruments, and obeying.

Directed Instruction ★

Distribute a copy of **BLM 4D Lesson 4 Test** to each student. Explain the instructions and format. Have students complete the test. When finished, read over the test, providing the answers for immediate feedback.

Notes:

Lesson Preparation
Moses Is Diligent — 5.0

Expected Student Outcomes

KNOW
Moses is diligent and courageous as he leads God's people to the Promised Land.

DO
Students will:
- recount God's faithfulness to the children of Israel
- differentiate between commandments that show love for God and love for others
- sequence events of the Bible truth and write ways to show diligence
- write a prayer, asking God for courage to do what is right

APPLY
Students will display diligence and courage as they obey God.

Lesson Outline
I. Israelites journey into the desert (Ex 15:22–17:16)
   A. Forgetting God's faithfulness
   B. Remembering God's faithfulness
II. The Ten Commandments (Ex 19:1–20:17, Eph 6:1–3)
   A. How to love God
   B. How to love others
III. The bronze serpent (Num 21:4–9)
IV. Courage to do what is right (1 Tim 4:12, Ex 15:22–17:16, Num 21:4–9)

♥ TEACHER'S HEART
It's easy to complain. When situations are hard or life is not easy, you may tend to grumble and let others know your displeasure. The Israelites had the same problem. Their discontent over not having the provisions needed showed not only their distrust of Moses, but their great distrust of God. The Israelites didn't value the deliverance from Egypt they had just experienced! Yet, God graciously made known to Moses His kindness and took notice of the people's complaints. He promised the Israelites an abundant and consistent supply of provision! God showed His unconditional love. He was faithful even though the Israelites were unsatisfied and murmuring.

Life will bring hardships. You may be very uncomfortable or feel forgotten. Isaiah 58:9 tells you that if you call upon God, He will answer. Psalm 22:3 says that God is enthroned in the praises of Israel. As His child, if you are to enter fully into His presence, then worshipping your Lord is the key. This applies even through life's hardships. When you walk in faith, you can rest in Him, satisfied as you watch His unconditional love and guidance provide what you need. The next time you're tempted to complain, praise Him for what He has done, is doing, and will continue to do!

Supplemental Materials are available to download. See Understanding Purposeful Design Bible at the front of this book for the Grade 2 URL.

MEMORY VERSE
Exodus 19:5

GLOSSARY WORDS
- manna
- diligence

MATERIALS
Day 1:
- Glass, dirty water
- BLM 5A Manna Recipe (*Extension*)

Day 2:
- VA 5A The Ten Commandments
- Poster board (*Extension*)

Day 3:
- DM-1 Character Traits
- DM-5 Map of Desert Journey
- Glass jar, uncooked egg in its shell, uncooked rice
- BLM 5B Practice Being Diligent (*Extension*)

Day 4:
- DM-1 Character Traits

Day 5:
- VA 5A The Ten Commandments
- BLM 5C Lesson 5 Test

♪ SONGS
Ten Commandments

TEACHER RESOURCES
Rose Book of Bible Charts, Maps, and Time Lines. Rose Publishing Inc., 2015.

STUDENT RESOURCES
Focus on the Family, ed., *Adventures in Odyssey, Life Lessons #1: Courage.* CD. Tyndale Entertainment, 2005.

Focus on the Family, ed., *Adventures in Odyssey, Life Lessons #4: Diligence.* CD. Tyndale Entertainment, 2005.

 Bible Grade 2

5.1 Moses Is Diligent
Focus: Israelites Journey into the Desert

MEMORY VERSE
Exodus 19:5

MEMORY WORK
- Encourage girl students to clap to each syllable as you say the Memory Verse. Ask boy students to snap their fingers or click their tongue to each syllable as you say the Memory Verse. Invite all students to stand and say the Memory Verse together.

PREPARATION
Fill a GLASS with DIRTY WATER. (*Introduction*)

EXTENSION
1A Note that in Psalm 78:25, manna is called *angels' food*. Use **BLM 5A Manna Recipe** to prepare the bread to be eaten with your students as you discuss God's provision. Tell the class that the children of Israel ate manna for 40 years, until they reached the border of Canaan, the land God had promised to Abraham.

Introduction ★
Display a GLASS that contains DIRTY WATER. Lead students to think about being in the desert with nothing else to drink. Tell them that in the Bible truth today, the Israelites face the problem of having nothing to drink.

Directed Instruction
Introduce the word **manna**, which was *food miraculously provided by God for the Israelites in the desert*. Read the following Bible truth adapted from Exodus 15:22–17:7:

> After Moses led the *Israelites*, who were also called the *children of Israel*, across the Red Sea, they journeyed into the desert, or wilderness. They traveled for three days in the desert and could not find any water. When they came to a place called *Marah*, there was water, but they could not drink the water because it was bitter. Forgetting what God had just done three days earlier, the Israelites cried out and complained to Moses. Moses cried out to God, and by following God's direction to throw a certain piece of wood into the water, Moses was able to make the water safe to drink.
>
> One month later, the children of Israel complained again to Moses and Aaron saying, "We wish we would have died in Egypt where we had plenty to eat. You brought us out into the wilderness to die of hunger!" Instead of remembering all that God had done to free them, they complained.
>
> God spoke to Moses and announced that He would rain down bread from heaven during the morning. The children of Israel called the bread *manna*. The manna looked like white, thin, flaky wafers. God instructed that the children of Israel were to gather only the amount of food that was needed for that day. On the sixth day, the children of Israel were to gather twice the amount of food so they would not have to work on the Sabbath. If the bread was not eaten as God commanded, the leftovers would stink and become wormy. God said that He would provide that day's food and was testing the obedience of His people. He was merciful to His people even though they had complained.
>
> Later, the Israelites again complained about not having water to drink. How forgetful they were! God had provided water and food and was gracious. God told Moses to take his walking stick, or rod, and strike a certain rock. God would make water come out of it. Moses did as God commanded, and the Israelites were able to drink. Moses continued to look to God and trust Him for help during the difficult situation.

Student Page 5.1
Have students complete the page.

Review

- How did God take care of the Israelites? (**Possible answers: He gave them good water and manna; He protected them.**)
- Why did the children of Israel complain? (**Possible answers: They were in a desert; they were thirsty and hungry.**)
- Why do you think the children of Israel forgot what God had done for them just a short time after leaving Egypt? (**They wanted good water; they were hungry and focused on that hunger; they were forgetful.**)

Notes:

APPLICATION

- Even though the children of Israel kept complaining, why did God keep providing? (**Possible answers: God loved them even when they were unthankful; God is patient.**)
- Why do you think people easily forget about what God has done for them? (**Answers will vary but should include that we tend to focus on the problem instead of trusting in God and remembering what He has done for us.**)
- In what ways can you remember to be thankful for what God has done for you? (**Possible answers: give thanks, write down blessings, praise Him**)

DAY 1

Name _____

Moses Is Diligent 5.1

In Exodus 15:22–17:16, the children of Israel left Egypt and wandered in the wilderness. They kept forgetting what God had done for them, but God was always with them. As He provided for them, He helped them remember His faithfulness.

1. Complete the sentences by using the following words: **manna, water, rock, stick, wafers**.

The children of Israel complained. They forgot God's faithfulness. They had no ___water___. God provided. The children of Israel complained again. God provided a bread called ___manna___. It looked like little, white ___wafers___. Later, the children of Israel needed water again. They complained. God told Moses to strike a ___rock___ with a ___stick___. God made water come out of the rock! God provided for the children of Israel. God was faithful.

2. How has God been faithful to you?
Possible answers: God is faithful to me because He is always with me; God is faithful to me because He provides food and shelter for me; God is faithful to me because He gives me peace when I am afraid.

5.2 Moses Is Diligent

Focus: The Ten Commandments

★ PREPARATION

Select **VA 5A The Ten Commandments**, and the "Ten Commandments" song from the Grade 2 URL. (*Directed Instruction*)

↻ EXTENSION

2A Brainstorm ideas with students on how to write the Ten Commandments in their own words. Examples could include the following:
• Honor God first.
• Don't misuse God's name.
• Respect your parents.
Distribute POSTER BOARD to students and have them cut rounded corners to produce the effect of a stone tablet. Encourage students to write each of the Ten Commandments in their own words on the poster board to make their own stone tablet.

Introduction

Allow students to play a game in any manner they choose. As students become frustrated because of a lack of rules, stop the game. Ask for reasons why the game was frustrating. (**Possible answers: Students may have played unfairly; students may have become upset with each other.**) In the Bible truth today, students will learn about rules God gives them to help them live well.

Directed Instruction ★ ↻

Display **VA 5A The Ten Commandments** and read the Bible truth on the back. Explain that God gave the Ten Commandments as a blessing to help people know how best to live. The Ten Commandments define what sin against God and others is. Emphasize that people should take these commandments seriously and do what they say (Deuteronomy 5:32–33).

The first four commandments direct people to love God.
1. You shall have no other gods before Me.
2. You shall not make for yourself a carved image; you shall not bow down to idols.
   (In the first two commandments, God is saying that people should love Him more than anyone, or anything else.)
3. You shall not take the name of the Lord your God in vain. (God wants people to not misuse His name as He is to be honored and respected.)
4. Remember the Sabbath day, to keep it holy. (When a person sets aside a day to worship God, it shows that he or she is putting God first above other things thought to be more important.)

The last six commandments direct God's people to love others.
5. Honor your father and mother. (God wants children to always treat their parents with honor and respect.)
6. You shall not murder. (God tells people to not be vengeful and kill anyone.)
7. You shall not commit adultery. (If a couple marries, God wants the two to be faithful to one another in all areas of life.)
8. You shall not steal. (This means that a person should not take what does not belong to him or her.)
9. You shall not bear false witness against your neighbor; you shall not lie. (God tells people to treat others appropriately. This means they should not hurt others by their words, lie to others, or lie about others.)
10. You shall not covet; you shall not desire other people's possessions out of jealousy. (God tells people to be happy for what others have and be content with what they themselves have.)

These commandments help people to live with others the way God intended. The more they follow these laws, the more peaceful their lives are. Many times people fail and do not keep all of the Ten Commandments. God knows people are not perfect, only He is perfect (Romans 3:23). Explain to students that breaking even one of God's rules hurts their relationship with God and others (James 2:10). When they break a

44

commandment, or a rule, they can go to God and ask for forgiveness. He still loves them even when they sin. God sent Jesus to die on the cross to pay for everyone's sin. When people believe in what Jesus did for them, they can ask His forgiveness and know God will forgive them. God will then give them the Holy Spirit to encourage them and help them do what is right.

Sing the song "Ten Commandments" from the Grade 2 URL.

Student Page 5.2
Read the directions and have students complete the page.

Review
- What do the first four commandments direct you to do? (**to love God**)
- What do the last six commandments direct you to do? (**to love others**)
- When you disobey a command, what should you do? (**I should ask God for forgiveness.**)
- Because God loves you, what did He give you to guide you and help you to obey? (**the Holy Spirit**)

APPLICATION
- Do the Ten Commandments apply to you today? If so, how? (**Possible answers: Yes, they teach us how to live and to love God more; they teach us right from wrong; they help us to live peacefully with others.**)
- Is it possible to follow all the commandments all the time? Why or why not? (**No, we cannot follow all of the commandments all of the time because only God is perfect.**)
- If we keep most of the commandments will that get us into heaven? Why or why? (**No, we cannot earn our way into heaven. Our sin separates us from God. We can only enter heaven by believing in Jesus' death on the cross, which paid for the forgiveness of sin.**)
- How will your life be different if you ask God to help you follow His commands? (**Possible answers: Our relationship with God won't be broken; we will live at peace with others; we will honor God and please Him.**)

DAY 2

5.2 *Moses Is Diligent*

God loves you. He helps you understand how to act toward Him and others. **Circle** the commandments that direct you to love God. **Underline** the commandments that direct you to love others.

1. You shall have no other gods before Me.

2. You shall not make for yourself a carved image; you shall not bow down to idols.

3. You shall not take the name of the Lord your God in vain.

4. Remember the Sabbath day, to keep it holy.

5. Honor your father and mother.

6. You shall not murder.

7. You shall not commit adultery.

8. You shall not steal.

9. You shall not bear false witness against your neighbor; you shall not lie.

10. You shall not covet; you shall not desire other people's possessions out of jealousy.

11. Read the situation. Write the number on the line to show which commandment was broken.

   • My dad and mom asked me to help, but I played instead. _____5_____

   • My friend got a new toy, and I was very jealous. _____10_____

12. Why did God provide the Ten Commandments?
   God gives us the Ten Commandments to help us know how to live.

18

5.3	# Moses Is Diligent
	Focus: The Bronze Serpent

★ PREPARATION

Select **DM-1 Character Traits**. (*Introduction*)

Select **DM-5 Map of Desert Journey**. (*Directed Instruction*)

Place an UNCOOKED EGG STILL IN ITS SHELL into a GLASS JAR. Fill the jar with UNCOOKED RICE. (*Directed Instruction*)

↶ EXTENSION

3A Encourage students to practice being diligent. Distribute **BLM 5B Practice Being Diligent** to students and direct them to document for five days the completion of a task of their choice from the *Choice Chart*. Collect the activity at the end of five days and discuss how being diligent makes a difference.

Introduction ★ ↶

Display **DM-1 Character Traits**. Instruct students to find the word *diligence* in their Glossary. Read the definition for **diligence**, which means *not giving up*. Tell students that the word *persistence*, which they learned in an earlier lesson, is very similar to the word *diligence*. Ask them who, in this week's lesson, exhibited great diligence. (**Moses**)

Directed Instruction ★

Read **Numbers 21:4–9**. Explain that the Israelites were walking a longer way than they had expected. They continued to complain and forget about God's faithfulness. In their frustration, they spoke against God and Moses. Explain that this passage highlights how lack of faith in God and complaining are sinful. The Israelites were saved from death only when they followed God's directions by looking at the bronze snake on the pole.

Display **DM-5 Map of Desert Journey**. Discuss the route Moses traveled as he diligently led the Israelites out of Egypt into the desert.

Tell students to participate in the review of this week's Bible truths by holding their thumbs up each time they hear the words *Moses was diligent*. Hold up the GLASS JAR filled with an UNCOOKED EGG IN ITS SHELL covered by UNCOOKED RICE. Read the following text. As you say *Moses was diligent*, gently shake the jar so the egg moves upward.

- Moses led the children of Israel through the Red Sea and into the wilderness. Everyone complained that that they were thirsty, but Moses did not give up. He went to God for help. Moses was diligent! (**Shake the jar; students hold up their thumbs.**) God gave them good water.

- The Israelites complained about having nothing to eat. They wanted to go back to Egypt! Moses spoke to God. Moses was diligent! (**Shake the jar; students hold up their thumbs.**) God gave them manna to eat.

- The children of Israel complained again about not having water. They were forgetful that God had been providing for them. Moses did not give up. He asked God what to do. Moses was diligent! (**Shake the jar; students hold up their thumbs.**) God told Moses to strike a rock with his walking stick and water came out.

- Moses went to meet God on Mount Sinai. Moses was diligent! (**Shake the jar; students hold up their thumbs.**) God gave Moses the Ten Commandments for the children of Israel follow.

- The children of Israel continued to wander and kept complaining to Moses. God sent snakes to remind the people to not complain. The children of Israel asked Moses to pray for God to take away the snakes. Moses was diligent! (**Shake the jar; students hold up their thumbs.**) God told Moses to make a bronze snake and lift it up on a pole for the Israelites to look at so they would not die from the snakebites.

At the end of the review, the egg will be on top of the rice. Explain that the rice represents the children of Israel who complained and were not diligent. The egg represents how Moses resolved to be a diligent leader, staying focused and doing what needed to be done. Remind students that a godly, diligent leader will obey God to do a specific job, even when others do not appreciate it. Express that God will help them to be diligent, when they ask Him to, even if others around them complain about what is going on.

Student Page 5.3
Have students complete the page.

Review
• What happened each time the Israelites complained? (**Possible answers: Moses went to God; Moses followed God's direction.**)
• How was Moses a diligent leader? (**Moses was diligent by continually asking God what to do. He trusted God for help, and did what God said to do.**)
• How did God help Moses to be a diligent leader? (**God helped Moses by giving Moses direction and providing what the Israelites needed.**)

APPLICATION
• Was it easy for Moses to be a leader? Why or why not? (**No, it had to have been hard to be so diligent because the Israelites complained a lot and kept forgetting God's faithfulness. Moses had to stand alone and rely on God.**)
• Are you willing to be diligent when things are difficult?
• In what ways can you be a diligent leader? (**Possible answers: I can read my Bible each day; I can ask God for help in doing something I'm supposed to be doing, even when others aren't; I can obey the first time I am told to do something.**)

REINFORCEMENT
The act of looking up at the bronze serpent, which Moses had made according to God's direction, brought healing from snakebites to the Israelites. However, by the time of King Hezekiah, the Israelites had turned the bronze serpent into an idol to which they burned incense. In an effort to do right in the sight of God and to stop the Israelites from continuing in this sin, King Hezekiah broke the bronze serpent into pieces (2 Kings 18:4). John refers to the purpose of the bronze serpent as a foreshadowing of salvation: Moses lifted up the bronze serpent. In like manner, Jesus was lifted up so that whoever believes in Him will not perish but have eternal life (John 3:14–15).

DAY 3

Name _____

Moses is Diligent `5.3`

Moses was a leader who showed diligence. He kept doing what God wanted him to do even when it was hard.

1. Number each phrase in the order it happened.

___5___ sharing the Ten Commandments

___3___ asking God for food

___2___ drinking good water that was once bitter

___4___ striking a rock for water

___6___ making a bronze snake to lift up on a pole

___1___ crossing the Red Sea

2. I can show more diligence by ___Answers will vary.___
_____
_____
_____

© Bible Grade 2   19

5.4 Moses Is Diligent
Focus: Courage to Do What Is Right

★ PREPARATION
Select **DM-1 Character Traits**. (*Introduction*)

↪ EXTENSION
4A Divide the class into four groups. Assign each group one of the following Scripture passages to read. Challenge students to find out how each Bible person showed courage. Have each group share about the verses.
- Joseph: Genesis 37:12–28 (**Joseph had to trust God and have courage after his brothers threw him into a pit and sold him as a slave.**)
- Jeremiah: Jeremiah 1:4–12 (**Jeremiah trusted God for courage to speak to the people when he didn't know what to say.**)
- Daniel: Daniel 6:1–10 (**Daniel showed courage when he continued to pray three times a day even though King Darius would not allow it.**)
- Peter: Matthew 14:22–33 (**Peter had courage to step out of the boat and walk on water to Jesus.**)

Introduction ★
Display **DM-1 Character Traits**. Review that *courage* means *doing the right thing even when afraid*. Write the following on the board and then discuss which choice would take the most courage to carry out:
- Read a book and tell about something you learned.
- Draw a picture and give it to a friend.
- Share about Jesus with someone who has never heard about Him.

Directed Instruction ↩
Discuss with students that Moses had to have courage out in the desert. There were many times when God asked Moses to do hard things. Moses must have felt afraid. He was leading a large group of people out into the desert where water was scarce. He was instructing them to listen to and follow God, even when they were ungrateful. All of these situations required Moses to have courage. Even though these jobs were tough, God helped Moses to not be fearful, to do the right thing, and to rest in Him for courage.

Instruct students that there will be times in their life in which God will have them do things that take courage. For example, it takes courage to tell the truth even if it means being punished.

Encourage students to listen to the following true-life story about Joshua, a seven-year-old boy who had courage to do the right thing:

Joshua had been saving his money for a year. All of the kids in the neighborhood had skates and Joshua so wanted to skate with his friends. He now had enough money and was going to buy that special pair of skates. Joshua wanted those skates more than anything! He asked his mom if they could go the next day to purchase the skates. His mom agreed. Joshua was so excited!

That evening, Joshua and some of his friends went to church. There was a guest missionary who spoke about people in a country called *Rwanda*. These people had to leave their homes quickly because of danger and had no food or clothes. The missionary was collecting money to give to these people. This touched Joshua's heart.

Afterwards, Joshua knew what he had to do. He told his mom and his friends he wanted to give all the money he had saved to the people in Rwanda. Some people thought Joshua should give away some of the money, and keep some to buy a less expensive pair of skates.

Joshua knew he wanted to give all of the money, but he was afraid he would never be able to save enough money again to get the skates. Joshua needed courage to do what he thought God wanted him to do, so he prayed and rested in God's strength. Joshua took courage in God and gave all his money.

The next day, Joshua's mom called him downstairs. She told him to go look outside the front door. There, in front of him, was a beautiful pair of skates! The note attached was from his grandparents saying, "Thank you for having the courage to do the right thing."

Student Page 5.4
Read the Scripture and directions together on the page. Have students complete the page.

Review

- What does it mean to have courage? (**Courage means doing the right thing even when I am afraid.**)
- How did Moses show courage? (**Possible answers: Moses led a very large group of people out into the desert where water was scarce; Moses told frustrated, angry people to listen to God; Moses made a bronze serpent and held it up so people wouldn't die.**)
- Joshua, the boy in today's story, had courage. How did his courage affect others? (**Possible answers: He helped people in Rwanda; God blessed him in a way he didn't expect.**)

APPLICATION

- When is it hardest to show courage? (**Possible answers: It is hard to show courage when others around you are not doing the same; it is hard to show courage when you are afraid and not trusting God.**)
- When you show godly courage, how does it affect others? (**Possible answers: When I show godly courage, people see how God's work is done; when I show godly courage, people are blessed by how God is working.**)
- How can you have more courage? (**Possible answers: I can rest in God's strength and not my own; I can trust in God to help me to not be afraid.**)

REINFORCEMENT

The nation of Edom, which descended from Esau, refused to allow the Israelites to pass through their land to reach Canaan, the Promised Land (Numbers 20:14–21:4, Deuteronomy 2:1–9). Moses asked graciously and promised not to harm any crops, or drink any of their water unless the Israelites purchased it, but Edom still refused. The Israelites had to travel a longer, more difficult way through a barren and sandy land. Obadiah is a book written about the judgment of Edom because of how Edom mistreated its relatives (Israel). According to some scholars, the nation of Edom was nonexistent by 100 AD.

DAY 4

5.4 Moses Is Diligent

Moses needed courage to trust God. Read 1 Timothy 4:12. Then, read the devotion written by Lydia, age 9. It is about how God helped someone to have courage.

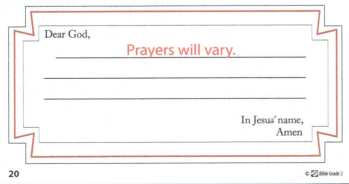

You can have courage and do what is right. Think about a time when you become afraid and need courage. Write a prayer to ask God for courage to do what is right. Spend time talking to God about courage.

Dear God,
Prayers will vary.

In Jesus' name,
Amen

5.5 Moses Is Diligent

Focus: Review and Assessment

★ PREPARATION

Select **VA 5A The Ten Commandments** for review.
(*Lesson Review*)

Make one copy of **BLM 5C Lesson 5 Test** for each student.
(*Directed instruction*)

Lesson Review ★

Use **VA 5A The Ten Commandments** to review the following Bible truths from this lesson:

• Moses was a leader who showed diligence as he led the children of Israel into the desert, or wilderness.
• *Diligence* means *not giving up*.
• Moses followed God's direction and turned bitter water into water safe to drink.
• The Israelites complained, and God sent a bread called *manna* to feed the people in the wilderness.
• God instructed His children to gather only certain amounts of food. He provided the manna and was testing the obedience of His people.
• After more complaining, God told Moses to take his walking stick and strike a rock so water would come out of it.
• God spoke to Moses on Mount Sinai and gave the children of Israel the Ten Commandments.
• God gave the Ten Commandments to guide people in how to recognize right from wrong and to know how to live well.
• The first four commandments direct us to love God.
• The last six commandments direct us to love others.
• God instructed Moses to make a bronze snake and lift it up on a pole. When the children of Israel looked at the snake, they would live and not die from snakebites.
• God wants us to have courage as Moses had.
• *Courage* means *doing the right thing even when afraid.*

Directed Instruction ★

Distribute **BLM 5C Lesson 5 Test** to each student. Have students complete the test.

Notes:

50

Lesson Preparation
Miriam and Aaron Learn Respect

6.0

Expected Student Outcomes

KNOW
Miriam and Aaron learn to respect authority.

DO
Students will:
- name the main theme and characters from the Bible truth
- identify authorities to respect and obey
- identify examples and reasons for disrespect
- find rewards promised in the Bible for obeying authorities
- examine possible consequences for disrespect
- define and apply respect in their lives

APPLY
Students will acknowledge the importance of respecting those in authority.

Lesson Outline
I. Miriam and Aaron challenge Moses (Num 12)
II. Respecting authority
  A. Who we should respect (Rom 13:1–2)
  B. How we should respect (Jer 42:6)
III. Disrespecting authority (Num 12)
  A. Reasons we disrespect
  B. Ways we disrespect (Titus 2:9–10)
IV. Consequences
  A. Rewards for obeying (Ex 20:12, Deut 5:29, Eph 6:5–8)
  B. Consequences for disobeying (Heb 13:17)

♥ TEACHER'S HEART

From the time they were born, the children of Cliff and Prew heard the following motto: "Obey now; ask later." Any command given by their parents, no matter how unpleasant, was to be followed immediately, and the *why* would be answered only after the command was completed. One day, in rural Indonesia, the reason for this motto was solidified. As the kids were crossing the path, Prew yelled, "Run!" With no hesitation, they ran. When safe, they turned to see what had caused the commotion: a horse had been spooked and was running down the path where the children had just been standing. There was no time for questions, only for obedience.

As you walk with God, He may tell you to do things that are unpleasant. Sometimes He may put people in authority over you that are unpleasant. In these situations, you may want to question, complain, or argue. Jeremiah 42:6 is a reminder to obey the voice of the Lord your God, regardless of whether what He says pleases you or not. God wants you to honor and love the authority leaders in your life, too. When you do, you are honoring and loving Him. Ask Him to give you a heart that obeys now and asks later.

📖 MEMORY VERSE
1 Peter 2:17

GLOSSARY WORDS
- authority
- respect

★ MATERIALS

Day 1:
- Brad fasteners
- VA 6A Miriam and Aaron Learn Respect, BLM 6A Readers Theater: Miriam and Aaron

Day 2:
- Umbrella
- BLM 6B Umbrella, card stock (*Extension*)

Day 3:
- No additional materials are needed.

Day 4:
- Building blocks or plastic building bricks (*Extension*)

Day 5:
- VA 6A Miriam and Aaron Learn Respect
- BLM 6C Lesson 6 Test

♪ SONGS
Books of the Bible (*Extension*)

TEACHER RESOURCES
Dobson, Dr. James. *The New Strong-Willed Child*. Tyndale House, 2007.
Leman, Dr. Kevin. *Making Children Mind without Losing Yours*. Baker, 2017.

STUDENT RESOURCES
Finn, Carrie. *Kids Talk About Respect*. Picture Window Books, 2007.

Supplemental Materials are available to download. See Understanding Purposeful Design Bible at the front of this book for the Grade 2 URL.

6.1 Miriam and Aaron Learn Respect
Focus: Miriam and Aaron Challenge Moses

📖 MEMORY VERSE
1 Peter 2:17

MEMORY WORK
- Provide students with the prepared viewer made from construction paper. Students should hold the viewer by one of the corners and turn the circle by grasping it at the window. Encourage students after they have read the verse several times, to try and recite it without looking.

⭐ PREPARATION
Cut out enough circles and squares from construction paper to make a viewer for each student. The circle should be big enough to fit the Memory Verse on the outer edge. The square should be big enough to cover and conceal the words on the circle. Cut a window on one side of the square large enough to allow one or more words to be read easily. Using the window on the square as a guide, write the Memory Verse on the outer edge of the circle. Keep the square over the circle and push a **BRAD FASTENER** through the midpoint of both pieces to complete the viewer. (*Memory Work*)

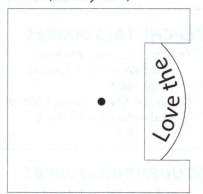

Select **VA 6A Miriam and Aaron Learn Respect**. Make four copies of **BLM 6A Readers Theater: Miriam and Aaron**. (*Directed Instruction*)

Introduction
Play the game Follow the Leader. Appoint one student as a leader to give commands that can be easily followed by the class. However, before the game begins, confidentially direct one student to complain about the directions, to disobey the directions, and to try to get other students to follow his or her lead. Allow the game to continue this way for a minute. Stop the game and discuss how students felt about the classmate who was complaining and seeking attention. Ask students why it is important to know who is in charge of the game. (**The game cannot be played correctly if people will not listen to the person in charge or it is unclear who is in charge.**) Today's Bible truth is about how Miriam and Aaron learned a very important lesson about respecting authority.

Directed Instruction ⭐
Have students locate *authority* and *respect* in the Glossary. **Authority** means *the power to enforce rules or give orders, or someone who has been given the power to enforce rules*. **Respect** means *a state of showing a proper attitude toward others, especially to those in charge*. Read **VA 6A Miriam and Aaron Learn Respect**. Reinforce the Bible truth by selecting students to read and act out the dialogue from **BLM 6A Readers Theater: Miriam and Aaron**.

Remind students that Miriam and Aaron were Moses' sister and brother. Miriam had watched Moses to keep him from drowning in the Nile River when he was a baby. Miriam had also led the women in singing praises to God after crossing the Red Sea. She had recognition and authority, but she wanted more. Likewise, Aaron had already helped Moses by speaking to Pharaoh in Egypt. He also was selected as *High Priest*, which means *the highest religious leader or pastor*. Aaron had authority and recognition. However, he was jealous of the amount of authority Moses had and the recognition Moses received. Jealousy drove Aaron and Miriam to grumble and complain disrespectfully against Moses.

Explain to students that God is the one who sets up authority. God had called Moses, so when Miriam and Aaron spoke against Moses, it was as if they were speaking against God Himself. Because of this, God spoke up in defense of Moses. Ask students what God said. (**God asked Miriam and Aaron why they weren't afraid to speak against Moses, His faithful servant.**) A result of Miriam's rebellion against Moses was *leprosy*, which is *a skin disease*. God does not take it lightly when people disrespect the authority He has put in place. It was clear that Miriam and Aaron showed that they did not respect Moses, the authority God had placed over them.

Explain that Jesus gave good examples of how to respect authority. Invite three volunteers to read **Luke 2:51**, **John 5:19–20**, and **Matthew 17:24–27**. Ask students what three types of authority figures Jesus obeyed and how He did it. (**He respected his parents by obeying them; He respected God by doing what He saw Him doing; He respected the government by paying His and Peter's taxes.**) Read **Matthew 28:18**. The Bible says that all authority was given by God to Jesus, His Son, and yet Jesus still respected earthly authority, leaving an example to follow.

Student Page 6.1
Assist students as needed to complete the page.

Review
- Why were Miriam and Aaron upset? (**They wanted recognition and credit; they were jealous.**)
- How did they express their feelings? (**They grumbled and complained against Moses.**)
- What did God say when He stood up for Moses? (**God told Miriam and Aaron that Moses was a faithful servant and they should have been afraid to speak against him.**)
- What happened to Miriam after God finished speaking to them? (**Miriam's skin turned leprous. Aaron asked Moses to forgive them. Moses prayed, and God forgave them and healed Miriam.**)
- What three sets of authority did Jesus respect and obey even though He was the Son of God? (**His parents, God, the government**)

APPLICATION
- How can you show respect? (**by listening, by obeying, by not complaining**)
- What could happen if you do not show respect or obey authority? (**Possible answers: We could get hurt; we could get in trouble.**)

REINFORCEMENT
Leprosy was one of the most dreaded diseases of the ancient world. It caused loss of sensation and deformity. In biblical times, it was believed to be highly contagious and hereditary. Those diagnosed by a priest as leprous were cast out of society for seven days, and then reevaluated. After that period, if they were deemed clean they were to offer a sacrifice and wash, allowing them readmission into society. As long as the priest determined that an individual was leprous, that person had to live outside the city. Whenever someone came near a leper, the leper was to shout out, "Unclean, unclean!" so that the person could pass by without getting too close.

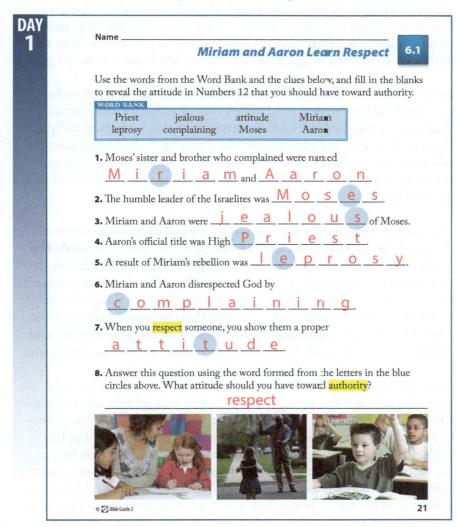

DAY 1

Name _____

Miriam and Aaron Learn Respect 6.1

Use the words from the Word Bank and the clues below, and fill in the blanks to reveal the attitude in Numbers 12 that you should have toward authority.

WORD BANK
| Priest | jealous | attitude | Miriam |
| leprosy | complaining | Moses | Aaron |

1. Moses' sister and brother who complained were named __M i r i a m__ and __A a r o n__.
2. The humble leader of the Israelites was __M o s e s__.
3. Miriam and Aaron were __j e a l o u s__ of Moses.
4. Aaron's official title was High __P r i e s t__.
5. A result of Miriam's rebellion was __l e p r o s y__.
6. Miriam and Aaron disrespected God by __c o m p l a i n i n g__.
7. When you respect someone, you show them a proper __a t t i t u d e__.
8. Answer this question using the word formed from the letters in the blue circles above. What attitude should you have toward authority? __respect__

6.2 Miriam and Aaron Learn Respect
Focus: Respecting Authority

★ PREPARATION
Have an UMBRELLA available to show the class. (*Introduction*)

EXTENSION
2A Duplicate enough copies of **BLM 6B Umbrella** onto CARD STOCK for each student. On one side of the umbrella, have students write the name of one authority they need to respect. Tell students to write on the other side how they should respect that authority figure. Encourage students to illustrate and color their umbrellas.

Introduction ★
Show students an UMBRELLA. Ask them what the purpose of an umbrella is. (**The umbrella provides protection from the rain or the sun's heat.**) Ask students what would happen if you decide to keep the umbrella closed, keep it away from your body, or turn it upside down, demonstrating each of these umbrella positions as you ask. (**It doesn't keep you protected from the rain or sun.**) Explain that an umbrella, if a person stays under it and uses it properly, protects him or her. In the same way, God has established authority so that if people stay under it and obey it, they will be protected.

Directed Instruction
Ask students to identify different kinds of authority that they need to obey. (**Possible answers: parents, teachers, church leaders, the government, the police**) Discuss with students how these authorities protect them. For example, police enforce the rules of the road so that driving is not a dangerous activity.

Explain that every person is under authority. Demonstrate this by creating a vertical flowchart on the board from the bottom up. Start with the direct authorities that students have in their lives, such as parents and teachers. Continue upward with the authorities above them. (For example, teachers have principals over them; parents have bosses and police over them.) Fill in the flowchart until students cannot think of any more authority figures.

Invite a student to read aloud **Romans 13:1–2**. Complete the flowchart by adding God at the very top. Explain that all authority comes from God and is set up by God. Lead students to see that when they complain about or disrespect any authority, it is as if they are complaining about and disrespecting God Himself. Conversely, when they obey and respect authority, it is as if they are obeying and respecting God. This honors and pleases Him.

Discuss that when people obey authority, law and order are maintained, the people know what to do, and they are protected. Read **Jeremiah 42:6**. Explain that sometimes respecting authority can be really displeasing, but God wants everyone to obey His voice, and obey the voice of the authority He has placed over them. Ask students to identify some things they might be asked to do that might be displeasing. (**Possible answers: doing chores when I'd rather play; sitting at a different desk because my teacher said to**) Discuss how they can show respect even though it may be unpleasant.

Note that there is such a thing as bad authority. Some students might already understand this by experience. Explain that occasionally in life they will be faced with authority that is unpleasant or even wrong. Sometimes bad people are put in charge and lead others to do bad things. Explain to students that they are supposed to obey and respect authority as long as the authority does not go against God's law. Explain that students must always obey God first, then people (Acts 5:29). Loyalty to God takes priority over human authority. Teach students to report the wrong actions of any authority figure to an adult they can trust, such as their parents or teachers.

Student Page 6.2
Allow students to work in pairs to complete the page.

Review
- Who establishes all authority? (**God**)
- Why are people given authority? (**Possible answers: to maintain law and order, to help us know what to do, to protect us**)
- When should you obey authority? (**We should obey authority all of the time unless it goes against God's law.**)

Notes:

> **APPLICATION**
> - Think of a time you were respectful even though it was hard. What helped you in the situation? (**Answers will vary but should include that we knew we were pleasing God.**)
> - What are specific ways you can show respect? (**by listening and obeying**)

6.3 Miriam and Aaron Learn Respect
Focus: Disrespecting Authority

↪ EXTENSION

3A Have students play the game Attitude Charades. Write different positive and negative attitudes on pieces of paper. Students are to enact the attitudes that are written on the pieces of paper. Their classmates should guess the attitude being enacted, and then should state the opposite attitude.

REINFORCEMENT

Miriam and Aaron began complaining first about Moses' wife. While this might have been ethnically driven, it is clear by what they said that this was merely a smoke screen, a diversion of the real issue at hand. What they tried to convey as constructive criticism was nothing more than jealousy. The lesson to be learned is the following: self-evaluation of heart motives helps to stem undue criticism of others.

Introduction

Select a student and quietly ask that student to role-play the act of talking back when you ask him or her to do something. In front of the class, ask the student to do something. When the student talks back, ask the class if they feel like the student did anything wrong and why it might be wrong. (**Answers will vary.**) Ask the class what should be done about this situation. (**Answers will vary.**) Explain to students that the talking-back interaction was staged. Inform them that today's lesson is about ways that authority is disrespected.

Directed Instruction ↪

Invite one student to summarize Numbers 12—Miriam and Aaron disrespect Moses. Ask students what actions Miriam and Aaron did that showed disrespect. (**They grumbled and complained against Moses.**) Explain that when a person complains about a leader, it shows that the person does not value the decisions made by the leader. The poor attitudes expressed distract others and set the example for others to also complain. Explain that complaining is toxic and quite infectious.

Complaining is not the only way people show disrespect to authority. Ask students to identify other actions and attitudes that might be disrespectful. (**Possible answers: lying, hating, jealousy**) Invite a student to read **Titus 2:9–10**. This passage is talking about slaves and masters, but the concept works with anyone who is under authority. Ask students in what two distinct ways the passage mentions how disrespect is shown. (**talking back and stealing**) People who show disrespect by talking back tend to do so if they do not like the person in authority over them, or do not want to do what is being asked of them. Regardless, *talking back*, which means *to verbally oppose or speak against authority*, is wrong.

Allow time for students to come up with ways they can express respect. Separate students into pairs, and instruct the pairs to write respectful actions or attitudes on a piece of paper. Let students present their ideas to the class. Explain that respecting authority involves proper thoughts, actions, and words.

Student Page 6.3
Read each of the following scenarios aloud, and let students identify how disrespect is being shown. Students are to draw a line between the picture and the action of disrespect on the page:
- Aaron's mom asked him to not swing the bat in the house. When she left the room, Aaron swung the bat anyway and broke a vase.
- When Andrew's older sister told him to get his pajamas on, he yelled at her and said, "I don't have to! It's not my bedtime yet!"
- The lesson they were doing in science was not interesting to Rebecca and Julie, so they started telling secrets and giggling in class.
- Mary came in to school chewing gum, even though it was against the rules. When the principal told Mary to spit out the gum, Mary was rude and rolled her eyes.

- When Anita's mom told her to eat her vegetables, she interrupted and complained with rude sounds and actions.
- The babysitter had asked Alex to play nicely. He disobeyed and acted unruly.

Review
- How did Miriam and Aaron show their disrespect? (**They grumbled and complained about their leader Moses.**)
- What two attitudes does Titus 2:9–10 tell you not to show toward your authorities? (**not to talk back or steal**)
- What are other ways you show disrespect with your actions? (**Possible answers: not listening, disobeying, expressing rude behavior with our body language, lying, interrupting, yelling**)

Notes:

APPLICATION
- What are ways you show disrespect with your attitudes? (**Possible answers: thinking badly about the person in authority, getting angry or frustrated, choosing not to listen**)
- Think of a time this week you have been disrespectful. What can you do to make that situation better? (**Possible answers: pray, ask for forgiveness, obey, listen**)

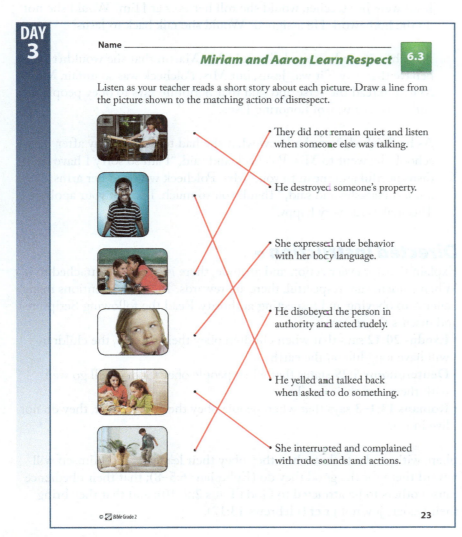

| 6.4 | # Miriam and Aaron Learn Respect
Focus: Consequences |

EXTENSION

4A Divide students into groups of three or four. Give each group a set of BUILDING BLOCKS or PLASTIC BUILDING BRICKS. Assign one leader per group. Each leader should determine what object will be built with the blocks. The group must listen to and obey the instructions of the leader and work together to build the object of the leader's choice. Remind students that sometimes they might want to be in charge or they might want to do things their own way. But, they are instructed to respect an authority figure, as long as the authority figure is not asking them to go against God's law.

4B As a review, practice locating books of the Old Testament by naming one out loud. Let the first student who locates it select and call aloud the next Old Testament book. Sing the song "Books of the Bible" from the Grade 2 URL.

Introduction

Read the following story to students:

Natasha thought her teacher Mrs. Polcheck gave students a lot of homework and didn't explain things well. Natasha soon started complaining about Mrs. Polcheck to her classmates at lunch. Many girls agreed that Mrs. Polcheck was unfair and started complaining too.

Natasha became so upset, she stopped doing her homework. When her teacher talked to her about the missing homework, Natasha crossed her arms and rolled her eyes. She didn't even look up at Mrs. Polcheck when she spoke. A few days later, when Natasha was corrected for a wrong answer, she talked back to Mrs. Polcheck with a bad tone in her voice, for which she was sent to the principal, Mr. Martin.

When Natasha got to Mr. Martin's office, she began to say how she didn't like her teacher Mrs. Polcheck. Mr. Martin stopped Natasha and opened his Bible. He read a verse about slaves obeying masters. He said that Christians are to obey people in authority just as they would obey Jesus, with respect and honest hearts. Mr. Martin asked Natasha if Jesus were her teacher, would she roll her eyes at Him? Would she not do the homework He assigned? Would she talk back to Jesus?

Natasha was embarrassed. She told Mr. Martin that she wouldn't behave that way if it was Jesus; but Mrs. Polcheck was so unfair. Mr. Martin reread the verse and said that Scripture says to obey people in authority as a way of honoring Jesus.

As he finished, Natasha knew what she had to do. That day after school, she went to Mrs. Polcheck and said, "I am so sorry I have been disrespectful and mean to you." Mrs. Polcheck wrapped her arms around Natasha and said, "Thank you so much. I accept your apology. This makes me very happy."

Directed Instruction

Explain that for every action and attitude, there is a reaction attached to it. When students are respectful, there are rewards. The Bible mentions many benefits to obeying and respecting authority. Read the following Scriptures and discuss the rewards:

- **Exodus 20:12** says that when children obey their parents, the children will have long life on the earth.
- **Deuteronomy 5:29** states that when people obey God, it will go well with them and their family.
- **Romans 13:1–3** says that when people obey the government, they do not live in fear.

Share with students that when they obey their leaders, God Himself will reward them for the good they do (Ephesians 6:5–8); that their obedience causes others to be attracted to God (Titus 2:9–10); and that they bring their leaders joy, not grief (Hebrews 13:17).

Brainstorm other possible benefits to obeying and respecting authority. (This is an opportunity to be more practical, mentioning things like good grades or physical rewards, such as a special privilege or treat.) Ask students to share ideas about what might happen if they disobey the different authorities in their lives, such as parents, teachers, principals, or the police. (**Possible answers: be harmed, get in trouble**) Record the answers given on the board. Show that the benefits of respecting authority far outweigh the consequences of not respecting authority.

Student Page 6.4
Read the directions. Allow students to independently complete the page.

Review
- What are some benefits you might have from respecting authority? (**Possible answers: We might have long life; we might get good things.**)
- What are some consequences of not respecting authority? (**We might be harmed or get in trouble.**)
- What does God promise you in Deuteronomy 5:29 if you obey Him? (**that life will go well for me and my family**)

APPLICATION
- Think of a time you were disrespectful to your parents or a teacher. What were some of the consequences because of that disrespect, and how did that make you feel? (**Answers will vary.**)
- Is there someone you have been disrespectful to? What can you do to make things right? (**Possible answers: pray, apologize, commit to being respectful**)
- How can you caution yourself to not be disrespectful in the future? (**Answers will vary but should include to remember Scripture says not to and to be willing to obey the Lord.**)

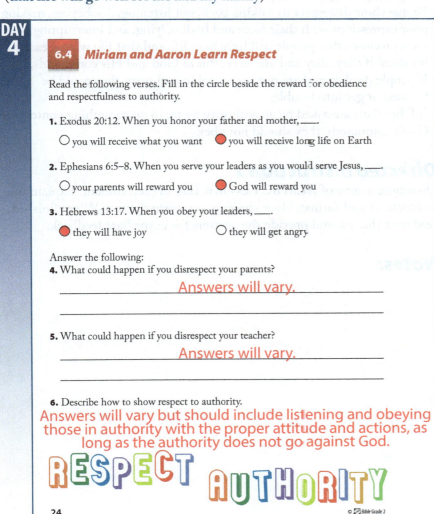

6.5 Miriam and Aaron Learn Respect

Focus: Review and Assessment

★ PREPARATION

Select **VA 6A Miriam and Aaron Learn Respect**. (*Lesson Review*)

Make one copy of **BLM 6C Lesson 6 Test** for each student. (*Directed Instruction*)

Lesson Review ★

Use **VA 6A Miriam and Aaron Learn Respect** to review the Bible truths from this lesson. Cover the following concepts:

- *Authority* means *the power to enforce rules or give orders, or someone who has been given the power to enforce rules.*
- *Respect* is defined as *a state of showing a proper attitude toward others, especially to those in charge.*
- Miriam and Aaron complained about Moses, their brother, and his authority.
- Miriam and Aaron were upset with Moses because they were jealous and wanted recognition.
- God told Miriam and Aaron that Moses was a faithful servant, and they should have been afraid to speak against him.
- After God finished speaking to Miriam and Aaron, He departed, and Miriam's skin became leprous.
- Aaron asked Moses for forgiveness; Moses prayed to God, and God forgave them and healed Miriam.
- God establishes all authority to maintain order and protect people.
- Scripture gives good examples of how to respect authority.
- People show disrespect by talking back, not listening, disobeying, making poor expressions with their faces and bodies, lying, and interrupting.
- God promises that people will have long life and that life will be easier for them if they obey and are respectful to God and His commands.
- If people disobey and are not respectful to authority, they could be harmed or get into trouble.
- If Christians are asked by an authority figure to do something contrary to God's commands, they should not obey.

Directed Instruction ★

Distribute a copy of **BLM 6C Lesson 6 Test** to each student. Explain the instructions and format. Have students complete the test. When finished, read over the test and provide the answers for immediate feedback.

Notes:

Lesson Preparation
Joshua Leads Israel
7.0

Expected Student Outcomes

KNOW
God commissions Joshua to lead the Israelites and emphasizes the need for Joshua to follow His Word.

DO
Students will:
- complete sentences about how God prepared Joshua and also prepares them
- write about an effective, godly leader
- discover God's encouraging promises
- learn a way to study and apply God's Word
- recall and practice how to share God's Word with others

APPLY
Students will read and study God's Word in order to understand how to follow Him.

Lesson Outline

I. Godly leaders are prepared (Num 27:15–23, Deut 34:1–6, Josh 1:1–9, Rom 13:1, 1 Tim 2:1–3)
II. Godly leaders trust God's promises (Deut 34:1–6, Josh 1:1–9, Isa 41:10, 1 Jn 2:25, Mt 11:28–29, Jn 14:27, Acts 1:8)
III. Godly leaders know God's Word (Ps 119:11)
   A. How to study the Bible (Josh 1:8–9)
IV. Godly leaders share God's Word (Mt 28:18–20)
   A. Sharing God's plan of salvation (Jn 3:16, 14:2–3; Rom 3:23; 1 Cor 15:3; Rom 6:23)

♥ TEACHER'S HEART

When God has work to do, He looks for willing servants to do it. Joshua succeeded Moses as the willing servant to lead the Israelites, and God used Moses to mentor and prepare Joshua for the task. Joshua, no doubt, learned much from Moses about loving God, following God's Word, and serving Him. Joshua watched what Moses did and began to develop his own faith walk with God. Moses influenced Joshua for good.

You are the model and mentor God has placed in the lives of your students. You want to influence them for the kingdom of God. What an awesome privilege! Allow them to see you loving God and following His Word. Think carefully about the things you value and how they reveal where your heart is. Students want to emulate leaders, so ask God to help you be the kind of example that will draw your students to the lordship of Jesus Christ. Esteem God's Word by making time in your class this year for reading and studying the Bible together.

MEMORY VERSE
Joshua 1:8

GLOSSARY WORDS
- commission
- disciple

★ MATERIALS

Day 1:
- VA 7A Joshua Leads Israel
- Time Line
- BLM 7A Friendly Letter Outline (*Extension*)

Day 2:
- Long rope, prizes
- VA 7A Joshua Leads Israel
- DM-6 Map of Canaan, the Promised Land (*Extension*)

Day 3:
- Paper bag, jar of honey, compact mirror, container of water, picture of a sword, flashlight (*Extension*)

Day 4:
- BLM 7B Sharing God's Word
- PP-3 Sharing God's Word (*Extension*)

Day 5:
- VA 7A Joshua Leads Israel
- BLM 7C Lesson 7 Test

♪ SONGS
Promised Land

TEACHER RESOURCES
Lucado, Max. *Outlive Your Life: You Were Made to Make a Difference*. Thomas Nelson, 2010.

STUDENT RESOURCES
Arthur, Kay, and Janna Arndt. *How to Study Your Bible for Kids*. Harvest House Publishers, 2001.

Supplemental Materials are available to download. See Understanding Purposeful Design Bible at the front of this book for the Grade 2 URL.

7.1 Joshua Leads Israel
Focus: Godly Leaders Are Prepared

 MEMORY VERSE
Joshua 1:8

MEMORY WORK
- Have students write the Memory Verse with different colors. Tell them to start by writing the verse in blue crayon; next, to trace around each blue letter of the verse in red crayon; and then, to finish by tracing around each blue and red letter of the verse in yellow crayon. Have students practice saying the multi-colored verse.

 PREPARATION
Select **VA 7A Joshua Leads Israel**. (Directed Instruction)

 EXTENSION
1A Instruct students to use **BLM 7A Friendly Letter Outline** to write a letter of thanks to a godly leader. Suggest that students also use Scripture for encouragement. Tell students to draw a picture in the box on the page.

1B Read **Luke 16:10a**. Discuss how Joshua had been faithful in little by being Moses' helper. When Joshua fought the Amalekites (Exodus 17:9), he was strengthened in warfare. When Joshua spent time in the tabernacle, which was a special tent in which Moses and others worshipped the Lord, he was strengthened in worship (Exodus 33:11). When Joshua stood up for Moses' leadership (Numbers 11:28), Joshua was strengthened in understanding how to govern the people. Because Joshua had been faithful and trustworthy in all these things, God gave him greater responsibility by choosing him to lead the Israelites into the Promised Land.

Introduction
Select a student to lead the game Leader Says. Invite the student to come to the front of the room, and tell the other students that you are giving this student authority. Remind students that *authority* means *the power to enforce rules or give orders, or someone who has been given the power to enforce rules.* Inform the class that they may choose to do things, such as clapping hands, jumping up and down, turning around, or following other directions, but only when the leader directs them to do so by saying, "Leader says …" (For example, "Leader says to clap.") The leader may also choose to describe an action without saying "Leader says." If students do the action when the leader has not stated "Leader says," those students must sit down. Students who listen carefully and follow the leader at the appropriate times will be standing at the end of the game.

As the game concludes, compare how you appointed a leader for the game with how God positions and prepares leaders to be in authority over you, the students, their parents, and others (Romans 13:1). Share that in the Bible truth today, God gives Joshua authority and prepares him to take over the leadership of God's chosen people, the Israelites.

Directed Instruction ★
Display **VA 7A Joshua Leads Israel** and read the back for today's Bible truth. Explain that God gave Joshua the special job of leading the children of Israel. As a person of authority, Joshua had to be courageous and trust God to help him lead the people the way God intended in order for the Israelites to take possession of the Promised Land.

God had prepared Joshua for a long time to be able to do what was needed to lead. Joshua was born in Egypt during the time the Hebrew people were enslaved by the Egyptians. Joshua witnessed firsthand the struggles and victories of Moses and God's chosen people. Joshua learned how to help Moses defend the Israelites in battles (Exodus 17:8–13) and was one of the spies sent into the land of Canaan (Numbers 13:8, 16). He was also a servant to Moses (Exodus 24:13). Joshua, filled with God's Spirit, had been under Moses' leadership, studying the Book of the Law, and helping the people just as Moses did. He was now ready to do what God had called him to do.

Share with students that just as God prepared Joshua, so they, too, need to be prepared to lead others the way God intends. Encourage your students to learn from godly leaders, as Joshua learned from Moses, in order to be prepared for what God calls them to do. To do this, they should study God's Word, rely on the Holy Spirit, pray for those in authority (1 Timothy 2:1–3), and spend time listening to godly leaders.

Student Page 7.1
Read the directions and have students complete the page.

Review
- Who prepared Joshua for leadership? (**God and Moses**)
- How was Joshua like Moses as a leader? (**Possible answers: They both followed God; they expected the people to know and follow God's Word; they trusted God to help them lead.**)
- How was Joshua prepared to be a godly leader? (**Possible answers: He helped Moses; he learned to trust God; he learned God's commands from Moses and the Book of the Law; he fought in battles.**)

Time Line
Guide students through the time line from Creation to Joshua. Ask students to share one fact about each event and person.

Notes:

APPLICATION
- Why do you think God picked Joshua to lead after Moses? (**Possible answers: Joshua had obeyed God for many years; he was filled with God's Spirit; he was prepared to do the job by having watched Moses; he expected the people to follow God.**)
- Do you think Joshua was fearful of leading? Why or why not? (**Answers will vary but should include that Joshua was trained and probably felt confident in his knowledge, but that he may have been fearful because he had never had the role of leading the people before.**)
- What are some qualities that godly leaders have? (**Possible answers: They trust God for guidance; they act courageously and with obedience; they are filled with God's Spirit; they are prepared by God for the job.**)
- How can you be prepared to lead others? (**Possible answers: I should pray for God's guidance; I should obey God and act courageously; I should be teachable and learn from godly leaders in authority; I should trust God to help me be prepared.**)

REINFORCEMENT
Joshua's name is appropriate for what God was doing in and through him. *Joshua* means *salvation* (Numbers 13:8). In the New Testament, Joshua's name is also the equivalent of *Jesus*, which means *Yahweh is salvation* (Matthew 1:21).

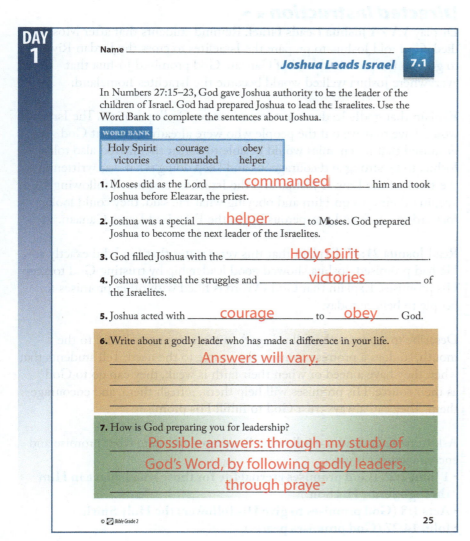

DAY 1

Joshua Leads Israel 7.1

In Numbers 27:15–23, God gave Joshua authority to be the leader of the children of Israel. God had prepared Joshua to lead the Israelites. Use the Word Bank to complete the sentences about Joshua.

WORD BANK
Holy Spirit   courage   obey
victories   commanded   helper

1. Moses did as the Lord __commanded__ him and took Joshua before Eleazar, the priest.
2. Joshua was a special __helper__ to Moses. God prepared Joshua to become the next leader of the Israelites.
3. God filled Joshua with the __Holy Spirit__.
4. Joshua witnessed the struggles and __victories__ of the Israelites.
5. Joshua acted with __courage__ to __obey__ God.
6. Write about a godly leader who has made a difference in your life.
   __Answers will vary.__
7. How is God preparing you for leadership?
   __Possible answers: through my study of God's Word, by following godly leaders, through prayer__

7.2 Joshua Leads Israel

Focus: Godly Leaders Trust God's Promises

★ PREPARATION

Have a LONG ROPE and TWO PRIZES on hand. (*Introduction*)

Select **VA 7A Joshua Leads Israel**, and the song "Promised Land" from the Grade 2 URL. (*Directed Instruction*)

⟳ EXTENSION

2A Display **DM-6 Map of Canaan, the Promised Land**. Ask students to find and point to Canaan, the Promised Land. God promised Joshua that everywhere he walked would become the Israelites' homeland. Encourage students to recount other biblical events and point to the areas on the map where those events occurred. (**Possible answers: the Hebrews leaving Egypt, crossing the Red Sea, wandering in the wilderness, crossing the Jordan River**)

2B Instruct students to draw something they value on a piece of paper. Explain that *value* means *something of great worth or importance*. Encourage each student to share briefly about their valued object. Challenge students to think about the Bible, which is the one object of greatest value to all of us. God and His promises will last forever.

Introduction ★

Stretch out a LONG ROPE on the floor. Invite two volunteers to stand on the rope and face the same direction. Tell the volunteers that you promise to give them a PRIZE if they can walk on the rope, keeping their eyes straight ahead, all the way to the end. Quietly ask a few students to distract the two volunteers by speaking loudly or offering a treat to their friends. If a volunteer gives in to the distraction or temptation and looks away or walks off the rope, tell that volunteer to return to his or her seat. If either volunteer completes what you asked, give him or her your promised prize.

Assuming at least one of the volunteers obeyed your directions, tell students that you fulfilled your promise of a prize for obedience. Likewise, God promised to give Joshua and the Israelites possession of Canaan if they were careful to do what God said. Read **Joshua 1:7** together. Compare the rope-walking activity (when the two volunteers tried to keep from looking to the right or left, away from distraction or temptation) to the obedience that God expected from the Israelites.

Directed Instruction ★ ⟳

Display **VA 7A Joshua Leads Israel**. Remind students that after Moses died, God told Joshua to prepare the Israelites to cross the Jordan River to go into the promised land of Canaan. God promised Joshua that everywhere Joshua walked would become the Israelites' homeland.

Explain that godly leaders trust in and act on God's promises. The Israelites would have to drive out the people who were already there, but God promised that no enemies would be able to defeat them. God also told Joshua to be strong and courageous and keep doing what was written in the Book of the Law. If Joshua and the Israelites continued following God, keeping their eyes on Him and obeying what He said, they could look forward to a safe and prosperous life in the Promised Land, Canaan.

Read **Joshua 21:45**. Explain that this verse states that God did exactly as He had promised. Joshua showed good leadership by trusting God to keep His promises. Explain that God's Word is filled with other promises for people to believe today.

Describe to students the following: As a straw connects liquid to the mouth, so does a promise connect the source to the need. Tell students that when they have a need or when their faith is weak, they can go to God as their source. His promises will help them, refresh them, and encourage them. They can always trust God to fulfill His promises.

Ask students to read the following Scriptures and state what promise and encouragement is given:
• 1 John 2:25 (**God promises eternal life for those who believe in Him through Jesus, His Son.**)
• Acts 1:8 (**God promises to give His followers the Holy Spirit.**)
• John 14:27 (**God promises peace.**)

- Isaiah 41:10 (**God promises to give us strength and help.**)
- Matthew 11:28–29 (**God promises rest for the weary.**)

Sing the song "Promised Land" from the Grade 2 URL.

Student Page 7.2
Allow students to work in collaborative pairs to complete the page.

Review
- What promises did God give to Joshua? (**Possible answer: God promised Joshua and the Israelites their homeland, to be with Joshua, to defeat the enemies of Joshua and the Israelites, and to be with Joshua wherever he went.**)
- What are some promises God gives to those who believe in Him? (**Possible answers: strength, help, eternal life, encouragement, rest, peace, the Holy Spirit**)
- What do all these promises tell you about God? (**Possible answer: He loves us, cares for us, provides for us, and we can trust Him.**)

APPLICATION
- How do you think Joshua and the Israelites felt when they experienced God's promises coming true? (**Answers will vary but should include that they would have felt an increase in trust and faith, and their relationship with God would have become stronger.**)
- How do you feel when someone fulfills a promise to you? (**Answers will vary.**)
- When God makes promises, how do you know He will keep them? (**Possible answers: God doesn't lie; He always keeps His promises; He cares about me.**)
- Which promise from God is most special to you? Why? (**Answers will vary but should include that because God always keeps His promises, if we believe in Jesus, we have eternal life with God.**)

REINFORCEMENT
The Israelites had to cross over the Jordan River to get into the Promised Land. This was not an easy feat because the river was in flood stage (Joshua 3:15). The Jordan River contains a large amount of water because several major tributaries flow into it. God used the Jordan River and the Jordan Valley for many significant events throughout the Old Testament and the New Testament. Elijah and Elisha performed miracles there. John the Baptist preached about Jesus coming to the Jordan River. Jesus was baptized and centered some of His ministry in the Jordan Valley.

DAY 2

7.2 Joshua Leads Israel

Joshua 1:1–9 and Deuteronomy 34:1–6 tell of promises from God to Joshua and the Israelites. Write **yes** beside each statement that is a promise from God. Write **no** beside each statement that is not a promise from God.

1. **yes** God promised Joshua the land of Canaan.
2. **no** God promised Joshua that he would receive many cattle and sheep when the Israelites arrived in Canaan.
3. **no** God promised the Israelites that there would be peace and no more fighting.
4. **yes** God promised Joshua that He would be with Joshua everywhere he went.

Isaiah 41:10 and John 3:16 are two of God's promises. Fill in the circle next to the word that best completes each sentence.

5. God promises to give His followers strength and _____.
   ○ money   ○ a lot of friends   ● help

6. God promises _____ to those who believe in Him.
   ○ no problems   ● eternal life   ○ no help

7. Choose one of these two promises and write why it encourages you.
   Answers will vary.

7.3 Joshua Leads Israel
Focus: Godly Leaders Know God's Word

EXTENSION

3A Fill a LARGE PAPER BAG ahead of time with a JAR OF HONEY, a COMPACT MIRROR, a SMALL CONTAINER OF WATER, a PICTURE OF A SWORD, and a FLASHLIGHT. Pull each item out of the bag, one at a time, and ask your students what these items have in common. In the following order, read the verses to your students to show how all of the items are related to God's Word: **Psalm 19:9–10** (honey), **James 1:23–24** (mirror), **Ephesians 5:26** (water), **Hebrews 4:12** (sword), and **Psalm 119:105** (light).

3B Inform the students about missionaries who translate Scripture and how important the missionaries' work is. Consider sharing a story about a specific translator, such as William Cameron Townsend, the founder of Wycliffe Bible Translators. Spend time praying for Wycliffe Bible Translators and missionaries from other Christian organizations who are translating and sharing God's Word.

Introduction

Instruct students to finish the following statements on a piece of paper:
• My greatest strength is …
• The thing I like to do most in my free time is …
• I feel most encouraged when …

Collect the answers. As you read a few aloud, ask the class to guess the person you are reading about. After students enjoy guessing a few times, have them guess who the following person is. Tell them he is someone from another school. Read the following statements:
• His greatest strength is helping others.
• The thing he likes to do most in his free time is to play soccer.
• He is most encouraged when someone tells him he did a good job.

Students will try to guess who the person is, but with no success. Inform students that the statements were describing a nice boy named *Jono*. Ask students why it was easier to guess about their classmates than about Jono. **(Possible answers: We don't know who Jono is; we know nothing about Jono; we have not spent any time with Jono.)** Share that just as they know about people because they spend time with them, so God wants them to spend time with Him so that they can get to know Him. They can do that by praying and studying and learning God's Word as Joshua did.

Directed Instruction

Joshua was prepared to be a leader. Joshua knew God's Word and had a close relationship with God. Joshua learned about following God's Word from Moses. God told Joshua that it was very important that he and the Israelites obey the Book of the Law. If they knew God's Word and obeyed it, they did not need to fear their enemies, because God would be with them everywhere they went.

Emphasize that God's Word is still important and valuable today. Tell students that when they love God, study His Word every day, and apply it to their lives, God guides them in life. When they spend time knowing God and learning from His Word, He helps them to know right from wrong and He comforts them. Read **Psalm 119:11**. Explain to students that being able to recall God's Word in all types of situations is a way to assure themselves of the Lord's presence and help in their life.

Tell students that whenever they study God's Word, they should first pray and ask God to teach them what they need to learn. Inform students that there are three questions that they can ask themselves when reading the Bible. Read **Joshua 1:9**, and ask the three questions as practice:
• What is this Bible verse saying? **(Possible answers: to not be afraid, to be strong and trust in God)**
• Why is this Scripture helpful? **(Possible answers: It reminds me to be courageous and bold even when I don't think I can do something; it encourages me to believe that God is with me.)**

- How will I respond? (**Possible answers: I can trust God when I am afraid; I will choose to believe that God is with me always.**)

Student Page 7.3
Read the directions. Have students complete the page independently.

Review
- What was important for Joshua to do as a leader? (**Answers will vary but should include to study and obey the Book of the Law in order to keep a strong relationship with the Lord.**)
- When is it important to study God's Word? Why? (**It is important to study God's Word every day so I can encourage myself in the Lord and so I can honor Him.**)
- Before studying God's Word, what should you do? (**pray and ask God to teach me new things**)
- State three questions to ask yourself when studying God's Word. (**What is the Scripture saying? Why is this Scripture helpful? How will I respond?**)

APPLICATION
- How is learning God's Word helpful? (**Possible answers: It shows me how to follow God; it comforts me.**)
- How does studying God's Word show that you love God? (**Possible answers: It shows I value God most; I choose to spend time with Him; I care about what God tells me.**)
- How will studying God's Word change your life? (**Possible answers: Studying God's Word helps me know God better and will help me not to do wrong things by reminding me of what's right; learning God's Word gives me the best way to encourage myself when I need it; knowing God's Word provides the guidance and answers I need.**)

DAY 3

Name _____

Joshua Leads Israel 7.3

God told Joshua and the Israelites to study and know His Word. Ask God to teach you what you need to learn from His Word. Pray. Read Joshua 1:8. Answer the three questions below to practice studying God's Word.

1. What does Joshua 1:8 tell you?
   Possible answers: to think about God's Word, to follow God's Word

2. Why is Joshua 1:8 helpful to you?
   If I know God's Word, it will help me through life.

3. How will you respond to Joshua 1:8?
   Answers will vary but should include a desire to read God's Word regularly.

4. Write a short prayer to the Lord, asking Him to help you study His Word.
   Answers will vary.

7.4 Joshua Leads Israel

Focus: Godly Leaders Share God's Word

★ PREPARATION

Make a copy of **BLM 7B Sharing God's Word** for each student. (*Directed Instruction*)

☞ EXTENSION

4A Show **PP-3 Sharing God's Word**. Motivate students to memorize the following Bible verses in order: John 3:16, 14:2–3; Romans 3:23; 1 Corinthians 15:3; Romans 6:23. Explain that these verses are helpful in sharing God's plan of eternal life with others. Offer an incentive to students who can recite all the verses by memory.

Introduction

Tell students to listen as you read this true story about a boy named *Ryan*: Ryan was listening to his second-grade teacher talk about knowing Jesus in a personal way and how God had changed her life. As Ryan listened, he realized that he had never really known God. Ryan thought that since his family believed in God and he went to a Christian school, he would automatically know God and go to heaven. As Ryan's teacher continued talking, the Holy Spirit excited Ryan's heart. Ryan wanted to know God in a personal way just like his teacher!

Later, Ryan asked his teacher if he could pray with her. She was delighted to pray with him. Ryan asked Jesus to forgive him of the wrong things he had done. He told Jesus he believed in what Jesus did for him when He died on the cross to pay for sin. Ryan was excited to have a personal relationship with God. Ryan told the rest of the class what he had done and the other students' lives were changed, too.

Directed Instruction ★ ☞

Share with students that Joshua had a personal relationship with God, and he put his trust in God. God gave Joshua a **commission**, which means *a job or task given to someone to do*. God entrusted Joshua to fulfill the commission of leading the Israelites.

Read **Matthew 28:18–20**. Explain that what is stated in this passage is called *the Great Commission*. Jesus was telling His disciples to go and help lead other people to know God and obey His commands. This commission was for all of Jesus' disciples. A **disciple** of Jesus is called *a follower of Jesus*. In order to fulfill the Great Commission, disciples should pray for people, share God's great love with everyone, and tell as many as possible of God's plan of eternal life. Then, they should be encouraged to know that the Holy Spirit will continue to draw those people closer to God.

Distribute **BLM 7B Sharing God's Word** to each student. Tell students to follow along on BLM 7B as you read the following explanatory statements, Scripture passages about eternal life, and student instructions:

1. God loves everyone and has a plan for every person. (Read **John 3:16**.) The heart represents God's love for people. Color the heart red.
2. Because God loves everyone, He has prepared a place for them to live with Him in heaven. (Read **John 14:2–3**.) The star represents God in heaven. Color the star yellow.
3. When people reject God, that sin separates them from God. (Read **Romans 3:23**.) The dark cloud represents sin. Color the cloud a dark color.
4. Jesus died on a cross to pay the price for sin, so that people do not have to be separated from God. (Read **1 Corinthians 15:3–4**.) The cross represents Jesus' payment for sin. Color the cross brown.
5. Because Jesus paid the price for sin and rose from the dead, anyone can receive His free gift of eternal life. When they do, they are not separated from God anymore. (Read **Romans 6:23**.) Color the gift any color.

Ask students to recount the symbols from this exercise without looking at BLM 7B. (**heart, star, dark cloud, cross, gift**) Tell students to use these symbols when they share God's Word and message of salvation with others.

Student Page 7.4
Read the directions. Assist students as needed to complete the page.

Review
- What did God commission Joshua to do? (**Possible answers: lead the Israelites, make sure the Israelites knew the Book of the Law**)
- What is a disciple of Jesus? (**a follower of Jesus**)
- What did Jesus commission His disciples to do? (**to share about God's plan of eternal life and to teach others His Word**)
- Name the symbols that can help you share God's Word with others. (**heart, star, dark cloud, cross, gift**)

APPLICATION
- Why is it important to share God's Word with others? (**Possible answers: God wants all people to receive eternal life; it is important to share God's Word so that others may know Him.**)
- Joshua showed courage in leading the Israelites. How might you show courage and obedience in doing your part of the Great Commission? (**Answers will vary.**)
- As a disciple of Jesus, how can you be ready to share God's Word? (**Possible answers: I can memorize God's Word to be ready when someone asks; I can be willing to tell about what Jesus did for me; I can learn ways to tell others about God's plan.**)
- What should you do if you tell someone about God and they do not accept God's Word? (**Possible answers: pray for them, knowing that the Holy Spirit will continue to draw them closer to God; keep showing them God's love**)

DAY 4

7.4 Joshua Leads Israel

God commissioned Joshua to lead and encourage the Israelites to follow God's Word. Jesus also gave a commission to His disciples to teach others about God's Word and His plan for eternal life. As God's disciple, you can share His plan with others.

Using the Scriptures as a guide, write beside each picture what you would say to tell someone about God's plan of eternal life.

1. John 3:16
God is love and He loves us.

2. John 14:2–3
God has prepared a place for us to live with Him in heaven.

3. Romans 3:23
Everyone has sinned and that sin separates us from God.

4. 1 Corinthians 15:3–4
Christ died on a cross to pay the price for our sin, so we do not have to be separated from God.

5. Romans 6:23
Since Jesus paid the price for our sin, we can receive His free gift of eternal life. We are not separated from God anymore.

7.5 Joshua Leads Israel
Focus: Review and Assessment

★ PREPARATION

Select **VA 7A Joshua Leads Israel** for review. (*Lesson Review*)

Make one copy of **BLM 7C Lesson 7 Test** for each student. (*Directed Instruction*)

Lesson Review ★

Use **VA 7A Joshua Leads Israel** to review the Bible truth. Cover the following concepts:
- Joshua was Moses' helper.
- Joshua observed Moses and learned from his leadership
- God prepared Joshua to take over leadership of the Israelites.
- Joshua was given authority by God to lead the Israelites after Moses died.
- Joshua courageously obeyed God and led the Israelites across the Jordan River into the land of Canaan, the Promised Land.
- God provided the land of Canaan to the Israelites.
- God promised Joshua He would be with Joshua wherever he went.
- A *commission* is defined as *a job or task given to someone to do.*
- God commissioned Joshua to lead the Israelites and encourage them to follow the Book of the Law.
- It is important to study the Bible daily and apply God's Word in life, just as Joshua did.
- God gives people many promises, such as eternal life, the Holy Spirit, peace, and rest and will fulfill these promises as the people put their faith in Jesus.
- *Disciples* are defined as *followers of Jesus.* They believe in Him and live to please Him.
- Disciples are given a commission by Jesus, called *the Great Commission.* Disciples are to obey this commission by telling others about God, His Word, and His plan of eternal life.
- The following symbols, meanings, and verses can help disciples share God's plan with others:
  heart = God's love (John 3:16)
  star = God in heaven (John 14:2–3)
  dark cloud = sin (Romans 3:23)
  cross = Jesus dying to pay for our sin; resurrection (1 Corinthians 15:3–4)
  gift = eternal life (Romans 6:23)

Directed Instruction ★

Distribute a copy of **BLM 7C Lesson 7 Test** to each student. Read the directions, and have students complete the test. When everyone has finished, give students an opportunity to practice sharing the Gospel with a partner, using the symbols and verses they have learned.

Notes:

Lesson Preparation
Joshua Obeys God

8.0

Expected Student Outcomes

KNOW
Joshua follows God's plan to conquer the city of Jericho.

DO
Students will:
- sequence the commands God gave Joshua to conquer Jericho
- identify God's two-fold big plan for everyone
- identify how God shows His specific plan to each person
- distinguish obedience and disobedience for Joshua and the Israelites
- read about children who, with God, have made a big difference and commit to doing the same

APPLY
Students will acknowledge that there is no problem too big for God as they follow His plan for their life.

Lesson Outline

I. Joshua obeys and conquers Jericho (Josh 6)
II. God's plan for His children (Jer 29:11)
    A. God's big plan (Jn 6:40)
    B. God's specific plan (1 Thess 4:3a)
III. Listening to and obeying God (Josh 6; 11:15)
IV. Nothing is impossible with God (Lk 1:37)

♥ TEACHER'S HEART

Jericho, a Canaanite city, was steeped in the lewd and sinful practices of that day. God brought judgment on the city through the obedience of Joshua and the Israelites. As surely as God judges the sin of a nation, He judges every individual.

Charles Spurgeon said, "All sin is contrary to the designs of eternal love, which has an eye to your purity and holiness. Do not run counter to the purposes of God. Each time you serve sin, you have crucified the Lord afresh, and put Him to an open shame. Can you bear that thought?"

Invite the Holy Spirit to search your attitudes and reveal those things that cannot continue to exist in your life. Allow God to cleanse you with hyssop and make you whiter than snow (Psalm 51:7, Isaiah 1:18). Let Joshua be an example. He stood in direct contrast to the behavior of the Canaanites of Jericho. He feared God; he dedicated his life to God; he obeyed God when it seemed ludicrous. Commit yourself afresh to obeying God. Make His purposes your own. God wants your life to totally reflect Him.

📖 MEMORY VERSE
1 John 3:22

GLOSSARY WORDS
- obedience

★ MATERIALS

Day 1:
- Envelopes
- DM-1 Character Traits, prize
- VA 8A Joshua Obeys God
- DM-7 Map of Israel and Jericho
- Sentence strips

Day 2:
- Package of cookies

Day 3:
- No additional materials are needed.

Day 4:
- VA 8A Joshua Obeys God
- Leather straps, beads (Extension)

Day 5:
- VA 8A Joshua Obeys God
- BLM 8A Lesson 8 Test

♪ SONGS
I Can Obey

TEACHER RESOURCES
Barna, George. *Transforming Children into Spiritual Champions*. Baker Books, 2016.
Willard, Dallas. *Hearing God*. CD. Hovel Audio Inc., 2005.

STUDENT RESOURCES
Mackenzie, Carine. *Wise Words to Obey: Words of Wisdom from the Book of Proverbs*. Christian Focus Publications, 2009.
Veggie Tales: Josh and the Big Wall. DVD. Universal Studios, 2018.

Supplemental Materials are available to download. See Understanding Purposeful Design Bible at the front of this book for the Grade 2 URL.

Joshua Obeys God
Focus: Joshua Obeys and Conquers Jericho

📖 MEMORY VERSE
1 John 3:22

MEMORY WORK
- Arrange students in groups to build a wall with the Memory Verse bricks made from construction paper. Encourage students to deconstruct and reconstruct the wall throughout the week for Memory Verse practice. Store the bricks in ENVELOPES as needed.

✷ PREPARATION
Cut brick shapes from construction paper. Write the words of the Memory Verse on the "bricks." Make several verse sets and store in ENVELOPES. (*Memory Work*)

Have **DM-1 Character Traits** ready to display. Select a SMALL PRIZE and hide it somewhere in your classroom. (*Introduction*)

Select **VA 8A Joshua Obeys God** and **DM-7 Map of Israel and Jericho** for use. Have SENTENCE STRIPS available. (*Directed Instruction*)

Introduction ★
Display **DM-1 Character Traits** and review the word **obedience**, which means *following directions wholeheartedly*. Explain to students that someone who obeys must listen to and follow directions promptly and with the right attitude. Ask a volunteer to come to the front of the class. Ask if the student is willing to obey. If the answer is yes, lead the student through a series of bizarre commands, such as quacking like a duck and touching every desk in the room. Eventually, lead the student to the hidden SMALL PRIZE. Explain that today's Bible truth is about God telling Joshua and the Israelites to obey some commands that did not make a lot of sense. Obedience for the student meant a prize; obedience for Joshua and the Israelites meant they got to see God do something absolutely amazing.

Directed Instruction ★
Read **VA 8A Joshua Obeys God**. Explain that Jericho was one of the earliest known cities. Throughout its history, it had multiple walls, with at least one that was very high and wide. Jericho's destruction was the result of its ungodly practices. It was the first city of many that would be overcome by the Israelites during their conquest of the land of Canaan.

Jericho was located in the central plains of Canaan. Show students **DM-7 Map of Israel and Jericho**. Explain how Jericho was a strategic location to begin the conquest of the Promised Land: it had natural springs of water; it had roadways and plains that would help mobilize great numbers of people; it would act as a divider between the northern and southern territories, separating the alliance between the Canaanite people. More important than being a strategic location, it was where God directed the Israelites to begin.

Review the very specific instructions God gave Joshua and the Israelites by writing them on SENTENCE STRIPS:
- March silently around the city once a day for six days.
- On the seventh day, march around the city seven times.
- Have seven priests blow horns, or trumpets, as they march in front of the ark of the covenant.
- At the long blast of the trumpets, have everyone shout.

Have students use the written instructions to reenact the Bible truth of Joshua and the Israelites conquering Jericho. Set up student desks in a large circle. Designate the following roles to students: *Joshua, priests to carry the ark of the covenant, seven priests to blow horns, soldiers as the front and rear guard, Israelites, citizens of Jericho.* Tell students designated as *citizens of Jericho* to stay within the walls and tell them to taunt and jeer the *Israelites* as they march around the "city." Have some kind of cue for the passing of days. Remind students that the people did not say a word when they were marching, until Joshua gave the command to shout.

Emphasize that these rules seemed odd and did not make much sense, but the people obeyed and the result was amazing. The entire wall collapsed

72

and they were able to take the city. It was a miracle to be sure, and God received all the credit.

Student Page 8.1

Remove the sentence strips from students' view. For Exercises 1–4, have students work in collaborative groups to sequence the instructions in order according to Joshua 6:2–5. Then, have students individually complete the remainder of the page.

Review
- Whom did God put in command over the Israelite army? (**Joshua**)
- How were the people to march around Jericho? (**They were to march without talking, and the soldiers were to be in front of the priests and behind the ark of the covenant.**)
- What were the Israelites to do on the seventh day after the seventh time around? (**The priests were to blow a long trumpet blast, and then at Joshua's command, the people were to shout.**)
- What was the result of the Israelites' obedience? (**The walls of Jericho collapsed and the Israelites were able to take the entire city.**)

DAY 1

Name _____

Joshua Obeys God 8.1

Read Joshua 6:2–5. Number each of the four commands that God gave to Joshua and the Israelites in the order given.

1. On the seventh day, march seven times. ____2____

2. At the long blast of the trumpets, have everyone shout. ____4____

3. March silently around the city once a day for six days. ____1____

4. Have seven priests blow horns, or trumpets, while marching in front of the ark of the covenant. ____3____

5. What was the result of the Israelites' obedience to God's instructions?
The walls collapsed and Israel conquered the whole city of Jericho.

6. Why do you think God gave such specific and strange commands?
Everyone would know that it was God in His power who brought the victory and not Israel in its power.

© Bible Grade 2   29

APPLICATION
- Why do you think God wanted the Israelites to march around the city instead of forcing their way inside? (**Possible answers: God was testing their obedience; God was showing the Israelites that it would be by His might and power that the walls would fall, not theirs; He wanted them to know He was in complete control.**)
- Read **Proverbs 3:5–6**. Use today's Bible truth as a point of reference to discuss this passage. Ask students to name things that God might ask them to do that might not make a lot of sense. (**Possible answers: pray for someone I don't know very well, give away some money I just received**)
- How can you make a commitment today to obey even if it does not make sense at the time, so that God can get the credit and glory? (**pray**)

REINFORCEMENT

Jericho is considered one of the oldest cities in the world. Archeological finds have been dated around 8,000 BC. Many people sought to settle in Jericho because of its perennial springs and oasis. In the Old Testament, *Jericho* is referred to as *the city of palm trees*. In New Testament times, its beauty attracted the eye and building skill of Herod the Great, who constructed a magnificent winter palace there. However, not everyone who settled in Jericho did so under friendly terms. There is archeological evidence that at many points in Jericho's history it had high and wide walls surrounding it, ostensibly to keep invaders out.

© Bible Grade 2   73

8.2 Joshua Obeys God
Focus: God's Plan for His Children

★ PREPARATION
Bring a **PACKAGE OF COOKIES** to class. (*Directed Instruction*)

⤴ EXTENSION
2A Encourage students to pray individually for things that might be in God's specific plan for them. Direct students to write about one or two things in their journal that they believe God is asking them to do.

Introduction
Discuss with students their weekend plans. Explain that sometimes they might have big plans to go to an amusement park. Once there, they might create smaller plans, such as going on a certain ride or eating at a certain place. Just like they make plans for things they want to do, God has special plans for each of His children. Today's lesson is about God's plans for His children. His desire is for each person to become His child.

Directed Instruction ★ ⤴
Review Lesson 8.1 by asking what God's big plan was for Joshua and the Israelites. (**to conquer Jericho**) God had a specific way to accomplish this task. Ask students for some of the specific commands the Israelites had to follow. (**Possible answers: march silently around the city once a day for six days; on the seventh day, march seven times**)

Read **Jeremiah 29:11**. Share that God has a good plan for His children. Next, read **John 1:12**. Explain that it is not until a person accepts Jesus as his or her personal Savior that he or she becomes a child of God.

Write in big letters on the board *God's Big Plan*. Read **John 6:40**. Explain that God's big plan starts with a desire for the entire world to *receive His gift of salvation*, which means *to hear about Jesus, believe in Him, and make a decision to follow Him*. This is a good time to make it personal for students, explaining that God wants each of them to have a relationship with Him through Jesus. Be sensitive to students who might need to talk individually about making this kind of decision. Allow the Holy Spirit to continue drawing closer those who are not already Christians. Ask students what needs to happen for the whole world to hear about Jesus. (**People who already believe in and follow Jesus need to talk about Him and share what they believe with people who do not yet belong to God's family.**)

Read **1 Thessalonians 4:3a**. The second part of God's big plan is *sanctification*, which means *the process of being set apart for a specific, holy purpose*. Show students a **PACKAGE OF COOKIES**. Ask students if there is anything special about those cookies. (**No.**) Discuss how they are the favorite cookie of someone in your family, and that person's birthday is coming up. This package of cookies is now being set apart as a special gift for that member of your family. Ask students to identify different things that are set apart for a specific purpose. (**Possible answers: toys to specifically be used in a pool, clothing set apart for special occasions**) Explain that sanctification, the second component to God's big plan for His children, is that they be set apart for the specific purpose of obeying God and living to please Him—essentially that they would live like Jesus.

Invite two volunteers to write the following under *God's Big Plan: 1) that you believe in Jesus (salvation),* and *2) that you live like Jesus (sanctification)*.

Explain that God has a specific plan for each one of His children. For Joshua and the Israelites, God's specific plan meant walking around a walled city for seven days. Discuss some specific plans God might have for you and your students. (**Possible answers: showing special kindness to a specific person, going to another country as a missionary, giving away a favorite toy**) The possibilities of God's specific plans are as varied as all the people in the world. Explain that to find out God's specific plan, God has provided tools of discovery: reading the Bible (Psalm 119:105), praying (Jeremiah 33:3), and listening to godly people (Proverbs 15:22). Using these tools can help anyone know what God wants him or her to do in life.

Student Page 8.2
Have students complete the page.

Review
- What are the two major parts of God's big plan? (**for people to receive the gift of salvation, and be set apart for a purpose—to live like Jesus**)
- What has to happen for the whole world to believe in Jesus as Savior? (**The whole world needs to hear about Jesus.**)
- What are three ways that will help you know God's specific plan for your life? (**reading the Bible, praying, and listening to godly people**)

APPLICATION
- Has there been a time when you have followed God's big plan to believe in Jesus as Savior? (**Answers will vary, but be sensitive to those who are considering their decision as well as those who are not quite ready.**)
- Who is someone you know who needs to hear about and believe in Jesus? (Lead students in prayer for those mentioned.)
- What are some ways you can live more like Jesus? (**Possible answers: pray for others; love unconditionally; care for others such as widows, orphans, and the poor; live how the Bible says to**)

REINFORCEMENT
According to recent studies, the most opportune time to reach people with the Gospel is between the ages of 5 and 12. The probability of someone believing in Jesus as their Savior in this age group is 32 percent. It goes down drastically to 4 percent for ages 13 to 18, and 6 percent for someone to believe in Jesus after the age of 19.

8.3 *Joshua Obeys God*

Focus: Listening to and Obeying God

★ PREPARATION

Select the song "I Can Obey" from the Grade 2 URL. (*Introduction*)

⟳ EXTENSION

3A Play the game Telephone. Have students sit in a line on the floor. Whisper into the first student's ear a short command only one time. Tell that student to then whisper the command into the ear of the next student, and so on, until your command gets to the end of the line. The last student must then perform the command that was passed down. At this point, the ending command will most likely not reflect the original command. Use this as an example of the importance of carefully listening in order to obey. If they do not carefully listen or cannot understand instructions, they cannot properly obey. All obedience must begin with listening.

Introduction ★

Sing the song "I Can Obey." Remind students that Joshua's obedience to God was necessary for the walls around Jericho to fall.

Directed Instruction ⟳

In the Bible truth about Joshua, God did something amazing, but it occurred in conjunction with Joshua's obedience. Joshua had to purpose to listen to and obey the instructions that God gave him. Today's lesson is about how God's children also need to listen and obey.

Explain that for God's children to obey Him, they have to listen first. Act out a small skit with a student. Pretend you are a second grader, and have the student pretend to be a parent repeatedly calling you to come do a chore. Pretend to be playing a game when the student calls your name. Ignore your name being called several times. Then, ask students what you should have done differently. (**You should have listened the first time your name was called and then completed the chore promptly.**) Explain that choosing to listen allows a person to obey quickly. Listening is the first step of obedience.

The second step is actually obeying what is being asked. To exemplify this, read the following story (adapted from Matthew 21:28–32):

> There were once two brothers named *Carlos* and *José*. One day, their dad came in and asked Carlos to take out the trash. Carlos said he didn't want to, but later changed his mind and took the trash out.
>
> The next week, their dad went to José and asked him to take out the trash. José said, "Sure, Dad, I'll do it in just a minute," but he kept playing his game and didn't do it.

Ask students which brother acted better or more honorably. (**Carlos**) Ask them why what Carlos did was better than what José did. (**Carlos said he didn't want to, which wasn't good, but he did eventually obey; José said he would complete the chore, but he chose not to. He didn't obey at all.**) Explain that sometimes people do the same thing when God, their parents, or teachers ask them to do something. They say they will, but they do not do it. That is disobedience. God wants His children to obey completely, not just with their words.

Remind students that *obedience* means *following directions wholeheartedly*. Emphasize that two key parts of obedience are doing things immediately and with the right attitude. If people drag their feet and take a long time in doing what is asked of them, they are not obeying the way they should. Likewise, if people do what is asked of them but have a bad attitude in the process, it shows their heart is not willing to be obedient.

Explain to students that sometimes obedience can be hard, but God will help when asked. Lead them in a prayer so that they can ask God to help them be to ready to listen and obey.

Student Page 8.3

Read instructions, and assist students as necessary to complete the page.

Review

- What is the first thing you need to do when your parents ask you to do something? (**listen**)
- When your teacher asks you to do something, how should you do it? (**promptly and with a willing attitude**)
- Who will help you obey if you ask? (**God**)

Notes:

DAY 3

Name _____

Joshua Obeys God   8.3

1. Read Joshua 6:1–5. Circle the words that show obedience to God's commands. Put an **X** over the words that show disobedience to God's commands.

people playing drums ✗	no priests ✗	tear down the gates of the city
talking ✗	(silent)	
(seven days)	dragging the ark ✗	(end with a loud shout)
end with clapping ✗	(soldiers in front)	soldiers in back ✗
five days ✗	(carrying the ark)	(playing horns, or trumpets)
(march around the city)	no soldiers ✗	

2. Look up obedience in the Glossary. Write the definition.

obedience: <u>following directions wholeheartedly</u>

3. Write a short prayer in which you ask God to help you listen and obey.

<u>Answers will vary.</u>

© *Bible Grade 2*   31

APPLICATION

- Which people in your life do you need to obey? (**Possible answers: God, parents, teachers, older family members**)
- Why is it important to obey? (**Possible answers: By obeying, I please God and can show I am responsible.**)
- Why is it hard to obey sometimes? (**I am not listening, or I am too excited, fearful, or greedy.**)
- How can you improve your obedience? (**I can choose to fully listen to what's being said and then promptly do what is asked of me.**)

REINFORCEMENT

In Exodus 23:16, God instructed the Israelites about first fruits. The Israelites were to give God the best of their soil, their crops, and their animals. Even their firstborn children were to be consecrated to the service of God.

Conquering Canaan was not to be any different. God said for the first and the best to be consecrated to Him. Jericho, located centrally in the plains of Canaan, was the first city to be conquered. It was also the best city in the land, with ample water and a tall, fortified wall. The Israelites were to take nothing for themselves; the city was to be dedicated solely to God. Thus, in conquering Jericho and leaving no survivors, the Israelites were obeying God's requirements completely.

© *Bible Grade 2*   77

8.4 Joshua Obeys God

Focus: Nothing Is Impossible with God

★ PREPARATION

Select **VA 8A Joshua Obeys God**. (*Introduction*)

Tear or cut pieces of construction paper into brick shapes. (*Directed Instruction*)

↻ EXTENSION

4A Use LEATHER STRAPS and COLORED BEADS to make wristbands for students to use as a reminder to pray all week for a problem they identified within their community or school. Use a different colored bead to encourage students to pray for each of the following categories: good ideas they can follow to implement change, a good attitude to care about the problem, courage to do whatever it takes, help to obey what God says to do.

4B Tell students to make a journal entry about how Hannah's story makes them feel and what it inspires them to do.

Introduction ★

Show students the picture on the front of **VA 8A Joshua Obeys God**. Ask students if there would ever be a time that they think God might ask them to walk around a wall seven times so that it will fall down. (**probably not**) Discuss how students might not have physical walls that need to come down, but there are other "walls"— problems in their families or communities that need help from God for change to occur. Read **Luke 1:37**, and share that today's lesson is all about how no problem is too big for God. He can tear down any "walls" in their life and in the life of their communities.

Directed Instruction ★ ↻

Lead a discussion with students about some major problems there might be in their school, their families, or their community, without identifying anything too personal. (**Possible answers: low funding for schools, a possible move, neighborhood crime**) Write down the problems on brick-shaped pieces of construction paper. Display the bricks as if they were a wall. Help students make the connection that these problems in their families and communities are like the big wall around Jericho, and with God's help those walls can come tumbling down. Tell students the following true-life story:

> When Hannah was five years old, she saw a man on the street eating out of a trash can. This made her sad and she wanted to help him. After talking to her mom, she found out that there are a lot of people who live on the street and who don't have money to buy food or clothes. This news caused her to not only want to help the man she saw on the street, but to help everyone who was homeless. Hannah wanted to end homelessness. She started an organization called *The Ladybug Foundation*. She began by decorating jars with ladybugs and taking the jars to businesses all over her city with notes asking for change to help homeless people. Now, Hannah travels all over the country to raise money and talk to homeless people. Her foundation has raised over half a million dollars, and she has seen many people who were living on the streets find a job and a place to live since she began. Hannah still believes that if everyone shares what they have, homelessness will be eliminated.

Work with students to select one problem written earlier on a paper brick. Have students think about some different ideas they might have to help their community with this problem. (**Possible answers: holding some fund-raising activities for school, making meals for elderly people, creating neighborhood patrol programs**) Remind students that there is no problem too big for God. Tell students that change can and does happen. Most often God uses a combination of His great power and people's willingness to obey and help. When these two are combined, God does amazing things. Lead students in prayer to ask God to help them with their selected project and to provide a miracle so change can happen.

78

Student Page 8.4

To further students' thinking on this subject, invite three volunteers to read these true stories of children who made a difference in their communities. Assist with the reading as needed. Encourage students to pray and ask God for an idea—a God-sized idea—that can knock down one of the "walls" in their community.

Review

- What are some problems in your community? (**Possible answers: homelessness and poverty, stray dogs or cats, people who are sick or have lost jobs, a park that needs to be cleaned up**)
- How did God take care of Joshua's big problem? (**God told Joshua to walk around Jericho, and God made the wall fall down.**)
- Is any problem impossible for God to solve? (**No, there is no problem too big for God.**)

Notes:

APPLICATION

- Read **Psalm 15**. Discuss with students how living righteously according to this psalm can be a way to help make positive change.
- Read **Isaiah 58:6–14** to your students and explain that it describes how to honor the Lord by caring for others. Discuss times when students have seen the oppressed, the hungry, and the poor and how that affected them. Discuss how compassion for others is a good motivation for trying to fix problems.

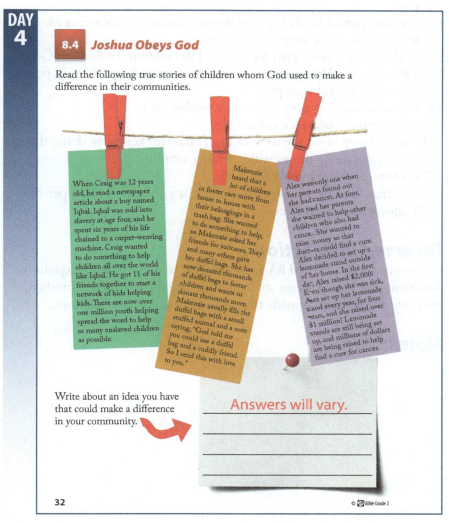

8.5 Joshua Obeys God

Focus: Review and Assessment

★ PREPARATION

Select **VA 8A Joshua Obeys God**. (*Lesson Review*)

Print a copy of **BLM 8A Lesson 8 Test** for each student. (*Directed Instruction*)

Lesson Review ★

Use **VA 8A Joshua Obeys God** to review the Bible truth. Cover the following concepts:

- Joshua had a strong relationship with God. He willingly listened to God and placed his faith in God. This relationship enabled Joshua to be an effective leader.
- God gave Joshua and the Israelites very specific instructions in order to conquer the city of Jericho: March around the city silently once a day for six days; have seven priests blow trumpets while marching in front of the ark of the covenant; on the seventh day, march seven times; at the long blast of the trumpets, have everyone shout.
- Jericho was an old, important city.
- Jericho had multiple walls, with at least one that was very high and wide.
- The Israelites obeyed, and the result was amazing. The huge wall collapsed and they were able to take possession of the city.
- God's big plan starts with a desire that the entire world would *receive His gift of salvation*, which means *to hear about Jesus, believe in Him, and make a decision to follow Him*.
- When a person accepts God's gift of salvation, he or she becomes a child of God.
- The second part of God's big plan is *sanctification*, which means *the process of being set apart for a specific, holy purpose.*
- God also has a specific plan for each of His children. To find out God's specific plan, God has given tools of discovery: reading the Bible, praying, and listening to godly people.
- *Obedience* means *following directions wholeheartedly.*
- The first step of obedience is listening.
- The second step of obedience is doing. It has two key parts: doing things promptly, and doing things with a willing attitude.
- There is no problem too big for God.
- Most often, God uses a combination of His great power and a person's willingness to obey and help.

Directed Instruction ★

Distribute a copy of **BLM 8A Lesson 8 Test** to each student. Explain the directions and format. Have students complete the test. When finished, read over the test, and provide the answers for immediate feedback.

Notes:

Lesson Preparation
Joshua Follows God

9.0

Expected Student Outcomes

KNOW
Joshua proclaims God's faithfulness and charges the Israelites to continue to follow Him.

DO
Students will:
- write about how Joshua followed God wholeheartedly
- recall Joshua's choice to remember God
- share a way that they can remember what God has done for them
- write a poem about God's faithfulness
- determine what to do when faced with temptation

APPLY
Students will recount God's faithfulness in their life and express confidence in His continuing faithfulness.

Lesson Outline

I. Joshua follows God wholeheartedly (Josh 23–24, Mk 12:30, Col 3:23)
II. Memorial to God (Josh 24:25–27, Gen 9:13, Deut 6:6, Josh 4:7, Lk 22:19–20)
III. God's faithfulness (Josh 24:1–15, Gen 1:1, 1 Jn 4:7–10, Rom 5:6, Mk 16:6, Jn 14:3, 28)
IV. Overcoming temptation (1 Jn 1:9, James 4:7–8)

♥ TEACHER'S HEART

Joshua led the people of Israel into a renewal of their covenant with God. The devotion of their hearts was waning severely as they encountered the temptations presented by the people living around them. Joshua was intently trying to refocus their affections on God. This was not an easy task. The Israelites saw Joshua's deep, personal commitment and service to God alone, which encouraged them to stay faithful.

At times your focus may need renewing too. Many things can pull you away from what is really important. Teaching year after year can sometimes become unfulfilling and mundane. The business of life, outside activities, and time constraints are all things that may draw you away from what is really important. Just as the Israelites renewed their covenant with God at Shechem, so you, as an educator, can renew your commitment to serve Him. Ask God for help and strength to carry out your commission. Look for ways to take your students from being on the sidelines of their faith, to being involved and serving God. This can happen by coming alongside, encouraging, and helping students to actively seek God in His Word. As the Israelites saw Joshua's commitment to serve God, students will see your commitment, which will encourage them to refocus their affections on God and renew their faith.

Supplemental Materials are available to download. See Understanding Purposeful Design Bible at the front of this book for the Grade 2 URL.

📖 MEMORY VERSE
Joshua 24:14

GLOSSARY WORDS
- wholeheartedly
- temptation

★ MATERIALS

Day 1:
- VA 9A Joshua Follows God
- BLM 9A Whole Hearts, envelopes (*Extension*)
- Leaf shapes (*Extension*)

Day 2:
- Box, personal items
- Piece of bread, cup, grape juice
- Smooth stones (*Extension*)
- Leaf shapes (*Extension*)

Day 3:
- DM-1 Character Traits
- Leaf shapes (*Extension*)

Day 4:
- Matches or lighter, candle

Day 5:
- VA 9A Joshua Follows God
- BLM 9B Lesson 9 Test

♪ SONGS
I Am Not Ashamed

TEACHER RESOURCES
Beers, Ronald A., and Amy E. Mason. *Bible Promises to Live By*. Tyndale House Publishers, Inc., 2007.

Rose, Shirley. *The Eve Factor: Resisting and Overcoming Temptation*. NavPress Publishing, 2006.

STUDENT RESOURCES
Lucado, Max. *With You All the Way*. Crossway Books, 2002.

9.1 Joshua Follows God
Focus: Joshua Follows God Wholeheartedly

MEMORY VERSE
Joshua 24:14

MEMORY WORK
- Divide students into two groups. Instruct each group to go to opposite sides of the room, and tell students that each group will be taking turns saying the Memory Verse. Direct the first group to recite the verse. When the first group is done reciting, the second group should begin reciting the verse. Repeat this procedure several times.

★ PREPARATION
Select **VA 9A Joshua Follows God** and the song "I Am Not Ashamed" from the Grade 2 URL. (*Directed Instruction*)

EXTENSION
1A Provide each student with a copy of **BLM 9A Whole Hearts** and an ENVELOPE. Ask students to name things they will commit to in order to follow God wholeheartedly. (**Possible answers: praying to God, learning God's Word, choosing friends well**) Read the directions. Instruct students to write ideas on each puzzle piece, cut the puzzle pieces apart, and place the pieces in their envelope. Tell students to give the puzzle to another student to solve.

1B Provide students with LEAF SHAPES cut from construction paper. Encourage students to write on the leaves how they will serve God wholeheartedly. On a classroom wall, create a construction paper tree, attaching the leaves to the trunk and limbs.

Introduction
Ask students to locate and read the word **wholeheartedly** in their Glossary. It means *with excitement, eagerness, and full purpose of heart*. Say the following phrases and tell students to stand when they hear a phrase that shows wholehearted action. Direct students to be seated if they hear an action that is performed *halfheartedly*, which means *with little interest or enthusiasm*.
- doing your best job with household chores because you love your parents (**students stand**)
- stuffing your clothes under your bed when asked to clean your room (**students sit**)
- walking to kick the ball, because you do not feel like helping your team (**students sit**)
- kicking the ball as hard as you can to help your team score a goal (**students stand**)
- asking a friend to church, even though your friend might not come (**students stand**)

Read **Mark 12:30**. Discuss what it means to love God with all your heart. (**Possible answers: to show God we love Him by everything we say, do, and think; to know God as a best friend; to think about God often**) Tell students that in today's Bible truth, they will learn how Joshua chose to follow God wholeheartedly.

Directed Instruction ★ ↻
Display **VA 9A Joshua Follows God**, and read the back. Explain that Joshua was a good leader because he followed God with his whole heart. He chose to love and serve God every day, all the way to the end of his life. He persevered in doing things God's way. Joshua kept seeking God's direction in battles, times of need, and times of blessing. He encouraged the Israelites to persevere in serving the Lord as well. Near the end of his life, Joshua asked the people to choose whom they would serve. Joshua had lived his life focused on doing the very best he could for God. Emphasize that making a commitment to God and keeping it is very important, no matter what others may think.

Read **Colossians 3:23**. Tell students that just as Joshua followed God wholeheartedly, they too can do things for God with all their heart. After all, what they do should please Him the most! No matter if they are doing school work, spending time with friends, or practicing an instrument, God wants them to do it wholeheartedly in a way that pleases Him—not just to please others. Encourage students to pray and ask God to help them persevere in following Him wholeheartedly in all they do.

Sing the song "I Am Not Ashamed" from the Grade 2 URL.

Student Page 9.1
Read the directions and have students complete the page.

Review

- Identify ways Joshua followed God. (**Possible answers: He followed God with his whole heart; he helped the Israelites possess the Promised Land; he chose to love and serve God every day; when he was a very old man, he called an important meeting to remind the Israelites to continue to love God.**)
- How did Joshua's behavior help the people of Israel? (**Possible answers: Joshua led the Israelites to Canaan, the Promised Land; Joshua set a good example of someone who loved God and served Him wholeheartedly.**)
- What decision did Joshua ask the Israelites to make? (**They had to choose whom they would serve from that moment on—God or the false gods of the people who lived around them.**)
- How can you tell if someone is persevering? (**Possible answers: He or she doesn't give up easily; that person continues doing what he or she set out to do, even if it's hard.**)

Notes:

APPLICATION

- Is it easier for you to follow God during times of hardship or times of blessing? Why? (**Answers will vary.**)
- Why might it be difficult to make a commitment to follow God wholeheartedly? (**Possible answers: It takes effort; I worry about what others think; I give up.**)
- What will help you follow God wholeheartedly? (**Possible answers: reading God's Word, praying to Him, doing what God thinks is important, being careful what I watch, choosing friends wisely, not worrying about what others think**)
- How do temptations get in the way of following God? (**If we give in to the temptations, they can cause us to do things that are not pleasing to God and sometimes cause us to forget about God.**)

REINFORCEMENT

Shechem was a very significant place of meeting for Joshua and the Israelites. Once Abraham reached Shechem, God promised to give the land to Abraham's descendants. In thanksgiving, Abraham built an altar to the Lord there. God multiplied Abraham's family in Shechem with the birth of Isaac, and later, Isaac's sons, Jacob and Esau. God spoke with Joshua at Shechem near Mount Ebal, as He renewed His covenant with His people. Joseph was also buried in Shechem.

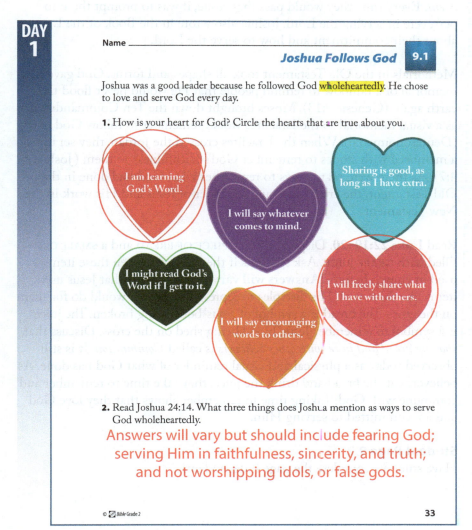

9.2 Joshua Follows God

Focus: Memorial to God

★ PREPARATION

Fill a SMALL BOX with PERSONAL ITEMS. (*Introduction*)

Select a SMALL PIECE OF BREAD, and fill a SMALL CUP with GRAPE JUICE for display. (*Directed Instruction*)

↶ EXTENSION

2A Give a SMOOTH STONE to each student. Have students use permanent markers to write a simple statement on the stones about being committed to serving God. Assist the students as needed. (For example: I will obey God; I will trust God; I will worship God.) Display the stones in the room to remind students to be committed to God.

2B Provide students with LEAF SHAPES cut from construction paper. Encourage students to write on the leaves a personal memorial of a time God worked in their life. Attach the leaves to the tree constructed in Lesson 9.1, Extension 1B.

Introduction ★

Display a SMALL BOX containing PERSONAL ITEMS that have special meaning to you. As you show these items to the students, discuss the memories you experience each time you look at these items. Tell students that when you take time to look at these items, it brings back special memories and makes you thankful for what God has done. Ask students if they have any place at home where they keep personal items to remember special times. (**Answers will vary.**) Tell them that in today's lesson, Joshua took time to set up a special visual way to remember what God had done.

Directed Instruction ★ ↶

Remind students that Joshua remembered God's faithfulness. He continually encouraged the Israelites to follow God. Joshua was a good leader. He held a meeting to personally challenge the Israelites to serve God only. The Israelites said they would. Joshua put a large stone under an oak tree near one of their places of worship as a visual reminder of the commitment they had made to God that day (Joshua 24:25–27). This stone was a *memorial*, which means *something that serves as a reminder of a certain event*. Every time they would pass that stone, it was to prompt them to persevere in serving the Lord. Joshua also wrote in the Book of the Law about their commitment and how to serve the Lord.

Memorials in the Old Testament took all shapes and forms. God gave the memorial of a rainbow to remind people that He would never flood the earth again (Genesis 9:13). Moses brought down the Ten Commandments as a visual memorial so the Israelites would remember to follow God (Deuteronomy 6:6). When the Israelites crossed the Jordan, they set up a memorial with stones to remember God's faithfulness to them (Joshua 4:7). As there were many ways to remember what God had done in the Old Testament, the cross is a visual reminder of Jesus and His work in the New Testament.

Read **Luke 22:19–20**. Display a SMALL PIECE OF BREAD and a SMALL CUP filled with GRAPE JUICE. Ask students if they have ever seen these items used in church before. (**Answers will vary.**) Tell students that Jesus used items like these with His disciples to represent what He would do for them on the cross. The bread is a symbol of Jesus' body being broken. The juice is a symbol to remember Jesus' blood being shed on the cross. Discuss that *sharing bread and juice with other believers* is called *Communion*. It is still observed today as a physical and visual reminder of what God has done. As believers eat the bread and drink the juice, they take time to remember and commune with God. Taking time to remember shows that they love God and are committed to serving Him.

Student Page 9.2
Have students complete the page independently.

Review

- What memorial did Joshua set up and why? (**Joshua put a large stone under an oak tree near one of the places of worship as a reminder of the Israelites' commitment to serve God only.**)
- Name some memorials that are mentioned in the Old Testament. (**Possible answers: rainbow, stones, Ten Commandments**)
- What did Jesus do to show His disciples how to regularly remember Him? (**He shared Communion with His disciples.**)
- Why is it important to remember what God has done? (**Possible answers: to prompt us to serve Him wholeheartedly, to help us persevere in the Lord's work, to show Him we love Him, to show God we want to obey Him**)

Notes:

APPLICATION

- Why do you think it is important to remember what God has done and is continuing to do? (**Answers will vary but should include that remembering God's power and faithfulness in the past helps us trust Him in the present.**)
- In what ways do you remember what God has done for you? (**I choose to think about how He has answered prayers in the past instead of worrying about what's going on now.**)
- How does remembering what God did for you make you feel? (**Possible answers: It makes me feel loved; it makes me feel cared for.**)

DAY 2

9.2 Joshua Follows God

Refer to Joshua 24. Write **T** for true and **F** for false.

1. **F** Joshua did not encourage the Israelites to follow God.
2. **F** Joshua put a large stone in a river as a memorial.
3. **T** Joshua wrote down the Israelites' promise to serve God wholeheartedly in the Book of the Law.
4. **F** Joshua set up a memorial to remind the Israelites of the Battle of Jericho.

Provide answers.

5. Joshua encouraged the Israelites to serve and follow God only. Read the choices below, and circle the choice you will make.

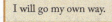 

I will go my own way.   I will serve God.   I will not decide.

6. Give an example of doing what God says and not giving up.

Answers will vary but should include a personal experience or a biblical account of obeying God diligently.

7. Write about something you can do to show God you remember what He has done for you.

Answers will vary.

9.3 Joshua Follows God
Focus: God's Faithfulness

★ PREPARATION
Select **DM-1 Character Traits**. (*Introduction*)

↪ EXTENSION
3A Provide students with **LEAF SHAPES** cut from construction paper. Encourage students to write on the leaves how God has shown Himself faithful in their life. Attach the leaves to the tree that was constructed in Lesson 9.1, Extension 1B and Lesson 9.2, Extension 2B.

Introduction ★
Refer to **DM-1 Character Traits**. Read the definition of *faithfulness*, which means *constant loyalty*. Have students share names of people in the Bible they have learned about this year who showed faithfulness. (**Answers will vary but should include Abraham, Joseph, Moses, and Joshua.**) Have students share names of faithful people alive today. (**Answers will vary.**) Today, students will review how God was faithful to His people.

Directed Instruction ↪
Review with students that Joshua met with the Israelites to remind them about God's faithfulness. Help students recount acts of God's faithfulness from what they have studied so far this year. Be sure to include the following:
- God led Abraham to the land of promise.
- God promised Abraham he would have many, many descendants.
- Abraham and Sarah had a son, Isaac.
- Isaac had two sons, Jacob and Esau.
- Jacob had 12 sons. Joseph was one of Jacob's sons.
- God protected Joseph from his brothers' evil actions. Joseph ended up rescuing the family from famine by asking them to come live in Egypt, where there was enough food to eat and land to live on. What his brothers meant for evil, God turned to good.
- Jacob's family grew and grew in the land of Egypt, continuing the fulfillment of God's promise to Abraham about his descendants.
- God sent Moses and Aaron to Pharaoh and delivered the children of Israel from slavery by sending 10 plagues.
- God guided the children of Israel through the Red Sea.
- God provided for the children of Israel in the desert.
- Moses led the Hebrews in the wilderness.
- God established Joshua as the leader after Moses.
- God helped the children of Israel cross the Jordan.
- The Israelites won the Battle of Jericho with God's help.
- The Israelites took possession of the land of Canaan that God had promised to them.

Have three volunteers read the following verses, and then ask the class to describe what the verses mean:
- **Psalm 18:25**—(**Faithful people experience the faithfulness of God.**)
- **Matthew 25:21**—(**People who are faithful in doing not-so-important things will be given more important things to do because they can be trusted.**)
- **Proverbs 3:3**—(**People should always live a life full of mercy and truth [faithfulness].**)

Student Page 9.3
Read the paragraph, and instruct students how to write a haiku. Review God's faithfulness depicted in the illustrations—the Battle of Jericho, parting of the Red Sea, rescuing Lot, and Joseph and his brothers. Have students to work individually or together to complete the page.

Review

- Compare and contrast obedience and faithfulness. (**Obedience can be a one-time action, faithfulness is obeying constantly.**)
- Compare wholeheartedness and perseverance. (**If I wholeheartedly follow God, I persevere to do all that He wants me to do. I don't give up and quit, nor do I obey Him just part of the time.**)
- What are some accounts from Scripture of God's faithfulness? (**Possible answers: God provided descendants of Abraham; God provided water, manna, and quail to the children of Israel when they were in the wilderness; God parted the Red Sea and stopped the Jordan River so that the Israelites could cross; God spared Rahab because of the help she gave to His people and the trust she had in Him.**)
- Is faithfulness something you are born with? (**No, I have to practice being faithful and ask God to help me.**)

Notes:

APPLICATION

- Name some ways God has been faithful to you. (**Possible answers: He created me; He loves me; He sent His Son to Earth for me.**)
- What does God's faithfulness remind you to do? (**Possible answers: fear God, honor Him, serve Him only**)
- Whom will you choose to serve? Why? (**Answers will vary.**)
- Why do the choices you make let others know who you are? (**My choices show others what is important to me.**)

DAY 3

Name _____

Joshua Follows God   9.3

A haiku is a special poem. Write a haiku that describes God's faithfulness. Use the example and the lines below to help you.

Answers will vary.

Title:	**Faithfulness**
5 syllables:	Jesus died for me.
7 syllables:	Jesus loves me all the time.
5 syllables:	I can count on God.

(Title) _____

(5) _____

(7) _____

_____

(5) _____

© Bible Grade 2   35

9.4 Joshua Follows God

Focus: Overcoming Temptation

★ PREPARATION

Have MATCHES or a LIGHTER, and a CANDLE available. (*Introduction*)

↻ EXTENSION

4A Have students role-play the following situations to show what they would do to overcome the temptation:

- Your mom leaves cookies she is saving for a party on the counter. They are your favorite kind and your brother thinks she will not miss a couple since there are so many. You want to eat some.
- Your friends are teasing a new student who is shy. You want to be cool like your friends and join in.
- You did not study for the spelling test. You worry about making a bad grade. You pretend you are sick so that you can stay home from school.
- You are playing a game at recess with several friends. Two of your friends are cheating and try to talk you into cheating to win the game. You really want to win.

Introduction ★

Use MATCHES or a LIGHTER to light a CANDLE. Ask students if it would be wise to run around the candle or get near it while playing. (**No.**) Discuss how a person can easily get burned when he or she gets too close to fire. Instruct students that it is the same with sin. God tells everyone to stay away from sin so they will not get "burned." God knows that sin can harm and even destroy, just like fire. Sometimes **temptation**, which means *a desire to do something even though it is wrong*, lures people to do wrong. God provides a way to help them overcome temptation because He loves them and does not want them to be hurt or harmed. Blow out the candle. Inform students that today's Bible truth teaches about how God helps people to overcome temptation.

Directed Instruction ↶

Remind students that the Israelites promised Joshua that they would only follow God. They said that they would not worship false gods. Joshua knew the people still living in the land of Canaan worshipped many false gods, and the Israelites might be tempted to do likewise.

Explain that everyone experiences temptations; however, being tempted is not a sin. Jesus was tempted in all things, yet He did not sin (Hebrews 4:15). Only when sin is acted upon, or given in to, does it become sin. With God's help, His children have the strength to overcome temptation (1 Corinthians 10:13). However, if they do sin but then are sorry, He will forgive their sin if they ask Him to (1 John 1:9).

Read the following story:

Heidi was seven years old. This was her first week to walk to school on her own. She didn't have one problem on the way to school. She remembered everything her parents had told her, including looking both ways before crossing the street.

Her walk home after school, however, was a very different story. Some of the older kids that walked home with her crossed the street very quickly without looking both ways. Heidi hesitated briefly, but when the other kids told her to hurry up and stop being slow, she ran right after them. Halfway across the street, she heard a car horn and looked up just in time to see a car come to a screeching halt.

Heidi realized that if she had taken the time to look both ways as her parents had told her, she would have known that it wasn't a good time to cross the street. She was very thankful that she was safe. Heidi also realized that she shouldn't listen to other kids when they tell her to do something that is wrong or dangerous.

Discuss with the students how Heidi gave in to temptation. Talk about what she could have done differently. (**Possible answers: obeyed her parents, stopped when she was tempted, not followed the other kids, remembered God's Word**) Read **James 4:7–8**. Help students understand

88

that Satan tries to tempt people to do the wrong things. Read the following phrase and sentences to help students remember what to do when tempted: Draw; Stand; Use; Flee.

- *Draw* near to God.
- *Stand* firm against the devil.
- *Use* God's Word to help you.
- *Flee* from temptation.

Student Page 9.4

Have students follow the directions and complete the page. Spend time in prayer with them asking God to help them overcome temptations.

Review

- How were Joshua and the Israelites tempted? (**They were tempted to serve false gods.**)
- Is it a sin to be tempted? Why or why not? (**No, it is only a sin when I give in to the temptation.**)
- What should you do if you sin? (**When I sin, I should realize I've done wrong, ask God for forgiveness, and do my best not to sin again.**)

APPLICATION

- Which do you think is harder: to give in to temptation, or to do what is right? (**Answers will vary but should include that it's easy to do the right thing when the temptation to do otherwise is not very strong.**)
- What temptations are hardest for you? (**Answers will vary.**)
- Why is it important to not give in to temptation? (**So that I won't sin or be harmed or hurt.**)
- What should you do when you are tempted? (**Possible answers: draw near to God, stand firm against the devil, flee from the temptation, pray for strength, use God's Word to help me.**)

REINFORCEMENT

In the days of Joshua, it was common and expected for people settling in a new land to begin participating in the religious practices of that area. It was also typical for people to worship many gods, adding the gods from the new land to the ones they currently worshipped.

The Canaanites worshipped Baal along with many other lesser gods. The Canaanites expected the Israelites to participate in the worship of their false gods and still worship Yahweh. That is why Joshua sternly warned the Israelites to serve God only. He knew the temptation they would face. Even though the Israelites committed to being faithful to God, they yielded to temptation after Joshua died and worshipped false Canaanite gods.

DAY 4

9.4 *Joshua Follows God*

1. Read James 4:7–8. Color the boxes containing sentences that tell what you should do when you feel temptation.

Stand firm against the devil.	Follow what others are doing, even if it is wrong.	
Draw near to God.	Do what I want to do.	Worry about what others might say.
	Use God's Word to help me.	Flee from temptation.

2. Write a prayer to God asking Him to help you overcome a temptation you may struggle with.

Answers will vary.

36

© Bible Grade 2

9.5 Joshua Follows God
Focus: Review and Assessment

★ PREPARATION

Select **VA 9A Joshua Follows God**. (*Lesson Review*)

Print a copy of **BLM 9B Lesson 9 Test** for each student. (*Directed Instruction*)

Lesson Review ★

Use **VA 9A Joshua Follows God** to review the Bible truths from this lesson. Cover the following concepts:

- Joshua's faithful leadership helped the Israelites possess Canaan, the Promised Land.
- Joshua reminded the leaders of Israel about God's faithfulness to them—how He delivered them from slavery in Egypt and helped them to occupy the Promised Land. (God multiplied Abraham's descendants. God sent Moses and Aaron to Pharaoh and delivered them from the plagues. He guided them through the Red Sea, and He provided for the Israelites in the desert. He made a way for them to cross the Jordan River, and He gave them victory in the Battle of Jericho.)
- The word *faithfulness* means *constant loyalty*.
- God was faithful to deliver the Israelites out of Egypt, and helped them win every battle to possess the land of Canaan.
- As a response to God's faithfulness, Joshua encouraged the Israelites to make up their minds to worship God wholeheartedly, as Joshua committed he would do.
- *Wholeheartedly* means *with excitement, eagerness, and full purpose of heart. Halfheartedly* means *with little interest or enthusiasm.*
- Joshua told the Israelites to be committed to following God with their whole heart. He knew they would be tempted to worship false gods.
- The Israelites made a choice to serve God.
- God wants everyone to love Him and serve Him with perseverence. He is faithful and loving.
- Joshua wrote down the Israelite's promise to serve God in the Book of the Law.
- A *memorial* is defined as *something that serves as a reminder of a certain event*.
- Joshua set up a special stone under a tree to remind the Israelites of their promise. Other memorials, such as the rainbow, the Ten Commandments, and the cross, serve as reminders of what God has done.
- *Temptation* means *a desire to do something even though it is wrong*.
- When God's children are tempted, they can remember the following: Draw; Stand; Use; Flee. (*Draw* near to God; *Stand* firm against the devil; *Use* God's Word to help you; *Flee* from temptation.)

Directed Instruction ★

Distribute **BLM 9B Lesson 9 Test** to each student. Read the directions and pronounce any difficult words. Have students complete the test.

Notes:

Lesson Preparation
Ruth Is Loyal
10.0

Expected Student Outcomes

KNOW
Ruth decides to remain with Naomi and serve God.

DO
Students will:
- differentiate between true and false statements about Ruth and Naomi
- define characteristics of a good friend
- recall a time when they have experienced being loyal
- describe the characteristics that make someone a good friend
- apply loyalty by naming specific friends and ways to express loyalty

APPLY
Students will identify examples of how they can be loyal.

Lesson Outline
I. Ruth is a loyal friend (Ruth 1, Gen 28:15, Deut 31:3)
II. Being a loyal friend (Prov 27:10)
III. Finding good friends (Prov 12:26, 1 Cor 15:33)
IV. Loyalty from God and to God (Prov 18:24, Deut 31:6, Jn 15:14)

♥ TEACHER'S HEART

The word *loyalty* has its roots in the French language. Originally it meant *the show of allegiance, faithfulness, devotion, commitment, consecration, and fidelity to one's king, ideals, causes, and friends*. Loyalty to God should be long lasting; however, the loyalty of Jesus' disciples vanished quickly when He was arrested. In spite of three years of intensive training and personal knowledge of the Son of Man, when faced with danger and disruption of their dreams, they all forsook Him. What a contrast to Paul's confession, "I have fought the good fight, I have finished the race, I have kept the faith" (2 Timothy 4:7).

There is no king greater than Jesus who calls for your loyalty. There is no greater purpose than allegiance to the claims of Christ in your life. There is no greater demand than your commitment to yield to the Holy Spirit so that He can transform your life. There is no greater purpose than your devotion to the Word of God and the will of God. And there is no greater calling for you than to nurture your students in the knowledge and admonition of the Lord. Reaffirm your loyalty to the Lord and His calling in your life. Let your students see your faithful devotion to the Lord. Your example will shape their life!

📖 MEMORY VERSE
Ruth 1:16

GLOSSARY WORDS
- loyalty
- famine

★ MATERIALS

Day 1:
- BLM 10A Neckwear Patterns, card stock, hole punch, string
- VA 10A Ruth Is Loyal, DM-1 Character Traits
- Time Line
- Piece of bread, flower, bitter herb, picture of friends (*Extension*)

Day 2:
- Various colors of yarn (*Extension*)

Day 3:
- BLM 10B Loyalty Cube (*Extension*)
- DM-3 Books of the Bible (*Extension*)

Day 4:
- Super glue, craft sticks
- Robe, scarf (*Extension*)

Day 5:
- VA 10A Ruth Is Loyal
- BLM 10C Lesson 10 Test

TEACHER RESOURCES
Ferguson, Sinclair B., *Faithful God: An Exposition of the Book of Ruth*. Evangelical Press, 2010.
McGinnis, Alan Loy. *The Friendship Factor*. Augsburg Books, 2004.

STUDENT RESOURCES
Mackenzie, Carine. *Ruth, the Harvest Girl*. CF4Kids, 2012.
Veggie Tales: Silly Little Thing Called Love. DVD. Big Idea, 2010.

Supplemental Materials are available to download. See Understanding Purposeful Design Bible at the front of this book for the Grade 2 URL.

10.1 Ruth Is Loyal
Focus: Ruth Is a Loyal Friend

MEMORY VERSE
Ruth 1:16

MEMORY WORK
- Give each student a copy of **BLM 10A Neckwear Patterns**. Have students write a small phrase from the Memory Verse on each shape. Direct students to lightly color and cut out each shape. Assist students by punching a hole in each shape with a HOLE PUNCH. Provide a STRING long enough to safely be tied around each student's neck. Instruct students to string the words of the verse in the correct order. Have students touch each shape and say each phrase to practice the verse.

PREPARATION
Make a copy of **BLM 10A Neckwear Patterns** onto CARD STOCK for each student. Have a HOLE PUNCH and STRING available for use. (Memory Work)

Select **VA 10A Ruth Is Loyal** and **DM-1 Character Traits**. (Directed Instruction)

EXTENSION
1A Read **Ruth 1**. Show a PIECE OF BREAD, and explain that *Bethlehem* means *house of bread*. The fact that no one had any food in a place where bread was typically available meant the famine was severe. Hold up a FLOWER. Explain that *Naomi* means *pleasant or lovely*. She was a pleasant person, but when her husband and sons died, she asked to be called *Mara*, which means *bitter*. Allow students to smell a BITTER HERB (like horseradish). Show a PICTURE OF FRIENDS. Inform students that *Ruth* means *friend or friendship*. Ruth lived up to her name.

Introduction
Draw seven large squares on the board at a height easy for students to reach comfortably. Inside each box create a dot-to-dot outline of each letter in the word **loyalty**. Inform students that each box contains a letter of a word they will learn about. Select students to complete the letters.

Directed Instruction ★
Invite a volunteer to look up the word *loyalty* in the Glossary and read the definition out loud. *Loyalty* is defined as *the character trait of showing faithfulness and devotion to someone or something*. Discuss with students different times that they might need to be faithfully devoted to or stick by someone. Explain that today's Bible truth is about a woman named *Ruth*, and how she showed loyalty. Read **VA 10A Ruth Is Loyal**. Explain that a **famine** means *a time when there is little to no rain, crops do not grow, and people have a hard time finding food*.

Inform students that women who lived during Ruth's time did not have the same privileges as men. When a woman lost her husband and became a widow, she often lost any recognition, property, and money she had from her husband. Without a husband, these women were often unable to support themselves with basic needs like food, shelter, or money. Because these women did not own property or work at a job, they had to depend on relatives or friends for help. Despite these circumstances, Ruth chose to remain loyal to Naomi and not return to her own family in Moab.

Show **DM-1 Character Traits**. While loyalty is not specifically mentioned on the chart, ask students what qualities loyalty is like. (**faithfulness, diligence, love**) Help students make the connection that when they show loyalty, they are behaving like Jesus—being faithful and diligent in His love for them. Read **Genesis 28:15** and **Deuteronomy 31:8**. Ask students what these verses say about God. (**He will never leave us; He is loyal.**)

Discuss how loyalty can cause one to feel. Express that being loyal can sometimes be scary. Loyalty requires a refusal to laugh at bad things said about another person. Loyalty may result in suffering, as when people make fun of a person for sticking up for someone they do not like. Help students understand that being loyal requires God's help.

Student Page 10.1
Read instructions to students, and direct them to complete the page.

Review
- What did Naomi, Orpah, and Ruth have in common? (**They were all related, and all three became widows.**)
- In what ways were these women different? (**They were different in age; Naomi was from the town of Bethlehem in Israel, and Orpah and Ruth were from the country of Moab; Orpah and Ruth made different decisions when Naomi told them she was returning to Bethlehem.**)

- Once Orpah left to return to her mother's house, how would her life be different from Ruth's? (**Answers will vary but should include that Orpah went back to live as she had growing up, worshipping idols, whereas Ruth chose to live with Naomi in a new country and worship the one, true God.**)
- How did Ruth show loyalty to Naomi? (**Ruth stayed with Naomi even though the future was uncertain.**)

Time Line

Direct students' attention to the **Time Line**. Point out what they have studied so far. Begin with Abraham, the man God promised to make into a great nation. Then, point out Moses and the Israelites leaving Egypt. Remind students that the Israelites entered into the Promised Land of Canaan with Joshua as their leader. Many years after Joshua died, Ruth married Boaz. Ruth became the great-grandmother of King David. The nation that God promised to Abraham continued to grow, and then many, many years later, Jesus was born into the family line of David.

APPLICATION

- What are ways you can show loyalty? (**Possible answers: by standing up for a friend, fulfilling my promises, not gossiping**)
- Who is someone you need to be loyal to? (**Answers will vary.**)
- Who is someone you know that displays loyalty regularly, and how does his or her loyalty affect you? (**Answers will vary.**)

REINFORCEMENT

The account of Ruth takes place around the time of Judges. It was a time when "there was no king in Israel, and everyone did what was right in his own eyes" (Judges 21:25). It was a time of repeated idolatry and immorality, a time when the nation did not follow God. During this dark time in Israel's history, a ray of light shone through a girl from a pagan country, who was loyal, kind, and self-sacrificing. Ruth modeled an earnest relationship with Naomi and God in the midst of gross immorality. Ruth became the great-grandmother to King David.

DAY 1

Name _____

Ruth Is Loyal 10.1

Read each statement below taken from Ruth 1. Decide if the statement is true or false. Circle the letter in the matching column.

Sentences	True	False
1. There was a great famine in the town of Bethlehem.	(R)	e
2. Ruth moved with Naomi and Elimelech to Moab.	b	(s)
3. Naomi's husband and two sons died in Moab.	(u)	i
4. Ruth and Orpah were cousins.	f	(a)
5. Ruth and Orpah were widows of Naomi's sons.	(l)	n
6. Naomi told the girls to go back to their homes.	(t)	k
7. Orpah stayed with Naomi all the way to Bethlehem.	c	(l)
8. Orpah continued to worship the one, true God.	v	(a)
9. Ruth stayed with Naomi even though she did not know what would happen.	(h)	p
10. Ruth was not happy moving with Naomi.	d	(o)
11. Ruth was loyal and kind.	(w)	j
12. Loyalty is the character trait of showing faithfulness and devotion to someone or something.	(y)	m

13. Solve the riddle. For each number, write the circled letter from above.

<u>R</u> <u>u</u> <u>t</u> <u>h</u>   <u>w</u> <u>a</u> <u>s</u>
 1   3   6   9   11 4   2

<u>l</u> <u>o</u> <u>y</u> <u>a</u> <u>l</u> !
 7   10 12 8   5

10.2 Ruth Is Loyal
Focus: Being a Loyal Friend

EXTENSION

2A Give each student SIX STRANDS OF VARIOUS COLORS OF YARN. Direct students to place their strands evenly side by side, and then tie one end of their strands into a knot. Tell them the knot is a symbol of friendship, and they are making a friendship bracelet. Inform students to design their bracelet for someone they want to be loyal to. Have students then twist the strands or braid them until the strand is long enough to fit around their chosen person's wrist. Tell them to finish by tying a knot at the other end of the strand. Their bracelet is then to be tied onto the wrist of the person they chose. Encourage students to determine to be a loyal friend and diligently love the person they want to give the bracelet to.

Introduction

Invite a volunteer to read **Proverbs 27:10** out loud. Write the word *friend* on the board. Direct students to share different character traits of a good friend. Write these traits on the board. (**Possible answers: loyalty, kindness, helpfulness, love, service**) Ask students what character trait Ruth showed as a sign of friendship to Naomi. (**Ruth showed loyalty.**)

Directed Instruction

To illustrate loyalty in friendship, read the following story to students:

Jessica and Katarina were so excited! Tonight was the big, school-wide skating party at the skating rink. They had been talking about it for what seemed like forever, and they hoped there would be a lot of races and prizes. They got to the rink about 6:30, and it seemed everyone was as excited as they were. Some were hurrying to get their skates on; others were crowding around the prize table to pick out the perfect prize for when they won a race; still others were gobbling down ice-cream cones.

Pretty soon, all the colored lights went on, the music started, and a man's voice called everyone onto the floor for the first skate of the night. Jessica and Katarina held hands as they skated around the rink. As they skated, they saw their friend Anna, and rushed to meet her. They all greeted each other with excitement. The man's voice then called the first graders onto the floor for the first race. Jessica and Katarina stood and watched.

"You're going to be my partner for the next race, right?" Jessica asked.

"Of course!" Katarina responded.

It was time; all the second graders were called to the floor. As Jessica and Katarina stood waiting for the race to start, Anna came up. "Katarina, I want you to skate with me," Anna said rudely.

"I'm sorry, Anna. But I asked Katarina to skate with me," said Jessica.

"You want a cool prize, right Katarina? We all know you won't win with Jessica. She always falls around the corners. If you want to win, you should skate with me," bragged Anna.

Ask students how they think Katarina responded to Anna. Discuss possibilities of what Katarina could do and why. Discuss how Jessica would feel if Katarina had decided to go with Anna instead. (**She would have felt sad or even mad.**) How would Jessica feel if Katarina chose to stay with her? (**She might feel happy and feel like her friend loves her.**)

Read the following scenarios, and discuss how second graders could display loyalty in these situations:

- At lunch, the cafeteria workers are giving out free ice cream. You and your friend are in line. The lunch supervisor hands you the last cone.
- Your friend comes to your house for a sleepover. In the middle of the night your friend wakes up with a stomachache.
- At recess, your friend asks you to play on the swings. But then some kids call out that there is a game of tag, and they want only you to join.

Student Page 10.2
Assist students in completing the page.

Review
- What is loyalty? (**the character trait of showing faithfulness and devotion to someone or something**)
- How could Katarina show loyalty to Jessica? (**by skating with Jessica even though she might not be the fastest or the best**)
- How can loyalty be seen in friendships? (**Possible answers: by staying with my friend when I want to do something else; by standing up for my friend when no one else will**)

APPLICATION
- How can you show loyalty to your friends? (**waiting for them, being patient, staying with them even when it might not be convenient for me, not saying unkind things about them**)
- What character traits do you need to show more of to your friends? (**Answers will vary.**)
- If a friend needed your help because he or she was being teased a lot, how could you show loyalty? (**Possible answers: by sticking up for him or her, by telling a teacher, by saying kind things about that friend**)

REINFORCEMENT
The book of Ruth is arguably the most familiar record of loyalty, but there are many others in God's Word that portray what it means to be faithful and devoted. The word *loyalty* is not prevalent in the Bible, but the Bible has much to say about what it means to be loyal. The friendship of Jonathan and David, found in 1 Samuel 18:1–4 and 1 Samuel 20, shows how Jonathan was loyal to David and helped him escape from King Saul. Another major example is Jesus and His loyalty to God. This strong devotion to His Father was not fully understood by many of His followers. Jesus often did things in ways that caused some to question His motives and methods. In doing so, though, Jesus was demonstrating God's will, not His own.

DAY 2

10.2 Ruth Is Loyal

1. Write how a good friend treats you and your other friends. How does a good friend behave? Start with every letter of the word **friend**.

   Example:

   F aithful

   R espectful

   I ntelligent

   E ncouraging

   N ever leaves

   D ependable

2. Describe a time when a friend was loyal to you and how it made you feel.

   Answers will vary.

10.3

Ruth Is Loyal
Focus: Finding Good Friends

⏎ EXTENSION

3A Copy **BLM 10B Loyalty Cube** for each student, and assist them in constructing the cube. Pair up students. Have students roll the Loyalty Cube and give an example of how they can show loyalty using the character trait they roll from the cube.

3B Display **DM-3 Books of the Bible** for students to reference while reviewing the books of the Old and New Testaments.

Introduction

Ask students to think, but not talk, about their best friend. Then lead a discussion about key traits of a good friend.

Directed Instruction ⏎

Ask students to describe how a friend should behave. (**Possible answers: help me, encourage me, support me, point me to follow Jesus**) Read **Proverbs 12:26** aloud. Explain that God cautions people to be careful in choosing their friends. Ask students why this might be important. (**If we have friends who are godly, they will help us be godly, too.**) The verse says that if someone has friends who are not godly, that person will be led astray. This means that the ungodly friends would convince that person to do things that do not honor God and are not good. To further illustrate this concept, read **1 Corinthians 15:33**. Ask students if they can say what this verse means. (**Even the best of people will be changed for the worse by being around ungodly people.**) Ask students how having ungodly friends could influence them to do bad things. (**Possible answers: I might copy their bad behaviors; I might learn to be disrespectful.**)

Ask student volunteers to write the following godly character traits on pieces of construction paper: *fears God, does not gossip, loves at all times, has a pure heart and kind speech, is not easily angered, helps you when you fall.* Discuss what these traits mean. In random order, post the papers for all to see. Direct students to look up the following verses and connect the Scriptures to the written character traits:
- **Psalm 119:63** (**fears God**)
- **Proverbs 16:28** (**does not gossip**)
- **Proverbs 17:17** (**loves at all times**)
- **Proverbs 22:11** (**has a pure heart and kind speech**)
- **Proverbs 22:24** (**is not easily angered**)
- **Ecclesiastes 4:10** (**helps you when you fall**)

Have students work in pairs to create a facial expression, gesture, or hand motion to go along with each trait. Tell each group of two students to come before the class and show their picture and their gesture. Encourage the rest of the class to say "A good friend …" along with the trait that is being illustrated; for example, "A good friend fears God."

Student Page 10.3

Direct students to think about their best friend as they fill in the page.

Review

- How should you pick your friends according to Proverbs 12:26? (**carefully or cautiously**)
- Why should you choose your friends carefully or cautiously? (**I learn from my friends and will eventually act like them. I want godly friends so that I will be influenced to behave in the same manner.**)

• What are some character traits of good friends according to the Bible? **(Good friends fear God, do not gossip, love at all times, have pure hearts and kind speech, are not easily angered, and help me when I fall.)**

Notes:

APPLICATION

• Are you careful in choosing your friends? (**Answers will vary.**)

• Are you aware of how friends can influence you in inappropriate ways? Do you need to forgive good friends sometimes? (**Answers will vary.**)

• Are you kind? Do you gossip? Do you love at all times? Are you pure in heart? Do you get angry easily? Are you a good friend? (**Answers will vary.**)

• Do you have kind friends? Do they gossip? Do they love at all times? Do they get angry easily? Are your friends good friends? (**Answers will vary.**)

DAY 3

Name _____

Ruth Is Loyal | 10.3

In the oval, draw a picture of a good friend. In the rectangle, write about why your friend is a good friend.

My Friend

Drawings will vary.

My friend is a good friend because ...
Answers will vary.

_____

_____

_____

_____

_____

_____

© *Bible Grade 2*

39

© *Bible Grade 2*

10.4 Ruth Is Loyal
Focus: Loyalty from God and to God

★ PREPARATION
Have a bottle of regular white glue, SUPER GLUE, and CRAFT STICKS available. (*Introduction*)

↻ EXTENSION
4A To review the Bible truth about Ruth, wear a ROBE and headpiece made from a SCARF. Place the questions below on slips of paper and designate a few students to interact with you. Ask each student to hold a pencil and pretend it is a microphone to use in his or her interview of you. Tell the students to ask you the questions on the slips of paper. Answer from Ruth's perspective.
- What is your name? (**Ruth**)
- Where do you live? (**I used to live in Moab, but I just moved to Bethlehem.**)
- What is your family like? (**Well, I was married, but my husband has died, and now it is just my mother-in-law and me.**)
- Why did you move to Bethlehem? (**Well, the famine is over, so there is food in Bethlehem now. Naomi wanted to return to her homeland.**)
- What was the most difficult thing about moving? (**Naomi, my mother-in-law, asked me to return home to my family in Moab, but I couldn't leave her. It was hard to leave my family, but I love Naomi and wanted to stay with her.**)
- How has God changed your life? (**I used to worship the false gods in Moab, but now I worship and serve the one true God. I understand now that He is real. He is loyal to me, and I do my best to be loyal to Him.**)

Introduction ★
Show students a bottle of regular white glue and a tube of SUPER GLUE. Ask what these two things are used for. (**to make things stick together**) Glue TWO CRAFT STICKS together with the regular, white glue, and TWO CRAFT STICKS with the SUPER GLUE. As you let the craft sticks dry for a couple of minutes, explain that when students are loyal to their friends, they are acting like glue sticking two things together. Discuss how sometimes your students may make choices that break their loyalty, like when they change plans because they get invited somewhere else, or they choose to spend time alone instead of with a friend as planned. To demonstrate this break in loyalty, pull apart the two craft sticks that were glued with the white glue. Explain that God is faithful and loyal forever. When He sticks things together, they do not come apart. Show the students the craft sticks glued with the super glue and try to pull them apart. Emphasize that these craft sticks represent God's faithfulness—completely binding.

Directed Instruction ↶
Read **Proverbs 18:24**. Ask students who is the one who sticks closer than a brother. (**God, or Jesus**)

Invite a student to read **Deuteronomy 31:6**. Define *forsake* as *to abandon or leave behind*. God promises that He will be with His people forever and not forsake them. Ask students how this promise makes them feel. (**Possible answers: good, safe, happy**) Lead students to discuss the implications of this promise and how they should act toward God. (**Possible answers: I should be loyal to God; I should never leave Him.**)

Invite a student to read **John 15:14**. Have students describe how to show God that they love Him and how to show that He is their friend. (**by obeying His commands**)

Read the following true-life story to illustrate how God's people should be loyal to Him because He is loyal to them:

Dr. David Livingstone lived during the 1800s. He was a man who knew that God would never leave him. Dr. Livingstone learned about many people in Africa who had never heard about Jesus and the salvation Jesus brings. He decided to spend His life serving God there.

In Africa, Dr. Livingstone saw people being cruelly treated as slaves. This made him sad. He knew helping them was what he was supposed to do. He traveled all over Africa, going places no other white man had been. He told people there about Jesus. He also charted out unknown places in Africa. Dr. Livingstone suffered a lot while in Africa—he was separated from his family, attacked by a lion, lived in constant pain, and contracted horrible diseases. Yet to him, serving God was more important.

Dr. Livingstone became famous in his home country of Great Britain for his explorations in Africa. He thought that his explorations would open the way for more people to come and preach the good news about Jesus to the people in the interior of Africa.

In 1873, Dr. Livingstone died while on his knees in prayer to the God who never left him, who would never leave the people of Africa.

Student Page 10.4
Have students complete the page independently.

Review
- Who will stick closer to you than a brother (Proverbs 18:24)? (**God, or Jesus, will stick closer than a brother.**)
- What promise has God given His people about His loyalty? (**God promises that He will never leave His people.**)
- How should you respond to the loyalty of God? (**I should be loyal to Him in return.**)
- How did David Livingstone show his loyalty to God? (**by spending his whole life serving God in Africa**)

APPLICATION
- Thank God for His promise to never leave you.
- How should you act toward God in light of His loyalty and faithfulness to you? (**be loyal to Him, obey His commands**)
- How can you personally show your loyalty to God? (**Answers will vary but should include spending time in prayer, reading the Bible, and choosing to live like He wants me to.**)

DAY 4

10.4 Ruth Is Loyal

Fill in the blank with the correct word from the Word Bank.

WORD BANK
leave   loyal   obeying

1. I will be __**loyal**__ to God. I will show Him my loyalty by __**obeying**__ His commands. God will never __**leave**__ those who choose Him.

Think of four people to be loyal to. Write each name on a blank.

2. If I am loyal to __**Answers will vary,**__ then I will keep my promises to him or her.

3. If I am loyal to __**Answers will vary,**__ then I will not speak badly about my friend when my friend is not with me.

4. If I am loyal to __**Answers will vary,**__ then I will be a friend when my friend is happy, sad, or even mad.

5. If I am loyal to __**Answers will vary,**__ then I will stick up for my friend if others make fun of him or her.

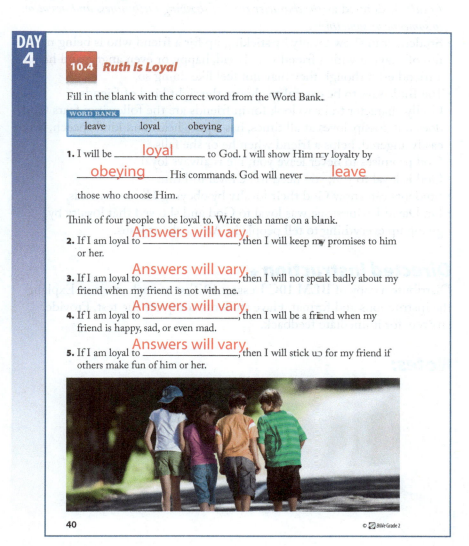

10.5 Ruth Is Loyal
Focus: Review and Assessment

★ PREPARATION

Select **VA 10A Ruth Is Loyal**.
(*Lesson Review*)

Make a copy of **BLM 10C Lesson 10 Test** for each student.
(*Directed Instruction*)

Lesson Review ★

Use **VA 10A Ruth Is Loyal** to review the Bible truth from this week's lesson. Cover the following concepts:

• Naomi and her husband, Elimelech, moved to Moab with their two sons to find food because there was a famine in Bethlehem.
• *Famine* means *a time when there is little to no rain, crops do not grow, and people have a hard time finding food.*
• Naomi's two sons married Moabite women, Ruth and Orpah.
• In Moab, Elimelech and both sons died.
• Naomi began the journey back to Bethlehem because she heard the famine was over.
• Ruth and Orpah began the journey with Naomi to Bethlehem.
• When Naomi encouraged the girls to return to their homes, Orpah returned to her family and to worshipping false gods, but Ruth vowed that Naomi's people would be Ruth's people and Naomi's God would be Ruth's God.
• Ruth showed great loyalty by staying with Naomi even though she was not sure what would happen.
• *Loyalty* is defined as *the character trait of showing faithfulness and devotion to someone or something.*
• Students can show loyalty by sticking up for a friend who is being made fun of; staying with a friend who is sad, happy, or even angry; and helping a friend even though they may not feel like doing so.
• The Bible says to be careful to choose the right kind of friends.
• Godly character traits to look for in friends are the following: fears God, does not gossip, loves at all times, has a pure heart and kind speech, is not easily angered, helps a friend when he or she falls.
• God promises to never leave you; He is always loyal.
• God is loyal to you; you need to be loyal to Him.
• Students can show God their loyalty by obeying His commands.
• Dr. David Livingstone was loyal to God and showed that loyalty by giving up everything to tell people in Africa about Jesus.

Directed Instruction ★

Distribute a copy of **BLM 10C Lesson 10 Test** to each student. Explain the instructions and format. Have students complete the test. Provide answers for immediate feedback.

Notes:

Lesson Preparation
Ruth Serves with Love
11.0

Expected Student Outcomes

KNOW
Ruth remains devoted to Naomi. Ruth meets Boaz and he becomes her kinsman-redeemer.

DO
Students will:
- match information about Ruth and Naomi's friendship
- identify and apply ways to serve others
- organize statements about what happened to Ruth
- compare ways that Boaz showed love to ways that they can show love

APPLY
Students will select ways to serve as a visible expression of love.

Lesson Outline
I. Ruth and Naomi (Ruth 2–4, Prov 17:17a)
II. Ruth serves Naomi (Deut 24:19–22)
　A. Serving others (Mt 25:34–45)
III. Boaz is a kinsman-redeemer (Ruth 4:1–10, Rom 5:6–11)
IV. Boaz loves Ruth (Ruth 3:11–12, 4:1–10)
　A. Unconditional love (1 Jn 4:7–11, 19; 1 Cor 13)

♥ TEACHER'S HEART

Titus 2:10b says that a servant's behavior can adorn the gospel of Jesus Christ. Simply put, others are attracted and won to the gospel by certain qualities of life, even among servants—qualities such as submission to authority, honesty, integrity, self-control, thoughtful speech, purity, kindness, hard work, devotion, joy, and confidence.

Thousands of godly servants have lived in obscurity quietly pouring out their lives in service to others. Few of us know the names of the care-giver for Corrie ten Boom or the person who led shoe salesman Dwight Moody to the Lord. Yet, like Ruth, they daily went about serving Christ as they served others. Without seeking fame or fortune, they simply adorned the gospel with their behavior.

What about you? Do you sometimes feel broken and spilled out as you respond to the needs of others? Ruth made a commitment to serve Naomi. This commitment made it possible for her to not consider the cost, but willingly sacrifice her future. Her dedication and love adorned the gospel and drew the attention of others. Your life also can attract others to the Savior. Integrate your witness with the life qualities that adorn the gospel as you daily minister in your classroom.

Supplemental Materials are available to download. See Understanding Purposeful Design Bible at the front of this book for the Grade 2 URL.

MEMORY VERSE
Galatians 5:14

GLOSSARY WORDS
- devoted
- love
- redeem

MATERIALS
Day 1:
- VA 11A Ruth Serves with Love

Day 2:
- Cup, grain cereal
- VA 11A Ruth Serves with Love
- DM-1 Character Traits
- Picture of people harvesting, sand, grass, seeds (*Extension*)

Day 3:
- BLM 11A Readers Theater: Ruth and Naomi, Part 1;
- BLM 11B Readers Theater: Ruth and Naomi, Part 2 (*Extension*)
- DM-8 Map of Moab and Bethlehem (*Extension*)

Day 4:
- Bowl, index cards, wooden spoon
- BLM 11C Gift of Character (*Extension*)

Day 5:
- VA 11A Ruth Serves with Love
- BLM 11D Lesson 11 Test

♪ SONGS
What Seems Impossible

TEACHER RESOURCES
Thompson, Janet. *Face-to-Face With Naomi and Ruth: Together for the Journey*. New Hope Publishers, 2009.

STUDENT RESOURCES
Taylor, Kenneth N. *Classic Bible Storybook*. Tyndale House, 2009.

11.1 Ruth Serves with Love
Focus: Ruth and Naomi

📖 MEMORY VERSE
Galatians 5:14

MEMORY WORK
- Read the Memory Verse several times together. Have students copy the verse on a blank sheet of paper. Encourage them to draw a picture under the verse about what the verse means.
- Assign hand signals that go along with the Memory Verse. For example, have students make a heart shape with their fingers to represent *love*, and point to someone to represent *neighbor*.

★ PREPARATION
Prepare the following for each of five groups of students: For one group member write *Jesus* on a piece of paper and then fold the paper in half. Write *selfish friend* and *unforgiving friend* on different pieces of paper for remaining group members. Fold papers in half. (*Introduction*)

Select **VA 11A Ruth Serves with Love**. (*Directed Instruction*)

↷ EXTENSION
1A Have students write a class letter from the perspective of Naomi to a friend to tell how Ruth has assisted her. Ask student volunteers to retell the Bible lesson one statement at a time, and record these statements on the board as a letter. When finished, reread the letter to the class.

Introduction ★
Direct students in the following activity to help them understand what a devoted friend would be like: Divide the class into five groups. Hand the prepared papers to one person in each group. Instruct each student to choose a piece of paper. Emphasize that each role indicated on the papers is to be kept a secret. Read the following scenarios out loud, asking students to role-play in their group how each person would react in each situation:
- You are sitting at the school lunch table. A student who calls you names is sitting at a table near you. He forgot his lunch. Your mom packed your favorite lunch.
- The friend who sits in front of you at school never gets work done. As your friend sits at a table during recess, she needs help with her schoolwork. You are having fun playing a game.

Ask students which classmate in the group would make the best friend? (**Students should identify the student playing the role of Jesus.**) Why? (**Possible answers: The student shared; the student showed kindness; the student was unselfish.**) In this activity, who do you think this student represents? (**Jesus**)

Tell students that it is not always easy to give help and support to friends, however they can learn from Jesus and the people in the Bible truth today about being **devoted**, which means *showing faithfulness and commitment to someone or something*.

Directed Instruction ★ ↷
Display **VA 11A Ruth Serves with Love**. Read the Bible truth. Remind students that Ruth had made a choice to leave Moab and her family and be devoted to Naomi and to Naomi's God. If Naomi died, Ruth would have had nothing; but, Ruth chose to help Naomi and be devoted to her no matter what happened. She helped Naomi at Naomi's greatest time of need.

A true friend does not desert someone when help is needed. Naomi and Ruth had become true friends. Ruth was selfless and loyal to Naomi. True friends should be devoted even when it is difficult. Boaz was God's blessing to Ruth for her devotedness to Naomi. Through this marriage, God provided her with a home where she learned more about the one true God.

As a devoted friend, Naomi sought protection for Ruth (Ruth 3:1). God blessed Naomi for her devotedness by giving her a son-in-law, Boaz. Eventually Ruth had a son and became the great-grandmother of King David. Jesus came from this family line.

At times, it can be hard to be a devoted friend. Scripture says that a devoted friend will love no matter what. Select a volunteer to read **Proverbs 17:17a** out loud.

102

Student Page 11.1
Tell students to read the directions and complete the page.

Review
- Where did Ruth move to with Naomi? (**Bethlehem**)
- What did Ruth do to show devotion to Naomi? (**Possible answers: She left Moab to take care of Naomi; she gleaned in the fields for Naomi.**)
- What did Naomi do to show devotion to Ruth? (**Naomi sought protection for Ruth and told her how to approach Boaz.**)
- How did God bless Ruth and Naomi for being devoted and loving friends? (**Possible answers: gave them a new home; helped Ruth learn more about the one, true God; gave Naomi a son-in-law, Boaz**)
- Compare the ways that Ruth and Naomi showed friendship to the ways that you and your friends show friendship. (**Possible answers: We both show kindness; we both help each other.**)

Notes:

APPLICATION
- How did Ruth's devotion and unselfishness affect both Naomi and Ruth? (**Possible answers: brought them together, helped them take care of each other, brought them blessings**)
- When you are devoted and unselfish, how does it affect your friendships with others? (**Answers will vary.**)

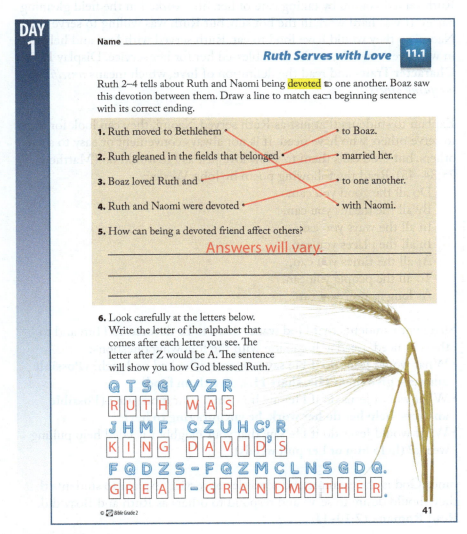

DAY 1

Name _____

Ruth Serves with Love 11.1

Ruth 2–4 tells about Ruth and Naomi being **devoted** to one another. Boaz saw this devotion between them. Draw a line to match each beginning sentence with its correct ending.

1. Ruth moved to Bethlehem — with Naomi.
2. Ruth gleaned in the fields that belonged — to Boaz.
3. Boaz loved Ruth and — married her.
4. Ruth and Naomi were devoted — to one another.

5. How can being a devoted friend affect others?
   Answers will vary.

6. Look carefully at the letters below. Write the letter of the alphabet that comes after each letter you see. The letter after Z would be A. The sentence will show you how God blessed Ruth.

QTSG VZR
RUTH WAS
JHMF CZUHC'R
KING DAVID'S
FQDZS-FQZMCLNSGDQ.
GREAT-GRANDMOTHER.

11.2 Ruth Serves with Love

Focus: Ruth Serves Naomi

★ PREPARATION

Fill a SMALL CUP with some GRAIN CEREAL. (*Introduction*)

Select **VA 11A Ruth Serves with Love** and **DM-1 Character Traits**. (*Directed Instruction*)

↻ EXTENSION

2A Give students an opportunity to serve others in practical ways. Provide them with a service project, such as picking up trash, raking leaves, cleaning an area, planting, or bringing food for someone in need.

2B Search online for a PICTURE OF MODERN-DAY PEOPLE HARVESTING VARIOUS TYPES OF GRAIN in a country like Cambodia or Vietnam. This will help students visualize what Ruth and the harvesters were doing. Provide each student with a large piece of construction paper. Direct students to draw a field to represent where Ruth gleaned. Have students look at the modern-day picture and then draw a picture of Ruth and others working in the field. Assist students in adding texture to their pictures by providing SAND, BLADES OF GRASS, and SEEDS to glue onto the paper. Display the dried 3-D artwork.

Introduction ★

Pass around the SMALL CUP filled with GRAIN CEREAL. Keeping students' allergies in mind, allow students to handle and taste the cereal. Explain what type of grain is in the cereal. Tell students that harvesting grains as a food source was an important part of life in Bible times, and still is today.

Directed Instruction ★ ↻

Display **VA 11A Ruth Serves with Love** to remind students of this week's Bible truth. Explain that God's law for the Israelites required that farmers leave behind some of their harvest for the fatherless and widows (Deuteronomy 24:19–22). Some selfish farmers may not have allowed a widow from a different country to come into their fields after the main harvesting was completed. However, Boaz was kind enough to allow Ruth, a widow and newcomer to his country, to take grains from the fields alongside his own workers. Boaz had heard about Ruth's kindness to Naomi, and God's law required that kindness be shown to widows. Boaz also told his workers to not bother Ruth in any way.

Ruth served Naomi by taking care of her. She worked in the field gleaning barley. It was hard work in the hot sun, but Ruth was willing to serve Naomi so they would have food to eat. Ruth served with love and helped in whatever ways she could. God blessed her for her service. Display **DM-1 Character Traits** and read the definition of **love**, which means *unselfishly accepting others*.

Explain to students that just as Ruth served Naomi, they can look for ways to serve others who have need. It is not always convenient or easy to serve others, but God calls them to show love just as He would do (Matthew 25:34–45). Read the following poem by John Wesley:

> Do all the good you can,
> By all the means you can,
> In all the ways you can,
> In all the places you can,
> At all the times you can,
> To all the people you can,
> As long as ever you can.

Share with students that God wants them to be devoted to Him and to others in need. Lead a discussion with the following questions:

- What would Jesus do if He saw someone who had no lunch? (**Possible answers: give them His, share His, give them food**)
- What would Jesus do if He saw how tired your mom was? (**Possible answers: help her do her work, be encouraging to her**)
- What would Jesus do if He saw that your neighbor needed help pulling weeds? (**help him or her pull weeds**)

Since God is the example and rewarder of service, explain to students that they should desire to serve and respond to others as Ruth and Boaz did. Read **Romans 12:10–11**.

Student Page 11.2

Have students read the directions and complete the page. Assist with reading as needed.

Review

- In what way did Ruth serve Naomi? (**She gleaned in the fields for her.**)
- What did Boaz do to help Ruth? (**Possible answers: allowed her to glean in his field, told his workers to not bother her**)
- Why was Boaz so kind to Ruth? (**Possible answers: He had heard of her kindness to Naomi; he wanted to honor God by obeying His law about taking care of widows; God prompted him to be kind and help.**)

Notes:

APPLICATION

- Do you think it is easy to serve others? Why or why not? (**Answers will vary.**)
- What motivates you to serve? (**Answers will vary.**)
- How does it make you feel to serve others? (**Answers will vary.**)
- Name ways God can use you to serve others. (**Possible answers: show compassion when needed, physically help those who need it, think about others more than myself**)

DAY 2

 11.2 Ruth Serves with Love

God wants you to be devoted to Him and serve others in need. God calls you to show love just as He would do.

1. Circle the boxes with the sentences that show service.

 Because Mr. Felton had a broken leg, Louis carried his groceries.

 Without being asked, Sunan cleared the table.

Mary didn't help her brother when he was struggling to read.

Read the devotion written by Juanita, age 8. Then, read the Scripture.

Serve It Up

One time my class went to the Rescue Mission. This is a place where people go to get some help. We sang Christmas carols and gave presents to the poor. Just seeing the joy on their faces really changed my life. It feels good to do things for others who have less than I do. Serving others is a cool thing to do. You could rake a yard, shovel a sidewalk, make a gift, or give help to others in need. Jesus was a wonderful example of this, and I want to be like Him.

2. Read Romans 12:10–11. What are some things you could do to serve others? Make your suggestions different from Juanita's.

Answers will vary.

42

11.3 Ruth Serves with Love
Focus: Boaz Is a Kinsman-Redeemer

★ PREPARATION
Select the song "What Seems Impossible" from the Grade 2 URL. (*Directed Instruction*)

↪ EXTENSION
3A Make a copy of **BLM 11A Readers Theater: Ruth and Naomi, Part 1** and **BLM 11B Readers Theater: Ruth and Naomi, Part 2** for each student. Tell students to read the script to review the Bible truth from this week's lesson.

3B Refer to **DM-8 Map of Moab and Bethlehem**. From Lesson 1.3, review the four directions of north, east, south and west. Ask students if they remember the sentence that can help them with directions. (**Never eat soggy worms.**) Have students identify the direction that Naomi and Ruth traveled to reach Bethlehem from Moab. (**west**)

Introduction
Have students locate **redeem** in the Glossary. *Redeem* means *to buy back and restore value and worth*. Discuss the definition. Read the following story:

Santiago worked hard to purchase a special soccer ball with his favorite player's signature on it. He loved playing soccer with his ball. One day during a game in his neighborhood, his ball was kicked so hard it landed in a nearby rushing stream. Santiago's heart was sad, as he watched his special ball float out of sight. He thought it was gone forever.

A month later, Santiago was at an outdoor market, and something caught his eye. It was his soccer ball on a table waiting to be sold! He knew it was his ball because the special signature was just as he remembered. Santiago worked hard and earned enough money to buy the ball back as his own. When he did, he once again cared for his ball, played with it, and cherished it because he valued it so much!

Explain that just as Santiago redeemed his ball by buying it back, Boaz redeemed something valuable to his family (Ruth 4:1–10).

Directed Instruction ★ ↪
Remind students that Naomi had been married to Elimelech. Ruth was Naomi's daughter-in-law and part of Elimelech's family. Ruth was married to one of Elimelech and Naomi's sons. Because of her husband's death, Ruth was not required to stay with Naomi; she could have gone back to her own family, who would have taken care of her. But she chose to go with Naomi and take care of her instead.

Recount that Boaz was a kinsman-redeemer. A *kinsman* is *a male relative*. A *kinsman-redeemer* was *a man who was willing to marry and care for a widow of one of his family members*. By marrying the widow, the kinsman-redeemer brought her back into the family. Inform students that Boaz bought the land that belonged to Elimelech. In doing this, Boaz gave Ruth the privilege of being in the family again by redeeming her. Read **Ruth 4:1–10**. Boaz redeemed Ruth by restoring her into the family. This action showed he valued her and gave her worth.

Explain to students that just as Boaz redeemed Ruth, so Jesus Christ paid the price to redeem all people. Even though sin separated everyone from God, He bought them back, or redeemed them, for a price. God was motivated out of love to restore people to Himself. Jesus paid the price when He came to the earth and died for them on the cross. His death paid the price for their sin and provided a way for them to receive all the blessings of being in His family. Emphasize that Jesus paid the price for salvation, but everyone is given the choice to accept or reject His gift of redemption. When they receive Christ's redemption for their sins, they "shall be saved by His life." At that point, they can rejoice in God, through their Lord Jesus Christ, because they are no longer separated from God (Romans 5:6–11).

Sing the song "What Seems Impossible" from the Grade 2 URL.

Student Page 11.3
Have students complete the page. Assist them as needed.

Review
• Why was Ruth no longer bound to stay with Elimelech's family? (**because of the death of Elimelech's son, who was Ruth's husband**)
• What does *redeem* mean? (**to buy back and restore value and worth**)
• When Boaz acted as kinsman-redeemer to Ruth, what privileges did that give her? (**She was cared for and became a member of the family again.**)
• Why did God send Jesus to redeem all people? (**because of His love for them**)

Notes:

DAY 3

Name _____

Ruth Serves with Love **11.3**

1. Use the sentences about Ruth to complete the graphic organizer.

• Boaz bought land and married Ruth.
• Ruth's husband had died.
• Boaz, her kinsman-redeemer, helped.

Ruth was poor and had no one to care for her.

Ruth's husband had died.	Boaz, her kinsman-redeemer, helped.	Boaz bought land and married Ruth.
Why?	Who helped?	How?

2. Boaz acted as kinsman-redeemer to **redeem** Ruth. Color the letters that complete the sentence: God _____ me through Jesus' sacrifice of death so I can be a part of His family.

p q r e d e e m e d e m

43

APPLICATION
• How do you know Boaz valued both God and Ruth? (**Boaz obeyed God's law as written in the Bible to provide food for widows. He acted as kinsman-redeemer to Ruth according to God's law, buying her family's land and marrying her.**)
• How do you know God values you? (**God paid the price for sin by dying on the cross to redeem me.**)
• What privileges do you have because Christ redeemed you? (**Possible answers: being part of God's family, being cared and loved for, living with God forever**)

REINFORCEMENT
Boaz was the son of Rahab, a Canaanite prostitute of Jericho (Matthew 1:5, Joshua 2). This made Boaz a half-Canaanite. King David's great-grandmother was Ruth, who was a Moabite. This means that King David's great-grandparents were part of the lineage of Jesus, yet they were not fully Jewish. This serves as a reminder that Jesus invites all people to be a part of His family. No matter where they are from, or what their past reveals, His redemption covers all.

11.4 Ruth Serves with Love

Focus: Boaz Loves Ruth

★ PREPARATION

Have on hand a LARGE BOWL, INDEX CARDS, and a WOODEN SPOON. (*Directed Instruction*)

↻ EXTENSION

4A Make a copy of **BLM 11C Gift of Character** for each student. Have students use BLM 11C as a prompt to demonstrate a devoted love to friends. Direct students to write a paragraph using all four character qualities.

4B Tell students to locate and read **Romans 8:38–39**. Make a class list of the ten things that can never separate them from God's love.

Introduction

Display a blank piece of paper and write the word *love* on it with a permanent marker. Inform students that the marker you used contained permanent ink. Display the paper, and ask students if doing any of the following things takes the word *love* away from the paper: Wad the paper in a ball; unwad the paper, and put pencil marks on it; throw the paper on the floor. (**No, the word *love* does not go away because it was written in permanent ink.**)

Explain to students that just as the word *love* was not taken away when things were done to the paper, so God's love works the same way. His love does not come and go according to what students look like or what they do. God's love is *unconditional*, which means *not based on what a person looks like, has, does, or says*. In the Bible truth today, students will see God's love lived out through Boaz as he loved Ruth unconditionally.

Directed Instruction ★ ↻

Remind students that Naomi instructed Ruth on how to approach Boaz and ask him for protection. Boaz complimented Ruth for her good character and behavior and told Ruth that he would care for her. Boaz said that there was another relative who was closer than Boaz that could care for Ruth, but that he would go and talk with him (Ruth 3:11–12). Boaz went to the leaders of the city to talk to the other relative. At first the man wanted to redeem the land that belonged to Naomi's family, but when he heard he would also be responsible for Naomi and Ruth, he asked Boaz to take on the responsibility. Boaz agreed (Ruth 4:1–10).

Explain that even though Ruth was a poor newcomer in the land, Boaz made the choice to love her. He chose to marry Ruth and care for her and Naomi. Boaz chose to love unconditionally the way God loves His children. Unconditional love is not given only when it is easy. Unconditional love happens even if the person being loved is poor, undesirable, or cannot give anything in return. Unconditional love happens when a person thinks about others more than himself or herself. That person chooses to see others the way God does. God loves His children, and values each of them no matter where they come from, how much they have, or what they look like. They are uniquely His own and He loves them just as they are. A person cannot have this kind of love for others without God. Remind students that because of God's love toward them and what He did for them on the cross, they can have the ability to love others unconditionally also (1 John 4:7–11, 19).

Display a LARGE BOWL. Tell students that God gave them a recipe to help them love others unconditionally. Read **1 Corinthians 13**. Tell students that God's Holy Spirit can help them to love others. Select a few "ingredients" from God's Word about love, and write them on the board. For example, *Love is patient* or *Love does not seek its own*. Hand out INDEX CARDS to volunteers. Have each volunteer write down an "ingredient" in the recipe for loving others unconditionally. Have students come up and place

108

their card in the bowl, stirring the "ingredients" with a WOODEN SPOON to make God's recipe for loving others. Keep this bowl displayed as a reminder all year and use it often to help students recall the characteristics of godly love.

Student Page 11.4
Assist students as needed to complete the page.

Review
- How did Boaz's willingness to be Ruth's kinsman-redeemer show unconditional love? (**He chose to love her regardless of what she had or where she was from.**)
- What is unconditional love? (**Possible answers: loving others with God's love, loving others even when you don't get anything in return**)
- How can you love others unconditionally? (**by asking God to help me love others as He loves them, with the Holy Spirit's help**)

APPLICATION
- When God looks at you, what does He see? (**Possible answers: a child of His, a unique creation, a special person He created**)
- Do you have to do anything to earn God's love? Why or why not? (**No, God loves me unconditionally.**)
- How should you see others? (**Possible answers: as God's children, as a special creation because God made everyone**)
- Name one way you can love someone unconditionally. (**Possible answers: caring for that person even when treated wrongly, not being concerned with what that person can give back, looking at the person as God would**)

REINFORCEMENT
Jesus showed the ultimate unconditional love by enduring the worst kind of death possible—crucifixion (Matthew 27:27–56). Like those who were victims of crucifixion, Jesus was forced to carry the crossbeam of the cross He would hang upon. The crossbeam weighed between 75 and 125 pounds. At crucifixion the victim's hands were usually tied to the wood. Jesus' hands were nailed to the wood. As others stood by and mocked Him, Jesus hung on a cross, taking on and paying for the sins of all, showing a love that goes beyond what anyone could imagine.

DAY 4

11.4 Ruth Serves with Love

1. Read Ruth 4:1–10. In each box on the top row, write one way that Boaz showed love to Ruth. In each box on the bottom row, write one way you can show love to others, as described in 1 Corinthians 13.

   Possible answers: Boaz married Ruth; Boaz cared for Ruth and Naomi; Boaz redeemed Ruth even though she was poor.

   Possible answers: show kindness, be unselfish, believe in others, be patient

2. How do you know Christ loves you unconditionally?
   Christ died on the cross to pay for my sins.

11.5 Ruth Serves with Love

Focus: Review and Assessment

★ PREPARATION

Select **VA 11A Ruth Serves with Love**. (*Lesson Review*)

Make a copy of **BLM 11D Lesson 11 Test** for each student. (*Directed Instruction*)

Lesson Review ★

Use **VA 11A Ruth Serves with Love** to review the Bible truth. Cover the following concepts:

- Ruth was devoted to Naomi, *Devoted* means *showing faithfulness and commitment to someone or something*.
- Ruth moved from Moab to Bethlehem to help care for Naomi after each of their husbands died.
- Ruth and Naomi had a loving, friendly relationship. They were devoted to serve and stay with each other.
- Ruth worked hard serving as she gleaned in fields that belonged to Boaz.
- *Redeem* means *to buy back and restore value and worth*.
- When Boaz chose to be Ruth's kinsman-redeemer, he bought the land that belonged to Elimelech. Boaz cared for her and took her as his wife.
- Ruth's marriage to Boaz gave her all the privileges and position of being a part of the family again.
- Boaz and Ruth had a son and named him *Obed*. Ruth became King David's great-grandmother through Obed. Boaz, Ruth, Obed, and King David are all part of the lineage of Jesus.
- To *love* means *to unselfishly accept others*.
- It is not always convenient or easy to serve others, but God calls His children to show love just as He would do.
- God's love is unconditional. This means that His love is not based on what a person looks like, has, does, or says.
- Boaz chose to love Ruth unconditionally as God loves unconditionally.
- Boaz showed unconditional love to Ruth. Unconditional love takes place when people think about others more than themselves and see others the way God does.

Directed Instruction ★

Distribute **BLM 11D Lesson 11 Test** to each student. Read the directions, and have students complete the test.

Notes:

Lesson Preparation
David Faces the Giant
12.0

Expected Student Outcomes

KNOW
David slays Goliath.

DO
Students will:
- identify key words in the Bible truth about David and Goliath
- identify good and bad forms of peer pressure
- understand that love destroys fear and brings courage
- write a letter to encourage someone who is facing a "giant" problem

APPLY
Students will speak out for God instead of yielding to peer pressure.

Lesson Outline
I. David faces Goliath (1 Sam 17)
  A. Courage
II. God uses the small
  A. God looks at the heart (1 Sam 16:1–13)
  B. What God has chosen (1 Cor 1:26–29)
  C. Peer pressure
III. Fear versus courage (2 Tim 1:7, 1 Jn 4:18)
IV. Giant problems (Mt 11:28–30)

♥ TEACHER'S HEART

Typically you are not called upon to slay giants. Rather it is the gnats that overwhelm you. Everyday stresses, correcting students, explaining to parents, completing your lesson plans, grading papers, always feeling like you are a day late and a dollar short—these are the things that do you in. David probably felt like his job as a shepherd was unbalanced and overwhelming at times. Isolated, unappreciated, too young for the real battle, he too could have given in and quit. However, during those years, he was being prepared for future experiences such as fighting the Philistine giant, Goliath.

Maybe those things you do day in and day out are preparing you for something God has ordained for your life. You must, in the midst of the "gnats," make consistent decisions to walk with Him, exhibiting love, joy, kindness, and perseverance. Faithfulness in these little things prepares you for opportunities of greater service. It also prepares you for the day you must face "the giant." Don't grow weary in doing your job well!

MEMORY VERSE
1 Samuel 17:47

GLOSSARY WORDS
- courage
- peer pressure

MATERIALS
Day 1:
- Beanbag
- Butcher paper, measuring tape
- VA 12A David Faces the Giant, DM-1 Character Traits
- Time Line
- Brown paper bags, aluminum foil (Extension)

Day 2:
- Butcher paper (Extension)

Day 3:
- Strips of cloth (Extension)

Day 4:
- Butcher-paper outline
- Butcher-paper outline, beanbags (Extension)

Day 5:
- VA 12A David Faces the Giant
- BLM 12A Lesson 12 Test

SONGS
Little Is Much

TEACHER RESOURCES
Lucado, Max. *Facing Your Giants: The God Who Made a Miracle Out of David Stands Ready to Make One Out of You.* Thomas Nelson, 2008.

STUDENT RESOURCES
Petach, Heidi. *David and Goliath.* Standard Publishing, 2005.
Mackenzie, Carine. *David: The Fearless Fighter.* CF4Kids, 2007.

Supplemental Materials are available to download. See Understanding Purposeful Design Bible at the front of this book for the Grade 2 URL.

12.1 David Faces the Giant
Focus: David Faces Goliath

📖 MEMORY VERSE
1 Samuel 17:47

MEMORY WORK
- Display the Memory Verse. Separate students into two groups. Direct each group to line up at the front of the classroom, facing one another. Hand a BEANBAG to one of the students. Direct the student to say or read a word in the verse and toss the beanbag to someone in the other group. The student who catches the beanbag then says the next word of the verse. Have students do this several times. When students have a good grasp of the verse, take the displayed verse down. Direct students to say the words and toss the beanbag again. If anyone makes a mistake, have him or her sit down.

★ PREPARATION
Have a BEANBAG available. (*Memory Work*)

Obtain a 9 ½' PIECE OF BUTCHER PAPER. Have a MEASURING TAPE on hand. Once the activity is completed, keep the drawing available for Lesson 12.4. (*Introduction*)

Select **VA 12A David Faces the Giant** and **DM-1 Character Traits**. (*Directed Instruction*)

EXTENSION
1A Direct students to create coats of armor by using LARGE BROWN PAPER BAGS and ALUMINUM FOIL. Ask students to volunteer to retell the Bible truth of David and Goliath as they dress in their coats of armor.

Introduction ★
Place the **9 ½' PIECE OF BUTCHER PAPER** flat on the floor. Select a volunteer to lie down on the butcher paper, and tell another student to trace out the volunteer's outline with a dark-colored crayon. Invite another student to measure the outline with a **MEASURING TAPE**. As students are sitting back down, draw the outline of a figure that is nine feet tall. (The nine-foot-tall figure should be on the same side as the student's.) Today's Bible truth is about a man who was taller than nine feet.

Directed Instruction ★
Read **VA 12A David Faces the Giant**. Point to the nine-foot figure on the butcher paper and note how much bigger this figure is compared to the student's. Ask students how they would feel if this man were trying to pick a fight with them. (**scared**) Goliath was about 9' 9" tall (1 Samuel 17:4). Further illustrate Goliath's size by selecting several students to portray a total weight of about 125 pounds. Explain that this was roughly how much Goliath's coat of armor weighed (1 Samuel 17:5). Stack books to approximate 15 pounds to show the weight of just the iron point at the tip of Goliath's spear (1 Samuel 17:7). Goliath was able to carry this extra weight easily and still be quick in battle. Ask students to describe in their own words Goliath's size. (**Possible answers: huge, enormous, crazy big**)

Discuss with students what they would do to prepare if they were going to fight someone like Goliath. (**Answers will vary.**) Highlight that Saul, who was the king and should have been leading his men, did not fight but had an idea of how David should get ready to fight. He had David put on the king's armor and take his sword. Explain that David was just a boy, about 17 years old, and a grown man's armor would not have fit him. David had also never practiced fighting in armor. He chose to use a sling and stones. Ask students who would have gotten the credit if David did things Saul's way and won. (**David and Saul**) Ask students who would more likely get the credit if David used a sling and stones. (**God**)

Invite a student to read **1 Samuel 17:45–47**. Everything that David did, he did to give God credit. David was probably scared and intimidated by this giant, but he still trusted God. David could have used Saul's armor, but instead he trusted God. And David could have said how great he was when he defeated the giant, but instead he gave God all the credit.

Display **DM-1 Character Traits**, and instruct students to locate **courage** in the Glossary and on DM-1. As a class, read the definition aloud. *Courage* is defined as *doing the right thing even when afraid*. Point out that after David showed courage, fought Goliath, and won, the Israelite army was no longer afraid. They then pursued the Philistines. Explain that this is usually what happens when God's people show courage and trust Him—everyone else will be encouraged to follow.

Student Page 12.1
Read the instructions to students, and assist them in completing the page.

Review

- What was Goliath's challenge to the people of Israel? (**for one man to fight him to determine the winner so that the Philistines would serve the Israelites or the Israelites would serve the Philistines**)
- What did David do when he heard Goliath's challenge? (**He went to King Saul and told him he would fight for Israel.**)
- How did David prepare for the battle? (**by choosing five smooth stones and his sling**)
- In whose name did David win the victory? (**in the name of God**)

Time Line
Refer to the **Time Line**, and identify where David fits in the history of Israel. Explain that David would soon become the most famous king in Israel. Review that David's great-grandmother was Ruth, who had been loyal to Naomi, and had faithfully served her. Remind students that Ruth and David are part of the lineage of Jesus.

APPLICATION

- If you were presented with a challenge to a battle like David, how would you prepare yourself? (**Answers will vary but should include choosing to remember what great things God has already done and asking Him for help through prayer.**)
- Has there been a time when you had to do something scary? How were you able to do it? (**Answers will vary.**)
- When you do something good, who do you want to get the credit? (**Answers will vary.**) Commit to allowing God to get the credit.

REINFORCEMENT

In today's society, Goliath's size is quite mind-boggling and might sound like something from a science-fiction movie. In David's day, however, giants were not the things of folklore and science fiction, but a part of life. In 2 Samuel 21:15–22, the exploits of David's mighty men are recorded in which they defeated real giants. Four men are mentioned in this passage, and three of them are described—one had a bronze spearhead that weighed 300 shekels (about 7.5 pounds); one had a spear with a shaft like a weaver's rod or beam; and one was a huge man with six fingers on each hand and six toes on each foot. All four of these giants were from a town called *Gath*, which was Goliath's hometown (1 Samuel 17:4).

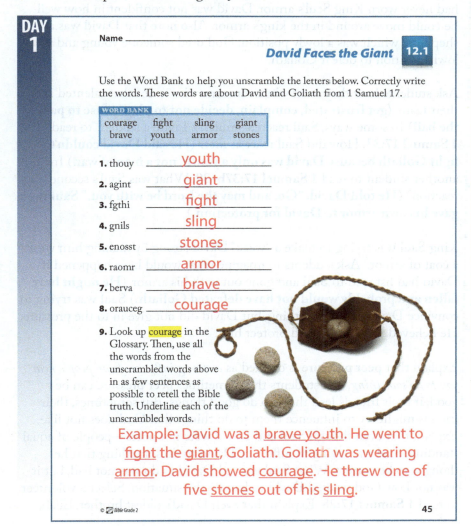

DAY 1

Name _____

David Faces the Giant 12.1

Use the Word Bank to help you unscramble the letters below. Correctly write the words. These words are about David and Goliath from 1 Samuel 17.

WORD BANK
| courage | fight | sling | giant |
| brave | youth | armor | stones |

1. thouy — youth
2. agint — giant
3. fgthi — fight
4. gnils — sling
5. enosst — stones
6. raomr — armor
7. berva — brave
8. orauceg — courage

9. Look up **courage** in the Glossary. Then, use all the words from the unscrambled words above in as few sentences as possible to retell the Bible truth. Underline each of the unscrambled words.

Example: David was a <u>brave youth</u>. He went to <u>fight</u> the <u>giant</u>, Goliath. Goliath was wearing <u>armor</u>. David showed <u>courage</u>. He threw one of five <u>stones</u> out of his <u>sling</u>.

12.2 David Faces the Giant

Focus: God Uses the Small

★ PREPARATION

Select the song "Little Is Much" from the Grade 2 URL. (*Introduction*)

⟲ EXTENSION

2A Divide a piece of BUTCHER PAPER into three equal sections. Have the class decide which three scenes should be depicted on a mural from the Bible truth about David and Goliath. Divide students into three groups and give each group a section of the butcher paper. Direct each group to draw and color its segment of the Bible truth. When each section is completed, reassemble the mural and display it in a prominent place.

2B Instruct students to write a journal entry on how they would have felt and responded if they were called upon to fight Goliath.

Introduction ★

Lead students in singing the song "Little Is Much."

Directed Instruction ⟲

To really understand how God uses the "little" things of this world, it is important to realize that the story of David begins before his victory over Goliath. Read **1 Samuel 16:1, 4–6**. Explain that Eliab was David's oldest brother. In fact, David had seven older brothers, but God had not chosen them to be king. Read **1 Samuel 16:7**. Tell students that God looks at their hearts, not what they look like, and not how big or strong they are. He does not choose like the world chooses. It was David, the youngest, whom God chose to be the next king of Israel. Read **1 Corinthians 1:26–29**. God often uses the unlikely and weak things of this world, instead of the wise and powerful, so that He gets glory. If God uses people who are weak, He can show how strong He is. This way, no one can boast about being great, only that God is.

When David went to fight Goliath, he was not only the youngest of eight boys; he did not have an adult body yet. Remind students that David had never worn King Saul's armor. David was not confident in how well he could move around in the king's armor. Also note that David was a shepherd, which was a lowly position. God used someone young and in a lowly position to defeat Goliath.

Ask students how they react when someone who is not that talented is on their team. (**get frustrated, complain, decide not to play, refuse to pass the ball**) In some ways, Saul reacted similarly. Invite a student to read **1 Samuel 17:33**. How did Saul react at first? (**He said David couldn't fight Goliath because David was only a youth, not a man of war.**) Invite another student to read **1 Samuel 17:37b–39**. What was Saul's second reaction? (**He told David. "Go, and may the Lord be with you." Saul then gave his own armor to David for protection.**)

King Saul was trying to make a "weak" David strong by making him wear a coat of armor. Ask students to imagine what would have happened if David had listened to Saul and gone out with his armor. (**He might have fallen and probably would not have defeated Goliath.**) Saul was trying to convince David to do something, but David did not give in to the pressure. He believed that God would protect him.

Explain that **peer pressure** is defined as *a strong influence from people near you to do something*. Tell students that sometimes peer pressure can be good, if their friends lead them to do good things. But sometimes, their friends might try to influence them to do things that God does not like. Explain that even though Saul and David were not peers—people of equal standing, Saul was trying to influence David to do something that he thought to be correct. What Saul wanted David to do was not bad, but it was not how God wanted David to handle the situation. Select a volunteer to read **1 Samuel 17:28**. Explain that even David's oldest brother, Eliab, was also pressuring David—he angrily questioned why David was there. Challenge students to think of different ways they can stand up for what is right instead of yielding to negative peer pressure. Pray with students to conclude the lesson.

Student Page 12.2
Students complete the page. Assist as needed.

Review

- How would David be considered too small, young, or weak? (**He didn't have an adult body; he was the youngest in his family; and he was a lowly shepherd.**)
- What did God say He looks at when He chooses people? (**God looks at the heart, not what a person looks like.**)
- How did Saul respond to God's choice? (**Saul said David couldn't do it, then he tried to get David to wear his armor.**)
- What is peer pressure? (**Peer pressure is a strong influence from people near you to do something.**)

APPLICATION

- Have you ever felt like you were too small, young, or weak for God to use you? (**Answers will vary.**)
- Take a moment and think about how God likes to use the small, young, and weak. Pray and ask God to use you to do whatever He wants you to do.
- When is a good time to give in to peer pressure? (**when friends influence you to do good things**)
- When is a time you have experienced bad peer pressure? What happened? (**Answers will vary.**)

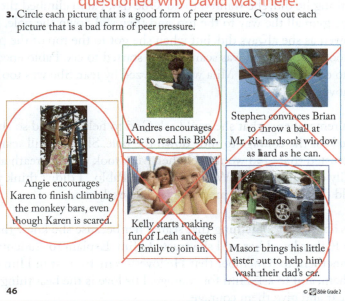

DAY 2

12.2 David Faces the Giant

1. Look up peer pressure in the Glossary. Write the definition.
   peer pressure: _a strong influence from people near you to do something_

2. How did Saul and Eliab show peer pressure toward David in 1 Samuel 17?
   Saul first told David that he could not fight Goliath because David was too young. Then, for protection, Saul tried to get David to wear his armor. Eliab angrily questioned why David was there.

3. Circle each picture that is a good form of peer pressure. Cross out each picture that is a bad form of peer pressure.

46

12.3 David Faces the Giant

Focus: Fear Versus Courage

⟲ EXTENSION

3A Solicit the help of parent volunteers to monitor this activity. Take students outside and match them in pairs. Explain to them that you will be blindfolding one student in each pair with a STRIP OF CLOTH. Instruct the other student to lead their blindfolded partner around the playground area. Explain that some obstacles might be scary or difficult to perform, but blindfolded students need to trust their partner to safely lead them. Allow students to lead each other through the playground. Caution the leaders to be careful to protect their blindfolded partner at all times. After several minutes, regroup and discuss how students felt. Ask if any were scared and what they did to conquer that fear.

3B Inform students that people who have accepted Jesus as Savior can be assured that God never leaves or abandons them (Hebrews 13:5), and that He will give them strength, or courage (Philippians 4:13). Teach them a simple pray for courage, such as "Lord, You are strong and in control. Thank You for always being with me. Please give me courage."

Introduction

Invite a volunteer to the front of the class. Ask the student to keep his or her legs straight and fall back in a "trust fall." If the student hesitates, promise that you will be there to catch the student. Ask what made the student finally fall backward. (**the promise to be caught, trust in you**) Tell students that sometimes in life they are faced with things that are really scary, and on their own they probably do not want to do them. But God is always with them, and from Him they can receive the courage to do the right thing, even when they are afraid.

Directed Instruction ⌐

Review with students the Bible truth about David and Goliath. Goliath was really scary. In fact, Saul and the rest of the Israelite army were so afraid that they would not go out and fight Goliath. Goliath was so confident, he came out and challenged the Israelite army for 40 days (1 Samuel 17:16). Ask students why David had the courage to go out and fight Goliath when trained military men did not. (**David trusted God because he had seen God's strength work through him before, and he fought in God's name.**)

Ask a student to read **2 Timothy 1:7**. (Note that some translations use *timidity* instead of *fear*, which might need to be defined for students.) Invite another student to read **1 John 4:18**. Ask what both of these verses have in common. (**They both talk about fear and love.**) Explain that when the person they love and trust is God, they can be sure that He is big enough and strong enough to handle any "giants" that may appear in their life. When they love and trust God, fear gets pushed aside by courage.

Read the following fictional story, which illustrates the connection between love and courage:

> Mila loved playing on the playground with her brother, Pablo. Anything he did, she wanted to do. One day, Pablo climbed the jungle gym all the way to the top, and then slid down the pole. Mila followed as she always did, but when she got to the top of the pole she looked down and was scared. Mila started to cry. Pablo encouraged her to come down, but Mila was paralyzed by fear. She was too scared to move.

> Mila remembered that she could ask God to help her, and so she prayed for the courage to slide down the pole. She was still scared, but she trusted that God would help her. Mila took a deep breath and slid shakily down the pole. "Wow, Mila!" said Pablo. "I didn't think you would do it!" "God gave me courage!" she exclaimed.

Mila was able to do something that scared her because she knew that her heavenly Father loved her, and she trusted Him. Explain to students that God wants them to remember that He loves them, to trust in Him to take care of them, and to ask Him for courage. His love is the best thing to destroy fear and give them courage.

Student Page 12.3
Direct students to complete the page.

Review

• Why did none of the Israelite soldiers or King Saul go out to fight Goliath? (**They were too afraid.**)
• Why was David not afraid to meet Goliath in battle? (**David trusted the Lord and knew from past experience that God would help him.**)
• What is the one thing that drives away fear? (**love**)

Notes:

APPLICATION

• Tell about a time you were really afraid of something. (**Answers will vary.**)
• What is something you can think of or do that will give you courage when you are in a scary situation? (**Possible answers: I can think about the great things God has done, that He loves me and will take care of me, and that I can trust in His love and not be fearful. Also, I can pray.**)

REINFORCEMENT

The fear of the Lord is a theme used often in the Bible. It is said that to fear God is the beginning of wisdom (Proverbs 9:10). Fear to an ancient Hebrew meant not only the emotional fear and trembling caused by something scary, but also the reverence shown to someone in high authority. To fear the Lord is to come to Him through the grace He extends, and to recognize His greatness and power and act accordingly in reverence.

DAY 3

Name _____

David Faces the Giant 12.3

1. Draw a picture of something you are afraid of.

Drawings will vary.

2. What can you do about this fear?

Possible answers: I can trust that God will help me with my fear because I know that I don't have to go it alone; I can tell my parents about the fear and ask for help.

3. Read 2 Timothy 1:7 and 1 John 4:18. What destroys fear and gives you courage?

Love can destroy fear, and as a result give us courage.

4. Your teacher read a story about Mila. God helped Mila when she was afraid. Draw a picture of how you can get courage when you are afraid.

Drawings will vary.

© Bible Grade 2   47

12.4 David Faces the Giant
Focus: Giant Problems

★ PREPARATION
Retrieve the BUTCHER-PAPER OUTLINE from Lesson 12.1. (*Directed Instruction*)

⤴ EXTENSION
4A Tape the BUTCHER-PAPER OUTLINE from Lesson 12.1 to the wall. Point to the phrases written on the butcher paper from today's lesson. These phrases are some of the big "giants" that second graders might face. Provide each student with a BEANBAG. Encourage them to throw the beanbag at the phrase that is their most difficult "giant." After each student has had a turn, lead a short discussion to help students identify ways that they can face these real-life "giants." Students may suggest strategies, such as prayer and talking to their parents.

Introduction
Instruct students to close their eyes, and listen to and visualize the following: *a hamster and a dog*, and *a kitten and a lion*. Tell students to open their eyes. Ask them to explain the difference in each phrase. (**The first animal was much smaller than the second animal.**) Direct students to close their eyes again and to visualize the following: *a mouse, a rooster, a goat, a horse*, and *an elephant*.

Explain to students that, in the last activity, you gave a list of animals in progression of size. So, each animal was smaller than the next one named. Explain that to a mouse, a rooster would be quite large, or a "giant" of sorts. But, to a rooster—the mouse's giant—a goat would be a "giant" and the rooster would be small in comparison. Use other animals from the sequence to further explain perspective. Tell students that the size of something depends on a person's viewpoint.

Directed Instruction ★ ⤴
Explain to students that you have been teaching them about David's situation with Goliath so they can know how to face difficult situations, or "giants," in their life. Lead students in a discussion to identify real-life giants. (**Possible answers: someone picking on me, parents divorcing, a relative struggling with a serious illness, confessing wrongdoing**) Write their answers on the BUTCHER-PAPER OUTLINE from Lesson 12.1. Tell students that God can help them face these "giants." Read **Matthew 11:28–30**. Explain that God wants them to go to Him in prayer. *Being yoked to Jesus* means *to do things His way*. Jesus is gentle and kind. He teaches His ways to people who are yoked to Him, and then their "giants" are not such big problems. In this Scripture, the word *rest* means *to stop and gather strength*. Going to God and trusting Him brings rest. His strength is given to those who trust Him. He can make difficult situations stop immediately. Having the viewpoint of God coming alongside to help them through a difficult situation can make the "giant" problem a small one. Discuss the following possible ways to defeat these "giants:"
- Pray for God's help.
- Talk to your parents or some trusted friends; ask them to pray with you.
- Recall and recite Bible verses.
- Determine to do the right thing, even when there is peer pressure.
- Ask someone to go with you when you must do something difficult.
- Practice doing right in less challenging times in order to be ready to do the right thing when a big problem comes.

Student Page 12.4
Read aloud the directions on the page, and then read the following dilemmas from which students are to select a topic for their letter:
- Susan is afraid to walk home from school by herself. What can she do?
- Phil has played with his dad's tools and one of them broke. He is scared about what his dad will say. What can he do?
- Ed wants to play with his older brother Peter, and Peter's friends. They keep telling him he is too little. What can he do?

• Robin has two friends who have asked her to do something that is wrong. What can she do?

Direct students to write a letter to one of the children from the scenarios. Encourage them to write about being strong and courageous, not giving into peer pressure, and learning what to do from Jesus. Ask some students to read their letters aloud if time permits.

Review

• What does God want you to do when you are faced with a "giant" in your life (Matthew 11:28–30)? (**God wants me to go to Him in prayer and rest in Him.**)
• What does it mean to "rest" in God? (**to stop and gather strength**)
• Is it always bad to follow peer pressure? (**No, it is only bad when I am influenced to do something that is wrong.**)

Notes:

APPLICATION

• What are some "giants" you and your family have had to face? (**Answers will vary.**)
• Do you trust that God can use you to face those giants and bring about something good? (**Answers will vary but should include that God's Word from this week's lesson encourages me.**)
• What does God want you to do with your burdens (Matthew 11:28–30)? (**He wants me to go to Him in prayer and let Him guide me. I will then have rest if I follow His guidance.**)
• What can you do to grow in courage? (**Possible answers: trust God, ask for help**)

DAY 4

12.4 *David Faces the Giant*

Write a letter to one of the children your teacher reads about. Help that boy or girl make a good and courageous choice.

_____,

Answers will vary but should include to trust in God, tell a parent how they feel, and to do the right thing even though they are scared.

_____,

48

© *Bible* Grade 2

© *Bible* Grade 2

119

12.5 David Faces the Giant

Focus: Review and Assessment

★ PREPARATION

Select **VA 12A David Faces the Giant**. (*Lesson Review*)

Make a copy of **BLM 12A Lesson 12 Test** for each student. (*Directed Instruction*)

Lesson Review ★

Use **VA 12A David Faces the Giant** to review the Bible truth. Cover the following concepts:
- The Philistine army wanted to fight the Israelites and King Saul.
- The Philistine's fiercest warrior, Goliath, challenged the Israelite army for 40 days in a row.
- Goliath was a 9' warrior whose shield weighed 125 pounds and whose spearhead weighed almost 15 pounds.
- *Courage* means *doing the right thing even when afraid.*
- No one had the courage to take on Goliath, not even Saul, the king.
- David came to the battlefield to bring food to his three older brothers. While he was there, he heard Goliath's challenge against God and the Israelites, His people.
- David went to King Saul and said he would fight Goliath.
- King Saul told David he was too young and small. David explained that he could fight Goliath because God would help him. King Saul wanted David to wear his armor.
- David did not have time to test King Saul's armor, so he chose five smooth stones and his sling.
- Through the power of God, David was able to defeat Goliath with a single stone.
- David was the youngest brother, smaller than an adult, and a mere shepherd, yet God used him in a great way.
- *Peer pressure* is defined as *a strong influence from people near you to do something.* David's oldest brother, Eliab, pressured David to go home. King Saul used pressure to try to convince David to wear his armor.
- Being yoked to Jesus brings rest. Jesus guides and teaches those who are yoked to Him to bring rest from "giants."
- Love and trust in God drive away fear.

Directed Instruction ★

Distribute a copy of **BLM 12A Lesson 12 Test** to each student. Explain the instructions and format. Have students complete the test. When students have completed the test, provide answers for immediate feedback.

Notes:

120

Lesson Preparation
Thanksgiving
13.0

Expected Student Outcomes

KNOW
David expresses thanksgiving to God for His provision and faithfulness.

DO
Students will:
- recount the event of King David leading the people in thanksgiving when the ark of the covenant arrived in Jerusalem
- describe who God is and God's promise to Abraham
- discover things to thank God for by using a code
- write about someone they are thankful for

APPLY
Students will express gratitude to God for His presence in their life.

Lesson Outline

I. David leads in thanksgiving (1 Chron 15:1–16:36)
II. David's song of thanksgiving (1 Chron 16:8–36)
   A. Who God is
   B. What God has done
III. Giving thanks to God (1 Chron 16:9; Ps 103:1–22, 105:1, 106:1, 47–48)
IV. Giving thanks for others (Col 3:15c)

♥ TEACHER'S HEART

Think of the times you have heard these two simple words: Thank you. How did those words make you feel? What did you say in response? When someone says thank you for nothing really in particular, it should fill your heart to overflowing.

When you are thankful, two things happen. First, your thankfulness pleases God and causes His heart to swell. If you are overjoyed when those you love and serve stop to say thank you, how much more is God overjoyed! Secondly, your thankfulness lifts your gaze from your circumstances and puts it on the Author and Perfecter of your faith. When you give Him thanks, your circumstances seem less challenging, your struggles much smaller, and God is greatly glorified in your life. Take time to thank Him for all He has done for you today, and allow your heart to overflow!

📖 MEMORY VERSE
Psalm 105:1

⭐ MATERIALS

Day 1:
- Flip chart or poster board
- DM-1 Character Traits
- VA 13A David Leads in Thanksgiving
- Time Line
- Cardboard box, gold wrapping paper, musical instruments (*Extension*)

Day 2:
- Time Line
- Globe (*Extension*)

Day 3:
- BLM 13A "All Things Bright and Beautiful" (*Extension*)

Day 4:
- Notebook
- Card stock (*Extension*)

Day 5:
- VA 13A David Leads in Thanksgiving
- BLM 13B Lesson 13 Test

♪ SONGS
It Is Good

TEACHER RESOURCES
DeMoss, Nancy Leigh. *Choosing Gratitude: Your Journey to Joy*. Moody Publishers, 2009.
Rainey, Barbara. *Thanksgiving: A Time to Remember*. Crossway Books, 2003.

STUDENT RESOURCES
Libby, Larry. *Someday Heaven*. Zonderkidz, 2001.
Veggie Tales: Madame Blueberry: A Lesson in Thankfulness. DVD. Big Idea, Inc., 2003.

Supplemental Materials are available to download. See Understanding Purposeful Design Bible at the front of this book for the Grade 2 URL.

© Bible Grade 2   121

13.1 Thanksgiving
Focus: David Leads in Thanksgiving

📖 MEMORY VERSE
Psalm 105:1

MEMORY WORK
- Read the Memory Verse together. Invite all students wearing brown to stand and read the verse. Have everyone wearing red stand and say the verse. Encourage everyone in the class to close their eyes and say the verse.

⭐ PREPARATION
Display the Memory Verse on a FLIP CHART or a piece of POSTER BOARD so students can see it all week. (*Memory Work*)

Write an encouraging note and secretly place it inside a student's lunch bag. Select **DM-1 Character Traits** (*Introduction*)

Select **VA 13A David Leads in Thanksgiving**. (*Directed Instruction*)

↪ EXTENSION
1A Tell students that the word *thanksgiving* is a compound word made up of *thanks* and *giving*. Invite students to share related forms of *thanksgiving*. Write them on the board. (**Possible answers: thank, thankful, thank you**)

1B Invite students to act out the celebration that David led. Wrap a CARDBOARD BOX with GOLD WRAPPING PAPER. Borrow as many MUSICAL INSTRUMENTS as needed. Select one student to be *David* leading the people, and four students to carry the gold box—the ark of the covenant. Get at least eight students to be the choir. Tell the remaining students to play the musical instruments. Have students sing a thanksgiving song and march around the room.

Introduction ⭐
At the beginning of class, ask the owner of the lunch bag with the hidden note to bring the lunch bag to you. Dramatically open the lunch bag and ask the student to retrieve the note and read it silently. Explain that the note was secretly placed in the student's lunch bag. Lead students to conclude that when someone does something for them, they should be thankful. Having an attitude of *thanksgiving* means *appreciating what you have*. It is the opposite of complaining and arguing. Display **DM-1 Character Traits** and have students chorally read the definition of thanksgiving.

Directed Instruction ⭐ ↪
Display **VA 13A David Leads in Thanksgiving**. Point to the ark of the covenant. The ark of the covenant was a gold-covered box that the Israelites had brought with them when they entered the Promised Land.

The ark of the covenant was a reminder to the Israelites of God's faithfulness and love. God spoke to the high priests from above the ark. Help students recall the following ways God provided for the Israelites:
- God spoke to Moses through the burning bush and wanted Moses to go to Egypt to rescue the Israelites from Pharaoh. God caused the 10 plagues to happen so Pharaoh would let the Israelites leave Egypt.
- The Israelites traveled toward Canaan, the Promised Land. God led the Israelites by a cloud during the day and a pillar of fire at night. He parted the waters of the Red Sea so the Israelites could cross on dry land. Pharaoh's army was destroyed. As the Israelites traveled, God helped Moses find water to drink and He sent bread (manna) from heaven.
- God spoke to Moses in front of the Israelites and later gave them the Ten Commandments. The Ten Commandments were written on tablets of stone and placed inside the ark of the covenant. God performed miracles through Moses. God protected, fed, and led His people.

Point out David leading the parade. Remind students that David grew up tending his father's sheep, wrote many psalms of worship, praise, and thanksgiving to God, and became king of Israel. Read the back of VA 13A for today's Bible truth. Share that David led the people in thanksgiving. The Levites, men from the family of Aaron, carried the ark. (Remind students that Aaron was Moses' brother.) After the ark of the covenant arrived in Jerusalem, David gave offerings to the Lord. Then David fed the Israelites. David gave each of them a loaf of bread, a piece of meat, and a cake of raisins. (Explain that a cake of raisins was a bar of raisins pressed together, not a cake with raisins inside.) There was music and singing! The Israelites remembered what God had done for them and were thankful.

Review
- What did the ark of the covenant help the Israelites remember? (**Possible answers: God's faithfulness and love, where the high priests heard from God**)

- What did David lead the people to do after the ark of the covenant arrived in Jerusalem? (**give thanks**)
- Who joined King David in moving the ark to Jerusalem? (**The Levites carried the ark of the covenant. There were singers and people playing musical instruments.**)
- Name one way God was faithful to the Israelites. (**Possible answers: leading the Israelites out of Egypt, leading them by a cloud during the day and a pillar of fire at night, giving them water and food**)

Student Page 13.1

Discuss the illustration at the top of the page. Read the text, and have students complete the page.

Time Line

Point to King David. Discuss the events surrounding King David's life in relation to Abraham, Moses, Joshua, and Ruth.

Notes:

APPLICATION

- When you remember God's faithfulness in your life, what should you do? (**Give thanks to God.**)
- Name one way God shows His faithfulness to you. (**Possible answers: God sent His Son to die on the cross and take my sins away; God brings people in my life to teach me about Himself; He keeps His promises found in His Word.**)

REINFORCEMENT

Psalm 105:1, the Memory Verse, is telling Christians to purposely remember what God has done for them in order to be thankful. *Make known His deeds* means *to tell others what God has done and to be thankful*. The word *thanks*, or a form of it, appears more than 100 times in the Bible.

DAY 1

Name _____

Thanksgiving 13.1

Match each sentence to the correct answer. Write the letter of the correct answer on each line.

1. The Israelites took the ark of the covenant to the Promised Land. Inside the ark were the stone tablets of the Ten Commandments that God gave Moses. The ark of the covenant helped the Israelites remember God's faithfulness and __b__.

2. King David wanted to keep the ark of the covenant in a __d__ place in the city of Jerusalem. The Levites moved the ark there.

3. The people of Jerusalem watched the arrival of the ark of the covenant to the special __a__ made for it. David led the people in a time of celebrating and __f__.

4. The ark arrived and it was placed inside the special tent. David gave offerings to the Lord. Then he gave each __g__ bread, meat, and __e__ to eat.

5. David selected some men to remember, praise, and __c__ the Lord God of Israel, who had been faithful to His children. There was music with stringed instruments, harps, cymbals, and trumpets.

a. tent

b. love

c. thank

d. holy

e. raisins

f. thanksgiving

g. Israelite

© Bible Grade 2   49

13.2 Thanksgiving

Focus: David's Song of Thanksgiving

★ PREPARATION

Select the song "It Is Good" from the Grade 2 URL. (*Introduction*)

⟡ EXTENSION

2A On the board, write *thank you* in the following languages:

Chinese—*xiè xiè*
French—*merci*
German—*danke schön*
Hebrew—*toda*
Portuguese—*obrigado*
Russian—*synkprya*
Spanish—*gracias*
Swahili—*asante*

Pronounce *thank you* in each language given. Use a GLOBE to point out the country where each *thank you* is spoken. Share that when someone says *thank you*, he or she is politely expressing gratitude. Explain that the heart of gratitude coming from the person saying *thank you* in any language conveys a message of appreciation. The person being thanked can sense the message. Mention that the words *thank you* are probably some of the first words they were taught to say and that saying *thank you* is a good habit.

2B Explain that David wrote about who God is in his song of thanksgiving, and he expressed his thankfulness for what God had done. God's Word tells believers to sing, clap, make music to the Lord, and to give thanks to the Lord. Lead the class to quote **Psalm 105:1**. Direct students to bow their heads and individually thank the Lord for something He has done for them.

Introduction ★

Sing the song "It Is Good" from the Grade 2 URL. Remind students that David led the people in thanksgiving after the ark of the covenant arrived in Jerusalem. David gave offerings to the Lord. Then David gave food to the Israelites. There was music and singing! David was so thankful that he wrote a song. Ask students if they remember what the song was about. (**Possible answers: thanksgiving, remembering what God had provided for the Israelites**) Instruct students to listen to the first verse in the song as you read **1 Chronicles 16:8**. Ask students what David tells the people to do. (**Give thanks to the Lord.**) Lead students to understand that giving thanks is important to God.

Directed Instruction ⟲

Introduce David's song of thanksgiving found in **1 Chronicles 16:8–36**. Write the reference on the board and give instructions for everyone to find the passage. Partners can assist each other in finding the passage. (If everyone has the same version of the Bible, give students the page number.) Lead students in reciting or singing the books of the Old Testament to remember where 1 Chronicles is found. Select students to read some of the beginning verses. Finish reading the song to the class.

Student Page 13.2

Tell students to complete Exercise 1. After they have finished, explain that David wrote about who God is—the true and living God, the Creator of the universe—and that God is always good. For Exercise 2, draw the graphic organizer found on the student page on the board. Explain that a graphic organizer is a drawing that shows how words or ideas fit together. Point out the arrows from one sentence to the other to show the connection. Tell students to complete Exercises 2–3. Afterward, remind them that in his song, David remembered God's promise to Abraham to make his family a great nation. The promise was being fulfilled when Abraham and Sarah had a son named *Isaac*, and Isaac and Rebekah had a son named *Jacob* who had many sons. Their descendants became a nation called *Israel*, and God was faithful to provide for the Israelites on their way to the Promised Land. Remind students that a *descendant* is defined as *a person who comes from a certain family line of parents, grandparents, and great-grandparents* and that many years later, Jesus was born in the nation of Israel. Jesus died for the sins of all people. God has been faithful to keep His promise of eternal life to Christians around the world.

Review

- Why did David write a song about thanksgiving? (**It was his expression of thanksgiving to God for faithfully providing for His people.**)
- How did David describe God in his song of thanksgiving? (**the true and living God, Creator of the universe, always good**)
- How did God keep His promise to Abraham to make his family a great nation? (**Abraham's descendants became a nation called *Israel* from which Jesus, the promised Savior of the world, was born.**)

124

Time Line

Point to King David on the **Time Line**. Locate and discuss how Jesus was born years later as a descendant in the same family.

Notes:

APPLICATION

- Read **1 Chronicles 16:8**; **Psalm 100**; and **Psalm 106:1, 47–48**. What do these verses say to do? (**Possible answers: give thanks to the Lord, worship Him, praise Him**)
- Why should you give thanks to the Lord? (**God's Word says to give thanks, and God deserves my thanks.**)
- Name one thing that God has provided for you that you are thankful for. (**Answers will vary but should include physical and spiritual provision.**)

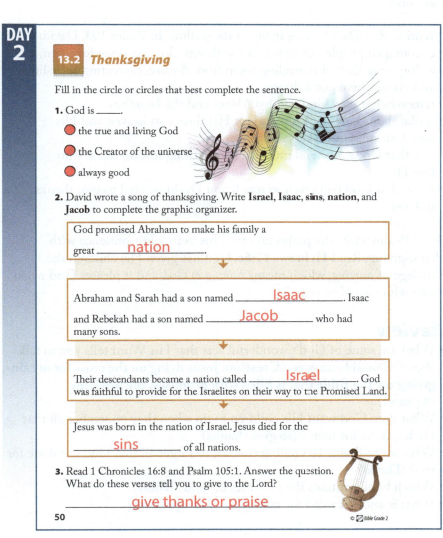

DAY 2

13.2 Thanksgiving

Fill in the circle or circles that best complete the sentence.

1. God is ____.
   - ● the true and living God
   - ● the Creator of the universe
   - ● always good

2. David wrote a song of thanksgiving. Write **Israel**, **Isaac**, **sins**, **nation**, and **Jacob** to complete the graphic organizer.

   God promised Abraham to make his family a great __nation__.

   Abraham and Sarah had a son named __Isaac__. Isaac and Rebekah had a son named __Jacob__ who had many sons.

   Their descendants became a nation called __Israel__. God was faithful to provide for the Israelites on their way to the Promised Land.

   Jesus was born in the nation of Israel. Jesus died for the __sins__ of all nations.

3. Read 1 Chronicles 16:8 and Psalm 105:1. Answer the question. What do these verses tell you to give to the Lord?

   __give thanks or praise__

13.3 Thanksgiving

Focus: Giving Thanks to God

EXTENSION

3A Obtain a copy of the song "All Things Bright and Beautiful" by Cecil Alexander and play it for the class. Distribute one copy of **BLM 13A "All Things Bright and Beautiful"** to each student. Direct students to select one verse of the song and illustrate the verse on the bottom of the page.

Introduction

Choose at least three students who have obeyed class rules well. Point out each of the three students, and thank them for a specific behavior, such as standing patiently in line to sharpen a pencil or raising a hand to answer or ask a question.

Ask students how it makes them feel when someone thanks them for doing something. (**Answers will vary but should include that it makes them happy when someone thanks them for doing something.**) Explain that God is also pleased when they say thank you to Him for something that He has done for them.

Directed Instruction

Read **1 Chronicles 16:9** and explain that this Scripture tells them to sing praises about God and to talk about all God's wonderful acts. Explain that some of the things they can thank God for are the Creation, God's Son Jesus who takes away the sins of the world, and the Bible that is filled with God's promises. God wants His children to thank Him for the things He has done.

Mention that David wrote many of the psalms. In Psalm 103, David:
- encouraged people not to forget the things God has done for them, such as forgiving their sins, healing them from disease, protecting their life, and giving them good things
- remembered how God had led Moses and the Israelites
- spoke about how the Lord had set His throne in heaven and His kingdom rules over everything
- saw that God's love and mercy are very strong toward those who fear Him
- knew that God had given so much and David wanted to give thanks to God

Read **Psalm 95:2**. The psalm says to come before His presence with thanksgiving. Read **Hebrews 11:6c**. God has given His children the privilege of *praying*, which means *talking to God*, and it pleases God when those who love Him pray.

Review

- What are some of God's wonderful acts that His Word tells you to talk about? (**Possible answers: Creation, Jesus dying on the cross for my sins, giving me the Bible that is filled with promises, the privilege of prayer**)
- What does God want His children to do when they remember all that He has done for them? (**to give thanks**)
- Who wrote Psalm 103 telling you not to forget all that God has done for you? (**David**)
- Which book contains the promises of God? (**Bible**)
- What is another word for talking to God? (**praying**)

Student Page 13.3

Read the directions. Demonstrate how to use the code by completing Exercise 1 together. Have students complete the page.

Notes:

APPLICATION

- Why is it important to thank God? (**It is a way to remember all that God has done.**)
- What is something you can thank God for right now? (**Answers will vary but should include physical and spiritual needs.**)

REINFORCEMENT

First Chronicles 16:9 is part of Psalm 105. David specifically wrote this psalm to give thanks to the Lord on the day the ark of the covenant was brought to Jerusalem. Many of the psalms exhort God's children to join in praise to Him. In 1 Chronicles 16:8–13 and Psalm 105:1–6, David lists a plethora of ways for one to glorify and praise God.

DAY 3

Name _____

Thanksgiving 13.3

Use the code to name things to thank God for.

Code:
a = drum, e = harp
i = violin, o = trumpet
u = maracas, l = butterfly
p = violin, r = bongo
s = xylophone, t = wreath

1. B i b l e
2. p r a y e r
3. J e s u s
4. c r e a t i o n

Use the code words above to complete the sentences.

5. Plants and animals are part of God's _____ creation _____.

6. _____ Jesus _____ is the Son of God.

7. The _____ Bible _____ is God's Word.

8. God's children talk to Him in _____ prayer _____.

9. Write about one thing God has provided for you that you are thankful for. Tell why. _____ Answers will vary. _____

© Bible Grade 2

51

13.4 Thanksgiving
Focus: Giving Thanks for Others

★ PREPARATION
Select a NOTEBOOK that could be used as a journal. (*Introduction*)

☞ EXTENSION
4A Distribute one sheet of CARD STOCK to each student. Demonstrate how to fold the paper lengthwise. Then tell students to turn the folded sheet so that the folded top half flips up. Instruct students to write a thank-you note to someone on the inside of the bottom half. Review where to put the date, greeting, body, closing, and signature. Instruct students to draw and color a design on the front of the card.

4B Direct students to find the table of contents in the front of their Bible to help with the correct order of the books in the Old Testament. Lead the class in singing or saying the books of the Old Testament. Call out the following Old Testament references, one at a time, for students to find: Psalm 96:4, 1 Chronicles 16:31, Psalm 106:1. The first student to find each verse gets to read it.

Introduction ★
Begin class by asking students to raise their hand if they have a journal that they write in regularly. Display the NOTEBOOK that could be used for a journal. Explain that a *journal* is defined as *a record of anything that someone wants to write about*. It could be a record of events, experiences, ideas, or anything they want to thank God for. Share that if someone scored the winning goal in a soccer game and does not want to forget it, he or she could write in a journal about the action that won the game and the date it happened. Maybe someone took a family vacation to see exotic animals and drew pictures and labeled them in a journal, so he or she could remember them for a long time. Perhaps someone has an idea for a new hopscotch game and writes about it in a journal, so friends can try it during recess. Encourage students to develop or continue the habit of writing or drawing in a journal.

Directed Instruction ☞
Ask a volunteer to assist you in front of the class. Hand him or her a piece of paper that has been ripped in half. Tell the class to imagine that this is a very important, valuable piece of paper, and that the volunteer is doing you a big favor by taping the pieces together, and giving it back to you. When the volunteer hands the paper to you, pretend not to notice for a while, and then take it absently (do not say thank you or acknowledge the student in any way until things get awkward). Ask the volunteer how it felt when you did not say thank you. (**Possible answers: annoying, rude**) Lead a discussion about how God feels when people are not thankful for the things He provides.

Remind students they have learned to thank God for the beautiful works of Creation that He has given them, for Jesus who died on the cross to take away the sins of the world, for the Bible, and for the privilege of prayer.

Teach that God provides for them through other people. Ask students to name people who provide for them every day. (**Possible answers: parents, relatives, friends, neighbors**) Quote **Colossians 3:15c**, "Be thankful." Help students recognize they need to thank God for others, especially parents or caregivers who take care of them. Share that they are also to be thankful for those who work to give them food, so they can have energy to move, work, and play. Discuss how community helpers work to keep them safe during the day and at night. Relate that friends are fun to be with and should help them make the right choices. Ask students to think of other people who God uses to provide for them. Help students to conclude that God uses other people in their lives, and students are to thank Him for His faithfulness and what He provides through those other people.

Review
• Who does God use to faithfully provide for you? (**Possible answers: parents, teachers, caregivers, community helpers, friends, others**)
• How do you know that God wants you to be thankful? (**The Bible tells me to be thankful.**)

- How can you let someone know that God has used him or her to be a blessing in your life? (**I can tell them thank you or write them a thank-you note.**)

Student Page 13.4

Mention that the page begins with a student named *Ursula*, who has written in her journal telling about people who provide for her and their faithfulness to her. Share that Ursula realizes that God uses many people in her life to bless her and she is thankful for them. Select different students to read the directions and each paragraph on the page. Have students complete the page. Assist as needed.

Notes:

APPLICATION

- Name one reason you are thankful for your friends. (**They help me make the right choices.**)
- Name someone who has blessed you and tell why you should thank that person. (**Answers will vary.**)

DAY 4

13.4 *Thanksgiving*

1. Ursula wrote in her journal about some people she is thankful for. Circle each word that tells about those people.

Giving Thanks for Others

I am thankful for my (family). We work together. We play together, and we pray together. Sometimes I have a (friend) over. We play games, build things, or just talk.

I try to learn something new every day. My classroom is a happy place. I learn to read and work hard so my (teacher) will put fun stickers on my papers. I pull the stickers off and collect them. At church, I listen to the (pastor). He helps me learn about God so I can tell others about Him.

The (farmer), the (truck driver), and the (grocery store worker) help to provide food for my meals and snacks. The (police officer) makes sure people obey laws. When I get sick, I see the (doctor), who gives me medicine. A (firefighter) rescues people and puts out fires. Every day I check the mail to see if the (postal worker) has delivered a letter to me.

I will try to say thank you or write a thank-you note to these people because they do nice things for me. God uses them to bless me.

2. Write about one person you are thankful for. Tell why.

Answers will vary.

52

13.5 Thanksgiving

Focus: Review and Assessment

★ PREPARATION

Select **VA 13A David Leads in Thanksgiving**. (*Lesson Review*)

Make one copy of **BLM 13B Lesson 13 Test** for each student. (*Directed Instruction*)

Lesson Review ★

Use **VA 13A David Leads in Thanksgiving** to review the Bible truth. Cover the following concepts:

• King David loved and served God with all his heart.
• King David was faithful and thankful to God.
• King David wanted the ark of the covenant to be kept in a holy place in Jerusalem.
• The ark of the covenant was a gold-covered box that the Israelites had brought with them when they entered the Promised Land.
• The Levites moved the ark of the covenant to the tent in Jerusalem.
• When the ark of the covenant arrived in Jerusalem, King David gave offerings to the Lord. Then King David gave food to the Israelites. There was singing, music, praise, and thanksgiving to God.
• God commands His people to be thankful.
• God provides for His children through other people. The Bible says to thank Him for His provision and faithfulness provided through others.
• God wants His people to thank Him for all He has done for them.

Directed Instruction ★

Distribute a copy of **BLM 13B Lesson 13 Test** to each student. Read the directions and pronounce any difficult words. Have students take the test. Read over the test, providing the answers for immediate feedback.

Notes:

Lesson Preparation
Elijah Trusts God

14.0

Expected Student Outcomes

KNOW
God meets the physical needs of Elijah, a widow, and her family.

DO
Students will:
- find Scriptures that remind them to trust God for courage
- apply benefits of trusting God
- complete sentences about God's provision
- draw conclusions about God's miracles

APPLY
Students will verbalize their trust in God to meet all their needs.

Lesson Outline

I. Elijah is encouraged (1 Kings 17:1–16, Mt 11:28–30)
II. Trusting God
    A. Path of direction (Ps 48:14, Prov 3:5–6)
    B. Peace (Rom 5:1, Phil 4:6–7)
    C. Provision (Phil 4:15–19)
III. God's ways (Rom 8:28–29)
IV. Miracles occur (1 Kings 17:1–16)

♥ TEACHER'S HEART

Elijah was alone. King Ahab and the Israelites were not following God's commands. Yet Elijah put his trust in God, and God gave Elijah courage. God came in Elijah's solitude and nourished him in the most unlikely ways. It was through the raven, a scavenger, and a widow who was on the verge of starvation that God gave Elijah satisfying provision at just the right time! Elijah's trust in God grew as he watched God nourish his soul and body each step of the way.

As a Christian teacher, you are not a stranger to trusting God. Sometimes, however, the cares of your classroom creep in and trials discourage you. You know that God is closer than your own breath, but in the turmoil of your days, you can become anxious and forget that your times are in His hands (Psalm 31:15).

Read Proverbs 3:5–6. God sometimes provides in the most unlikely and unexpected ways. Many times He provides in small ways through a kind word, a change of heart, or a surprise act of kindness that lifts you up. As Elijah courageously trusted God to constantly satisfy him, ask your loving Father today for the courage to trust Him to provide for you each step of the way.

MEMORY VERSE
Philippians 4:19

GLOSSARY WORDS
- provision
- prophet

MATERIALS

Day 1:
- VA 14A Elijah Trusts God, backpack, rocks

Day 2:
- Magazines (*Extension*)

Day 3:
- BLM 14A Widow's Bread Recipe (*Extension*)

Day 4:
- VA 14A Elijah Trusts God
- Jar (*Extension*)

Day 5:
- VA 14A Elijah Trusts God
- BLM 14B Lesson 14 Test

♪ SONGS
All Things Work Together

TEACHER RESOURCES
Men of Courage: A Study of Elijah and Elisha. Christian Focus Publications, 2004.
Swindoll, Charles R. *Elijah: A Man of Heroism and Humility*. Thomas Nelson, 2008.

STUDENT RESOURCES
DeStefano, Anthony. *This Little Prayer of Mine*. Waterbrook Press, 2010.
Mackenzie, Carine. *Elijah: God's Miracle Man*. CF4Kids, 2012.

Supplemental Materials are available to download. See Understanding Purposeful Design Bible at the front of this book for the Grade 2 URL.

14.1 Elijah Trusts God
Focus: Elijah Is Encouraged

 MEMORY VERSE
Philippians 4:19

 MEMORY WORK
- Have students locate the Memory Verse in their Bible. After reading and practicing the verse, have students answer who, what, when, and why about the verse.

 PREPARATION
Select **VA 14A Elijah Trusts God**. Have an EMPTY BACKPACK and THREE LARGE ROCKS available. (*Directed Instruction*)

EXTENSION

1A Divide the class into three groups. Tell students that they will be given information about someone from the Bible who showed courage through difficult situations. Use the following information:
- Moses courageously told Pharaoh to let God's people go from Egypt. Moses followed God's direction. God then sent the ten plagues. Exodus 10:21–11:1 tells about the last plagues.
- Joshua courageously obeyed God, even though the situation seemed impossible, and God brought down the walls of Jericho. Joshua 6:2–5 tells about the directions God gave Joshua.
- David courageously faced Goliath in God's name and for God's people. David defeated the champion of the Philistines. 1 Samuel 17:42–51 tells of this confrontation.

Have each group think of three clues to share with the class. Challenge students to guess the Bible character assigned to the other groups.

Introduction
Read the following true-life experience to the class:
> You wake up in the morning, and there is nothing for breakfast. You give your baby brother a hug and walk to school. School is two miles away. The road is dusty. At school, your growling stomach distracts you from paying attention. During recess, you get in an argument with another student over a piece of bread that was on the ground. You put the bread in your pocket. When school is over, you run home to your baby brother. He is crying, alone, and hungry. Because your parents are gone, you have to take care of him. You give him the piece of bread, and tell him it will be okay. You go to bed and hope tomorrow will be a better day.

Share with students that the above story is a common occurrence in many parts of the world. Many people face hardships, and many of these people are children. It is understandable that in tough situations, people can feel *discouragement*, which means *a feeling of hopelessness*. Explain to students that when they are discouraged, they should put their trust in God, and believe in His **provision**. *Provision is defined as a supply of something needed*. In today's Bible truth, students will learn about how Elijah trusted in God for provision.

Directed Instruction ★
Display **VA 14A Elijah Trusts God**. Read the back for today's Bible truth. Elijah loved God, listened to God, and wanted others to follow God. He was a true **prophet**, defined as *someone who has special knowledge from God*.

Invite a volunteer to come to the front of the class. Place an EMPTY BACKPACK on the student's back. Place THREE LARGE ROCKS, one by one, inside the backpack while reading each of the following reasons that could have discouraged Elijah:
- There was a wicked king named *Ahab* who would not listen.
- The wicked king convinced the Israelites to worship false gods.
- Elijah told them to change their ways and King Ahab became angry, so God told Elijah to flee and hide by the brook Cherith.

Ask the volunteer how the bag feels. (**Possible answers: heavy, weighted down**) Share that discouragement can feel like a big, heavy weight. Remind students that when they are discouraged, they need to trust God for help.

Explain that Elijah put his trust in God. Elijah knew God's will and God's ways because he had spent time listening to God and learning from Him. Remove the three large rocks, one by one, from inside the backpack while reading each of the following reasons why Elijah was encouraged by God:
- God sent ravens to feed Elijah every morning and evening.
- When the brook dried up, God sent Elijah to a widow.
- The widow gave Elijah water and bread. God provided food for Elijah, the widow, and the widow's family for many days.

Ask the volunteer with the empty backpack how the bag feels. (**Possible answers: lighter, not heavy**) Share with students that if they listen to God, trust Him, and allow Him to encourage them during hardships, He will lift the heaviness of their burdens. Select a volunteer to read **Matthew 11:28–30**. Remind students that just as Elijah trusted God, they also can trust God to give them courage and to meet their needs each day (Philippians 4:19, Matthew 6:11).

Student Page 14.1
Assist students as needed to complete the page.

Review
- What is a prophet? (**someone who has special knowledge from God**)
- How did Elijah the prophet show courage? (**Possible answers: He told King Ahab about the drought; he asked the widow for water and bread.**)
- How did Elijah know about God? (**Elijah spent time listening to God and learning from Him.**)
- What is provision? (**Provision is a supply of something needed.**)

DAY 1

Name _____

Elijah Trusts God 14.1

In 1 Kings 17:1–16, the prophet Elijah was courageous. Elijah listened to God's direction. God brought provision to Elijah. Read each situation and color the box with the reference that reminds you to trust God.

1. Michael is shy and afraid of being teased by the children at school.

| Psalm 18:2 | Psalm 38:14 |

2. Sherinna's father lost his job and is looking for a new place to work.

| Proverbs 12:10 | Philippians 4:19 |

3. Tyesha's family moved to a new city, and she feels alone.

| Psalm 2:2 | 1 Peter 5:7 |

4. How did God encourage Elijah?

Possible answers: God sent ravens to feed Elijah every morning and evening; God sent Elijah to a widow after the brook dried up; God provided food for Elijah, the widow, and the widow's family.

5. Write a short prayer to God. Ask Him to give you the courage to listen to Him and trust Him.

Answers will vary.

© Bible Grade 2   53

APPLICATION
- Take time to thank God for His provision for you and your family.
- Ask God for His courage in a situation that is difficult in your life. Make the effort to diligently pray about the situation.

REINFORCEMENT
John Newton was born in London in 1725. His mother died in 1732, and his father, a merchant service commander, drowned in 1751. After his father's death, Newton deserted his ship, was later captured, and became a servant to a slave trader. He suffered brutal persecution and inhumane treatment. Newton lost all sense of religious conviction, which his mother had first instilled in him. He went on to become a captain of slave ships. Steering homeward through a storm, full of discouragement and fear, Newton gave his life to God. It was at this point that he wrote in his journal words that later inspired him to pen the well-loved hymn "Amazing Grace." When John Newton was most discouraged, God gave him an appreciation of His amazing grace. The hymn is still loved and sung today.

© Bible Grade 2   133

14.2 Elijah Trusts God
Focus: Trusting God

★ PREPARATION
Select the song "All Things Work Together" from the Grade 2 URL. (*Directed Instruction*)

↪ EXTENSION
2A Provide each student with a MAGAZINE and a sheet of construction paper. Explain what a collage is. Ask students to look through the magazine to find pictures of things God provides for them. Encourage students to cut out and glue the selected pictures onto their sheet of construction paper. Display the collages that represent God's provision.

Introduction
Read the following paragraph:
> You are stuck on a rooftop! Below you are firefighters holding a very large net. The firefighters are encouraging you to jump into the net. It looks so far down! Would you trust them to catch you?

Discuss the concept of trust with students. Explain that just as firefighters are people they can trust, God is someone they can always trust for help. Today, students will learn what Elijah gained from trusting God and what they will gain from trusting God.

Directed Instruction ★ ↪
Explain to students that sometimes they may find it hard to completely trust God when they are in a difficult circumstance. Trusting in God involves agreeing with Him that He wants the best for them, even if they don't understand His methods. Trusting in God yields many benefits, which are mentioned in the Bible. To help students remember, share about these benefits that begin with the letter *p*: **p**ath of direction, **p**eace, **p**rovision.

Path of direction:
- Elijah: God told Elijah to go to the brook Cherith. After the brook dried up, God directed him to the widow (1 Kings 17:2–9).
- Students: God will also give them direction and continued guidance when they put their trust in Him (Psalm 48:14, Proverbs 3:5–6).

Discuss ways that God has given direction. (**Possible answers: showed my family where to live, guided my dad or mom to a job**)

Peace:
- Elijah: God told Elijah that He had commanded a widow to take care of him. Elijah trusted God, journeyed on from the brook, and came upon the widow (1 Kings 17:9–10).
- Students: Trusting in God also brings peace in their time of need (Romans 5:1, Philippians 4:6–7).

Discuss ways that God has given peace. (**Possible answers: helped me not to be afraid when my family didn't have enough money, helped me not to worry when I was sick**)

Provision:
- Elijah: God sent ravens to bring food to Elijah in the morning and evening. God supplied food for Elijah, the widow, and the widow's family by keeping the flour bin full every day (1 Kings 17:4–6, 14–16).
- Students: God provides for them as they trust Him to meet their needs (Philippians 4:15–19).

Discuss ways that God has provided. (**Possible answers: gave me food, gave me a home, gave me friends**)

Sing the song "All Things Work Together" from the Grade 2 URL.

Student Page 14.2
Have students read the directions and complete the page. Assist as needed. Encourage students to share their answers when completed.

Review
- How did Elijah benefit from trusting God? (**Possible answers: God gave him direction where to go; God gave him peace; God provided the food he needed.**)
- Name the benefits you can receive from trusting God. (**path of direction, peace, provision**)
- Compare the ways that Elijah benefited from trusting God to ways that you benefit from trusting God. (**Answers will vary but should include that I benefit by knowing His path of direction, having His peace, and receiving His provision, just as Elijah did.**)

Notes:

DAY 2

14.2 *Elijah Trusts God*

Elijah always benefited from trusting God. You can also benefit from trusting God. Answer each question.

1. **P**ath of direction: Read Psalm 48:14 and Proverbs 3:5–6. When has God directed your path?

Answers will vary.

2. **P**eace: Read Romans 5:1 and Philippians 4:6–7. When has God given you peace?

Answers will vary.

3. **P**rovision: Read Philippians 4:15–19. When has God given you provision?

Answers will vary.

4. Circle every third letter to find the answer to the question. Write the answer on the line.

How can you be like Elijah?

A Y I p e c d m a g r n c c l u m i y q s o o t a v e w b n p j t u r o g n a a k n y c d z g p i o u h m t n u m a l y h p t e r r g q u y p s d d t u u i v b n L K G w j o l h d

I can listen to and put my trust in God.

54

© Bible Grade 2

APPLICATION
- Name a difficult time when you needed to trust in God. (**Answers will vary.**)
- What is the hardest thing about trusting God? (**Possible answers: I have to put my faith in Him and not myself; I have to agree with Him that He wants the best for me.**)
- Why is it better to trust God than to try to do things on your own? (**If I trust in God, He will give me direction, peace, and provision.**)

REINFORCEMENT
In Bible times, widows had no way of providing for themselves when their husbands died. Many lived in poverty, never receiving an inheritance. The Bible gives guidance on the treatment of widows. The Old Testament states that God sustains the fatherless and widows (Psalm 146:9), that widows are not to be afflicted, and that God hears their cries (Exodus 22:22–24). In the New Testament, Jesus commended and showed compassion to widows in the account of the widow giving two mites (coins) in Mark 12:42–44 and in the account of the widow's dead son who was raised to life in Luke 7:11–17. In 1 Timothy 5:3–16, Paul gave principles to guide the Church on how widows are to be treated. James 1:27 challenges believers to demonstrate true faith by showing compassion and kindness toward widows who have nothing with which to reciprocate.

14.3 Elijah Trusts God
Focus: God's Ways

⟳ EXTENSION

3A Select **BLM 14A Widow's Bread Recipe** and prepare the bread. Provide a snack for students and explain that the bread is similar to something the widow may have made.

Introduction

Write the following statements on the board and select volunteers to read them aloud:
- A bear helped a bee find honey.
- A fish helped an otter build a dam.
- A friend in first grade helped you study for a test.
- A student that you do not know helped you find your lost puppy.

Ask students what is strange about all these statements. (**The one helping is one who is least likely to assist.**) Tell students that just as all these animals and people were the least likely to help, so God gave Elijah the least likely helpers to assist and provide what he needed.

Directed Instruction ⟳

Explain that God does not always provide in expected, probable, and likely ways. Elijah had to trust God to provide for him during the drought. God did provide by way of ravens. A raven is a *scavenger*, which is defined as *an animal that feeds on dead animals or discarded food*. A raven would have been one of the least likely birds to bring Elijah food. It would have been scavenging for its own food to hoard for itself! Bringing food to Elijah would have been a very strange thing for a raven to do. Yet, God provided for Elijah in this unexpected way.

After the brook dried up, God told Elijah to go to a city on the coast. God led Elijah to a widow from this city. A widow at that time would have had no way to make money after her husband died. A widow may have been the least likely person to give Elijah food. Yet, this widow gave what little she had, and God used her in an unexpected way to provide for Elijah!

Explain to students that when God provides for them, He may do it in ways they would never expect. God may bring an unexpected person their way to give them what they need. Or, God may use strange circumstances to help the students through hard situations. Many times they may not understand how God works, but they should know He is always working things together for good to those who love Him. The unexpected way God provides is always better than their own plans to provide for themselves. Select a volunteer to read **Romans 8:28–29** aloud.

Allow students to share about how God could provide in unexpected ways. (**Possible answers: A new friend could bring encouragement to a sad friend; a neighbor could take a meal to a sick friend.**) Tell students to earnestly look for ways in which God works. Remind them that it is important to not get discouraged if God does not work things out the way they expect. They can know that God will always be there in their time of need, just as He was with Elijah.

Student Page 14.3
Direct students to work in pairs to complete the page.

Review

- Why did Elijah need provision? (**There was a drought.**)
- Why was it strange for a raven to feed Elijah? (**Ravens are scavengers and they would usually not give food away.**)
- What was unusual about a widow providing food for Elijah? (**Widows did not have a way to make money to provide for their needs after their husbands died.**)

Notes:

APPLICATION

- What do you learn about God from the way He provided for Elijah? (**He does not always do things the way we expect. He is powerful.**)
- Why do you think God provided for Elijah in the least likely ways? (**God provided in these ways so we would know it only happened because of Him.**)
- Name a time God provided for you in an unlikely way. (**Answers will vary.**)

REINFORCEMENT

God chose ravens—scavenger birds often associated with death and disease—to bring life and nourishment to Elijah. Like falcons and hawks, ravens are superb fliers. They eat carrion and will prey on sick or injured animals. They were once targeted for extermination as pests. It was only through God's power that this unlikely source could have fed Elijah.

DAY 3

Name _____

Elijah Trusts God `14.3`

The Bible truth in 1 Kings 17:1–16 tells how God provided for Elijah. Write a word from the Word Bank that best completes each sentence.

WORD BANK

| widow | raven | scavenger | unlikely | food |

1. God provided for Elijah in _____unlikely_____ ways.

2. A _____raven_____ brought Elijah food at the brook Cherith.

3. This was strange because a raven is a _____scavenger_____.

4. God told Elijah to go to a _____widow_____ for help.

5. The widow shared what little _____food_____ she had with Elijah, and God provided a constant food supply.

6. Color the smiley face if the statement is true.

☺ God provides for everyone in the same way.

☺ Because there was a drought, God provided for Elijah.

☺ It was common for ravens to bring food to people.

☺ Even though God may work in unlikely ways, it is for your good.

© Bible Grade 2

55

14.4 Elijah Trusts God

Focus: Miracles Occur

★ PREPARATION

Select **VA 14A Elijah Trusts God**. (*Directed Instruction*)

↻ EXTENSION

4A Give students time to think of a personal prayer request. Allow ample time for students to pray aloud or silently for the requests. Encourage students to pray in faith for God to do miracles.

4B Provide an EMPTY JAR for students to fill with earned coins. When the jar is full, pray with the class about where the money should go to provide help to someone in need. Repeat this activity throughout the year.

Introduction

Write the words *magic trick* and *miracle act* on the board. Select a volunteer to read the words aloud. Ask students to share how they would define a *magic trick*. (**an illusion or a trick that can be learned and performed by someone**) Remind students that a *miracle* is *an act of God that is impossible by human or natural causes.*

Tell students that God performed many miracles in the life of Elijah. They were not tricks, but things that only could happen through God!

Directed Instruction ★ ↻

Explain to students that just as God performed miracles for Elijah, God performs miracles in their lives today. Read the following true-life story about a boy named *James*:

> James limped while walking to class. He had a sore on his ankle, but he didn't think much of it. By lunch time his ankle was very swollen and red. The teacher noticed and told James to see the school nurse. The nurse was concerned, but she instructed James to stay off of the ankle and to come back if it continued to swell.
>
> As James sat in class that afternoon, his ankle became more swollen. He returned to the nurse, who called his mom to come immediately to the school. After that, things happened so fast! The next thing James knew was that he was surrounded by doctors in the hospital! He had a severe infection that was spreading quickly through his young body.
>
> That night all of James' family and friends prayed. By morning, the infection was worse. The doctor told James' parents that his body was not accepting the medicine to help the infection. James' family prayed, as there was nothing else they could do. As they prayed, James felt God's presence as he trusted God to help him. The next morning, the swelling had gone down! God had performed a miracle!

Display **VA 14A Elijah Trusts God**. Remind students that Elijah was courageous, and he chose to put his trust in God. In doing so, God provided for Elijah through unlikely methods. Recount for the students the following actions and ways of provision that showed God's mighty hand in Elijah's life:

- To get the Israelites' attention, Elijah prayed and God sent a drought that would last for many years (1 Kings 17:1).
- Ravens fed Elijah at the brook (1 Kings 17:4–6), even though they are naturally scavengers.
- God kept filling the flour bin and the oil jar for Elijah, the widow, and the widow's family (1 Kings 17:13–16).

Using these points of review, emphasize that each scenario describes a miracle from God in Elijah's life. Only the one, true God can provide in such miraculous ways. This is because only God is all-powerful, or omnipotent.

Student Page 14.4
Have students read the directions and complete the page.

Review

- Review the definition of a miracle. (**A miracle is an act of God that is impossible by human or natural causes.**)
- Compare a miracle to a trick. (**Humans can learn and perform tricks, but only God can perform a miracle.**)
- Name a miracle God performed for Elijah. (**Possible answers: sent years of drought, provided food through ravens, provided an unending supply of food during the drought**)

Notes:

APPLICATION

- When something special happens, how do you know it is a miracle? (**It is a miracle when the only way possible for something special to have happened is by God's power.**)
- What do you think Elijah did before each miracle happened? (**prayed, listened to, and did what God wanted him to do**)
- Have you seen God do a miracle in your life? If so, what did He do? (**Answers will vary.**)
- Why does God perform miracles? (**Possible answers: to demonstrate His power; to give provision; to show He is the one, true God**)

DAY 4

14.4 Elijah Trusts God

1. Draw a picture of a miracle God did for Elijah.

Drawings will vary but could include a raven feeding Elijah, jars of oil and bins of flour, or rain falling.

2. Draw a picture of another miracle you have seen or heard about.

Drawings will vary.

3. Circle **T** if the statement is true and **F** is the statement is false.

T (F)   A miracle can be performed by anyone.
(T) F   Magic tricks can be performed and learned by anyone.
(T) F   Miracles only come from God.
(T) F   God performs miracles to show His power

4. What do God's miraculous ways of provision show you?

God's miraculous ways of provision show me that He is the one, true God.

14.5 Elijah Trusts God
Focus: Review and Assessment

★ PREPARATION

Select **VA 14A Elijah Trusts God**. (*Lesson Review*)

Make a copy of **BLM 14B Lesson 14 Test** for each student. (*Directed Instruction*)

Lesson Review ★

Use **VA 14A Elijah Trusts God** to review the Bible truth. Cover the following concepts:
- A *prophet* is defined as *someone who has special knowledge from God*.
- Elijah was a prophet of God. God used Elijah to tell King Ahab and the Israelites to stop worshipping false gods and breaking His commands.
- After Elijah prayed, there was a terrible drought with no little to no rain for a long period of time.
- King Ahab became very angry, so God told Elijah to flee and hide by the brook Cherith.
- Elijah trusted in God and His provision.
- A *provision* means *a supply of something needed*.
- God provided for Elijah in an unlikely way. He sent ravens to bring Elijah food in the morning and evening.
- When God provides in the least likely way, it can only be from Him.
- Elijah trusted God to take care of him when he was discouraged. Three benefits from trusting God are path of direction, peace, and provision.
- After the brook dried up, God sent Elijah to the home of a widow.
- The widow shared her last meal with Elijah. God supplied for her, her family, and Elijah by filling the flour bin and the oil jar with a constant food supply.
- God performed many miracles in Elijah's life.
- A miracle is an act of God that is impossible by human or natural causes.
- Miracles can only happen with the one, true God.

Directed Instruction ★

Distribute a copy of **BLM 14B Lesson 14 Test** to each student. Verify that students understand the directions and any difficult words. Have students complete the test.

Notes:

Lesson Preparation
Elijah Is Bold
15.0

Expected Student Outcomes

KNOW
Elijah challenges the prophets of Baal and is victorious.

DO
Students will:
- retell the Bible truth of Elijah boldly defeating the prophets of Baal
- identify things that can distract them from their relationship with God
- ask God's forgiveness for not keeping Him first
- identify verses having to do with boldness
- express how they can show boldness, like Elijah

APPLY
Students will pray in faith and speak boldly about the Lord to others.

Lesson Outline

I. Elijah continues in courage (1 Kings 18:1–45, 2 Kings 2:1–11)
II. Hearing God (Ps 46:10)
   A. Have a heart toward God (Mt 6:19–21)
   B. Still small voice (1 Kings 19:11–12)
   C. Idols (1 Kings 18:1–45, Ex 20:2–6)
III. Boldness (Phil 4:13)
   A. Speaking boldly (2 Cor 3:7–12)
   B. Acting boldly
   C. Praying boldly
IV. Disciples
   A. Elijah's disciple (2 Kings 2:1–11)
   B. Making disciples (Mt 28:18–20, Acts 1:8, Eph 6:19)

♥ TEACHER'S HEART

Elijah's life was amazing. Though he was in close communion with God and a central figure in miraculous events, he was a person with emotional highs and lows common to everyone (James 5:17). Regardless of Elijah's emotional state, God never changed. He was still God, able to speak to Elijah's soul with His voice alone. God spoke—sometimes gently, sometimes powerfully—providing physical rest, good food, direction for the future and assurance of His presence. Elijah's committed relationship with God allowed him to develop boldness and a deep trust in God.

Speak and live like Elijah before your students. To live a godly life in a world full of sin and idol worship requires great boldness. Your students will notice you living for God, boldly taking a stand against evil, and humbly confessing your sin. Pray for your students with a faith like Elijah's—that they may know God and receive wisdom and revelation through their knowledge of Him (Ephesians 1:17). So, be bold! Speak boldly; live boldly; and pray boldly!

📖 MEMORY VERSE
2 Corinthians 3:12

GLOSSARY WORDS
- idol

★ MATERIALS

Day 1:
- Crepe paper
- Container of bold coffee beans
- VA 15A Elijah Is Bold
- Stones, clear baking dish, twigs, sand or dirt, water (*Extension*)

Day 2:
- Pictures of a television, video games, food, friends, and toys

Day 3:
- BLM 15A Boldness
- PP-4 Boldness (*Extension*)
- BLM 15B Be Bold, stickers, various craft materials (*Extension*)
- Time Line

Day 4:
- Beanbag (*Extension*)

Day 5:
- VA 15A Elijah Is Bold
- BLM 15C Lesson 15 Test

TEACHER RESOURCES

Bartel, Blaine. *7 Absolutes to Pray Over Your Kids*. Harrison House, 2005.

Strobel, Lee, and Mark Mittelberg. *The Unexpected Adventure: Taking Everyday Risks to Talk with People About Jesus*. Zondervan, 2009.

STUDENT RESOURCES

Benge, Janet and Geoff. *Rachel Saint: A Star in the Jungle*. YWAM Publishing, 2005.

Supplemental Materials are available to download. See Understanding Purposeful Design Bible at the front of this book for the Grade 2 URL.

15.1 Elijah Is Bold
Focus: Elijah Continues in Courage

📖 MEMORY VERSE
2 Corinthians 3:12

MEMORY WORK
- Read the Memory Verse to students, and tape the prepared "rocks" to the floor (in the correct order) inside the creek area. Direct students to take turns stepping on the rocks as the rest of the class repeats the verse. Allow each child to have a second turn, this time jumping from rock to rock while individually saying each word of the Memory Verse.

★ PREPARATION
Cut rock shapes from construction paper and write each word of the Memory Verse onto one rock shape. Twist BLUE CREPE PAPER and tape it to the floor, creating a perimeter of a "creek area." (*Memory Work*)

Obtain a CONTAINER OF BOLD COFFEE BEANS. (*Introduction*)

Select VA 15A Elijah Is Bold. (*Directed Instruction*)

↻ EXTENSION
1A Provide students a visual of Elijah's challenge to the prophets of Baal by piling 10–12 STONES in a LARGE, CLEAR BAKING DISH. Put a few small TWIGS on top of the stones and some SAND or DIRT around the base. Create a trench in the sand or dirt. Pour WATER on top of everything, enough to fill the trench. Ask students what usually happens when fire and water come in contact with each other. (**Water usually puts out fire.**) Be sure students understand that nothing could have burned on that wet altar built by Elijah unless it was a miraculous act of God.

Introduction ★
Show students a CONTAINER OF BOLD COFFEE BEANS. Invite them to look at, smell, and describe the beans. Students might use words such as *strong*, *dark*, or *smelly*. Explain that you are holding bold coffee beans. *Bold* describes coffee beans that are stronger and darker than other coffee beans. Ask students what *bold* means when describing a person. (**strong, courageous, not fearful, says things without worry**) Explain that the Bible truth today is about a man who was very bold in standing up for God.

Directed Instruction ★ ↻
Distribute two pieces of construction paper to each student. Direct students to write *The Lord is God* on one piece of construction paper, and *You shall not worship idols* on the other piece. Instruct students to listen carefully as you read **VA 15A Elijah Is Bold**. To sharpen students' listening skills, direct them to raise the paper with *The Lord is God* every time they hear Elijah's name. Have students raise the paper with *You shall not worship idols* when they hear Baal or the prophets of Baal mentioned. As you read VA 15A, pause to give students enough time to respond by raising the appropriate piece of paper.

Explain that in Old Testament times, people often made images of animals and men. The people would then worship these images as gods—bowing down to the images, giving sacrifices, and promising that they and their children would serve these false gods. God wanted the Israelites to only do those things for Him and not for the hand-crafted images. The Israelites stopped worshipping God, because they forgot God's laws and everything He had done for them. Most Israelites were worshipping a false god named *Baal*, and only a few people were still following the one, true God. Because of this, Elijah could have been killed for his devotion to God, which was a strong reason for him to be fearful. Instead, Elijah showed great boldness and courage. Ask students how Elijah showed boldness in the Bible truth. (**His boldness was seen in challenging the prophets of Baal, in his covering the entire altar with water, and in his prayer that God would light the altar on fire.**)

Student Page 15.1
Have students review the Bible truth by completing the page.

Review
- Why do you think some of the Israelites stopped worshipping God and started worshipping false gods? (**They forgot about God's laws and what He had done for them.**)
- What happened to the altar of the prophets of Baal? (**nothing**)
- Why did Elijah pour so much water on the altar to the Lord? (**to show that it would have been impossible for the altar to catch on fire, unless God made it happen**)
- Why do you think God burned everything around the altar? (**so that everyone would know without any doubt that He was God**)

- Why was Elijah able to be so bold when he challenged the prophets of Baal? (**Elijah had a strong relationship with God. He knew that God was with him and that he could be bold in what he did.**)

Notes:

APPLICATION

- Think of a time when you saw someone being bold. How did that person's boldness make you feel? (**Answers will vary.**)
- When should you speak and act bravely for what is right? (**when I see someone doing or saying something that isn't right**)

REINFORCEMENT

The Hebrew noun *ba'al* means *master*, *possessor*, or *husband*. When used as a proper name, *Baal* refers to *the storm-god or sun-god who was the most important deity of all the Canaanite gods*. Because of this storm-god reference, Baal was often symbolized as lightning, and consequently, this false god was known as *the lord of fire*. When Elijah staged the contest against the prophets of Baal, the challenge was between the god who was said to create fire through lightning and the God who is a consuming fire and whose presence is accompanied by fire.

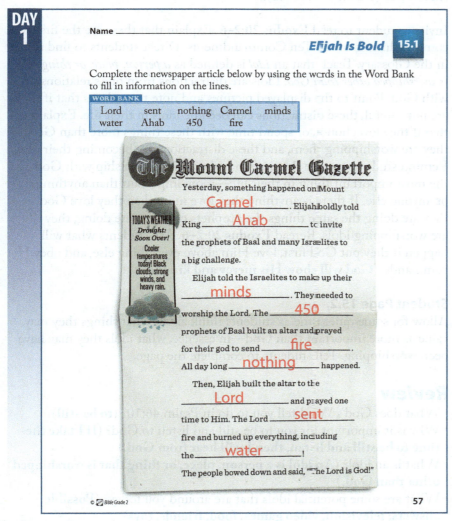

DAY 1

Name _____

Elijah Is Bold 15.1

Complete the newspaper article below by using the words in the Word Bank to fill in information on the lines.

WORD BANK
| Lord | sent | nothing | Carmel | minds |
| water | Ahab | 450 | fire | |

The Mount Carmel Gazette

Yesterday, something happened on Mount ____Carmel____. Elijah boldly told King ____Ahab____ to invite the prophets of Baal and many Israelites to a big challenge.

Elijah told the Israelites to make up their ____minds____. They needed to worship the Lord. The ____450____ prophets of Baal built an altar and prayed for their god to send ____fire____. All day long ____nothing____ happened.

Then, Elijah built the altar to the ____Lord____ and prayed one time to Him. The Lord ____sent____ fire and burned up everything, including the ____water____!

The people bowed down and said, "The Lord is God!"

TODAY'S WEATHER
Drought: Soon Over!
Cooler temperatures today! Black clouds, strong winds, and heavy rain.

15.2 Elijah Is Bold
Focus: Hearing God

★ PREPARATION
Select PICTURES OF A TELEVISION, VIDEO GAMES, FOOD, FRIENDS, and TOYS. (*Introduction*)

☛ EXTENSION
2A Separate students into groups of two or three so that they can interview each other to review the Bible truth. Name one student to play the role of the *interviewer*, one to play the role of *Elijah*, and one to play the role of *one of the prophets of Baal*. If the group is a pair, the student playing *Elijah* can also be *a prophet of Baal*. Allow students to switch roles, so that they each have a turn answering or asking questions. Prepare for this activity by writing the following interviewers' questions on the board or on a piece of paper:

Questions to ask *Elijah*:
1. Why were you on Mount Carmel today?
2. Who were all those people jumping around?
3. Why did you ask for water to be dumped on your altar?
4. Were you confident God would answer you? Why?

Questions to ask *a prophet of Baal*:
1. Why were you on Mount Carmel today?
2. Why did you yell and jump?
3. How did you feel when the altar to your god didn't burn?
4. Why did Elijah's altar to God burn even soaked with water?

Introduction ★
Display PICTURES OF A TELEVISION, VIDEO GAMES, FOOD, FRIENDS, and TOYS so students can see them. Ask them what these pictures all have in common. (**Answers will vary but might include that they are all things we enjoy.**) Discuss with students how the pictures represent things that can distract them from their relationship with God. When they have a good, strong relationship with God, they are confident in Him and His promises. With this confidence comes a boldness from knowing who God is. Through this boldness, they can live for Him, doing what is right, regardless of circumstances.

Directed Instruction ☛
Invite a volunteer to locate and read **Psalm 46:10**. Explain that God's Word reminds them to take time to be still. Select another volunteer to read **Matthew 6:19–21**. Explain to students that when they make God their "treasure," and want a close relationship with Him, they will be more likely to take the time to be still and hear from Him. Emphasize that if they take the time to listen, God will speak to them in a gentle way—a still small voice (1 Kings 19:11–12).

Invite a student to read **Exodus 20:2–6**. Explain that these are the first two commandments of the Ten Commandments. Direct students to find **idol** in the Glossary. Teach that an *idol* is defined as *a person, place, or thing that is worshipped other than God*. Idols are distractions from one's relationship with God. Point to the displayed pictures and note to students that if they are not careful, these distractions can become idols in their life. Explain that if they love, honor, or spend time with these things more than God, they are worshipping them, and these distractions are becoming their idols. Remind students to take the time to make their relationship with God the most important thing in their life—more important than anything or anyone else. If there is anything they love more than they love God, they are doing the same things the prophets of Baal were doing; they are worshipping idols. Reread **Exodus 20:2–6**. Ask students what will happen if they put God first, love Him above everything else, and obey His commands. (**God will show His mercy and kindness.**)

Student Page 15.2
Allow for some quiet time as students think about what things they may value as more important than God—in essence, what idols they may have been worshipping. Tell students to complete the page.

Review
- What does God's Word tell you to do in Psalm 46:10? (**to be still**)
- Why is it important for you to be still and listen to God? (**If I take the time to be still and listen, then I will hear from God.**)
- What is an idol? (**An idol is a person, place, or thing that is worshipped other than God.**)
- What are some potential idols that are around you today? (**Possible answers: television, video games, food, friends, toys**)

144

- Why does God want you not to worship idols? (**He wants me to worship and honor Him above everything else.**)

Notes:

APPLICATION
- What do you spend the most time doing? (**Answers will vary.**)
- What is your most prized possession? (**Answers will vary.**) Do you love this more than God? (**Answers will vary.**) If so, ask God for forgiveness and for help to not allow things, or idols, to be more important to you than He is.

DAY 2

15.2 *Elijah Is Bold*

1. Circle the pictures of things that distract you from your relationship with God. In the last box, draw a picture of something that could take too much of your attention from God.

   Answers will vary.

Drawings will vary.

2. **Idols** distract people from God. Write a prayer to ask God's forgiveness for any idol you may have. Ask Him to help you worship Him only.

   Answers will vary.
   _____
   _____

15.3 Elijah Is Bold

Focus: Boldness

★ PREPARATION

Make one copy of **BLM 15A Boldness** and follow the directions on the blackline master. (*Directed Instruction*)

⤴ EXTENSION

3A Show **PP-4 Boldness** in order to review other Bible truths and to make personal connections on how to be bold. Discuss with students how they can show boldness in praise, obedience, and courage.

3B Duplicate **BLM 15B Be Bold** for each student. Read the directions and assist students as needed. Allow students to use markers, STICKERS, and VARIOUS CRAFT MATERIALS to decorate their posters.

Introduction

Direct students to think about a situation that might make them fearful or discouraged. Invite a few students to share their ideas. Ask the whole class what it would look like to be bold in those situations. (**Answers will vary but should include defending someone, praying for courage, and speaking even when afraid.**)

Directed Instruction ★ ⤴

Review the Bible truth with the class. Remind students that Elijah had a close relationship with God, and it was because of this close relationship that Elijah could be bold. Ask students how Elijah showed boldness of faith when he faced the prophets of Baal. (**He challenged them to a contest; he poured water on the altar to the Lord; he asked the Lord to light the altar.**)

Share about three ways that Elijah showed boldness. The first was in the way he spoke to the prophets. He challenged them to a contest, and then boldly asked questions about where their god was and why he did not light the altar they built. Second, Elijah was bold in the way he acted. It would be a miracle for the altar he built to catch on fire, but Elijah went further—he dug a trench and poured water all over the altar until it filled the trench. Third, Elijah prayed boldly for the fire of the Lord to fall on the altar. This really would take a miracle, and Elijah boldly asked for one. Share with students that God also wants them to be bold in faith—in how they speak, act, and pray.

Divide students into small groups and distribute the different scenarios cut out from **BLM 15A Boldness**. Direct students to read each scenario, role-play the scenario, and demonstrate how boldness might look in a specific situation.

Read **2 Corinthians 3:7–12**. Explain this passage to students by stating that when people believe that Jesus died for their sins, they are accepted by God. Emphasize that believing in this truth enables them to speak boldly. Invite a student to read **Philippians 4:13**. Explain that because Jesus died for everyone, those who accept His salvation have hope, and He gives them power to be strong in Him no matter how scared they are. Therefore, they can be very bold in their speech, actions, and in their prayers.

Student Page 15.3
Direct students to complete the page. Assist as needed.

Review

- In what three ways did Elijah show boldness? (**in his speech, in his actions, and in his prayer**)
- In what three ways should you show boldness? (**in my speech, in my actions, and in my prayers**)

146

- How do Christians become bold? (**Because Christians believe in Jesus, they are no longer separated from God. They have hope in Jesus, and Jesus gives each Christian strength to handle all kinds of situations. Christians, then, choose to trust God for the strength to do what is right and then they do it.**)

Time Line

Point to where King David is on the Time Line. Explain that David was a good king, in fact he was described as *a man after God's own heart* (Acts 13:22). King Solomon, who was King David's son, ruled after King David. However, Solomon started to follow idols. Because of that, God split the kingdom, and David's descendants were given only a small portion named *Judah*. The greater portion of the kingdom was called *Israel*. Israel was led by many evil kings. These evil kings all worshipped idols. King Ahab was one of the most evil kings of Israel, and his wife, Jezebel, led the entire nation to follow idols. It was during their reign that Elijah challenged the 450 prophets of Baal.

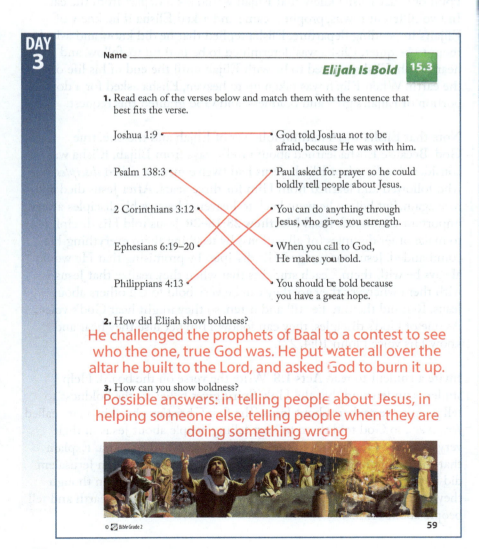

APPLICATION

- Why is it important to be bold and stand up for God? (**God has done so much for me, so I should be bold for Him. As Christians, we are part of His family.**)
- In what ways might you be bold for God? (**Possible answers: telling people about Jesus, in helping someone else, telling people when they are doing something wrong**)
- Pray and ask God for help to be bold and stand up for Him.

REINFORCEMENT

In 1956, a group of five men went deep into the jungle of Ecuador with the intent to preach the gospel to a violent tribe called the *Huaorani*. (The *Huaorani* are also known as the *Auca* people.) They had been warned not to go, but they believed that God had called them to tell this tribe about Jesus. At first the Aucas seemed interested and friendly, but the tide soon turned and the tribe killed all five men. Two years later, Rachel Saint and Elisabeth Elliot boldly went to live with the same tribe. Rachel's brother Nate had been one of the five men killed by the Aucas, along with Elisabeth's husband, Jim. In 1959, these two unarmed women and Elisabeth's daughter were able to move into the Auca settlement. It was not long before they were able to share the message of the gospel in a way their brother and husband had not been able to. As a result, the whole tribe gave their life to God and followed Jesus. Rachel lived and worked with the Huaorani people until she died of cancer in 1994.

15.4 Elijah Is Bold
Focus: Disciples

⤷ EXTENSION

4A To reinforce Acts 1:8, introduce students to the game Target Prayers. Use chalk to draw a target on the ground outside. (Note that the target should be very large so that each student can easily hit a ring on the target.) Tell students that the center represents family, the next ring represents relatives, the next represents friends, and the outer ring represents neighbors. Have a student toss a **BEANBAG** at the target. Ask the student to name (or give the initials of) an unsaved person he or she knows in the category in which the beanbag landed. Placing a time limit on each student will help keep the game moving along. Allow each student a turn. Conclude the activity with an opportunity for students to pray for the people they have "targeted" in the game.

Introduction

Direct students to stand in a line and play the game Follow the Leader. Identify yourself as the leader, and direct students to do exactly what you do as you perform a few different gestures. Explain that today's lesson is about people who follow a leader.

Directed Instruction ⤷

Tell students that some time after Elijah challenged the 450 prophets of Baal, Elijah's time of serving God was coming to an end. The Lord told Elijah to anoint Elisha as a prophet, and Elijah did so by placing his mantle, which is a sleeveless coat, on Elisha (1 Kings 19:16, 19). Elisha would become the main prophet of Israel after Elijah's departure. Remind students that a true prophet is someone who has special knowledge from God. The placement of the mantle symbolized God's choice of Elisha to receive the authority and power of being a prophet of the one, true God. Read **2 Kings 2:1–11**.

Point out that Elisha knew that Elijah would soon depart from the earth. In two different towns, prophets came and asked Elisha if he knew of Elijah's impending departure. Elisha replied that he did know and asked them to be quiet. Elisha was determined to be faithful to, follow, and stay near Elijah. Elisha wanted to be with Elijah until the end of his life on the earth. When Elijah was taken up to heaven, Elisha asked for a double portion of Elijah's gifts and boldness, and God granted this request.

Note that Elisha was a faithful follower of Elijah and the one, true God. Because Elisha learned about God's ways from Elijah, Elisha was considered a *disciple* of Elijah. Jesus had twelve men he called *disciples* who followed and learned from Him for three years. After Jesus died and rose again, but before he went back to heaven, He gave his disciples a very important command. Read **Matthew 28:18–20**. Jesus told His disciples to make other disciples (of all nations) by teaching them everything He commanded. Jesus encouraged His disciples by promising that He would always be with them. Teach students that when they realize that Jesus is with them wherever they go, they can be very bold to tell others about Jesus. Remind them to be still and listen, so they might hear God's voice. As one of God's disciples, they can follow Him because they hear and know His voice (John 10:4, 27).

Invite a student to read **Acts 1:8**. Write the verse on the board. Help students understand that the Holy Spirit gives believers the boldness to tell people everywhere about Jesus. The first Christians lived in a city called *Jerusalem*, so God told them to start telling people about Jesus in their very own city. God then told them to go to Judea and Samaria. Explain that these were regions near the city of Jerusalem. People from Jerusalem did not get along very well with the people from Samaria, even though they were neighbors. Last, Jesus said to go to the ends of the earth and tell people about Him.

148

Tell students that the Holy Spirit will help all Christians, no matter what age, tell people everywhere about Jesus. He will help them tell first their family, which is their "Jerusalem." Then, he will help them tell their neighbors and friends, which is their "Judea and Samaria." Lastly, the Holy Spirit will help Christians go to people all over the world. Explain that this is what full-time missionaries do.

Student Page 15.4
Direct students to work in collaborative pairs to complete the page.

Review

- Who was a faithful follower of the one, true God and Elijah? (**Elisha**)
- What command did Jesus give His disciples before He went back to Heaven? (**to make more disciples and teach them Jesus' commands**)
- Why can Christians be bold in making disciples? (**because the Holy Spirit promises to be with them**)
- Where can Christians go to make disciples? (**to their family, their friends, their neighbors, the whole world**)

APPLICATION

- Make a list of people you know who do not yet know Jesus as Savior. Pray that God will give you the boldness to share with them about Jesus so that they too can be His disciples. (For students who do not feel comfortable making a list, partner them with another classmate who is able to make a list.)

REINFORCEMENT

The apostle Paul was in many ways the epitome of boldness. He preached the gospel in over 15 cities where he was often met with open hostility and violence. Yet he spoke with great courage before Jews and Greeks, philosophers, workmen, and kings. He boldly sang the praises of God in jail. He suffered beatings, whippings, shipwrecks, and much more, and yet he boldly proclaimed the gospel. Even so, Paul still asked for prayer for boldness in speech, so he could share the gospel message (Ephesians 6:19).

DAY 4

15.4 *Elijah Is Bold*

Read Acts 1:8. Then in each circle, write the name of a person or a group of people whom you can pray for and boldly tell about Jesus.

You shall be my witnesses ...

to the ends of the earth
(the world)
Answers will vary.

in Judea and Samaria
(my neighbors and friends)
Answers will vary.

in Jerusalem
(my family)
Answers will vary.

60
© *Bible Grade 2*

© *Bible Grade 2*

149

15.5 Elijah Is Bold

Focus: Review and Assessment

★ PREPARATION

Select **VA 15A Elijah Is Bold**.
(*Lesson Review*)

Make one copy of **BLM 15C Lesson 15 Test** for each student.
(*Directed Instruction*)

Lesson Review ★

Use **VA 15A Elijah Is Bold** to review the Bible truth. Cover all of the following concepts:

- Elijah was a man of God during a time when very few people were following God.
- Many people in Israel were bowing down to and worshipping Baal and other idols.
- Elijah challenged 450 prophets of Baal to a contest to see who was the one, true God. Elijah and the false prophets would each build an altar. Then the prophets of Baal would ask their god to send fire to burn the sacrifice, and Elijah would ask the one, true God to do the same.
- The prophets of Baal begged and pleaded with their god to send fire, but no fire came.
- Elijah dug a trench around the altar to the Lord. Then, he had water poured all over the altar. He asked God to send fire. God sent a fire that burned everything on the altar, including the water and the rocks. He is the real God. He alone is all-powerful.
- A close relationship with God produces a boldness and confidence in Him and His promises. Christians can live for God and stand up for what is right because of this boldness.
- Scripture says not to worship idols, but to serve and worship God only.
- An *idol* is defined as *a person, place, or thing that is worshipped other than God.*
- Elijah was bold in what he said to the prophets and in how he acted and prayed to God.
- God wants all Christians to be bold in how they speak, act, and pray.
- Elijah taught Elisha, his disciple, how to be bold.
- Jesus wants Christians to go everywhere and make disciples of their family, friends and neighbors, and people all over the world.
- Christians can be very bold in making disciples because Jesus promised to be with them forever.

Directed Instruction ★

Distribute a copy of **BLM 15C Lesson 15 Test** to each student. Have students complete the test. When finished, read over the test and provide the answers for immediate feedback.

Notes:

Lesson Preparation
Nehemiah Leads

16.0

Expected Student Outcomes

KNOW
Nehemiah leads others as they begin rebuilding the wall of Jerusalem.

DO
Students will:
- recognize ways Nehemiah showed good leadership
- discover ways to cooperate
- describe how Nehemiah responded to mockers and how students should also respond
- read and write about a real-life scenario involving perseverance

APPLY
Students will cooperate with one another when completing tasks.

Lesson Outline
I. Nehemiah leads as God directs (Neh 1–3, 7:1–12)
II. Cooperation (1 Cor 12:12–21)
III. Resistance from mockers (Neh 2:19–20; Prov 13:1b, 29:8)
IV. Nehemiah perseveres (Phil 1:5–6)

♥ TEACHER'S HEART

Stress. Nearly every book written for teachers addresses this topic. Nehemiah seems a likely candidate for experiencing stress-related problems. Yet, the key to his success was his reliance on God's help and his ability to organize and delegate work to people as they completed the task of rebuilding the walls of Jerusalem. Just like you, he had two choices: do or delegate.

It's been said that it is better to let 10 people do the work versus doing the work of 10 people. Stress and burnout happen when you try to do too much. Ask yourself what generally keeps you from delegating tasks. Is it a sense that no one else will complete the task correctly? In other words, it won't be done like you would do it. By doing this, you take on more and more responsibility, which creates more stress, which makes you less gracious and less effective. What is God's message to you as you study Nehemiah? Wouldn't your second graders love to help you? It makes them feel significant to accomplish assigned tasks and adds to the well-being of your class. Will you trust that they can help you? You need only to delegate. Ask the Lord to help you delegate today!

📖 MEMORY VERSE
Nehemiah 4:6

GLOSSARY WORDS
- defense
- mock

★ MATERIALS

Day 1:
- Index cards
- Picture of the Great Wall of China, VA 16A Nehemiah Leads, DM-1 Character Traits, Time Line
- DM-9 Map of Persia (*Extension*)

Day 2:
- Simple puzzles
- VA 16A Nehemiah Leads, shoe with laces
- Milk cartons, shoe boxes (*Extension*)

Day 3:
- Paper clips
- BLM 16A Actions for Rebuilding (*Extension*), DM-3 Books of the Bible (*Extension*)

Day 4:
- VA 16A Nehemiah Leads
- BLM 16B Wall of Jerusalem with Gates (*Extension*)

Day 5:
- VA 16A Nehemiah Leads
- BLM 16C Lesson 16 Test

♪ SONGS
What Seems Impossible

TEACHER RESOURCES
MacArthur, John. *Nehemiah: Experiencing the Good Hand of God*. Word Publishing, 2001.

STUDENT RESOURCES
Ross, Neil H. *Nehemiah: Builder for God*. CF4Kids, 2014.

Supplemental Materials are available to download. See Understanding Purposeful Design Bible at the front of this book for the Grade 2 URL.

© Bible Grade 2   151

16.1 Nehemiah Leads
Focus: Nehemiah Leads as God Directs

📖 MEMORY VERSE
Nehemiah 4:6

MEMORY WORK
- Practice saying the Memory Verse several times together. Divide the class into four groups. Distribute a set of prepared INDEX CARDS to each group. Instruct students to shuffle the cards on the floor or desk in front of their group. Challenge each group to cooperate quickly to place the cards in correct order to show the verse.

★ PREPARATION
Write each of the words from the Memory Verse on an INDEX CARD. Do this to make four sets of cards. (*Memory Work*)

Have on hand a PICTURE OF THE GREAT WALL OF CHINA. (*Introduction*)

Select **VA 16A Nehemiah Leads** and **DM-1 Character Traits**. (*Directed Instruction*)

↪ EXTENSION
1A Display **DM-9 Map of Persia** to show how far the Israelites were taken away from the Promised Land during their captivity, from Jerusalem to Babylonia.

1B Instruct students to write a journal entry on how they would approach cooperating with others to complete a difficult task.

Introduction ★
Show a PICTURE OF THE GREAT WALL OF CHINA. Explain to students that this wall was originally about 5,500 miles long. It took over 2,000 years to build the wall. Ask students why a country would build a wall such as this. (**for protection from invasion by people from other countries or areas**) Walls around countries and cities are used as a **defense**, which is *a means of protection*. Ask students how countries today usually protect their land. (**Possible answers: army, police**) Explain that the ancient Israelites rebuilt a wall that was used as a defense to protect their city, Jerusalem.

Directed Instruction ★ ↪
Instruct students to listen as you read **VA 16A Nehemiah Leads**. Explain that cities in Nehemiah's time usually had a wall built around them for protection. A wall made it difficult for robbers to get in at night and also made it hard for armies to quickly capture a city. When Nehemiah heard that the city of Jerusalem had no protection, God led him to rebuild the walls around the city.

Nehemiah was a good leader, and the people liked his idea to make the city strong again. The people listened to Nehemiah because Nehemiah cared deeply for them, and he looked to God as he planned ahead what to do.

It would have been difficult for Nehemiah to rebuild this wall by himself. He knew it would take a lot of people and would be very hard work. Nehemiah had courage to go before King Artaxerxes and ask for his help. Nehemiah did not give up. He encouraged others, planned, and helped do anything he was able to do in order to complete what God had led him to do. Nehemiah showed good *leadership*, which means *the ability to guide and influence others*. Refer to **DM-1 Character Traits**.

Nehemiah showed good leadership because he:
- fasted, prayed, repented, and trusted God's direction (Nehemiah 1:4–11)
- helped to protect and take care of others (Nehemiah 1:11–2:1)
- received assistance from others (Nehemiah 2:1–9)
- encouraged others (Nehemiah 2:17–18)
- answered God's way when others insulted him (Nehemiah 2:19–20)
- worked hard, cooperated, and delegated work (Nehemiah 3)
- was faithful to see the work done (Nehemiah 7:1–2)

Teach students the following acronym to help them remember attributes of Nehemiah being a good leader:
- **N** ever doubted what God wanted him to do
- **E** ncouraged others
- **H** elped protect others
- **E** xpected others to offer assistance
- **M** ade prayer a priority
- **I** nitiated cooperation
- **A** nswered God's way when insulted
- **H** ad a hardworking and faithful character

Discuss ways students can show good leadership as Nehemiah did. (**Possible answers: help others, cooperate, make godly decisions**)

Student Page 16.1
Have students complete the page. Upon completion, pray with students for God to help them be good leaders.

Review
- Why did Nehemiah want to rebuild a wall around Jerusalem? (**Possible answers: God led him to do so; he wanted to help provide protection.**)
- To whom did Nehemiah go to ask for help? (**King Artaxerxes**)
- Name one way Nehemiah was a good leader. (**Possible answers: Nehemiah made good decisions; he initiated cooperation; he was hardworking and never doubted God.**)

Time Line
Identify the biblical characters students have studied so far in the Old Testament, ending with Nehemiah. Encourage students to recall one fact about each character.

APPLICATION
- What kind of person was Nehemiah? (**Possible answers: faithful to God, caring, helpful, cooperative, hardworking**)
- Would you want Nehemiah to lead a project you were working on? Why or why not? (**Answers will vary.**)
- What do you think is the most important thing about being a good leader? (**Answers will vary but should include being a good example to show others a good way to behave.**)
- How could you be a good leader to others? (**Possible answers: pray, speak the truth, do what is right**)

REINFORCEMENT
Nehemiah, a Jew living in exile in Persia, had the trust and ear of Artaxerxes, the king of Persia. As a cupbearer, Nehemiah had the privileged position of taste testing the king's wine before he drank it, which could have been a fatal role. God placed Nehemiah in this important role for a reason. During Old Testament times in Israel and surrounding nations, this job was an honored position in the royal courts. The Persians called the cupbearer or king's butler *Saky*. The Hebrew name is *Mashkeh*, and is written about in Genesis 40:9–13, where Joseph interpreted the dream of Pharaoh's cupbearer. The term is also included in 1 Kings 10:3–7, where the queen of Sheba is talking about King Solomon's prosperity and wisdom, and Solomon's cupbearers are listed as part of his royal household.

DAY 1

Name _____

Nehemiah Leads 16.1

Nehemiah showed good leadership in rebuilding the wall around Jerusalem.

1. Color the layers in the wall that show how Nehemiah gave good leadership.

trusted and prayed to God for help

gave up

tried to do the work by himself

encouraged others

made good decisions

Write **T** for true and **F** for false.

2. __T__ Cities in Nehemiah's time usually had a wall built around them for defense.

3. __F__ The people did not like Nehemiah's idea to rebuild the wall.

4. __T__ It took courage for Nehemiah to ask King Artaxerxes for help.

© *Bible Grade 2*   61

© *Bible Grade 2*

16.2 Nehemiah Leads
Focus: Cooperation

★ PREPARATION

Obtain FOUR SIMPLE PUZZLES and remove one piece from each puzzle. (*Introduction*)

Select **VA 16A Nehemiah Leads** and have on hand a SHOE WITH LACES. (*Directed Instruction*)

↻ EXTENSION

2A Display the following labels in the classroom:
- *North side*: Eliashib the high priest and his team
- *West side*: many workers, including sons of Jerusalem's district leaders
- *South side*: leaders of the southern districts and their sons
- *East side*: Levites, other leaders, goldsmiths, and merchants

Instruct students that each label represents one area of the wall and the different people who probably worked on that area. Assign students to different areas of the room. Give students EMPTY PAPER MILK CARTONS and EMPTY SHOE BOXES. Direct them to build a wall within a short, allotted time frame, just as the Israelites worked together to accomplish rebuilding the wall in 52 days.

2B Read aloud and discuss **Philippians 2:3–4** with the class. Pray with students for God to help them live unselfishly.

2C Plan with students a service project the class could work on together for 52 days, the same time frame for rebuilding the wall around Jerusalem.

Introduction ★

Divide the class into four groups. Give each group one of the FOUR SIMPLE PUZZLES to put together. As students complete the puzzle they may ask you for the missing piece. Instruct students to try to complete the puzzle without the missing piece. When students are done, ask them if their puzzles are complete. (**No.**) Remind students that as each piece was important to complete the puzzle, so each person working in a group is important to complete a job.

Directed Instruction ★ ↻

Explain to students that in putting the puzzle together they had to *cooperate*, which means *to work together to achieve a common goal*. When they cooperate, many times they have to give up the exact way they want to do things, allowing others to complete a task in their own desired way. Ask students for ideas about how to cooperate. (**Possible answers: share, plan ahead, support other's ideas, assist others**)

Tell students that the Israelites had to cooperate to rebuild the wall around Jerusalem. The workers needed to plan, share tools, assist others, encourage those around them, and ignore or stop anyone who was preventing progress. Remind students that different people helped to build various areas of the wall all at the same time. The workers were people with different abilities, yet they all cooperated. Refer to **VA 16A Nehemiah Leads** to show how the people contributed to the work and cooperated to rebuild the wall in 52 days (Nehemiah 6:15).

Share with students that just as the Israelites needed to work together, so they, too, can accomplish more if they do not work alone. Read **1 Corinthians 12:12–21**. Explain to students that each body part is important. Every part of the body is useful and helps the other parts. And, with all the parts working together with the power of the Holy Spirit, they can accomplish a task more easily.

Invite a volunteer to use only one hand to tie a SHOE WITH LACES. Explain that it is possible to tie the shoe with one hand. Some people are able to do this, but if people use two hands at the same time, the task is easier to complete. Allow the volunteer to use both hands to tie the shoe. Share with students that just as it is easier if both hands tie a shoe, so it is easier when they help each other to complete a job or task.

Explain that it is the same way with the body of Christ, or believers. God made each believer unique and different, yet all can work together to complete the job God has asked them to do. It is good to listen and let each person help because everyone can help in some way.

Discuss how projects are easier to do when each person in the class is helping in some way. Cite examples, such as cleaning the classroom, planning a chapel, and carrying boxes or supplies.

Student Page 16.2
Direct students to work in collaborative pairs or trios to complete the page. Encourage students to pray and ask God to give them a cooperative spirit.

Review

- What does it mean to cooperate? (**to work together to achieve a common goal**)
- How did Nehemiah help the Israelites to cooperate when building the wall? (**He inspired them; he set up areas for different people to work on at the same time.**)
- How did the Israelites finish the work in only 52 days? (**They all cooperated and followed Nehemiah's leadership and his directions.**)

Notes:

DAY 2

16.2 Nehemiah Leads

1. Use Nehemiah 1–3 as a reference. What did the Israelites do to cooperate when rebuilding the wall?

   Possible answers: split up to work in different areas, helped each other, encouraged each other

2. What can you do to help cooperate when working with others?

   Possible answers: share, plan ahead, assist others, support others' ideas

3. Circle every phrase that describes an activity in which cooperation would be helpful.

   (playing on a team) — watching television — reading a book

   (raking a yard)

   (cleaning a classroom) — (singing in a choir)

   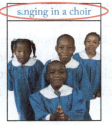

APPLICATION

- Why is it important to cooperate? (**Cooperation makes it easier to complete a job and help others.**)
- What can you do to make cooperation work? (**Listen to God and to others and plan to be helpful.**)
- What is special about the body of Christ according to 1 Corinthians 12:12–21? (**Each person is unique and different, yet important, and working together in unity with the Holy Spirit is God's design.**)
- Since you are made in a special way, think of ways that you can use your special gifts to help others. (**Answers will vary.**)

REINFORCEMENT

Nehemiah delegated tasks and instructed where people should work on the wall. People were assigned to work near their home so they would not have to go far. In case of attack, they could also protect their home and family. The whole family could also help out in the effort. Priests rebuilt the gate through which animals were brought for sacrifice. They also rebuilt the parts of the wall close to the temple. Commuters who lived and worked outside of Jerusalem were assigned areas with few homes. Even rulers of districts and half-districts were given assignments on the building project.

16.3 Nehemiah Leads
Focus: Resistance from Mockers

⭐ PREPARATION

Have on hand an abundance of PAPER CLIPS. Select two volunteers and secretly tell them to disrupt the class's efforts to gather paper clips. These two volunteers could complain and do things to counteract the other students' work. (*Introduction*)

↻ EXTENSION

3A Distribute a copy of **BLM 16A Actions for Rebuilding** to each student for a review on how to cooperate and not hinder others from doing God's work.

3B Display **DM-3 Books of the Bible** for students to reference while reviewing the books of the Old and New Testaments.

Introduction ⭐

Scatter PAPER CLIPS across the floor. Select five volunteers to pick up the paper clips while being timed. Scatter the same number of paper clips and have the entire class gather them while being timed. However, during this second activity, alert the two previously selected volunteers to cause a disturbance. Compare the times of both tasks—the second timed activity will have a shorter time. Remark that as more people worked together, the task was finished more quickly. However, it was frustrating to have the two volunteers not cooperating during the second activity.

Remind students that they had to cooperate to complete the task. Ask them what was frustrating about completing the task during the second activity. (**Two classmates were causing trouble and complaining.**) Tell students that as the Israelites cooperated to rebuild the wall, people tried to stop the work by mocking the Israelites. Direct students to locate the word **mock** in the Glossary. *Mock* means *to make fun of*.

Directed Instruction ↻

Remind students that workers had all come together to cooperate and rebuild the wall. As they were working Sanballat, Tobiah, and others mocked them—teasing them about what they were doing, and accusing them of going against the king, which was not true. These mockers were trying to scare the Israelites to stop them from rebuilding the wall.

Nehemiah did not become angry or try to mock them in return. He chose his words wisely in responding. Nehemiah told the mockers that God would help the Israelites do well, because God's servants would cooperate and go forward to rebuild the wall. The mockers would not have any right to blessings in Jerusalem because of their behavior. Nehemiah continued after that to organize workers in different areas to begin the work, refusing to listen to those who mocked them. Read **Nehemiah 2:19–20**.

Explain to students that people may mock them when they are trying to complete a task, especially a task for the Lord. Discuss what it feels like to be mocked. (**Possible answers: degrading, uncomfortable, sad, hurtful**) Remind students that though it is hurtful to be mocked, they have a choice of whether to get angry and quit, or respond positively and keep going. Remind them that they can trust that God will help them succeed, just as He helped Nehemiah.

The Bible addresses mockers and those around them. Locate and read the following verses:
• A mocker does not listen to instruction (**Proverbs 13:1b**).
• A mocker resents someone who tries to help (**Proverbs 15:12**).
• A mocker is disliked (**Proverbs 24:9**).
• People are blessed when they avoid mockers (**Psalm 1:1**).

Have four groups cooperate to act out a short skit to show what the Bible says about how to respond to mockers. Skits will be based on the following:
- Even though mockers tease, you are not to become angry (Proverbs 29:8).
- It is right to not allow a mocker to be a part of what is happening, because he or she is stirring up trouble (Proverbs 22:10).
- Choose words wisely when answering a mocker (Proverbs 15:28).
- Pray for mockers because they need to be prayed for (Proverbs 15:29).

Student Page 16.3
Read the directions and have students complete the page.

Review
- What happened to Nehemiah and the Israelites as they started rebuilding the wall? (**Sanballat, Tobiah, and others began to mock them.**)
- What did Nehemiah tell the mockers? (**God would help the Israelites; they would continue the work; the mockers wouldn't be blessed.**)
- How did the people respond after Nehemiah talked to the mockers? (**They did not listen to the mockers, but they cooperated and followed Nehemiah's leadership.**)

APPLICATION
- Why did people mock Nehemiah and those trying to rebuild the wall? (**They wanted to scare them and slow down the work.**)
- Why do people mock others today? (**Possible answers: to make themselves look better, to stop others from doing what God wants them to do**)
- How should you respond to a mocker? (**Possible answers: do not become angry, do not listen, choose words wisely, pray for the mocker**)
- What happens when you respond in the right way when you are mocked? (**Possible answers: God helps you complete the task; others follow your example; the mocker may realize he or she was wrong.**)

REINFORCEMENT
Jesus received the ultimate mocking as He died on the cross. Soldiers mocked Jesus as they took away His clothes and gave Him a scarlet robe and crown of thorns, taunting Him as "King of the Jews" (Matthew 27:27–44). They placed Jesus between two robbers as if He were nothing more than a common criminal. People passing by mocked Him by saying, "If you are the Son of God, come down from the cross" (Matthew 27:40). The chief priests mocked Jesus by saying that He saved others, but He could not save Himself (Matthew 27:42). One of the robbers even made fun of Jesus. Jesus was stripped, cursed at, spit at, and insulted, yet He chose to forgive the mockers (Luke 23:34). After Jesus' death, the Roman guards who had mocked Him proclaimed, "Truly this was the Son of God" (Matthew 27:54). Jesus rose from the dead in victory (Acts 2:24)!

DAY 3

Name _____

Nehemiah Leads 16.3

In Nehemiah 2:19–20, some people chose to Nehemiah during the rebuilding of the wall.

1. Look carefully at the letters written below. Write the letter of the alphabet that comes after each letter you see. The letter after Z would be A. The phrases you decode are from Proverbs 15:28 and Proverbs 29:8. They tell how God wants you to behave when someone is mocking you.

B G N N R D   L X   V N Q C R   V H R D K X .

C N   M N S   A D B N L D   Z M F Q X .

2. Why should you respond God's way when someone mocks you?
Possible answers: God will help me complete the task; God will bless me for doing what is right.

16.4 Nehemiah Leads
Focus: Nehemiah Perseveres

★ PREPARATION

Select **VA 16A Nehemiah Leads**, and the song "What Seems Impossible" from the Grade 2 URL. (*Directed Instruction*)

⟳ EXTENSION

4A Distribute one copy of **BLM 16B Wall of Jerusalem with Gates** to each student. Remind them how Nehemiah trusted God to complete the wall. Share the following information about the gates that were repaired:

• Sheep Gate (Nehemiah 3:1): This gate exited from the Bethesda Pool area into the Kidron Valley. Also called the *Benjamin Gate*.
• Fish Gate (Nehemiah 3:3): This gate was the place where people purchased and sold fish. It is also called the *Ephraim Gate*.
• Old Gate (Nehemiah 3:6): This gate was on the west wall. It is also called the *Jeshanah Gate*.
• Valley Gate (Nehemiah 2:13, 15; 3:13): This gate was where Nehemiah's inspection began and finished.
• Refuse Gate (Nehemiah 3:14): This gate led to the valley where trash was dumped. It is also called the *Dung Gate*.
• Fountain Gate (Nehemiah 3:15–16): This gate was near the King's Garden on the east wall. It most likely gave access to the Pool of Siloam.
• Water Gate (Nehemiah 3:26): This gate was located across from the Valley Gate and led to the Kidron Valley.
• Horse Gate (Nehemiah 3:28): This gate was where horses may have entered the city.
• East Gate (Nehemiah 3:29): This gate was located on the east side of the temple complex.
• Inspection Gate (Nehemiah 3:31): This gate was located where the wall turned at an angle. It was also known as the *Muster Gate* or *Miphkad Gate*.

Introduction

Write the word *perseverance* on the board and its definition—*not giving up*. Note that another word for *perseverance* is *persistence*. Have students make as many words as possible using letters in the word *perseverance*. Students may try to form a few words and want to stop, but encourage them to keep going as there are many words to be formed. (**Possible answers: an, can, creep, par, pear, pen, persevere, prance, ran, seen, verse**) See who has the most perseverance to keep trying until you ask them to stop. Discuss actions that take perseverance to complete. (**Possible answers: memorizing Bible verses, homework, learning to play an instrument, sports**)

Directed Instruction ★ ⟳

Read this following real-life story to students:

Paul sat in a circle with all the other students in his third-grade class. As other students sat with their legs crossed, Paul sat with his legs straight out. Paul was born with a rare problem—his knees would not bend correctly. There were times when people laughed at and mocked Paul, but Paul trusted God to help him through each day. As Paul grew, he felt God's calling to be a runner. Despite pain, hardship, and humiliation, Paul kept practicing and trying to run the best he could.

Paul joined the track team and trained hard for a race. When race day came, Paul ran the race with all his might. His teammates cheered as he gave it all he had. All the other runners had come across the finish line, but Paul was still completing his last lap. All of a sudden Paul's teammates stood and cheered him on. Soon the entire crowd stood and cheered as they watched Paul come across the finish line with a smile on his face. Fans celebrated as they saw the testimony of perseverance and knew that God had helped Paul complete what he had started.

Refer to **VA 16A Nehemiah Leads**. Remind students that Nehemiah showed perseverance by going to Jerusalem to inspect the city gates and wall so he could know how to help. He persevered when others mocked him. Nehemiah also persevered in organizing workers and helped in doing the hard work of rebuilding. He never gave up despite difficulties. Nehemiah stayed committed to the task God had led him to do.

Point out to students that God may lead them to do a hard job that requires perseverance. Read the following sentences aloud, and ask students to hold their thumbs up when a statement is read that shows perseverance:

• God was leading Tika to tell a friend about Jesus. She kept praying and showing love to her friend even though her friend did not want to hear about it. (**thumbs-up**)
• God led Yuri to help his little brother with a hard job each day. Yuri did not listen and obey; he watched television instead.
• God led Deon to help organize a chapel program with his class. All the kids were arguing about who would do each job. One student mocked Deon. Deon prayed for God to help him and came up with a plan to involve everyone using their unique talents. (**thumbs-up**)

Read **Philippians 1:5–6**. Remind students that when God leads them to persevere in different, and sometimes difficult circumstances, they can trust Him to help them complete the work He began in them.

Sing the song "What Seems Impossible" from the Grade 2 URL.

Student Page 16.4
Assist students as needed to complete the page.

Review
- What does perseverance mean? (**not giving up**)
- How did Nehemiah show perseverance? (**Possible answers: going to Jerusalem to inspect the city gates and wall, organizing workers, helping in the work, not allowing mockers to discourage him from completing the work**)
- How does Philippians 1:5–6 encourage you? (**It says that I can trust God to help me complete a work that He began, even when the circumstance may be difficult.**)

APPLICATION
- What would have happened if Nehemiah had quit halfway through his task of rebuilding? (**The wall would not have been completely rebuilt, and Jerusalem would not have been fully protected.**)
- What should you do when you feel like giving up? (**I should ask God for help and strength to keep going because He will help me to complete the work.**)

DAY 4

16.4 *Nehemiah Leads*

1. Read Colossians 3:23. Then read what Elyse, age 9, wrote in a devotion about perseverance.

   Do you ever NOT want to do your homework, or your chores? I definitely have this problem, as sometimes I get lazy and tired. At times I just feel like doing what I want to do, but then I realize that I need to persevere because whatever I am doing is for the Lord. When I persevere and do the right thing, I am pleasing and glorifying God. Next time I think about being lazy, I will think about Colossians 3:23. This verse helps me to persevere and remember to trust God to help me.

2. Write about a time you changed your mind about being lazy and you persevered instead.

   Answers will vary.

3. Draw a picture below of what you think Jerusalem's wall looked like after Nehemiah persevered for 52 days.

   Drawings will vary.

16.5 Nehemiah Leads

Focus: Review and Assessment

★ PREPARATION

Select **VA 16A Nehemiah Leads** for reference. (*Lesson Review*)

Make a copy of **BLM 16C Lesson 16 Test** for each student. (*Directed Instruction*)

Lesson Review ★

Use **VA 16A Nehemiah Leads** to review the Bible truth. Cover the following concepts:

• Nehemiah had a strong relationship with the Lord.
• God led Nehemiah to rebuild the wall around Jerusalem. It took courage for Nehemiah to go before King Artaxerxes and ask for help.
• The city wall was a means of defense and protection. *Defense* is defined as *a means of protection*.
• Nehemiah showed good leadership, which means he had an excellent ability to guide and influence others.
• Nehemiah was a good leader because he worked hard, cooperated, prayed, and encouraged others.
• Attributes of Nehemiah being a good leader are:
    N ever doubted what God wanted him to do
    E ncouraged others
    H elped protect others
    E xpected others to offer assistance
    M ade prayer a priority
    I nitiated cooperation
    A nswered God's way when insulted
    H ad a hardworking and faithful character
• *Cooperate* means *to work together to achieve a common goal*.
• The Israelites had cooperated with one another to rebuild the wall around Jerusalem. The workers were split into specific areas and had to plan, share tools, and assist others.
• Just as the Israelites needed to work together, every Christian can accomplish more when fellow believers within the body of Christ help each other. Everyone is unique and needed.
• As Nehemiah worked, others mocked him and tried to get him to stop. *Mock* means *to make fun of*.
• When mocked, Christians have a choice to get angry and quit or respond positively and keep going, knowing that God will help them succeed just as Nehemiah did.
• Nehemiah showed perseverance by completing the job God had him to do, even though it was difficult.
• The word *perseverance* means *not giving up*. Another word for *perseverance* is *persistence*.
• Christians can trust God to help them complete the work He leads them to do. They should include prayer as a part of completing the work.

Directed Instruction ★

Distribute a copy of **BLM 16C Lesson 16 Test** to each student. Verify that students understand the directions and any difficult words. Have students take the test.

Notes:

Lesson Preparation
Christmas

17.0

Expected Student Outcomes

KNOW
The angel Gabriel foretells the birth of Christ. The Messiah is born. The shepherds and wise men worship Him.

DO
Students will:
- identify the main individuals in the Christmas narrative and the names of Jesus from Isaiah 9:6
- create a birth announcement for Jesus
- identify the means of communication God used to share His exciting news of Jesus' birth
- give examples of how people responded to Jesus' arrival

APPLY
Students will share the true meaning of Christmas, the celebration of Christ's birth.

Lesson Outline
I. Jesus' birth announced (Lk 1:26–38, Mt 1:18–25)
II. Jesus' birth (Lk 2:1–7)
III. The shepherds worship (Lk 2:8–20)
IV. The wise men worship (Mt 2:1–12, 25:40)

♥ TEACHER'S HEART
One quiet night near the town of Bethlehem, shepherds were watching over their flocks. They yawned as they gazed at the stars twinkling in the dark sky. Suddenly an angel appeared before them in dazzling raiment, announcing the birth of a savior in the City of David. Trembling with fear, the shepherds listened as the angel declared to them, "I bring you good news of great joy!" Then a host of angels filled the skies, praising the God of heaven who had imparted peace and goodwill to people on the earth.

What a message of hope to people living in darkness and despair! In the City of David, the Savior was born! God sent His Son to redeem the human race, to set everyone free from sin and the Law's impossible demands (Galatians 4:4–5). Stop for a moment and consider the impact this good news has had on your life. Where would you be without this Savior?

Because Jesus came, you are no longer under condemnation for your sin, unable to sufficiently keep the requirements of a holy God. No longer are you alienated from your Creator, having only an obscure knowledge of His nature and will. No longer are you a stranger to His ways, a foreigner to His covenant of love (Ephesians 2:12). Through faith in Him, your troubled heart can experience an intimate relationship with God. Let the angel's message fill you with great joy, renew your soul, and encourage you today!

MEMORY VERSE
Isaiah 9:6

★ MATERIALS

Day 1:
- VA 17A Jesus Is Born
- Book of baby names
- BLMs 17A–D Nativity Stick Puppets, Parts 1–4; card stock; craft sticks

Day 2:
- Stick puppets from Lesson 17.1
- Time Line

Day 3:
- DM-10 Shepherd and Sheep
- Stick puppets from Lesson 17.1

Day 4:
- Wrapped Christmas gift
- Piece of gold jewelry, incense, jar of olive oil or perfumed oil
- Stick puppets from Lesson 17.1
- PP-5 The Good News of Christmas (*Extension*)

Day 5:
- VA 17A Jesus Is Born
- BLM 17E Lesson 17 Test

♪ SONGS
First Christmas Day
Away in a Manger/Silent Night (*Extension*)
Glory

TEACHER RESOURCES
Rich, Mike, and Catherine Hardwicke. *The Nativity Story*. DVD. New Line Home Video, 2007.

STUDENT RESOURCES
McCaughrean, Geraldine, and Sophy Williams. *The Nativity Story*. Lion UK, 2009.

Supplemental Materials are available to download. See Understanding Purposeful Design Bible at the front of this book for the Grade 2 URL.

17.1 Christmas
Focus: Jesus' Birth Announced

 MEMORY VERSE
Isaiah 9:6

MEMORY WORK
- Encourage students to create, in pairs, their own tune to the Memory Verse and present the tune to the class.

 PREPARATION
Select **VA 17A Jesus Is Born**. (Directed Instruction)

Bring a **BOOK OF BABY NAMES** to class. (Directed Instruction)

Make copies of **BLMs 17A–D Nativity Stick Puppets, Parts 1–4** on VARIOUS COLORS OF CARD STOCK to construct one complete set of nativity puppets. Affix puppets to CRAFT STICKS for ease of use. When complete, select the following three puppets for today's lesson: ANGEL GABRIEL, MARY, JOSEPH. (Directed Instruction)

 EXTENSION
1A Cut red, green, and white strips of construction paper approximately 2" x 8" in size. Instruct students to write one word of the Memory Verse on the center of each strip. Create a chain by linking strips together with glue, making sure each word is visible. Alternate colors for added beauty and to help students associate the color patterns with the words of the verse.

Introduction
Have students share about some things that might seem absolutely impossible. Ask students what it would take for them to believe that the things they mentioned would actually happen? (**Possible answers: if the person who promised was capable of making it happen, if I had a lot of money, if it were a miracle**) Share that today's lesson is about some people who heard news that seemed impossible.

Directed Instruction ★ ↻
The focus each day this week will be on a different aspect of Jesus' birth. Read **VA 17A Jesus Is Born**, making the story come alive for students who may already be familiar with the Bible truth about Christmas. Explain that Mary was a teenager when she learned that she would become a mother. She wondered about the news and thought it was impossible for her to have God's Son. But the angel Gabriel told her not to be afraid, because God was pleased with her. Read **Luke 1:37**. Ask students to use this verse to explain why Mary could trust what the angel said. (**God can do the impossible.**)

Remind students of the impossible things they shared earlier. Ask how they might react if someone told them that God would make those things happen. (**Possible answers: wouldn't believe it, would believe but be cautious, would believe wholeheartedly**) Explain that Mary could have doubted, but instead she believed what the angel said. Mary offered herself as God's servant and willingly accepted His plans for her.

Remind students that Mary was not the only one to receive news. Joseph was told in a dream that he should not be afraid to take Mary as his wife, and that the child she carried was the Son of God. Joseph obeyed God and became Mary's husband.

Refer to the **BOOK OF BABY NAMES** to help students discover what their names mean. Ask students why names are important. (**Names tell others who we are; they can even tell things about us.**) Read **Matthew 1:21–23** aloud. Ask students what name Joseph was to give God's Son and what the name means. (**Jesus, the one who saves**) What other name would people use to refer to Jesus? (**Immanuel**) What does this name mean? (**God with us**) Ask students what Jesus came to save them from. (**sin**)

Select the ANGEL GABRIEL, MARY, and JOSEPH from the stick puppet collection made from **BLMs 17A–D Nativity Stick Puppets, Parts 1–4**. Invite a volunteer to come to the front of the room and use the puppets to retell the part of the Bible truth about Mary and Joseph receiving the news that they were going to have a son and were to name Him *Jesus*.

Student Page 17.1
Read instructions and assist students as needed.

Review

- What news did the angel give to Mary? (**The angel told Mary that she was going to give birth to God's Son.**)
- How did Mary respond? (**Mary said that she was the Lord's servant and that she wanted God's plan spoken by Gabriel to come true.**)
- What name was Joseph to give the child and what did the name mean? (**Jesus, the one who saves**) What is another name people would call Jesus, and what did this name mean? (**Immanuel, God with us**)

Notes:

APPLICATION

- How does it make you feel to know that Jesus is God's Son? (**Answers will vary but should include the feeling of being secure because with God, nothing is impossible.**)
- How would you respond if you received amazing news like Mary did? (**Answers will vary.**)

REINFORCEMENT

Around 1,000 years before the birth of Jesus, King David received a wonderful promise: God would raise up a ruler from David's royal lineage and David's kingdom would be established forever (2 Samuel 7:12–13). This promised King would reign as God's Son, and His Father's love would never be removed from Him (2 Samuel 7:14–15). When the angel Gabriel appeared to Mary and declared that she would bear a son, he echoed the words of this promise. Mary's firstborn would be called *the Son of the Highest* (Luke 1:32). He would reign over Israel on the throne of His ancestor David, and His kingdom would never end. The ancient prophecy spoken to King David was fulfilled 1,000 years later with the birth of Christ. God had kept His promise!

DAY 1

Name _____

Christmas **17.1**

Write the word or words that best answer each question from the Word Bank. One word will be used twice.

WORD BANK

| Jesus | Mary | angel Gabriel | Joseph |

1. Who appeared to a young woman to tell her that she would become the mother of God's Son? _____angel Gabriel_____

2. What was this young woman's name? _____Mary_____

3. Who saw an angel in a dream who told him not to be afraid? _____Joseph_____

4. What was one of the names given to God's Son? _____Jesus_____

5. What name means "the one who saves?" _____Jesus_____

6. Read Isaiah 9:6. Fill in the circle next to each name that describes what Jesus would be called.

○ Man   ● Mighty God   ● Wonderful   ● Everlasting Father

○ Coach   ○ Teacher   ● Counselor   ● Prince of Peace

7. What does **Immanuel** mean?

God with us

© *Bible Grade 2*   65

17.2 Christmas

Focus: Jesus' Birth

★ PREPARATION

Write each of the following prophecies fulfilled at Jesus' birth on six strips of paper:
- born of a virgin, call His name Immanuel (Isaiah 7:14)
- a descendant of Abraham (Genesis 22:18)
- of the tribe of Judah (Isaiah 37:31)
- a descendant of David (2 Samuel 7:11–16)
- born in Bethlehem (Micah 5:2)
- from Nazareth in Galilee (Isaiah 9:1–2)

(Directed Instruction)

Select the song "First Christmas Day" from the Grade 2 URL. (Directed Instruction)

Select the BABY JESUS, the MANGER, and the DONKEY from the stick puppet collection made in Lesson 17.1 (Directed Instruction)

↪ EXTENSION

2A Select the song "Away in a Manger/ Silent Night" from the Grade 2 URL to sing with students. Ask them how singing carols can be a good way to share the true meaning of Christmas with others. Encourage students to sing these carols to others during Christmas.

Introduction

Share with students that today's lesson is about the very special circumstances surrounding Jesus' birth.

Directed Instruction ★ ↪

Explain that in the Old Testament, God had given many promises about Jesus, the Messiah. At least six of these were fulfilled at the time of Jesus' birth. Invite six students to read the prepared strips of paper containing the prophecies.

Ask students for the two names of Jesus found in Matthew 1:21 and 1:23 and learned in Lesson 17.1. (**Jesus and Immanuel**) Remind them that *Immanuel* means *God with us*. Explain that the God of the universe came to Earth as a small baby. Ask students how they would expect Jesus, the Son of God and the King of kings, to come down to the earth for the first time. (**Possible answers: Jesus would come to the earth and live in a palace or mansion; many people would clap and cheer to announce Jesus' arrival.**)

Explain to students that the Roman emperor, Caesar Augustus, had ordered a census, so everyone had to return to the town where their family line began to be counted and pay taxes. When Mary and Joseph arrived in Bethlehem, there was no room for them in the inn, so they had to stay elsewhere. They probably slept in a stable, because the Bible says that when Jesus was born, Mary laid Him in a manger, a box used to hold hay for animals to eat. Invite students to close their eyes and imagine the scene: how it would have felt to sleep in a stable, how it would have smelled, what it would have looked like. Discuss with students why God would choose to send His Son to the earth this way and not the way they would expect. (**Possible answer: God wanted to change the way we think about Jesus.**)

Sing the song "First Christmas Day" from the Grade 2 URL with students.

Select BABY JESUS, the MANGER, and the DONKEY from the stick puppet collection made in Lesson 17.1. Invite a volunteer to come to the front of the room and use the puppets to tell about Mary and Joseph arriving in Bethlehem and baby Jesus being born. Remind students that when they look at the donkey puppet and the manger, they should think about Jesus being born in a stable. Explain that people call the day of Jesus' birth *Christmas*.

Student Page 17.2
Help students complete the page as needed.

Review

- What promises did God give in the Bible about Jesus and His birth? (**Jesus would be born of a virgin and called Immanuel; He would be a descendant of Abraham and David, from the tribe of Judah; He would be born in Bethlehem.**)

- Why did Mary and Joseph travel to Bethlehem? (**The Roman emperor, Caesar Augustus, had ordered a census to be taken and taxes to be paid.**)
- Where did Mary place Jesus after He was born? (**in a manger**)

Time Line
Point out Jesus' birth. Then begin at Creation and review the events and people covered thus far in the school year.

Notes:

APPLICATION
- What do you think it might have been like to be there right after Jesus was born in Bethlehem? (**Answers will vary.**)
- What is your favorite Christmas carol or song, and what do the words tell you about Jesus? (**Answers will vary.**)

REINFORCEMENT
Christ's birth is traditionally celebrated on December 25, but was He really born on that date? Luke 2:1–4 states that at the time of Jesus' birth, Caesar Augustus ruled the Roman Empire and ordered a census for tax purposes. Quirinius, the governor of Syria, spearheaded the census in Israel, where Mary and Joseph lived. However, the biblical narrative offers no specific information on the timing of Jesus' birth. Some scholars believe that the reference to the shepherds caring for their flocks in the fields means that the birth took place in the spring instead of the rainy month of December. Other scholars maintain that the sheep may have been a special flock of sacrificial animals for the temple that shepherds tended year-round. This latter view would support the traditional date of Jesus' birth.

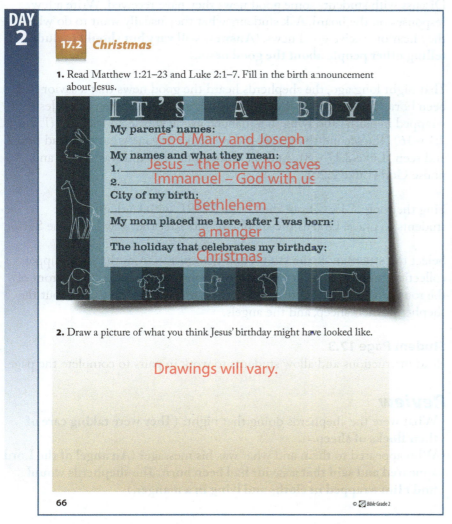

17.3

Christmas
Focus: The Shepherds Worship

★ PREPARATION

Select **DM-10 Shepherd and Sheep**. (*Introduction*)

Select the song "Glory" from the Grade 2 URL. (*Directed Instruction*)

Select the SHEPHERDS, the SHEEP, and ANGELS from the stick puppet collection made in Lesson 17.1. (*Directed Instruction*)

Introduction ★

Show students **DM-10 Shepherd and Sheep**. Ask them what they know about sheep. (**Possible answers: They have wool; they smell bad; they eat grass.**) Explain to students that a *shepherd* is defined as *a person who takes care of sheep*. Today's lesson is about shepherds who heard some exciting news.

Directed Instruction ★

Explain that shepherds often spend a lot of time by themselves. Their job is to watch over and take care of their sheep, lead them to pastures where the sheep can eat, and protect them from predators, such as lions and wolves.

Recount that when Jesus was born, shepherds were taking care of their flocks nearby. Suddenly an angel appeared to the frightened shepherds and announced the birth of Jesus. When the angel finished speaking, the whole sky was filled with angels singing and praising God. The glory of God surrounded them. Teach that Jesus was to be called the *Lamb of God*, because God accepted His sacrifice on the cross to pay for the sins of all.

Discuss with students some good news they have received. Write a few responses on the board. Ask students what they usually want to do when they hear or receive good news. (**Answers will vary but should include telling other people about the good news.**)

That night long ago, the shepherds heard the good news that a savior had been born. The first thing they did was to go to Bethlehem to find Jesus wrapped in cloths and lying in a manger, just as the angel had said (Luke 2:15–16). The second thing they did was tell everyone what they had heard and seen (Luke 2:17–18). And the third thing they did was glorify and praise God (Luke 2:20).

Sing the song "Glory" from the Grade 2 URL with students. Invite students to praise God as the shepherds did after they saw Jesus, the Savior.

Select the SHEPHERDS, the SHEEP, and the ANGELS from the stick puppet collection made in Lesson 17.1. Invite a volunteer to come to the front of the room and use the puppets to tell the part of the Bible truth about the shepherds, their sheep, and the angels.

Student Page 17.3

Read instructions and allow students to work in pairs to complete the page.

Review

- What were the shepherds doing that night? (**They were taking care of their flocks of sheep.**)
- Who appeared to them and what was his message? (**An angel of the Lord appeared and said that a savior had been born. The shepherds would find Him wrapped in cloths and lying in a manger.**)

- What three things did the shepherds do in response to the news? (**They went to find Jesus, they told everyone what they had heard and seen, and they glorified and praised God.**)

Notes:

APPLICATION
- Have you believed the good news that Jesus is your Savior, who forgives your sin once and for all? (**Answers will vary.**)
- Write down the names of people you can share the good news of Jesus' birth with. (**Answers will vary.**)

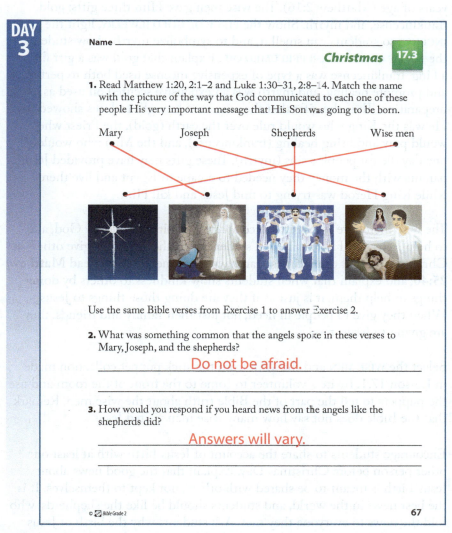

| 17.4 | # Christmas
Focus: The Wise Men Worship |

★ PREPARATION

Have ready a WRAPPED CHRISTMAS GIFT. (*Introduction*)

Have available a PIECE OF GOLD JEWELRY, INCENSE, and JAR OF OLIVE OIL OR PERFUMED OIL. (*Directed Instruction*)

Select the WISE MEN and the STAR from the stick puppet collection made in Lesson 17.1. (*Directed Instruction*)

↻ EXTENSION

4A Review the Bible truth for this week by showing students **PP-5 The Good News of Christmas**. As you show the slides, ask students to retell the events of the first Christmas.

4B Give students the opportunity to take gifts to needy people at a retirement home, a soup kitchen or homeless shelter, or some other community venue. Explain that when Christians give gifts to needy people, it is as if they are giving them to Jesus, and that is a wonderful way to worship God (Matthew 25:40).

Introduction ★

Show students the WRAPPED CHRISTMAS GIFT. Ask students to think about the best gift they have ever received. Then ask them to think about the best gift they have ever given. Discuss why gifts are given at Christmas. (**Possible answers: to celebrate Jesus' birth, to show others I care for them**) Share with students that today's lesson is about some people who gave Jesus very special gifts.

Directed Instruction ★ ↻

The focus of today's lesson is the wise men who came to worship Jesus. The wise men were considered wise because they studied everything, including the stars. These wise men were from the East, which could have been Persia, Arabia, or Mesopotamia. One day these wise men noticed a new star. They knew that this new star announced the birth of the promised Messiah, Jesus.

The wise men followed the star to the home of Mary and Joseph, where they found young Jesus. By this time, Jesus was older, perhaps one or two years of age (Matthew 2:16). The wise men gave Him three gifts: gold, frankincense, and myrrh. Show the PIECE OF GOLD JEWELRY, light the INCENSE so students can smell it, and to symbolize myrrh, show students the JAR OF OLIVE OIL OR PERFUMED OIL. Explain that gold was a gift fit for a king, frankincense was a type of expensive incense used both to perfume and promote healing, and myrrh was an expensive scented oil used as burial preparation. Thus the gifts that the wise men brought to Jesus showed that He was the King who would rule over the earth (gold), the Priest who would pray and bring healing (frankincense), and the Man who would one day die for people's sins (myrrh). These gifts may have provided Jesus' parents with the money they needed to escape to Egypt and live there while King Herod was trying to find Jesus and kill Him.

The wise men gave Jesus gifts to celebrate His birth, to glorify God, and to help Jesus and His family. Tell students that the gifts they give others at Christmas (and at other times) can have the same purpose. Read **Matthew 25:40**, and explain that when students show kindness to others by doing things to help them, it is just as if they are doing those things to Jesus. When they give to people in need, not just their family and friends, they are giving to Jesus, too.

Select the WISE MEN and the STAR from the stick puppet collection made in Lesson 17.1. Invite a volunteer to come to the front of the room and use the puppets to tell the part of the Bible truth about the wise men. Remark that the Bible does not say how many wise men visited Jesus.

Encourage students to share the account of Jesus' birth with at least one other person before Christmas Day. Explain that the good news about Jesus' birth is meant to be shared with others, not kept to themselves. It is the best news in the world, and students should be like the shepherds, who told the news to everyone they met. Ask students why the birth of Jesus

168

is the best news they have ever received. (**because Jesus came to be our Savior, who forgives our sins and gives us new life**)

Student Page 17.4
Have students complete the page.

Review

- What gifts did the wise men present to Jesus? (**gold, frankincense, and myrrh**)
- What should be the reason you give gifts at Christmas? (**to celebrate Jesus' birth, to glorify God, to help people**)
- Why is it important to share the truth about Jesus' birth with people? (**because people need to know that Jesus came to the earth to save them from their sins**)

Notes:

DAY 4

17.4 *Christmas*

God used different ways to announce the arrival of His Son, Jesus. Some people heard an angel or a group of angels. Others saw a star in the sky. One had a dream. How did each person or group of people respond to the news?

Mary 1. Possible answers: "I am the Lord's servant. Let it be according to your word."

Joseph 2. Possible answers: took Mary as his wife, named the baby Jesus

Shepherds 3. Possible answers: "Let us go to Bethlehem ... "; they sang and told everyone about Jesus.

Wise men 4. Possible answers: rejoiced, gave gifts to Jesus

68 © Bible Grade 2

APPLICATION

- Whom can you tell about the birth of Jesus this Christmas? (**Answers will vary.**)
- What gifts can you give to loved ones to celebrate Jesus' birth? (**Answers will vary.**)
- Each person responded to the news of Jesus' birth by worshipping God through obedience, telling others, and giving gifts. What ways can you worship and thank God for sending Jesus? (**Answers will vary.**)

REINFORCEMENT

After visiting suffering children on the Korean island of Kojedo, Bob Pierce wrote in his Bible, "Let my heart be broken with the things that break the heart of God." This prayer was the guiding force behind Bob's vision for Samaritan's Purse, a ministry he established in 1970. His mission and ambition were to enable Christians to bring the love of Jesus to poor and suffering people all over the world. Franklin Graham has expanded upon Bob Pierce's vision and mission as president of the organization. One of the ministries of Samaritan's Purse is Operation Christmas Child, which collects shoe boxes filled with toys, school supplies, and other items packed by families, churches, and others—including many Christian schools. The boxes are sent to needy children around the world. Since the program began in 1993, Christmas shoe boxes have been sent to children in more than 130 countries. In 2010, an estimated 8 million children received shoe boxes around the world.

© Bible Grade 2

17.5 Christmas

Focus: Review and Assessment

★ PREPARATION

Select **VA 17A Jesus Is Born**.
(*Lesson Review*)

Make one copy of **BLM 17E Lesson 17 Test** for each student.
(*Directed Instruction*)

Lesson Review ★

Use **VA 17A Jesus Is Born** to review the Bible truth. Cover the concepts that follow:

- The angel Gabriel told Mary she was going to give birth to God's Son.
- Mary could trust that what the angel said was going to happen because God can do the impossible.
- Joseph was told in a dream not to be afraid to take Mary as his wife, because the child she carried was the Son of God.
- Joseph responded in obedience. He married Mary.
- Two names of God's Son are *Jesus*, which means *the one who saves*, and *Immanuel*, which means *God with us*.
- After Jesus was born, Mary wrapped Him in cloths and laid Him in a manger.
- The Old Testament prophesied that Jesus would be born of a virgin, He would be a descendant of Abraham and David from the tribe of Judah, and He would be born in Bethlehem.
- An angel told shepherds the good news that the Savior had come.
- The shepherds ran to find Jesus. After the shepherds found Jesus, they told everyone what they had heard and seen and returned to their fields, glorifying and praising God.
- The wise men were considered wise because they studied everything, including the stars.
- The wise men noticed a new star that was a sign the promised Messiah, Jesus, had been born.
- The wise men followed the star to Bethlehem, where they found young Jesus.
- The wise men gave Jesus three gifts: gold, frankincense, and myrrh.
- Giving to people in need is like giving to Jesus (Matthew 25:40).

Directed Instruction ★

Distribute a copy of **BLM 17E Lesson 17 Test** to each student. Explain the instructions and format to students. Have students complete the test. When they are finished, read over the test, providing the answers for immediate feedback.

Notes:

Lesson Preparation
Nehemiah Stands Firm

Expected Student Outcomes

KNOW
Nehemiah and the Israelites face opposition as the Israelites continue rebuilding the wall of Jerusalem.

DO
Students will:
- list Nehemiah's fears and use Scripture to identify what to do when they are afraid
- evaluate their own integrity in making godly decisions
- complete the sentences about the armor of God
- contrast instances of pleasing God against instances of pleasing others

APPLY
Students will make godly decisions when faced with opposition.

Lesson Outline

I. Nehemiah does not fear opposition (Neh 1–4, Ps 46:1)
II. Nehemiah shows integrity (Neh 5, Prov 10:9)
III. Nehemiah deals with adversaries (1 Pet 5:8, Neh 4:13–23)
  A. Armor of God (Eph 6:10–18)
IV. Nehemiah finishes despite pressure (Neh 6, 1 Cor 16:13–14, Phil 4:6–7)
  A. Positive peer pressure
  B. Negative peer pressure

♥ TEACHER'S HEART

As the rebuilding of the wall continued, Nehemiah stood firm. Fear of failure, fear of those who opposed him, and fear of his own inadequacies could have overwhelmed him. Yet, Nehemiah chose to face his fears and stand firm against complaints, unfair treatment, and pressure to quit.

Nehemiah stood strong in building his foundation on God before he thought about building the wall (Nehemiah 1:4–11). Nehemiah's strength and determination came from an inner peace from his relationship and commitment to God. He continually encouraged others and kept a watchful eye out for the opposition.

Does fear grip you at times? You may feel that others oppose or misunderstand you. The pressure can be overwhelming. You may want to give up. As Nehemiah showed how to stand firm in his faith and not be afraid, you too can go to Christ, who is your firm foundation (1 Corinthians 3:10–11). As you teach and do the job God called you to do, ask Him to help you keep a watchful eye for the schemes of the enemy, and pray for His wisdom and strength to be in you. In doing so, you'll begin to operate in the power, love, and sound mind offered by God to bring about His results (2 Timothy 1:7).

📖 MEMORY VERSE
Matthew 19:26

GLOSSARY WORDS
- opposition
- integrity

★ MATERIALS

Day 1:
- VA 18A Nehemiah Stands Firm

Day 2:
- Bowl, individually wrapped treats
- BLM 18A Who Am I (*Extension*)

Day 3:
- BLM 18B Armor of God
- BLM 18C Sword, poster board (*Extension*)

Day 4:
- BLM 18D Salt Dough Recipe, BLM 18E Wall of Jerusalem Outline, paper plates, watercolor paints (*Extension*)

Day 5:
- VA 18A Nehemiah Stands Firm
- BLM 18F Lesson 18 Test

♪ SONGS
Armor of God

TEACHER RESOURCES

Fields, Don. *Nehemiah: The Courage to Face Opposition*. InterVarsity Press, 2002.
Hybels, Bill. *Who You Are When No One's Looking*. InterVarsity Press, 2010.

STUDENT RESOURCES

Hyman, Frieda Clark. *Victory on the Walls: A Story of Nehemiah*. Bethlehem Books, 2016.
Lehman, Dana. *I Double Dare You!* Lehman Publishing, 2008.

Supplemental Materials are available to download. See Understanding Purposeful Design Bible at the front of this book for the Grade 2 JRL.

18.1 Nehemiah Stands Firm
Focus: Nehemiah Does Not Fear Opposition

📖 MEMORY VERSE

Matthew 19:26

MEMORY WORK

- Have students read the Memory Verse in unison. Then repeat the following directions until every student has practiced the verse at least one more time: Everyone with brown eyes say the verse. Everyone wearing something blue say the verse. Everyone who did chores before school today say the verse. Everyone who has a brother or sister say the verse. Everyone who likes to sing say the verse. Everyone in second grade say the verse.

★ PREPARATION

Select **VA 18A Nehemiah Stands Firm**. (*Directed Instruction*)

↩ EXTENSION

1A Read and discuss the following Scriptures in which God says not to fear:
- **Genesis 26:24, Isaiah 41:10–11** (Do not fear, God will be with you.)
- **1 Kings 17:13–14** (Do not fear, God will provide.)
- **Isaiah 43:1–4** (Do not fear, God will be with you in hard times.)
Divide students into three groups to make "Fear Not" posters on construction paper.

Introduction

Ask students to think about what the following things have in common: the dark, an enemy, a storm, new experiences, difficult responsibilities, being left out. Point out that all of these represent something people may be afraid of. Lead a short discussion of some fears that students may have. Tell students that Nehemiah also had to face some fears when rebuilding the wall of Jerusalem. This is the focus of today's Bible truth.

Directed Instruction ★ ↩

Display **VA 18A Nehemiah Stands Firm** and read the Bible truth on the back. Before Nehemiah could start rebuilding the wall of Jerusalem, he had to have a firm foundation in God. Nehemiah needed to make godly decisions when faced with **opposition**, which means *someone or something that is resistant to a situation.* Instead of worrying about all the things that could happen, he trusted in God.

Nehemiah could have been afraid of
- the possibility that King Artaxerxes might not grant him permission to return to Jerusalem (Nehemiah 2:1–9);
- what mockers and other people were saying (Nehemiah 2:19);
- Sanballat, Tobiah, and other enemies who were trying to stop him (Nehemiah 4:1–11); and
- not being successful or not completing the job (Nehemiah 1:11).

Nehemiah did not choose fear but demonstrated courage and boldness as he
- prayed to God for help (Nehemiah 1:4–11, 2:4);
- stood firm against mockers (Nehemiah 2:20, 4:1–15);
- took refuge in God (Nehemiah 1:4);
- set guards against the enemy (Nehemiah 4:13–23); and
- encouraged the people to work together and remember God when they were discouraged (Nehemiah 4:14).

Remind students of the fears they mentioned during the Introduction. Explain that they may be afraid of what will happen in the future, of what others might say about them, or of not being big or strong enough to do a job. At times they may even fear opposition. But just as Nehemiah did, they can turn to God in prayer and trust Him to help them. Read **Psalm 46:1**. Point out that God will show them how to stand strong and guard against their enemies as they take refuge in Him. Tell them it takes boldness and a willingness to keep at something.

Teach students the following poem to help them remember what to do when they are afraid. If you wish, you may sing the poem to a familiar tune or a simple melody.

> When you're afraid and don't know what to do,
> Be still and pray, for God will see you through.
> Build your faith on God's Word, which is true,
> He'll help you stand and show you what to do.

When enemies mock and come against you,
In God you can trust and take refuge!

Student Page 18.1
Assist students in completing the page. Then spend time praying together for boldness and perseverance in fearful situations that students may be experiencing. Encourage students to remember how faithful and powerful God is. Remind them that standing together and trusting in God will increase their boldness.

Review

- Name something Nehemiah could have been afraid of. (**Possible answers: mockers, enemies, not completing the job**)
- Who stayed angry with Nehemiah as he continued rebuilding the wall? (**Sanballat, Tobiah, and other enemy leaders**)
- What did Nehemiah say to the people when others around him were afraid of the mockers? (**Nehemiah reminded the Israelites to remember God and how great and awesome He is.**)

APPLICATION

- What did Nehemiah choose to do when he could have let fear stop him? (**Possible answers: prayed, trusted God, stood firm**)
- How did these choices help Nehemiah? (**God gave Nehemiah the strength and confidence to finish rebuilding the wall.**)
- Do your fears ever get in the way of doing what God asks you to do? Why or why not? (**Answers will vary.**)
- What should you do when you are afraid? (**Possible answers: pray, trust in God, stand firm**)

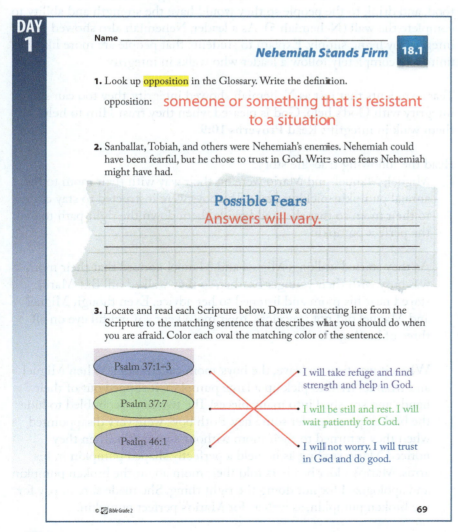

18.2
Nehemiah Stands Firm
Focus: Nehemiah Shows Integrity

★ PREPARATION

Have a BOWL of SMALL, INDIVIDUALLY WRAPPED TREATS on hand. Privately select two students to disrupt the Introduction activity by taking as many treats as they would like, to the point of emptying the bowl. (*Introduction*)

↷ EXTENSION

2A Write the following names on the board: David, Elijah, Jesus, Joshua, Moses, Nehemiah, Ruth. Print a copy of **BLM 18A Who Am I** to review which people in the Bible showed integrity by taking a stand and doing what was right in spite of opposition. Instruct students to look at the names on the board and raise their hand if they know the person you are describing as you read each statement aloud.

Introduction ★

Place a BOWL of SMALL, INDIVIDUALLY WRAPPED TREATS in front of the room. Inform students that they are permitted to choose one treat from the bowl. As students come to the front of the room, walk to the back of the room, facing away from them. Quietly signal the two previously selected students to begin taking handfuls of treats from the bowl. Wait for students to notice their behavior and complain. When complaints are voiced, calm students by telling them that you told their two classmates to misbehave. Instruct the two students to return the extra treats to the bowl, keeping one treat apiece. Lead a discussion on **integrity**, which means *the state of being completely honest and showing respect for others*. Tell students that Nehemiah showed integrity as he worked with others in rebuilding the wall. This is the focus of today's Bible truth.

Directed Instruction ↶

Remind students that even though others treated Nehemiah unfairly, he stayed strong in doing what God told him to do. Nehemiah met with the nobles and leaders of Israel who were treating their own people unfairly. Nehemiah told these leaders to return land, olive groves, houses, money, food, and drink to the people so they would have the strength and ability to complete the wall (Nehemiah 5). As a leader, Nehemiah also showed great integrity by living simply. Explain to students that people are more likely to unite and completely follow a leader who walks in integrity.

Teach students that just as Nehemiah showed integrity, they too can show integrity with God's help. God is pleased when they trust Him to help them walk in integrity. Read **Proverbs 10:9**.

Read the following true-life story:

Miguel, Manuel, and Mario were on their way with their mom to the annual pumpkin-picking event. The boys were instructed to stay close to their mom so that she could guide them down the right path to pick the perfect pumpkin.

As they started walking, Miguel and Manuel noticed that their mom was busy with their younger brother, so they walked off. But Mario stayed near his mom and listened to her advice. Even though Miguel and Manuel did not stay close, their mom kept a watchful eye on all three of her boys.

When it was time to leave, the boys' mom called them. When Miguel and Manuel tried to pick up a large pumpkin, it slipped out of their hands and smashed into many pieces! The two boys scrambled to hide the broken pieces under some hay. Both boys were very disappointed when they returned to their mom without a pumpkin. Then they noticed Mario smiling as he held a perfectly shaped pumpkin in his arms. Mario's older brothers told their mom about the broken pumpkin and apologized for not doing the right thing. She made sure to pay for the broken pumpkin, as well as for Mario's perfect pumpkin.

Ask which boy(s) showed integrity and why. (**Mario showed integrity because he stayed close to his mom and did what was right. Miguel and Manuel showed integrity when they told their mom about the broken pumpkin, even though they knew there would be consequences for their actions.**) Tell students to stay close to God and walk with Him. He will give them direction. They can trust God to help them to have integrity, because He is reliable and will not take them down the wrong path.

Student Page 18.2
Have students complete the page. Encourage them to pray for integrity.

Review
• What is integrity? (**the state of being completely honest and showing respect for others**)
• How did Nehemiah show integrity? (**Nehemiah stayed strong in doing what God told him to do even though others treated him unfairly. He lived simply.**)
• What happens if you stay close to and walk with God? (**God will guide me and give me direction.**)

APPLICATION
• What do you think people remembered about Nehemiah after meeting him? (**Possible answers: He was a caring leader; he had integrity; he followed God.**)
• When people think of you, what do you want them to remember? (**Answers will vary.**)
• Name ways you can show integrity toward others. (**Possible answers: follow God and those in authority; complete what I start; be honest; do what is right, even when no one is watching**)
• How are people who work together stronger than those who argue about everything? (**Possible answers: work gets done faster; everyone does what they are supposed to do, even when no one is watching; enemies can't get past them.**)

DAY 2

18.2 *Nehemiah Stands Firm*

1. Look up integrity in the Glossary. Write the definition.

integrity: the state of being completely honest and showing respect for others.

2. Nehemiah showed integrity by living simply. Fill in each box in the **Yes** column beside sentences that show integrity. Fill in each box in the **No** column beside sentences that do not show integrity.

Yes	No	
■	□	I pray to God and choose to obey, even when no one is looking.
■	□	I try to follow God, even when it is difficult.
□	■	I sometimes borrow things and do not give them back.
■	□	I live in a way that other people can trust me.
□	■	I sometimes hide to avoid obeying my parents.
■	□	I do not take advantage of people who are kind to me.

3. Write a short prayer to God that says how you want to live a life of integrity.

Answers will vary.

70   © Bible Grade 2

18.3 Nehemiah Stands Firm

Focus: Nehemiah Deals with Adversaries

★ PREPARATION

Make copies of **BLM 18B Armor of God** for each student. (*Directed Instruction*)

Select the song "Armor of God" from the Grade 2 URL. (*Directed Instruction*)

↪ EXTENSION

3A Provide copies of **BLM 18C Sword** to each student. Direct them to cut and trace the sword outline onto POSTER BOARD. Cut out the poster-board sword. Remind students that the workers on the wall had to be ready with a sword, or another weapon, in one hand as they worked with the other hand. They did this to guard against an enemy attack. Ask students to hold their sword in one hand for part of the day as they do their schoolwork or help others. Point out that this exercise illustrates the importance of always being ready to use the sword of God's Word to guard against Satan's schemes and attacks. Express that as they all resolve to stand firm and follow God, their unity advances the kingdom of God.

3B Show students how to use the sword of the Spirit, God's Word, to pray. Encourage students to make a prayer request more personal by adding their own or a classmate's name to the Scripture as they pray. Allow students to choose any of the following Scriptures:
• Philippians 1:3–6
• Colossians 3:17, 4:6
• 1 Thessalonians 5:16–17
• 2 Thessalonians 3:5
• 1 Peter 5:7

Introduction

Read the following scenario to students:

The blazing sun scorched the dry, cracked earth. A lion peered out from behind a bush in anticipation as an antelope approached a water hole. As the antelope bent down for a drink, the lion took the opportunity to attack. The antelope was caught off guard and could not escape.

Ask students what the antelope could have done differently to ward off the attack? (**been more alert**) Read **1 Peter 5:8**. Explain to students that Satan is like a roaring lion looking for someone to attack. Satan will lie to them to stop them from doing what God wants them to do.

Directed Instruction ★ ↪

Teach students that as believers they also have adversaries, or enemies, coming against them to stop the work God has called them to do. Read **Ephesians 6:10–18**. Point out to students that they can use these "weapons," just as Nehemiah and the workers used physical weapons to guard against their enemies while they rebuilt the wall.

Provide a copy of **BLM 18B Armor of God** to each student. Direct students to color each of the armor pieces as you read the following aloud:

• the belt of truth: A soldier wears a belt to hold his weapons. This belt represents Jesus, who is the Truth. Jesus made a way for everyone to come to God. By drawing near to Him, a child of God can find security and protection in spiritual battles (John 14:6).

• the breastplate of righteousness: A breastplate is a protective covering to guard a soldier's heart and other vital organs. This breastplate represents the righteousness that comes from Jesus alone. He gave His life to cover and protect those He loves (1 Corinthians 1:30).

• feet fitted with the gospel of peace: A soldier's feet must be prepared and ready for action. In the same way, before children of God can do spiritual battle, they need to be prepared and ready to share the good news about Jesus with others (Romans 10:15).

• the shield of faith: A shield protects a soldier when someone attacks with a weapon. This shield stands for faith in Jesus Christ. As children of God hold firmly to faith in Jesus, God enables them to stand strong in Him (Galatians 2:20, Proverbs 30:5).

• the helmet of salvation: A helmet protects a soldier's head. This helmet stands for the hope of salvation in Jesus (1 Thessalonians 5:8). Without hope it is easy to give in to thoughts of fear, discouragement, and despair, but God is the God of hope, who gives joy and peace (Romans 15:13).

• the sword of the Spirit: A sword is a powerful weapon, ready to be used at any time. The sword of the Spirit stands for God's Word. Children of

God need to be ready at any time to use God's Word as the Holy Spirit guides them (Psalm 119:105, Hebrews 4:12).

Explain to students that they do not need to fear the spiritual battle, because God won the victory when Jesus died on the cross for them and rose from the dead, conquering sin and death. Believers are to pray and be alert so they will be ready to stand firm when Satan tries to deceive them.

Student Page 18.3
As students complete the page, play the song "Armor of God" from the Grade 2 URL.

Review
• Why did Nehemiah and the workers have to carry weapons in one hand and tools in the other? (**so they would be ready to fight their enemies as they worked on the wall**)
• What enemy do you fight against as a believer? (**Satan and his followers**)
• Name each piece of armor that God tells you to wear for battle. (**belt of truth, breastplate of righteousness, feet fitted with the gospel of peace, shield of faith, helmet of salvation, sword of the Spirit**)

APPLICATION
• Why is it important to put on the armor of God every day? (**It is important to put on the armor of God, because God has the power to help me fight any battles I have.**)
• Do you need to be afraid of the spiritual battle against evil? (**No.**) Why or why not? (**God has already won the battle and will give me all I need to overcome the enemy.**)
• What should you do to prepare for spiritual battles? (**Possible answers: pray, read God's Word, trust in God's salvation, tell others about His peace, know that God will show me the right thing to do and then I will choose to do it**)

REINFORCEMENT
In Old Testament times, soldiers used long-range, medium-range, and close-range arms as offensive weapons in battle. Long-range arms included the bow and arrow and slingshots. Medium-range arms included javelins or spears. For close-range, hand-to-hand combat, swords were used. Although swords came in a variety of shapes and sizes, there were only two basic types: the single-edged sword, with a straight or curved edge, and the double-edged sword, used for piercing.

Defensive armor included helmets, breastplates, and shields. Helmets were made of metal or leather, and the shape of a helmet indicated which army a soldier belonged to. Breastplates were heavy, with as many as 700 to 1,000 small metal plates sewn onto cloth. Shields were made of wicker or of leather stretched over wooden frames.

DAY 3

Name _____

Nehemiah Stands Firm   18.3

Read Ephesians 6:10–18. God gives you armor to fight spiritual battles. Complete the sentences with words from the Word Bank.

WORD BANK

shield	breastplate	feet
sword	helmet	belt

1. The _____**belt**_____ of truth stands for Jesus. He is the truth. This armor is worn by soldiers to hold weapons around their waist.

2. The _____**breastplate**_____ of righteousness reminds me that righteousness comes only from Jesus. This armor is worn by soldiers to protect their body.

3. The _____**feet**_____ fitted with the gospel of peace reminds me to be ready to go and share about Jesus with others. A soldier must be ready for battle with good footwear.

4. The _____**shield**_____ of faith stands for faith in God. He helps me to stand strong in Him. Soldiers use this armor for protection from other weapons.

5. The _____**helmet**_____ of salvation reminds me that God is the God of hope. He gives me joy and peace. He does not give me thoughts of fear and despair. This armor protects a soldier's head.

6. The _____**sword**_____ of the Spirit stands for God's Word. This armor is used by soldiers as a weapon for attacking. I should know and use God's Word.

© Bible Grade 2   71

18.4 Nehemiah Stands Firm

Focus: Nehemiah Finishes Despite Pressure

EXTENSION

4A Using **BLM 18D Salt Dough Recipe**, make enough dough for each student to construct a miniature version of the wall of Jerusalem. Provide each student with a copy of **BLM 18E Wall of Jerusalem Outline** and a LARGE PAPER PLATE. Have each student form the finished wall of Jerusalem with the salt dough, using the plate as the wall's foundation and the blackline master as an outline. Direct students to decorate their finished wall with WATERCOLOR PAINTS.

Introduction

Review the definition of *peer pressure* by writing the following words on the board: *a strong influence from people near you to do something*. Instruct students to read the definition aloud together. Explain that peer pressure can be positive or negative. Positive peer pressure involves an influence to do something good. When Christians work together to bring about something good, the positive peer pressure they place on one another brings glory to God. What Nehemiah and the Israelites did in rebuilding the wall resulted in honoring God.

Negative peer pressure involves an influence to do something wrong. Ask students if they have ever felt pressure to do wrong things that their peers were doing. (**Answers will vary.**) Point out that they may often give in to peer pressure because they do not want to appear different from others. In some instances, others may even try to trick them into doing something they do not want to do. This is the focus of today's lesson.

Directed Instruction

Remind students that Nehemiah had to stand strong against negative peer pressure from Sanballat, Tobiah, and the crowd around him (Nehemiah 6). He had to act wisely, be brave, and follow God's instructions for rebuilding the wall, even though others were pressuring him to stop. Nehemiah's enemies tried to trick him by lying to him, taunting him, and writing false things about him. They even tried to convince Nehemiah to hide in the temple for fear of being killed. If Nehemiah had listened to them, they would have called him *a coward*. But he did not give in to the pressure. Instead, he chose to stand firm and please God rather than others. When the wall was finished, Nehemiah remembered to praise God for giving him the strength to complete the task.

Read the following scenarios to your students. Instruct them to raise their hand each time the situation involves negative peer pressure. When it involves positive peer pressure, tell students to keep their hands down.
- a friend wants you to steal and lie (**hands up**)
- a neighbor asks you to help rake her yard (**hands down**)
- classmates are cheating on a test while the teacher is not looking (**hands up**)
- students are trying to get you to do something you do not think is right (**hands up**)
- some boys and girls ask you to help them clean up the trash on the playground (**hands down**)

Read **1 Corinthians 16:13–14**. Lead a discussion on how students can stand firm against negative peer pressure by doing everything in love. Encourage them to talk about instances of positive peer pressure. Remind students that just as God helped Nehemiah to stand strong, He will also help them to stand strong when negative peer pressure comes. Select a volunteer to read **Philippians 4:6–7**. Explain to students that they are not to worry; instead, they are to go to God in prayer, and He will give them the peace and strength to make godly choices, even when others are not doing so. When they accomplish what God wants them to do by following His guidance, they need to remember to praise and thank Him for the way He helped them, just as Nehemiah did when he finished the wall.

Student Page 18.4
Assist students as needed to complete the page.

Review

- What kind of negative peer pressure did Nehemiah experience? (**A number of people tried to consistently stop Nehemiah from rebuilding the wall.**)
- How did Nehemiah respond to negative peer pressure? (**Nehemiah stood strong and finished rebuilding the wall.**)
- What did Nehemiah remember to do when God gave him strength? (**Nehemiah remembered to thank God, because God helped him complete the task.**)

APPLICATION

- Compare the ways Nehemiah was pressured to the ways you can be pressured. (**Answers will vary.**)
- How does it feel when others pressure you to do something wrong (negative peer pressure)? (**Answers will vary.**)
- What should you do when you are feeling pressure from friends (peers) to do the wrong thing? (**Go to God in prayer, stand strong, and do what is right.**)
- Tell about a time you experienced negative peer pressure but chose to do what was right. (**Answers will vary.**)

REINFORCEMENT

The modern city of Jerusalem is of key importance to Christianity, Judaism, and Islam. It is surrounded by seven mountains, including Mount Zion, Mount Moriah, and Mount Ophel. Psalm 125:1–2 states that those who trust in God are like Mount Zion, for they will not be moved but will endure forever. The Lord surrounds His children as the mountains surround Jerusalem. *Jerusalem* means *City of Peace*, a name that reflects its historical significance as one of the oldest continuously inhabited cities in the world. The original name for Jerusalem, referred to in Genesis 14:18, is *Salem*, which means *peace*. Psalm 122:6–7 calls for those who love Jerusalem to pray for peace and prosperity within its walls. Today there are eight gates leading into Jerusalem. The Refuse (or Dung) Gate to the south retains the name it had in Nehemiah's day (Nehemiah 3:14). In 2007, archaeologists from Hebrew University excavated the area surrounding this gate, uncovering what is believed to be part of the wall Nehemiah and the Israelites rebuilt.

DAY 4

18.4 Nehemiah Stands Firm

Peer pressure can be positive or negative. If you ask Him, God will help you make correct choices when your peers pressure you.

1. Fill in the circle next to each phrase that describes a **positive** peer pressure. Positive peer pressure influences you to do what pleases God.
    - ● pray often
    - ● listen to God's voice
    - ○ listen to and follow anyone
    - ● trust God
    - ● tell others about God's Word
    - ○ keep quiet about God's Word

2. Fill in the circle next to each phrase that describes a **negative** peer pressure. Negative peer pressure influences you to please others instead of God.
    - ● do what is popular at the moment
    - ● always follow the crowd, even when it is wrong
    - ○ pray to God often
    - ○ behave and listen to your parents
    - ● listen to and follow wrong advice
    - ● give up when it is hard

3. Write a short prayer. Ask God to help you put on His armor and stand strong when faced with negative peer pressure.

   Answers will vary.

18.5 Nehemiah Stands Firm

Focus: Review and Assessment

★ PREPARATION

Select **VA 18A Nehemiah Stands Firm** for reference. (*Lesson Review*)

Print a copy of **BLM 18F Lesson 18 Test** for each student. (*Directed Instruction*)

Lesson Review ★

Use **VA 18A Nehemiah Stands Firm** to review the Bible truth. Cover the following concepts:

- Sanballat, Tobiah, and others were angry and continued trying to stop Nehemiah from rebuilding the wall.
- *Opposition* means *someone or something that is resistant to a situation*.
- Nehemiah needed to make wise decisions when faced with opposition.
- Each person boldly worked on the wall with one hand while holding a weapon in the other to guard the city.
- *Integrity* is defined as *the state of being completely honest and showing respect for others*.
- Nehemiah stayed strong and had integrity, doing what God told him to do even though others threatened him and tried to trick him.
- Nehemiah prayed, asking God to strengthen the Israelites to band together in unity against their enemies.
- God gives His children armor to help them fight spiritual battles. They do not need to fear the spiritual battle, because God has already won the victory through Jesus Christ.
- The armor of God is made up of the belt of truth, the breastplate of righteousness, feet fitted with the gospel of peace, the shield of faith, the helmet of salvation, and the sword of the Spirit.
- Nehemiah had to be brave and do what God directed, even though he felt peer pressure to quit.
- When students experience negative peer pressure, they should be on guard, stand firm, and trust God to help them do what is right. Then they should follow God's guidance.
- Nehemiah and the Israelites completed the wall after 52 days of working from morning until evening.
- Nehemiah remembered to give God praise and thanks because He granted Nehemiah the strength to complete the task.

Directed Instruction ★

Distribute a copy of **BLM 18F Lesson 18 Test** to each student. Read the directions and go over any difficult words on the page before students begin the test.

Notes:

Lesson Preparation
Esther Listens to Wise Advice
19.0

Expected Student Outcomes

KNOW
Esther becomes queen and heeds wise counsel.

DO
Students will:
- identify the wise advice Mordecai and the king's servant gave Esther
- identify Esther's action in response to the wise advice she received
- determine whose instruction they are to follow
- write a prayer to God, asking Him for wisdom
- identify ways to delight in the Lord
- choose wise advice they could give to someone

APPLY
Students will discern who or what to listen to and identify wise advice.

Lesson Outline
I. Esther listens and obeys (Esth 1–2)
II. Choosing wise advice (Prov 1:8–9, 19:20)
III. Wisdom's rewards (Ps 1, Prov 8:32–35)
IV. Giving wise advice (Ps 111:10; Prov 9:10, 15:33)

♥ TEACHER'S HEART

Sometimes situations arise in your classroom which seem to need the experience and wisdom of someone who has been teaching for a lifetime. A seasoned teacher or administrator usually has the ability to pull solutions "out of the air." In other words, their expertise and experience have become knowledge applied—wisdom. Think of someone whom you see in this light. People like this have the ability to draw out the best in you. You respect them for their knowledge and their care. They have learned the lesson of James 3:17—that wisdom from above is pure, peaceable, gentle, willing to yield, full of mercy and good fruits, impartial, and sincere.

God invites you to come to Him, especially when you are in need of wisdom. He promises to provide generously to all who ask even with the simplest faith (James 1:5). Ask God for His wisdom today as you seek to give good counsel and encouragement to your students. Some of them are experiencing difficult times and need your encouragement, just as you need God and wise counselors to advise and encourage you.

MEMORY VERSE
Proverbs 19:20

GLOSSARY WORDS
- submission
- wisdom

MATERIALS

Day 1:
- VA 19A Esther Listens to Wise Advice, poster boards, paper crowns

Day 2:
- Semi-transparent blindfold
- Ornate piece of jewelry

Day 3:
- No additional materials are needed.

Day 4:
- DM-11 Advice Alphabet, coin
- Note cards, box

Day 5:
- VA 19A Esther Listens to Wise Advice
- BLM 19A Lesson 19 Test

TEACHER RESOURCES
Moore, Beth. *Esther: It's Tough Being a Woman*. Lifeway Press, 2008.
Saibel, Michael O. *One Night with the King*. DVD. 20th Century Fox, 2007.

STUDENT RESOURCES
Mackenzie, Carine. *Esther: The Brave Queen*. Christian Focus Publications, 2006.
Veggie Tales: Esther, the Girl Who Became Queen. DVD. Universal Studios, 2018.

Supplemental Materials are available to download. See Understanding Purposeful Design Bible at the front of this book for the Grade 2 URL.

19.1 Esther Listens to Wise Advice
Focus: Esther Listens and Obeys

MEMORY VERSE
Proverbs 19:20

MEMORY WORK
- Separate students into groups of three or four. Direct them to create hand motions for the main words of the Memory Verse. Allow each group to teach their hand motions to the rest of the class while reciting the verse. Lead students to collectively recite the verse once each group has had a turn.

★ PREPARATION
Select **VA 19A Esther Listens to Wise Advice**. (*Directed Instruction*)

Have on hand THREE POSTER BOARDS. (*Directed Instruction*)

Prepare TWO PAPER CROWNS. (*Directed Instruction*)

Introduction
Write the word *advice* on the board, and ask a volunteer to say the word aloud. Explain that *advice* is defined as *a suggestion about what another person could do*. Another word for *advice* is *counsel*. Point out to students that someone's advice can be good or bad. They should only follow the advice of people whom they respect and trust. Today's Bible truth is about a woman who listened to and followed the advice of people she respected.

Directed Instruction ★
Read **VA 19A Esther Listens to Wise Advice**. Explain that Esther followed the advice of Mordecai because she respected him and was loyal to him, as if he were her own father. Direct students to look up *loyalty* in their Glossary and review the following definition: *the character trait of showing faithfulness and devotion to someone or something*. Review the three pieces of wise advice Esther listened to and obeyed. Write them on the board, as follows:
- Mordecai instructed Esther not to tell anyone about her family background—of her being a Jew.
- The king's servant Hegai told Esther what to do to prepare herself to see the king.
- Mordecai told Queen Esther to notify King Ahasuerus of the evil plan to murder him.

Separate students into three groups. Give each group one of the THREE POSTER BOARDS. Assign one of the three pieces of advice for Esther to each group. Instruct students to copy the advice onto the poster board. Allow time for each student in every group to write part of the advice on the poster board. Afterward, display the poster boards in a prominent place in front of the room.

Select four students to pantomime the Bible truth about Esther and Mordecai for the class. Ask a female student to be *Esther*, and three male students to be *Mordecai*, *King Ahasuerus*, and the king's servant *Hegai*. Place one CROWN on King Ahasuerus's head. Allow students in the "audience" to take turns reading the Bible truth about Esther from **VA 19A Esther Listens to Wise Advice**. As students read, *Esther* should nod her head, heeding the advice displayed on the poster boards. When *King Ahasuerus* makes *Esther* queen, he should place the other CROWN on *Esther's* head.

Explain that Esther had a choice to make when Mordecai advised her to keep her family background a secret. Point out that Esther showed **submission** to Mordecai by being humble and obedient. Define *submission* as *the act of accepting the authority or decision of someone else*. Esther's respect for her relative Mordecai and the king's servant made it easier for her to follow their advice.

Discuss why Esther might have followed the advice of these men. (**Answers will vary but should include she respected them, was loyal to Mordecai, and she knew they were wise. Esther was humble and**

182

submitted, or yielded, to Mordecai's advice, and she trusted God to guide her.)

Student Page 19.1
Assist students as needed to complete the page. Allow them to look up the word *submission* in the Glossary to answer Exercise 6.

Review

• To whom was Esther loyal? (**Mordecai**)
• What three pieces of advice did Esther receive? (**to not tell anyone about her Jewish family background, to follow Hegai's instructions to prepare for the king, to tell the king of the evil plot against him**)
• How did Esther respond to this advice? (**She listened and obeyed the advice each person gave her.**)
• Why did Esther follow the advice she received? (**She trusted and respected Mordecai and the king's servant. She was loyal to Mordecai and responded in obedience, humility, and submission.**)

APPLICATION

• What is some excellent advice you have received? Why was it such good advice? (**Answers will vary.**)
• Would you have displayed loyalty if you were in Esther's position? (**Answers will vary.**)
• To whom should you be loyal? (**Possible answers: God, my parents, my authority figures**)

REINFORCEMENT

According to Greek historians, King Ahasuerus, or Xerxes, reigned over the Persian Empire from 486–465 BC. Before Esther became queen, the king's wife, Vashti, or Amestris, was queen. Vashti had likely incurred the king's anger before the banquet mentioned in Esther 1:10–12, but her refusal to obey his summons to attend the event further infuriated him.

The Bible and other historical documents provide little information about the reign of King Ahasuerus, the father of Artaxerxes, who was the king Nehemiah served. The identity of the queen seated beside Artaxerxes in Nehemiah 2:6 remains a mystery as well.

DAY 1

Name _____

Esther Listens to Wise Advice **19.1**

Solve the math problems. Match your answer to the word in the Code Box. Use the five words to make a sentence about Esther in Exercise 5.

Code Box

11 = wise	22 = listened	34 = Esther	45 = advice	56 = to

1. Mordecai was Esther's relative. He gave her wise __advice__.
$12 + 21 + 12 =$
He told her not to tell anyone about her family background.

2. __Esther__ was loyal to Mordecai. She obeyed him because
$23 + 11 =$
she respected him. She knew that Mordecai was __wise__.
$37 − 26 =$

3. Esther also __listened__ to the king's servant. He told
$12 + 10 =$
her how to prepare herself for the king.

4. Mordecai told Queen Esther __to__ tell King Ahasuerus
$69 − 13 =$
that there was an evil plan to kill him.

5. __Esther listened to wise advice.__
_____

6. Write the definition of submission: __the act of accepting the authority or decision of someone else__

© *Bible Grade 2*   73

19.2 Esther Listens to Wise Advice

Focus: Choosing Wise Advice

★ PREPARATION

Have a SEMI-TRANSPARENT BLINDFOLD available. Select two students and direct them to purposefully give both good and bad directions during the obstacle-course activity. (*Introduction*)

Have available an ORNATE PIECE OF JEWELRY. (*Directed Instruction*)

⟳ EXTENSION

2A Direct students to think of one person who has given them wise advice or counsel. Allow students to write a short letter or e-mail of thanks to that person. Encourage students to pray for that person, and assist students in mailing or e-mailing the letters.

Introduction ★

Introduce the following activity to help students see the importance of listening to good advice: Assist students in setting up a simple obstacle course by using objects in the room, such as wastebaskets, books, desks, and chairs. Instruct students to remain seated during the activity. Show them the SEMI-TRANSPARENT BLINDFOLD without mentioning that the fabric is partially see-through (for safety). Inform students that you will wear the blindfold and trust them to verbally guide you through the obstacle course. Proceed with the activity, reminding students to be very clear in their directions. Allow students to take turns directing you around the obstacles. The two previously selected students should purposely give you both good and bad directions. After finishing the course, discuss with students what happened when you followed their advice. (**Possible answers: When you followed our good advice, you did not run into anything in the obstacle course; when you followed our bad advice, you ran into different obstacles and strayed off the safe path.**) Explain to students that God has placed people in their life whom they can trust and who can give them wise advice that they should listen to and follow.

Directed Instruction ★ ⟳

Direct students to locate **wisdom** in the Glossary. Invite a volunteer to read the definition aloud. (**using what you know in the best way**) Review with students what wise advice Esther listened to and immediately obeyed. (**to not tell anyone about her Jewish family background, to follow Hegai's instructions to prepare for the king, to tell the king of the evil plot to kill him**) Remind students that when someone gives them advice, they must first pray about it and then determine whether that advice is wise. If it is not wise, they should not follow it. Discuss with students different factors to consider when determining whose advice to listen to:

- Consider whether the person has given good or bad advice in the past. Explain that if a person has led them to do something that later got them in trouble, then that person probably does not give the wisest advice.
- Consider the person's age. Generally, the older a person is, the more life experience that person has, so he or she will probably give wise counsel. However, there are many young people who are also able, with God's guidance, to give wise counsel.
- Consider whether the person is loyal to God. The person should believe in and follow God's leading. That individual's walk with God will affect his or her ability to give wise advice.

Invite a student to read **Proverbs 1:8–9** aloud. Ask students what two people God's Word says they should listen to. (**father and mother**) Show students an ORNATE PIECE OF JEWELRY. Explain that these Bible verses teach that the counsel and teaching of their parents are like fine jewelry and make life more beautiful and abundant. Select a volunteer to read or recite **Proverbs 19:20**, the Memory Verse. Discuss what happens when a person is willing to listen to advice or counsel and accept discipline or receive instruction. (**The person will be wise, or considered wise, when he or she is older.**)

Student Page 19.2

Direct students to complete the page. Afterward, lead students in a prayer asking God to give them wisdom as to whose advice they should follow.

Review

- What does *wisdom* mean? (**using what you know in the best way**)
- How did Esther show that she believed the advice from both Mordecai and Hegai was wise? (**Esther immediately acted upon the different pieces of advice.**)
- Name some ways you can determine whose advice to listen to. (**Pray, consider whether the person has given good or bad advice in the past, consider the person's age, and consider whether the person is loyal to God and believes in and follows His leading.**)
- Whose teaching does the Bible say you should follow? (**my father's and my mother's**)
- What happens when you are willing to listen to and accept good advice? (**I will be wise, or considered wise, when I am older.**)

APPLICATION

- Who are some wise advisers or counselors in your life? (**Answers will vary.**)
- Are you quick to listen to and obey the teachings and instructions of your parents? (**Answers will vary.**)
- Do you follow wise advice, or do you try to do things your way? (**Answers will vary.**)
- How can you display loyalty to others who need wise advice? (**Answers will vary but should include that I can pray for wisdom to give wise advice.**)

REINFORCEMENT

God created everything with wisdom (Psalm 104:24–26, 136:4–9). In Hebrew, the word for *wisdom* is *chakam,* and in Greek, wisdom is expressed by the words *sophia* and *phronesis. Sophia* refers to *philosophical insight into the true nature of things, the concept of knowing right from wrong. Phronesis* means *the practicality of acting rightly or wrongly.*

The Bible states that wisdom begins with the *fear of the Lord* (Job 28:28, Psalm 111:10, Proverbs 9:10). The righteous and humble are blessed with wisdom (Proverbs 2:7, 11:2), which in turn produces kindness (Proverbs 31:26). Solomon gained worldwide acclaim for the great wisdom God gave him (1 Kings 4:29–34), and even today, his legendary wisdom is known throughout the world. But Jesus' wisdom was far greater than Solomon's (Matthew 12:42). When the apostle Paul prayed for the Ephesian believers, he boldly and affectionately asked God to give them the spirit of wisdom and revelation to know Him better (Ephesians 1:17).

DAY 2

19.2 Esther Listens to Wise Advice

1. Look up wisdom in the Glossary. Write the definition.

wisdom: ___using what you know in the best way___

Read Proverbs 1:8–9 to help you answer Exercises 2–3.

2. Name two people who can give you good advice.

my ___Answers will vary.___ and my ___Answers will vary.___

3. Follow their advice and teaching. When you do, it will be like you are wearing fine jewelry. What are the two pieces of jewelry mentioned in the verses? Circle them.

Fill in the circle next to the word that best completes each sentence.

4. If you listen to good advice and follow it, then you will be ___.

○ lied to ● wise ○ tricked

5. You should ___ if you want wisdom.

○ walk ○ sleep ● pray

74

19.3 Esther Listens to Wise Advice

Focus: Wisdom's Rewards

⟳ EXTENSION

3A Draw a vertical line down the center of the board. On the left side write *Wise Advice,* and on the right side write *Rewards.* Ask students to think of some wise advice their parents, other adults, or dependable friends have given them. Invite students to share the advice and the reward or protection that followed. Write responses on the corresponding sections of the board. Use the following examples if students have difficulty beginning this activity:

• *Wise Advice*: Wear boots and a raincoat when it is raining. *Rewards*: Staying dry and warm.

• *Wise Advice*: Listen to God's Word. *Rewards*: Learning to be like Christ.

Introduction

Read **Psalm 1**. Discuss with students that the friends they choose can influence their decisions. A child of God is to live in a distinct way, set apart from the world. Write the following acronym on the board, describing the attributes of a person who has wisdom:

W onders what is best
I s intelligent
S eeks God
D oes what is right
O beys and is humble
M editates on God's Word

Directed Instruction ⟲

Remind students that Esther knew that Mordecai was wise and followed God's ways. Out of loyalty to Mordecai, she followed his advice. In doing this, he received a reward—his name was written in the king's record book.

Read the following to students:

> There was once a young prince whose father left him his kingdom. The prince did not know what to do, so he prayed. One night, God came to the king and told him He would give the king anything he asked for. The king realized that he didn't even have enough wisdom to ask for the right thing, so he decided to ask for wisdom itself. God was very pleased. He granted his request and made him the wisest man on Earth. In fact, God was so pleased that He gave the king wealth, popularity, and power, too.
>
> When another young man became king, he was also scared and didn't know what to do. The young king decided to seek the advice of his father's advisers. These men were wise and had given his father good counsel in the past. They told the young king that he should be kind to the people so that his kingdom would grow. The young king did not like this advice, so he asked his friends what he should do. His friends said that he should be cruel and demand more work from the people. The king liked this advice. But when he followed it, the people became angry. They rebelled, and the king lost most of his kingdom.

Explain that the two kings are Solomon and his son Rehoboam (1 Kings 3:1–15, 12:1–24). Share that Solomon showed wisdom because he prayed and asked God for help. As a result, he received wisdom as well as wealth, popularity, and power. Discuss how the other king, Rehoboam, received good counsel at first, but he did not follow it. He then acted foolishly, which made everyone angry, and he lost almost all of his kingdom. Explain to students that wisdom and foolishness have rewards and consequences. Students may not gain great wealth or lose a kingdom as a result of their wise or foolish choices, but they will often experience positive outcomes when they heed wise advice, and great negative consequences when they listen to foolish advice. Explain to students that when they ask God for wisdom, He will make them wise as they follow His guidance.

Chorally read **Proverbs 8:32–35**. Explain to students that *blessed* can mean *happy*. Discuss how following instruction and wise advice could make someone happy. (**Answers will vary.**) Note that Esther was blessed as she found favor in the eyes of King Ahasuerus. Ask students what other rewards will be given to a wise person. (**They will enjoy life more and obtain or receive God's favor.**)

Student Page 19.3
Read the directions and assist students in completing the page.

Review
- Name some attributes of a person who has wisdom. (**Possible answers: intelligent, does what is right, obedient, humble, makes good choices**)
- What does *blessed* mean? (**happy**)
- What are some results of living in wisdom? (**Possible answers: being happy, obtaining or receiving God's favor, enjoying life more**)

APPLICATION
- Think of a time when you or a friend listened to wise advice. What was the result? (**Answers will vary.**)
- Think of a time when you or a friend did not listen to wise advice. What was the result? (**Answers will vary.**)
- Contrast Esther and Rehoboam. (**Possible answers: Esther listened to and followed an older, wiser person's advice, but Rehoboam did not follow advice from his father's older and wiser advisers; Esther remained loyal to Mordecai; Rehoboam became disloyal to his father's advisers.**)

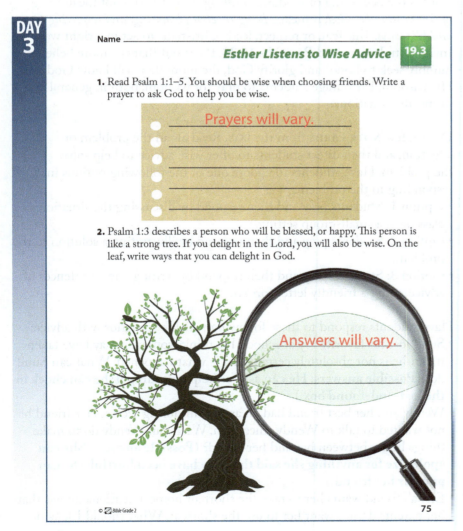

19.4 Esther Listens to Wise Advice
Focus: Giving Wise Advice

★ PREPARATION
Have **DM-11 Advice Alphabet** and a COIN available. (*Introduction*)

Write on NOTE CARDS some typical problems that second graders might face, and then place the cards in a BOX. (*Directed Instruction*)

⤴ EXTENSION
4A Give each student a piece of construction paper. Instruct them to write a statement of good advice or wisdom that a parent, teacher, family member, friend, or classmate has shared with them. Have students to illustrate their page of advice. Bind the finished pages into a class book titled *The Book of Good Advice*.

Introduction ★
Display **DM-11 Advice Alphabet** and select students to read each letter of advice. Show students a COIN. Ask how many sides the coin has. (**two**) Explain that just as a coin has two sides, wisdom also has two sides. The first "side" of wisdom is to know what is true and right. The second "side" of wisdom is to know what needs to be done.

Directed Instruction ★ ⤴
Explain that because of Mordecai's loyalty to God, Mordecai knew what was true and right. He knew what needed to be done—telling Esther to protect her family background and to warn the king of the evil plan against him. And, out of loyalty to Mordecai, Esther listened to his wise advice.

Direct students to think about whether wisdom is something everyone has. Ask if some people are born with wisdom, and if someone can grow in wisdom. (**Answers will vary but should include that not everyone is born wise, but everyone can grow in wisdom.**) Read **Psalm 111:10** and **Proverbs 9:10**. Explain that the Old Testament says that "the fear of the Lord is the beginning of wisdom." *Fearing the Lord* does not mean *being afraid or scared of God*; it means *being reverent, honoring, and respecting God and His ways*. This fear, or respect, leads Christians to act in a right way. Invite a student to read **Proverbs 15:33**. Point out that the more believers humbly seek to honor and glorify God, the more they will know God and His wisdom. Encourage students to pray for wisdom, both in general and in specific situations.

Draw a few NOTE CARDS from the BOX. Read aloud the problem or situation, and then direct students to offer wise advice to help solve the problem. Have students to choose one of the following options in responding to the problems:
- Option 1: Students pray and then respond by discussing the situation as a class or in a small-group setting.
- Option 2: Students pray and then respond by illustrating a solution to the problem.
- Option 3: Students pray and then respond by writing a few sentences of advice, using a friendly letter format.

Have students respond to these following real-life scenarios with advice:
- Sunil lost his favorite toy at school. He thinks someone may have taken it, but he is not absolutely certain that is what happened. What can Sunil do? (**Possible answers: He can ask for help in finding it; he can check in the lost-and-found box.**)
- Wendy and her best friend had an argument during recess. Her friend has not wanted to talk to Wendy since then. What can Wendy do to make things better between her and her friend? (**Possible answers: She can apologize for anything she said that may have been hurtful; she can pray for her friend.**)
- Elena's friend wants her to take the shortcut home, but Elena knows that her parents do not want her to use the shortcut. What should Elena do?

(**Possible answers: She can try to convince her friend to take the usual way home; she can obey her parents out of loyalty, love, and respect for them, no matter what other people want her to do.**)

Student Page 19.4
Have students complete the page.

Review
- What are the two sides of wisdom? (**knowing what is true and right, knowing what needs to be done**)
- Were you born with wisdom? (**No, but I can grow in wisdom by honoring and respecting God and His ways, and asking Him for wisdom.**)
- In giving advice, how can you show loyalty to someone? (**I should pray and ask God for the wisdom that is needed.**)
- Who was Mordecai loyal to? (**God**)

Notes:

APPLICATION
- Think of someone you could give good advice to. Pray and ask God to give you the wisdom to do so.

DAY 4

19.4 Esther Listens to Wise Advice

Read each situation below. Fill in the circle next to the advice that you would give to help the person. You may choose more than one piece of advice.

1. Kurt is not enjoying school. Some students have been laughing at him. Kurt wants them to stop. What should he do?
   - ● Kurt could pray about the situation.
   - ○ Kurt could tell lies about the students to get even.
   - ● Kurt could ask an adult to help.
   - ● Kurt could talk to the students and ask them to be nice.

2. Hong's best friend, Tai, moved away. Hong misses playing soccer with his friend. He feels alone. What should he do?
   - ○ Hong could call Tai to talk, without his parents' permission.
   - ● Hong could sit down and write a letter or e-mail to Tai.
   - ○ Hong could refuse to be friendly and remain alone.
   - ● Hong could pray and ask God to help him be friends with other teammates.

3. Unscramble the letters to complete the sentence.

I should _____pray_____ to God and ask Him for daily wisdom.

19.5 Esther Listens to Wise Advice

Focus: Review and Assessment

★ PREPARATION

Select **VA 19A Esther Listens to Wise Advice**. (*Lesson Review*)

Print **BLM 19A Lesson 19 Test** for each student. (*Directed Instruction*)

Lesson Review ★

Use **VA 19A Esther Listens to Wise Advice** to review the Bible truth. Cover the following concepts:

- Esther was given three pieces of advice: to not tell anyone about her Jewish family background, to follow Hegai's instructions to prepare for the king, to tell the king of the evil plot to kill him.
- Esther responded to the advice she received by following it.
- Esther followed the counsel she received because she trusted and respected Mordecai and the king's servant.
- Esther was loyal to Mordecai and responded to him in obedience, humility, and submission.
- *Loyalty* means *the character trait of showing faithfulness and devotion to someone or something.*
- *Submission* means *the act of accepting the authority or decision of someone else.*
- *Wisdom* means *using what you know in the best way.*
- If people are willing to listen to good advice, they will be wise, or considered wise, when they are older.
- God's Word says to follow the instruction of one's father and mother.
- Attributes of a person with wisdom:
  - **W** onders what is best
  - **I** s intelligent
  - **S** eeks God
  - **D** oes what is right
  - **O** beys and is humble
  - **M** editates on God's Word
- The Bible says that people are blessed, or happy, when they listen to and follow wise advice.
- Another reward of living in wisdom is receiving God's favor.
- The two sides of wisdom are to know what is true and right, and to know what needs to be done.
- A Christian should love, honor, and respect God and His ways, and pray and ask God for wisdom in all things.

Directed Instruction ★

Distribute a copy of **BLM 19A Lesson 19 Test** to each student. Have students complete the test. When they have finished, read over the test, providing the answers for immediate feedback.

Notes:

Lesson Preparation
Esther Is Unselfish — 20.0

Expected Student Outcomes

KNOW
Esther unselfishly risks her life to save God's people.

DO
Students will:
- choose ways to be unselfish
- compare and contrast Mordecai and Haman's actions
- identify three key words to help them remember the joy of putting others first
- write about a friend who is kind
- order events in Esther's life

APPLY
Students will explore and put into practice ways to act unselfishly.

Lesson Outline
I. Esther shows unselfishness and resolve (Esth 3–5, Phil 2:3–4, Jn 3:16)
II. Mordecai is rewarded (Esth 6–10, Mt 16:27)
III. Honor God and others first (Mt 7:12, Jn 13:34)
IV. Prepared by God (Rom 8:28–29, James 1:2–3, Esth 4:14)

♥ TEACHER'S HEART
You might be sitting at your desk at this moment wondering if all the time you have spent planning and preparing lessons these past few weeks is really making a difference for your students. It may seem that the time spent behind the scenes doesn't matter to anybody. Be assured that your commitment and expenditure of time are making a difference! It may not be measurable at this moment, but valuable seeds are being planted in the lives of your students. Galatians 6:9 reminds you to be patient and not become weary in performing your duties because in time you will see the results of your labor. Most importantly, be reminded that everything done for Christ does matter and will be rewarded in His time.

As Esther gave up her own concerns and acted to help save others, you too can put aside your concerns and tend to the matter of showing students how they can be saved through Jesus Christ. You can go before King Jesus, and know He will listen as you intercede on your students' behalf. As you are integrating God into every part of your lessons, know you are doing something that really matters.

Supplemental Materials are available to download. See Understanding Purposeful Design Bible at the front of this book for the Grade 2 URL.

MEMORY VERSE
Philippians 2:4

GLOSSARY WORDS
- unselfish
- resolve
- patience

★ MATERIALS
Day 1:
- VA 20A Esther Risks Her Life
- Money (*Extension*)

Day 2:
- Trophy, ribbon, certificate, or medal
- BLM 20A Mordecai Reward (*Extension*)
- Love Bowl from Lesson 11.4 (*Extension*)

Day 3:
- No additional materials are needed.

Day 4:
- BLM 20B My Life Time Line (*Extension*)

Day 5:
- VA 20A Esther Risks Her Life
- BLM 20C Lesson 20 Test

♪ SONGS
Books of the Bible (*Extension*)
All Things Work Together

TEACHER RESOURCES
A Walk Thru the Book of Esther: Courage in the Face of Crisis. Baker Books, 2010.
Rigby, Jill. *Raising Unselfish Children in a Self-Absorbed World.* Howard Books, 2008.

STUDENT RESOURCES
Pulley, Kelly. *Queen Esther Helps God's People.* Zonderkidz, 2008.

© Bible Grade 2   191

20.1 Esther Is Unselfish
Focus: Esther Shows Unselfishness and Resolve

MEMORY VERSE
Philippians 2:4

MEMORY WORK
- Practice a Sword Drill, calling out the Memory Verse reference and seeing how quickly students can locate the verse in their Bible. Tell the student who finds the verse first to stand. As a reward, invite this student to the front of the room to lead the other students in reciting the Memory Verse. Repeat the activity several times.

★ PREPARATION
Select **VA 20A Esther Risks Her Life**. (*Directed Instruction*)

EXTENSION
1A Read **Matthew 25:14–29**, where the parable of the talents is mentioned. Explain that a *talent* is defined as *an ancient monetary unit that was worth about $1,000*. Today, a *talent* is *an ability that God has given someone to do well*. The parable, or story, Jesus told teaches that people should use the gifts and abilities God has given them in wise ways. Encourage students to use the talent God has given them to benefit others. Point out that putting others first will draw students into a closer relationship with God. Give each student a SMALL AMOUNT OF MONEY and challenge them to multiply it. Discuss ideas that might work, such as buying ingredients for cookies to bake and sell or buying supplies for a car wash. Designate a date for students to bring the multiplied money back to class. Together, decide upon a ministry to donate the money to, demonstrating the act of living unselfishly.

Introduction
Point out that selfish people tend to think only of themselves and ignore the feelings or needs of others. Explain that when someone is **unselfish**, or shows selflessness, it means *showing concern for others more than oneself*. An unselfish person thinks about the needs of others more than his or her own.

Directed Instruction ★
Divide the class into four groups so that each group represents one of the following people: Esther, King Ahasuerus, Haman, and Mordecai. Tell students that you are going to read about each of these people in the Bible truth and they are to make the following motions when they hear the name of the person that their group represents. Read **VA 20A Esther Risks Her Life** and guide students to make the corresponding motions:
- Group 1: place a crown on their head each time they hear *Esther*
- Group 2: hold an imaginary scepter high each time they hear *king*
- Group 3: shake their fist when they hear *Haman*
- Group 4: clasp their hands when they hear *Mordecai*

Explain that Haman was a very proud and selfish person. He liked being powerful and making people bow down before him. He thought only of himself and not about the welfare of the Jews. He asked the king to write a law that would kill all the Jewish people for not obeying the customs and laws of the king. He had no idea that Queen Esther was Jewish, because she had kept it secret. The king gave Haman his signet ring to stamp the wax so that the law could not be changed.

When Esther heard about Haman's evil plan, she wanted to help the Jews. But the king had not asked to see her for a whole month! She knew that if she went to the king without an invitation, he could have her killed. Fear or selfishness could have kept Esther from acting on behalf of her people. But Esther showed **resolve**, which means *a determination to do or not do something*. She trusted Mordecai's advice to act and not miss out on the privilege to do what God wanted her to do. He reminded her that she, too would die if she did nothing. She resolved to be courageous and unselfish, risking her own life to help her people. Through Esther, God delivered His people from certain death.

Explain to students that they can choose to be selfish like Haman or unselfish like Esther. Read **Philippians 2:3–4** and discuss how a child of God can live unselfishly, valuing others above himself or herself. Encourage students to show resolve to be unselfish at all times. Read **John 3:16**. Remind students that Jesus showed the greatest unselfishness by putting their need for a savior ahead of Himself, and giving His life for them.

Divide the class into two groups. Assign one of the following scenarios to each group. Ask the groups to discuss unselfish ways to solve the problem and then share their ideas with the other group.
- At a class party, one of the cupcakes falls on the floor. Now there are not enough cupcakes for everyone. What can be done? (**Answers will vary.**)

- On a special day at school, students are invited to honor their grandparents. Some students do not have any grandparents, and they feel embarrassed and sad. What can be done? (**Answers will vary.**)

Student Page 20.1
Have students independently complete the page.

Review

- How was Haman proud and selfish? (**Haman liked that people bowed down to him and praised him.**)
- What would have happened if Esther had not been courageous or had chosen to be selfish? (**The Jewish people would have died, God would have chosen someone else to save His people.**)
- What does it mean to be unselfish? (**showing concern for others more than oneself**)
- Why did Esther choose to be unselfish? (**Possible answers: She placed her security in God; she cared more about others than herself.**)
- What does it mean to show resolve? (**to have a determination to do or not do something**)

APPLICATION

- What do you learn when you compare the way Haman acted with the way Esther acted? (**Haman's selfishness caused trouble and hardship; Esther's resolve and unselfishness helped others.**)
- What do you think others would learn from the way you act? (**Answers will vary.**)
- What is an unselfish thing someone has done for you? (**Answers will vary.**)
- Name some things you can do to show selflessness toward others. (**Answers will vary.**)

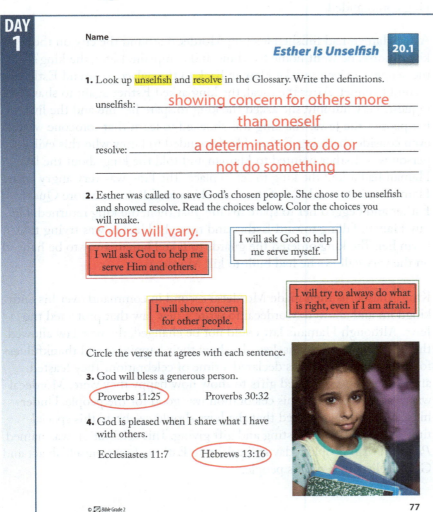

20.2 Esther Is Unselfish
Focus: Mordecai Is Rewarded

★ PREPARATION
Have a TROPHY, RIBBON, CERTIFICATE, or MEDAL available. (*Introduction*)

☞ EXTENSION
2A Print **BLM 20A Mordecai Reward** for students as needed. In the spirit of Purim, a Jewish celebration that Mordecai established as a law, plan a surprise celebration to reward students in your class who practice obedience in these areas: selflessness, wise leadership, and patience. Challenge students to practice unselfishness by looking for other students to whom you could give a Mordecai Reward.

2B To review the characteristics of godly love, invite students to select and read a card from the LOVE BOWL introduced in Lesson 11.4.

2C Use the song "Books of the Bible" from the Grade 2 URL to review the books of the Old and New Testaments.

Introduction ★
Display a TROPHY, RIBBON, CERTIFICATE, or MEDAL. Ask students to share about a time when they received a reward. (**Answers will vary.**) Discuss why rewards are given. In today's lesson, students will hear how Mordecai was rewarded.

Directed Instruction ☞
Read the following from Esther 6–10 to the students:

After Queen Esther's first banquet, the king could not sleep. So he asked his servant to read his record book to him. When the servant read the part about Mordecai saving the king's life, King Ahasuerus realized that nothing had been done to reward Mordecai for his good deed. So the king called for Haman and asked him to think of a special reward for someone he wanted to honor. Haman assumed that he was the person the king wanted to honor, so he proposed a fine reward: Dress the one being honored in royal robes, place him on one of the king's horses, and lead him around the city, announcing to everyone how honorable he was. The king was pleased with the idea and ordered Haman to do everything he had suggested for Mordecai. Haman was humiliated but did as the king commanded.

After Haman had finished leading Mordecai around the city on the king's horse, he went home to whine and complain. Later, the king's messengers arrived to take Haman back to the palace to attend Esther's second banquet. After the meal, the king asked Esther again to share her request. Very humbly, she asked the king to spare her life and the lives of her people, the Jews. The king was shocked to learn that someone would even consider harming Esther. He demanded to know who this evil person was. Esther pointed to Haman and told the king about the law Haman had asked the king to set in place. The king was very angry with Haman and stormed out of the room. Haman fell down before Queen Esther and begged her to spare his life. Just then, the king returned. He saw Haman falling toward Esther and thought Haman was trying to harm her. The king ordered the guards to take Haman away to be hanged on the very gallows he had built to kill Mordecai.

King Ahasuerus then made Mordecai second in command over his entire kingdom and allowed Mordecai to write a new law that protected the Jews. Although Haman's law could not be changed, the new law allowed the Jews to defend themselves. To show their happiness and thankfulness for the new law, the Jews declared a time of celebration. They feasted, and some even exchanged gifts to show how happy they were. Mordecai was wise and saw that this celebration was good for the people. Under his leadership, he declared that the Jews should celebrate this special time every year with feasting and gift giving. This celebration was named *Purim.* Jewish people today still celebrate Esther's brave, unselfish act and God's deliverance of His people.

Point out to students the differences between Mordecai and Haman by noting the following:
- Mordecai was humble and did what was right in God's eyes.
- Haman was proud and expected others to recognize and reward him.

Read **Matthew 16:27**. Explain to students that God sees who follows Him and will reward each person in His own way and time. God allowed Mordecai to be honored for his choices to follow and obey Him.

Student Page 20.2
Have students work in pairs to complete the page.

Review
- Who did Haman think should be rewarded? (**himself**)
- Whom did King Ahasuerus want to honor? (**Mordecai**)
- How was Mordecai rewarded? (**The king made him second in command and allowed Mordecai to write a new law protecting the Jews.**)
- What is the celebration of this new, protective law for the Jews called, which commemorates the deliverance of the Jewish people? (**Purim**)

APPLICATION
- If you were King Ahasuerus, or Xerxes, whom would you have wanted to reward? Why? (**Answers will vary.**)
- Whom does Jesus, your King, choose to reward? (**those who humbly follow Him**)
- Why is it more important to humbly follow God than to look for rewards? (**I should do things not to be recognized or rewarded but because I love God.**)

REINFORCEMENT
The celebration of Purim, commemorating God's deliverance of the Jewish people in Queen Esther's time, is still one of the most joyous holidays on the Jewish calendar, celebrated in February or March each year. Mordecai proclaimed Purim as a time of feasting and gladness. On this day, people exchanged delicacies and also gave gifts to the poor (Esther 9:22). During Purim celebrations today, participants also wear costumes and listen to a traditional reading of the book of Esther. The word *purim* means *lots*, which refers to the lots Haman cast to determine the day when the Jewish people would be put to death (Esther 9:24–26). Before celebrating Purim, Jews observe a fast—the Fast of Esther—in remembrance of the three-day fast Queen Esther and the Jewish people held before her audience with King Ahasuerus.

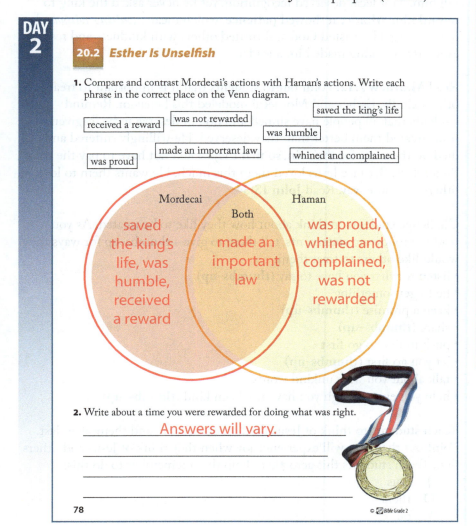

20.3 Esther Is Unselfish

Focus: Honor God and Others First

↻ EXTENSION

3A Have students sacrifice a recess period to put the needs of someone else first. Some suggestions include cleaning classrooms, planning a surprise, supervising younger kids on the playground, helping someone study for a test, or writing an encouraging note to someone.

3B Choose students to play the different roles in the Bible truth from Luke 10:25–37, the parable of the good Samaritan. Narrate as students act out the Scripture verses. Challenge students to think about ways the Good Samaritan was thinking about others more than himself.

Introduction

Allow students to chat quietly in small groups. Walk around the room and interrupt conversations by talking loudly and changing the subject. Do this several times until you have everyone's attention. Ask students if something like this has ever happened to them. Discuss how it feels to be treated poorly. (**Possible answers: frustrating, sad, lonely**)

Directed Instruction ↻

Esther and Mordecai knew how to treat others because they knew how God treated people, and they wanted to do the same. Esther put God first by honoring Him in all she did. She also honored others, like Mordecai, by following his advice and going before the king, even though saving her people seemed impossible. Esther put the Jewish people first even though she knew she might be killed. She showed what she believed by her actions.

Mordecai put God first no matter what the cost. He showed wisdom and did not bow down to anyone but God. Mordecai put others first by refusing to say bad things about Haman, even though Haman wanted to kill him. Mordecai deserved recognition, yet he never asked the king to reward him. Mordecai showed **patience**, which means *waiting without complaining*. He trusted God and treated others with kindness and respect, even after the king made him a leader.

Read **Matthew 7:12**. Point out to students that it is important to treat others kindly. Esther and Mordecai modeled this behavior. Remind students that all people have sinned and do not deserve to be forgiven. Jesus treated them better than they deserved. He willingly suffered and died on the cross for their sin, so that they would not have to pay the price themselves. Because Jesus loved them this much, He wants them to love others the same way. Read **John 13:34**.

Challenge students to think about how they like to be treated. As you read the following statements, tell them to give a thumbs-up for ways they would like others to treat them:
- listen to what you have to say (**thumbs-up**)
- lie to get something
- keep a promise (**thumbs-up**)
- share (**thumbs-up**)
- push in line to go first
- let you go first (**thumbs-up**)
- talk about you with unkind words
- help you even though you have not been kind (**thumbs-up**)

Teach students to think of Jesus first, others second, and themselves last. Point out that they will experience joy when they think of Jesus and others first. Teach students this acrostic to help them remember to do this:

J esus
O thers
Y ou

Student Page 20.3

Direct students to complete the page. Look for opportunities to pray with students about treating others the same way they would want to be treated.

Review

- How did Esther and Mordecai treat others? (**They thought of others more than themselves.**)
- What does *patience* mean? (**waiting without complaining**)
- In what way did Jesus treat you better than you deserve? (**Even though I am a sinner, He died on the cross for me.**)

Notes:

APPLICATION

- In what ways can you show patience toward others? (**Answers will vary.**)
- Name some ways you can honor God and others first. (**Answers will vary.**)

DAY 3

Name _____

Esther Is Unselfish   **20.3**

1. Look up **patience** in the Glossary. Write the definition.

patience: _____ waiting without complaining _____

_____

2. Joy comes when you think of Jesus and others before yourself. Fill in the lines to remember how to think first about others.

Jesus _____   **O**thers _____   **Y**ou _____

3. Read Ephesians 4:32. Simon, age 8, wrote a devotion to tell how two children brought him joy. Read his devotion:

> Have you ever wanted new friends? One day at school, I made two new friends. They were very kind to me. They thought of me before themselves. They played nicely, shared their lunches with me, and even invited me to the movies! We had fun spending time together. They both reminded me that when we treat others kindly, it brings joy!

Write about a friend who treats you kindly.

Answers will vary.

© *Bible Grade 2*

79

© *Bible Grade 2*

20.4 Esther Is Unselfish

Focus: Prepared by God

★ PREPARATION

Select the song "All Things Work Together" from the Grade 2 URL. (*Introduction*)

⤾ EXTENSION

4A Copy **BLM 20B My Life Time Line** for each student and distribute the copies. For an example of what they are to do, share events that have happened chronologically in your life. Tell students to complete the activity. Remind students that God has a purpose for everything that has happened in their life. Encourage them to look back on these events and realize God's protection and leading in their life.

4B Instruct students to write a journal entry describing ways they have seen God's hand at work in their life or have them describe a situation in which they do not understand why certain events or situations are occurring, but how they are trusting God in the meantime.

Introduction ★

Ask students to write briefly about a problem they have faced in the past or are currently facing. Collect the papers and read them silently. Then take some time to pray aloud for students, making sure to respect their privacy. Explain to students that they will face many difficult events in life, but the Lord will uphold them, use each experience to help them grow, and prepare them to help others, if they let Him. Read **Romans 8:28–29**. Discuss how God can make all things work out for good, but remind students that God's promise is for those who belong to Him and love Him. When students give themselves wholeheartedly to God, He promises to work out everything for the best, no matter how hopeless things may appear. Trusting that He will do this is part of being a child of God.

Sing the song "All Things Work Together" from the Grade 2 URL.

Directed Instruction ⌒

Remind students that *patience* means *waiting without complaining*. Read **James 1:2–3**. Tell students that trials, or problems, are tests of faith, and these trials can produce patience in their life. Esther's life was not easy, but God worked through every circumstance to prepare her for what He called her to do. The events in her life brought her to a time and place—"such a time as this"—when God used her to save her people. Read **Esther 4:14**.

Review the following events that show how God prepared Esther, placed her in specific situations for His glory, taught His people patience in their trials, and caused all things to work together for good:

- Esther's parents died when she was young, so her relative Mordecai adopted her and raised her. God chose Mordecai to care for Esther, and she became a beautiful young lady.
- When Queen Vashti disobeyed King Ahasuerus, he decided to select a new wife as queen. Esther was chosen to go before the king, but Mordecai told her not to reveal her Jewish family background. Esther did as Mordecai told her because she respected him and was loyal to him. God worked in the king's heart to select Esther and make her queen.
- Mordecai was sitting near the king's gate one day and happened to hear two guards making plans to kill King Ahasuerus. Mordecai sent a message to Queen Esther, and she told the king about this evil plan. God used Mordecai and Esther to save the king's life.
- Mordecai refused to bow down to Haman, one of the king's officials, and this made Haman very angry. Haman discovered that Mordecai was Jewish and that Jewish people only worshipped God. Haman convinced the king to set up a law to kill all of the Jewish people. When Mordecai heard about Haman's evil plan, he was very upset and sent word to Esther. Esther chose to show resolve and unselfishness. She risked her life to help her people. God used Esther to deliver His people from death.

The events in Esther's life—losing her parents as a child, being raised by Mordecai, hiding her Jewish family background, becoming the wife of a foreign king, and risking her life for her people—did not prevent God from using her in mighty ways.

Point out to students that just as God prepared Esther, so He is preparing them for what He wants them to do. God knows the beginning, the middle, and the end of their life. He brings people and events into their life at just the right time.

Student Page 20.4
Have students work in collaborative pairs or trios to complete the page.

Review
- What can trials in your life produce in you (James 1:2–3)? (**patience**)
- Who adopted Esther when she was young? (**Mordecai**)
- How did Esther become queen? (**Queen Vashti disobeyed the king, so he chose Esther as his new queen.**)
- What were the events in Esther's life preparing her for? (**to save the Jewish people**)

APPLICATION
- Which difficult events in Esther's life did God use for good? (**Possible answers: losing her parents and then being adopted by Mordecai, learning about Haman's plan to kill the Jews, risking her life to go before the king**)
- What was the importance of God's timing in Esther's life? (**Everything that happened in her life led up to her becoming queen and helping the Jews.**)
- How do you know that God has a good purpose for your life? (**Answers may vary but should include that His Word tells me so.**)
- How can God use what has happened in your life to help others? (**Answers will vary.**)

REINFORCEMENT
Ahasuerus is the Hebrew name for the king of Persia; *Xerxes* is the Greek name. King Ahasuerus died 13 years after Esther became queen. When Esther approached the king to intercede on behalf of her people, she had been queen five years. Even after all this time, Esther still intrigued the king, and he responded favorably to her request to speak with him. It was no coincidence that God had prepared Esther "for such a time as this" (Esther 4:14) and had placed her in a position of influence and authority.

God also placed another queen, King Belshazzar's wife, in a position of influence at just the right time. When she learned that the king's advisers could not interpret the strange writing on the wall, she told the king about Daniel's gifts of interpretation. The king listened to his wife and summoned Daniel, who interpreted the message from God (Daniel 5:10–17).

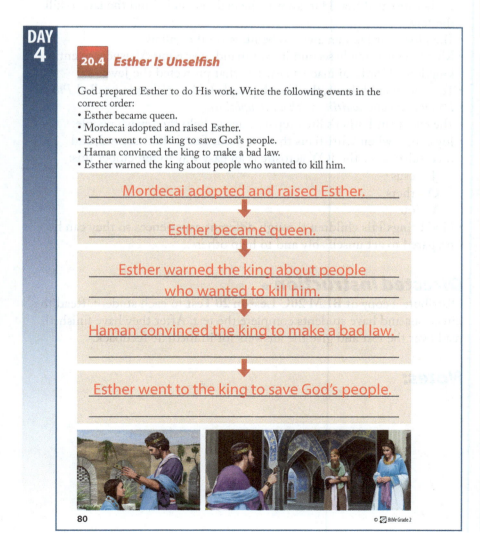

DAY 4

20.4 Esther Is Unselfish

God prepared Esther to do His work. Write the following events in the correct order:
- Esther became queen.
- Mordecai adopted and raised Esther.
- Esther went to the king to save God's people.
- Haman convinced the king to make a bad law.
- Esther warned the king about people who wanted to kill him.

Mordecai adopted and raised Esther.
↓
Esther became queen.
↓
Esther warned the king about people who wanted to kill him.
↓
Haman convinced the king to make a bad law.
↓
Esther went to the king to save God's people.

20.5 Esther Is Unselfish

Focus: Review and Assessment

★ PREPARATION

Select **VA 20A Esther Risks Her Life**. (*Lesson Review*)

Copy **BLM 20C Lesson 20 Test** for each student. (*Directed Instruction*)

Lesson Review ★

Use **VA 20A Esther Risks Her Life** to review the Bible truth. Cover the following concepts:

- King Ahasuerus had many advisers. He looked to Haman for advice even though Haman was proud and selfish.
- Haman was angry with Mordecai because Mordecai did not bow down to him. When Haman discovered that Mordecai was Jewish, he convinced the king to put a law in place to have the Jews killed for not obeying the king's customs and laws.
- Mordecai did what was right in God's eyes. Haman was proud and expected others to bow down to and honor him.
- The king rewarded Mordecai for protecting him from being murdered.
- To be *unselfish* means *showing concern for others more than oneself*.
- *Resolve* is defined as *a determination to do or not do something*.
- Esther acted unselfishly, showed resolve, and risked her life by going before the king to plead for the lives of her people.
- The king listened to Esther and honored her request. Through Esther, God delivered His chosen people.
- Esther revealed that Haman was the evil person behind the law to kill the Jews.
- The king sent Haman away to be hung on the gallows.
- Mordecai was made second in command over King Ahasuerus's entire kingdom. Mordecai made a new law that protected the Jews.
- To show thankfulness, the Jewish people had a celebration called *Purim*.
- *Patience* means *waiting without complaining*.
- The events in Esther's life prepared her to help the Jewish people.
- Joy comes when Christians think of Jesus first, others second, and themselves last. The JOY acrostic is an easy way to remember this:
    - **J** esus
    - **O** thers
    - **Y** ou
- God brings His children through different experiences so they can be prepared to act unselfishly and to help others.

Directed Instruction ★

Distribute a copy of **BLM 20C Lesson 20 Test** to each student. Read the directions and have students complete the test. After they have finished, read over the test and give the answers for immediate feedback.

Notes:

Lesson Preparation
Job Is Patient — 21.0

Expected Student Outcomes

KNOW
Job is patient in the face of adversity.

DO
Students will:
- sequence the events in the Bible truth about Job
- exemplify how they can show patience in various situations
- identify ways words can be powerful
- mark graphs to rate how patiently they wait for things

APPLY
Students will demonstrate patience.

Lesson Outline
I. Patience defined (Job 1–2, 42)
II. Patience shown (James 5:7–11)
III. Patiently control your words (Job 1:20–22, 42:1–6; James 3:5–6)
IV. Eagerly waiting (Jn 14:1–4, Rev 21)

❤ TEACHER'S HEART

Today, Western society seems to prize efficiency, speed, and productivity over everything else. Microwaves and fast-food restaurants focus on immediate gratification, and mealtimes are no longer a leisurely affair. Waiting in line or in traffic can bring out the worst in people. If people must wait in line longer than a few minutes, they begin to shift their weight, look at their watches, roll their eyes, make snide comments, and even be rude to the sales staff. People don't like to wait.

The Bible, however, emphasizes patience. In fact, few of God's promises were fulfilled immediately. Abraham had to wait more than 20 years to receive his promised son. Moses waited 40 years to be ready for leadership, and another 40 years to catch a glimpse of the much-awaited Promised Land. Jacob worked 14 years to fulfill an agreement he made to marry the woman he loved. Even the apostle Paul waited 3 years after his conversion before he spoke to anyone about the gospel. The early Church waited eagerly for Christ's return, and 2,000 years later, believers are still waiting. God values patience. It is through patient endurance that the promises of God are fulfilled. He wants His people to wait on Him without complaining, to endure hardships, and to persevere as Job did.

What are you patiently enduring today? How can you model patience for your students so that they will be able to see God at work in your life? Endure patiently, and expect to see God guiding, sustaining, and bringing victory in your life and in your classroom!

📖 MEMORY VERSE
Ephesians 4:2

GLOSSARY WORDS
- repentance

⭐ MATERIALS

Day 1:
- Sidewalk chalk
- DM-1 Character Traits
- VA 21A Job Is Patient
- BLM 21A Patience Scenarios
- Poster board (*Extension*)

Day 2:
- Apple, knife
- Bean seeds, jars, cotton (*Extension*)
- BLM 21B Apple Tree (*Extension*)

Day 3:
- No additional materials are needed.

Day 4:
- BLM 21C Letter to Jesus (*Extension*)

Day 5:
- VA 21A Job Is Patient
- BLM 21D Lesson 21 Test

TEACHER RESOURCES
Sutherland, Robert. *Putting God on Trial: The Biblical Book of Job*. Trafford Publishing, 2004.
Swindoll, Charles R. *Job: A Man of Heroic Endurance*. Thomas Nelson, 2009.

STUDENT RESOURCES
Peterson, Doug. *Ben Hurry: A Lesson in Patience*. Zonderkidz, 2005.

Supplemental Materials are available to download. See Understanding Purposeful Design Bible at the front of this book for the Grade 2 URL.

21.1 Job Is Patient
Focus: Patience Defined

📖 MEMORY VERSE
Ephesians 4:2

MEMORY WORK
- Use SIDEWALK CHALK to draw a hopscotch grid on the ground. In each square, write a portion of the Memory Verse. Have students take turns hopping from one end of the grid to the other, saying a portion of the Memory Verse on each square.

★ PREPARATION
Have SIDEWALK CHALK available. (*Memory Work*)

Select **DM-1 Character Traits**. (*Introduction*)

Select **VA 21A Job Is Patient**. (*Directed Instruction*)

Make a copy of **BLM 21A Patience Scenarios**, and cut the scenarios apart. (*Directed Instruction*)

EXTENSION
1A Help students write a class story about patience on POSTER BOARD. Write a story starter sentence on the poster board. For example, "There was a boy named _____. He had a loose tooth that just wouldn't come out." As students take turns adding to the story, write their contributions on the poster board. As you do this, guide them through logical sequencing. Be sure the word *patience* and examples of patience are included in the story. Point out that waiting for a turn to add to the story is another example of patience. Let everyone make illustrations for the story, and use the illustrations as a border around the story. Display in a prominent place.

Introduction ★
Show **DM-1 Character Traits**. Review the definitions of *patience*, *diligence*, and *humility*. Remind students that diligence and perseverance are very similar. Let students discuss ways these traits were seen in the lives of Abraham and Moses. (**Possible answers: Abraham showed humility by patiently waiting for God to fulfill His promise to give Abraham and Sarah a son; Moses patiently trusted God while he persevered 40 years in the wilderness and humbly led the Israelites.**) Explain that the person in today's Bible truth showed all three traits.

Directed Instruction ★
Read **VA 21A Job Is Patient**. Explain that Job was a good man who loved God. Sometimes bad things happen to good people, and they don't understand why. It is not because God does not love people or because He causes to bad things to happen. The choices people make in those situations help build their trust and faith in God, or tear it down. Point out that Job's wife wanted him to say hateful words to God. She chose to be angry with God. Job did not. Highlight that Job did not understand why he was suffering, but he patiently endured and had confidence that God would not leave him. In the end, God restored Job's health, rewarded him with a double portion of his possessions, and gave him more sons and daughters.

Emphasize that patience is a quality God has in abundance. He is extremely patient with His children, and that should inspire them to be patient with others! Remind students to turn to God and ask Him for help being patient.

Discuss a variety of situations that require patience. Ask students to share about times when they have needed patience. Do not let students judge one another for being impatient in a situation. The emphasis should be on the variety of real-life situations that require patience. Take time to pray, and let students ask God to help them become more patient.

Invite students to role-play situations that require patience. Assign students to one of four groups. Give each group one of the scenarios from **BLM 21A Patience Scenarios**. Direct students to act out their group's scenario, as well as several ways they could show patience in that situation.
- You are the last person in line waiting for a drink of water on a very hot day. What could you do to help yourself wait patiently? (**Possible answers: Count to a certain number slowly; pray for each person in line ahead of me; think of something nice about each person in line.**)
- You are at a carnival and want to get on a busy and popular ride. How could you wait patiently for your turn? (**Possible answers: Do something else until the line is shorter; stand in line without complaining.**)
- Your parents have promised to take you swimming after they finish the yard work. How can you wait patiently until it is time to go? (**Possible answers: Help do some yard work; don't pester them about the time.**)
- You have to wear a cast on your broken arm for six weeks. How can you be patient until it is time for the doctor to take off the cast? (**Possible**

202

answers: Follow all the doctor's instructions so the arm will heal; don't complain about the length of time.)

Student Page 21.1
Read the directions and help students complete the page.

Review
- What bad situations happened to Job? (**He lost all his children, servants, crops, and animals.**)
- How did Job show patience? (**He patiently trusted God, even when his wife and friends told him to blame God for the bad things that happened to him.**)
- How did Job show diligence? (**He did not give up.**)
- How did Job show humility? (**He knew he could not completely understand his suffering—only God is all-knowing and all-powerful.**)
- What happened as a result of Job's patience? (**God healed Job sores, allowed him to have 10 more children, and gave him back double the possessions he had lost.**)

APPLICATION
- In what situations is it hard for you to show patience? (**Possible answers: when someone is unfair to me; when I'm tired, hungry, or bored; when I'm in a hurry**)
- How do you think you would have reacted to the kind of suffering Job experienced? (**Answers will vary.**)

REINFORCEMENT
It is uncertain who wrote the book of Job and when. Some scholars claim it is the oldest book in the Bible, while others maintain that it must have been written in the days of King Solomon. Although the date and authorship are unknown, the story vividly portrays a centuries-old question that asks why a person who fears God and shuns evil experiences suffering. The narrative begins with a heavenly debate between God and Satan, which Job is unaware of, and shows Satan as the mastermind behind Job's suffering. The book of Job explains that God is mighty in power, wisdom, and knowledge. Job accepted that he could not fathom God, and he never blamed God for his suffering. In the end, God rewarded him by restoring a double portion of the possessions that Satan had taken from him. God also gave Job more sons and daughters.

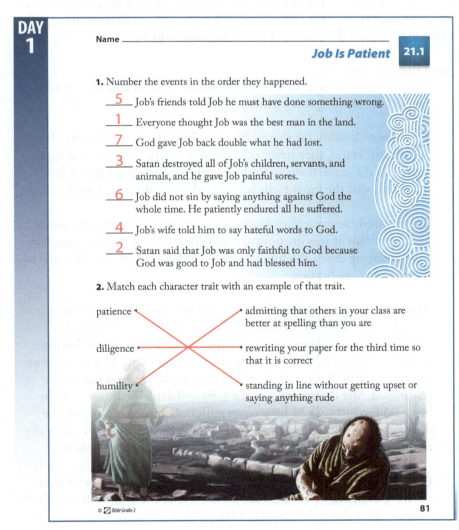

| 21.2 | # Job Is Patient
| | **Focus: Patience Shown**

★ PREPARATION

Bring in an **APPLE** and a **KNIFE**. (*Introduction*)

↻ EXTENSION

2A Help students understand the concept of patience as they wait for their plants to grow. Each student will need a handful of **BEAN SEEDS**; a **SMALL JAR**, such as a baby-food jar; and a small bit of **COTTON**. Show students how to wet the cotton and wrap the beans in it. Place the cotton in small jars on a window sill. As the week goes on, chart the progress of the sprouts. Discuss how it takes time and patience to wait for the results.

2B Have students draw the stages of growth of an apple tree on **BLM 21B Apple Tree**. Explain that an apple tree starts as a seed, grows into a shoot, becomes a tree, and finally bears fruit. Remind students that it can take up to 10 years for an apple tree to bear any fruit. That kind of waiting requires patience!

Introduction ★ ↻

Show students the **APPLE**. Using a **KNIFE**, cut the apple open and show students the seeds. Discuss the growth process by explaining that an apple tree starts as a seed, produces a shoot, grows into a tree, and then later bears fruit. It can take up to 10 years for a tree to grow and produce any fruit. Waiting for that fruit to be ready can take quite a bit of patience!

Review the story of Job. Remind students how he showed patience by trusting God and enduring through hard times. Explain that just like waiting for an apple to grow and produce fruit, sometimes students must wait a long time before they see good things happen.

Directed Instruction

Read **James 5:7–11**. Ask students what farmers wait for. (**They wait for rains and for their crops to grow.**) Ask whether farmers can do anything to make the rains come faster. (**No.**) Ask students what will happen if a farmer worries about the lack of rain. (**Answers will vary but should include that he will get frustrated, angry, or anxious.**) Explain that when students wait impatiently, it affects them negatively. Not only that, it affects others around them negatively. Choosing to be patient while waiting will help students and those around them stay calm and happy.

Read the following story:

After weeks and months of thinking about it, Beth and Kira would finally have their eighth birthday party!

The cousins had always shared the same birthday, but since they lived in different states, they never celebrated it together. Ever since Kira moved to the same town as Beth several months earlier, the girls thought about the great birthday party they would have together.

They invited everyone they knew, and they planned really fun games. Their excitement was uncontrollable. When the day finally came, they were counting down the minutes until all their friends would come to the birthday celebration.

About half an hour before the party, the neighbor who had recently moved from Japan, Mrs. Sato, came running to the door with her son in her arms. Riku was very sick and needed to go to the hospital, and Mrs. Sato didn't have a car. Beth's mom quickly phoned everyone to pray for little Riku, and she said that the party would have to be postponed. She then turned to the girls and explained the situation. She said the girls would have to wait. Beth became very angry. She didn't want to wait. She yelled at her mom that it wasn't fair. Then she ran to her room, sat on her bed, and began to cry and complain.

Kira remembered that her Sunday-school teacher talked about how showing patience pleased God. She knew that she and Beth were both disappointed about the party, but Riku's health was more important.

204

Kira decided to comfort her cousin by suggesting that she spend the night with Beth.

The next morning, the girls woke up and went downstairs. The living room was decorated for the party, and all of their friends were there! Beth's mom told the girls that their friends decided to surprise them. Beth apologized to her mom for yelling and being impatient. The party ended up being even better than they had imagined.

Student Page 21.2
Direct students to complete the page.

Review

- Which cousin showed patience while waiting for the party? (**Kira**)
- How could Beth have responded with more patience? (**Possible answers: She shouldn't have yelled at her mom; she could have prayed for Riku; she shouldn't have complained.**)
- How does a farmer show patience? (**by waiting for the rains to come and the crops to grow**)

DAY 2

21.2 Job Is Patient

On the lines beside each picture, write a short phrase about how you could show patience in that situation.

1. **Answers will vary.**

2. **Answers will vary.**

3. **Answers will vary.**

82

APPLICATION

- How can being patient please God? (**Answers will vary but should include being patient shows love, respect, and concern for others, and this pleases God.**)
- What can you do to help yourself remember to be patient the next time you start to feel impatient? (**Answers will vary but should include praying before I speak, waiting a few seconds before doing or saying anything, and remembering to quote this week's Memory Verse.**)
- How does complaining make you feel? (**Answers will vary but should include angry, frustrated, and not in control.**)
- How does being patient in a bad situation make you feel? (**Answers will vary but should include peaceful, content, and in control of myself.**)

REINFORCEMENT

God told Satan he could harm and destroy Job's possessions, but not take Job's life. Job suffered greatly but chose not to blame God. Interestingly, the name *Job* in Hebrew means *persecuted*.

Christians in many countries around the world today are being persecuted for their faith in God, and like Job, they choose to trust in God's love and faithfulness rather than blame Him for their difficulties. Several organizations track and report the countries with the most persecution. Christians in these countries are in need of prayer to endure and praise God throughout their persecution.

21.3 Job Is Patient

Focus: Patiently Control Your Words

⟳ EXTENSION

3A Help students locate the book of Psalms in their Bible. Tell them that they will find verses related to how they use their tongue while they wait patiently. Divide students into two teams. Have them mark the beginning and the end of the book of Psalms with small pieces of paper so that they will know their search parameters. Explain that when you call out a Scripture reference, everyone should quickly try to locate it in their Bible. Tell the first student who finds the verse to stand and read the verse aloud to receive a point for his or her team. After each verse is read, ask students to explain what the verse means. Place the emphasis on everyone locating the verse, reading it, and understanding its meaning. Use the following references: Psalm 19:14, 145:2, 51:15, 35:28, 145:6, 49:3, 34:13.

3B Read **Job 40:4b**. Have students trace their own hand onto paper and cut out the shape. Instruct students to write the Bible verse on the paper hand as a reminder to control the words they say.

Introduction

Read and discuss the following verses about the tongue:
- **Psalm 39:1**—Explain to students the idea of muzzling their mouth to keep from saying impatient words.
- **Psalm 137:6**—Have students try to keep their tongue on the roof of their mouth as they talk. Explain that it is difficult to say anything good or bad without using their tongue.
- **Psalm 141:3**—Draw a picture of a mouth with a soldier at each side. Discuss this word picture about guarding words.

Explain to students that it is possible to control the words that come out of their mouth, but it is not natural or easy. God can and will help them, if they cooperate with Him!

Directed Instruction ↶

Invite a volunteer to read **Job 1:20–22**. Ask students how Job's words showed what was in his heart. (**His words showed that his heart was focused on God, because he praised God and didn't blame God for his suffering.**) Remind students that during times of suffering, it is easy to get angry and complain. But Job did not do either of these things; he controlled his tongue and used his words to bring glory to God.

Point out that when suffering continues, a natural response is to ask God why it is happening. Job reminded God how good he had been throughout his life, and that he didn't deserve suffering. But Job quickly changed his attitude after a conversation with God. God discussed with Job how He had created everything without Job's help. Job was wanting to know things that only God knows and can understand. Ask a student to read **Job 42:1–6**. Job displayed humility and an attitude of **repentance**. Ask students to locate the word *repentance* in their Glossary, which means *being sorry for sin, confessing the sin, and changing my actions*. Job realized that God was all-powerful and all-knowing, and Job's human mind could never fully understand God or the reasons bad things happen. Explain that after Job waited patiently and refused to get angry at God, God restored his possessions twice over and gave him more sons and daughters!

Read **James 3:5–6**. The Bible compares the tongue or spoken words to a fire. Discuss helpful uses of fire, such as heat from a fire in a fireplace, light from a flame on a candle, or power from a rocket engine at takeoff. Explain that when it is controlled, fire is powerful and good. Likewise, students' controlled words can have power to bring life and energy to others. Discuss destructive fires, such as a house fire or a forest fire. Students' out-of-control words can be quite hurtful, too. Discuss the importance of controlling destructive words. Ask students to share some examples of when they needed to repent after speaking rashly. (**Answers will vary.**)

Student Page 21.3
Read **James 3:3–5**. Explain the purpose of the bit, the rudder, and the spark. Have students circle that part of each picture as it is mentioned.

206

Explain that a bit, a rudder, and a spark are all very small in comparison with the rest of the picture, but each is very powerful.

Have students read the story and then write a prayer of repentance. Allow time for students to share their prayer with the class.

Review
- How can your words be like a fire? (**When they are controlled, they can help, and when they are uncontrolled, they can be destructive.**)
- How did Job patiently control his words when he was going through a hard time? (**He didn't complain; he controlled his tongue used his words to glorify God.**)
- What did Job show repentance for? (**for thinking that he didn't deserve suffering because of his goodness, and for thinking he could understand things only God can understand**)

Notes:

APPLICATION
- Who do you get most impatient with? (**Answers will vary.**) What do you say to this person when you are feeling impatient? (**Possible answers: Move out of the way; stop bugging me; I don't want to do that now.**)
- How do impatient words affect your relationship with that person? (**Answers will vary but should include that it hurts my relationship.**)
- How will controlling your words help your relationship with that person? (**Answers will vary but should include that it shows respect and kindness.**)
- Take a moment to determine to set a guard over your mouth so that when you are feeling impatient, your words will still be kind and respectful.

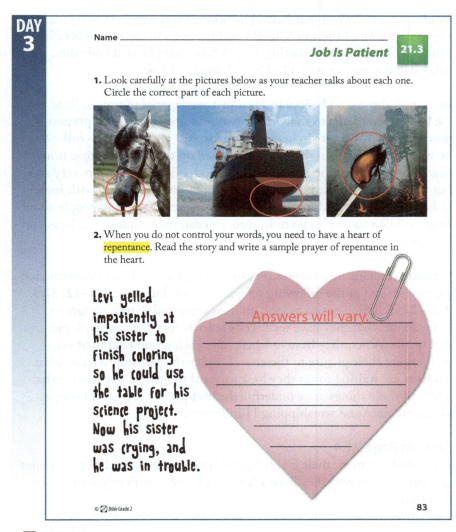

21.4 Job Is Patient

Focus: Eagerly Waiting

★ PREPARATION

Write the following Scriptures and their reference on separate pieces of construction paper: Revelation 7:9, 11–12; 21:3, 4, 21, 27. (*Directed Instruction*)

↱ EXTENSION

4A Using **BLM 21C Letter to Jesus**, direct students to write a letter to Jesus telling Him how they are waiting for Him to return and looking forward to spending eternity in heaven with Him. Help students think about how they feel and what they are most looking forward to about heaven.

Introduction

Ask students to name some things that are so good, they are worth waiting to receive. (**Possible answers: a new bike, a fun vacation, a visit with grandparents**) Talk about waiting for Christmas morning. Students may want the day to come so badly, but there is nothing they can do to make it come sooner. Invite students to share some of the things they do to help them wait patiently for Christmas. Explain that Jesus gave those who believe in Him two promises to look forward to with excitement and joy.

Directed Instruction ★ ↱

Ask students why the Jewish people were waiting for Jesus' birth. (**Jesus was the promised Messiah who would save them.**) Explain how Jesus' birth began the events that would lead to salvation. Remind students that Adam and Eve sinned soon after they were created. This sin separated all people from God. God does not want people to be separated from Him. He wants them to be close to Him. A perfect sacrifice was the only way to take away the separation. Only Jesus has never sinned; no one else has ever been perfect. There is no way for people to save themselves.

In His goodness, God sent Jesus, His Son, to die instead. When Jesus died, He took the sin of the whole world on Himself. People who believe in Him have eternal, or everlasting, life. When their physical body dies, their spirit will live forever with God in a place called *heaven*.

Jesus gave those who believe in Him two very special promises. Read **John 14:1–4**. Ask students to share those two promises. (**Jesus will prepare a place for His followers in heaven, and He will return for His followers to be with Him.**) Explain that after Jesus died on the cross and rose from the dead, He went up to heaven to be with God. His disciples were very sad, but they looked forward to His return and to someday being with Jesus in heaven. While the disciples waited, they were busy telling people about Jesus. While you wait to go to heaven, you can tell people about Jesus and heaven too!

Separate students into six groups. Give each group a piece of construction paper with one of the following references: **Revelation 7:9, 11–12; 21:3, 4, 21, 27**. Tell each group to look up their verse and draw a picture or write about what they have read. Tell students they may use both pictures and words. When they have finished, have each group read their verse and present their picture to the class. Display the pictures to show what students are waiting for as they look forward to heaven. Emphasize that while all these things are wonderful, the best part of heaven is being in God's presence and worshipping Him forever.

Student Page 21.4

Have students mark their graph. Spend time reviewing each topic, and let students explain why they have a hard or easy time patiently waiting for that thing.

Review

- God rewarded Job's patience by restoring double the possessions he lost and by giving him more sons and daughters. How will God reward a Christian's patience? (**I will feel peace and contentment now, I will become a stronger Christian, and there will be rewards for me in heaven.**)
- What two things did Jesus promise to people who believe in Him? (**Jesus will prepare a place for His followers in heaven, and He will return for His followers to be with Him.**)
- What is Jesus preparing for His followers according to John 14:1–4? (**a room or mansion in heaven**)
- What will you see in heaven? (**Possible answers: Jesus and God, people from every tongue and tribe, angels, throne, elders, four living creatures, God wiping away tears, gates of pearls and a great street of gold, people whose name is written in the Lamb's Book of Life**)
- What will be the best part about heaven? (**Answers will vary but should include worshipping God and being with Jesus.**)

APPLICATION

- Name something that is hard to wait patiently for. (**Answers will vary.**) Name something you can wait patiently for. (**Answers will vary.**)
- The Bible teaches that only those who have believed in Jesus will enter heaven. Has there ever been a time when you believed in Jesus as your Savior? (**Answers will vary.**) (Let students have an opportunity to talk about salvation and pray with you or someone who is available.)
- What are you most looking forward to about heaven? (**Answers will vary but should include worshipping God.**)

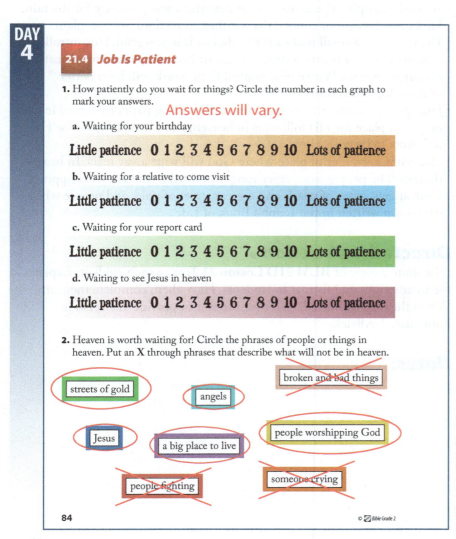

21.5 Job Is Patient

Focus: Review and Assessment

★ PREPARATION

Select **VA 21A Job Is Patient**. (*Lesson Review*)

Make one copy of **BLM 21D Lesson 21 Test** for each student. (*Directed Instruction*)

Lesson Review ★

Use **VA 21A Job Is Patient** to review the Bible truth. Cover the following concepts:

- Job was a good man who loved God.
- Satan caused events that destroyed Job's possessions and killed all of Job's children, servants, and animals. Job then got painful sores all over his body and used a piece of broken pottery to scrape his skin.
- Job's wife told him to say hateful words against God.
- Job's three friends told him that he must have done something wrong, and that God was punishing him.
- Job did not blame God for his suffering.
- The word *repentance* means *being sorry for sin, confessing the sin, and changing my actions.*
- Job was repentant. He realized that his knowledge of the Lord had been weak, and that God truly is all-powerful and all-knowing.
- In the end, God blessed Job with double the possessions he had lost and gave Job more sons and daughters.
- Job showed loyalty and patience by trusting God and not giving up, even though he went through terrible suffering.
- A good example of patience is a farmer who waits patiently for the rain. He knows he cannot control the weather, so he does not complain.
- The tongue is a small part of the body, but it is powerful. Uncontrolled or impatient words can destroy, but controlled and patient words can encourage others. People who control their words will have better relationships with others.
- Jesus promised two things that are worth waiting patiently for—He will prepare a place for His followers in heaven, and He will return for His followers to be with Him.
- Heaven is a wonderful place where God will wipe away tears. In heaven there will be people from every tongue and tribe who are worshipping God, angels, gates of pearls and a great street of gold, and people whose names are written in the Lamb's Book of Life.

Directed Instruction ★

Distribute a copy of **BLM 21D Lesson 21 Test** to each student. Explain the instructions and format to students. Have them complete the test. When they have finished, read over the test to provide answers for immediate feedback.

Notes:

Lesson Preparation
Daniel Is Faithful

22.0

Expected Student Outcomes

KNOW
Daniel makes godly decisions when faced with negative consequences. God gives Daniel the ability to interpret King Nebuchadnezzar's dream.

DO
Students will:
- make good choices and identify Scripture verses that show faithfulness to God
- recall and recount selected portions of the Bible truth
- demonstrate an understanding of prayer
- identify ways to help lead others to make right choices

APPLY
Students will acknowledge that doing things God's way demonstrates faithfulness, and that being faithful is a deliberate choice.

Lesson Outline
I. Daniel shows faithfulness (Dan 1)
II. The king's dream (Dan 2)
III. Faithfulness in prayer (Dan 2:17–18, 20–23; Ps 34:17; Jn 14:14; Phil 4:18–19)
IV. Pressure to choose (1 Cor 10:13)

♥ TEACHER'S HEART

Faithfulness, remaining true to God even in the face of adversities, can be extremely difficult at times. It helps to remember that God is faithful and can never be anything but faithful. Hudson Taylor worked to bring the gospel to China in the 1800s. As one of China's pioneer missionaries, he was able to accomplish much by trusting in God's faithfulness. He said, "Holding His faithfulness, we may go into every province of China. Holding His faithfulness, we may face, with calm and sober but confident assurance of victory, every difficulty and danger …. Let us not give Him a partial trust, but daily, hourly serve Him."

Being a teacher carries the weight of many responsibilities. How wonderful to know that as you fulfill these many responsibilities, you can count on God's faithfulness to be with you, help you, guide you, and strengthen you. Maybe you experience great faith in God in some areas of your life, and then find yourself lacking faith in other areas. A reminder about God's faithfulness in the midst of any faithlessness you may have is found in 2 Timothy 2:13—God remains faithful because this is His very nature. Set a daily example before your students that encourages them to rely on God and His faithfulness. They need to know that you trust God, you ask for His help through prayer, and you follow Him. Your example of being faithful to God can speak more loudly and clearly than any lesson you could ever teach on faithfulness.

📖 MEMORY VERSE
Psalm 138:3

GLOSSARY WORDS
- faithfulness

★ MATERIALS

Day 1:
- Time Line
- Name tags, food (*Extension*)

Day 2:
- VA 22A King Nebuchadnezzar
- BLM 22A Nebuchadnezzar's Statue, DM-12 Nebuchadnezzar's Statue

Day 3:
- Wrapped gift
- BLM 22B Write Your Own Prayer (*Extension*)

Day 4:
- PP-6 Peer Pressure (*Extension*)
- BLM 22C Readers Theater: Peer Pressure (*Extension*)

Day 5:
- VA 22A King Nebuchadnezzar
- BLM 22D Lesson 22 Test

♪ SONGS
Only God Can Do
Praying (*Extension*)

TEACHER RESOURCES
Ironside, H.A. *Daniel: An Ironside Expository Commentary*. Kregel Publications, 2005.
Prince, Derek. *Secrets of a Prayer Warrior*. Chosen Books, 2009.

STUDENT RESOURCES
MacBeth, Sybil. *Praying in Color Kids' Edition*. Paraclete Press, 2009.

Supplemental Materials are available to download. See Understanding Purposeful Design Bible at the front of this book for the Grade 2 URL.

22.1 Daniel Is Faithful
Focus: Daniel Shows Faithfulness

 MEMORY VERSE
Psalm 138:3

 MEMORY WORK
- Write the verse on the board and practice saying it several times. Direct the students to find the previously hidden pieces of paper on which the words of the verse are written, and tell students to put the words in order as quickly as possible.

★ **PREPARATION**
Write each word of the Memory Verse on a separate piece of paper and hide the pieces of paper around the classroom. (Memory Work)

 EXTENSION
1A Provide NAME TAGS and prepare a new name or a name used in another country for each student. On the board, write some directions that are in a different language or are nonsense words. Provide a NEW FOOD that you think students might not have tasted. Give students the name tags and a sample of the new food, keeping allergies into consideration. Discuss the forced changes that Daniel and his friends endured, and how it would feel for Daniel and his friends to move to a new place without their families and experience new names and foods.

Introduction
Write the heading *Do Not Use Words* on the board and list these words under the heading: *the, my, and, it, is*. Instruct students to think of a sentence about their friends without using the words on the board. As students share answers, let them discuss the difficulty of the challenge.

Explain that choosing not to use the forbidden words showed that the students had *resolve—a determination to do or not do something*. In today's Bible truth, Daniel and his friends showed resolve to remain faithful to God. Let students use the Glossary to look up **faithfulness**, which means *constant loyalty*. In today's Bible truth, it took a lot of boldness for Daniel and his friends to be faithful to God.

Directed Instruction
Read the following Bible truth paraphrased from Daniel 1:

Long ago, the city of Jerusalem was invaded by the king of Babylon and his army. The king's name was *Nebuchadnezzar*. When the king took over Jerusalem, he captured many of the Jewish people who lived there and took them to Babylon. Daniel and three of his friends were some of those taken captive. They were teenagers when they were taken from their homes and made to go live in the king's palace.

When Daniel and the three boys arrived in Babylon, the king chose them to be his very special servants and gave them each a new name. Daniel was called *Belteshazzar*. Daniel's friends were named *Shadrach, Meshach,* and *Abed-Nego*. For three years, the boys would study the Babylonian language and learn all the wisdom of the land. When they finished their training, they would spend the rest of their lives serving the king as wise men, advisers close to the king.

Daniel and his three friends had been raised to be faithful to God, to worship God only, and to obey His laws. As part of their training, King Nebuchadnezzar required them to eat foods that were forbidden by God's law. The four boys now had a choice—to be faithful to God or to please the king. They chose to be faithful to God.

Daniel boldly asked permission for himself and Shadrach, Meshach, and Abed-Nego to eat only vegetables and to drink only water for 10 days. At the end of that time, if they looked any worse than the others who were also in training, they would agree to eat the king's food. So for 10 days, Daniel and his friends ate only vegetables and drank only water. At the end of those days, they looked better than all the other boys! As a result, they were given permission to keep eating the food listed in God's law.

God honored the boldness and faithfulness of Daniel and his friends. He blessed them and gave them special abilities to learn and understand all the things they needed to know to serve the king. When all the new servants appeared before King Nebuchadnezzar, none compared to Daniel, Shadrach, Meshach, and Abed-Nego.

Daniel and his friends were taken captive together, and together, they boldly decided to remain faithful to God. Their unity helped them make a choice to follow God's ways.

Student Page 22.1
Read the directions and let students work in pairs to look up the Scriptures.

Review

- How did Daniel and his friends show faithfulness to God? (**not wanting to eat food forbidden by God's law, by following God's way of eating**)
- How did Daniel show boldness? (**He asked that he and his friends be allowed to eat only vegetables and drink water for 10 days.**)
- What was the result of the boys' faithfulness in eating foods listed in God's law? (**They looked better than all the others.**)

Time Line
Refer to the **Time Line** and review ways God rewarded faithfulness in the lives of the various Bible people studied in previous lessons this year.

APPLICATION
- Tell about a time when God has shown faithfulness to you. (**Answers will vary.**)
- Tell about a time when you showed faithfulness to God. (**Answers will vary.**)
- Why is it important to show faithfulness to God? (**Possible answers: He wants to have a relationship with me; He wants me to obey because I love Him; God has been faithful to me.**)
- Daniel and his friends were bold to request not to eat the king's food. When have you shown boldness? (**Answers will vary.**)

REINFORCEMENT
The placement of the books in the Bible does not always follow chronological order. The book of Esther is in the Old Testament before the book of Daniel; however, the book of Daniel was written in the sixth century BC and Esther was likely written sometime between 470 BC and 424 BC.

Daniel was taken captive by King Nebuchadnezzar in 605 BC when he was around the age of 15. This all happened before Esther became queen. Daniel and Esther lived close in time to each other in history. Both chose to serve and follow the one, true God.

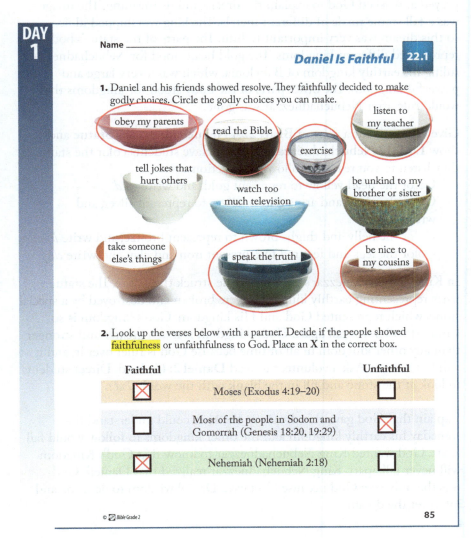

22.2 Daniel Is Faithful
Focus: The King's Dream

★ PREPARATION

Select **VA 22A King Nebuchadnezzar**. (*Directed Instruction*)

Print a copy of **BLM 22A Nebuchadnezzar's Statue** for each student and prepare **DM-12 Nebuchadnezzar's Statue** for display. (*Directed Instruction*)

Select the song "Only God Can Do" from the Grade 2 URL. (*Directed Instruction*)

↻ EXTENSION

2A King Nebuchadnezzar's dream was about kingdoms. Let students imagine they have a kingdom. Have students get in groups of two or three and discuss their kingdoms. Use the following questions to guide their thinking: What does your kingdom look like? What buildings would be in your kingdom? Where will your kingdom be located? Who will live in your kingdom?

After a few minutes in their small groups, gather the students together again. Tell students that the Bible gives some ideas of what God's kingdom in heaven is like. Review things learned about heaven in Lesson 21.4, such as a main street of gold and gates of pearl, no crying, worshipping God, and people whose names are written in the Lamb's Book of Life.

Introduction

Explain that dreams are thoughts, pictures, or images in a person's mind during sleep. Lead a discussion by asking students the following questions:
- Have you had a strange dream?
- Did you tell someone else your dream?
- Did that person try to explain the dream to you?

In today's Bible truth, Daniel needed wisdom and he needed it quickly. He and his friends did what everyone should do in a difficult situation—they prayed to God! Daniel had faith that God would help him understand what the king's dream meant. During the time when Daniel lived, the Babylonians considered dreams to be messages from their false gods. King Nebuchadnezzar did not know anything about Daniel's God. Because Daniel and his friends were taken as captives to Babylon, they had an opportunity to tell King Nebuchadnezzar about God's power.

Directed Instruction ★ ↻

Read **VA 22A King Nebuchadnezzar**. Explain that God used Daniel to help Nebuchadnezzar understand the meaning of his dream. Daniel wisely prayed and asked God to explain the dream and its meaning. The image was a tall statue made of different metals. The king worshipped idols, so this dream was very important to him. The parts of the statue's body represented different kingdoms. The gold head stood for Nebuchadnezzar ruling his earthly kingdom of Babylonia, which was a very large and powerful kingdom. The other parts of the body stood for kingdoms that would rule after Nebuchadnezzar was gone.

Give each student a copy of **BLM 22A Nebuchadnezzar's Statue** and show **DM-12 Nebuchadnezzar's Statue**. Have students color the statue as they listen to you read the following directions:

Color the head yellow to represent gold, and write *gold*.
Color the chest and arms gray or silver to represent silver, and write *silver*.
Color the belly and thighs brown to represent bronze, and write *bronze*.
Color the legs and feet red to represent iron and clay, and write *clay*.

In King Nebuchadnezzar's dream, a stone struck the statue. The statue parts representing earthly kingdoms were broken and destroyed by a special stone, which represented God and His kingdom. God's kingdom is so strong it will never fall apart. God's kingdom is much greater and stronger than any other kingdom in all of time because God is ruler over it, and it will last forever. Ask a volunteer to read **Daniel 2:44** aloud. Direct students to look at the stone and fill in the blank with the word *God's*.

Explain that God gave this dream so the king could understand that someday his earthly kingdom and the other kingdoms to follow would fall apart. God wanted King Nebuchadnezzar to know that God's Kingdom will never fall apart. King Nebuchadnezzar realized that Daniel's God was the only true God because God gave Daniel wisdom to describe and interpret the dream.

214

Sing the song "Only God Can Do" from the Grade 2 URL. Let students volunteer to pray and thank God for doing things that seem impossible, such as giving Daniel the ability to explain the king's dream.

Student Page 22.2
Read the directions and have students complete the student page.

Review
• Who could not explain King Nebuchadnezzar's dream? (**the king's own wise men**)
• How did the king react when the wise men could not explain the dream? (**The king became very angry and wanted all wise men in the kingdom to be killed.**)
• How did Daniel react to the news that he would be killed? (**He boldly volunteered to interpret the dream; he and his friends prayed and asked God to give Daniel wisdom to describe and interpret the dream.**)
• How did God respond to Daniel's faith? (**God revealed both the dream and the meaning to Daniel.**)

APPLICATION
• Instead of worrying, Daniel prayed to God. When have you chosen to pray instead of worry? (**Answers will vary.**)
• Daniel showed boldness to speak to the angry king. How do you think Daniel felt when he told King Nebuchadnezzar his dream? (**Possible answers: nervous, afraid the king might be mad about the interpretation, happy that God gave the answer to him**)
• When have you boldly spoken the truth to someone, not knowing how they would react to what you said? (**Answers will vary.**)

REINFORCEMENT
The statue in Nebuchadnezzar's dream represented four different kingdoms. Nebuchadnezzar ruled the kingdom of Babylonia, which was the richest and most powerful kingdom at that time. This was represented by the golden head of the statue. The silver chest and arms represented the kingdom of Medo-Persia, which would rise second in power and rule after Babylonia. The bronze belly and thighs represented the kingdom of Greece, which was the third kingdom to rule over the earth. The last earthly kingdom, represented by the legs and feet, was a kingdom made up of a mixture of people who were strong and weak. This mixture of clay and iron would not hold together. Although the Bible does not specifically say, some scholars suggest this was the Roman Empire. The Roman Empire fell in 476 AD because of conflicts inside and outside its borders.

DAY 2

22.2 Daniel Is Faithful

1. Match the person or people to the correct phrase.

King Nebuchadnezzar — could not tell the king what he wanted to know

The king's wise men — had a dream he could not understand

Daniel and his three friends — told the king that God knew the answer

Daniel — all prayed that God would tell Daniel the dream and its meaning

2. Pretend you are Daniel. Tell King Nebuchadnezzar what his dream meant (Daniel 2). Choose your words carefully. Remember, you are talking to a king!

Answers will vary but should include: The gold head on the statue stands for you and your kingdom. The chest, arms, belly, legs, and feet stand for other kingdoms (Persia, Greece, and Rome). All these kingdoms will fall apart, but the stone is God's kingdom and it will never be destroyed.

86
© Bible Grade 2

© Bible Grade 2
215

22.3 Daniel Is Faithful

Focus: Faithfulness in Prayer

★ PREPARATION

Prepare a WRAPPED GIFT.
(*Introduction*)

↻ EXTENSION

3A Make copies of **BLM 22B Write Your Own Prayer** for each student. Guide students to write a prayer to God by using the prompts.

3B Ask students to share about problems or situations that worry them. Read **Philippians 4:6–7**. Remind students when they have a problem or need, they can go to God in prayer. Select and sing the song "Praying" from the Grade 2 URL.

Introduction ★

Display the WRAPPED GIFT and tell students the gift is for someone. Invite a student to come and stand beside you. Wait for the student to ask for the gift. If the student asks, give it freely. If the student does not ask, graciously invite another student to come without giving the gift away. Continue until a student finally asks for the gift. If no one asks, inquire why the students think no one has received the gift yet. Explain that sometimes they do not receive because they do not pray and ask. God has special things for them, but many times they need to ask.

Prayer can also be a gift that is given to someone. Explain that each time they pray for someone, they are giving the gift of taking that person's needs to God! Pass the gift to a volunteer to hold while praying for someone.

Directed Instruction ↩

Review the Bible truth from Lesson 22.2 about King Nebuchadnezzar's dream. Remind students that Daniel and his friends were faced with being killed, but they made a choice to have faith in God. Ask a volunteer to read **Daniel 2:17–18**. Explain that Daniel and his friends united together in prayer and asked God for wisdom for Daniel to be able to interpret the dream. After Daniel and his friends prayed, God gave Daniel wisdom to understand the king's dream. Daniel immediately praised God for who God is and thanked God for revealing the dream to him. Ask a volunteer to read **Daniel 2:20–23**.

Tell students that Daniel demonstrated his faith in God by going to God in prayer. Explain to students that God longs to have a relationship with them. Prayer is an immediate and powerful way to communicate with God. They can talk to God when they are at home, school, on the playground, in a car, or anywhere. God wants them to ask for help and trust Him to take care of them. God will give them wisdom when they do not know what to do, peace when they have fear, boldness when they need it, comfort when they are sad, and understanding when they are confused. God always hears their prayers and will help them. Read **Psalm 34:17**. God is never too busy to hear anyone's prayers. God values the prayers of all people—a person's age does not matter to Him either!

Discuss the following aspects that can be included in a prayer and why:
- Praise God for who He is, He is Holy, He is the Provider, He is Love and He is the Creator. Explain that when a prayer starts by praising God, it is easier to keep the prayer focused on God and His power to take care of the needs being mentioned to Him.
- Confess any failing to do things God's way. Prayers are more powerful when sins are admitted.
- Ask God to provide for your needs and the needs of others. God promises to meet your needs according to John 14:14 and Philippians 4:18–19. Remember that the most important need is for a person to believe in Jesus as his or her Savior. Point out the difference between needs and wants.

216

- Thank God for things He has done. This helps believers remember God's faithfulness to them.

Spend a few minutes in prayer together.

Student Page 22.3
Have students complete the first part of the page on their own and then talk with a partner about the prayer pictures.

Review
- How did Daniel respond to his problem? (**He went to God in prayer.**)
- Who did Daniel ask to join him in prayer? (**Daniel asked Shadrach, Meshach, and Abed-Nego**)
- How did God answer Daniel and his friends' prayer? (**God gave Daniel wisdom to describe and interpret the king's dream and saved them all from death.**)

APPLICATION
- Tell the class about a prayer that God answered. (**Answers will vary.**)
- Who do you sometimes pray with? (**Answers will vary.**) How do you feel when you pray with someone? (**Possible answers: happy, nervous, shy, glad to have someone to pray with**)
- Daniel and his friends showed faith in God's ability to answer their prayer. Do you have faith that God will answer your prayers? Why or why not? (**Answers will vary but should include an example of God's faithfulness in answering prayers.**)
- God responded to the prayers of Daniel and his friends in a mighty way. What does this tell you about God? (**Answers will vary but should include that God is all-knowing, He is wise, and He answers prayer.**)

REINFORCEMENT
After Daniel prayed and God revealed the king's dream to him, Daniel received many honors. The king made him ruler over the province of Babylon and chief administrator over all the wise men. Daniel used his privilege to facilitate jobs in the government for Shadrach, Meshach, and Abed-Nego—his fellow captive friends who had joined him in refusing the king's food and prayed with him for wisdom. Together, they were able to introduce the king and people of Babylon to God's great power (Daniel 2:46–49). God can use every situation, even negative ones, to further His Kingdom!

DAY 3

Name _____

Daniel Is Faithful 22.3

1. Mark with a check the sentence that is true about prayer.

    _____ God hears the prayers of adults more than children.

    _____ God is too busy to hear your prayers.

    ✓ God is faithful to hear your prayers and will answer them.

2. Discuss with a partner how you could pray for the people in each picture. On the line below each picture, write a word that will help you remember how to pray for people in that situation.

Answers will vary but should include peace or love.

Answers will vary but should include happy or cheerful.

Answers will vary but should include healing.

Answers will vary but should include friends.

| 22.4 | **Daniel Is Faithful**
Focus: Pressure to Choose |

EXTENSION

4A Show **PP-6 Peer Pressure** as a review. Discuss situations in which students have led their group of friends to make good choices. Let students tell about times when they have been a part of a group that was making wrong choices and how they handled the situation.

4B Assign parts and have students act out **BLM 22C Readers Theater: Peer Pressure**. Talk with students about times when they have felt pressure to do something because their friends were doing it. Help students recognize that they can be bold and have resolve to follow God's ways even if their friends are not.

Introduction

Read the following fictional story to the class:

Yun finished eating her snack and threw the wrapper on the ground because it was easier than walking all the way to the trash can. Yun's friends noticed her throw the wrapper on the ground and they knew that she might get in trouble for littering. Her friends did not want her to get in trouble. They decided to start a "Keep It Clean" group and asked everyone in the class to join the group. Each day they took a few minutes of recess time to clean up the playground together. Yun wanted to do things with her friends, so she joined them. After cleaning up the playground together, Yun was excited about how good it felt to help her friends make the playground look great.

How did Yun's friends help her? (**They started a group that helped Yun change her bad habit of littering.**)

Directed Instruction

Review the Bible truth about how King Saul pressured David to wear his armor to fight the giant Goliath, and how David boldly chose to trust in God's protection—not the king's. David decided not to give in to pressure from King Saul. Remind students that *peer pressure* means *a strong influence from people near you to do something*. Peer pressure can be good or bad. Friends can pressure you to do something that is not following God's ways. This pressure can be bad and lead to trouble. Discuss ways that peers can influence students to do the wrong thing. (**Possible answers: by giving pressure to say bad words, by not listening to the teacher, by cheating**) Tell students that when someone pressures them to do the wrong thing, they should get away from the situation and ask God for help. Then they should do the right thing, trusting God for His strength to obey Him. Ask a volunteer to read **1 Corinthians 10:13**.

Remind students that peer pressure can also help them to make good choices to follow God's ways and please Him. Friends can encourage each other to work together, have good attitudes, and serve others. Daniel's friends practiced a good kind of peer pressure. When Daniel and his friends were told they had to eat King Nebuchadnezzar's rich food instead of following God's law, they were faithful to help each other follow God. Also, when Daniel needed wisdom to interpret the king's dream, he asked his friends to pray for him. They joined him in doing the right thing.

Read each scenario listed and choose volunteers to role-play how the friends can show good peer pressure.

- You and your friends are at church waiting for the adult choir rehearsal to finish. You look out the window and notice an elderly friend of the family needs help in her garden. Your friends are ready to start playing a board game. What should you do? (**Possible answers: Ask everyone to join you in helping her; make a game to see who can pull the most weeds; pray for the neighbor.**)

- During recess, some students playing a game on the playground are cheating. You and your friends are afraid others will join in the cheating. What can you do? (**Possible answers: Play and do not cheat; remind them to follow the rules; pray for them**)
- A new girl in your class thinks you and your friends are strange because you go to church. She invites you and your friends to her house on Sunday morning. What can you do? (**Possible answers: Invite her to church; go to her house after church; pray for her**)

Student Page 22.4
Complete the page together and discuss answers as a class.

Review

- Compare good peer pressure and bad peer pressure. (**Good peer pressure turns you toward doing the right thing, and bad peer pressure influences you to go away from doing what is right.**)
- How did Daniel and his friends show positive peer pressure? (**Together they did not want to eat the king's food, and they prayed to God for Daniel to be able to know and interpret the king's dream.**)

APPLICATION
- Tell about a time when you have been influenced by your friends to make a wrong choice. (**Answers will vary.**)
- Tell about a time when you have been influenced by your friends to make a right choice. (**Answers will vary.**)
- When have you and someone else decided to help each other to be faithful to God's ways? (**Answers will vary.**)
- How might your friends react if you looked for ways to pray, encourage, and help others when you are with them? (**Answers will vary but should include that they might be motivated to make good choices also.**)

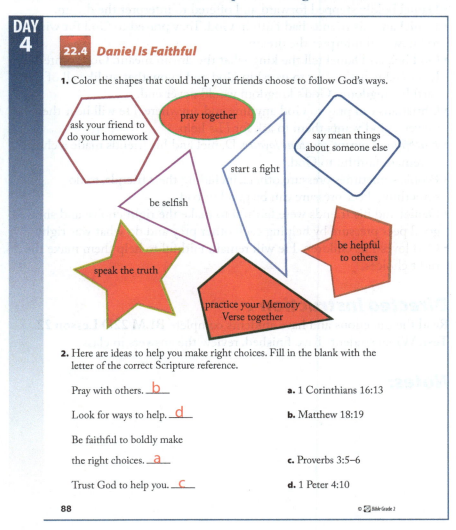

22.5 Daniel Is Faithful
Focus: Review and Assessment

★ PREPARATION

Select **VA 22A King Nebuchadnezzar**. (*Lesson Review*)

Print **BLM 22D Lesson 22 Test** for each student. (*Directed Instruction*)

Lesson Review ★

Use **VA 22A King Nebuchadnezzar** to review the Bible truths from this lesson. Cover the following concepts:

• When King Nebuchadnezzar took over the city of Jerusalem, he captured many of the Jewish people who lived there and took them to Babylon.
• The king chose Daniel and his three friends to study and learn to be his wise men. Their names were changed. Daniel was called *Belteshazzar*. Daniel's friends were renamed *Shadrach*, *Meshach*, and *Abed-Nego*.
• King Nebuchadnezzar required them to eat foods that were forbidden by God's law.
• Daniel and his friends did not want to disobey the king, but they chose to be faithful to God. They boldly asked permission to eat only vegetables and drink water.
• God honored the faithfulness of Daniel, Shadrach, Meshach, and Abed-Nego and blessed them with good health and special abilities to understand all they needed to serve the king.
• Nebuchadnezzar's wise men could not interpret the king's dream. He became angry and ordered all the wise men to be killed, including Daniel and his friends.
• Daniel boldly stepped forward and offered to interpret the dream.
• Daniel and his friends had faith in God. They prayed to God for wisdom to know and interpret the dream.
• God helped Daniel tell the king what the dream meant. God wanted King Nebuchadnezzar to worship God and know that, unlike all of the earthly kingdoms, God's kingdom would never end.
• Christians can pray to God anytime and anywhere. He will hear their prayers. God wants them to ask for His help.
• *Faithfulness* means *constant loyalty*. Daniel and his friends made a choice to remain faithful to God.
• People sometimes pressure others, including their friends, to do something. Peer pressure can be good or bad.
• Daniel and his friends were faithful to make the right choice and showed good peer pressure by helping each other pray and do what was right.
• God loves His children. He will remain faithful to help them make the right choices.

Directed Instruction ★

Read the directions and have students complete **BLM 22D Lesson 22 Test**. When students have finished, review the answers in class.

Notes:

220

Lesson Preparation
Daniel's Friends Are Faithful

23.0

Expected Student Outcomes

KNOW
Daniel's friends stand firm in their commitment to God. They are thrown into the fiery furnace.

DO
Students will:
- identify and correct mistakes in the retelling of the Bible truth
- choose actions that show resolve to obey God
- solve a code to supply the missing words
- write about showing faithfulness to God

APPLY
Students will recognize the need for prayer and faithfulness to God even when confronted with persecution.

Lesson Outline
I. Faithfulness to God (Dan 3, Deut 31:6)
II. Resolve to obey God (Dan 3:13–18)
III. Courage and deliverance (Ps 91:14–16)
IV. Others praise God (Ps 34:1–3, Dan 3:28–30, Mt 5:14–16)

♥ TEACHER'S HEART

Faithfulness to God is often easier when things are going well and there are no negative consequences. In many cases, people have suffered much for their faithfulness to God. This week's Bible truth focuses on three young Hebrew men who were taken as captives to Babylon. Their friends and family back home might never have heard of their choice to be faithful to God or their refusal to bow to King Nebuchadnezzar's golden statue. Throughout the Old Testament, the children of Israel were often quick to abandon God and worship idols. Yet these three men resolutely obeyed God rather than the earthly king who wanted to be worshipped as a god. Faithfulness does not require an audience. Faithfulness is being constantly loyal even if no one else knows.

Think about a time when someone showed faithfulness to you and consider how that made you feel. This week, you have the opportunity to model faithfulness to God in your choices, words, and actions. Your example will show your students that you love and trust God. Remember, you never know who is watching you. It is best to have the habit of faithfulness to God in the little things as well as the big things. You can trust that God is always faithful to love you, to be with you, and to keep all of His promises!

📖 MEMORY VERSE
Psalm 34:4

GLOSSARY WORDS
- deliverance

⭐ MATERIALS

Day 1:
- VA 23A The Fiery Furnace

Day 2:
- No additional materials are needed.

Day 3:
- DM-1 Character Traits
- BLM 23A Pray for Romanians (*Extension*)

Day 4:
- Lighter or matches, candles

Day 5:
- VA 23A The Fiery Furnace
- BLM 23B Lesson 23 Test

♪ SONGS
I Can Obey
What Seems Impossible (*Extension*)

TEACHER RESOURCES
Torchlighters: The Richard Wurmbrand Story. DVD. Vision Video, 2008.
Wiersbe, Warren W. *Be Resolute: Daniel*. David C. Cook, 2008.

STUDENT RESOURCES
Veggie Tales *Rack, Shack, and Benny: A Lesson in Peer Pressure*. DVD. Universal Studios, 2018.
Verdicchio, Jacey. *A King's Decree and the Brave Three*. Tate Publishing, 2008.

Supplemental Materials are available to download. See Understanding Purposeful Design Bible at the front of this book for the Grade 2 URL.

23.1 Daniel's Friends Are Faithful
Focus: Faithfulness to God

MEMORY VERSE
Psalm 34:4

MEMORY WORK
- Practice the Memory Verse together several times. Divide students into two groups seated on the floor. Recite the verse, but say it correctly sometimes and purposely make mistakes at other times, such as adding, deleting, or substituting words. Each time you make a mistake, teams compete to have a student be the first to jump up and correct the mistake. If a student jumps up and corrects the mistake, his or her team gets a point. If you say the verse correctly and a student jumps up to correct the mistake, his or her team loses a point. Repeat this process several times.

★ PREPARATION
Select **VA 23A The Fiery Furnace**. (*Directed Instruction*)

Introduction
Have students state the names of Daniel's three friends. (**Shadrach, Meshach, and Abed-Nego**) Ask students what they remember about them. (**Possible answers: They were taken captive from Jerusalem; they were trained to be advisers to the king; they refused to eat the king's rich foods and chose to eat vegetables and drink water; they prayed together for Daniel to have wisdom to know and interpret the king's dream.**) Tell students that today's Bible truth is about these three friends who experienced a miracle because they chose to obey God instead of the king.

Explain that these young men had already chosen at least once to trust God and courageously follow God's ways, but they were about to have another test. Ask students how they would feel if they finished what they thought was the last math test in second grade, only to find out they had another one to take. (**Possible answers: frustrated, mad, disappointed**) Life is full of choices. Just because a student chooses well once does not guarantee that he or she will choose well the next time. Tell students that faithfulness to God is the right choice to make each day of their lives!

Directed Instruction
Read **VA 23A The Fiery Furnace**. Explain to students that Shadrach, Meshach, and Abed-Nego learned they had to constantly choose to obey God and follow God's ways even when it meant they might suffer. Point out that the king made them change their names, work for him, and learn another language. They had done all of these things with great obedience, and the king rewarded them with good jobs. Ask students why Shadrach, Meshach, and Abed-Nego would not obey the command to bow down and worship the king's gold statue. (**because they wanted to faithfully obey God**)

Explain to students that the Bible says they are to obey those in authority over them, such as parents, coaches, teachers, pastors, and other adults. But God is an authority greater than any other authority. Rarely will an authority ask them to do something that goes against what God's Word says. But if that happens, students need to obey God.

Explain that Shadrach, Meshach, and Abed-Nego followed God, even though doing so meant they might be killed. God wants His children to be faithful to Him—even in difficult situations. Ask students how they typically react when faced with tough choices. (**Answers will vary but should include that they pray and follow God's ways.**) Let students tell some of the thoughts that Shadrach, Meshach, and Abed-Nego might have had in the following situations:
- when they heard the music playing as a signal to bow down to the gold statue
- when the king ordered them to be thrown into the furnace
- when the Son of God was with them in the fire

Challenge students to choose faithfulness to God today and each day. Remind them that God rewards faithfulness.

Student Page 23.1
Read the instructions to students. Assist students as necessary.

Review
- Why was the king angry with Shadrach, Meshach, and Abed-Nego? (**They would not bow down to his statue.**)
- What did they say that God would do for them? (**God would deliver them from the furnace.**)
- How did the king respond to what they said? (**He became angrier and ordered the furnace heated seven times hotter.**)
- What happened when they were thrown into the fiery furnace? (**The three friends were not hurt, and a fourth man, the Son of God, stood in the fire with them.**)
- When is the only time you should disobey people in authority? (**when they tell me to do something that goes against what God tells me to do**)

APPLICATION
- Read **Deuteronomy 31:6**. God was with Shadrach, Meshach, and Abed-Nego—even in the middle of the fire. How do you feel knowing that God is always with you? (**Answers will vary but should include that I feel like being faithful to God because He is faithful to me.**) In what situations have you felt God was with you? (**Answers will vary.**)
- Have you faced a difficult situation recently? (**Answers will vary.**) How did you choose to be faithful to God through it? (**Answers will vary but should include that I prayed or chose to follow God's ways.**)
- What does today's Bible truth tell you about God? (**Possible answers: He is all-powerful; He protects me.**)

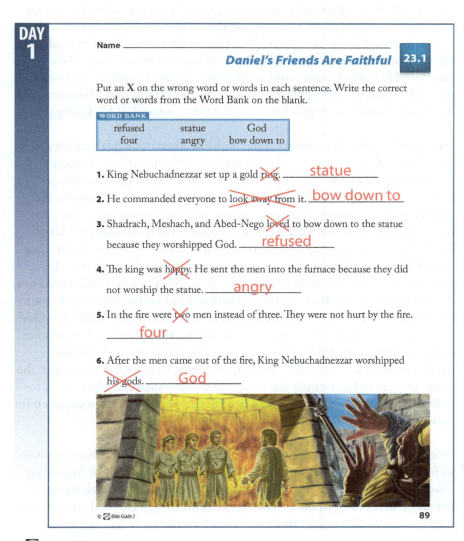

23.2 Daniel's Friends Are Faithful
Focus: Resolve to Obey God

★ PREPARATION
Select the song "I Can Obey" from the Grade 2 URL. (*Introduction*)

↻ EXTENSION
2A Ask students to write a journal entry about what they would have done if they were in the crowd standing next to Shadrach, Meshach, and Abed-Nego when the music signaled everyone to bow down to the king's statue.

2B Explain that students should have a strong resolve to be faithful to God in any situation. Play a game of naming situations from A to Z in which students can decide to show faithfulness to God, such as **a**t the store, **b**eing with my friends, **c**hurch, and so forth.

Introduction ★
Sing the song "I Can Obey" from the Grade 2 URL. Explain that learning God's Word will help students know God's ways so that students can obey them. Have students find and read the following verses and discuss what each one teaches about God's ways: **Exodus 20:3** (no other gods), **Exodus 20:12** (honor or obey parents), **Exodus 20:15** (do not steal), **John 13:35** (love one another), and **Galatians 5:13b** (serve one another in love).

Directed Instruction ↻
Ask students to turn to Daniel 3. Select a student to read **Daniel 3:13–15**. Explain that Shadrach, Meshach and Abed-Nego faced a very difficult situation. King Nebuchadnezzar was angry and had the men brought before him to personally explain the command to them. Ask students why the king might have given them a second chance. (**Possible answers: They might not have understood the command; he wanted them to live; he did not want to lose them as his advisers.**) Let students read together the question that King Nebuchadnezzar asked at the end of verse 15. (**He asked what god would save them.**) On the board, write the words *god* and *God*. Point to the word *god* as you explain that King Nebuchadnezzar worshipped many gods that were powerless. Point to the word *God* and ask students if God is powerless. (**No, God is all-powerful.**) Let students tell you some of the things they know that are true about God. (**Possible answers: He is the Creator and is all-powerful, all-knowing, and pure love; He is our provider.**) The king did not understand that Shadrach, Meshach, and Abed-Nego's God was different from all of his false gods.

The three friends chose not to argue with the king, but explained they would serve God no matter what happened to them. Ask a volunteer to read **Daniel 3:16–18**. These three men responded with great resolve to show their faithfulness to God. Invite a student to look up *resolve* in the Glossary, which means *a determination to do or not do something*. Explain that when the men said they knew God could save them from the king's hand, they also recognized that God might choose not to save them. They would show faithfulness without a guarantee that God would save them. Ask students what these three men had decided they would and would not do in this situation. (**They decided to follow God and to not bow down to the statue.**) Ask students what the men's resolve to remain faithful to God could have cost them. (**their lives**) Explain that following God sometimes means making very difficult decisions to obey God's ways, and those decisions could lead to suffering. Invite students to tell what they think the men's prayers to God might have been. (**Possible answers: They asked for deliverance, thanked God for His promise to be with them, and asked for courage to remain faithful to God.**)

Ask students to describe tough situations in which they can show resolve to follow God's ways. (**Possible answers: when friends are not following God's ways, when I will miss out on something fun or special, when someone makes fun of me for doing the right thing**) Remind students to pray and ask God for help whenever they find themselves in difficulties.

They may never face life-or-death consequences for following God, but they can resolve to follow God because they know that He will be with them and help them.

Student Page 23.2

Read the scenarios on the page. After students mark their answers, let them explain why each answer shows resolve to obey God.

Review

- What did King Nebuchadnezzar say that showed he did not understand God's power? (**He asked what god would save or deliver them.**)
- Why were Shadrach, Meshach, and Abed-Nego so confident before the king? (**They believed that God could deliver them. They had seen God answer their prayers in the past.**)
- Explain in your own words the answer the three men gave the king. (**Answers will vary but should include that their God would save them but if He didn't, they still would not worship the king's statue.**)

APPLICATION

- When have you shown resolve to follow God's ways? (**Answers will vary.**) (After students share their answers, congratulate them and affirm their decisions to show faithfulness to God.)
- How do you feel when you show resolve to be faithful to God? (**Answers will vary but should include it feels good to please God.**)
- In what situations is it hardest for you to obey God? (**Answers will vary.**)

REINFORCEMENT

When Hananiah, Mishael, and Azariah were taken captive from Jerusalem to Babylon, they were given Chaldean or Babylonian names. Their new names most likely reflected names of Chaldean gods. Hananiah's name in Hebrew meant *gift of God* or *Jehovah has given*, but became *Shadrach*, which meant *command of Aku*. Aku was the moon god worshipped by the Babylonians. Mishael's Hebrew name meaning *who is what God is*, was changed to *Meshach*, which meant *guest of a king*. The name *Azariah* in Hebrew means *whom Jehovah helps*. In Babylon he was given the name *Abed-Nego*, meaning *servant of Nego*. Nego most likely referred to Nebo, the god of wisdom, writing, and agriculture. The names given to the young Hebrew men did not turn them away from being faithful to the one, true God.

DAY 2

23.2 *Daniel's Friends Are Faithful*

Circle the answer that best shows resolve to obey God.

1. When others make fun of me for doing the right thing, I will
   a. get angry at them for not joining with me.
   b. pray for my friends to want to do the right thing, too.

2. When I am in a store and I see something I want, I will
   a. wait until I can buy it with my money.
   b. sneak it into my pocket.

3. When my friend is angry at me, I will
   a. say something mean to him or her.
   b. pray that I will not be angry with him or her.

4. When I feel like disobeying my parents, I will
   a. hide so I do not have to obey them.
   b. choose to obey them.

5. How can you obey God's Word? Write down three ways to do what God's Word says to do.

   a.
   b. Possible answers: worship no other gods, honor and obey parents, do not steal, love one
   c. another, serve one another in love

90

© Bible Grade 2

225

23.3 Daniel's Friends Are Faithful

Focus: Courage and Deliverance

★ PREPARATION

Select **DM-1 Character Traits**. (*Introduction*)

↻ EXTENSION

3A Make a copy of **BLM 23A Pray for Romanians** for each student. After students fill in their answers, have them get together with a partner and pray for the children in Romania.

3B Sing the song "What Seems Impossible" from the Grade 2 URL. Discuss with students different situations in the Bible that seemed impossible, but from which God delivered His people, such as Moses leading the Israelites out of Egypt and crossing through the Red Sea, and the battle of Jericho.

Introduction ★

Show **DM-1 Character Traits**. Review the definitions of *courage*, *faithfulness*, and *obedience*. Let students give examples of people from the Bible truths studied this year who demonstrated strong examples of these traits. (*courage*: **Moses and David;** *faithfulness*: **Joshua, Ruth, Daniel, Shadrach, Meshach, and Abed-Nego;** *obedience*: **Abraham and Joshua**)

Directed Instruction ↝

Invite students to find the word **deliverance** in the Glossary. Ask a volunteer to read its meaning, which is *saved or rescued from a difficult situation*. Explain to students that God is able to save and rescue. Read **Psalm 91:14–16**. Remind students to show faithfulness to God's ways and ask God to deliver them from difficult things.

To further illustrate God's deliverance read the following true story:
Richard Wurmbrand was happily ministering to his Romanian people when the government of his country became Communist. The new Communist leaders asked pastors, like Richard, to tell everyone to be faithful to the new government even though that government did not want anyone to believe in God.

Richard could not do that! He stood up and spoke before a large group, promising to be loyal to God. The government officials were very upset, but his wife was very proud of Richard's faithfulness to God. Later, Richard was arrested by the secret police and put in prison. His wife was put in a different prison. Their son was left homeless and alone. The Wurmbrand family suffered because of their faithfulness to God.

In prison, Richard was treated badly and beaten. It took courage to remain faithful to God in prison, but he knew that his choice to follow God was the right choice. Eight years later, Richard saw God's deliverance when the government surprisingly decided to let him go free, but he was warned not to preach again. Reunited with his family, Richard had to decide what he would do. If he preached about God, he would go back to prison. If he didn't preach about God, he would be free, but he would know that he was unfaithful to God. Richard chose to continue to tell people about Jesus. He was arrested again and told he had to spend 25 years in jail.

God saw Richard's faithfulness. After Richard had been in prison for five years, another miracle took place and he was set free! A group of Christians in another country paid $10,000 to the Communist government in Romania to let Richard and his family leave Romania. They were finally free to tell people about Jesus and God's power to deliver! Richard and his wife began a ministry of telling people about the Christians who suffer because of their faithfulness to God. Although Richard and his wife are now in heaven, their ministry still continues and helps Christians know how to pray for Christians around the world who suffer for Jesus.

Lead students in prayer to ask for the resolve and courage to show faithfulness to God in any and all situations they encounter.

Student Page 23.3
Have students complete the page. Tell students to share their drawing.

Review
• What does the word *deliverance* mean? (**Deliverance means saved or rescued from a difficult situation.**)
• Why was Richard Wurmbrand arrested and put into prison? (**He chose to be faithful to God and not the Communist government.**)
• What happened after his first eight years in prison? (**God delivered him and he was released.**)
• Did Richard obey the government warning not to preach again? Why or why not? (**No, he knew God wanted him to continue to preach and teach others about God.**)
• What happened after he was sent to prison again? (**God delivered him again and he was released.**)

APPLICATION
• Tell about a time when God delivered you out of a difficult situation. (**Answers will vary.**) You might not have known at the time it was God who helped you. Take a minute to thank God that He delivered you, that He is always with you, and that He loves you.
• Who do you know that is going through a tough time right now? (**Answers will vary.**) What could you pray for that person? (**Answers will vary but should include that God will give him or her courage to do what is right.**)

DAY 3

Name _____

Daniel's Friends Are Faithful **23.3**

Use the Code Box to figure out the missing words.

Code Box					
1 = a	2 = c	3 = d	4 = e	5 = g	6 = i
7 = l	8 = n	9 = o	10 = r	11 = u	12 = v

1. God saw Shadrach, Meshach, and Abed-Nego's

c o u r a g e
2 9 11 10 1 5 4

2. They saw God's

d e l i v e r a n c e
3 4 7 6 12 4 10 1 8 2 4

3. Look up deliverance in the Glossary. Write the definition.

deliverance: ___saved or rescued from a___ ___difficult situation___

4. Shadrach, Meshach, and Abed-Nego experienced God's deliverance. Draw a picture to show how they might have looked when they came out of the fiery furnace.

Drawings will vary.

© Bible Grade 2

91

© Bible Grade 2

23.4 Daniel's Friends Are Faithful
Focus: Others Praise God

★ PREPARATION
Obtain a LIGHTER or MATCHES, and FOUR CANDLES. Place the candles at different locations in the classroom. (*Directed Instruction*)

⌒ EXTENSION
4A Ask students to write a short journal entry from the perspective of King Nebuchadnezzar. Invite students to imagine how he would have felt when the three men were still in the furnace and walking around unhurt. Tell students to think about how it would have felt to see a fourth man in there. Let students wonder what the king thought when the men came out of the furnace and their clothes did not even smell like smoke. Ask students how they would have felt if they were Nebuchadnezzar. (**Possible answers: amazed, astonished, afraid**)

4B Invite students to role-play this week's Bible truth in groups of three and portray Shadrach, Meshach, or Abed-Nego. Provide a narration as each group pantomimes the actions.

Introduction
Choose two or three praise songs that students know and sing them together. Discuss why people who love God spend time praising and worshipping God. (**Answers will vary but should include that people want to tell God how much they love Him.**)

Read **Psalm 34:1–3**. Explain that David had experienced God's deliverance many times in his life and he wanted everyone to join him in praising God. Ask students to explain why they think everyone does not worship God. (**Possible answers: They have not heard about Him; they do not know He loves them; they have not seen His power.**) Remind students that their actions and choices to obey God can help others see God's love and power.

Directed Instruction ★ ⌒
Read **Daniel 3:28–30**. Ask students what Nebuchadnezzar's reaction was when the three men came out of the fiery furnace. (**He praised God.**) Explain that Shadrach, Meshach, and Abed-Nego's faithfulness to God created a situation where God delivered them in an amazing way. They did not know how or even if God might save them. They decided to follow God no matter what happened to them. They did not know their choice to follow God would affect other people, but it did. The king saw how they believed in God and how God delivered them, and as a result, he worshipped God. The king even made a command that no person in his kingdom should say anything bad about God because no god could deliver like the God of Shadrach, Meshach, and Abed-Nego.

Explain to students that sometimes people are watching them to see their actions and reactions. Some of the people may not know Jesus as their Savior and are looking to see how the students handle difficult situations. When students show resolve to be faithful to God, He may use the situation to do amazing things and show His faithfulness. When God delivers believers from harm, other people see God's power and might choose to follow God, too.

Invite a student to read **Matthew 5:14–16**. Explain that their faithfulness and obedience to God can be seen in the good things they do. Turn out the lights to make the room dark. Use a LIGHTER or MATCHES to light ONE CANDLE at the front of the classroom to illustrate how a small flame lights up a dark place. Explain that Christians shine God's light by showing faithfulness and obeying God's ways. When they do, others might want God's light to shine in their lives also. As you talk, light one of the other candles in the room. Remind students that they are helping others to see God's love and power, and maybe others will choose to praise and worship God also. Continue until all four candles are lit. Talk about how much light the four candles give off in the dark room. The four candles can represent the four compass directions to show that God's light needs to spread to all the areas of the earth. Explain that God desires everyone in the whole world to be part of His family and worship Him. People can see God's love and power when believers in God faithfully obey Him.

Student Page 23.4
Read the instructions and give students time to complete the page.

Review

- King Nebuchadnezzar had to order the men to come out of the furnace. Why do you think they might have wanted to stay in there? (**Answers will vary but should include that God Himself was there with them.**)
- How did Nebuchadnezzar respond when the three men came out of the fiery furnace? (**He praised God.**)
- What might happen when others see you do what is right? (**Others will notice and might praise God.**)
- What is a goal God has for the whole world? (**He wants the whole world to know Him and worship Him.**)

Notes:

APPLICATION

- What are some ways you have felt like Shadrach, Meshach, and Abed-Nego? (**Possible answers: when I chose to follow God's ways instead of doing something wrong that someone else wanted me to do; I knew God was going to deliver me.**)
- Tell about a time when your faithfulness to God led others to praise Him. (**Answers will vary.**)

REINFORCEMENT

Miracles help people to believe in God and His power. Missionaries often recount instances of a healing or a deliverance that inspired people to place their faith in God. The amazing deliverance of Shadrach, Meshach, and Abed-Nego from the furnace saved their lives, but the ultimate goal was for King Nebuchadnezzar to worship God. Although God loves His children, their comfort and happiness are not His priority. People worshipping God is the top priority. Nebuchadnezzar immediately praised God and commanded all people of all languages not to speak against God. The Bible tells the story of God's desire to be worshipped by all people and in all languages. The wonderful scene around God's throne in Revelation 7:9 shows that people from every nation, tribe, people, and language will worship God.

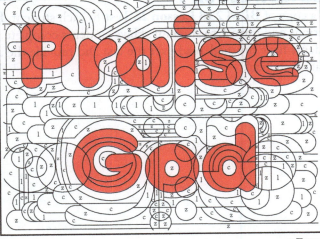

DAY 4

23.4 Daniel's Friends Are Faithful

1. Think about Shadrach, Meshach, and Abed-Nego's faithfulness to God. How can you show faithfulness to God? Write three sentences to answer the question.

   Answers will vary.

2. Use an orange crayon to color every shape that has a letter **f**. What might people do when they see your faithfulness to God and His faithfulness to you?

23.5	**Daniel's Friends Are Faithful**
	Focus: Review and Assessment

★ PREPARATION

Select **VA 23A The Fiery Furnace**. (*Lesson Review*)

Print **BLM 23B Lesson 23 Test** for each student. (*Directed Instruction*)

Lesson Review ★

Use **VA 23A The Fiery Furnace** to review the Bible truths from this lesson. Cover the following concepts:

• King Nebuchadnezzar was angry with the three young men—Shadrach, Meshach, and Abed-Nego—because they would not bow down to his gold statue.

• Shadrach, Meshach, and Abed-Nego knew that God could deliver them from the fiery furnace. They did not know if God would chose to save them, but they decided to still be faithful to God no matter what happened to them.

• When they were put in the furnace, they were not hurt, and a fourth man, the Son of God, was with them.

• Shadrach, Meshach, and Abed-Nego showed courage and faithfulness to God. They believed God is who He says He is and will do what He says He will do.

• When the three men came out of the fire, Nebuchadnezzar responded by worshipping God.

• *Deliverance* means *saved or rescued from a difficult situation.*

• Richard Wurmbrand chose to be faithful to God even though he was put in prison.

• When God delivered Richard from prison, he was told never to preach about God. Even though he might suffer in prison again, Richard kept preaching.

• God delivered Richard out of prison a second time. He spent the rest of his life helping people learn about the Christians suffering around the world because they had chosen to be faithful to God.

• The only time to disobey people in charge is when the authority goes against what God says to do.

• When Christians show faithfulness to God in difficult situations and God shows faithfulness to them, others will notice and might choose to worship God.

• God's goal is for the whole world to know Him. He desires for all to worship and praise Him.

Directed Instruction ★

Distribute a copy of **BLM 23B Lesson 23 Test** to each student. Explain the instructions and format to students. Have students complete the test. When students have finished, read over the test and provide the answers for immediate feedback.

Notes:

Lesson Preparation
Daniel Is Confident
24.0

Expected Student Outcomes

KNOW
Daniel's confidence in God brings God honor. Daniel interprets the writing on the wall and is later protected in the lions' den.

DO
Students will:
- match the words of the message on the wall and its interpretation
- identify how God protected Daniel
- apply things Jesus taught about prayer
- draw pictures to make a time line of Daniel's life

APPLY
Students will express confidence in God's guidance, provision, and protection. They will affirm that God's kingdom is forever.

Lesson Outline
I. God reveals the answer (Dan 5)
II. God delivers Daniel (Dan 6, Ps 32:7)
III. Daniel prays
   A. The Lord's Prayer (Mt 6:9–13)
IV. God's faithfulness to Daniel (Dan 1, 2, 5, 6)

♥ TEACHER'S HEART

Jesus said that anyone who wanted to be great in His kingdom, or considered successful, must be the servant of all (Mark 10:43–44). While the world counts riches, beauty, proficiency, position, and power as true marks of success, Christ followers are called to a different way of life—a life of surrender, selflessness, and service. Daniel left a wonderful example to follow. Surrounded by political intrigue, peer influence, and direct mandates, he could have chosen the easy path of compliance. Daniel showed faithfulness to God and God was faithful to him and delivered him from many difficult circumstances. Daniel relied on God through every situation he encountered, whether he was endangered or honored. Daniel's life was threatened more than once and he was even sentenced to execution. In spite of the dangers, he remained true to God. God delivered Daniel and rewarded him publicly under each king of the Babylonian Empire.

Pray that you and your students will honor God in tough times and experience God's type of success. As you humbly model going to God and consistently surrendering to Him through prayer, students will see God's protection, provision, and power in your life. Confidently rely on Him to do what needs to be done no matter what path you find yourself on throughout your life.

Supplemental Materials are available to download. See Understanding Purposeful Design Bible at the front of this book for the Grade 2 URL.

📖 MEMORY VERSE
Joshua 1:9

GLOSSARY WORDS
- confidence
- prophecy

★ MATERIALS

Day 1:
- Soft object or ball
- Blindfold
- Love Bowl from Lesson 11.4 (*Extension*)

Day 2:
- VA 24A Daniel in the Lions' Den
- BLM 24A Daniel's Rap (*Extension*)

Day 3:
- BLM 24B Prayer Puzzle, DM-13 Prayer Puzzle
- Large sheet of paper (*Extension*)

Day 4:
- Large sheet of paper, beanbag

Day 5:
- VA 24A Daniel in the Lions' Den
- BLM 24C Lesson 24 Test

♪ SONGS
Praying
Books of the Bible (*Extension*)
I Am Not Ashamed

TEACHER RESOURCES
DeMuth, Mary E. *You Can Raise Courageous and Confident Kids: Preparing Your Children for the World They Live In.* Harvest House Publishers, 2011.
Omartian, Stormie. *The Power of a Praying Life.* Harvest House Publishers, 2010.

STUDENT RESOURCES
Storyteller Café: The Lion's Den. DVD. Vision Video, 2007.

24.1 Daniel Is Confident
Focus: God Reveals the Answer

📖 MEMORY VERSE
Joshua 1:9

MEMORY WORK
- Review Joshua 1:8, the Memory Verse from Lesson 7.1, and then introduce this week's verse. Toss the SOFT OBJECT or BALL to any student in the room. Tell the student who catches it to say the first word of the verse. Have that student toss the ball to another student to say the second word. If the ball is dropped or the wrong word is said, have the first student toss it to a different student to say the correct word. Continue until all students have had a turn.

★ PREPARATION
Provide a SOFT OBJECT or BALL. (Memory Work)

Select a BLINDFOLD for student use. (Introduction)

 EXTENSION
1A Review the characteristics of godly love by inviting students to pick and read a card from the LOVE BOWL introduced in Lesson 11.4.

Introduction ★
Use a BLINDFOLD to cover a volunteer's eyes. Ask the volunteer to write his or her name on the board. Ask if he or she is absolutely sure it is spelled correctly. Remove the blindfold for the volunteer to see how he or she did.

Have students locate and read the definition of **confidence** in their Glossary. *Confidence* means *total trust or faith in someone or something*. Ask students if they thought the volunteer had confidence that the name was spelled correctly even with a blindfold on. Explain to students that their actions can show others they have confidence in someone or something.

In today's Bible truth, Daniel's actions showed he had confidence that God would give him the correct explanation of a message.

Directed Instruction
Read the following Bible truth adapted from Daniel 5:

After King Nebuchadnezzar's reign, a new king came into power. His name was *Belshazzar*. After many years as king, he decided to have a banquet for 1,000 of the country's leaders. During the banquet, King Belshazzar asked his servants to use the silver and gold drinking cups that Nebuchadnezzar's soldiers had taken from the temple of God in Jerusalem. As they admired the cups, the king and the leaders began to worship their false gods of gold, silver, iron, wood, and stone.

Suddenly, the fingers of a human hand appeared on one of the walls and began writing a message that no one could read. King Belshazzar was so terrified by what was happening that his knees and legs were shaking! The queen came into the banquet hall, and she was amazed by the writing on the wall. When she realized that even the wise men could not tell the king what the message meant, she reminded King Belshazzar that Daniel had been able to solve many difficult problems for King Nebuchadnezzar. King Belshazzar sent for Daniel right away.

When Daniel arrived, King Belshazzar promised to reward him if he could explain what the writing meant. Daniel replied that King Belshazzar did not need to give him a reward. Daniel promptly and confidently told the king what he wanted to know. It was not a good message. The message said that the one, true God judged King Belshazzar because he failed to honor God and worshipped false gods instead. King Belshazzar would soon lose his kingdom, and a new king from a different country would take his place.

King Belshazzar was amazed at Daniel's ability to solve the mystery. He rewarded Daniel just as he had promised, even though Daniel did not want the reward. That very evening, King Belshazzar was killed, and a new king named *Darius* took over the kingdom of Babylonia.

Explain that Daniel showed confidence in God's omniscience—His ability to know everything—in guiding Daniel to interpret the words written on the wall. Daniel did not question the interpretation or wonder if it was correct. Daniel courageously told the king the message that God had revealed to him, even though the message might have made the king very angry. The message was a **prophecy**, which means *a message or instructions given directly by God to a prophet and told about something that would happen in the future.* Daniel did not want the king's rewards because he knew his ability to interpret the writing came from God and not his own wisdom.

Student Page 24.1
Allow students to work in pairs to complete the page.

Review
- What were King Belshazzar and the leaders doing at the banquet? (**having a party, drinking out of the golden cups from God's temple, worshipping false gods**)
- What was the meaning of the message on the wall? (**It was a prophecy that meant Belshazzar would lose his kingdom.**)
- How did Daniel know the meaning of the message? (**God revealed it to him because He is all-knowing.**)

APPLICATION
- Why can you have confidence in God? (**Possible answers: God knows everything; God is faithful to answer me when I pray; God promises to help me.**)
- God is all-knowing. How can this fact help you with a problem or difficult situation? (**Answers will vary but should include that I can pray and know that God will help me because He knows everything about the situation.**)

REINFORCEMENT
The name *Belshazzar* means *Bel has protected the king.* Bel was one of the many gods worshipped by the Babylonians. King Belshazzar was unconcerned about attack from the Persian army because his confidence was in his city's massive walls. The great banquet may have been given to show his people that there was nothing to fear from the Persians. During the banquet they used 5,400 gold and silver vessels taken from the temple in Jerusalem (Ezra 1:9–11). While Belshazzar was celebrating, the Persian army dug a canal to divert the Euphrates River and entered the city through the riverbed.

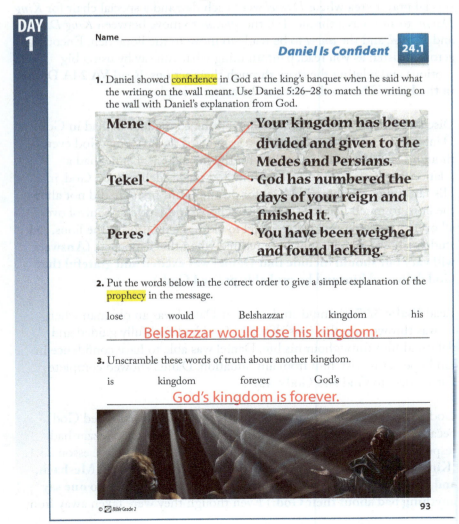

24.2 Daniel Is Confident
Focus: God Delivers Daniel

★ PREPARATION
Select **VA 24A Daniel in the Lions' Den**. (*Directed Instruction*)

⟲ EXTENSION
2A Make a copy of **BLM 24A Daniel's Rap**. As you read the rap, have students snap their fingers to create a rhythm.

2B Remind students that Daniel showed confidence in God to deliver him. Let students find and read the following Scriptures that show why they can have confidence in God:
- God knows them very well. (**Psalm 139:14**)
- God wants to provide good things for them. (**Matthew 7:11**)
- God knows when they are afraid. (**Psalm 56:3**)
- God wants to be their strength. (**Psalm 28:7**)

Introduction
Ask the class what is needed in each of these situations (**protection**):
- a hurricane is coming and you are standing on the beach
- you are on a trail in the woods and a bear approaches you
- lightning is striking all around and you are in an open field
- the car you are in swerves out of control on ice as you ride to school

Ask students to think of situations in which they might need God's protection. Discuss how courage and prayer are important in difficult situations. Point out that they should listen to God and let Him guide them through His Word. Inform students that in today's Bible truth, God protects Daniel in a dangerous situation.

Directed Instruction ★ ⟲
Ask volunteers to silently act out these roles during the reading of the Bible truth: *King Darius*, *Daniel*, *officials*, *lions*, and an *angel*. Before you read the Bible truth, designate an area for the lions' den where the *lions* can be pacing and waiting for their prey. Emphasize how hungry the lions must have been waiting for a prisoner to become their dinner. Also designate a special prayer area where *Daniel* went each day, and a special chair for *King Darius* to sit on as a throne. Tell the *officials* to move between *King Darius* and *Daniel*, and the *angel* to be ready to move to the lions' den. Encourage actors to listen as you read, pantomiming what you say by using big motions and relating the story through their actions. Read **VA 24A Daniel in the Lions' Den** to the class as the actors role-play.

Discuss Daniel's need for protection and the confidence he had in God. Daniel knew God wanted him to keep praying and trusting God even though Daniel would be shut in with the fierce lions. Daniel had a relationship with God and trusted in God for his deliverance. God, in His faithfulness, honored Daniel for putting Him first. He did not allow the lions to touch Daniel! God created lions, and God has control over all of nature. God provided an angel to close the mouths of the lions. Ask students how Daniel might have reacted when this happened. (**Answers will vary but should include that Daniel was excited and grateful that God delivered him and he probably praised God.**)

Read **Psalm 32:7**. Remind students that Daniel was an old man when he was thrown into the lions' den, and God had faithfully guided and delivered him throughout his life. Daniel was able to have confidence in God's power to save him from any situation. Daniel showed complete faithfulness to God and God's ways.

God protected Daniel from harm, and King Darius worshipped God because of it. Ask students to explain how King Nebuchadnezzar had responded after Daniel's friends remained faithful to God in Lesson 23.1. (**King Nebuchadnezzar saw God's power protect Shadrach, Meshach, and Abed-Nego in the fiery furnace and commanded that no one say anything bad about their God.**) Even though they were taken away from their homes to a new land, Daniel, Shadrach, Meshach, and Abed-Nego remained faithful to God. The kings and people in the new land of God's power and praised God for His ability to guide, provide, and protect.

Student Page 24.2
Read the directions and have students complete the page. Discuss how God also protects students in tough circumstances, as he did with Daniel.

Review

- Why were the officials looking for something Daniel had done wrong? (**They were jealous of Daniel.**)
- What did the officials do to trick King Darius? (**They talked him into making a new law that said everyone had to pray to the king only.**)
- How did Daniel honor God after the law was made? (**He kept praying to God three times a day by his open window.**)
- What was King Darius' response to the way God protected Daniel? (**He made a new law that everyone should honor the God of Daniel.**)

APPLICATION

- Why do you think God chose to protect Daniel? (**Answers will vary but should include that God wanted people to know of His power to deliver those who trust in Him.**)
- When have you needed protection from God? (**Possible answers: in a storm, in the dark, when tempted to do something wrong**) How did God help you? (**Answers will vary.**)
- What are some things that you will do the next time you need courage and deliverance? (**Answers will vary but should include praying and confidently trusting God to help.**)

REINFORCEMENT

Lions are carnivores known to kill other animals as large as elephants and giraffes. They readily eat any meat they can find, usually feeding at sundown and sleeping during the day. A full grown male lion is six to seven feet long, and weighs between 370 and 500 pounds. Lions typically consume more than 75 pounds of meat at a single meal and then rest for a week before eating again. They are well-muscled animals and formidable predators. Biblically, Satan is compared to a roaring lion seeking whom he may devour (1 Peter 5:8).

24.3	# Daniel Is Confident
	Focus: Daniel Prays

⭐ PREPARATION

Print **BLM 24B Prayer Puzzle** for each student. Select **DM-13 Prayer Puzzle**. (*Directed Instruction*)

Select the song "Praying" from the Grade 2 URL. (*Directed Instruction*)

↻ EXTENSION

3A Place a LARGE SHEET OF PAPER on the wall. Write the following titles on the paper: *praise, guidance, provision, forgiveness, deliverance.* Ask students to write under the appropriate title the things they would like to ask God or say to God. (**Possible answers: I praise God for His love; I need guidance about how to tell a friend about Jesus.**) Use this as a guide at prayer time each day.

3B Select the song "Books of the Bible" from the Grade 2 URL to sing together.

Introduction

Divide students into small groups. Have each group make a list of things they like to talk about with their friends. Next, ask them to make a list of all the things they talk about to God. Gather the class together. Discuss the similarities and differences of the two lists and why they may not talk to God like they talk to their friends.

Directed Instruction ⭐ ↻

Daniel knew the importance of praying to God and he prayed three times each day. God does not require a certain number of times to pray to Him each day—He hears and answers any and all prayers! Prayer is talking to God. Prayer is not a special way to say something to get what you want from God. It is a way to share your thoughts and needs with Him.

Explain that Jesus gave an example of how He talked with God because His followers wanted to know how to pray. Distribute a copy of **BLM 24B Prayer Puzzle** to each student. Display **DM-13 Prayer Puzzle** to aid students. Read **Matthew 6:9–13**. Explain each of the following parts of the Lord's Prayer, and direct students to write each of the words listed in the space provided on the puzzle pieces:

1. **Praise**: God wants everyone to recognize His holiness and to honor Him with praise (verse 9). Discuss words to use to praise God by describing who He is. (**Possible answers: holy, all-powerful, Creator, loving**)
2. **Guidance**: Students can expect that God will guide them to do things that follow God's ways and will help others come to know about God and His kingdom, which lasts forever (verse 10). Discuss how to express what living for God looks like. (**Possible answers: reading the Bible, praying, serving others, loving others with God's love**)
3. **Provision**: God wants His children to not worry about their daily needs, but to ask Him to provide for them. Just as Jesus trusted God to take care of what He needed every day, students should confidently look to God for their needs, too (verse 11). Discuss things that God provides. (**Possible answers: food, a place to live, a loving family**)
4. **Forgiveness**: Because all have sinned, everyone needs God's forgiveness. No one could pay the price for sin, so Jesus paid that price, or debt, when He died on the cross. Since Jesus forgives and has paid that debt, He wants His followers to forgive others (verse 12). Discuss times when forgiveness is needed or given to others. (**Possible answers: when someone lies, when someone disobeys, when someone is unkind**)
5. **Deliverance**: God wants His children to ask for help to courageously fight against evil. He has complete power over Satan and gives Christians the power to fight against evil (verse 13). Discuss times when students are tempted to do what is wrong. (**Possible answers: when others choose to do wrong, when it seems like doing wrong has good rewards**)

Discuss ways Daniel also followed the prayer examples from the Lord's Prayer. (*praise*: **He gave praise to God for giving him the interpretations of Nebuchadnezzar's dream and the writing on the wall;** *guidance*: **He** prayed to understand the king's dream; *provision*: God provided health to Daniel and his friends as they ate foods that followed God's laws; *forgiveness*: Daniel probably forgave the king for taking him from his country; *deliverance*: Daniel was delivered from the lions' den.)

Sing the song "Praying" from the Grade 2 URL and spend a few minutes letting students pray with a partner.

Student Page 24.3
Read the text and directions and have students complete the page.

Review

• How did Daniel show he had a relationship with God? (**He talked and listened to God regularly.**)
• What was Daniel's prayer habit? (**Three times a day he knelt to pray in front of an open window that faced Jerusalem.**)
• How did Jesus teach His followers to pray? (**He gave an example that is now known as the Lord's Prayer.**)

APPLICATION

• Why do you think Jesus gave an example of how to pray? (**Answers will vary but should include that Jesus wants everyone to understand what prayer is and some of the things that can be part of a prayer.**)
• Name the five things from the example of the Lord's Prayer that could be included in your prayer. (**praise, guidance, provision, forgiveness, and deliverance**)
• Which part of the Lord's Prayer example is the easiest for you to remember to include in your prayer? Why? (**Answers will vary.**)

DAY 3

Name _____

Daniel Is Confident 24.3

Jesus taught His disciples how to pray in Matthew 6:9–13. Complete the sentences below. Use them as a prayer guide when you pray.

1. I can praise God for _Answers will vary._
2. I want God's guidance to help me _Answers will vary._
3. I see God's provision in my life in _Answers will vary._
4. I can give forgiveness to _Answers will vary._
5. I need God's deliverance when _Answers will vary._

6. Read Psalm 4:1, 8. Jennifer, age 9, wrote a devotion about prayer. Read it and then answer the question at the end of the devotion.

God loves you very much. If you are ever scared and need protection, you can always ask God for help. One night I was frightened by a big storm. I prayed to God and asked Him, "What should I do?" He answered, "Do you believe I love you? Then I will protect you." When the Lord told me that, it made me feel safe and loved. Just as God answered when I needed protection, God will always answer you no matter what you ask Him. Usually He answers "Yes, no, or maybe later." God talks to you, but He also likes it when you talk to Him! If you are listening, He can talk to you in many ways, like through words of Scripture, a song, or talking to another person. Keep looking to God and spend time talking to Him!

What will you talk to God about?
_____ Answers will vary. _____
_____

© Bible Grade 2   95

© Bible Grade 2   237

24.4 Daniel Is Confident

Focus: God's Faithfulness to Daniel

★ PREPARATION

Select the song "I Am Not Ashamed" from the Grade 2 URL. (*Introduction*)

Obtain a BEANBAG. Write the following words in a tic-tac-toe grid on a LARGE SHEET OF PAPER: *resolve, faithfulness, deliverance, peer pressure, courage, obedience, prophecy, revelation, prayer.* (*Directed Instruction*)

⤼ EXTENSION

4A Explain to students that Daniel served three different kings in his lifetime. In chapters 1–4, he served Nebuchadnezzar. In chapter 5, he served Belshazzar, and in chapter 6, he served Darius the Mede. Write each king's name on the board. Direct students to find the following passages: Daniel 2:46–48; 5:29; 6:1–3. Write the reward Daniel received from each king under his proper name. (*Nebuchadnezzar*: **high position and many gifts;** *Belshazzar*: **purple robe, gold chain, and third most-powerful ruler;** *Darius*: **one of three administrators placed in charge of the entire kingdom**)

4B Write the word *Daniel* down the side of the board. Let students suggest phrases or sentences about Daniel's life that start with each letter in his name.

Introduction ★

Sing the song "I Am Not Ashamed" together. Discuss why Daniel was not ashamed to worship God. (**Possible answers: He knew God was powerful; he knew God was faithful; he had experienced God's guidance and deliverance.**)

Directed Instruction ★ ⤼

Invite a volunteer to toss the BEANBAG onto the LARGE SHEET OF PAPER. Use the word on which the beanbag lands to discuss how that aspect of God's care was demonstrated in Daniel 1 below. Then have another student toss the beanbag again and discuss Daniel 2. Repeat for Daniel 5 and 6.

From Daniel 1: Daniel and his friends were captured by King Nebuchadnezzar and had to move to Babylon. They were told to eat the king's rich foods like everyone else. Even though they could have been punished, they asked permission to eat vegetables and drink water in order not to disobey God's law. They needed God to help them remain faithful to Him in a new land. God provided them with good health. God also blessed them by giving them special abilities and wisdom to serve the king.
- resolve and faithfulness to obey God's law
- peer pressure to eat different food than others
- courage for Daniel to ask for permission to eat foods different from the king's rich foods
- obedience to God's law

From Daniel 2: King Nebuchadnezzar had a dream that his advisers could not interpret. The king became angry and wanted all the advisers killed. Daniel asked his friends to pray. God provided the knowledge for Daniel to know and interpret the dream. The king was amazed and recognized Daniel's God was the one, true God.
- prayer for God to give wisdom about the dream
- revelation of the dream and its meaning
- courage for Daniel to tell the king what his dream meant
- prophecy of what would happen to the king's kingdom

From Daniel 5: During King Belshazzar's banquet, fingers of a hand wrote a message on the wall. King Belshazzar asked Daniel to interpret the message. God provided revelation for Daniel to know exactly what the words meant.
- courage for Daniel to tell the king what the message meant
- revelation of the meaning of the writing on the wall
- obedience to tell the king the message from God
- prophecy of what would happen to the king's kingdom

From Daniel 6: Daniel was faithful to pray to God even though King Darius was tricked into making a law that said anyone who bowed down to something other than the king would be thrown into the lions' den. God protected Daniel by sending an angel to close the lions' mouths. King Darius made a new law that said everyone should honor Daniel's God.

- resolve, faithfulness, courage, and obedience to pray even when it was against the law
- peer pressure against praying to God when everyone else was praying to the king
- prayer three times a day in front of an open window

Student Page 24.4

Read the directions. Complete the activity together to review Daniel's life.

Review

- Name one way God provided for Daniel. (**Possible answers: God gave him good health; God gave him wisdom to interpret dreams and the message on the wall; God gave him protection.**)
- Name the kings who saw Daniel be faithful to God. (**King Nebuchadnezzar, King Belshazzar, and King Darius**)
- How did the kings react to God's faithfulness to guide and deliver Daniel? (**King Nebuchadnezzar and King Darius both made laws to praise and honor God.**)

APPLICATION

- Why did Daniel choose to trust God throughout his life? (**He had a relationship with God and knew God would provide for him.**)
- What does Daniel's life teach you about God? (**Possible answers: God wants me to have a close relationship with Him; God is faithful; nothing is too difficult for God.**)

DAY 4

24.4 *Daniel Is Confident*

Draw pictures of different events in Daniel's life that match the Scriptures given below. Drawings will vary but should include

DANIEL 1 — eating vegetables and looking healthy

DANIEL 2 — interpreting Nebuchadnezzar's dream of a statue

DANIEL 5 — interpreting the writing on the wall at the king's banquet

DANIEL 6 — being protected in the lions' den

96

© *Bible Grade 2*

© *Bible Grade 2*

239

24.5 Daniel Is Confident

Focus: Review and Assessment

★ PREPARATION

Select **VA 24A Daniel in the Lions' Den**. (*Lesson Review*)

Make a copy of **BLM 24C Lesson 24 Test** for each student. (*Directed Instruction*)

Lesson Review ★

Use **VA 24A Daniel in the Lions' Den** to review the Bible truths from this lesson. Cover the following concepts:

- King Belshazzar had a banquet with his leaders. At the banquet, they used silver and gold items taken from the temple in Jerusalem to worship their false gods.
- At the banquet, fingers of a human hand began writing on the wall. Daniel was asked to interpret the message on the wall.
- Daniel did not want the rewards King Belshazzar offered.
- *Confidence* means *total trust or faith in someone or something*.
- Daniel had confidence that God was all-knowing and would reveal the interpretation of the writing.
- *Prophecy* means *a message or instructions given directly by God to a prophet and told about something that would happen in the future*.
- The message was a prophecy that King Belshazzar would lose his kingdom because he failed to honor God. Only God's kingdom lasts forever.
- When Daniel worked as an adviser to King Darius, other officials were jealous of Daniel's success.
- King Darius' officials tricked the king into making a law that said everyone had to pray to the king only.
- Daniel continued to pray three times a day in front of an open window, even though he knew he could be thrown into the lions' den for not obeying the king's law.
- Daniel chose to honor God by praying to Him rather than praying to King Darius.
- God protected Daniel and delivered him from the lions by sending an angel to shut the lions' mouths.
- Daniel prayed to God throughout his life. Jesus gave an example of how to pray, known as the *Lord's Prayer*. When Jesus prayed, He praised God, asked for guidance, asked for provision, asked for and gave forgiveness, and asked for deliverance from evil.
- God provided help for Daniel in each situation in his life, and God will also provide help to those who love Him.

Directed Instruction ★

Distribute copies of **BLM 24C Lesson 24 Test**. Read the directions and explain any vocabulary students need help understanding. When everyone is finished, review test answers for immediate feedback.

Notes:

240

Lesson Preparation
Mary and Joseph Obey God

25.0

Expected Student Outcomes

KNOW
Mary and Joseph submit to and willingly participate in God's plan of redemption through Jesus.

DO
Students will:
- write Mary's and Joseph's responses to messages from the Lord
- choose obedient responses to real-life experiences
- use a chart showing Old Testaments prophecies and their fulfillment to complete sentences
- read real-life scenarios of humility and submission

APPLY
Students will demonstrate a willingness to act on God's Word. They will display humility and submission.

Lesson Outline

I. God sends an angel (Mt 1, 2:13–15, 19–23; Lk 1:26–38, 46–56, 3:23–38)

II. God knows everything
 A. Mary and Joseph obey God (Mt 1:20–25, 2:13–14, 19–21; Lk 1:31–38)

III. Prophecies about the Messiah
 A. Nathan and Isaiah (2 Sam 7:16–17; Is 7:14, 9:6–7)

IV. Humility and submission
 A. Mary and Joseph participate in God's plan
 B. Personal humility and submission

❤ TEACHER'S HEART

"Tell me a story!" Children of all ages like to hear a good story. We share stories with our friends, we watch them on television, and we read them in books. It should not surprise us that God chose a story as a means by which to reveal Himself. Jesus also used stories as an effective way to teach.

The Bible is God's story. It contains glimpses of His perfect plan for the world, a plan we cannot quite comprehend. It shows us God's character, which has not changed. It records stories of how God reached out to reveal His will and His love to humanity. The birth, death, and resurrection of Jesus Christ marked a turning point in the story of God's plan for the world. God pursues a relationship with us and invites us to participate in His plan each and every day. Be on the lookout for these opportunities. Remind yourself that you are a dynamic part of God's story and count it a privilege to participate in His plan! You DO make a difference!

📖 MEMORY VERSE
Matthew 1:21

GLOSSARY WORDS
- Trinity

✻ MATERIALS

Day 1:
- VA 25A Mary and Joseph Obey God
- Time Line
- BLM 25A God's Plan Cube, card stock (*Extension*)

Day 2:
- Poster board (*Extension*)
- Magazines (*Extension*)

Day 3:
- Brochure
- Time Line

Day 4:
- Colored strips of paper (*Extension*)

Day 5:
- VA 25A Mary and Joseph Obey God
- BLM 25B Lesson 25 Test

♪ SONGS
I Can Obey

TEACHER RESOURCES
House, H. Wayne and Randall Price. *Charts of Bible Prophecy*. Zondervan, 2003.

STUDENT RESOURCES
Larsen, Carolyn. *What Does the Bible Say About That?* Crossway Books, 2009.

Supplemental Materials are available to download. See Understanding Purposeful Design Bible at the front of this book for the Grade 2 URL.

25.1 Mary and Joseph Obey God
Focus: God Sends an Angel

📖 MEMORY VERSE
Matthew 1:21

MEMORY WORK
- Write the Memory Verse on the board. Randomly, erase 10 of the words. Write each word that was erased on a piece of paper—one word per piece of paper. Distribute each piece of paper to different students. Instruct students to tape their word in the correct spot on the board. Direct the class to read the verse.

★ PREPARATION
Select **VA 25A Mary and Joseph Obey God**. (*Directed Instruction*)

EXTENSION
1A Write the acrostic for the word *obey* as shown below. Use each horizontal word in a phrase that describes the word *obey*. For example: Telling others about God is a way **of** obeying Him.
Each person there did his or her best to do what the Bible says.
Of
Be
Each
You

1B Duplicate copies of **BLM 25A God's Plan Cube** on CARD STOCK for each student. Demonstrate how to follow a plan to make the cube, and instruct students to complete the cube. Invite partners to roll their cubes, read the word on top, and say the complete message: "Obey God and follow His plan." Reiterate that God has a plan for each person. Assure students that as they grow and obey God, He helps them to follow His plan for their life.

Introduction
Invite three volunteers to come to the front of the room. Give one student the message to stand in any corner of the room with a book on his or her head. Tell another student to put his or her backpack on and stand by the door. Tell the third student to write his or her name on the board and stand near the name.

Share how each student received a message and all three students did what they were instructed to do. Comment on how each response was an obedient one.

Directed Instruction ★
In Old Testament times, there were people called *prophets* who spoke prophecies. Review that *prophecy* means *a message or instructions given directly by God to a prophet and told about something that would happen in the future*. Because God is all-knowing and all-powerful, He knows what will happen in the future. Introduce Nathan and Isaiah as Old Testament prophets. They said that God had a plan for a baby to be born to take away the sins of the world.

Display and read **VA 25A Mary and Joseph Obey God**.

Share that Mary was pregnant before she was married to Joseph. Be sensitive to the needs of your class when discussing the significance of the virgin birth. Explain that the baby's father was the Holy Spirit, who is part of the **Trinity**. The *Trinity* is defined as *one God in three Persons—God the Father, God the Son, and God the Holy Spirit*. Explain that each part of the Trinity has a different function and purpose in a believer's life, yet they are all one God. God the Father sent God the Holy Spirit to Mary so God the Son could be born. God the Father loved the world so much He sent His Son to save it. He also sent the Holy Spirit to be a companion to believers always.

State that Mary and Joseph obeyed God. They willingly accepted and were happy to be a part of God's plan. Ask students to name the promised Savior that was born to take away the sins of the world. (**Jesus**) Explain that Jesus provides a way for people to have a right relationship with God.

Conclude the lesson by stating that Nathan's and Isaiah's prophecies were fulfilled in the New Testament.

Review
- What was Mary's response when the angel told her she was favored among women? (**Mary said, "Let this happen to me just like you have said." She praised the Lord.**)
- What was Joseph's response to each of his three dreams? (**Joseph married Mary. Joseph took the young child and Mary to Egypt. Joseph, the young child, and Mary stopped in a region of Israel and settled in a city of Galilee called Nazareth. Joseph obeyed God.**)

- How were Mary and Joseph part of God's plan? (**They obeyed and became Jesus' earthly parents.**)
- How was God's promise of a savior fulfilled? (**Jesus was born and paid the price necessary to bring people back to God. His death and resurrection provided the way for people to be accepted into a right relationship with God.**)

Student Page 25.1
Read the directions and have students complete the page.

Time Line
Inform students that today's lesson introduces the transition from the Old Testament to the New Testament. Show the break between BC and AD. Locate Mary, Joseph, and Jesus. Help students comprehend that the record of Mary, Joseph, and Jesus appears in the New Testament.

Notes:

APPLICATION
- What is one way to find God's plan for your life? (**Possible answers: by praying, and by learning Scripture and doing what it says**)
- How can God use you? (**Possible answers: I can tell others about Jesus so they can have a right relationship with God; I can show others the love of God in what I say and what I do.**)

REINFORCEMENT
In Isaiah 7:14 God's omniscience was evident when He gave the Israelites a sign about the Messiah coming to Earth, when they did not even know to ask for a sign. The word *virgin* used in this Scripture refers to a young girl of marriageable age. Other places in the Old Testament use the word to refer to young men also (1 Samuel 17:56, 20:22). When Joseph learned of Mary's pregnancy during the time of betrothal, he should have divorced Mary, according to both Jewish and Roman customs. He could have profited by keeping her dowry while divorcing her. Instead, Joseph chose to obey the angel's message (Matthew 1:20–21), even though he might have endured shame from others who were not aware of the angel's revelation about Mary's conception.

DAY 1

Name _____

Mary and Joseph Obey God 25.1

Write Mary's or Joseph's response to the message from the Lord.

1. An angel of the Lord came to Mary and told her not to be afraid, because she had found favor with God.

Answers will vary but should include Mary said, "Let this happen to me just as you said." Mary realized she was blessed and she praised the Lord. Mary obeyed God.

2. The angel told Joseph not to be afraid to take Mary as his wife.

Answers will vary but should include Joseph married Mary. Joseph obeyed God.

3. The angel told Joseph to take Jesus and Mary to Egypt.

Answers will vary but should include Joseph took the young child and Mary to Egypt during the night. Joseph obeyed God.

4. The angel told Joseph to take Jesus and Mary to Israel where it was safe for them.

Answers will vary but should include Joseph, the young child, and Mary went to Israel and settled in a city of Galilee called Nazareth. Joseph obeyed God.

5. Who are the three Persons of the Trinity?

God the Father, God the Son, and God the Holy Spirit

| 25.2 | # Mary and Joseph Obey God
Focus: God Knows Everything |

★ PREPARATION

Select the song "I Can Obey" from the Grade 2 URL. (*Introduction*)

⌔ EXTENSION

2A Invite students to make a list of rules for the game of kickball or any other game they often play. Write the rules on a piece of POSTER BOARD and post them. Challenge students to understand that when just one rule in a game is not obeyed, the game gets confusing and some people are not happy because the game seems unfair. Read one of the rules and ask, "What would happen if this rule were not obeyed?" Help students discover that when everyone obeys the rules in a game, it is fair and the end results are more easily accepted.

2B Distribute some MAGAZINES to students. Have students find and cut out pictures of people in positions of authority. Instruct each student to glue his or her pictures on a sheet of paper. Invite students to share the different authority figures. Make a list of them on the board and read the list out loud.

Introduction ★

Sing the song "I Can Obey" from the Grade 2 URL. Remind students that Mary and Joseph obeyed God. Discuss how they became part of God's plan for Jesus to be born. Share that God has a plan for each of them. God wants believers to obey Him so they can follow His plan for their lives.

Directed Instruction ⌒

Explain that just as parents requires their children to be obedient, even if the child does not understand the reasons, so God requires people to be obedient even though they do not understand God's plans. God's plan is far better than any plan a human being can come up with. After all, He is God. He is all-knowing and all-powerful. He asks believers to remember that He loves them, and to trust Him and obey willingly because His plan is perfect. It cannot be improved upon.

Read **Jeremiah 29:11.** God promises believers that His plans are good, and for their benefit.

Read **Psalm 100:5.** God reminds believers that He is a loving God, and asks them to remember all that He has done for them throughout history.

Read **Isaiah 55:8–10.** God reminds people that they cannot understand his thoughts and plans fully, and that they must trust and obey even though they do not understand. When God told Noah to build an ark, it must have seemed ridiculous. But Noah obeyed, and as a result he and his family were saved and played a part in God's great plan. When God told Moses to go back to Egypt, where he was wanted for murder, that must have seemed dangerous to Moses. But Moses obeyed God, and God used him to bring the Israelites out of Egypt and slavery. Mary and Joseph obeyed God, even though what He asked of them seemed impossible. Because they were obedient, they played a major part in God's perfect plan to save the world from sin.

Ask students if they think that they should obey in small, everyday ways, or only when it really matters. (**They should obey in both.**) Discuss how obeying in the small things builds trust, which leads to more responsibilities, and larger blessings.

Present these scenarios and ask what each person should have done:
* Brooke likes to eat strawberries for an afternoon snack. Her mother told her not to eat the berries in the bowl because she wanted to use them in a fruit salad. Brooke was all alone in the kitchen and saw the strawberries. They looked delicious and Brooke thought that she would eat just one of them. She picked out the biggest one and ate it. (**Brooke should not have eaten the strawberry even when her mother was not there.**)
* Latisha and Bree were playing in the park and ran by a bench that had a sign on it. The sign read WET PAINT—KEEP OFF. They did not know if the paint was wet or not, so they touched the bench. The girls got paint all over their hands, and they had nothing to clean their hands with.

244

(Latisha and Bree should not have touched the freshly painted bench. The posted sign stood for authority even though no one was there.)

Lead a discussion on how important it is to obey even when no one is looking. Invite students to share times they have obeyed when their mother, father, babysitter, or teacher was not there looking at them. Reinforce that doing the right thing makes each of them a happy person and helps them to best follow God's plan for their life.

Review

- Why should people obey God? (**so they can please Him, be part of His plan**)
- How would you describe God's plans? (**God's plans are perfect, loving.**)
- Why is it important to obey when no one is looking? (**because it builds trust, I get more responsibilities and blessings**)

Student Page 25.2
Read the directions and have students complete the page.

APPLICATION

- Name some people God tells you to obey. (**Possible answer: those who have authority over me such as parents, pastors, teachers, and police officers**)
- If a parent told you to clean your room and then he or she walked away, should you clean your room? Why or why not? (**Answers will vary.**)
- Tell about a time when you obeyed someone but that person was not looking to see if you were obeying. (**Answers will vary.**)

DAY 2

25.2 Mary and Joseph Obey God

Read each real-life experience. Circle the letter next to the words that show an obedient response. More than one answer is correct.

1. Griffin's mom and dad have been praying about what God wants them to do. Now the family will move far away.
   - **a.** Griffin can get ready to move while praying for his future friends. *(circled)*
   - b. Griffin can pout and whine about leaving his friends.
   - **c.** Griffin can realize that God will use him to share the gospel with his new neighbors. *(circled)*

2. A missionary is coming to visit Savannah's family. She has to give up her room for a week.
   - a. Savannah can grumble and complain.
   - **b.** Savannah can cheerfully clean her room. *(circled)*
   - **c.** Savannah can be willing to hear about the missionary's work. Maybe she can serve God as a missionary too. *(circled)*

In each box, write the letter of the alphabet that comes after each letter you see.

3. FNC JMNVR DUDQXSGHMF.
   GOD KNOWS EVERYTHING.

98

25.3 Mary and Joseph Obey God
Focus: Prophecies About the Messiah

★ PREPARATION
Select a BROCHURE from the location where a future field trip is planned. (*Introduction*)

↻ EXTENSION
3A Instruct students to turn to the Table of Contents in their Bibles. Lead students in naming the books of the Old Testament and then singing them. Continue the process with the books of the New Testament.

Introduction ★
Ask students if they can remember a trip that their family planned and then took. Share that a special field trip is planned for the class and display a BROCHURE from the location. Tell when, where, and why the class is going. Discuss the event enthusiastically. Relate that you are speaking like a prophet who tells something that is going to happen in the future.

If a field trip cannot be planned, discuss something that is looked forward to, such as an art festival, a science fair, an end-of-the-year awards program, a special event, or a chapel.

Directed Instruction ↶
Remind students that prophets spoke prophecies, and when the event happened, the prophecy was fulfilled.

Today's lesson makes the transition from the Old Testament to the New Testament. Students have studied about men and women in the Old Testament up to this point. As students are introduced to prophets who prophesied in the Old Testament, they will understand that many prophecies were fulfilled in the New Testament.

Read **2 Samuel 7:16–17**. Explain that the prophet Nathan told David that his kingdom would last forever. Share that David had a descendant named *Joseph*. Years later, Mary and Joseph had a son named *Jesus*. Jesus was born into David's family. Jesus would be King and rule over the world forever.

Read **Isaiah 7:14**. Teach that the prophet Isaiah said that someday a virgin would have a son and His name *Emmanuel* would mean *God with us*. Years later, Mary was blessed by the Holy Spirit and she had a son whose name was *Jesus*, which means *God is salvation*. He would save His people from their sins.

Read **Isaiah 9:6–7**. Relate that the prophet Isaiah said a child would be born and a son given who would rule on the throne of David. Years later, Jesus was born in the city of David. Jesus was the promised Savior.

Time Line
Identify the biblical characters students have studied in the Old Testament. Ask students to recall one fact about each character. Encourage students to discern the truth of the prophecies God gave to Nathan and Isaiah. Share that Nathan and Isaiah said that someday Jesus would be born, save His people from their sins, and rule over the world forever. Jesus was the expected King, the Messiah. God had a plan and it was fulfilled.

Review
• What was Nathan's prophecy? (**David's kingdom would last forever.**)
• How was Nathan's prophecy fulfilled? (**David had a descendant named Joseph. Jesus was born to into Joseph's family, which means He was a**

246

part of David's family line. Since Jesus lives forever, David's kingdom lasts forever.)

- What were some of Isaiah's prophecies? (**Someday a virgin would have a son, and this Son would rule on the throne of David.**)
- How were Isaiah's prophecies fulfilled? (**Mary was blessed by the Holy Spirit and had a son named Jesus. Jesus was the promised Savior, and He was born in the city of David.**)
- Name two people in this lesson who obeyed God and were part of God's plan in fulfilling some of the Old Testament prophecies. (**Mary and Joseph**)

Student Page 25.3
Read the directions and have students complete the page.

Notes:

APPLICATION

- Why is it important for you to obey God? (**so that I can be a part of fulfilling His plan**)
- Think of a situation where it was very difficult to obey, but you did the right thing by obeying. How does your obedience compare to that of Mary and Joseph? (**Answers will vary but should include that even though the situation was difficult, obedience was the right response in God's eyes.**)

REINFORCEMENT

The Bible records many instances when people received heavenly messages from angels. Both Mary and Joseph were visited by angels who brought them messages about their roles in the life of Jesus. Luke 1:26 specifically names Gabriel as the angel who spoke to Mary. The angel Gabriel is noted as the angel who appeared with messages about the Messiah—both His birth and His mission. Gabriel appeared to Daniel with end-time prophecies (Daniel 8:16, 9:21–27) and to Zacharias with news about John's birth and role in preparing the way for the Messiah (Luke 1:11).

DAY 3

Name _____

Mary and Joseph Obey God   **25.3**

OLD TESTAMENT PROPHECY		NEW TESTAMENT FULFILLMENT
Nathan: David's kingdom would last forever.	God had a plan.	Jesus' kingdom is forever.
Isaiah: A virgin would have a son. His name would mean **God with us.**	God had a plan.	Mary was blessed by the Holy Spirit. She had **Jesus.**
Micah: The Messiah would come from Bethlehem.	God had a plan.	Jesus was born in Bethlehem.

Write **Jesus, Isaiah, Nathan, Savior,** and **plan** to complete the sentences.

1. The prophet ____Nathan____ prophesied that David's kingdom would last forever. The prophet ____Isaiah____ prophesied that someday a virgin would have a son who would rule on the throne of David.

2. The prophets told about God's ____plan____. Years later, Mary and Joseph obeyed God and He used them to complete His promise. ____Jesus____ was born. The promised ____Savior____ provided a way for people to have a relationship with God.

© *Bible Grade 2*   99

© *Bible Grade 2*   247

25.4 Mary and Joseph Obey God
Focus: Humility and Submission

⟲ EXTENSION

4A Observe students and identify those who demonstrate humility and submission during their daily activities. When a student has demonstrated humility or submission, share with the class what the act of humility or submission was. Write a sentence describing the act on a COLORED STRIP OF PAPER, and the name of the person displaying humility or submission, and tape it to the wall. Add strips for every act of humility and submission you witness. Continue taping the strips end to end to see how far around the room the strips of paper can go.

Introduction

Write the word *humility* horizontally on the board. Then write the word *submission* vertically so that the letter *i* in each word intersects.

```
        s
        u
        b
        m
h u m i l i t y
        s
        s
        i
        o
        n
```

Explain that Mary and Joseph submitted to God out of humility to His plan. They knew that God's plan was more important than any plan they might have. They showed submission to God by recognizing His plan and giving themselves to God's authority.

Directed Instruction ⟲

Share that in life there are times when God wants us to demonstrate humility and submission. State that a person who has humility is a person who has the attitude of not being proud. Remind students that humility means thinking and caring about God and others first. It means listening for His guidance. Humility refers to the attitude or willingness a person has. Review that submission is the act of accepting the authority of someone else or surrendering your own will to someone else's. Explain that it takes humility to be truly submissive in a God-honoring way.

Read the following scenarios and ask students to name who showed humility and submission and tell how they were displayed:

- Mrs. Carter told Landon and Derek it was garbage day and to take out the garbage. Landon did not like taking out the stinky can full of trash. He went upstairs and packed his book bag to get ready for school. All of a sudden Derek heard the garbage truck coming up the street. He ran out of the house and put the trash can in the driveway just in time to get picked up. (**Derek showed humility by taking out the stinky trash can. He showed submission by doing what his mother said.**)

- Mr. Miller took his class to the computer lab to work on a math game. Everyone had access to a computer except Lena and Breanne. A computer became available because someone had finished. Instead of rushing ahead to get to the computer first, Lena told Breanne to use the computer. Breanne was happy to take her turn at the math game. (**Lena showed humility because she didn't mind being last. She showed submission by letting someone else go before her.**)

- There was a basketball game between the two second-grade teams. Ethan was on one team. Cole was on the other team. Cole's team was only two points ahead when he ran into Ethan accidentally, knocking Ethan down. The referee blew the whistle and the game stopped. Cole reached out his hand to help Ethan get up. (**Cole showed humility by helping Ethan up. Ethan showed submission by allowing Cole to help him up.**)

Remind students that if they do not listen for God's voice, they will miss out on many blessings. If they do not listen, they cannot hear Him speak. If they cannot hear Him speak, then they will not do what He wants. If they do not do what He wants, then they cannot be a part of God's plan, and they miss out on the privilege of carrying out God's work.

Review

- How did Mary and Jesus show humility and submission? (**They were willing to be a part of God's plan of redemption through Jesus.**)
- What was Mary's response when she was told she would have a baby but she did not understand why? (**Mary submitted to God's plan even though she didn't understand it all.**)
- Name some situations when others have shown humility and submission. (**Answers will vary.**)

Student Page 25.4

Read the directions and text for each question aloud. Have students complete the page. Review each life experience in Exercises 1–3 and ask how each person showed humility and submission. (**Answers will vary.**)

Notes:

APPLICATION

- Name one way you can show humility and submission to another person. (**Answers will vary.**)
- How can you show the Lord that you want to be a part of His plan? (**Possible answers: by obeying God, by showing humility and submission to others**)

DAY 4

25.4 Mary and Joseph Obey God

Mary and Joseph showed humility and submission by willingly being a part in God's plan. When Mary was told that God had chosen her to be the mother of Jesus, she said, "Let this happen to me just as you have said." Even though Mary did not understand why this was happening to her, she showed humility and submission to God.

Read each life experience. Write the name of the person who shows humility and submission.

1. At the breakfast table Mrs. Thomas reminded her sons, Joe and Dionte, to make their beds before going on an outing to the zoo. Dionte stopped reading an action-packed book to make his bed. Joe had to be reminded a second time before he made his bed.

   _____Dionte_____

2. Mr. Barnes bought some flowers for Mrs. Jonas, an elderly neighbor. Mr. Barnes wanted his daughters, Mandy and Cynthia, to go with him to take the flowers to Mrs. Jonas. Cynthia did not go to Mrs. Jonas' house. Mr. Barnes and Mandy went to Mrs. Jonas' house and gave her the flowers. Mrs. Jonas was so happy.

   _____Mandy_____

3. Abby's mother asked her to put the books that she and her friends had been reading back on the bookshelf. Just then, her older brother Seth pulled all the books off the shelf and ran off. Abby was upset with Seth, but put all the books on the shelf.

   _____Abby_____

25.5 Mary and Joseph Obey God

Focus: Review and Assessment

★ PREPARATION

Select **VA 25A Mary and Joseph Obey God**. (*Lesson Review*)

Make one copy of **BLM 25B Lesson 25 Test** for each student. (*Directed Instruction*)

Lesson Review ★

Use **VA 25A Mary and Joseph Obey God** to review the Bible truths from this lesson. Cover the following concepts:

- The *Trinity* is defined as *one God in three Persons—God the Father, God the Son, and God the Holy Spirit.*
- God had a plan for the promised Savior of the world to be born.
- Prophets Nathan and Isaiah spoke of God's promise for a baby boy to take away the sins of the world.
- The prophecies spoken by the prophets were fulfilled.
- Mary and Joseph submitted to and willingly participated in God's plan of redemption through Jesus.
- God used Mary and Joseph to fulfill His promise.
- Jesus the Messiah was born.
- The promised Savior of the world would redeem people, providing a way for them to have a restored relationship with God.
- God's plans are perfect, and we cannot fully understand them
- God promises believers that His plans are good, and for their benefit.
- Because God is all-powerful and all-knowing, He knows what will happen in the future.
- Listening for God's voice means you will be able to hear His instructions. Hearing enables you to do His will, which means you become a part of God's perfect plan.

Directed Instruction ★

Distribute a copy of **BLM 25B Lesson 25 Test** to each student. Read the directions and pronounce any difficult words. Have students complete the test. When everyone is finished, read over the test, providing the answers for immediate feedback.

Notes:

Lesson Preparation
Jesus Is Merciful
26.0

Expected Student Outcomes

KNOW
Jesus demonstrates His power and mercy by healing people.

DO
Students will:
- define and illustrate an example of mercy
- explain how Jesus showed mercy to a blind man
- write a letter to Jesus from the perspective of a man healed from a sickness
- illustrate the sequence of sin, confession, and forgiveness as seen in 1 John 1:9
- describe being merciful in a personal and practical way

APPLY
Students will conclude that God is merciful. They will extend mercy to others.

Lesson Outline
I. Jesus heals the blind (Lk 18:35–43, Mt 9:27–31)
II. Jesus heals the sick (Mk 1:40–45, Jn 5:1–15)
III. God shows you mercy (Ps 136:1–9, 1 Jn 1:9)
IV. Showing mercy to others (1 Jn 4:7–11, Mt 5:7)

♥ TEACHER'S HEART

Justice is getting what you deserve; mercy is not getting what you deserve. Most of the time sin and wrong decisions must be punished; justice calls for it. However, the lessons learned when a punishable offense is met with mercy is that the giver of that mercy is doing something good, in spite of the wrong that needs to be punished. Mercy fills a soul with relief and gratitude. It is undeserved and unexpected. In Victor Hugo's famous novel *Les Misérables*, Jean Valjean, a convict, steals silver plates from a good and kind bishop. When Valjean is arrested, the bishop does not give Valjean the justice he deserves; instead, he gives him silver candlesticks outright and says, "Jean Valjean, my brother: you belong no longer to evil, but to good. It is your soul that I am buying for you. I withdraw it from dark thoughts and from the spirit of perdition, and I give it to God!" That one act of mercy changed the wretched convict into a good man. While this is just a story, it is a picture of the wonderful mercy you have received at the hands of a merciful God. The mercy that flows from the cross is incomprehensible. Mercy changes you. Mercy will change your students. Ask God to give you wisdom to recognize when to show your students mercy instead of the justice they deserve.

Supplemental Materials are available to download. See Understanding Purposeful Design Bible at the front of this book for the Grade 2 URL.

© Bible Grade 2

📖 MEMORY VERSE
Micah 6:8

GLOSSARY WORDS
- mercy

★ MATERIALS
Day 1:
- BLM 26A Memory Squares, envelopes
- VA 26A Jesus Heals a Blind Man, PP-7 The Life of Jesus
- Large box (*Extension*)

Day 2:
- Envelopes (*Extension*)

Day 3:
- DM-1 Character Traits
- Scientific balance, two objects of equal size and weight (*Extension*)

Day 4:
- DM-14 Mercy Cycle
- Pretzel twists, string or ribbon (*Extension*)

Day 5:
- VA 26A Jesus Heals a Blind Man
- BLM 26B Lesson 26 Test

♪ SONGS
Love with the Love of Jesus

TEACHER RESOURCES
Stanley, Charles F. *Surviving in an Angry World: Finding Your Way to Personal Peace.* Howard Books, 2010.

STUDENT RESOURCES
Anderson, Dan and Kristin Blegen. *Jonah: A Veggie Tale Movie.* DVD. Lionsgate, 2003.
Hastings, Selina. *The Children's Illustrated Bible.* DK Publishing, 2005.

251

26.1 Jesus Is Merciful
Focus: Jesus Heals the Blind

MEMORY VERSE
Micah 6:8

MEMORY WORK
- Supply each student with a copy of **BLM 26A Memory Squares**. Instruct students to write a few words of the Memory Verse into each of the squares, until all of the squares contain a portion of the verse. Then direct students to cut out each square. Have students mix up the paper squares on their desk. Challenge them to independently arrange the word squares so they match the order of words in the Memory Verse. Encourage students to repeat the activity several times, working together in groups. Provide each student with an ENVELOPE to store the squares.

★ PREPARATION
Duplicate copies of **BLM 26A Memory Squares** for each student. Have ENVELOPES available. (*Memory Work*)

Select **VA 26A Jesus Heals a Blind Man** and **PP-7 The Life of Jesus**. (*Directed Instruction*)

EXTENSION
1A One way to show mercy is through giving. Share about a local soup kitchen or homeless shelter. Teach that these places help people who do not have homes or money to buy food and who may be sick. Place a LARGE BOX in a prominent location in your classroom. Encourage students to bring items throughout the week to add to the box. Suggest items such as canned goods, coats, and blankets. Tell students that these items will be donated at the end of the week to people in need.

Introduction
Direct students to close their eyes and imagine that they are blindfolded and cannot see. Have them visualize the following:
- You are standing on a busy street corner and hear a loud crash.
- You have to walk down a long flight of stairs by yourself.
- You are confused and do not know how to find your way home.
- You have to find a specific office in an unfamiliar, large building.

Have students open their eyes. Ask them how these scenarios made them feel. (**Possible answers: scared, worried, anxious, thankful for their sight**) Discuss with students how wanting someone to help them during times of need is normal. Today's lesson is about a blind man who was in desperate need of help.

Directed Instruction ★ ⌒
Read **VA 26A Jesus Heals a Blind Man**. Explain that the blind man had heard that Jesus was able to heal. The blind man wanted so much to see that he cried out to Jesus as He was passing by. Share with students that when they cry out to Jesus, He hears them, just as He heard the blind man on the side of the road. When Jesus healed the man, He said that the man's faith had healed him. This man believed with his whole heart that Jesus could and would make him see.

Share the following from Matthew 9:27–31:
> At another time, two blind men followed Jesus, crying out, "Son of David, have mercy on us!" He asked them, "Do you believe that I am able to do this?" They answered, "Yes, Lord." Jesus then touched their eyes and said, "Because of your faith, it will happen." Suddenly they could see! Jesus showed His power and mercy by healing the blind men.

Instruct students to look up the definition of **mercy** in the Glossary. Write the definition on the board: *kindness and compassion*. Jesus was kind and compassionate (caring) to the blind men. Explain that every person needs mercy. Mercy includes showing both kindness and compassion, but it can also involve forgiving people when they do not deserve it.

To bridge the gap between Lessons 25 and 26, show **PP-7 The Life of Jesus** to teach students about the life of Jesus, starting with His birth. Share that Jesus was the Son of God when He was born, throughout His entire life, and when He died and rose again. Explain to students that God's ultimate act of mercy was to send Jesus to die for their sins. Teach students that Jesus is able to heal because of His *omnipotence* which means *the quality of being all-powerful*.

Student Page 26.1
Direct students to independently complete the page.

Review

- What does *mercy* mean? (**kindness and compassion**)
- Who did Jesus show mercy to in today's Bible lesson? (**blind men**)
- How did Jesus show mercy? (**He healed the blind men.**)
- What did Jesus say was the reason that all three blind men were healed? (**their faith**)

Notes:

APPLICATION

- Do you have faith that God can fix a problem in your life? (**Answers will vary.**) Ask God to give you more faith so that you will see Him do greater things in your life.
- Why was Jesus able to heal the blind men? (**Answers will vary but should include He is omnipotent, He is God.**)

DAY 1

Name _____

Jesus Is Merciful 26.1

1. Look up mercy in the Glossary. Write the definition.

mercy: <u>kindness and compassion</u>

_____

2. Write and draw a picture about a time that someone showed mercy to you.

Answers will vary.

_____

_____

_____

_____

Drawings will vary.

3. How would you show kindness and forgiveness to someone who tripped you at recess?

Answers will vary but should include I won't get mad, I won't tattle, I will forgive.

4. Read Luke 18:35–43. How did Jesus show mercy to the blind man?

Jesus showed mercy by healing the blind man instantly.

© Bible Grade 2

101

© Bible Grade 2

253

26.2 Jesus Is Merciful

Focus: Jesus Heals the Sick

EXTENSION

2A Instruct students to draw the main events of today's Bible truth in comic-strip format. Prepare an ENVELOPE for each student by slitting open the sides and cutting a square viewing hole in the front. Give each student an envelope. Direct students to slide their comic-strip pictures through the envelope as they practice retelling the story of Jesus healing the lepers to a classmate.

Introduction

Ask students to think of how they feel when they are sick. Have students describe some symptoms of being sick, and discuss some possible remedies. (**Possible answers: prayer, medicine, a warm bath, a gentle touch from Mom**) Ask students how long it might take for medicine to work and make them feel better. (**Answers will vary but should include that it depends upon the kind of illness.**) Share that today's lesson is about how Jesus instantly healed some men who were sick.

Directed Instruction

Remind students that leprosy is a horrible skin disease. People with leprosy may have sores or deformed limbs, lose feeling in their bodies, and suffer from bad infections. During Jesus' time, most people with leprosy were forced to leave their families and communities and live in the countryside by themselves or with a group of lepers.

One day when Jesus was in Galilee, a man with leprosy came to Him and begged Jesus to heal him (Mark 1:40–45). "Lord, if You are willing, You can make me clean [from my disease]," the man said. Jesus felt compassion, love, and pity for the man and placed His hands on the man's damaged body. Then Jesus said, "I am willing; be cleansed." Immediately the leprosy disappeared, and the man was healed! Jesus told the man to go to the local priest, tell him what had happened, and offer a gift to God, which the Law of Moses required. The priest would then allow the man to return to his family. Jesus not only healed the man, but He made it possible for the man to return to his family and friends.

Explain to students that lepers were often treated as outcasts and ignored. But when Jesus saw these men, He had mercy on them and was not afraid to touch them. He accepted them and did not ignore them. Jesus immediately healed them. Remind students that Jesus was able to heal lepers because of His *omnipotence,* which means *the quality of being all-powerful.* He also showed kindness and compassion when He healed them.

On a different day, Jesus was in the city of Jerusalem, and He passed by the Pool of Bethesda (John 5:1–15). *Bethesda* means *house of mercy.* Many sick, blind, lame, and paralyzed people waited beside the pool. They went there so that they could be placed into the water for healing when the water began to bubble.

On the day that Jesus passed by the pool, He saw a man lying there who had been sick and weak for 38 years. Jesus knew how long the man had suffered, so He asked the man, "Would you like to be made well?" The man replied, "I cannot get well because I don't have anyone to help me get into the bubbling water." In response, Jesus said to the man, "Stand up, pick up your sleeping mat, and walk!" Instantly the sick man was healed! He rolled up his mat and began walking. This man was living proof of Jesus' mercy and power!

Student Page 26.2
Select volunteers to read aloud the Scriptures on the page. Have students complete the page.

Review
- What is leprosy, and how were lepers treated? (**Leprosy is a horrible skin disease. Lepers were cast out of society.**)
- What did Jesus do for the lepers? (**He showed kindness and compassion toward them. He touched them and healed them instantly.**)
- What was the man by the pool waiting for? (**He was waiting for the water to bubble so he could go into the water and be healed.**)
- What did Jesus do for him? (**He spoke to him and healed him instantly.**)

Notes:

APPLICATION
- How would you have felt if Jesus had healed you instantly like these two men? (**Answers will vary.**)
- How should you respond if Jesus heals you? (**I should show thankfulness.**)

REINFORCEMENT
Leprosy in the Old Testament was classified as any infection or malformation of the skin. The priest diagnosed the disease and then sent the leper out of the community for seven days. If at the end of that time, the skin was unchanged, the leper was ostracized seven more days as a precaution against spreading the disease throughout the community. By New Testament times, leprosy was no longer considered just a physical disease; it was also seen as a hereditary and highly contagious moral or spiritual defect.
Lepers were cast out of society completely and went about like mourners. Living in solitary perdition, they were forced to call out "unclean, unclean" when anyone approached. The way the religious community dealt with lepers stands in stark contrast to the Savior's behavior. He spoke to lepers; He got close to them; He touched them. He saw them not as lepers but as people.

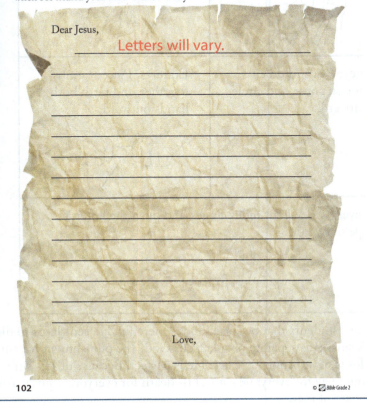

DAY 2

26.2 Jesus Is Merciful

Read Mark 1:40–45 and John 5:2–9. Imagine that you are the leper or the sick man at the pool. Write a letter to thank Jesus for healing you. Answer these questions: What was your life like before Jesus healed you? What did He do when He healed you? How did it make you feel?

Dear Jesus,

Letters will vary.

Love,

26.3 Jesus Is Merciful
Focus: God Shows You Mercy

★ PREPARATION
Select **DM-1 Character Traits**. (*Directed Instruction*)

↻ EXTENSION
3A Obtain a SCIENTIFIC BALANCE to show students. Make sure the balance is calibrated correctly. Have TWO OBJECTS OF EQUAL SIZE AND WEIGHT, one labeled *mercy* and the other labeled *justice*. Explain that because God is just, He cannot be near sin. His justice means satisfactory payment must be made for the sin. Place the object labeled *justice* on the scale and explain that the satisfactory payment for sin is death. Teach that God is not only completely just, He is also completely merciful. Place the object labeled *mercy* on the scale; this will balance the scale. Explain that it is through God's undeserved love and favor that people receive His mercy. By His mercy, the justice everyone deserves—death, or eternal separation from God—is withheld from those who accept what Jesus accomplished through His death, burial, and resurrection.

Introduction
Write the word *mercy* on the board and explain that *mercy* means *kindness and compassion*. Discuss with students what God has done to show them mercy. (**Possible answers: He takes away my sins; He forgives me; He loves me unconditionally; He does not remember any of my sins.**)

Directed Instruction ★ ↻
Invite students to read **Psalm 136:1–9** responsively. Explain that you will read the first part of each verse, and students should respond by reading the second part of each verse. Note that their response will always be the same. Point out that different translations use the words *love* and *mercy* interchangeably. Teach that true kindness and compassion need to be motivated by love and shown with love. God shows love, or mercy, because He cares for His children. Note that this psalm reminds His children to be thankful, demonstrating an attitude of thanksgiving to the Lord for all He has done and for who He is. Display **DM-1 Character Traits** and remind students that *thanksgiving* means *appreciating what you have*.

Teach students sign language to use as they say their part of Psalm 136. Direct them to say and sign the response.

• God's (His): Place palm out and move hand upward from shoulder toward heaven.	• Love: Cross arms in front of chest.
• Mercy: Place middle finger on chest, and circle it outward.	• Endures: Place thumbs together, and push both hands outward. 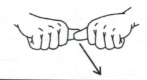
• Forever: Circle bent index finger, and push the letter Y shape outward. 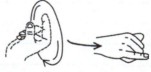	

Explain to students that because God is merciful, He sent Jesus to die for people's sins. Sins separate people from God. The punishment for sin is death. Jesus never sinned because He is perfect. Because of His sinlessness, Jesus could pay for everyone's sins. His death for everyone's sins was the ultimate act of mercy.

Student Page 26.3
Challenge students to quickly locate **1 John 1:9** in their Bible, and read the verse aloud in unison. Direct students to complete the page independently.

Review
- Who gives you unconditional mercy? (**God**)
- What are some ways that God has shown you His mercy? (**Answers will vary but might include that He forgives me, He cleanses me, and He sent Jesus to die for me.**)
- How long will God's mercy, or love, endure? (**forever**)

Notes:

APPLICATION
- When do you need to be shown mercy? (**Answers will vary but should include when I have sinned or am in trouble.**)
- How has God shown you mercy? (**Answers will vary.**)
- How should you respond to mercy? (**I should show thankfulness to God or the person who shows me mercy.**)

REINFORCEMENT
The belief in a benevolent God who is unconditionally merciful is unique to Christians and Jews (Hebrews in the Old Testament). Buddhists and New Age practitioners believe that the universe and God are identical (*pantheism*), and that people can create their own reality. Consequently, people are not guilty of any sin that a god or gods need to forgive. Hindus believe in a multitude of gods (*polytheism*) who have to be appeased before they will show mercy. In the monotheistic faith of Muslims, Allah is a distant God of justice who expects righteous behavior and submission to the divine will.

Mercy is mentioned hundreds of times in the Bible. Throughout the Old Testament, "His mercy endures forever" is proclaimed repeatedly. God in His mercy led the Hebrews out of the land of Egypt and across the Red Sea (Exodus 15:13). Jesus demonstrated supreme mercy by His sacrificial death on the cross, shedding His blood to forgive sin and save people from God's deserved judgment. Those who receive Jesus' sacrifice as payment for their sins are reconciled to God and are invited to His throne of grace, where they can find mercy in their time of need (Hebrews 4:16).

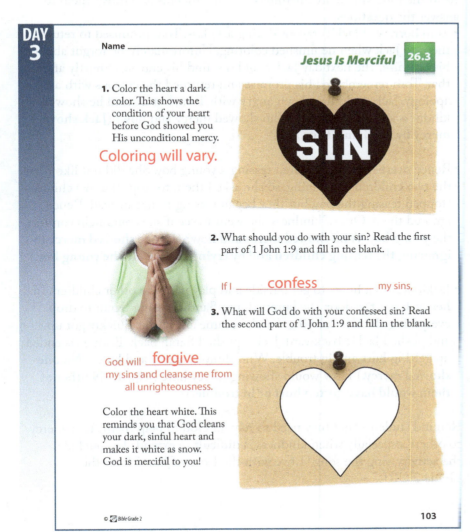

26.4 Jesus Is Merciful

Focus: Showing Mercy to Others

★ PREPARATION

Have **DM-14 Mercy Cycle** available.

Select the song "Love with the Love of Jesus" from the Grade 2 URL. (*Directed Instruction*)

↻ EXTENSION

4A Display a BAG OF PRETZEL TWISTS. Discuss the shape of a pretzel. Explain that some historians believe the intertwined pieces originally illustrated arms folded in prayer. This can remind students to pray for people who cross their path or whose lives are intertwined with theirs. Encourage students to pray and ask God to help them show mercy to people He has placed in their lives, especially in hard situations. Supply each student with a few pretzels and a STRIP OF STRING OR RIBBON long enough to make a slip-on necklace. Direct students to thread the string or ribbon through one of the pretzels. Assist students in tying a knot in the string or ribbon.

4B Look through the large box of mercy items collected during week from Lesson 26.1, Extension 1A. If possible, organize a field trip to a local soup kitchen or a homeless shelter to deliver the items. Another option would be to give the items to an invited guest from a local charitable organization who can share with students about the organization.

4C Discuss how God feels about those who refuse to show mercy. Read **Matthew 18:23–35** and point out that the servant who refused to show mercy did not get any mercy himself.

Introduction

Read the following scenarios aloud and ask students what they should do to show mercy, or kindness and compassion to others:

- Someone told a lie about you. What should you do? (**show the person mercy by forgiving him or her**)
- Someone is unkind to you. What should you do? (**show the person mercy by being kind to him or her**)

Discuss how showing mercy is sometimes difficult, especially when one is hurt by someone else's actions. Encourage students to ask God to help them show mercy, even when they do not feel like doing so.

Directed Instruction ★ ↻

Read **1 John 4:7–11**. Point out to students that they should be merciful because God has shown them love and mercy. Read **Matthew 5:7**. Display **DM-14 Mercy Cycle**. Select students to read each sentence to reinforce the concept of the "cycle" of mercy.

Read the following daily dilemmas to your students and direct them to answer the questions:

- Tom borrowed Jack's crayons during art class. Tom promised to return them to Jack when he finished coloring. Unfortunately, he forgot about his promise. The next day Jack could not find his crayons. Shortly after that, Tom remembered his promise and returned the crayons with an apology. Jack could have been angry with Tom, but instead he showed kindness and forgave him. Who showed mercy and how? (**Jack showed mercy by forgiving Tom.**)

- Renee overheard two children teasing a young boy. She did not like what the two children were doing, so she asked them to stop. The two children stopped teasing the boy, but they began teasing Renee instead. Renee ignored them. Out of kindness she went to see if she could help comfort the young boy. Who showed mercy and how? (**Renee showed mercy by ignoring the teasing children and by trying to console the young boy.**)

- Jackie was in a hurry to get outside and play with the other children. In her rush out the door, she bumped into Sarah, causing Sarah to drop everything she was carrying. Sarah became angry. She quickly got up and pushed Jackie backward. Jackie pushed Sarah back. Both girls ended up getting hurt and in trouble. Who showed mercy and how? (**No one showed mercy.**) How would showing mercy have helped? (**Neither of them would have gotten hurt or in trouble.**)

Remind students that they need to rely on God to help them show mercy to others, especially when kindness is difficult to extend. To conclude the activity, sing the song "Love with the Love of Jesus" from the Grade 2 URL.

Student Page 26.4
Have students work in groups to complete the page.

Review

• What are two reasons why you should show mercy to others? (**God has shown me mercy. When I show mercy to others, others may also be merciful to me.**)
• What are some ways you can extend mercy to others? (**Possible answers: be kind and caring, be forgiving, not get angry**)
• Who can you rely on to help you show mercy to others, even if you do not feel like being kind and compassionate? (**God**)

Notes:

APPLICATION

• In what specific ways can you show mercy to others? (**Answers will vary.**)
• Who are some people to whom you could show mercy? (**Answers will vary but should include people who have physical needs as well as any other needs.**)

DAY 4

26.4 *Jesus Is Merciful*

Write phrases to describe being merciful. Use each word provided.

More _Answers will vary but should include a description of what it is to be merciful._____

Ever _____

Really _____

Careful to _____

Instantly _____

Faithful to _____

Usually _____

Letting others _____

104

© *Bible* Grade 2

26.5 Jesus Is Merciful

Focus: Review and Assessment

★ PREPARATION

Select **VA 26A Jesus Heals a Blind Man**. (*Lesson Review*)

Make one copy of **BLM 26B Lesson 26 Test** for each student. (*Directed Instruction*)

Lesson Review ★

Use **VA 26A Jesus Heals a Blind Man** to review the Bible truth. Cover the following concepts:

- *Mercy* means *kindness and compassion*.
- Mercy can also involve forgiving people when they do not deserve or request it.
- A blind man begged Jesus to have mercy on Him. Jesus showed mercy by healing the blind man instantly.
- Jesus said that the man was healed because of his faith. Jesus knew the man believed that Jesus could heal him.
- Jesus is able to heal because of His *omnipotence*, which means *the quality of being all-powerful*.
- *Leprosy* is defined as *a horrible skin disease*. Lepers were cast out of society.
- Jesus showed mercy and touched the lepers. They were instantly healed.
- True kindness and compassion should be motivated by love and shown with love.
- God has shown His mercy by sending Jesus to die for everyone's sins so that they could be forgiven and cleansed.
- The Bible says to be thankful to the Lord for all He has done and for who He is.
- God's mercy (love) endures forever.
- Christians should show mercy to others because God has extended mercy to them.
- Christians can show mercy to others by being kind and caring, by forgiving others even when they do not deserve or request it, and by not getting angry or being mean.

Directed Instruction ★

Distribute a copy of **BLM 26B Lesson 26 Test** to each student. Have students complete the test. When they have finished, read over the test, providing the answers for immediate feedback.

Notes:

Lesson Preparation
Jesus Is Compassionate

27.0

Expected Student Outcomes

KNOW
Jesus teaches compassion toward others.

DO
Students will:
- identify traits and actions of sheep and people
- describe what Jesus, the Good Shepherd, does for them
- write about ways to stay close to Jesus
- complete exercises about Jesus' parable of the prodigal son

APPLY
Students will acknowledge that God is compassionate. They will show compassion toward others.

Lesson Outline
I. A shepherd shows compassion (Mt 9:35–38, Jn 10:11–16, Lk 15:1–7)
II. Jesus, the Good Shepherd (Ps 23, Is 53:6, Jn 10:11)
III. A gracious father (Lk 15:11–32)
IV. God shows compassion (Ex 34:6; Ps 118:1–4, 72:12–14; Deut 4:31; 1 Jn 4:10–11)

♥ TEACHER'S HEART

Have you ever noticed that the word *passion* is in the word *compassion*? The root meaning of *compassion* is *with passion* or *with deep, heartfelt, wrenching, crushing desire*. As Jesus went through the cities and villages, His heart was moved with compassion because the people were like sheep without a shepherd (Matthew 9:35–36). From quiet, remote villages to bustling cities, He sought out the most discouraged, weary souls and was moved to heal and bring them close to Him.

It is interesting to also note that *compassion* contains the word *compass*—a tool for keeping travelers on course. Jesus was always concerned about the spiritual needs of people. His actions caught the attention of people and His life was the way to hope and salvation.

You are challenged to be the compass that will point your students to Jesus. But you can't do that unless you also share His passion. As you pray with a heartfelt desire for these precious souls to be moved and drawn near to Jesus, think about the compassion Jesus has for you.

MEMORY VERSE
Matthew 9:36

★ MATERIALS

Day 1:
- DM-10 Shepherd and Sheep
- VA 27A Jesus Is the Good Shepherd

Day 2:
- DM-15 Psalm 23
- BLM 27A Lost Sheep (*Extension*)
- Poster-board strips, yarn, hole punch, small Bibles (*Extension*)

Day 3:
- Balloons, streamers, snacks (*Extension*)

Day 4:
- First-aid kit, emergency number, adhesive bandages, gauze or tape, ointment
- Poster board (*Extension*)

Day 5:
- VA 27A Jesus Is the Good Shepherd
- BLM 27B Lesson 27 Test

♪ SONGS
Walk Like Jesus (*Extension*)

TEACHER RESOURCES
Keller, Timothy. *The Prodigal God: Recovering the Heart of the Christian Faith*. Penguin Books, 2011.
Keller, W. Phillip. *A Shepherd Looks at Psalm 23*. Zondervan, 2008.

STUDENT RESOURCES
Lollar, Phil. "BTV: Compassion." *Adventures in Odyssey*. Audiobook. Focus on the Family, 2008.
Toscano, Charles. *Papa's Pastries*. Zonderkidz, 2010.

Supplemental Materials are available to download. See Understanding Purposeful Design Bible at the front of this book for the Grade 2 URL.

27.1 Jesus Is Compassionate
Focus: A Shepherd Shows Compassion

 MEMORY VERSE
Matthew 9:36

MEMORY WORK
- Encourage students to lightly tap their feet to each syllable as you say the Memory Verse. Have them repeat this action as they say the Memory Verse. Then direct all students to stand and say the Memory Verse together.

★ **PREPARATION**
Select **DM-10 Shepherd and Sheep**. (*Introduction*)

Select **VA 27A Jesus Is the Good Shepherd**. (*Directed Instruction*)

 EXTENSION
1A Select and sing together the song "Walk Like Jesus" from the Grade 2 URL. Brainstorm ways students can walk like Jesus and show compassion by helping meet the physical and spiritual needs of students their age.

Introduction ★
Display **DM-10 Shepherd and Sheep**. Write the following characteristics of sheep on the board:
- not very smart
- stubborn
- lose their way easily, have no sense of direction
- tend to wander, go astray (off the correct path)
- unaware of dangers, such as cliffs or wild animals
- hard for them to get up once they have fallen over
- helpless and totally dependent

Discuss these characteristics, noting that sheep cannot survive without a shepherd's protection and compassion. Another word for *compassion* is *caring*. Remind students that compassion and kindness are aspects of mercy. Teach that *compassion* is *caring that often includes the desire to help*. Ask students: Do the characteristics of sheep also describe people? (**Yes.**) Today's lesson is about Jesus, the Good Shepherd.

Directed Instruction ★ ⟳
Read **VA 27A Jesus Is the Good Shepherd**. Explain that Jesus had compassion for people. He cared not only for their physical needs, but He also saw and cared for their spiritual needs. Jesus described Himself as a shepherd because people, like sheep, need guidance and help.

Share with students that Jesus knows what they need. Explain that just as a shepherd searches for lost sheep to bring them back to safety, Jesus searches for spiritually lost people to bring them back to Him. Jesus is always watching over them to heal them, provide for them, and forgive them, because every person is valuable to Him. When a child of God goes astray, Jesus longs for that person to come back to Him with a heart of repentance. Review that repentance is being sorry for sin, confessing the sin, and changing one's actions.

Read the following true story about Kripa:
> Four-year-old Kripa watched as the sky lit up with fireworks at a huge celebration. Thousands of people were there enjoying the festivities, game booths, and different ethnic foods. As Kripa's family walked around, Kripa saw a fun game and wandered off the path. Her parents had told her to stay close to them, but Kripa disobeyed them. The next thing Kripa knew, she could not see her family. At the same time, her family realized that Kripa was missing, but they could not find her in the large crowd. It became dark, and everyone in Kripa's family was very worried. They stopped and prayed to God for help and guidance. After looking for Kripa for quite some time, they found her sitting on a blanket with someone who was watching over her. This person had calmed Kripa's fears about being away from the protection of her parents. Kripa was very sorry for disobeying her parents. Her parents hugged her tight and carried her home.

Discuss with students what it feels like to be away from the protection of someone who cares for them. (**Possible answers: frightening, lonely, scary, sad**)

Student Page 27.1
Have students complete the page. When complete, discuss the one characteristic of people listed in Exercise 1 that is different from sheep. (**people show repentance**)

Review
• Why did Jesus have compassion on the crowds of people around Him? (**He knew the people were lost like scattered sheep, and they needed someone to protect, lead, and care for them.**)
• What did Jesus know about the people that caused Him to want to help them? (**They were lost and needed His help to find hope and salvation.**)
• How is the story of Kripa like the description of Jesus as a shepherd searching for His lost sheep? (**Possible answers: Just as Kripa's parents searched for her after she wandered off, Jesus my Shepherd searches for me when I wander off; He does not want me to go astray or get lost.**)

APPLICATION
• In what ways are you like sheep? (**Possible answers: I go my own way; I tend to wander off the path I should be on; I am unaware of and ignore danger; I need a shepherd.**)
• Why did Jesus call himself *the Good Shepherd*? (**because He knows and cares for His sheep**)
• How has Jesus been a good shepherd to you? (**Answers will vary.**)

REINFORCEMENT
Sheep in Bible times represented wealth. They provided people with food and milk, wool for clothing, and leather skins that were used as protective coverings like tents or blankets. Shepherds kept careful watch over their sheep because they were highly valued possessions.

DAY 1

Name _____

Jesus Is Compassionate | 27.1

1. Write the words from the Word Bank under the correct heading. Some words will be used more than once.

WORD BANK

| go astray | unaware of danger | show repentance |
| need help | are valuable | |

Sheep	People
go astray	go astray
need help	need help
unaware of danger	unaware of danger
are valuable	are valuable
	show repentance

2. Who is the Good Shepherd? _____ Jesus _____

3. Tell about a time when you needed someone to show you compassion.

Answers will vary.

© *Bible Grade 2*
105

© *Bible Grade 2*

27.2 Jesus Is Compassionate
Focus: Jesus, the Good Shepherd

★ PREPARATION
Secretly ask three students to say, "I am your teacher" when silently prompted. (*Introduction*)

Select **DM-15 Psalm 23**. (*Directed Instruction*)

↻ EXTENSION
2A Before class, make one copy of **BLM 27A Lost Sheep**. Write Psalm 23 on a section of the board. Choose five words from the psalm—such as *leads* or *comforts*—that describe what the Good Shepherd does, and write each word on the five sheep from BLM 27A. Cut out the sheep and place them around the room. During class, explain that some of the words from the psalm were written on sheep that are "lost" in the classroom. Direct students to be like a shepherd who goes to find his lost sheep. When all the lost sheep (the missing Scripture words) have been found, rejoice as a class and give thanks to God. Conclude the activity by reciting Psalm 23 together, incorporating the lost words.

2B Cut 3" × 6" POSTER-BOARD STRIPS and a 6" PIECE OF YARN for each student. Encourage students to demonstrate compassion by making bookmarks for children who are ill at home or in a hospital. Direct students to write a verse from Psalm 23 on the bookmark and design a border. Use a HOLE PUNCH to make a hole at the top of the bookmark, and loop the yarn through the hole to make a tassel. If possible, obtain a supply of SMALL BIBLES to send with the bookmarks. Spend time praying for those who are sick and need comfort.

Introduction ★
Direct students to close their eyes, to listen carefully, and to raise their hand when they hear a voice saying a true statement. First, silently prompt the three previously selected students to say "I am your teacher" one at a time. (**Students should not raise their hand.**) Then say the sentence yourself. (**Students should raise their hand.**) Ask students how they knew which voice was telling the truth. (**They knew who was telling the truth because they recognized the voices, even with their eyes closed.**)

Directed Instruction ★ ↻
Read **Psalm 23**, which describes what Jesus does as the Good Shepherd. Just as sheep can trust their shepherd to take care of them, students can fully trust Jesus, their Good Shepherd, to care for them. They need to listen to and know His voice. He will lead them down the right paths in life.

Display **DM-15 Psalm 23**. Read each verse from **Psalm 23** again, discussing the following points and asking students how each verse relates to them:

- **Psalm 23:1**—Jesus supplies their needs. Because the Lord is their Shepherd, students can be sure that He will supply everything they need. He will protect and take care of them, like a shepherd does for his sheep.

- **Psalm 23:2**—Jesus keeps them safe. Just as a shepherd provides his sheep with calm waters to drink and a safe place to eat nourishing grass, the Lord provides safe pastures for God's children. Explain to students that Jesus knows their needs and will supply each one. They can lie down and rest because Jesus will keep them safe.

- **Psalm 23:3**—Jesus leads and guides them. Just as a shepherd leads sheep through winding paths to safe, open fields, Jesus will lead God's children to safe places where they can learn and grow. Explain to students that they can feel calm and secure because they can fully trust God's leading. He guides them daily in ways that are right and bring honor to Him.

- **Psalm 23:4**—Jesus comforts them. Every student will walk through difficult times and not understand why certain things are happening. The problems they face may seem confusing and overwhelming, and they may feel as if they are walking through a deep valley in the dark. Tell students they do not need to be afraid when they go through difficult times, because the Good Shepherd is with them and will comfort them.

- **Psalm 23:5**—Jesus protects them. Teach students that shepherds lead their sheep to the high pastures for protection and nourishment during the warm season. Point out that shepherds also used oil to protect sheep from insects and to treat wounds. In the same way, students need the Lord's anointing to protect them from things that hurt them.

- **Psalm 23:6**—Jesus gives them hope. Share with students that Jesus will lead them and give them hope not only for their life on Earth but for eternity with Him. They can look forward to promised future blessings.

Read **Isaiah 53:6** and **John 10:11**. Explain to students that people have all gone astray and sinned. Share that Jesus, their Shepherd, wants to bring them back to God. He died on the cross to pay the price for their sins, and He rose again so they could have a right relationship with Him, as if they had never sinned. They all need Jesus' help to show repentance, receive His gift of salvation, and look to Him as their Shepherd for guidance.

Student Page 27.2
Direct students to work in pairs to complete the page.

Review

- Share one way that Jesus is like a good shepherd watching over a flock of sheep. (**Possible answers: He protects; He leads; He comforts.**)
- How can you show Jesus that He is important to you? (**by listening to and reading His Word, by knowing His voice**)
- How are you like sheep? (**I go astray.**)
- What is one main characteristic that shows how you are different from sheep? (**I have sinned and need to show repentance.**)

APPLICATION

- What happens when a sheep stays close to the shepherd? (**He is protected from harm, watched over, and provided with food to eat.**)
- What happens when you stay close to Jesus, the Good Shepherd? (**Answers will vary but should include that He provides for my needs.**)
- How can you stay close to the Good Shepherd? (**Answers will vary but should include that I can pray and ask Him to remind me that He is near.**)

REINFORCEMENT

The Hebrew word for *shepherding* is often translated *feeding*. The Israelites understood shepherding, or sheep herding, quite well because it had been a chief occupation of their ancestors, dating back to Abraham (Genesis 12:16, Genesis 30:31–40, Exodus 3:1). Shepherds knew each of their sheep by name (John 10:3–5), and every day they led the sheep to fresh water and pasture to feed. Shepherds continually kept track of their sheep, counting each one, caring for the weakest of the flock, protecting them from wild animals, and leading them to safety. Shepherds kept their flocks together, though they separated the sheep from the goats (Matthew 25:32). Jesus called Himself the Good Shepherd because He knew His sheep by name and would lay down His life for them (John 10:11–18). Jesus is also referred to as "that great Shepherd of the sheep" (Hebrews 13:20).

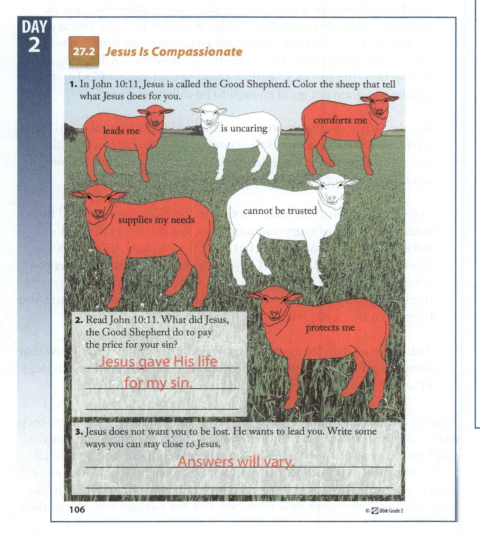

27.3 Jesus Is Compassionate
Focus: A Gracious Father

EXTENSION

3A Celebrate God's compassion and forgiveness as a class. Help students decorate the room with **BALLOONS** and **STREAMERS**. Give each of them a piece of paper to write down an example of when God showed compassion or forgave them. Post the papers around the room and encourage students to share with one another what they wrote while they enjoy a **SNACK** together.

Introduction

Invite students to share about a time they disobeyed their parents. Ask how it affected their relationship with their parents. (**Answers will vary.**)

Directed Instruction

Read aloud the following Bible truth based on Luke 15:11–32 in which Jesus told this story:

A man had two sons. The younger son said, "Father, give me what you're planning for me to receive after you die." Although this was unusual, the father divided his goods between his sons.

The younger son moved away to another country. He lived very recklessly, spending everything he had. A famine came, and very little food grew. To survive, the younger son began working for a man, feeding husks of corn to pigs. The son would gladly have eaten the husks himself! He was starving, but no one gave him anything.

The younger son knew that his father's servants had plenty of bread to eat, so he decided to return home to work as a servant. He understood that he couldn't expect to be treated like a son anymore because he had been selfish, left his father, and lived recklessly. As he journeyed home and was still a long way off, his father saw him coming and felt compassion for him. The father ran to meet his son, hugging and kissing him. The son said, "Father, I have sinned against God and against you. I am not good enough to be called your son."

But the father said to his servants, "Hurry. Get the best robe and put it on my son. Put a ring on his finger and sandals on his feet. Kill the fat calf. Let's have a feast and celebrate! My son was dead but is now alive again! He was lost, but now he has been found!"

The older son, who had been working in the fields, came toward the house. He was very angry and refused to join the celebration. His father begged him to come in, but the older son said, "Listen, Father. I have served you all my life. I never did anything wrong, and yet you never even gave me a young goat so I could have a party with my friends. But now that this reckless son of yours has returned home, you have given him a big feast!"

The father replied, "Son, you have always been with me. You know that everything I own is yours. We should celebrate. Your brother was dead to us and now is alive. He was lost, but now he is found."

Explain to students that Jesus told this story and the story of the lost sheep to the same religious leaders. In this story, Jesus was pointing out that the religious leaders were like the older son who stayed home and obeyed all his father's rules. But just like the older son, they only obeyed God out of duty, not because they loved Him or wanted a relationship with Him. The sinners whom Jesus spent time with were like the younger son. When they repented of their reckless living and turned to God, He welcomed them home and celebrated.

Share with students that just as the father showed compassion for his lost son, God has compassion for them. When they confess their sin and repent, God shows them mercy because of what Jesus did for them on the cross. God, who is all-powerful, has provided a way to bring everyone who is lost to Him.

Student Page 27.3
Direct students to independently complete the page.

Review
- What made the younger son decide to come home after living recklessly? (**His life was horrible; he knew his father was kind; he repented and wanted a loving relationship with his father again.**)
- How did the father react to his son's return? (**welcomed his son in love**)
- How did the older brother react when he learned about the celebration his father ordered? (**He was angry and refused to join in.**)

APPLICATION
- What do you think the younger son learned? (**Answers will vary but should include that he understood that he had sinned against God and his own father.**)
- How did the father show compassion to the older son? (**Answers will vary but should include that the father cared for his older son, too, and wanted to help the older son realize that the son was basing his relationships on works and duty, not love.**)
- How is God your Father like the father in the story? (**He has compassion on me. He forgives me when I repent of my sin.**)

REINFORCEMENT
According to Jewish law, the eldest son would receive twice as much inheritance as the other sons (Deuteronomy 21:17). Even though it was legal for the younger son to ask for his share of the inheritance any time during his life, he dishonored his father and showed that he valued things more than people if he requested it before the appointed time. The younger son in Jesus' story, knowing the kindness of his father, decided to return home with a heart of repentance. But before he could even confess his sin and ask his father to forgive him, his father ran to meet him—which was considered undignified and not a customary to do—took his son in his arms, and kissed him, showing unconditional love, compassion, and grace to his wayward son.

DAY 3

Name _____

Jesus Is Compassionate 27.3

1. Trace and color pictures about the father and his younger son from Luke 15:11–32. Tracing and coloring will vary.

The son asked his father for money and went far away.	The son spent all the money and had to feed pigs.
The son saw his mistake and returned home.	The father had compassion on his son when he returned.

2. Why was the older son angry about the party?

because he always obeyed and never got a party like the younger son

3. What did his father tell him was the right thing to do?

Celebrate, because your brother, who was lost, is now found.

© Bible Grade 2   107

© Bible Grade 2

27.4 Jesus Is Compassionate

Focus: God Shows Compassion

★ PREPARATION

Have on hand a FIRST-AID KIT with the following items inside: an EMERGENCY NUMBER, ADHESIVE BANDAGES, GAUZE OR TAPE, and OINTMENT. (*Directed Instruction*)

↻ EXTENSION

4A Divide the class into four groups. Instruct students to read the following Scriptures and discuss how compassion was shown in each situation. Allow groups to share their observations with the entire class.

• Genesis 6:5–8, 9:12–17 (**God saved Noah's family and set a rainbow in the sky as a sign of His promise to all people.**)
• Luke 10:25–37 (**The Good Samaritan helped a wounded man.**)
• Mark 1:40–45 (**Jesus healed a man with leprosy.**)
• Matthew 14:13–21 (**Jesus fed 5,000 people.**)

4B Discuss with students 10 ways they can show compassion to others. Write ideas on a POSTER BOARD, and display it in the classroom to remind students to put their ideas into practice.

Introduction

Give students a piece of paper and ask them to draw a picture of whatever comes to mind when you read the following descriptions:
• a person who does not get angry easily
• a person showing kindness to someone who does not deserve it
• a person caring for another person in need

Ask a few students to share their drawings. Explain that everyone you described was compassionate. Today they will learn how God shows compassion to them and how they can show compassion to others.

Directed Instruction ★ ↻

Display the FIRST-AID KIT. Explain that a person may use a first-aid kit to show kindness and compassion to others.

Display the items one by one as you share the following information:
• EMERGENCY NUMBER: An emergency number is necessary to contact important people during a crisis. Read **Exodus 34:6**. One way to help others and show compassion is to call upon (or pray to) God, who shows the most compassion.

• ADHESIVE BANDAGES: Bandages offer protection. God continually gives His children mercy and protection. Students should thank God for His everlasting mercy. Read **Psalm 118:1–4**. Students should also show mercy and love during the day through their attitudes and actions.

• GAUZE OR TAPE: Gauze or tape is used to wrap, cover, or protect something. God chooses to wrap His compassion around His children and protect them because He knows their needs. Read **Psalm 72:12–14**. In the same way, students can extend compassion as they see the needs of others.

• OINTMENT: Just as ointment helps to keep out infection and heal wounds, God wants to help students keep the infection of sin out of their life. God showed mercy and love to His children by fulfilling His promise to send a savior. Read **Deuteronomy 4:31** and **1 John 4:10–11**. Because God forgives their sins, students can show mercy and forgiveness to others.

Inform students that it is hard to show compassion to others on their own, but they can do it with the Holy Spirit's help. Others will see God's presence through their actions.

Student Page 27.4

Assist students as needed to complete the page.

Review

- What has God shown you? (**mercy, love, compassion, protection**)
- In what ways does God want you to show compassion to others?
  (**Possible answers: by praying for others, by showing mercy and love, by encouraging others to turn to God**)
- Who did your all-powerful God send to fulfill His promise of a savior?
  (**God sent Jesus, His Son, to fulfill His promise of a savior.**)

Notes:

APPLICATION

- Why is it important to show compassion to others? (**Because God shows compassion to me.**)
- When is it most difficult for you to show mercy and forgiveness to others? (**Answers will vary.**)
- Describe a time when you showed someone that he or she is special to God. (**Answers will vary.**)

DAY 4

27.4 *Jesus Is Compassionate*

1. How can you show compassion? Read each sentence. Mark true or false.

T	F	
☒	☐	I can forgive. I can choose not to become angry easily.
☒	☐	I can treat people with kindness and mercy.
☒	☐	I can be thoughtful of others.
☒	☐	I can ask God to help me show compassion to others.
☒	☐	I can help others in need.

2. Circle ways God shows you compassion.

sends people to take care of me

teaches me about Him

forgives me

heals me

sent Jesus to die for my sins

guides me

108

© *Bible Grade 2*

27.5 Jesus Is Compassionate

Focus: Review and Assessment

★ PREPARATION

Select **VA 27A Jesus Is the Good Shepherd**. (*Lesson Review*)

Print **BLM 27B Lesson 27 Test** for each student. (*Directed Instruction*)

Lesson Review ★

Use **VA 27A Jesus Is the Good Shepherd** to review the Bible truth. Cover the following concepts:

- As Jesus taught people, He saw they needed compassion. Another word for *compassion* is *caring*.
- Compassion and kindness are aspects, or types, of mercy.
- Jesus described Himself as a shepherd because people, like sheep, need guidance and help.
- A shepherd's job was to protect and care for his sheep. Sheep are easily frightened, they need protection, and they tend to go astray.
- Jesus, the Good Shepherd, cares deeply for God's children. He will protect and lead them.
- People are like sheep; they all have gone astray and sinned. But Jesus, the Good Shepherd, died on the cross to pay the price for their sins and bring them back to God.
- People need Jesus' help, strength, and guidance to be able to show repentance, receive the gift of salvation, and look to Him as their Shepherd.
- Jesus told the story of two sons. The younger son asked for his part of his father's money and lived recklessly. The son valued fun and material things more than relationships.
- When this younger son ran out of money, he remembered his father's kindness and showed repentance by admitting his sin.
- The father still loved his younger son and had compassion on him in spite of what the son had done. When the father saw his younger son coming home, he ran to meet him.
- The father rejoiced that his son had come to him, and he had a great feast to celebrate.
- When the older son became angry about the celebration, the father showed compassion to him by stating that he wanted to help the older son realize that the son was basing his relationships on works and duty, not love.
- Just as the father showed compassion and forgiveness to his younger son, God shows compassion and forgiveness to His children. God loves His children and shows them mercy because of what Jesus did for them on the cross.
- God rejoices when people repent and turn to Him. He restores their relationship with Him when they accept His gift of salvation.
- Just as God shows compassion to His children, they can show compassion to others.

Directed Instruction ★

Distribute a copy of **BLM 27B Lesson 27 Test** to each student. Read the directions and assist with any difficult words. Have students complete the test. Afterward, provide answers for immediate feedback.

Lesson Preparation
Martha Grows in Faith
28.0

Expected Student Outcomes

KNOW
Martha's faith in Jesus grows stronger after the death of Lazarus.

DO
Students will:
- define *mourn* and sequence the events when Jesus raised Lazarus from the dead
- identify statements that Jesus said about Himself
- recognize the I AM statements of Jesus and know what they mean
- select words that illustrate Jesus' omnipotence
- identify the fruit from John 15:5 in a believer's life

APPLY
Students will express their trust in Jesus, knowing that He is capable of doing anything.

Lesson Outline
I. Martha's faith grows (Jn 11:1–45)
II. Believing in Jesus (Jn 11:25–27, 3:16; Rom 10:9–10)
III. Telling others about Jesus (Jn 14:6, 1 Cor 15:3–4, Acts 4:12)
IV. Jesus is all-powerful (Mk 10:27, Phil 4:12–13, Jn 15:1)

♥ TEACHER'S HEART

Luke 10:38–42 records that Jesus went to Martha's house. Martha was distracted and busy serving. She was also worried and troubled about many things, including that her sister Mary was not helping. Mary was peacefully listening to Jesus, resting at His feet and taking in all that He said. When Martha voiced her grievance to Jesus, He responded that Mary was doing the right thing—spending time with Him. In fact, Jesus had a similar habit of resting in the presence of His Father and learning from Him (John 5:19).

Martha noted what Jesus was teaching her and reprioritized her life. By the time the events in John 11:1–45 occurred, Martha was a woman of greater faith. She called for Jesus when Lazarus, her brother, was sick. She acknowledged to Him that Lazarus would not have died had Jesus been with him, and she made the boldest statement of faith, "I believe that You are the Christ, the Son of God."

As a teacher and a "can do" person, one who is proactive for your students, you can be like Mary and Martha. Make God's Word your priority. From this position of resting in and learning from God, the tasks serving your students will follow without worry. As you are encouraged to do in Hebrews 4:11, labor to enter His rest! And as Mary and Martha discovered, you will see the glory of God (John 11:40)!

Supplemental Materials are available to download. See Understanding Purposeful Design Bible at the front of this book for the Grade 2 URL.

📖 MEMORY VERSE
John 11:25

GLOSSARY WORDS
- mourn
- plan of salvation

★ MATERIALS

Day 1:
- VA 28A Martha Grows in Faith
- DM-1 Character Traits

Day 2:
- BLM 28A I Believe Hand (*Extension*)

Day 3:
- BLM 28B What I Believe (*Extension*)

Day 4:
- Branch
- Love Bowl from Lesson 11.4 (*Extension*)

Day 5:
- VA 28A Martha Grows in Faith
- BLM 28C Lesson 28 Test

♪ SONGS
For I Am Not Ashamed
Jesus Can
Books of the Bible (*Extension*)

TEACHER RESOURCES
Strobel, Lee. *The Case for the Resurrection*. Zondervan, 2009.
Wolgemuth, Robert, and Bobbie Wolgemuth. *How to Lead Your Child to Christ*. Tyndale House, 2005.

STUDENT RESOURCES
MacArthur, John. *A Faith to Grow On*. Thomas Nelson, 2000.
Mackenzie, Carine. *Martha and Mary: Friends of Jesus*. CF4Kids, 2014.

28.1 Martha Grows in Faith
Focus: Martha's Faith Grows

📖 MEMORY VERSE
John 11:25

MEMORY WORK
- Direct students to write every other word of the Memory Verse on the top half of a sheet of paper while quietly saying each alternate word aloud. Next, instruct students to repeat the activity, but this time, have them say every other word of the verse aloud while writing each alternate word on the bottom half of the paper. When finished, students will have written the complete verse on two halves of the paper. Invite students to chorally read their completed verse.

★ PREPARATION
Select **VA 28A Martha Grows in Faith** and **DM-1 Character Traits**. (*Directed Instruction*)

Introduction
Direct students to visualize a large airplane, and ask how they know it will take off. (**Possible answers: The plane is designed to take off; I've seen one take off before; I've been on a plane that has taken off.**) Explain that believing that a huge airplane will take off demonstrates faith in the plane and the people who made it and operate it. When people get on a plane, they believe that the plane will do what it was designed to do. Some people might be afraid and have only a little faith in airplanes. But even a little faith gets them onto a plane and up in the air. Today's lesson is about a woman who grew in her faith in Jesus.

Directed Instruction ★
Read **VA 28A Martha Grows in Faith**. Martha demonstrated several stages of faith. First, she and her sister, Mary, sent for Jesus because Martha believed that He could heal Lazarus (John 11:3). When Jesus arrived too late, she expressed her belief that if Jesus had been there, her brother would not have died (John 11:21). She also had faith that Lazarus would rise from the dead when Jesus came back someday to take everyone to heaven (John 11:24). Read **John 11:25–27**. Martha knew that Jesus could perform miracles and she may have had some understanding that Jesus is God's Son, but in the end, she said that she fully believed He was the Son of God, who had the power to give life and raise the dead.

Explain that when someone dies, those who loved that person feel a deep and intense sadness. To **mourn** means *to feel deep sadness due to someone's death or because of a loss.* When Jesus saw Martha and Mary crying because their brother had died, He also felt sad and cried (John 11:35). Jesus loved Lazarus, and He loved the sisters, too. When He saw how sad they were, He felt compassion for them. Explain to students that Jesus loves them, too, and understands when they are sad. And for those who have accepted Him as Savior, He sent the Comforter—the Holy Spirit—to be with them and help them (John 14:16–18, 26; 16:7). Display **DM-1 Character Traits**, and review the trait of *love*, which is defined as *unselfishly accepting others.* Jesus unselfishly accepted everyone and died for their sins.

Explain that in Bible times, people were often buried in caves called *tombs*. A large stone was usually rolled in front of the entrance to protect the body from animals, weather, or robbers. Once the body was laid inside the tomb and the stone was set in place, it was not moved for at least a year. Lazarus' body had been in the tomb four days, and the smell would have been really bad. According to Jewish tradition, it was long past the time when a person might be resuscitated, or brought back to life. Teach that a dead body would have been wrapped in strips of cloth or grave clothes. These strips would have been tightly wrapped around the main part of the body, and the arms and feet tied together. A smaller cloth would have covered the head. Point out that Jesus showed just how powerful He is when He commanded a dead man to get up and walk out of the tomb. Teach that *divinity* means *the quality of being God.* Jesus was able to raise Lazarus from the dead due to His divinity and omnipotence—the quality of being all-powerful.

Student Page 28.1

Assist students as necessary to complete the page.

Review

- How did Martha's faith grow? (**At first she said she believed that Jesus could heal her brother, but later she said she fully believed that Jesus was the Son of God.**)
- How did Jesus feel when He spoke to Martha and Mary about Lazarus' death? (**He was sad and cried. He loved Lazarus and the sisters, so He had compassion.**)
- What does *mourn* mean? (**to feel deep sadness due to someone's death or because of a loss**)
- What does *divinity* mean? (**the quality of being God**)
- How could Jesus resurrect Lazarus after he had been dead four days? (**Jesus is God. He is omnipotent, or all-powerful.**)

Notes:

APPLICATION

- When was the last time you felt really sad? (**Answers will vary.**) Remember that whenever you feel really sad, Jesus looks at you with compassion, and the Holy Spirit is there to comfort you and help you.
- When you are sad, what can you say to Jesus to show Him that you trust Him? (**Answers will vary but should include I believe that He is God's Son and that He'll take care of me.**)

DAY 1

Name _____

Martha Grows in Faith | 28.1

1. Look up mourn in the Glossary. Write the definition.

mourn: to feel deep sadness due to someone's death or because of a loss

2. Number the events in the order they happened.

4	Jesus cried and had compassion.
5	Jesus commanded that the stone be moved away from Lazarus' tomb.
1	Lazarus became very sick. Martha and Mary sent word to Jesus that Lazarus was sick.
2	Lazarus died. Jesus traveled to Martha and Mary's home.
7	Lazarus was raised from the dead and many believed in Jesus.
3	Martha told Jesus that if He had been there, Lazarus would not have died.
6	Jesus thanked God and called for Lazarus to come out of the tomb. Lazarus came out in his grave clothes.

3. Read John 11:40. Write what Jesus said Martha would see if she believed.

the glory of God

© *Bible Grade 2*

109

28.2

Martha Grows in Faith
Focus: Believing in Jesus

↻ EXTENSION

2A Make a copy of **BLM 28A I Believe Hand** for each student. Explain that to receive eternal life, students need to believe five statements about Jesus. Invite students to follow along as you read each statement. Encourage them to come to you at any time if they want to receive Jesus as their personal Savior. If a student comes to you, review each point on the diagram, and ask the student if he or she believes each statement. Invite the student to read the statements aloud, saying "I believe" at the beginning of each one. Then lead the student in a prayer to receive Jesus as his or her Savior.

2B Instruct students to write a journal entry on how they feel about Lazarus' death and Martha's faith in Jesus. Would they have responded like Martha, or in a different way? Encourage students to write a prayer to God asking Him for a strong faith in Him.

Introduction

Ask students to share the most important question anyone has ever asked them. (**Answers will vary.**) Explain that today's lesson is about a very important question Jesus asked Martha. In fact, it is the most important question ever asked.

Directed Instruction ↻

Encourage students to think about the question Jesus asked Martha. Be prepared to pray with any student who appears ready to receive Jesus as his or her personal Savior.

Read **John 11:25–27**. Use the following questions to lead a discussion about the question Jesus asked Martha:

- What did Jesus say? (**Jesus said that He is the resurrection and the life, and whoever believes in Him will have eternal life.**)
- What did Jesus ask Martha? (**if she believed what He said**)
- What was Martha's response to Jesus? (**Martha believed that Jesus is God's Son.**)

Assist students in recalling what Jesus did after He spoke with Martha and Mary. (**He proved to everyone that He had power over death by resurrecting Lazarus from the dead.**)

Tell students that every person who reads Jesus' words in John 11:25–26 must someday answer that same question. Ask students if they believe Jesus is able to give eternal life to anyone who believes in Him. Pause for a moment, allowing time for students to think before responding. Then ask them if they believe Jesus can give them eternal life right now. Give students ample time to respond. (**Answers will vary.**)

Invite a volunteer to read **John 3:16**. Explain to students that God sent Jesus to die for their sins because He loves them so much. God's **plan of salvation** is defined as *God's plan to send His Son to die on the cross to pay for the sins of all people*. This gift of eternal life is offered to anyone who believes in Jesus. Invite another volunteer to read **Romans 10:9–10**. Explain that to receive this gift, students must believe in their heart that Jesus is God's Son and came to die for them. Then they need to *confess with their mouth*, which means *to say out loud*. Explain to students that they need to truly believe in the truth about Jesus and not just confess with their mouth because someone tells them to do so.

Allow for time for students to think about God's plan of salvation. Again, be prepared to pray with those who express a desire to receive Jesus. Be aware of students who seem confused or may be trying to please you by giving the "right" answer. Pray for wisdom to know how best to talk with your students about faith in Jesus. Some students may not respond right away but will be ready at another time. Continue to sow the Word of God in their hearts, and pray that the Holy Spirit will bring them to faith.

Announce that this week, students will learn more about believing in Jesus. They will also learn how to share the good news about Jesus with others.

Student Page 28.2

Share that it is important to know what Jesus said in order to believe in Him. Direct students to read the page and assist them in completing the crossword puzzle. Point out that each clue will help them learn something about Jesus and the reason He came to Earth. When the mystery word *life* is unscrambled, it will complete the verse at the bottom of the page. Emphasize that God wants everyone to have the free gift of eternal life and that believing in Jesus is the only way a person can receive this gift of life.

Review

- Why did God send Jesus? (**He loves the world.**)
- What is God's plan of salvation? (**God's plan to send His Son to die on the cross to pay for the sins of all people**)
- What must you do to receive eternal life? (**I need to confess with my mouth that Jesus is Lord, and believe in my heart that God raised Jesus from the dead.**)

APPLICATION

- Has there been a time when you believed in your heart that Jesus is Lord and confessed with your mouth so that you could receive eternal life? (**Answers will vary.**)
- Take time to pray and thank God for His plan of salvation.

REINFORCEMENT

After His resurrection, Jesus appeared in bodily form not only to His disciples but also to several hundred witnesses (Acts 1:3, 1 Corinthians 15:5–6). During that time, Jesus reminded His followers of the words He had spoken before His death (Luke 24:7), and He opened their minds to understand the truth concerning His death and resurrection (Luke 24:45-46). But for more than 2,000 years, people have tried to refute the death, burial, and resurrection of Jesus Christ. The apostle Paul tried to discredit the faith and kill Christians until he encountered the risen Jesus on the road to Damascus and believed (Acts 9). Likewise, C. S. Lewis, author of The Chronicles of Narnia, set out to debunk the gospel, but his search led to an encounter with the risen Christ that transformed his life.

If Jesus was not raised from the dead, faith in Him is futile, and no one is truly free from sin. But Jesus is alive (1 Corinthians 15:17–20)! His death and resurrection are inseparable elements of the gospel. Everyone can put their hope in Christ, who paid the penalty for sins on the cross and reconciled people to God. He conquered sin and death when He rose from the grave, and He lives forever to intercede for believers in Him (Romans 6:5–10, 8:34)!

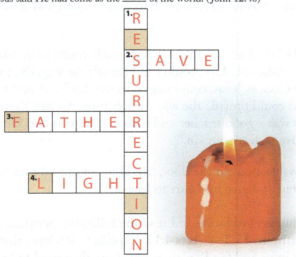

28.3 Martha Grows in Faith
Focus: Telling Others About Jesus

★ PREPARATION
Select the song "For I Am Not Ashamed" from the Grade 2 URL. (*Introduction*)

↪ EXTENSION
3A Make a copy of **BLM 28B What I Believe** for each student. Invite students to spend some quiet time thinking and praying about what they really believe about Jesus. When they are ready, have them write their response on their copy of BLM 28B.

Introduction ★
Sing with students the song "For I Am Not Ashamed" from the Grade 2 URL.

Directed Instruction ↩
Remind students that as they listened to the Bible truth earlier in the week, they saw that Martha's faith in Jesus grew. Tell students that God wants their faith to grow, too. He also wants them to believe the right things about Him.

Read the following fictional story to students:

"Dad! Dad!" Michael and Jake rushed into their dad's study. "We were talking to Katie, Bruce, and their parents about coming to church with us this Sunday, and Mr. Ericson said something we don't understand!"

"What was that?" asked Mr. Duncan as he put down the book he was reading. Jake plopped down in the chair across from his father's desk and said, "Mr. Ericson said that Jesus was a good teacher, but that really He was just a man, nothing more."

Michael added, "Doesn't the Bible say that Jesus is God?"

Mr. Duncan opened his Bible. "Let's see what the Bible says. That's what we need to know and believe. If people don't know God's Word, they believe whatever they want to believe. Maybe Mr. Ericson has never heard what the Bible says about Jesus."

"So, what's the answer?" Jake asked. "Was Jesus just a man like you and Mr. Ericson?" Dad replied, "He was a man, Jake, just like we are. He had a body with hands, arms, and feet. He got hungry and thirsty. He got tired and needed to rest. He hurt and laughed and cried, just like we do.

"But God's Word tells us that He was much, much more than just a man. See, kids, only God could call Himself the way, the truth, and the life. Only God, as Jesus, could rise from the dead and never die again. Only God could provide the way for salvation. So Mr. Ericson is right that Jesus was a good teacher and man, but Jesus is also God, and only He can save us from our sin."

As the boys dashed out the door, Mr. Duncan prayed that Mr. Ericson would listen and give his heart to Jesus.

Ask three volunteers to locate and read the following Scriptures: **John 14:6, 1 Corinthians 15:3–4, Acts 4:12**. Explain to students that to tell their friends about Jesus and God's plan of salvation, they need to know His Word and believe the right things about Him.

Student Page 28.3
Direct students to work in pairs or trios to complete the page.

In each of the following Scriptures, Jesus was telling a truth about Himself:
- A loaf of bread gives you energy and life. Jesus gives you life.
- A vine is needed so fruit can grow. You need Jesus to grow.
- A lamp gives you light. Jesus is your light.
- His empty tomb means He is more powerful than death. Through Jesus you can have eternal life.
- A traffic sign shows you where to go. Jesus guides you in life.
- A gate allows sheep into their pen. Jesus is the only way into heaven.
- A good shepherd takes care of his sheep. Jesus takes care of you.

Review

- Why were Michael and Jake upset? (**Mr. Ericson said that Jesus was a good man and teacher, but nothing more.**)
- What three truths from the Bible did Mr. Duncan point out to the boys that meant Jesus is more than just a good man? (**Jesus said He was the way, the truth, and the life; Jesus died, was buried, and rose from the grave; Jesus is the only way to be saved.**)
- What do you need to know in order to share about God's plan of salvation? (**know God's Word, believe the right things about Him**)

APPLICATION

- Who do you know who has not yet received Jesus as his or her Savior? (**Answers will vary.**) Commit today to tell this person about Jesus so that he or she can also have eternal life.
- What can you do for someone who does not know Jesus as his or her Savior? (**I can pray for the person to believe in Jesus as Savior.**) Read **Matthew 9:35–38**. Explain that Jesus taught His followers to pray for God to send workers (Christians) to those who did not know Him so that the gospel message would be shared.
- What do you believe about Jesus? (**Answers will vary but should include that He is the only way to salvation.**)

DAY 3

Name _____

Martha Grows in Faith 28.3

Jesus compared Himself to many things. He did this to help people understand who He is. Read these Bible verses. Write the correct verse under the matching picture.

John 6:35
John 8:12
John 10:7
John 10:11
John 14:6
John 15:1
John 11:25

1. John 6:35

2. John 15:1

3. John 8:12

4. John 11:25

5. John 14:6

6. John 10:7

7. John 10:11

© Bible Grade 2

111

28.4 Martha Grows in Faith
Focus: Jesus Is All-Powerful

⭐ PREPARATION

Make rough sketches of the following events of this week's Bible truth on separate sheets of construction paper: a messenger coming to Jesus, Jesus traveling, Jesus meeting Martha, Jesus meeting Mary, Jesus standing before Lazarus' tomb. (*Directed Instruction*)

Cut a SMALL BRANCH off a potted plant or a tree. (*Directed Instruction*)

Select the song "Jesus Can" from the Grade 2 URL. (*Directed Instruction*)

↻ EXTENSION

4A To review the characteristics of godly love, invite students to pick and read a card from the LOVE BOWL introduced in Lesson 11.4.

4B Use the song "Books of the Bible" from the Grade 2 URL to review the books of the Old and New Testaments.

Introduction

Invite a strong volunteer to come to the front of the classroom. Place a chair close to the volunteer. Explain to students that you will prove the volunteer's strength. Begin by placing a heavy book in the student's hands. Keep piling on more books until the volunteer cannot bear the weight anymore and has to drop the books onto the chair. Invite other volunteers to the front if they think they are strong enough to carry the books. Repeat the activity a few more times. Tell students that today's lesson is about strength.

Directed Instruction ⭐ ↻

Display the rough sketches of the Bible truth for this week. Invite several students to come forward and tell what happened in each of the sketches.

Remind students that the Introduction activity was about strength. Ask them to name the strongest people they know. (**Answers will vary.**) Ask if those strong people could lift heavy objects, such as a desk, a large couch, or a small car. Explain that everyone's strength has a limit. Even the strongest people in the world cannot do some things. Ask students if they think a really strong person could make someone dead come back to life. (**Answers will vary.**) Point out that this is impossible for normal human beings, but that Jesus did it. He raised Lazarus from the dead four days after he died. Ask students what this tells them about Jesus. (**He was really strong.**) Remind students that Jesus is omnipotent, or all-powerful. Nothing is impossible for Him or for God. Read **Mark 10:27**. State that Jesus has power over the strongest force on Earth—death.

Invite a student to read **Philippians 4:12–13**. Explain to students that Jesus can give them the strength and power to do anything, even things that are very hard for them to do on their own, such as doing the right thing, not saying mean words, listening and obeying, and not telling lies. If they remain in Jesus, they will see His power in their lives.

Read **John 15:1**. Ask students what Jesus called Himself. (**the true vine**) Show them the SMALL BRANCH. Ask them what will happen to that branch in a couple of days, now that it has been cut off from the plant. (**It will die.**) Ask what would have happened if the branch had not been cut off but had remained connected to the plant. (**It would have continued living and might have produced fruit.**) Explain to students that like a branch, if they stay connected to Jesus by praying, learning about God and reading the Bible, they will grow spiritually and produce good fruit. Explain that good fruit is showing others the goodness of God through words and actions pleasing to Him (Colossians 1:10) and displaying the fruit of the Spirit (Galatians 5:22–23). Warn students that if they become disconnected from Jesus, they will wither and die spiritually. They need to stay connected to Him to grow.

Sing together the song "Jesus Can" from the Grade 2 URL. Explain that Jesus is all-powerful and nothing is too difficult for Him.

278

Student Page 28.4
Assist students as needed to complete the page.

Review

- Jesus showed He had power over something that no one else did. What was it? (**death**)
- What does Jesus is omnipotent mean? (**He is all-powerful.**)
- What will happen if you believe in Jesus? (**His power will be in me, and I will be able to do all things through Him.**)
- How can you stay connected to Jesus? (**by learning about and reading the Bible, praying, and trusting Him**)
- What will happen if you stay connected to Jesus? (**I will produce good fruit, which means I will show others the goodness of God through my words and actions. I will display the fruit of the Spirit.**)

Notes:

APPLICATION

- What situations have you experienced when you needed Jesus' power? (**Answers will vary.**)
- What can you do to rely on Jesus' power rather than your own? (**I can pray to Him and ask Him to help me. I can remember that Jesus is omnipotent, and all things are possible through Him.**)

REINFORCEMENT

Since Old Testament times, the vine has been a well-known symbol in Israel (Psalm 80:8–9). Israeli farmers care for their vines meticulously, tending each branch to ensure that it produces high-quality fruit. A gardener also prunes each branch so that it will produce even more fruit. In John 15:1–10, Jesus identified Himself as the true, life-giving vine, God the Father as the gardener, and believers as the branches. Just as a gardener prunes the branches of a vine so that they will produce quality fruit, God carefully prunes the lives of believers so that they will bear fruit for Him. The Greek word for pruning (*kathairei*) can also refer to cleansing. Being pruned can be painful, but it's the only way believers can be truly fruitful. When a branch fails to bear fruit, the gardener lifts it off the ground—*airei* in the Greek—so it can get more sun and become fruitful. Branches need to abide in, or stay connected to, the life-giving vine to bear fruit. If they are cut off from the vine, they wither and die. Likewise, when believers abide in Christ and His love by keeping His commandments, their lives overflow with high-quality fruit.

DAY 4

28.4 Martha Grows in Faith

1. Each sentence tells about how God is all-powerful. He can handle anything. Write the best choice for each sentence on the lines.

   God can ___**heal**___ you if you are sick.
   remain   allow   heal

   God can ___**help**___ you when you are hurting.
   help   place   weep

   God raised Jesus from the dead to give you eternal ___**life**___.
   lists   light   life

2. Read Philippians 4:13. Who can help you have faith and be strong in all things? ___**God**___

3. In John 15:5, Jesus describes Himself as the vine. If you have accepted Jesus as your Savior, you are a branch of Jesus, the Vine. Write about what being a branch of Jesus means.

Answers will vary but should include that I will do the good works that God wants me to do, and I will show the fruit of the Spirit.

28.5 Martha Grows in Faith

Focus: Review and Assessment

★ PREPARATION

Select **VA 28A Martha Grows in Faith**. (*Lesson Review*)

Print one copy of **BLM 28C Lesson 28 Test** for each student. (*Directed Instruction*)

Lesson Review ★

Use **VA 28A Martha Grows in Faith** to review the Bible truth. Cover the following concepts:

• Jesus loved Martha, Mary, and Lazarus.
• Martha's faith grew the more she listened to and trusted Jesus. At first she believed Jesus could heal her brother. Then she came to the conclusion that Jesus is God's Son. Because of her trust in Him, she saw the glory of God.
• Martha and Mary mourned when Lazarus died. To *mourn* means *to feel deep sadness due to someone's death or because of a loss.*
• Jesus had compassion for Martha and Mary when He saw how sad they were over their brother's death. Jesus cried with them.
• Even though Lazarus had been dead four days, Jesus asked for the stone to be rolled away from the tomb.
• Jesus showed that He is all-powerful when He raised Lazarus from the dead.
• *Divinity* means *the quality of being God.* Through His divinity and omnipotence, Jesus was able to raise Lazarus from the dead.
• God sent His Son because He loves the world and does not want anyone to perish. God's *plan of salvation* is defined as *God's plan to send His Son to die on the cross to pay for the sins of all people.*
• To receive eternal life, people must believe in their heart that Jesus is Lord and confess it with their mouth. They should truly **believe in Jesus and not just confess because someone says to do so.**
• Jesus said that He is the resurrection and the life. He asked Martha if she believed this. She did not just say yes, she confessed it with her mouth.
• God's Word says that Jesus was more than just a good man. Jesus said He is the way, the truth, and the life; He died and rose from the grave; He is the only way to be saved.
• If anyone believes in Jesus, that person will have the power of Jesus and will be able to do all things through Him.
• A believer can stay connected to Jesus by reading the Bible, learning about Him, praying, and trusting Him.
• Jesus called Himself the true vine. If a believer stays connected to Jesus, he or she will produce good fruit.

Directed Instruction ★

Distribute a copy of **BLM 28C Lesson 28 Test** to each student. Review the instructions and format with students. Have students complete the test. When they have finished, read over the test, providing the answers for immediate feedback.

Notes:

Lesson Preparation
Easter 29.0

Expected Student Outcomes

KNOW
Jesus is arrested, crucified, and raised from the dead.

DO
- write words to match clues in order to review Jesus' triumphal entry
- answer questions about Jesus' last meal
- order the events of Jesus' arrest and trial
- determine true statements regarding the resurrection

APPLY
Students will celebrate that Jesus achieved victory over sin and death by His own death and resurrection.

Lesson Outline

I. Jesus' triumphal entry (Jn 2:12–19, 13:1–11)
  A. Enters Jerusalem as the Messiah
  B. Washes the disciples' feet
II. Jesus' last supper (Mt 26:17–30, Jn 17)
  A. Celebrates the Last Supper with His disciples
  B. Prays for all believers
III. Jesus' arrest, crucifixion, and burial (Mk 14:43–50, 14:53, 15:1–47; Jn 19)
IV. Jesus is risen (Mt 28:1–10, Mk 16:12–20, Lk 24:1–49, Jn 20:1–18, 1 Cor 15:3b–8)
  A. Mary Magdalene, disciples on the road to Emmaus, other witnesses

♥ TEACHER'S HEART

When was the last time you thought about the cross? Through the ages, crosses have been erected or torn down, ornamented, worn as jewelry or tossed aside. There's only one thing that has not been true of the cross; it has never been ignored. Why? Because the cross demands a decision. Every generation since that first Easter has had to look at the cross and make the same fundamental choice—to acknowledge what Jesus did for the world on a cross to pay for their sins, or to walk away.

Jesus told His followers what to do with the cross. Believers must daily die to self, take up their cross and follow Him (Luke 9:23). You are called to teach your students to do the same. This is the heart of Christian education: to teach students to take up their own cross and become sold-out followers of the risen Savior, Jesus Christ.

Ask the Lord to give you the strength to lead your students by example, to die daily to self, take up your cross, and wholeheartedly follow Him.

Supplemental Materials are available to download. See Understanding Purposeful Design Bible at the front of this book for the Grade 2 URL.

MEMORY VERSE
Matthew 28:6

★ MATERIALS

Day 1:
- VA 29A Jesus' Triumphal Entry
- Tissue paper (*Extension*)
- PP-8A Jesus Rides into Jerusalem (*Extension*)

Day 2:
- VA 29B Jesus' Last Supper
- PP-8B The Last Supper and Jesus' Prayer (*Extension*)

Day 3:
- A cross, VA 29C Jesus' Arrest, Crucifixion, and Burial
- PP-8C Jesus' Arrest, Crucifixion, and Burial (*Extension*)
- BLM 29A Jesus Prays for Others (*Extension*)

Day 4:
- Plastic Easter eggs
- VA 29D Jesus Is Risen
- Time Line
- PP-8D Jesus Is Risen (*Extension*)
- BLMs 29B–C Easter Scene, Parts 1–2; card stock (*Extension*)

Day 5:
- VAs 29A–D
- BLM 29D Lesson 29 Test

♪ SONGS
Create in Me
Easter Rise Up

TEACHER RESOURCES
Lucado, Max. *Six Hours One Friday: Living the Power of the Cross.* Thomas Nelson, 2012.

STUDENT RESOURCES
Sproul, R. C. *The Prince's Poison Cup.* Reformation Trust Publishing, 2008.
The Story of Jesus for Children. DVD. Inspirational Films, 2005.

29.1 Easter
Focus: Jesus' Triumphal Entry

📖 MEMORY VERSE
Matthew 28:6

MEMORY WORK
- Write the Memory Verse reference on the board. Write the words *angel*, *Jesus*, and *women* on the board. Challenge students to find the Memory Verse in their Bible, tell who spoke the words (**angel**), about whom the words were spoken (**Jesus**), and to whom the words were addressed (**women**). Circle the appropriate word as each person is identified. Recite the verse several times until students can say it with their eyes closed.

⭐ PREPARATION
Select **VA 29A Jesus' Triumphal Entry**. (*Directed Instruction*)

EXTENSION
1A Act out Jesus' triumphal entry into Jerusalem. Make palm branches by having each student roll an **18" × 24" SHEET OF GREEN TISSUE PAPER** and tape it together. When rolled, have students use their scissors to make three cuts down the side of the tube. Gently pull the paper up from the center of the tube and spread it out to resemble a palm branch.

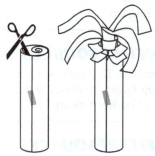

1B Present **PP-8A Jesus Rides into Jerusalem** to review the Bible truth.

Introduction
Ask students if they have ever watched or participated in a parade. (**Answers will vary.**) Whom did they see; what did they hear; and what did it feel like to march down the street or to watch the people in the parade? (**Answers will vary.**) Explain today's lesson has an event like a parade. It was an exciting time when the people of Jerusalem celebrated Jesus as the Messiah, the promised Savior of the world.

Write the word *hosanna* on the board. Explain that this is a Hebrew word that means *save us* or *praise God*. The people who were shouting "Hosanna!" were acknowledging that they needed someone who would be able to save them. Remind students that God sent Jesus to die for their sins because He loves them so much. He alone is worthy of praise (Psalm 18:3). Explain to students that in praising God, the people were describing God's many qualities and telling Him and others of His greatness.

Directed Instruction ★
Display **VA 29A Jesus' Triumphal Entry** and read the back for today's Bible truth. Review the meaning of the words *prophecy* and *Passover*, while encouraging students to look up the definitions in the Glossary. Explain that it was the custom of many Jewish families to go to Jerusalem to celebrate the Passover. Jesus and His disciples were following this tradition.

Point out that as the people praised Jesus, shouting "Hosanna!" they also called Him their *King*. Jesus, the King, came to save God's people from eternal separation from Him.

Ask students if they have noticed how dirty their feet become when they walk barefoot. Explain that there were few paved roads in Jesus' time, and people wore sandals or went barefoot, so everyone's feet were quite dirty after a day of walking everywhere. It was normally the job of the youngest or most lowly servant in the household to wash people's feet, but Jesus chose to wash His disciples' feet. By this action, Jesus demonstrated to His disciples that they needed to love and serve others. Explain to students that they, too, need to love and serve others. Encourage students to think about different ways that they can follow Jesus' example of love and service as they go about their daily routine. Share with students that they will experience *joyfulness*, which means *celebrating God's goodness*, while loving and serving others. Ask students to share about a time they felt joy while loving and serving others. (**Answers will vary.**)

Explain to students that many Christians celebrate Jesus' triumphal entry into Jerusalem every year. This annual celebration is called *Palm Sunday*, and it is celebrated one week before Easter. Invite students to share ways that Palm Sunday is celebrated at their church. (**Answers will vary.**)

Student Page 29.1
Allow students to work in collaborative pairs or trios to complete the page.

Review

- What miracle had Jesus performed before He rode into Jerusalem? (**Jesus had raised Lazarus from the dead.**)
- What prophecy did Jesus fulfill on the day He rode into Jerusalem? (**Zechariah's prophecy that the Messiah would ride into Jerusalem on a donkey**)
- What did Jesus teach His disciples by washing their feet? (**He taught them to love and serve others.**)
- Why did Jesus take the time to teach love and servanthood? (**Answers will vary but should include that because Jesus made love and servanthood a priority, Christians should follow His example to joyfully love and serve others.**)

Notes:

APPLICATION

- Read **Matthew 21:1–11**. This is the story of Jesus' triumphal entry into Jerusalem from Matthew's Gospel. Point out the fact that Jesus knew exactly where the donkey and her foal would be. Ask students is there anything the Lord does not know. (**No.**) Is it possible to keep anything from Him? (**The Lord knows everything about me. I can't hide anything from Him.**)
- Why did Jesus wash the disciples' feet? (**Possible answers: to set an example of love and being a servant; washing feet was one of the lowliest jobs a servant could have; Jesus did not want his disciples to think of themselves as too important to love and serve.**)
- Pray and ask God to show you how to love and serve others today. Thank Him for opportunities to joyfully love and serve.

REINFORCEMENT

On Palm Sunday in the south Indian state of Kerala, flower petals are tossed inside most sanctuaries following the reading of Scripture. First the congregation hears the words shouted by the crowd welcoming Jesus, "Hosanna! Blessed is He who is come and is to come in the name of the Lord God." These words are read to the congregation three times. The worshippers then repeat, "Hosanna!" and the flower petals are scattered. This Syrian Christian tradition reminds worshippers of the honor shown to Jesus upon His entry into Jerusalem.

29.2 Easter

Focus: Jesus' Last Supper

★ PREPARATION

Select the song "Create in Me" on the Grade 2 URL. (*Introduction*)

Select **VA 29B Jesus' Last Supper** (*Directed Instruction*)

⌐ EXTENSION

2A Present **PP-8B The Last Supper and Jesus' Prayer** to review the Bible truth.

Introduction ★

Play the song "Create in Me" from the Grade 2 URL, and ask students not to sing along, but just to listen. Ask them to share their feelings as they listen to the song. (**Possible answers: thoughtful, quiet, respectful**) Explain that Jesus' last meal was a very serious occasion for Jesus and His disciples. Jesus knew that it would not be long before He would have to die on the cross. It was a time for the disciples to remember what He had taught them. Following this explanation, invite the students to sing the song "Create in Me."

Directed Instruction ★ ⌐

Display **VA 29B Jesus' Last Supper** and read the back for today's Bible truth. Remind students that the Passover was celebrated to remember when God had given the Hebrews special instructions so death would pass over their homes. This act of obedience saved the life of the firstborn child in each Hebrew family, when they were still under Pharaoh's rule in Egypt. Explain that it was customary for families to share this traditional meal together and to recall the events of the first Passover.

When Jesus shared the Passover meal with His disciples for the last time before His death on the cross, He instituted the tradition of including the Lord's Supper as an act of worship. Sharing the Lord's Supper is one way to remember Jesus' death on a cross, the sacrificial act that saves all believers from eternal separation from God. Jesus Himself took the place of the sacrificial lamb of the Passover. His shed blood cleanses people from their sins (1 John 1:7). Teach students that Jesus' sacrificial act reconciles, or restores their relationship to God. Because of God's love and grace, He had a plan to reconcile people to Him. Remind students of God's plan of salvation: He sent Jesus to die for their sins, because He loves them (John 3:16).

Teach students that because Jesus is the Son of God, He is all-knowing. He knew that His time on the earth was coming to an end, and He knew that one of His disciples would betray Him. Explain that the word *betray* means *to turn against a friend*. Judas, one of Jesus' disciples, chose to betray Jesus by telling the Jewish leaders where Jesus could be found.

Point out to students that Jesus devoted a lot of time to prayer. He prayed for Himself, He prayed for His disciples, and He also prayed for people who would come to know Him. Through prayer, or talking to God, Jesus humbly made His requests known to the Father.

Student Page 29.2

Have students independently complete the page. Invite them to spend some time in prayer, thanking God for His love, grace, and plan of salvation.

Review

• What Jewish tradition were Jesus and His disciples celebrating as they ate

together? (**They were celebrating the Passover.**)
- Why was it important for Jesus to celebrate the Passover with His disciples? (**He wanted them to remember Him and all that He had taught them during His time on Earth.**)
- What did Jesus use to represent His body? (**a piece of bread**) What did He use to represent His blood? (**a cup of wine**)
- What did Jesus explain as the reason for shedding His blood? (**Forgiveness of sins came through His death.**)
- What is God's plan of salvation and what does His plan do for you? (**God sent Jesus, His Son, to die for my sins. God did this because He loves me. Through Jesus' sacrificial act, He has reconciled, or restored my relationship to God.**)

Notes:

APPLICATION

- Early Christians established the tradition of celebrating the last Passover meal that Jesus had (1 Corinthians 11:23–26). Churches today call this tradition the *Lord's Supper*, *Communion*, or *Holy Communion*. Why is it important for you to remember what Jesus has done for you? (**Answers will vary but should include that I will forget what the Lord has done for me if I do not purposefully remember His love and sacrifice.**)
- Jesus prayed for His disciples and for all believers. Tell about a time when you prayed for someone else. (**Answers will vary.**)
- Jesus prayed for His disciples to work together and not be separated by disagreements. Is it important for Christians to stick together? Why? (**Answers will vary.**)

DAY 2

29.2 Easter

Read the paragraph about Jesus' last meal. Answer the questions.

> Jesus knew that His time on Earth with the disciples was coming to an end. He wanted to give them a way to remember Him because He would soon go back to heaven. Jesus took some of the bread from the table. He broke the bread and blessed it. Then He gave a piece of the bread to each of the disciples to eat. Jesus explained that the bread was like His body. He said that He would soon die for their sins. Then Jesus took a cup of wine. He shared it with the disciples and explained that the wine was like His blood. He was going to shed His blood for them so that they could be forgiven from all their sins.

1. Why did Jesus share His last meal with His disciples?
   Answers will vary.

2. What did Jesus say the bread stood for? _His body_

3. What did Jesus say the wine stood for? _His blood_

4. How do you think Jesus felt during this last meal with His disciples? Explain your answer.
   Answers will vary.

5. How do you feel when you think about Jesus dying for you? Explain your answer.
   Answers will vary.

114

29.3

Easter
Focus: Jesus' Arrest, Crucifixion, and Burial

★ PREPARATION

Bring in a CROSS that is large enough for all students to see. (*Introduction*)

Select **VA 29C Jesus' Arrest, Crucifixion, and Burial**. (*Directed Instruction*)

⤷ EXTENSION

3A Present **PP-8C Jesus' Arrest, Crucifixion, and Burial** to review the Bible truth.

3B Find an audio or video recording of the spiritual "Were You There?" online. Allow quiet time for students to listen to the words and/or watch the video. Explain that the song was written more than 100 years ago, but it is still sung in churches today. Ask students to share their thoughts about the lyrics and the music. Sing the song together.

3C Make copies of **BLM 29A Jesus Prays for Others** for each student. Challenge students to read verses from **John 17** to complete the page.

Introduction ★

Hold up a CROSS. Ask students to name various places that they have seen crosses. Ask what they think about when they see a cross. (**Answers will vary but should include that Jesus died on a cross.**) Tell students that a cross is more than just a symbol of the Christian faith. It is a reminder of God's love and Jesus' sacrificial death for them. When they think about how great a sacrifice it was for Jesus to die for them, it should move them to love, gratitude, and righteous living. The Cross challenges them to live out their faith daily (Luke 9:23).

Directed Instruction ★ ⤷

Display **VA 29C Jesus' Arrest, Crucifixion, and Burial** and read the back of it for today's Bible truth. Teach that *crucifixion* means *death by being hung on a cross*. Jesus' crucifixion was part of God's plan of salvation—an ultimate display of His love, grace, and mercy. All people have sinned, are separated from God because of their sin, and are in need of forgiveness. Through Jesus' sacrificial act on the cross, those who believe in Jesus have forgiveness of sins and everlasting life with Him in heaven.

Ask students to imagine that they are watching the scene of Jesus' arrest. Remind them that the Jewish leaders were afraid of Jesus' popularity and that they did not believe His claim to be the Messiah, the promised Savior of the world. Their solution was to have Jesus arrested and put on trial, even though Jesus did nothing to deserve such treatment. Explain to students that fear or unbelief can lead to sin if they do not stand firm in their faith.

Tell students to imagine Jesus carrying His heavy cross after being severely beaten. Remind them that Jesus suffered pain, harsh treatment, and humiliation on their behalf. Explain to students that even though they may go through some difficult times, it is hard to completely understand what Jesus endured for them.

Teach that some Christians call the day that Jesus died *Good Friday*, *Great Friday*, or *Holy Friday*. Remind students that Jesus went through the agony of dying on a cross because He loves each one of them so much. Lead the class in prayer, thanking and praising Jesus for His sacrifice for their salvation. Allow students to have a time of silent prayer, being aware that thinking about Jesus' death may be a very emotional experience for some students.

Student Page 29.3

Direct students to independently complete the page.

Review

- Why did the Jewish leaders want to kill Jesus? (**Possible answers: He was attracting many followers; they did not believe His claims to be the Son of God; they did not want to accept that Jesus was the Messiah.**)
- Where was Jesus crucified? (**Golgotha, or Calvary**)

- What did Jesus do for you on Good Friday? (**Jesus died for me and through His death, He provided forgiveness of my sins.**)
- Why did God willingly send Jesus to die for you? (**because He loves me, and shows me grace and mercy**)

Notes:

APPLICATION

- Read **Luke 22:54–62**. Why do you think Peter denied, or said that he did not know, Jesus? (**Possible answers: Peter was afraid; he lacked faith.**)
- Read **Luke 9:23**. What do you think it means to take up your cross and follow Jesus? (**Answers will vary but should include that I am to daily set aside my will to do what God wants me to do.**)
- What part do you have in God's plan of salvation? (**God sent Jesus to die for my sins. To be forgiven, I need to confess my sins, recognize that I need a savior, and have faith in Jesus.**)

REINFORCEMENT

Christians around the world celebrate Easter in a variety of interesting ways. Hot cross buns, pastries with a cross marked on the top, are sold in the United Kingdom during the Easter season. Christians in the Ukraine decorate eggs with elaborate designs called *pysanky*. The red coloration of these eggs reminds Ukrainians of the blood of Christ.

Many symbols are associated with Easter, including eggs and lambs. Some of these symbols came from pagan traditions to which Christian missionaries gave new meaning. The egg is a symbol of new life; it also resembles the tomb that could not hold the risen Lord. Lambs are also frequently seen as symbols of Easter because of the association of the sacrificial lamb with Jesus, the Lamb of God.

DAY 3

Name _____

Easter 29.3

1. Number the events of Jesus' arrest in the order that they happened.

[2] Jesus prayed for the disciples.   [5] Jesus was taken away.

[1] Judas arranged for Jesus' arrest.   [3] A disciple drew his sword.

[4] Jesus questioned the leaders.   [6] The disciples ran away.

2. Complete the sentences with **governor**, **wrong**, **crucify**, and **priest**.

After Jesus was arrested, He was taken to the high

_____priest_____ for a trial before the Jewish leaders.

Because the Jewish leaders could not sentence a prisoner to death, Jesus was

taken to Pontius Pilate, the Roman _____governor_____

for trial. Pontius Pilate could not find anything that Jesus had done

_____wrong_____. Even so, Pilate allowed the Jewish

leaders to _____crucify_____ Jesus.

3. Christians call the day that Jesus died **Good Friday**. Think about why this day is good. Color the picture.

Coloring will vary.

© *Bible Grade 2*

115

29.4 Easter

Focus: Jesus Is Risen

★ PREPARATION

Prepare a **PLASTIC EASTER EGG** for each student. Make copies of the Memory Verse and place one inside each egg. Hide the eggs around the classroom for students to find. (*Introduction*)

Select the song "Easter Rise Up" from the Grade 2 URL. (*Introduction*)

Select **VA 29D Jesus Is Risen** (*Directed Instruction*)

↪ EXTENSION

4A Present **PP-8D Jesus Is Risen** to review the Bible truth. Choose one of the suggestions for a class celebration on the last slide.

4B Make enough copies of **BLMs 29B–C Easter Scene, Parts 1–2** on **CARD STOCK** for each student. Direct students to color, cut out the figures, and assemble the scene to retell the Bible truth about Easter.

Introduction ★

Have students search around the classroom to find the hidden **PLASTIC EASTER EGGS**. Instruct students to return to their desks after finding one egg each. When all the students are seated, direct them to open the eggs and chorally read the Memory Verse. Explain that opening the egg should remind them of Jesus' empty tomb. Death could not keep Jesus in the tomb. Jesus is risen from the dead!

Play and sing the song "Easter Rise Up" from the Grade 2 URL.

Directed Instruction ★ ↪

Display **VA 29D Jesus Is Risen** and read the Bible truth on the back. Ask students who Jesus had raised from the dead just days before. (**Lazarus**) Jesus was able to do this because of His omnipotence—the quality of being all-powerful. God again showed his omnipotence by resurrecting Jesus.

Ask students what Mary Magdalene and other women noticed when they went to Jesus' tomb to finish wrapping Jesus' body in spices and cloth strips. (**the large stone had been rolled away from the tomb**) As they were wondering what could have happened, angels appeared. An angel reminded the women that Jesus said He would rise from the dead. Ask students to share how they would have reacted in this situation. (**Possible answers: I would have been afraid; I would have been amazed.**) The women remembered what Jesus had said. They ran to tell the disciples that Jesus was alive.

Review the following events that occurred after the women ran to tell the disciples the news of Jesus rising from the dead:
- Peter ran to the tomb and saw that Jesus was not there.
- Jesus appeared to Mary Magdalene.
- Jesus appeared to two believers on the road to Emmaus. The two men did not recognize Him until He prayed and blessed the food at supper.
- As the two men shared the news of His appearance with the disciples, Jesus appeared and showed all of them that He was alive.
- Jesus appeared to many others, at many different times. One time, He appeared to over 500 people.
- Jesus told His disciples to share the good news about God's love and His plan of salvation for everyone.

Teach students a traditional Easter greeting by saying, "He is risen!" Prompt them to respond, "He is risen indeed!" Pair students and have them take turns repeating the greeting.

Explain that Jesus' resurrection from the dead is the most significant miracle in the Bible. Because Jesus conquered death, believers will rise again to live with Him in heaven forever.

Student Page 29.4
Have students complete the page independently.

Review

- Why did Mary Magdalene and the other women go to the tomb on Sunday morning? (**They wanted to finish wrapping Jesus' body with spices and linen cloths for burial.**)
- What did the angel say to the women after they noticed that the stone had been rolled away from the entrance to the tomb? (**The angel asked the women why they were looking for a living person in a tomb. The angel announced that Jesus was no longer there; He had risen.**)
- How did Jesus rise from the dead? (**God, who is omnipotent, resurrected Jesus from the dead.**)
- What significance does Jesus' resurrection have in your life? (**Since Jesus took the punishment for my sins by dying on the cross, I am reconciled to God and will live with Him in heaven forever.**)

Time Line

Point out the resurrection of Jesus. Explain that all the events discussed in this week's lesson took place over the course of eight days, beginning with Jesus' triumphal entry into Jerusalem on a Sunday and ending with Jesus' ressurrection the following Sunday.

APPLICATION

- How do you think Mary Magdalene felt when she realized that Jesus was alive? (**Answers will vary.**)
- Why is the miracle of the resurrection the most important miracle in the Bible? (**Answers will vary but should include that because Jesus lives, I will live with Him in heaven forever.**)
- Tell about how you would share the Bible truth about Easter with a friend or family member. (**Answers will vary.**)

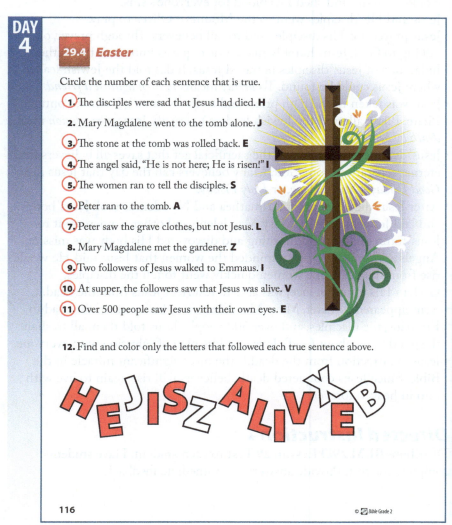

DAY 4

29.4 *Easter*

Circle the number of each sentence that is true.

1. The disciples were sad that Jesus had died. **H**
2. Mary Magdalene went to the tomb alone. **J**
3. The stone at the tomb was rolled back. **E**
4. The angel said, "He is not here; He is risen!" **I**
5. The women ran to tell the disciples. **S**
6. Peter ran to the tomb. **A**
7. Peter saw the grave clothes, but not Jesus. **L**
8. Mary Magdalene met the gardener. **Z**
9. Two followers of Jesus walked to Emmaus. **I**
10. At supper, the followers saw that Jesus was alive. **V**
11. Over 500 people saw Jesus with their own eyes. **E**

12. Find and color only the letters that followed each true sentence above.

H E J S Z A L I V X E B

29.5

Easter

Focus: Review and Assessment

★ PREPARATION

Select **VA 29A Jesus' Triumphal Entry**, **VA 29B Jesus' Last Supper**, **VA 29C Jesus' Arrest, Crucifixion, and Burial**, and **VA 29D Jesus Is Risen**. (*Lesson Review*)

Make one copy of **BLM 29D Lesson 29 Test** for each student. (*Directed Instruction*)

Lesson Review ★

Use **VAs 29A–D** to review the Bible truths. Cover the following concepts:

- Jesus rode a donkey into Jerusalem. This was a fulfillment of Zechariah's prophecy in the Old Testament.
- Believers annually celebrate Jesus' triumphal entry into Jerusalem. This celebration is called *Palm Sunday*, and is celebrated one week before Easter.
- The people who saw Jesus riding into Jerusalem shouted praises to Him. They shouted "Hosanna!" *Hosanna* means *save us* or *praise God*. The people were acknowledging the need for someone to save them from their sins.
- God sent Jesus to die for people's sins because He loves them—this is God's plan of salvation. Because of this ultimate display of love, grace, and mercy, He alone is worthy of praise. Praising God describes God's many qualities and tells Him and others of His greatness.
- In washing their feet, Jesus demonstrated to His disciples the need to love and joyfully serve others.
- Jesus shared a last meal with His disciples. He knew that His time on the earth was coming to an end. Jesus used a piece of bread to represent His body, and a cup of wine to represent His blood. Jesus explained that He would soon die and shed His blood for everyone's sins.
- Jesus and His disciples went to the Mount of Olives to pray.
- Jesus prayed for His disciples and for all believers. Through prayer, or talking to God, Jesus humbly made His requests known to the Father.
- Judas, one of Jesus' disciples betrayed Jesus. Judas told the Jewish leaders where Jesus could be found. To *betray* means *to turn against a friend*.
- Jesus was taken to the high priest and to the Roman governor, Pontius Pilate. Pilate allowed the Jewish leaders to crucify Jesus. *Crucifixion* means *death by being hung on a cross*.
- Jesus' death on the cross was the sacrificial act that saves all believers from eternal separation from God. Many believers call the day that Jesus died *Good Friday*, *Great Friday*, or *Holy Friday*.
- After Jesus died, Joseph of Arimathea and Nicodemus took Jesus' body and laid Jesus in a tomb. Mary Magdalene and other women went to Jesus' tomb on the third morning and discovered His body was missing! Angels appeared, and one reminded the women that Jesus said He would rise from the dead. The women quickly went to tell the disciples.
- God, in His omnipotence, was able to resurrect Jesus from the dead.
- Jesus appeared to Peter, Mary Magdalene, two believers on the road to Emmaus, the disciples, and over 500 people. Jesus told them all to share the good news about God's love and His plan of salvation with everyone.
- Jesus' resurrection from the dead is the most significant miracle in the Bible. Since Jesus conquered death, believers will rise again to live with him in heaven forever.

Directed Instruction ★

Distribute **BLM 29D Lesson 29 Test** to each student. Have students complete the test. Provide answers for immediate feedback.

Lesson Preparation
Peter Acts Boldly
30.0

Expected Student Outcomes

KNOW
Peter learns to overcome his fears and failures through the power of the Holy Spirit.

DO
Students will:
- complete activities to identify facts about the Bible and write about ways to show growth in their faith in God
- recognize that the Holy Spirit is their helper and describe a way they would like the Holy Spirit's help
- solve a coded message to retell the Bible truth
- sequence events from Peter's life

APPLY
Students will act boldly when afraid and when their faith is challenged. They will acknowledge their ongoing dependence upon the Holy Spirit.

Lesson Outline
I. Peter's fearful reactions (Jn 18:1–12, 15–18; Lk 22:47–62; Eph 3:12)
II. The Holy Spirit (Acts 1:3–9, 2:1–41, 4:1–31; Jn 21:15–19)
III. Amazing deliverance (Acts 12:1–11)
IV. Power in Peter's life (Jn 18:10; Lk 22:51–62; Acts 4:1–12, 12:1–17)

♥ TEACHER'S HEART

Your stomach is in knots because you know you're going to be late. Your fingers tense up and your head is pounding. You overreact and cut in front of another car. You say a few unkind words about the driver in front of you, which brings a look of surprise to your passenger's face. Your heart sinks, and you realize that you just revealed your lack of self-control.

Sometimes wayward moments like this pop up in your classroom as well. Your students will certainly identify with Peter's struggles to control his reactions. Many of them constantly strive to rein in their impulses, as you know very well. How encouraging for students to see that Peter made mistakes just like they do. But Peter's behavior changed when he repented and was reconciled to Christ. Then he was filled with the power of the Holy Spirit, and acted with courage and confidence.

Let students see the Holy Spirit's power in your life. Let Him teach and temper you in the area of self-control. Challenge yourself and your students to ask the Holy Spirit daily for His powerful help.

📖 MEMORY VERSE
2 Timothy 1:7

GLOSSARY WORDS
- reconcile
- persecute

★ MATERIALS
Day 1:
- Time Line

Day 2:
- BLM 30A Holy Spirit Helper
- PP-9 The Holy Spirit (*Extension*)
- Hard-boiled egg (*Extension*)

Day 3:
- VA 30A Peter Acts Boldly

Day 4:
- DM-1 Character Traits (*Extension*)

Day 5:
- VA 30A Peter Acts Boldly
- BLM 30B Lesson 30 Test

♪ SONGS
Create in Me
What Seems Impossible

TEACHER RESOURCES
Chan, Francis. *Forgotten God: Reversing Our Tragic Neglect of the Holy Spirit*. David C. Cook, 2009.
Swindoll, Charles R. *So, You Want to Be Like Christ: Eight Essentials to Get You There*. Thomas Nelson, 2007.

STUDENT RESOURCES
Baker, Rod. *Real Power for Kids: Knowing the Holy Spirit as Your Friend*. Harrison House, 2005.
Lepley, Lynne M. *Three in One: A Book About God*. Abingdon Press, 2013.

Supplemental Materials are available to download. See Understanding Purposeful Design Bible at the front of this book for the Grade 2 URL.

30.1 Peter Acts Boldly
Focus: Peter's Fearful Reactions

📖 MEMORY VERSE
2 Timothy 1:7

MEMORY WORK
- Have students locate the Memory Verse in their Bible and read the verse together several times. Divide the class into two groups. Invite students in the first group to say the first half of the verse in a fearful and timid voice. Then have the other group say the second half of the verse in a bold and confident voice. Have the groups switch roles. Continue until students show mastery of the verse.

↻ EXTENSION

1A Read **Proverbs 25:28**. Ask students to describe problems a city might have if its walls were broken down. (**Possible answers: unsafe, danger of enemy attacks, robbers stealing things, wild animals can get in**) Remind students how Nehemiah and the Israelites worked to rebuild the walls of Jerusalem. Explain that the people felt safer when the walls were complete and strong. Ask how a person who does not show self-control is like a city without walls. (**Possible answers: That person can be taken advantage of; people do not feel safe around someone who is out of control.**) Discuss how a city needs a builder and designer to construct it well. In the same way, students can trust in God as their Master builder and designer. Following His plan for their life is a display of self-control.

Introduction

Describe what it would feel like to be in a boat during a storm at sea. Tell students to imagine themselves in the boat. Ask what would help them feel less afraid. (**Possible answers: someone steering the boat, help from someone who has saved boats from storms before, for the storm to stop**) Explain that sometimes students can be like that boat—out of control and tossed about by fear. God wants them to look to Him for help to steer them to safety and help them to be calm and in control.

Directed Instruction ↻

Remind students that one of Jesus' followers was a disciple named *Peter*. Read the following Bible truth paraphrased from John 18:1–12, 15–18, and Luke 22:47–62:

> The chief priests and Pharisees sent some officials and soldiers to arrest Jesus in the garden of Gethsemane. Peter wanted to stop the arrest, so he drew his sword and swung it at Malchus, the high priest's servant. Instead of killing Malchus, Peter ended up cutting off Malchus' right ear. After Jesus healed Malchus, Peter followed the Jewish officials and soldiers as they led Jesus away. Peter waited in the high priest's courtyard to see what would happen. Three different times people asked Peter if he knew or followed Jesus. Three times Peter lied because he was afraid. Later, he was deeply sorry and cried bitterly.

Explain that Peter reacted poorly when Jesus was arrested. Jesus did not want him to fight. Later, he was afraid of being recognized as Jesus' follower, and so he lied. Explain that fear causes people to do things they did not plan to do. This kind of fear does not come from God (Ephesians 3:12). In fact, fear is the opposite of what God wants for His children. He wants His children to have faith in Him. Ask students for ways to grow in godly faith. (**Possible answers: learn God's Word, pray, think about what the Bible says and then do it, remember what God has already done**)

Peter recognized that he was wrong to deny that he knew Jesus. He was very upset with himself and sorry for his lack of self-control. Being sorry is the first step in repentance. The other two elements of repentance are confessing the sin and changing the actions. While spending time with Jesus, Peter had learned to trust and put his faith in Jesus, which allowed his faith to grow. But, when Jesus was arrested, Peter gave in to fear.

Tell students that when things are out of control and they are afraid, they must realize that God has the power to guide, help, and give them the boldness to do what is needed. In the following activity, instruct students to hold their thumbs down when you read about a fearful reaction, and to hold their thumbs up when you read about a reaction showing self-control and God's peace.

Read the following:
- You lie about having your homework done because you are afraid you will get in trouble. (**thumbs down**)

292

- You tell the truth and accept the consequences for your actions because you are sorry and plan to do better next time. (**thumbs up**)
- You encourage and build up others because each person is precious to God. (**thumbs up**)

Student Page 30.1
Read the directions and assist as needed.

Review
- How did Peter show a lack of self-control? (**He cut off Malchus' ear.**)
- How did Peter show fear when questioned about Jesus? (**He lied and said he didn't know Jesus.**)
- How did Peter show repentance? (**After he denied Jesus three times, he felt sorry and cried.**)

Time Line
Point to Jesus' resurrection on the **Time Line**. Only 40 days later was Pentecost, when God sent the Holy Spirit to Jesus' followers in Jerusalem. This marked the beginning of the Church.

APPLICATION
- Why do you think Peter was fearful? (**Possible answers: He felt unsafe; he did not want to be recognized as one of Jesus' followers; he did not fully accept Jesus' love and acceptance of him.**)
- Tell about a time when you allowed fear to cause you to do something out of control or that surprised you. (**Answers will vary.**)
- Have you felt fearful recently? (**Answers will vary.**) How did you overcome your fear? (**Possible answers: through prayer, by trusting in God's help, by saying memorized Bible verses**)

DAY 1

Name _____

Peter Acts Boldly   30.1

Unscramble the letters to complete each of the three sentences.

1. The officials and soldiers came to ___**arrest**___ Jesus.
   a t r e s r

2. Peter became scared and cut off Malchus' ___**ear**___.
   r e a

3. Peter should have used self-___**control**___.
   n o t r c o l

4. Peter said he was not a follower of Jesus. Solve the math problems. Circle the ones that tell how many times Peter denied Jesus.

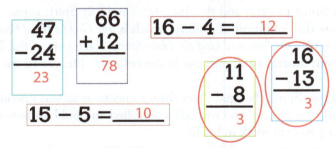

$47 - 24 = 23$ $66 + 12 = 78$ $16 - 4 = 12$

$15 - 5 = 10$ $11 - 8 = 3$ $16 - 13 = 3$

5. Faith is the opposite of fear. Write two or more things you can do to help your faith in God grow.

___**Answers will vary.**___

30.2 Peter Acts Boldly
Focus: The Holy Spirit

★ PREPARATION
Make copies of **BLM 30A Holy Spirit Helper** for each student. (*Directed Instruction*)

↻ EXTENSION
2A Show **PP-9 The Holy Spirit** to help explain the Holy Spirit's role in the life of a believer in Christ.

2B Describe the Trinity by displaying a HARD-BOILED EGG to your class. Explain that an egg has three parts. The shell protects the egg. The white part is nourishment for the chicken while it is growing and the yoke is where the chicken is formed. Explain that even though all three parts are different and have different functions, they are all part of making up one egg. In a similar way, God is one God in three different forms—God the Father, God the Son, and God the Holy Spirit.

Introduction
Talk about how some people take vitamins or protein drinks to help their bodies have extra strength and health. A person can live without the extra vitamins or protein, but some believe these things help boost energy and give the body more power. Believers in Christ have something much more powerful than a vitamin pill or powdered drink, they have a gift from God—the Holy Spirit! Peter and the disciples knew that the extra power they had from the Holy Spirit within them gave them power and boldness, and helped them grow in their faith in Christ.

Directed Instruction ★ ↻
Read the following Bible truth paraphrased from John 21:15–19 and Acts 1:3–9, 2:1–41, 4:1–31:

> After Jesus died on the cross, He rose from the dead and appeared to His disciples over a period of 40 days. During one of these times, Jesus renewed and restored His relationship with Peter. Then, just prior to Jesus ascending, or going up, into heaven, He told the disciples to wait in Jerusalem so that they could be baptized with the Holy Spirit—a gift from God the Father. Peter and the other disciples were empowered by the Holy Spirit to do all that God had called them to do. Peter was able to speak boldly to others, explaining who Jesus was and sharing God's plan of salvation. Thousands came to believe in Jesus as the Savior because of what Peter said and because of the change in Peter and the other disciples. Even when the elders of Israel arrested Peter and John and then commanded them not to speak of Jesus, these two disciples didn't become fearful. Instead, Peter and John and other believers prayed for boldness to speak more about the Lord, and they asked the Lord to use them to heal others and perform signs and wonders.

Reiterate that when Jesus returned to heaven, God the Father sent the Holy Spirit to Peter and the disciples. The Holy Spirit is part of the Trinity. Review the definition of *Trinity*, which is *one God in three Persons—God the Father, God the Son, and God the Holy Spirit*. Each part of the Trinity has a different function and purpose in the believer's life, yet all are one God.

The Holy Spirit changed Peter from someone who was uncontrolled and fearful to someone who was self-controlled and bold. Others could see God's power at work in his life.

Denominations may differ in opinion over some of the gifts of the Holy Spirit, but the power and guidance of the Holy Spirit are gifts from God. They are available to all believers in Christ.

Distribute copies of **BLM 30A Holy Spirit Helper**. Have students work with a partner to complete the page. Correct the page together by discussing each way the Holy Spirit can help believers in Christ. End by asking volunteers to pray and thank God for giving the gift of the Holy Spirit.

Student Page 30.2
Read the poem together with students. Emphasize *Holy Spirit, be my Helper* in each stanza and have students circle the phrase. Upon completion, allow time for students to share answers that explain how they would like the Holy Spirit's help.

Review
- Who was given to guide and help Peter and the disciples? (**the Holy Spirit**)
- Explain the Trinity. (**Answers will vary but should include that the Trinity is God in three different Persons—God the Father, God the Son, and God the Holy Spirit.**)
- What are some things the Holy Spirit does to help you? (**Possible answers: grows my faith in Christ, helps me know God's voice, helps me tell others about Jesus, gives me self-control, helps me not be fearful, prays for me**)

APPLICATION
- How had Peter's relationship with Jesus changed since Jesus' resurrection? (**He no longer denied Jesus, but repented and was renewed and restored in his relationship with Jesus.**)
- What can you do when you need to renew and restore your relationship with Jesus? (**Possible answers: repent, ask the Holy Spirit to help me grow to be more like Christ, learn from the Bible**)
- How did Peter's life change because of the Holy Spirit? (**Possible answers: He received power from the Holy Spirit; the Holy Spirit helped him be bold; the Holy Spirit helped him with self-control.**)
- As a follower of Jesus, how do you see the Holy Spirit working in your life? (**Possible answers: I feel closer to God; I have more boldness to tell others about Jesus; I have more self-control.**)

REINFORCEMENT
The word *Trinity* does not appear in the Bible. Theophilus, a bishop in Antioch, Syria, first used the word *Trinity* in 168 AD. Patrick, bishop of Ireland and known also as St. Patrick, used the shamrock to explain the Trinity in 432 AD. He illustrated it by showing one shamrock with three lobes of equal size representing each Person of the Godhead. Thereafter, Christians began using the word *Trinity* regularly to describe the relationship between the Father, Son, and Holy Spirit. There are more than 60 Bible passages that talk about the three Persons in the Bible, such as Matthew 28:19, Ephesians 4:4–6 and Titus 3:4–6.

DAY 2

30.2 Peter Acts Boldly

1. Read the poem. Draw a circle around the words **Holy Spirit, be my Helper**.

When I know that I should listen,
I fear recess I'll be missin',
My teacher doesn't give permission,
Holy Spirit, be my Helper!

When I have to wait in line,
I'm worried we may run out of time,
Others may receive what's mine,
Holy Spirit, be my Helper!

When I want to be strong,
Telling of Jesus to whom I belong,
I fear others may think I'm wrong,
Holy Spirit, be my Helper!

2. Write how you would like the Holy Spirit to help you.

Answers will vary.

30.3 Peter Acts Boldly

Focus: Amazing Deliverance

★ PREPARATION

Select the song "Create in Me" from the Grade 2 URL. (*Introduction*)

Select **VA 30A Peter Acts Boldly**. (*Directed Instruction*)

⟳ EXTENSION

3A Read **Matthew 5:10–12**. Explain that people are not usually happy about being persecuted, but God has rewards for people who are persecuted because of their faith in Him. Talk about some of the places around the world where Christians currently suffer persecution. Take time to pray for the believers to remain bold in sharing their faith with those who persecute them.

3B Instruct students to write a journal entry on how they would have felt and responded after praying for Peter's release from prison and then having him show up after God delivered him from prison.

Introduction ★

Sing the song "Create in Me" from the Grade 2 URL. Review that Peter's heart changed when he repented of denying his relationship to Jesus. Tell students to look up **reconcile** in their Glossary, and let a volunteer read that it means *to restore a relationship*. Explain that Jesus reconciled his relationship with Peter. Talk about times when students have felt disappointed, betrayed, or offended by someone, but then were able to renew or restore the relationship. Explain that Jesus never holds a grudge; He is always willing to reconcile.

Review how Peter changed from being fearful and uncontrolled to being empowered by the Holy Spirit to boldly tell others about Jesus. Because of Peter's boldness, he was persecuted. Ask a volunteer to read the Glossary definition of **persecute**, which means *to treat someone in a cruel way*. Persecution can happen for many different reasons, but Peter was persecuted because of his bold witness for Jesus.

Directed Instruction ★ ⟳

Read **VA 30A Peter Acts Boldly**. Ask students how they might have felt if they had been in Peter's situation in prison. (**Answers will vary.**) Point out that the Holy Spirit gave Peter the power to be patient and calm—unlike his reaction the night Jesus was arrested. Peter had grown immensely in his faith in Christ and in self-control since the night of Jesus' arrest, so much so that the angel actually had to wake him and tell him to get up and go!

Explain that a vision is like a dream but with open eyes. Ask why Peter thought he might have been dreaming. (**Answers will vary but should include that seeing an angel was not normal or something that ordinarily happened.**) Remind students that while Peter was in prison, the Church had been praying for him. It may have seemed like a hopeless situation since many of the other followers of Jesus had been persecuted and some had even been killed. Let students give examples of the Church's prayers. (**Possible answers: Please set Peter free; help Peter boldly talk about Jesus in prison; keep Peter safe; remind Peter of all that Jesus said.**) Encourage students to show the surprised reactions of the believers when Peter appeared. Remind students that they should not be surprised when God answers prayers in really big ways!

Student Page 30.3

Direct students to work with a classmate to solve the code about the Bible truth. Have them complete the rest of the page independently.

Review

- Why was Peter persecuted? (**He was boldly telling people about Jesus. King Herod did not like that and had Peter thrown in prison.**)
- How might Peter have reacted differently in prison if he did not have the power of the Holy Spirit in him? (**Possible answers: He might have tried to escape; he might have fought with the guards; he probably would have been afraid of being killed.**)

296

- Explain what happened when the angel appeared in Peter's prison cell. (**The angel told him to get up, the chains fell off, Peter was told to dress and follow the angel past the guards, and then Peter went out through the open iron gate.**)

Notes:

APPLICATION

- Peter and Jesus reconciled their relationship. Who is someone you might need to reconcile with? (**Answers will vary.**)
- How can the Holy Spirit help you reconcile with someone? (**Possible answers: help me know the words to say, help me be bold to ask forgiveness, help me want to do what is right and reconcile**)
- You might be teased or bullied because of your faith in Christ. Tell about a time when you or someone you know has been persecuted for faith in Christ. (**Answers will vary.**)

REINFORCEMENT

Herod Agrippa I was the grandson of Herod the Great, who ordered the children of Bethlehem to be murdered. He was also the nephew of Herod Antipas, who beheaded John the Baptist. Herod Agrippa I had already beheaded James and now Peter was under heavy guard in prison, waiting for trial and a sure death sentence. Four soldiers at a time watched over Peter—two beside him and two at the guard posts. Herod was determined to destroy the Church, but God had different ideas. The believers were constantly praying and God's power prevailed over the decision of an evil ruler. God's deliverance of Peter was amazing and inspired many to put their faith in God.

DAY 3

Name _____

Peter Acts Boldly `30.3`

1. Use the clues in the Code Box to figure out the missing words in the retelling of the Bible truth.

Code Box

a = 1	b = 2	d = 3	e = 4	g = 5	h = 6
i = 7	l = 8	n = 9	o = 10	p = 11	r = 12
s = 13	t = 14	v = 15	w = 16	y = 17	

After Peter r e p e n t e d and reconciled
          12 4 11 4 9 14 4 3

with Jesus, the H o l y   S p i r i t
               6 10 8 17   13 11 7 12 7 14

gave him p o w e r to b o l d l y
         11 10 16 4 12   2 10 8 3 8 17

tell others about Jesus. King Herod b e g a n to persecute
                                     2 4 5 1 9

the Church and put Peter in p r i s o n . Many people
                            11 12 7 13 10 9

p r a y e d God sent an a n g e l
11 12 1 17 4 3   1 9 5 4 8

to d e l i v e r Peter from prison.
    3 4 8 7 15 4 12

2. Peter's example can help you to be bold for Jesus. Write about a time when you might speak or show boldness for Jesus.

Answers will vary.

_____

_____

_____

© Bible Grade 2

119

30.4 Peter Acts Boldly

Focus: Power in Peter's Life

★ PREPARATION

Select the song "What Seems Impossible" from the Grade 2 URL. (*Introduction*)

↻ EXTENSION

4A Display **DM-1 Character Traits**. Point out that *patience* means *waiting without complaining*. Explain how the Holy Spirit helped Peter show patience in prison—a very different reaction from when he cut off Malchus' ear during Jesus' arrest. Discuss other character traits Peter showed after he was reconciled to Jesus and empowered by the Holy Spirit. Talk about how the Holy Spirit can empower students to exhibit all of these good character traits.

4B Draw a vertical line on the board and label it *Peter's Spiritual Growth Chart*. At the bottom of the chart, have students write some of the things Peter did based on fear and uncontrolled behavior. (**Possible answers: cut off Malchus' ear, denied knowing Jesus three times**) Moving upward on the line, invite a volunteer to mark when Jesus and Peter reconciled. Next, ask another volunteer mark when the Holy Spirit filled Peter. Last, at the top of the line, request that another volunteer mark some of the changes that showed Peter was growing in his faith because of the power of the Holy Spirit. (**Possible answers: spoke boldly about Jesus, healed others, did miracles, stayed calm in prison, continued to trust in God**)

Introduction ★

Sing the song "What Seems Impossible" from the Grade 2 URL. Let students name some of the seemingly impossible things God has done in their lives. (**Answers will vary.**) After students share examples, encourage them to thank God for delivering them and doing the impossible.

Directed Instruction ↻

As volunteers act out portions of Peter's life, encourage students to watch for ways he changed and how the Holy Spirit's power was shown in his life. Ask two students to read **John 18:10** and **Luke 22:51**. Select students to play the parts of *Jesus*, *Peter*, *Malchus*, *the crowd*, and some of *the other disciples*. Direct *Jesus* and *the other disciples* to stand together. Tell *the crowd* to pretend to hold swords and clubs and rush toward *Jesus* saying, "Come with us!" Have *Peter* gently brush *Malchus'* ear with an imaginary sword. Direct *Jesus* to the touch the ear. Tell *the crowd* to say, "Malchus is healed!" Discuss how Peter's life showed fear and a lack of self-control.

Appoint two students to read **Luke 22:54–62**. Select a girl to play *the servant girl*, some students to sit around an imaginary fire, someone to be *Peter*, and someone to be *the rooster*. Encourage *the servant girl* to question *Peter* about being with Jesus. Tell the students around the fire to identify *Peter* as a follower of Jesus. Direct *Peter* to say he does not know Jesus all three times. Have *the rooster* crow. Tell *Peter* to look alarmed and begin to cry, hurrying away. Discuss how Peter immediately felt repentant because he was disloyal to Jesus. Tell students after Jesus rose from the dead and appeared to the disciples several times, he talked with Peter, and acknowledged Peter's love for Him. He showed forgiveness to Peter by giving him the job of caring for his people. Their relationship was restored.

Remind students that after Jesus went back to heaven, God gave the Holy Spirit to be a helper. Peter, by the Holy Spirit's power, healed people and did other amazing things that Jesus told His followers to do.

Choose several students to read **Acts 4:1–12**. Select two students to be *Peter* and *John*. Choose students to be members of *the crowd*. Select *a spokesperson* and *guards*. Have *Peter* and *John* preach to *the crowd*. Have *the spokesperson* approach and order that they be arrested. *The guards* can take them to prison. Discuss how Jesus' followers were persecuted because they boldly spoke about Jesus.

Choose several students to read **Acts 12:1–11**. Select students to play *Peter*, *two soldiers*, *guards*, and *an angel*. Tell *Peter* to sit in prison between the *two soldiers* with *the guards* standing by the door of the prison. Direct *Peter* to act as if he is sleeping. Have *the angel* walk in and touch *Peter's* shoulder and tell him to get up. The *two soldiers* can look surprised. Tell *the angel* to walk past *the guards* with *Peter* following. Tell *Peter* to look curious and a bit confused, as if what he had just seen and done was a dream, but then realize that God sent an angel to deliver him from prison. Discuss how God can do things that are impossible for people to do.

Student Page 30.4
Read the directions and have students order the events in Peter's life. Upon completion of the questions, allow time for students to discuss their answers with a partner.

Review
- Compare how Peter acted before and after he received the Holy Spirit. (**Before Peter received the Holy Spirit, he was fearful and acting uncontrolled. After he received the Holy Spirit, he became bold.**)
- Give examples of how Peter behaved fearfully and showed a lack of self-control before he had the Holy Spirit. (**Possible answers: cut off Malchus' ear, denied knowing Jesus three times**)
- What are some of the ways that Peter showed he grew in his faith? (**Possible answers: became bold, preached about Jesus to others, showed the Holy Spirit's power**)

Notes:

APPLICATION
- What can you learn from Peter's life? (**Possible answers: to desire the power of the Holy Spirit in my life, to be bold in sharing my faith, to control myself and trust Jesus**)
- How can the Holy Spirit help you? (**Answers will vary but should include that the Holy Spirit's power can help in every area of my life.**)

DAY 4

30.4 Peter Acts Boldly

1. In the boxes below, write each sentence in the correct order as it happened.

- Peter was sorry he lied about knowing Jesus.
- Peter was set free from prison by an angel.
- Peter cut off Malchus' ear.
- Peter boldly preached about Jesus.

Peter cut off Malchus' ear.

Peter was sorry he lied about knowing Jesus.

Peter boldly preached about Jesus.

Peter was set free from prison by an angel.

2. How did Peter's life change?
The Holy Spirit's power helped Peter become bold for Christ.

3. How can God change your life?
Answers will vary.

30.5 Peter Acts Boldly
Focus: Review and Assessment

★ PREPARATION

Select **VA 30A Peter Acts Boldly**. (*Lesson Review*)

Make copies of **BLM 30B Lesson 30 Test** for each student. (*Directed Instruction*)

Lesson Review ★

Use **VA 30A Peter Acts Boldly** to review the Bible truths from this lesson. Cover the following concepts:

• Peter fearfully reacted to Jesus' arrest by cutting off Malchus' ear.
• Several people asked Peter if he knew Jesus and he denied it three times.
• Peter repented immediately and was deeply sorry for acting uncontrollably. He cried bitterly.
• After Jesus died on the cross, He rose from the dead and appeared to the disciples over a period of 40 days.
• During that time, Jesus reconciled his relationship with Peter.
• To *reconcile* means *to restore a relationship.*
• Before Jesus went to heaven, the disciples were promised the gift that God would send—the Holy Spirit.
• The Holy Spirit is part of the *Trinity*, which means *one God in three Persons—God the Father, God the Son, and God the Holy Spirit.*
• The Holy Spirit was given to help believers in Jesus in many different ways; by reminding them about things Jesus said, guiding them to know truth, giving them strength, helping them tell others about Jesus, praying for them, and providing the fruit of self-control.
• The Holy Spirit's power helped Peter grow in his faith.
• Peter was able to speak boldly to others about God's plan for salvation and thousands came to believe in Jesus as their Savior.
• Peter, John, and other believers got together to speak boldly and pray that God would use them to do amazing things.
• To *persecute* means *to treat someone in a cruel way.* Persecution can happen for many different reasons, but Peter was persecuted because of his bold witness for Jesus.
• King Herod persecuted Peter. Peter was arrested and put in prison, but God delivered him by sending an angel to free Peter from his chains and open the doors of the prison.
• The Church was praying constantly for Peter. The believers were surprised when he appeared to them after being set free by the angel.
• Peter was changed from being a fearful follower of Christ to one who boldly told others about Jesus and performed miracles.
• God wants followers of Jesus to trust in the Holy Spirit, as Peter did, to help them speak boldly to others about Jesus, even if they are persecuted.

Directed Instruction ★

Distribute a copy of **BLM 30B Lesson 30 Test** to each student. Read the directions and pronounce any difficult words. Once students have completed the test, provide answers for immediate feedback.

Notes:

Lesson Preparation
Peter Accepts Others — 31.0

Expected Student Outcomes

KNOW
Peter shares God's plan of salvation at Cornelius' home.

DO
Students will:
- use their own words to retell the Bible truth of Peter sharing the gospel with Cornelius
- recognize the similarities and differences between themselves and another student
- discover Scriptures that mention the Body of Christ and identify their role in the Body
- identify words to explain the plan of salvation
- practice telling another student about Jesus

APPLY
Students will demonstrate a teachable heart, accept others regardless of their differences, and freely share the plan of salvation.

Lesson Outline
I. Peter accepts Cornelius (Acts 10)
II. Accepting others (Col 3:11, James 2:1–10)
III. The body of Christ (Mk 16:15; 1 Cor 12:12–27; Ps 139:14; Rom 10:13–15)
IV. Go and tell (Lk 10:2)

♥ TEACHER'S HEART

Patty spent the first seven years of her life as an orphan in a Guatemalan village before she was adopted by an American family. Patty was old enough to understand what her adoptive family had brought her out of, and she was grateful. She didn't have to worry anymore about when she would eat next or if the holes in her clothes would get bigger. However, life in the United States wasn't as easy as she first thought it would be. She discovered that she was different. Her accent and dark skin brought ridicule. One day she heard a speaker talk about God as Father. Patty tearfully cried out to God, "I want to be part of Your family; I want to be accepted by You." For Patty, the truths of God became real that day: that God loves the whole world (John 3:16), that Christ died for everyone (Romans 5:8), that He does not want anyone to perish (2 Peter 3:9), and that anyone who believes in Him is adopted into the family of God and receives the gift of eternal life (1 John 5:11–12).

These truths are for everyone! People of all ages and all races are desperate to be accepted into God's family. Some of those are children in your classroom. Pray for each student to respond positively to God's offer to become His child. Encourage those students who do belong to Jesus to invite others to join the family of God!

MEMORY VERSE
1 John 3:23

GLOSSARY WORDS
- favoritism

MATERIALS

Day 1:
- VA 31A Peter and Cornelius
- Bed sheet, safety pins, pictures of various animals

Day 2:
- Magazines (Extension)

Day 3:
- BLM 31A Body Parts
- BLM 31B Shapes (Extension)

Day 4:
- BLM 31C People Group Profile (Extension)

Day 5:
- VA 31A Peter and Cornelius
- BLM 31D Lesson 31 Test

♪ SONGS
Love with the Love of Jesus

TEACHER RESOURCES
Dunagan, Ann. *The Mission-Minded Child: Raising a New Generation to Fulfill God's Purpose.* Authentic Publishing, 2007.

Morgan, Elisa. *"I Can" Evangelism: Taking the "I Can't" Out of Sharing Your Faith.* Revell, 2008.

STUDENT RESOURCES
Morgan, Robert J. *Knowing, Showing, Growing: My John 3:16 Discovery Book.* B&H Publishing Group, 2010.

Supplemental Materials are available to download. See Understanding Purposeful Design Bible at the front of this book for the Grade 2 URL.

31.1 Peter Accepts Others
Focus: Peter Accepts Cornelius

MEMORY VERSE
1 John 3:23

MEMORY WORK
- Draw a 3' × 3' grid on the board. Divide students into two teams. Use *X*s and *O*s to represent each team. Each time a team member says the verse correctly, that team gets to place its symbol on the grid. The next turn then goes to the other team. If that team member says it correctly, that team gets to put its symbol on the grid. The winner is the first team to get three symbols in a row vertically, horizontally, or diagonally.

PREPARATION
Select **VA 31A Peter and Cornelius**. (*Directed Instruction*)

Obtain a **LARGE BED SHEET**, **SAFETY PINS**, **PICTURES OF KOSHER ANIMALS** (chickens, sheep, goats, cows) and **PICTURES OF NONKOSHER ANIMALS** (snakes, horses, pigs). (*Directed Instruction*)

Introduction
Begin a discussion about the worst-tasting or most unhealthy foods that students have ever eaten. Ask them why they did not like those foods. If some students like the foods that other students did not enjoy, let them explain why. (**Answers will vary.**) Point out that people can have different opinions about food and some opinions are based on family preference or cultural eating habits. Explain that today's Bible truth is about a man whom God challenged to change his thinking.

Directed Instruction ★
Read **VA 31A Peter and Cornelius**. Explain that in the Old Testament Jewish people were God's chosen people. The Jewish people loved the fact that they were God's chosen people, so they did not often interact with people who were *Gentiles*, which means *non-Jewish people*. When Jesus came, He said that God loved the whole world, not just Jewish people. Jews did not that like very much; they liked being special and they wanted the Messiah to come just for them.

Show students a **LARGE BED SHEET**. Use **SAFETY PINS** to attach **PICTURES OF KOSHER ANIMALS** to the sheet. Explain that based on the Old Testament laws, these were the foods that Jewish people ate. Hold up the **PICTURES OF NONKOSHER ANIMALS**. Explain that the Jews never ate these animals or wanted to be friends with people who ate them. Discuss some of the animals that are typically eaten in your locale and are acceptable in your culture. Then mention some animals that people might eat in a different area or culture. God wanted His followers to focus on telling people about Jesus and not let disagreements about food or nationality stop them from sharing the gospel.

Point out that what Peter was shown in the vision was very different from what the religious law said. God's message had to be repeated three times before Peter understood and was willing to accept the change. Ask students to describe something that had to be repeated to them several times before they understood it. (**Possible answers: a math concept, the definition of a word, directions explaining how to do a chore at home**) Peter needed to obey, so it was important that he listen to God and clearly understand the message. God understood that this was a big change for Peter, and He was willing to repeat the vision so that Peter understood how important it was. Because Peter listened and obeyed, he was able to help Gentiles learn of God's love for them and guide them into God's family.

Pin the **PICTURES OF NONKOSHER ANIMALS** onto the bed sheet. Explain that Peter could now eat the animals that had not been allowed and God would not be upset. However, other Jews, who did not see the vision and hear the voice, were upset because Peter was breaking Jewish religious law. Invite students to tell how Peter might have felt as he spent time with Gentiles and ate some of their foods. (**Possible answers: happy to share the gospel with Gentiles since God had told him to do so, afraid that other Jews would be upset, uncomfortable**) It would take time for other Jewish followers of Jesus to understand what Peter understood. Eventually, all of Jesus' followers agreed that the gospel message was for everyone, not just the Jewish people. They began to preach the gospel to everyone.

Student Page 31.1
Read the directions and help students complete the page as needed.

Review
• What did the angel tell Cornelius? (**to send servants to get Peter who would explain God's plan of salvation**)
• What was Peter's vision? (**He saw a sheet with animals that God told him could now be eaten.**)
• What did the vision mean? (**God wanted everyone to hear the gospel, not just the Jewish people; Peter was to no longer call dirty what God had made clean.**)

Notes:

DAY 1

Name _____

Peter Accepts Others `31.1`

1. In each of the spaces, write a small phrase indicating what happened in the Bible truth from Acts 10.

> Cornelius, a man who loved God, saw ...
> **an angel**
>
> who told him to ...
> **send servants to get Peter.**

> Meanwhile, Peter went to a rooftop where he saw ...
> **a vision of a sheet with all kinds of animals.**
>
> He was told to no longer call dirty what God had ...
> **made clean.**

> Cornelius' servants came to where Peter was and said ...
> **go with us to Cornelius' house.**
>
> Peter went with them to Cornelius' house where he told them ...
> **about Jesus and they all received the Holy Spirit.**

2. Read Acts 10:34–35 and write in your own words what Peter shared at Cornelius' house.

Answers will vary but should include Peter realized the gospel was for everybody.

© Bible Grade 2   121

APPLICATION

• Peter changed his eating habits because he had a vision from God. On a scale from 1 to 5 with 5 being highest, how willing are you to change your eating habits if it would help others learn about God's plan of salvation? (**Answers will vary.**)

• What might have happened if Peter had not been willing to accept Cornelius as a believer in Jesus? (**Possible answers: God would have sent someone else; Cornelius and his friends might not have heard about God's plan of salvation and then been filled with the Holy Spirit; Peter would have missed baptizing Cornelius and his household.**)

REINFORCEMENT

Most Jewish people in Peter's time kept kosher laws pertaining to what foods could and could not be eaten. Peter's vision would have been more than troubling; it would have been mortifying to any Jew. In the Old Testament, God had given the prophet Ezekiel a similar command to eat something unclean, and Ezekiel responded equally indignantly (Ezekiel 4:13–14). Likewise, laws existed in Jewish culture pertaining to Gentiles—namely that Jews did not go to a Gentile's home, allow a Gentile to enter their home, or eat with a Gentile. Peter may have been disgusted at the thought of eating unclean food, but the message that the gospel was for everyone was loud and clear. He did the unlawful thing and invited the Gentile servants into the home of his Jewish host to stay the night (Acts 10:23), traveled with the Gentiles, and stayed a few days at Cornelius' house.

© Bible Grade 2

303

31.2 Peter Accepts Others
Focus: Accepting Others

EXTENSION

2A Provide students with MAGAZINES and a piece of construction paper. Instruct them to cut out three pictures of people who are like them in some characteristic and three pictures of people who are not like them. Tell students to separate their paper into two parts by making a line down the middle. Have them label each side *Like Me* and *Not Like Me* and glue their pictures under each heading. Discuss how differences are not bad; in fact they can be really good. Give personal examples of things that are different, which you have discovered are good, such as foods, ways of doing a task, or a certain route to a favorite place.

2B Write the following Scripture references on the board. Invite students to find and read them aloud. Ask students to explain what each verse says about how important people are to God and why students should accept everyone.
- **Psalm 139:14 (People are wonderfully made.)**
- **John 3:16 (God loves everyone.)**
- **Acts 10:34–35 (God loves everyone equally and is not partial.)**
- **Romans 5:8 (Jesus died for all people.)**

Introduction

Lead a game by placing spaces on the board to represent a word. Separate the class into two teams. Have teams take turns guessing letters. When the first team gets something right, cheer. When the second team gets something right, look annoyed. When the first team, the favored team, is incorrect look sad; but when the second team, the ill-favored team, is incorrect look joyful. When the game has finished, discuss with students how they felt about your reactions during the game. (**Answers will vary but should include that the members of the first team felt special and the members of the second team felt rejected.**)

Directed Instruction

God loves everyone. Invite a student to look up **favoritism** in the Glossary and read aloud the definition, which is *treating a person or a group better than others*. Let students explain how they felt in situations where they experienced favoritism shown to someone else. (**Answers will vary.**) Explain that accepting others and showing favoritism are opposites. Read **Colossians 3:11**. Explain that this verse mentions some groups of people that were very different from others. Tell students to notice that God does not show favoritism toward any of them—He does not want anyone to be separated from Him. This wonderful new way for Jewish believers to love and accept Gentiles began with Peter going to Cornelius' home.

Invite a student to read **James 2:1–10**. Discuss how it is sometimes difficult to love others who are different. Remind students that sin is sin and although favoritism is not like stealing or killing, God calls favoritism a sin. Encourage students to follow Peter's example and accept others because that is what God wants. Sometimes they will be surprised how much they enjoy being with people who are different and learning new things from them.

Explain that people are hurt by the favoritism in some Christians' words and actions. It can be very difficult for these people to hear and accept the good news about God's love and plan of salvation after having been treated so poorly. Read the following situations aloud and encourage students to think of ways to solve each problem. (**Solutions will vary.**)
- Alex was injured in a car accident and must use a wheelchair. Mark and Feng are assigned to be his helpers. They dislike having to wait for Alex. Sometimes they yell at him to hurry up. How can the other students encourage these two to be more accepting of Alex?

- Naledi is from South Africa. Although she speaks and understands English, the other students in her class sometimes have trouble understanding what she says. Sometimes they ignore her questions. This hurts her feelings. What can help Naledi feel accepted?

- Hayley is allergic to many kinds of food. She must eat special kinds of food, and some of these foods do not smell very good. Because of this, many students avoid sitting with her at lunchtime. She feels very lonely and wishes somebody would sit with her and be her friend. What can be done to make Hayley feel less lonely?

Explain to students that by accepting and loving others, they will show God's acceptance and love in a way that helps others desire to be part of His family.

Student Page 31.2
Place students in pairs to complete the page.

Review
- What does the Bible say about showing favoritism? (**Believers in Jesus Christ must not show favoritism.**)
- Why does Jesus want His followers to accept others? (**to tell them about God's love and plan of salvation**)
- If you accept and love others who do not know Jesus, what might happen? (**You might have a part in leading them to accept Jesus as savior.**)

APPLICATION
- Think of someone who is hard for you to accept and is not in your class. Do not name the person. Why do you think it is hard to accept this person? (**Possible answers: They do things differently; they are not like me.**)
- How might accepting that person help him or her learn about God? (**Possible answers: They might understand that God accepts them; it helps them understand God's love.**) (Encourage students to pray that God will help them see that person just as He sees them. Pray that God will give students courage to accept that person and to share God's love and acceptance with him or her.)
- Tell about a time when you showed favoritism toward someone and how you might act differently now that you know that God does not want you to show favoritism. (**Possible answers: I saved the swing for my friend, but now I would let anyone use the swing next to me; I only invited friends with fun video games to my house, but now I would invite all of my friends.**)

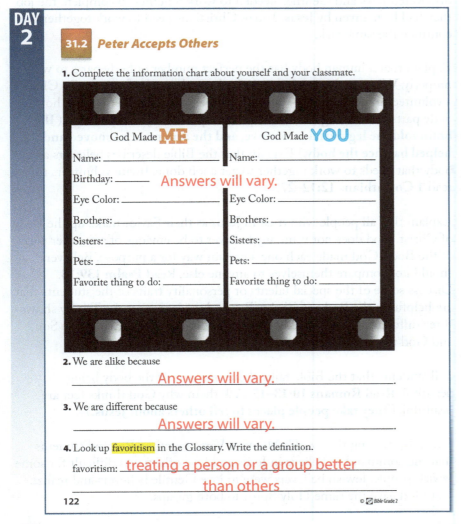

31.3 Peter Accepts Others
Focus: The Body of Christ

★ PREPARATION
Duplicate **BLM 31A Body Parts**. *(Introduction)*

↪ EXTENSION
3A Make a copy of **BLM 31B Shapes** for each student. Ask students to follow the instructions on the paper to color and cut out the shapes. Collect all of the pieces in groups of the same shape and color. Divide your students into six groups and give pieces of the same colored shape (for example, blue triangles) to each group. Ask each group to create a picture of a car by using the single colored shapes. After a few minutes stop and have each group share the design it created. Ask if they had trouble being creative. (**Yes, because we were limited to only one shape and color.**) Brainstorm what it would be like if everyone in the classroom was the same. On the board, make this drawing that shows the shapes that, when put together, form a car. Encourage each group to obtain the shapes they need in an orderly manner to complete the car. Ask what this activity teaches about accepting others. (**Possible answers: Differences are important and necessary; we can do more with different pieces.**)

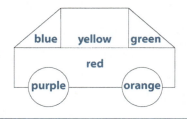

Introduction ★
Display **BLM 31A Body Parts** while walking around the classroom. Allow students to pick which body part they would like to be and gather in groups to make up a whole body. (There might be several groups.) Ask students what body parts are missing. (**Possible answers: stomach, mouth, ears, nose**) Discuss what would happen if a real body did not have those body parts. (**Possible answers: could not survive without a place to digest food, could not talk, could not smell anything, could not hear what others are saying**)

Directed Instruction ↩
Review the Bible truth about how the Jewish people viewed Jesus and the Messiah as belonging to them and not the Gentiles. The Jewish people acted like they were a body that did not want any other people group to be part of that body. Peter's vision showed that God wanted all people to be part of God's family. Explain that it was not easy for Jews to change the way they thought about Gentiles. Read **Mark 16:15**. Jesus gave His followers a big job; they were to tell everyone about Him. Peter did this when he went to Cornelius and told him about Jesus. The early Church discovered Jews and Gentiles needed to work together to complete the job they had been given by Jesus. Today, Christians need to work together to continue the same task.

Explain that a human body has the perfect number of body parts to work properly. When each part does its job, the body works fantastically. Choose a volunteer to demonstrate walking. Then let the volunteer explain how body parts worked together to help accomplish the job of moving. (**The brain told the leg muscles to move, and the arm muscles moved and helped balance the body.**) Explain that the Bible describes believers as a body that needs to work together to get a job done. Invite volunteers to read **1 Corinthians 12:12–27**.

Explain that all people who trust in Jesus as their Savior make up the Body of Christ. God does not want any believer to be envious of any other part of the Body. God made each one a certain way for a purpose. Believers should not compare themselves to anyone else. Read **Psalm 139:14**. Discuss some of the special talents or personality traits of the students that are helpful to the Body of Christ. Remind students that the Trinity shows three different Persons working together: God the Father, God the Son, and God the Holy Spirit.

Tell students that the Bible talks about one part of the body being beautiful. Read **Romans 10:13–15**. Ask them why God thinks feet are beautiful. (**They take people places to tell others about Jesus.**)

Finish by reciting this week's Memory Verse together. Remind students that the command to believe in Jesus and love others was difficult for some Jewish people. Jewish believers were to love Gentile believers and realize that God gave the same Holy Spirit to both groups.

Student Page 31.3

Help students find the Bible verses and circle ones that mention the Body of Christ. Invite students to share the part of the body where they see themselves fitting best.

Review

- What does it mean when the Bible compares Christians to a body? (**Christians make up the Body of Christ. Each Christian has a different part in the Body of Christ; all parts are necessary.**)
- How should each part of the Body of Christ treat the other parts? (**Possible answers: Each part should respect other parts; everyone has a job to do and should do it; no one should be envious.**)
- What are some of the different things each part of the Trinity does? (**Possible answers: God is the Creator and Father; Jesus came to the earth to die for everyone's sins and is God the Son; the Holy Spirit guides, comforts, and reminds believers of what Jesus said.**)

APPLICATION

- How do you feel knowing that God has a unique place and job for you? (**Answers will vary.**)
- What job do you think God has for you right now? (**Possible answers: learning about Jesus more, telling my friends and family about Jesus, showing that I accept others by playing with them at recess**)

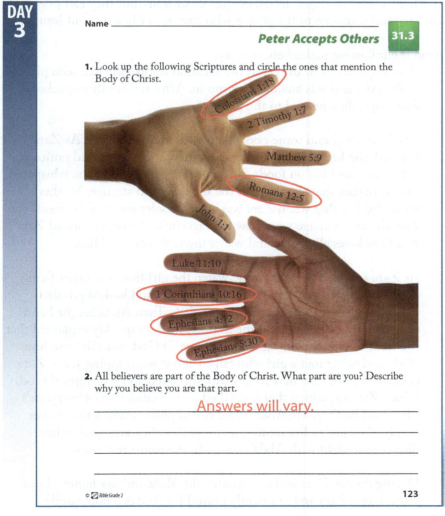

31.4 Peter Accepts Others

Focus: Go and Tell

★ PREPARATION

Select the song "Love with the Love of Jesus" from the Grade 2 URL. (*Introduction*)

EXTENSION

4A Make a copy of **BLM 31C People Group Profile** for each student. Let students use reference books or missions materials and websites to find information about a people group and write it on their paper. Invite students to share the results of their research with the class. Have the class pray that God would send Christians to these countries to tell those people about Jesus.

4B Pray for unreached people groups. Look online or in current missions-focused resources to learn facts about groups of people who probably have not heard and learned about Jesus. Use the facts as points to pray for that people group.

Introduction ★

Sing the song "Love with the Love of Jesus" from the Grade 2 URL. Remind students that not everyone knows about the love of Jesus. Let students share their experiences of telling others about Jesus.

Directed Instruction

Explain that Peter was one of the first Jewish believers to go to the Gentiles with the message of the gospel. Tell students that they should be like Peter, who was willing to go wherever God wanted him to go. Peter preached the good news of Jesus to whomever he met. Explain that God wants everyone to know about Jesus. There are many wonderful things to tell about Jesus, but the most important is His plan of salvation. Ask students to read and review the definition in the Glossary: God's plan to send His Son to die on the cross to pay for the sins of all people. Remind students that the angel appeared to Cornelius and said that Peter would explain God's plan of salvation. Both Peter and Cornelius obeyed God and many Gentiles became a part of God's family.

Let a student read **Luke 10:2**. Explain that right now they might not go to another country or region to tell people about Jesus, but they can pray for God to send someone to the people who have never heard about Jesus.

Read the following make-believe story:

Zara hopped out of the car at the vacation resort. She had seen pictures of the pool and was anxious to jump in. After the family unpacked their bags, they headed to the pool.

Zara's family found some pool chairs near another family. As Zara listened, she heard them talking in a different language and noticed they were snacking on foods she had never seen before. She whispered to her mother that she thought the foods looked strange. Mother reminded her that when Zara was a preschooler some of the foods she thought were strange were now her favorites. Mother reminded Zara that God loves all people and wants them to worship Him.

As Zara splashed her feet in the water, the girl from the other family sat down next to her. Zara introduced herself and looked puzzled when the girl said that her name was *Abda*. Then Abda laughed and explained that her name meant *worshipper*. Zara quickly explained that she went to church and was a worshipper of God and His Son, Jesus. Abda had never met a girl who talked about worshipping Jesus. Zara continued to tell her new friend why she loved and worshipped God. When Zara explained that Jesus died on the cross so that everyone's sins could be forgiven, Abda asked her to please explain that to her family. Zara ran to her mother and together they arranged to have dinner that night with Abda's family in the resort restaurant.

During dinner, Zara and her family told Abda and her family about Jesus. Later, Zara and her family prayed for Abda's whole family.

They prayed that other believers in Jesus would be friends with the family and tell them more about Jesus. As Zara climbed into bed, Mother rubbed Zara's feet and mentioned how beautiful they were because they took her to the place where she told Abda about Jesus. Zara giggled, "My feet did not need to go to another country to be beautiful—they became beautiful on our vacation!"

Student Page 31.4

Have students complete the page independently. Direct them to select a classmate and practice telling each other about Jesus.

Review

• Explain God's plan of salvation. (**It is God's plan to send His Son to die on the cross to pay for the sins of all people.**)
• What must happen before people can believe in Jesus? (**They must hear, which means someone must tell them about Jesus.**)
• Why were Zara's feet beautiful? (**They took her to a place where she told someone about Jesus.**)

APPLICATION

• How would you respond if God asked you to go and tell people who are different from you about Jesus? (**Possible answers: be excited and go, start learning about that people group, be scared and not go**)
• Choose a country where you would like to go and tell people about Jesus. Explain why. (**Answers will vary.**)
• What things would you tell someone about Jesus? (**Answers will vary but should include that Jesus died, rose again, and offers forgiveness for sins so that he or she does not have to be separated from God anymore.**)

REINFORCEMENT

Jesus' command to go into all the world is known as *the Great Commission*, found in Matthew 28:19–20, Mark 16:15, Luke 24:46–48, John 20:21–22, and Acts 1:8. Does this mean that believers need to become full-time missionaries and go to lands far away, or witness to people around them, wherever God has directed them to serve? Jesus said to share the gospel first with people nearby, and then reach outward in scope until the whole world has heard the good news. Students can fulfill Jesus' command as they go to their family, friends, and neighbors and share God's love and message of salvation. Developing this habit prepares them to fulfill the Great Commission throughout the rest of their life, bringing people from every tribe, tongue, people, and nation to give praise and worship to God (Revelation 5:9).

DAY 4

31.4 Peter Accepts Others

Imagine that you are telling someone about Jesus.

1. What country is the person from? _____Answers will vary._____

2. Where did you meet the person? _____Answers will vary._____

How will you tell that person about Jesus? Look up the Scriptures and circle the correct word or words that explain God's plan of salvation.

ABCs of Faith

3. A _____ that you sin. (Romans 3:23)

Anoint
(Admit)
Ask

4. B _____, repent, and receive eternal life. (Mark 1:15, Romans 6:23)

Baptize
Be ready
(Believe)

5. C _____ Jesus as Lord. (Romans 10:9)

(Choose)
Check
Chase

6. What else would you tell that person about Jesus?

_____Answers will vary._____

_____

_____

7. Find a classmate and practice telling each other about Jesus.

124   © Bible Grade 2

© Bible Grade 2

31.5 Peter Accepts Others

Focus: Review and Assessment

★ PREPARATION

Select **VA 31A Peter and Cornelius**. (*Lesson Review*)

Make one copy of **BLM 31D Lesson 31 Test** for each student. (*Directed Instruction*)

Lesson Review ★

Use **VA 31A Peter and Cornelius** to review the Bible truths from this lesson. Cover the following concepts:

- Cornelius was a Gentile who loved God, prayed every day, and gave money to the poor.
- An angel told Cornelius to send servants to get Peter who would explain God's plan of salvation—God's plan to send His Son to die on the cross to pay for the sins of all people.
- Peter had a vision of a sheet full of animals that were eaten by Gentiles, but not Jewish people.
- God told Peter to eat the animals. Peter answered that he would not eat them because they were unclean according to Jewish law.
- The voice said that God had made the animals clean. Peter saw this vision three times before the sheet disappeared.
- The vision meant God wanted Gentiles, as well as Jewish people, to hear about Jesus and the plan of salvation.
- Everyone can now be part of God's family no matter their background, culture, education, or possessions.
- *Favoritism* means *treating a person or a group better than others.*
- When people show favoritism, they are treating a person or a group better than others.
- God loves every people group and is not partial.
- God wants believers to accept others so they can explain to anyone God's love and plan of salvation.
- The Bible compares Christians to a body, which means everyone has a place and a purpose.
- One body part should not be envious of other body parts. Each should do its job and should show respect to other parts.
- In Romans 10:15, God says the feet of people who share the good news of Jesus with others are beautiful.
- God wants everyone to be saved from their sins by believing in Jesus as their Savior. Before people can believe in Jesus, they must first hear the gospel message.
- Although students might not be able to go to different people groups right now, they can pray that God will send people to share the gospel with those who have never heard it.

Directed Instruction ★

Distribute a copy of **BLM 31D Lesson 31 Test** to each student. Explain the instructions and format to students. Have students complete the test. When they are finished, read over the test and provide the answers for immediate feedback.

Notes:

Lesson Preparation
Paul and Barnabas Encourage
32.0

Expected Student Outcomes

KNOW
Paul and Barnabas encourage others in the faith.

DO
Students will:
- write about what happened to Paul and Barnabas, relating it to encouragement in their own life
- match acts of exhortation in the life of Paul and Barnabas
- identify key words and ways to encourage others
- apply how to encourage a missionary in various ways

APPLY
Students will identify acts of encouragement and discover ways in which they can encourage others.

Lesson Outline
I. Barnabas encourages Saul (Acts 4:32–36, 9:1–30)
II. A journey of exhortation (1 Thess 5:12–14, Acts 11:22–30)
III. Encouragement encounters (1 Thess 5:11, Heb 10:24–25)
IV. Encouragement to missionaries (2 Thess 1:11–12)

♥ TEACHER'S HEART

Who was one of the most famous encouragers of the Bible? A man named *Joseph*—or perhaps you know his nickname, *Barnabas*. Apparently Barnabas' father was also an encourager. What a wonderful gift from the Lord—to be able to surround people with love that reduces hurt and helplessness. An encourager is a kind person who speaks gentle words that can make others feel accepted, purposeful, and enabled to accomplish a task. God used Barnabas to introduce Paul to the fellowship of believers and set Paul on the path of ministry. Do you need encouragement today?

As the school year draws to an end, many additional tasks require your attention—evaluations, report cards, practices for special activities, and more! In the interest of getting things accomplished, it is easy to spend more time in isolation, cut off from the encouragement and support of other Christians. If your year-end duties are drawing you away from others and into yourself, resolve to find the time to be with other believers so you can receive and give encouragement (Hebrews 10:24–25). Take a moment and consider your colleagues, as well. If you haven't seen much of them in the workroom or hallways during the past few weeks, check in with them. A kind word encourages a heart that is discouraged during this hectic time. Ask the Lord to give you a heart of encouragement today, so you can be encouraged and be an effective encourager to your students and colleagues!

Supplemental Materials are available to download. See Understanding Purposeful Design Bible at the front of this book for the Grade 2 URL.

📖 MEMORY VERSE
1 Thessalonians 5:11

GLOSSARY WORDS
- apostle
- missionary

★ MATERIALS

Day 1:
- VA 32A Paul and Barnabas Encourage Others
- Butcher paper (*Extension*)

Day 2:
- DM-16 Map of Antioch to Jerusalem
- Love Bowl from Lesson 11.4 (*Extension*)

Day 3:
- Note cards
- BLM 32A Signs of Encouragement (*Extension*)

Day 4:
- World map
- BLM 32B Prayer Hanger, card stock (*Extension*)
- Special foods, pictures (*Extension*)

Day 5:
- VA 32A Paul and Barnabas Encourage Others
- BLM 32C Lesson 32 Test

♪ SONGS
What Seems Impossible (*Extension*)

TEACHER RESOURCES
Roehlkepartain, Jolene L. *Teaching Kids to Care and Share: 300+ Mission and Service Ideas for Children*. Abingdon Press, 2000.

STUDENT RESOURCES
Andrews, Andy. *The Boy Who Changed the World*. Tommy Nelson, 2014.

32.1 Paul and Barnabas Encourage
Focus: Barnabas Encourages Saul

MEMORY VERSE
1 Thessalonians 5:11

MEMORY WORK
- Write the Memory Verse on the board, and read it aloud. Rewrite it again and make a number of deliberate mistakes. See if students can spot all the mistakes and correct them.

PREPARATION
Select **VA 32A Paul and Barnabas Encourage Others**. *(Directed Instruction)*

EXTENSION
1A Hang a LARGE SHEET OF BUTCHER PAPER on the wall. Write *Encouragers!* at the top of the paper. As you see or hear your students encourage others by their actions or words this week, write brief descriptions on the chart. Ask students to add to the list, noting the encouraging words or actions of others, until everyone in the class is encouraged!

Introduction
Read the following fictional story to the class:

> Devin came to school wearing the same clothes for a few days, and a lot of his classmates noticed. One day, Lila said mean things to Devin. The next day, the class found out that Devin's parents had been in a car accident, and they were hurt very badly. Lila felt terrible for saying mean things to Devin. She told Devin she was sorry and quietly asked him to forgive her. When Lila went home that afternoon, she asked her parents if they could help Devin's family.
>
> The next day, Lila still felt bad. Mr. Sakawa, her teacher, noticed that she was sad and asked her what was wrong. After hearing what she had to say, Mr. Sakawa reminded Lila that God had forgiven her. He encouraged Lila, commending her for recognizing that what she did was wrong, for apologizing to Devin, and for trying to help his family.

In today's Bible truth, students will learn about people who encouraged others. *Encourage* means *to support, strengthen, and show confidence in someone.*

Directed Instruction ★ ↵
Read **VA 32A Paul and Barnabas Encourage Others**. Point out that Joseph's name was also *Barnabas*, which means *Son of Encouragement* (Acts 4:36). Barnabas encouraged others to accept Jesus and his friend Saul. Saul, also known as *Paul*, witnessed to others and encouraged them to accept Jesus too. Barnabas and Paul served the Lord wholeheartedly.

Read and discuss the following Scriptures:
- **Acts 9:1–2:** Remind students that disciples are followers of Jesus Christ. Ask students why they think Saul was trying to harm the disciples of his day. (**Possible answers: He did not understand what Jesus had done; He thought the disciples were wrong to follow Jesus.**)

- **Acts 9:3–6:** Why did Saul not know that Jesus was speaking to him? (**He didn't know Jesus' voice because he didn't belong to Jesus.**)

- **Acts 9:26:** Why was it difficult for Jesus' disciples to trust that Paul had become a believer? (**because Saul had persecuted believers and had been an enemy of Christ**)

- **Acts 9:27:** Explain that an **apostle** is defined as *one of the twelve men chosen by Jesus to tell others about Him.* What did Barnabas tell the apostles to help them trust and accept Paul? (**He explained that Jesus had spoken to Paul and changed him, so Paul began preaching boldly for Christ.**) Note that Barnabas gently but clearly explained to the apostles how God had changed Paul's heart. By standing up for Paul, Barnabas encouraged him in his new life. He also encouraged the apostles to believe that God had truly changed Paul's heart. Paul eventually became known as the *apostle Paul* and began to powerfully preach the good news about Jesus and His love (Acts 9:19–22).

- **Acts 9:28–30:** What happened to Paul after he became a follower of Christ? (**He stayed with the disciples and preached boldly about Jesus in Jerusalem.**) Explain that since the disciples had a relationship with Barnabas, they trusted him and were willing to believe that Paul had changed. Barnabas, Paul, and other disciples spent time with one another and shared the good news about Jesus with many people.

Student Page 32.1
Have students work in pairs or trios to complete the page.

Review
- Who encouraged Saul? (**Barnabas**)
- What does it mean to encourage someone? (**to support, strengthen, and show confidence in someone**)
- What happened to Paul because Barnabas trusted him? (**Paul was encouraged, and the other disciples saw the change in Paul's life and began trusting him too.**)

APPLICATION
- Would you have trusted Paul after he became a follower of Jesus? Why or why not? (**Answers will vary.**)
- What would you have said to Paul to encourage him? (**Answers will vary.**)
- Think of simple ways to encourage others around you, showing them kindness by your words and actions. Pray and ask God to help you follow through with these acts of kindness.

REINFORCEMENT
In Acts 13:9, the New Testament records that Saul was also called *Paul* following his conversion. In Bible times, people were often referred to by more than one name. Names in Jewish culture typically had special meanings or significance. *Saul* was a Jewish name, taken from King Saul, and *Paul* was a Roman name that Gentiles used. The apostle Paul was not only a Jew; he was also a Roman citizen (Philippians 3:4–6, Acts 22:25–28). Before his conversion, Saul identified himself primarily as a pious Jew and a member of the elite sect of Pharisees. But following his dramatic conversion on the road to Damascus, he began using the name *Paul*, which signified his new faith in Christ and his apostolic ministry to the Gentiles (1 Timothy 2:7).

DAY 1

Name _____

Paul and Barnabas Encourage 32.1

1. Look up **apostle** in the Glossary. Write the definition.

   apostle: *one of the twelve men chosen by Jesus to tell others about Him*

2. Paul and Barnabas encouraged others. Locate each Bible verse and complete each sentence.

Acts 4:36
Saul heard from Jesus and believed in Him!
Barnabas encouraged Saul. He took Saul to the apostles and explained what God had done.

Acts 13:9
Saul was also known as Paul. He was filled with the Holy Spirit. He became an apostle and shared the good news of Jesus.

3. How can you encourage others in the same way Barnabas encouraged Paul?
   Answers will vary.

© *Bible Grade 2*   125

32.2 Paul and Barnabas Encourage
Focus: A Journey of Exhortation

★ PREPARATION
Select **DM-16 Map of Antioch to Jerusalem**. (*Directed Instruction*)

↪ EXTENSION

2A Sing the song "What Seems Impossible" from the Grade 2 URL.

2B To review the characteristics of godly love, invite students to select and read a card from the LOVE BOWL introduced in Lesson 11.4.

2C Instruct students to write a journal entry about how they would feel if they had been Barnabas or Paul. Would they have encouraged Paul as Barnabas did? Would they have responded the same way Saul did when Jesus spoke to him? Encourage students to write a prayer to God, asking Him to help them encourage others.

Introduction
Write the following encouraging statements on the board:
- Super!
- Great job!
- Excellent!
- You shine!
- Star performance!
- Neat work!
- Ecstatic!
- You can do it!

Have students think of other encouraging statements to add to the list. Ask them if hearing these phrases would help them repeat their choice or behavior. (**Answers will vary but should include it does help to hear words of encouragement when I face hard choices.**) Explain that students can encourage others not only by saying kind words but also by reminding people to behave in a way that pleases the Lord. Read **1 Thessalonians 5:12–14**. Today's lesson will discuss ways Barnabas encouraged Paul after he became a follower of Jesus.

Directed Instruction ★ ↪
Barnabas not only encouraged Paul with his words, but he taught others to behave in ways that would draw them closer to God. Explain that this kind of teaching is called *exhortation—words or actions that encourage others and urge them to do the right thing*. Write the word *exhortation* and its definition on the board. Read the word and definition a few times in unison.

Display **DM-16 Map of Antioch to Jerusalem**. Divide students into four groups. Instruct each group to answer the following questions by reading Scriptures about places Barnabas and Paul traveled to exhort and encourage others in their faith. Have each group share answers as they find and point to each location on the map.

- Group 1: Read **Acts 11:22–24**. What did Barnabas do while he was in Antioch? (**He spent time in fellowship with believers and encouraged them to continue following Jesus. He shared about Jesus' love with people who didn't know the Lord. Many came to faith in Jesus through Barnabas' encouragement.**) Note that the Church of Jerusalem sent Barnabas to Antioch because a great number of people were turning to Jesus and believing in Him there.

- Group 2: Read **Acts 11:25**. Why did Barnabas go to Tarsus? (**Barnabas went to Tarsus to look for Paul.**)

- Group 3: Read **Acts 11:26**. Why did Barnabas bring Paul to Antioch? (**He wanted Paul to help him teach and exhort the believers there.**) How long did they stay in Antioch? (**one year**) Share that the followers of Christ were first called *Christians* in Antioch.

- Group 4: Read **Acts 11:27–30**. Why did Barnabas and Paul go to Jerusalem in Judea? (**They were bringing aid from believers in Antioch to the believers in Jerusalem, who were suffering from a terrible famine.**) Review that a famine is a time when there is little to no rain, most crops do not grow, and people have a hard time finding or buying food. The disciples exhorted and encouraged believers in Jerusalem during the famine by giving food and other gifts to provide for their needs.

Student Page 32.2
Assist students as needed to complete the page.

Review
- What is exhortation? (**words or actions that encourage others and urge them to do the right thing**)
- Briefly describe where Barnabas and Paul traveled to encourage others. (**Barnabas was sent to encourage believers in Antioch, and he brought Paul from Tarsus to help him teach for a year. When a famine occurred in the region of Judea, believers in Antioch sent Barnabas and Paul to take aid to the believers in Jerusalem and provide for their needs.**)
- Name one way Barnabas and Saul exhorted or encouraged other believers. (**Possible answers: They taught believers; they traveled and brought food and gifts to believers.**)

DAY 2

32.2 *Paul and Barnabas Encourage*

Your words can encourage others to draw closer to God. You can also remind others to act in ways that please God.

1. List some ways you can encourage others to do the right thing.

Answers will vary.

2. Match Paul and Barnabas with their encouraging words and actions by writing the correct letter in the box.

Paul and Barnabas

a. Paul was a new believer and needed to grow. The believers in Jerusalem were afraid of him.

b. Paul was sent to Tarsus after teaching in Jerusalem. Barnabas went to Tarsus to find Paul.

c. The believers in Jerusalem were hungry because of a famine.

Encouraging Words and Actions

c Paul and Barnabas took food and gifts to them.

a Barnabas took Paul to the apostles. He spoke about how Paul became a believer after Jesus spoke to him from heaven.

b Barnabas took Paul to Antioch. Together they encouraged believers by teaching them.

126

© *Bible Grade 2*

APPLICATION
- How do you feel when others exhort you? (**Answers will vary.**)
- How can words of exhortation help you behave in ways that please God? (**The words encourage me to do what is right.**)
- How can you use exhortation to encourage someone else? (**Answers will vary.**)

REINFORCEMENT
The apostle Paul was born a Roman citizen but given the Jewish name *Saul*. He was raised in a well-respected Jewish family and was immersed in the Jewish faith and culture. He studied under Gamaliel, a Pharisee and a renowned expert in the Law (Acts 22:3), and became a zealous young Pharisee. He developed a hatred for Christians, even giving his approval when Stephen was stoned to death (Acts 7:57–8:1). Saul believed that Jesus and His disciples were heretics and was determined to annihilate all followers of Christ (Acts 8:1–3), until Jesus appeared to him on his way to Damascus and radically transformed his life. Now using the name Paul, he went from persecuting believers to preaching boldly about Christ, passionately seeking to convince people that Jesus had died for them and risen from the dead (Acts 13:9). Paul suffered greatly for the sake of the gospel. He was shipwrecked, stoned, beaten, treated as an outcast, imprisoned, starved, whipped, and threatened (2 Corinthians 11:23–28). Yet he continued to boldly declare the gospel, encouraging believers in his letters to follow Jesus wholeheartedly.

32.3 Paul and Barnabas Encourage
Focus: Encouragement Encounters

★ PREPARATION
Have available NOTE CARDS for each student. (*Directed Instruction*)

↪ EXTENSION
3A Make a copy of **BLM 32A Signs of Encouragement** for each student. Teach students some sign language to encourage others.

3B Review the order of the books of the Bible. Line up students into two evenly matched teams. Let one team member say the first book of the Bible, and then go to the back of the line. The next student in line says the next book, and then goes to the end of the line, and so on. If a student misses a book, the preceding player must return to the front of the line and begin with that book while other students prompt him or her. Play until all books have been named successfully. The two teams can compete against each other to see how fast they can name the books, or each team can try to beat its own time by using a time clock.

Introduction
Read the following true-life story:
> Ricardo went on a mission trip with his family to a far-away country. The people in this country didn't have many material things, and yet they seemed very happy. Ricardo became friends with another boy named Manuel, who lived with his family. The boys enjoyed talking together. One day Ricardo found some coins on the ground and decided to give them to Manuel. Ricardo thought that the little bit of money might encourage Manuel, because he seemed very poor. Manuel was very thankful and smiled brightly. He told Ricardo, "I know just what I am going to do with this money!" Later as they were walking down the street, Manuel took Ricardo into a small store and bought him a snack and drink with the money. Manuel told Ricardo that he was so encouraged by Ricardo's kindness, he wanted to show kindness in return. Ricardo's act of encouragement inspired Manuel's act of encouragement. They realized that they had encouraged each other by their actions! Both of the boys smiled. They walked along as they shared a special snack together.

Ask students who was encouraged. (**Both boys were encouraged because they thought about the other person.**)

Directed Instruction ★ ↪
Remind students that the early believers shared what they had with each other and encouraged one another by helping provide for each person's needs. Read **1 Thessalonians 5:11** and **Hebrews 10:24–25** aloud together. Explain to students that these verses are reminders from God's Word that believers are to encourage one another often. The early Church grew because believers helped and encouraged one another. Tell students that there are many ways to encourage others, depending on the situation.

Discuss various ways to encourage others by asking students to complete the following statements:
- Mom is tired. You can encourage Mom by …
- Dad has a big project to complete. You can encourage Dad by …
- Your sister lost a book. You can encourage your sister by …
- A neighbor is sick. You can encourage your neighbor by …
- Your friend is moving and is sad. You can encourage your friend by …
- A grandma is by herself and feeling lonely. You can encourage the grandma by …
- A family across the street is out of food because the parents lost their jobs. You can encourage the family by …
- A new classmate at school is struggling with math. You can encourage the new classmate by …

Share with students that one way to encourage others is by writing notes. Give each student a NOTE CARD. Tell students to think of someone they would like to encourage, and write that person's name on the front of the card. Allow time for students to write a brief, encouraging message on the back of the card. Challenge them to ask a trusted adult to help them deliver their note. Urge them to also pray for the person they wanted to encourage.

Student Page 32.3
Direct students to complete the page.

Review
• What does God's Word say about encouraging others? (**I should encourage others often.**)
• What happened when believers in the early Church encouraged others? (**The early Church grew when believers encouraged others.**)
• Name one way you can encourage others. (**Possible answers: pray for someone, write a note, say kind words, spend time with someone, help someone complete a task**)

Notes:

APPLICATION
• How do you like to be encouraged? (**Answers will vary.**)
• What happens when you encourage others? (**They feel blessed and want to encourage others in return.**)
• What is your favorite way to give encouragement? (**Answers will vary.**)
• Pray and ask God to help you encourage someone today in a specific way.

DAY 3

Name _____

Paul and Barnabas Encourage 32.3

Read the sentence and color the letters that spell the answer.

1. God wants you to be an _____.

en p cour t ager z

2. Circle the words that give encouragement.

(wonderful)   go away   (congratulations)

(neat)   (fantastic)   hurry up

3. Draw a picture of yourself encouraging others.

Drawings will vary.

4. Use some of the circled words above to write a sentence about your picture.

Answers will vary.

© Bible Grade 2   127

© Bible Grade 2

32.4 Paul and Barnabas Encourage

Focus: Encouragement to Missionaries

★ PREPARATION
Have available a LARGE WORLD MAP. (*Introduction*)

EXTENSION

4A Make a copy of **BLM 32B Prayer Hanger** on WHITE CARD STOCK for each student. Direct students to write the names of missionaries they can pray for. Instruct students to color and cut out the hanger. Encourage students to display the prayer hanger at home as a reminder to pray for missionaries around the world.

4B Raise money to support a selected missionary by organizing a bake sale or another type of fund-raiser. In addition to the financial support, gather SPECIAL FOODS and PICTURES, and write encouraging notes to send in a package to the missionary.

Introduction ★
Display the LARGE WORLD MAP. Indicate various locations on the map. Ask students if they know of anyone in these various locations who is a **missionary**, which means *someone devoted to spreading the good news of Jesus Christ*. Explain that believers and missionaries who live in other places around the world need encouragement just as missionaries at home do.

Directed Instruction
Teach students that Paul and Barnabas, as followers of Christ, were missionaries. They traveled to many places to tell others about Jesus Christ and His plan of salvation. Ask students to recall and share the name of another missionary who shared the message of the gospel to the Gentiles. (**Peter**) At times, these missionaries were in dangerous situations and needed prayer for protection. Remind students that the Church had prayed for Peter, and God had rescued Peter from prison.

Read **2 Thessalonians 1:11–12**. As believers prayed for Paul, Barnabas, the apostles, and the disciples, the Holy Spirit encouraged the believers. In turn, they were strengthened, and the Church grew in numbers (Acts 9:31, Philippians 1:3–6). Explain to students that just as believers in the early Church prayed for missionaries, students can also encourage and pray for missionaries they know today. Whether missionaries serve in areas nearby or far away in other countries, praying for them encourages them and unleashes God's power.

Read the following true-life story:
> Derrick and a team of missionaries were traveling through Africa. As they went through the country of Ethiopia, they needed to pass through a dangerous area to reach an orphanage that desperately needed the supplies they had brought. All of a sudden, the missionaries' van became stuck in a large pothole, and a mob of angry men appeared. The men began to yell at the missionaries and rock the van back and forth. Even though the missionaries were frightened, they immediately began to pray. Just when they thought their situation could not get any worse, their van broke free from the muddy hole and started moving forward! The missionaries were able to escape the angry crowd and safely drive away. Later on, Derrick and his team were greatly encouraged when they heard believers at home say that the Holy Spirit had prompted them to pray for the missionaries at the exact moment they were in danger! Their prayers not only encouraged the missionaries but helped them escape a dangerous situation. The missionaries felt loved and cared for because other believers had been praying for them.

Read and discuss the following ways to encourage missionaries:
- Pray for them. Ask about their concerns, and let them know you are praying for them often.
- Write to them regularly, and encourage them with Scripture. Send them birthday cards and holiday greetings.

- Send pictures or packages of meaningful specialty items.
- Support them financially, if possible, to meet physical needs.

Student Page 32.4
Divide students into small groups to pray for different local missionaries and those around the world. Direct students to work in these groups to complete the page.

Review
- What is a missionary? (**someone devoted to spreading the good news of Jesus Christ**)
- What did believers in the early Church do to encourage missionaries? (**They prayed for and supported the missionaries.**)
- What happened when believers in the early Church prayed faithfully? (**The believers were strengthened, and the Church grew in numbers.**)
- Why is it important to pray for missionaries? (**Possible answers: to encourage them, to ask God to keep them safe, to strengthen them, to help unleash God's power**)

APPLICATION
- One way to serve the Lord is to be faithful in prayer. Pray and ask God to help you be committed to pray faithfully for a specific missionary. Ask God to give you different ideas of ways you can encourage the missionary.

REINFORCEMENT
When Jesus sent out His disciples to preach the good news in the regions beyond Jerusalem, He told them not to go to the Gentiles but to preach first to the "lost sheep" of Israel (Matthew 10:5–6). Believers in the early Church continued to preach primarily to the Jewish people after Jesus' death and resurrection. But then God called Paul to preach the gospel to the Gentiles so that they, too, might come to faith in Christ (Acts 9:15, Romans 15:15–16). God brought Barnabas and Paul together as missionaries to preach the gospel to both Jews and Gentiles throughout Asia Minor (Acts 11:22–30; 13–14). When Paul and Barnabas separated, Paul continued his ministry to the Gentiles, as well as to his own people, before his imprisonment in Rome (Acts 16–28). As the Jews and Gentiles heard and responded to the gospel, they experienced persecution and were scattered throughout the world as missionaries for Christ. Because of this, people from all over the world heard the gospel, and many became followers of Jesus.

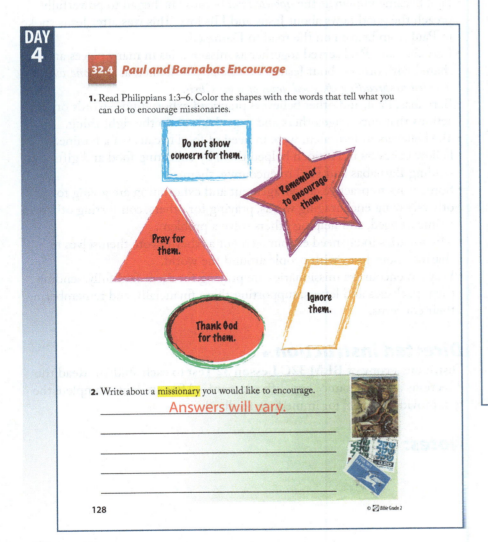

32.5 Paul and Barnabas Encourage

Focus: Review and Assessment

★ PREPARATION

Select **VA 32A Paul and Barnabas Encourage Others**. (*Lesson Review*)

Make a copy of **BLM 32C Lesson 32 Test** for each student. (*Directed Instruction*)

Lesson Review ★

Use **VA 32A Paul and Barnabas Encourage Others** to review the Bible truths. Cover the following concepts:

- Believers in Jerusalem shared what they had with one another in love, and the Church began to grow.
- Joseph, who was also called *Barnabas*, sold his land and gave the money to the Church. Barnabas was helpful, cheerful, and encouraging.
- To encourage is to support, strengthen, and show confidence in someone.
- A man named *Saul* tried to arrest and kill believers.
- As Saul was traveling to a town named *Damascus* to harm believers, Jesus spoke to him from heaven. God changed Saul's heart that day, and Saul became a follower of Jesus.
- Saul, also known as *Paul*, had been known to threaten and harm believers in the past, so followers of Jesus were afraid of him at first.
- Barnabas explained to the apostles what had happened to Paul and encouraged them to trust him.
- An *apostle* is defined as *one of the twelve men chosen by Jesus to tell others about Him*.
- Paul became known as the *apostle Paul* because he began to powerfully preach the good news about Jesus and His love. This was after Jesus spoke to Paul from heaven on the road to Damascus.
- Barnabas and Paul served together as missionaries in many places and shared with others about Jesus. A *missionary* is defined as *someone who is devoted to spreading the good news of Jesus Christ*.
- Barnabas, Paul, and other believers practiced exhortation—words or actions that encourage others and urge them to do the right thing.
- The believers in Jerusalem were in need of food because of a famine. Fellow believers in Antioch helped them by collecting food and gifts and sending Barnabas and Paul to encourage them.
- Some ways to practice encouragement and exhortation are giving to others, saying encouraging words, praying for others, comforting others in a time of need, and helping others solve a problem.
- Missionaries today need encouragement as they devote themselves to sharing about Jesus with people around the world.
- Ways to encourage missionaries are praying for them faithfully, sending them packages and letters, supporting them financially, and remembering their concerns.

Directed Instruction ★

Distribute a copy of **BLM 32C Lesson 32 Test** to each student. Read the directions and pronounce any difficult words. After students complete the test, provide answers for immediate feedback.

Notes:

Lesson Preparation
Paul and Silas Witness

33.0

Expected Student Outcomes

KNOW
Paul and Silas share their faith in prison.

DO
Students will:
- define *witness* and identify examples of witnessing
- write John 16:33 and 1 Thessalonians 5:17 in their own words
- draw pictures or write words to represent various situations of prayer
- review the three ways that Paul and Silas worshipped God
- write a prayer of praise in the form of a song

APPLY
Students will realize that they can pray to God, praise God, and share the good news of Jesus with others, regardless of their circumstances.

Lesson Outline

I. Paul and Silas share their faith (Acts 16:16–34)
II. Reactions to persecution (Acts 16:16–34, Jn 16:33)
III. Prayer as a lifestyle (Eph 6:17–18, 1 Thess 5:17)
IV. Ways to praise God (Mt 28:18–20)

♥ TEACHER'S HEART

Jeannine is a missionary in Medellín, Colombia, a city known for drug cartels and violence. Jeannine first started working in Colombia teaching Hebrew in a seminary. She soon felt God calling her to go into a prison and preach the gospel. As a single woman, she was terrified to go into the overcrowded, all-male prison that housed some of the most hardened criminals. However, she put aside her fear, followed God's calling, and went to Bellavista prison. When she began teaching the gospel, an average of two murders were committed at the prison each day. Through Jeannine's continuing faithful witness, lives are being transformed; in fact, the whole prison is being transformed. The number of inmates murdered has fallen to one per year, and thousands have accepted Jesus as their Lord and Savior.

Sometimes, when you work in a Christian environment, you might forget that there are many hurting people seeking the solutions God offers. How sensitive have you been recently to share the gospel outside the walls of your school and church? In Matthew 28:19, Jesus commanded His followers to share the gospel throughout the world. Paul fulfilled this commission time after time throughout his ministry. Pray, as Paul prayed in Ephesians 6:18–20, that you might be bold in sharing the gospel. Encourage your students daily to look for places to shine the light of the gospel in a dark world.

📖 MEMORY VERSE
Acts 16:31

GLOSSARY WORDS
- witness

★ MATERIALS

Day 1:
- Cardboard or wooden dowels
- VA 33A Paul and Silas Witness
- BLMs 33A–B Paul and Silas, Parts 1–2

Day 2:
- Shoe boxes, index cards (*Extension*)

Day 3:
- Paper lunch bags (*Extension*)

Day 4:
- Coin
- Magazines (*Extension*)
- DM-3 Books of the Bible (*Extension*)

Day 5:
- VA 33A Paul and Silas Witness
- BLM 33C Lesson 33 Test

♪ SONGS
For I Am Not Ashamed
You Are My God
Books of the Bible (*Extension*)

TEACHER RESOURCES
Duncan, Ken. *In the Footsteps of Paul*. Thomas Nelson, 2009.
Strobel, Lee. *The Case for the Real Jesus*. Zondervan, 2014.

STUDENT RESOURCES
DeMasi, Kacee. *Sharing God Kid Style*. DVD. Got GOD Films, 2008.
Mackenzie, Carine. *Paul: Journeys of Adventure*. CF4Kids, 2014.

Supplemental Materials are available to download. See Understanding Purposeful Design Bible at the front of this book for the Grade 2 URL.

33.1 Paul and Silas Witness
Focus: Paul and Silas Share Their Faith

MEMORY VERSE
Acts 16:31

MEMORY WORK
- Give each student a piece of paper. Instruct students to fold their paper in half vertically and cut along the fold. Help them tape the two pieces end to end. Direct students to write the Memory Verse along the length of the paper. Tape one end of the paper to a CARDBOARD or WOODEN DOWEL, and roll it around the dowel. Students can practice saying the verse one word or one phrase at a time as they unroll the scroll. Allow adequate time for students to learn the verse.

★ PREPARATION

Have available a CARDBOARD or WOODEN DOWEL for each student. (*Memory Work*)

Select the song "For I Am Not Ashamed" from the Grade 2 URL. (*Introduction*)

Select **VA 33A Paul and Silas Witness**, and make copies of **BLMs 33A–B Paul and Silas, Parts 1–2** for each student. (*Directed Instruction*)

↪ EXTENSION

1A Work with students to create interview questions for today's Bible truth from Acts 16:16–34. Separate students into pairs, and have them interview each other using the prepared questions.

Introduction ★
Sing the song "For I Am Not Ashamed" with students. Explain to students that it is through the good news about Jesus that they are saved. The gospel is such good news that they should never be ashamed to share it with everyone they meet. Today's lesson is about two men who were mistreated and imprisoned because they were not ashamed to share with others about Jesus.

Directed Instruction ★ ↪
This week, you will share God's plan of salvation with students. You may have opportunities to lead some students to Christ. Be sensitive to those who may need more one-on-one time to talk and ask questions. Pray and ask God to give you the right words to say and to make His timing clear for each student in these final days of the school year.

Write the word **witness** on the board. Invite students to locate the word in the Glossary and follow along as you write the definition on the board: To *witness* means *to share about the good news of Jesus with others*. Witnessing is part of God's plan for every Christian. Remind students of this often, and tell them that they are never too young for God to use them to witness for Him. Explain that there are a variety of ways to tell others the good news. Teach that *a person who shares about the good news of Jesus with others* is also called a *witness* for Him.

Read **VA 33A Paul and Silas Witness**. Distribute copies of **BLMs 33A–B Paul and Silas, Parts 1–2** to each student and have students complete them with a partner. Afterward, review the answers as a class.

Teach that Paul and Silas were able to rejoice in that dark prison because their joy came from the Lord. They knew that God would help them, so they continued witnessing to others about Jesus while they were in prison. As they prayed and sang hymns, other prisoners heard the good news about Jesus. Encourage students to pray and ask God to give them words of wisdom when they witness to others about Jesus.

Ask students why they think Paul and Silas stayed in prison after they were freed from their chains. (**Possible answers: They knew God was in charge of their situation; they knew God had them in prison to witness for Him.**) Discuss why the prison keeper asked Paul and Silas how to be saved instead of locking them up again. (**Possible answers: He knew why Paul and Silas had been put in prison, and he believed their message about salvation was true because they didn't run away; the prison keeper saw that they were honest men who practiced what they believed.**) Ask students what they can learn about witnessing from Paul and Silas' example. (**Possible answers: that God wants me to use words and actions when I witness, that God wants me to always be ready to share the good news about Jesus, that I can witness even in hard situations**)

Student Page 33.1
Have students complete the page independently.

Review
- When you witness to someone, what are you doing? (**sharing about the good news of Jesus with others**)
- To whom were Paul and Silas witnessing when they were in prison? (**the other prisoners and the prison keeper**)
- How did Paul and Silas witness to others? (**by praying and singing hymns to God**)
- How can you witness to others? (**through my words and actions**)
- What should you do before you witness to someone? (**pray and ask God for wisdom**)

Notes:

APPLICATION
- Ask God to help you find joy in Him and to give you wisdom as you witness to others.
- How would you have felt after the earthquake shook your chains loose and flung open the prison doors? (**Answers will vary.**)
- The all-powerful God who was involved and active in the lives of Paul and Silas is the same God who loves you and is involved in your life. Take a moment to pray and thank God for being involved and active in your life.

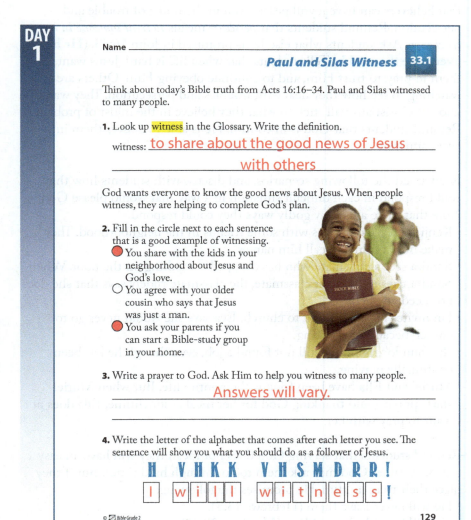

DAY 1

Name _____

Paul and Silas Witness 33.1

Think about today's Bible truth from Acts 16:16–34. Paul and Silas witnessed to many people.

1. Look up **witness** in the Glossary. Write the definition.

   witness: *to share about the good news of Jesus with others*

God wants everyone to know the good news about Jesus. When people witness, they are helping to complete God's plan.

2. Fill in the circle next to each sentence that is a good example of witnessing.
   - ● You share with the kids in your neighborhood about Jesus and God's love.
   - ○ You agree with your older cousin who says that Jesus was just a man.
   - ● You ask your parents if you can start a Bible-study group in your home.

3. Write a prayer to God. Ask Him to help you witness to many people.
   Answers will vary.

4. Write the letter of the alphabet that comes after each letter you see. The sentence will show you what you should do as a follower of Jesus.

   H VHKK VHSMDRR!
   I will witness!

33.2 Paul and Silas Witness
Focus: Reactions to Persecution

EXTENSION

2A Provide each student with a SHOE BOX. Direct students to use crayons, markers, and colored paper to design a diorama depicting a scene from this week's Bible truth. Distribute an INDEX CARD to each student. Instruct students to write a brief summary of the scene.

Introduction

Brainstorm with students some difficult situations they could face as second graders. (**Possible answers: family illnesses, monetary hardships, family problems, difficulties in school**) Then ask what is the most natural way to respond to these bad situations. (**to be sad or angry, or to question why**) Today's lesson is about responding to difficult situations.

Directed Instruction

Review with students why Paul and Silas were thrown in prison. (**Paul commanded an evil spirit to come out of a slave girl. The slave girl's owners were angry that they could no longer make money with her.**) Ask students if Paul did something good or bad. (**something good**) Note that even though Paul did something good, he and Silas were put in prison.

Explain to students that there may be times in life when they do what is right, but bad things still happen. Invite a student to read **John 16:33**. Point out that as long as people live on the earth, they may experience trouble, sickness, poverty, or other kinds of suffering. But Jesus promised that believers can have joyful peace, even in the midst of trouble and persecution. Remind students that *persecute* means *to treat someone in a cruel way*. Ask students what else Jesus promised in John 16:33. (**He has overcome the world.**) Tell students that when life is hard, Jesus wants them to pray, to trust Him, and to continue obeying Him. Others are watching to see how they deal with troubles and persecution. They want to know if Christians will stick to what they believe in the midst of problems. Remind students that God is in control. He is able to deliver them in every situation.

Read aloud the following scenarios, and discuss with students how they could respond in each difficult situation in a way that would please God. Note that there are many godly ways they could respond.
- Kenji shares about Jesus with some friends in the neighborhood. They make fun of him and call him names.
- Sondra sees a classmate who has dropped something on the floor. When Sondra tries to help her classmate, the classmate rudely says that she does not need any help.
- Ian invites his cousin Eva to church. Eva says she would never go to church because it is boring.
- Raymundo's mom has still not found a job, even though he has been continually praying.
- Muriel and Ella have been friends their entire life. But when Muriel starts praying and thanking God for her meal at lunchtime, Ella does not want to pray with her.

Remind students that serving God does not mean they will have an easy life. Sometimes God may ask them to go through hard times. But if they place their trust in Him, He promises the following:
- He will never leave them (Hebrews 13:5).
- He will be with them always (Matthew 28:20).

- He has overcome the world (John 16:33).
- He will work everything out for their good (Romans 8:28–29).

Student Page 33.2
Assist students as necessary while they complete the page.

Review

- Why were Paul and Silas thrown in prison? (**Paul commanded an evil spirit to come out of a slave girl, and her owners were angry with them.**)
- Even though Paul and Silas did not do anything bad, they still ended up in prison. How did they respond while they were in prison? (**They prayed, worshipped God, and witnessed to the prisoners and prison keeper about Jesus.**)
- What two promises does Jesus give you in John 16:33? (**In this world I will have trouble, but He has overcome the world.**)
- What does God want you to do when times are hard? (**Possible answers: I can pray; I can trust and praise Him; I can trust that He will be with me and can deliver me.**)

APPLICATION

- Who benefited when Paul and Silas prayed and praised God in the prison? (**Paul, Silas, other prisoners, prison keeper**)
- Pray and ask God for the strength and courage to trust, praise, and worship Him the next time you face trouble. Acknowledge that He is all-powerful and is able to deliver you.

REINFORCEMENT

If anyone knew about hard circumstances, it was Paul. He had been in prison, flogged severely, and exposed to death. He received 39 lashes five times. He was beaten with rods and stones. He had been shipwrecked and left adrift in the open sea for a night and a day. Paul faced danger from rivers, robbers, fellow Jews, Gentiles, and false believers. Wherever he was, whether in the city, in the country, or at sea, he faced countless hardships and dangers. He labored through many sleepless nights and experienced hunger, thirst, cold and nakedness (2 Corinthians 11:23–28). Of course, Paul's experiences were a little extreme. Most Christians do not go through this kind of hardship. But the point is that Paul did not give up or get angry. He rejoiced in the things that showed his weakness, because his weakness revealed God's power (2 Corinthians 12:9–10). Paul knew that God could use all of these experiences to spread the gospel and bring glory to Himself through Paul (1 Corinthians 9:19–23).

DAY 2

33.2 Paul and Silas Witness

Jesus wants you to find peace in Him.

1. Read John 16:33. Write what this verse means to you.

Answers will vary but should include that Jesus said there would be problems in the world. Jesus said believers should have joyful peace in these times of trouble knowing that He has overcome the world.

To persecute means to treat someone in a cruel way. Read the following story about persecution.

Kai sat down for lunch at his new school. He bowed his head to thank God for his food. Some students began to make fun of him. One student came by and pushed Kai's bowl of soup. Kai said nothing and began to clean up the mess. The students said mean words and made fun of Kai for praying. Kai finished cleaning up the spilled soup. He silently prayed for the students as he left the lunch room and thanked God for helping him remain calm.

2. Would you respond in the same way Kai did? Write about how you would respond.

Answers will vary.

3. Match the following Scriptures to the correct description.

Matthew 28:20 — Jesus will never leave you.
John 16:33 — Jesus will be with you always.
Romans 8:28–29 — Jesus has overcome the world.
Hebrews 13:5 — Jesus will work everything out for good.

130

33.3 Paul and Silas Witness
Focus: Prayer as a Lifestyle

↪ EXTENSION

3A Give each student a **PAPER LUNCH BAG**. Instruct students to write a prayer to God on the bag. Prayers may begin with phrases such as the following:
- "Thank You for … "
- "Help me with … "
- "I praise You for … "

Allow time for students to decorate their bags. Encourage students to bring a snack or their lunch in the bag the following day. While they are eating, they can remember to pray the prayer they wrote to God.

Introduction

Have students write a paragraph about a good friend. Tell them to describe that friend and explain why they are so close. Invite volunteers to read their paragraph aloud. Ask students if they would be able to stay such close friends if they never talked to their friend. (**No, it is hard to be someone's friend if you never talk or communicate.**) Explain to students that today's lesson is about talking to God. He wants to be their good friend, and that is why He wants them to talk to Him every day. Remind students that prayer is simply talking to God.

Directed Instruction ↩

Invite a few volunteers to review what happened in the Bible truth this week. (**Possible answers: Paul and Silas witnessed for Jesus; Paul and Silas were thrown into prison; Paul and Silas witnessed to the prisoners and prison keeper by praying and worshipping God; the prison keeper's family believed in Jesus, and all of them were baptized; Paul and Silas were set free from their chains.**) Ask what Paul and Silas did first when they were put in prison. (**They prayed to God.**) Explain that it would have been easy for Paul and Silas not to pray. They might have been angry that they were beaten and put in prison for telling others about Jesus, even though they had done nothing wrong. They might have felt so sad that they were in this situation that they forgot to pray. But Paul and Silas remembered to pray.

Read **Ephesians 6:17–18** and **1 Thessalonians 5:17**. Using the following chart, review with students how to pray and things for which to pray:

• for enemies	Matthew 5:44
• in secret	Matthew 6:6
• to not be tempted	Matthew 26:41
• in faith	Mark 11:24
• to forgive	Mark 11:25
• with others	Acts 1:14
• for new believers	Acts 8:15
• with singing	Acts 16:25
• for safety	Romans 15:30–31
• for others to be restored	2 Corinthians 13:9
• with thanksgiving	Ephesians 1:16
• for others to be strengthened	Ephesians 3:16
• to fearlessly witness	Ephesians 6:20
• with joy	Philippians 1:4
• to not be anxious	Philippians 4:6
• for wisdom and knowledge of Jesus	Colossians 1:9
• to share the gospel	Colossians 4:2–4
• night and day	1 Thessalonians 3:10
• in trouble	James 5:13
• in sickness	James 5:14
• for weather	James 5:17–18

Note that the reason Paul and Silas could pray even in prison is because they had devoted themselves to pray on all occasions with all kinds of prayers. Explain to students that God wants them to be devoted to praying too. This is the way they will get to know Him and what He wants them to do. Through prayer, students will see God's hand at work in their life.

Student Page 33.3
Remind students that God wants them to pray at all times, without giving up. Have students complete the page.

Review
• Why should you pray? (**It's the way I can talk to God and get to know what He wants me to do.**)
• When should you pray? (**all the time, without giving up**)
• What kind of prayers should you pray? (**I should pray all kinds of prayers for every situation.**)

APPLICATION
• Do you have a special place where you go to pray and worship God? (**Answers will vary.**) You can pray in many different places, including your room, a quiet park, a corner of a room, a closet, or even under your bed. Find a place where you can be alone and talk to God. Remember that He has promised that He will never leave those who trust Him (Hebrews 13:5). If you are His child, thank Him for being with you always. Take time to pray for others too.

REINFORCEMENT
More than 25 verses in the New Testament mention Jesus praying. Although the Bible records the prayers He prayed for His disciples, for Himself, and for others, the majority of Jesus' prayer life is not revealed in the Bible. Very little is known about what Jesus prayed, but there is no doubt that prayer was a priority for Him. He often would go to quiet places early in the morning and late at night (Matthew 14:23, Mark 1:35, Luke 5:16). He fervently wanted to do God's will (Luke 22:42) and spent many sleepless nights conversing with His Father (Luke 6:12). If Jesus, the Son of God, considered prayer so important in His own earthly life and ministry, how much more should His followers make prayer a priority?

DAY 3

Name _____

Paul and Silas Witness **33.3**

God wants you to talk to Him every day.

1. Read 1 Thessalonians 5:17. Write what this verse means to you.

Answers will vary but should include I should never stop praying, I should continually talk to God, and God wants me to pray in all situations.

2. Draw pictures of the times and places you can pray. Or write a prayer you would pray at that time or place.

I can pray ...

Drawings and answers will vary.

in the morning	at nighttime	when I am happy
when I am sad	at school	at home

© *Bible Grade 2*   131

© *Bible Grade 2*   327

Paul and Silas Witness
Focus: Ways to Praise God

★ PREPARATION
Select the song "You Are My God" from the Grade 2 URL. (*Introduction*)

Have a COIN available. (*Directed Instruction*)

↪ EXTENSION
4A Provide students with MAGAZINES to find pictures of community places where they can praise and worship God, including the local swimming pool, the library, parks, sporting venues, neighborhoods, or bicycle trails. Have students cut out and glue various pictures onto a piece of construction paper titled *I Will Praise God Everywhere*. Display these collages throughout the classroom to remind students that they can praise God with their words and actions everywhere they go.

4B Using **DM-3 Books of the Bible** and the song "Books of the Bible" from the Grade 2 URL, review the books of the Old and New Testaments.

Introduction ★
Sing the song "You Are My God" from the Grade 2 URL. Explain to students that when they sing songs like this from their heart, they are worshipping God.

Directed Instruction ★ ↪
Teach students that God wants them to praise and worship Him, no matter what. He wants them to praise Him when they are happy and when they are sad. Paul and Silas knew how to praise God even in prison. They worshipped God in three ways: by praying, singing, and witnessing.

First, Paul and Silas prayed. When they prayed, they showed that they trusted God to deliver them from prison. They praised and worshipped God as they talked to Him. Teach students that when they talk to God, they are praising and worshipping Him too. And just like Paul and Silas, they are telling God that they trust Him.

Second, Paul and Silas sang. When they sang, they were focusing on God and His omnipotence. Explain to students that the Bible talks over and over about singing to God. When students worship God by singing and playing instruments, it helps them stop thinking about themselves and start focusing on God, His love, and His power. Share that the book of Psalms is made up of songs and poems that the people of God used to praise and worship Him.

Third, Paul and Silas witnessed to others about Jesus. Before the earthquake, they witnessed by singing about God's love and power while the other prisoners listened. Immediately after the earthquake, Paul and Silas shared the gospel with the prison keeper when he asked them what he must do to be saved. Read **Matthew 28:18–20**. Before He ascended into heaven, Jesus commanded His disciples to go and make disciples of all nations. He promised to always be with them. Explain that *making disciples* means *sharing your belief in Jesus with others and helping them grow in their personal relationship with Him*. Teach students that they too can witness for Jesus. And by witnessing, they are praising and worshipping God.

Tell students that they need to know where and to whom they might witness. Divide the class into two teams. Explain that you will toss a COIN into the air, and when it lands, the teams will take turns responding. The team designated *heads* will respond by giving the *name of a person* or *a category of people* they can witness to. The team designated *tails* will respond by naming *a place* where they can witness. Each time the coin is tossed, write either the name or category of people on the board in one column or the name of a place in the other column. Note that the purpose of this activity is to broaden students' awareness of ways to witness. Specify a time to complete the activity.

Student Page 33.4

Direct students to work in pairs to complete Exercises 1–4. Have them complete Exercise 5 independently. When students finish the exercises, give them time to share their song of praise with their partner.

Review

- What were the three ways Paul and Silas worshipped God in prison? (**They worshipped God by praying, singing, and witnessing to the other prisoners and the prison keeper.**)
- How is praying a way to worship and praise God? (**It tells God that I love Him and trust Him, no matter what.**)
- What does it mean to make disciples? (**Making disciples means sharing my belief in Jesus with others and helping them grow in their personal relationship with Him.**)

Notes:

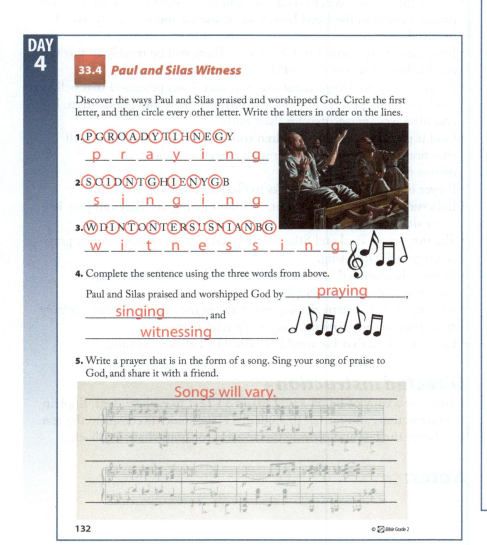

APPLICATION

- Take a minute to praise and worship God by praying and singing to Him.
- Write down the names of three people you know who do not know Jesus. Commit to praying for them all week long. Also pray that God will give you an opportunity to share the good news about Jesus with them.

REINFORCEMENT

One of the biggest evidences of the resurrection is the radical transformation of Jesus' disciples from fear-filled men to bold, faith-filled witnesses for Christ. Their fearful actions are well documented. When Jesus was arrested, they deserted him and fled (Matthew 26:56, Mark 14:50). And on the day Jesus rose from the grave, He found them behind closed doors, hiding in fear of the Jewish leaders (John 20:19). But in a matter of days, these fearful men turned into champions of the resurrected Christ, boldly preaching about Him and telling of His power at work in them (Acts 4:31, 33). What brought about this amazing transformation? Encountering the risen Savior, realizing that He had fulfilled every promise and prophecy, and being empowered by the Holy Spirit made them willing to risk their lives for the gospel. If Jesus had not been raised from the dead, His followers would not have laid down everything to preach about Him. In fact, if the resurrection had not taken place, people who follow Christ should be pitied more than anyone (1 Corinthians 15:12–21). But Jesus has indeed conquered death, and His disciples boldly shared the gospel with others!

33.5 Paul and Silas Witness
Focus: Review and Assessment

★ PREPARATION
Select **VA 33A Paul and Silas Witness**. (*Lesson Review*)

Print **BLM 33C Lesson 33 Test** for each student. (*Directed Instruction*)

Lesson Review ★
Use **VA 33A Paul and Silas Witness** to review the Bible truth. Cover the following concepts:
- Paul and Silas were not ashamed to share the good news about Jesus with other people.
- To *witness* means *to share the good news about Jesus with others*.
- Witnessing is part of God's plan for every Christian.
- Paul and Silas boldly witnessed for Jesus, and told others about God's plan of salvation.
- Paul commanded an evil spirit to come out of a slave girl. Paul and Silas were severely beaten and sent to prison because the slave girl's owners were angry that they could no longer make money with her.
- Paul and Silas prayed and sang praises to God while they were in prison. The other prisoners listened to them while they worshipped God.
- A great earthquake shook the prisoners' chains loose and opened the prison doors, but Paul, Silas, and the other prisoners did not leave.
- The prison keeper thought the prisoners had escaped and was going to kill himself, but Paul told him to stop, because they were all still there.
- When the prison keeper asked Paul and Silas how to be saved, Paul told him to believe in the Lord Jesus Christ, and he and his family would be saved.
- Jesus gave two promises in John 16:33: There will be trouble in this world, but He has overcome the world.
- *Persecuted* means *being treated in a cruel way*. Jesus promised that believers can have joyful peace, even in the midst of trouble and persecution. Paul and Silas were persecuted for their faith.
- God is pleased when His children trust Him and praise Him in all situations. He will see them through everything and is able to deliver them.
- Prayer is the way a believer talks to God and hears from Him.
- Believers should pray at all times, without giving up. They can pray in every situation.
- The three ways Paul and Silas worshipped God in prison were by praying, singing, and witnessing.
- Before He ascended into heaven, Jesus told His followers to go everywhere and make disciples.
- *Making disciples* means *sharing your belief in Jesus with others and helping them grow in their personal relationship with Him*.
- Jesus promised that He would be with His believers always.

Directed Instruction ★
Distribute a copy of **BLM 33C Lesson 33 Test** to each student. Explain the instructions and format to students. Have students complete the test. Read over the test and provide the answers for immediate feedback.

Notes:

330

Lesson Preparation
Review 34.0

Expected Student Outcomes

KNOW
Students will review details of what God did in and through the lives of biblical characters presented this year.

DO
Students will:
- give examples of character qualities of the one, true God
- identify how Bible characters worshipped God, and how students can worship God
- correctly sequence Bible truths
- reflect upon what they have learned this year and write about how to apply it

APPLY
Students will express a desire to follow the example of the godly Bible characters they have studied.

Lesson Outline
I. Who God is
  A. Omnipotent, provider, salvation through Jesus (Phil 4:18–19, Rom 10:9–10)
II. Responses to God
  A. Worshipping, listening, obeying (Ps 145:3)
III. Relationship to God
  A. Prayer, faith, boldness (Heb 4:16, 1 Cor 3:5–9, Phil 1:6)
IV. Relationship to others
  A. Love, service and respect, evangelism and missions (1 Jn 4:7–11; Mt 22:36–40, 28:19–20)

❤ TEACHER'S HEART
The school year is coming to an end. Soon the last bell will ring, students will clean out their desks, and summer vacation will begin. As you spend time with your students during this final week, a bittersweet feeling may come over you. You've poured your life into your students and shared many precious moments, but now your students are moving on. You may wonder how much they've learned or whether their lives will change for the better as a result of your investment. Be encouraged! The Bible truths you've presented this year are seeds you've planted in their hearts that will produce fruit in God's time. Your students have learned about men and women of faith who trusted God in the midst of victory and failure and serve as life examples for each student. These same men and women are now witnesses in heaven, calling your students to "lay aside every weight, and the sin which so easily ensnares [them], and … run with endurance the race that is set before [them], looking unto Jesus, the author and finisher of [their] faith" (Hebrews 12:1–2). So take heart, dear teacher, you've done what the Lord has called you to do!

Supplemental Materials are available to download. See Understanding Purposeful Design Bible at the front of this book for the Grade 2 URL.

📖 MEMORY VERSE
Philippians 1:6

★ MATERIALS
Day 1:
- Balloons
- Scrapbook or photo album
- BLM 34A Name Cards, card stock
- VAs 8A, 14A, 23A, 25A, 26A, 28A
- Love Bowl from Lesson 11.4

Day 2:
- BLM 34A Name Cards
- VAs 4A, 13A, 33A
- BLM 34A Name Cards (*Extension*)
- BLMs 34B–D Who Are They Cards, Parts 1–3; card stock (*Extension*)

Day 3:
- BLM 34A Name Cards
- DM-1 Character Traits
- VAs 15A, 16A, 21A, 22A, 30A

Day 4:
- Gifts
- BLM 34A Name Cards
- VAs 2A, 6A, 10A, 20A, 31A, 32A; BLM 34E They Serve, I Serve
- Time Line
- PP-10 God's People in Review (*Extension*)

Day 5:
- BLM 34F Lesson 34 Test

♪ SONGS
Only God Can Do
You Are My God

TEACHER RESOURCES
Kohlenberger III, John R. *Read Through the Bible in a Year.* Moody Publishers, 2008.

STUDENT RESOURCES
Henley, Karyn. *Day by Day Begin-to-Read Bible.* Tyndale Kids, 2007.

© *Bible* Grade 2

331

34.1 Review
Focus: Who God Is

📖 MEMORY VERSE
Philippians 1:6

MEMORY WORK
- Separate students into two groups. Give each group a BALLOON. Have students take turns stomping on the balloon until it pops. Then tell them to assemble the pieces of paper and chorally recite the verse.

⭐ PREPARATION
Secure TWO BALLOONS. Copy this week's verse onto a piece of paper. Cut the paper into smaller pieces. Insert the smaller pieces of paper into a balloon. Inflate the balloon. Repeat process for a second balloon. (Memory Work)

Have available a SCRAPBOOK or PHOTO ALBUM. (Introduction)

Print two copies of **BLM 34A Name Cards** on CARD STOCK. Cut the cards apart. Laminate each set of cards, if possible, and bind each set with a rubber band. The name cards will be used throughout the week. Select the following name cards from one set for today's activity: JOSHUA; ELIJAH; SHADRACH, MESHACH, AND ABED-NEGO; MARY AND JOSEPH; JESUS; MARTHA. (Directed Instruction)

Select **VA 8A Joshua Obeys God, VA 23A The Fiery Furnace, VA 26A Jesus Heals a Blind Man**, and **VA 28A Martha Grows in Faith**. Select the song "Only God Can Do" from the Grade 2 URL. (Directed Instruction)

Select **VA 14A Elijah Trusts God.** (Directed Instruction)

Select **VA 25A Mary and Joseph Obey God**. Have available the LOVE BOWL that was introduced in Lesson 11.4. (Directed Instruction)

Introduction ★
Show students a SCRAPBOOK or PHOTO ALBUM of your family or friends, and ask them what this item is for. (to remember people and events) Talk about how looking at the photos reminds you of things God has done, godly character traits of the people, and memorable times that make you feel thankful and glad. Remind students that they have studied the lives of Bible characters throughout the year. Each character has shown them something very valuable about living God's way.

Directed Instruction ★
Hand out the following name cards from one set of **BLM 34A Name Cards** to selected students: JOSHUA; ELIJAH; SHADRACH, MESHACH, AND ABED-NEGO; MARY AND JOSEPH; JESUS; MARTHA. Ask students to come forward, read their name card aloud, and share one thing they recall about that Bible character. Review that God is the one, true God who revealed Himself to these people. Ask students to share some of the characteristics of God they learned from the Bible truths this year. (**Possible answers: God is powerful; God loves me; God is forgiving.**)

First, review that because God is the one, true God, He is all-powerful, or omnipotent. Separate students into four groups, and give each group one of the following visual aids: **VA 8A Joshua Obeys God, VA 23A The Fiery Furnace, VA 26A Jesus Heals a Blind Man, VA 28A Martha Grows in Faith**. Select one student in each group to hold the visual aid while others in the group take turns sharing excerpts of the Bible truth that they recall from the VA. Ask each group to share with the rest of the class one or two things over which God has power, according to the Bible truth. Write students' responses on the board, and then have them chorally repeat "God has power over … ," using each of their responses to complete the sentence. (**Possible answers: sickness, death, obstacles, fire, danger**) Sing the song "Only God Can Do" from the Grade 2 URL.

Second, explain that because God is the one, true God, He provides for His people. Read **Philippians 4:18–19**. God will supply not just *some* of their needs but *all* of their needs. Display **VA 14A Elijah Trusts God**. Note that God miraculously used ravens and a poor widow to supply food for Elijah.

Finally, remind students that because God is the one, true God, He gives them salvation through Jesus. Display **VA 25A Mary and Joseph Obey God**. Note that Mary and Joseph willingly accepted their role in God's plan of salvation. God sent His Son, Jesus, to die on the cross to pay for the sins of all people. Read **Romans 10:9–10**. God wants everyone to have faith in Jesus because He loves everyone. Invite students to pick a card from the LOVE BOWL and read aloud the characteristics of godly love. God also wants His children to witness, or share, about the good news of Jesus. To do this, they need to hear, read, know, and understand His Word. They need to believe the right things about Him so they can correctly share the truth with others in love (2 Timothy 2:15).

Student Page 34.1
Display all visual aids used in today's lesson as students complete the page.

Review

- What three things can you remember from the Bible truths about the one, true God? (**Possible answers: God is all-powerful; God has provided salvation for me through Jesus; God provides for my needs.**)
- Which events from the Bible truths show you that God is all-powerful, or omnipotent? (**Possible answers: God causing the walls of Jericho to fall down; God saving Daniel's friends from being burned; Jesus healing the blind man; Jesus resurrecting Lazarus**)
- How does the Bible truth about Elijah show you that God provides for you? (**Possible answers: God took care of Elijah's needs by supplying food and water; God will take care of my needs, too.**)
- Whom did God send to Earth to offer you salvation? (**Jesus**) What does God want you to do with His plan of salvation? (**He wants me to accept it for myself and tell others about what Jesus did for them.**)

APPLICATION

- Take some time to pray and thank God for His omnipotence. Thank Him for His power in all situations, for His provision for your needs, and for His plan of salvation through Jesus, His Son.
- Ask God to give you the boldness and courage to share the good news of Jesus with those who do not know Him. Make a commitment to diligently pray for those people.

DAY 1

Name _____

Review 34.1

1. Because God is the one, true God, He is all-powerful. Look at the pictures of each Bible truth. Select and circle two pictures. Write about how the Bible characters in these Bible truths show you that God is all-powerful.

Possible answers: God was powerful when He made the walls of Jericho fall down. God was powerful when he saved Daniel's friends from the fiery furnace. God was powerful when Jesus healed the blind man. God was powerful when Jesus raised Lazarus from the dead.

2. Because God is the one, true God, He provides for your needs. Write about how God provided for Elijah.

God provided for Elijah's needs first by having ravens bring him food by the brook. God also provided for Elijah's needs through a widow and her food supply.

3. Because God is the one, true God, He gives you salvation through Jesus. Mary and Joseph obeyed God and His plan. Write about God's plan of salvation.

Jesus, God's Son, came to the earth. He was perfect. He was arrested, crucified, and buried. Three days later, He rose from the dead, proving He was the Savior. God's plan was for His Son to die on the cross to pay for the sins of all people.

34.2 Review

Focus: Responses to God

★ PREPARATION

Select the song "You Are My God" from the Grade 2 URL. (*Introduction*)

Have available one set of name cards from **BLM 34A Name Cards**. Select one of each of the following name cards for today's activity: ABRAHAM, MOSES, MIRIAM, DAVID, PAUL, SILAS. (*Directed Instruction*)

Select **VA 4A The Red Sea Crossing**, **VA 13A David Leads in Thanksgiving**, and **VA 33A Paul and Silas Witness**. (*Directed Instruction*)

↻ EXTENSION

2A Using name cards from both sets of **BLM 34A Name Cards**, place one set of name cards face up in a circle on the floor. Have students stand outside the circle. (If you have more than 20 students, use blank cards so every student has a place to stand.) Direct students to walk around the circle as music plays, and stop when the music stops. Read aloud a name card from the second set of cards. The student standing next to the matching card should state a fact about the character. If the statement is incorrect, select volunteers to answer until a correct response is given. Play long enough to name each character at least once.

2B Print one copy each of **BLMs 34B–D Who Are They Cards, Parts 1–3** on CARD STOCK. Hide the cards in the classroom, and challenge students to locate all 40 cards. Instruct students to pair up with the student who has their matching card. One card will list the Bible character's name. The other will describe what the character did.

Introduction ★

Sing the song "You Are My God" from the Grade 2 URL. Explain that because God is the one, true God, His people should respond to Him in certain ways. Tell students that today's lesson will review three ways they should respond to God: worshipping and praising Him, listening to Him, and obeying Him.

Directed Instruction ★ ↻

Hand out the following name cards from **BLM 34A Name Cards** to selected students: ABRAHAM, MOSES, MIRIAM, DAVID, PAUL, SILAS. Invite students to come forward, read their name card aloud, and write on the board one thing they recall about that Bible character. Emphasize that all of these Bible characters worshipped the one, true God. Read **Psalm 145:3**. Remind students that God alone is worthy of praise.

Separate students into three groups, giving each group one of the following: **VA 4A The Red Sea Crossing, VA 13A David Leads in Thanksgiving, VA 33A Paul and Silas Witness**. The selected visual aids give reasons for worshipping God or describe situations when God's people worshipped Him. Give each group a few minutes to prepare a short skit based on their VA. Select a leader from each group to facilitate the skit planning. Each skit must include how and why the people in the Bible truth worshipped God. (**Moses and Miriam worshipped and praised God in song after He parted the Red Sea; David worshipped God and danced before Him as the ark of the covenant was brought into Jerusalem; Paul and Silas worshipped God in prison by praying and singing praises to Him.**) Students may use the Bible truth on the back of the VA to help them prepare their skit. After each group has performed, tell students that these three Bible truths are good reminders to worship God for who He is and what He has done, and to praise Him at all times.

In addition to worshipping the one, true God, students also need to listen to Him. After reading the following three clues, ask students for the name of the person being described:
• God spoke directly to him and called him to go to a new land.
• He listened to God and left his home to follow God's command.
• He trusted that God would take care of him. (**Abraham**)

Explain to students that God may not speak to them directly as He did to Abraham, but He always speaks through His Word, the Bible. Emphasize that they can trust in the truthfulness of God's Word.

Teach students that when they listen to God, they must take the next step and obey Him. Sometimes it may be difficult to obey Him because they may want to do things their own way. But God wants them to obey Him and do His will. Remind students that they should obey willingly. Moses is an example of someone who needed to learn this. Remind students that Moses did not want to do what God asked him to do—to go back to Egypt—but God taught him to obey with the right attitude. God even sent Aaron along to help Moses obey God.

Student Page 34.2

Have students independently complete the page, reviewing how each Bible character worshipped, listened to, and obeyed God.

Review

- What are three ways you can respond to God? (**I can worship and praise Him, listen to Him, and obey Him.**)
- Why do you worship God and praise Him? (**because He is God, and for what He has done**)
- How did Abraham listen to God? (**When God told Abraham to move to a new land, he left his home, went where God told him, and trusted God to take care of him.**)
- What is the main way God communicates with you and helps you listen to Him? (**His Word, the Bible**)
- What can you learn from Moses about obedience? (**God wants me to obey willingly.**)

Notes:

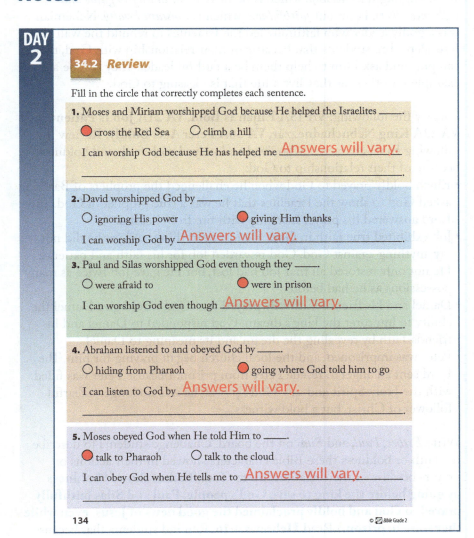

APPLICATION

- Ask God to give you a heart to listen to Him and praise Him, even if He asks you to do something you do not want to do.
- How can you personally obey God better? (**Answers will vary.**)
- What are some things God has done in your life for which you can worship Him? (**Answers will vary.**)

REINFORCEMENT

The order and balance of the earth and the universe reveal the power of God. The balance of gravitational force, the speed of light, the distance between the stars, and the polarity of the water molecule are evidence of His omnipotence. They declare that a purposeful intelligence created this world; for if balance did not exist in these areas, life could not exist.

Romans 1:20 states that since the creation of the world, God's invisible attributes, including His eternal power and Godhead, have been clearly seen through what He made. In addition to all that God created, He made man and woman in His image and likeness (Genesis 1:26–27). Psalm 139:14 testifies that every person has been "fearfully and wonderfully made" by the Creator, who is worthy of praise and worship. The greatest revelation of God's power is Jesus, the Son of God, the visible image of the invisible God (Colossians 1:15).

34.3 Review
Focus: Relationship to God

★ PREPARATION

Have available one set of name cards from **BLM 34A Name Cards**. Select one of each of the following name cards for today's activity: ELIJAH, NEHEMIAH, ESTHER, JOB, DANIEL, PETER, PAUL, SILAS. (*Directed Instruction*)

Select **DM-1 Character Traits** and **VA 16A Nehemiah Leads**. (*Directed Instruction*)

Select **VA 15A Elijah Is Bold**, **VA 21A Job Is Patient**, **VA 22A King Nebuchadnezzar**, and **VA 30A Peter Acts Boldly**. (*Directed Instruction*)

☞ EXTENSION

3A Distribute pieces of construction paper to students. Direct them to cut the paper into 3" × 5" rectangles. Ask them to write short prayers to God. Assist students in stapling together a few pieces of paper to create a mini booklet of prayers.

3B Invite students to work in small groups or pairs to mime the Bible truths to one another.

Introduction

Ask students to share about what it takes to be someone's best friend. (**Possible answers: spend time with that person, be kind to that person**) Explain to them that today's lesson is about God's friendship with them and how they are to behave in their relationship with Him.

Directed Instruction ★ ☞

Hand out the following name cards from **BLM 34A Name Cards** to selected students: ELIJAH, NEHEMIAH, ESTHER, JOB, DANIEL, PETER, PAUL, SILAS. Ask students to come forward, read their name card aloud, and share one thing they recall about the Bible character. Explain that these Bible characters had a consistent relationship with God. God wants to be in a relationship with all people. Teach that communication is very important in a relationship. Ask students how they can communicate with God. (**pray**)

Display **DM-1 Character Traits** and **VA 16A Nehemiah Leads**. Review all the character traits that should be found in a person who follows God. Highlight *leadership*, which is defined as *the ability to guide and influence others*. Point out *faithfulness*, which is *constant loyalty*. Nehemiah was a godly leader who faithfully led the Israelites to rebuild the wall in Jerusalem. Tell students that because of their relationship with God, they can pray and ask Him to help them be a faithful leader. They will be an example for others as they live a life that is pleasing to God.

Display the following: **VA 15A Elijah Is Bold**, **VA 21A Job Is Patient**, **VA 22A King Nebuchadnezzar**, **VA 30A Peter Acts Boldly**. Review the following Bible characters who lived and prayed with faith and boldness because of their relationship to God:
- Elijah boldly prayed to God when he challenged the prophets of Baal. He asked God to show the Israelites that he was a true prophet of God. The Lord answered his prayer instantly with fire from heaven.
- Job exhibited true faith in God. He lost everything, and yet he did not say anything against God. God rewarded Job for his faith and patience. He not only restored all that Job had lost, but He gave Job twice as many possessions as he had before.
- Daniel and his friends faithfully prayed that God would give Daniel the ability to interpret the king's dream. God responded to Daniel and his friends' faith by revealing the dream and its meaning to Daniel.
- Peter was imprisoned, and the local church began praying for him. The Lord sent an angel to rescue Peter from prison. Because Peter was filled with the Holy Spirit and saw God's power, he was no longer a fearful follower of Christ, but a bold witness.

Write *Esther*, *Paul*, and *Silas* on the board. Challenge students to describe the faith or boldness these Bible characters showed in their actions or prayers because of their relationship to God. (**Esther showed boldness by going before the king to save God's people; Paul and Silas faithfully prayed to God and boldly proclaimed the good news of Jesus, even while they were in prison.**) Read **Hebrews 4:16**. Remind students that because

336

of their relationship to God, they can pray boldly, knowing that He will hear. They can trust God and be bold in telling others about Him, and do what God has called them to do. Read **1 Corinthians 3:5–9** and point out that God gives different tasks to believers, such as planting and watering, but the important thing to know is that it is God who gives the growth.

Student Page 34.3
Direct students to work in groups as they sequence the Bible truth events.

Review

- How can you communicate with God? (**by praying**)
- How can you be a godly leader? (**by praying and asking God for wisdom and doing what He guides me to do**)
- What will others notice as they look to you as a leader? (**They will see my example as I live a life that is pleasing to God.**)
- What does God want you to do in your relationship with Him? (**pray, trust and have faith in Him, be bold for Him**)
- When you are in a relationship with God, what will He replace your fear with? (**boldness**)

APPLICATION

- Take some time to thank God for your relationship with Him. Thank Him for the gift of prayer. Ask Him to give you wisdom to be a godly leader.
- Ask God to transform your fears about sharing the good news about Jesus with others into boldness, as He did for Peter.
- Read **Philippians 1:6**. Who has begun a good work in you? (**God**) Will He leave His work unfinished? (**No, He will complete it.**)

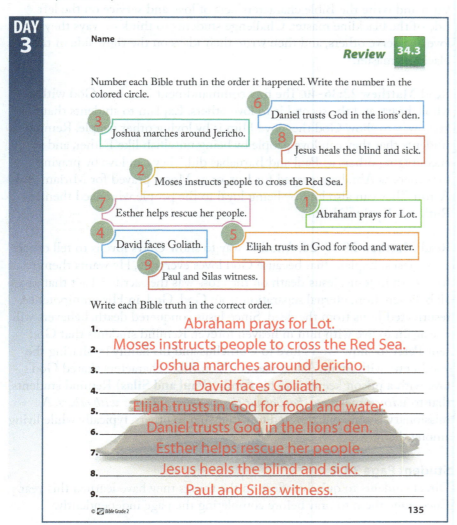

34.4 Review

Focus: Relationship to Others

★ PREPARATION

Prepare a SMALL GIFT for each student, such as CANDY, STICKERS, or an ENCOURAGING NOTE. (*Introduction*)

Have available one set of name cards from **BLM 34A Name Cards**. Select one of each of the following name cards for today's activity: ABRAHAM, MOSES, MIRIAM, AARON, RUTH, ESTHER, PETER, PAUL, BARNABAS. (*Directed Instruction*)

Select **VA 2A Abraham Prays**, **VA 6A Miriam and Aaron Learn Respect**, **VA 10A Ruth Is Loyal**, **VA 20A Esther Risks Her Life**, **VA 31A Peter and Cornelius**, and **VA 32A Paul and Barnabas Encourage Others**. Make a copy of **BLM 34E They Serve, I Serve** for each student. (*Directed Instruction*)

☛ EXTENSION

4A To review the Bible truths taught this year, show students **PP-10 God's People in Review**.

4B Ask students to write a journal entry about a favorite Bible character and a memorable Bible truth they learned this year.

4C Select a student to sit on a chair facing away from the board. Write the name of a Bible character on the board. Explain that the rest of the class will give clues to this "contestant." Tell students to raise their hand and wait to be selected before providing a clue. Limit clues to a one- or two-word description from the Bible truth. Simple actions or facial expressions are also allowed. The contestant is allowed three guesses. If he or she guesses incorrectly, read the answer on the board. Play until all who wish to be a contestant have a turn.

Introduction ★

Give each student a SMALL GIFT. Tell students that you are giving them a gift because of your love for God and your love for them. Explain that God has called them to love each other. Read **1 John 4:7–11**. Believers show that they are God's children by loving others because God loves them.

Directed Instruction ★ ☛

Hand out the following name cards from a set of **BLM 34A Name Cards**: ABRAHAM, MOSES, MIRIAM, AARON, RUTH, ESTHER, PETER, PAUL, BARNABAS. Invite students to read their name card aloud, and write one thing on the board that they recall about that person. Explain to students that each Bible character served others or showed love for others. Today's lesson is about how God wants His children to love, to serve, and to respect others.

Place students in six groups. Give each group one of the following: **VA 2A Abraham Prays, VA 6A Miriam and Aaron Learn Respect, VA 10A Ruth Is Loyal, VA 20A Esther Risks Her Life, VA 31A Peter and Cornelius, VA 32A Paul and Barnabas Encourage Others**. Give each student a copy of **BLM 34E They Serve, I Serve**. Ask each group to review the Bible truth and write the Bible characters' acts of love and service on the left side of the blackline master. Challenge students to think of ways they can love and serve others, and then write their ideas on the right side of the blackline master.

Read **Matthew 22:36-40**. The first commandment is to love God with a whole heart, and the second is to love others. Explain to students that a great way to show God they love Him is by loving other people. Remind students that they can love people by being unselfish like Esther, and by encouraging others as Paul and Barnabas did. They can love by praying for others as Abraham prayed for Lot, or as Moses prayed for Miriam and Aaron. They can also love by being loyal to the people who need them, as Ruth was loyal to Naomi.

Read **Matthew 28:19–20**. Another way to show God's love is to tell others about Jesus. Explain that because God loves everyone, He wants them to have faith in Jesus. Jesus' death on the cross was the sacrificial act that saves all believers from eternal separation from God. God, in His omnipotence, resurrected Jesus from the dead. Since Jesus conquered death, believers will rise again to live with him in heaven forever. Remind students that God sent Peter to show God's love to Cornelius and his family by sharing the good news with them. Ask students which Bible characters shared God's love with a prison keeper and his family. (**Paul and Silas**) Remind students that to *witness* means *to share about the good news of Jesus with others*. A missionary is someone devoted to witnessing to others, typically while living among them.

Student Page 34.4

Direct students to quietly reflect on the things they have learned this year. Encourage them to pray before completing the page independently.

Review

- God wants His children to love, to serve, and to respect others. What are the first and second greatest commandments (Matthew 22:36-40)? (**to love God with my whole heart and to love people**)
- What are some ways you can show love to people? (**by serving, encouraging, being loyal, praying, sharing the good news about Jesus**)
- What does it mean to witness? (**to share about the good news of Jesus with others**) What do you call someone who is devoted to witnessing about Jesus? (**a missionary**)
- Why should you tell people about Jesus? (**God wants everyone to know about His Son, Jesus. I show God that I love Him and others when I tell others about Jesus.**)

Time Line
Select name cards from both sets of **BLM 34A Name Cards** that correspond to the Bible characters on the **Time Line**. Hand out these name cards to various students. Instruct them to stand beneath the appropriate place on the Time Line. Remind students that those who share a Bible character's name should stand side by side.

APPLICATION
- Pray and ask God to give you a heart to love, serve, and respect others.
- What are some ways you can love and serve people? (**Answers will vary.**)
- Who can you love and serve this week? (**Answers will vary.**)

REINFORCEMENT
Youth With A Mission, YWAM, is an outreach ministry that began in 1960. The main focus of YWAM is "to know God and to make Him known." Their Mercy Ministry teams show the love of Jesus through numerous programs, such as agricultural assistance, health care, and micro-enterprise development. Through these programs, YWAM aims to ease suffering and provide hope for those affected by poverty, disease, and injustice. The ministry of YWAM helps with long-term community development when natural disasters strike, including hurricanes, tsunamis, and earthquakes. YWAM also uses music, performance arts, and sports as opportunities to connect and share the gospel with people from many different cultures.

In Burma, YWAM has set up a tiny children's library called *the Rice Seeds Library*. Many Burmese children stop attending school around the age of 12 in order to work and contribute financially to their families. YWAM team members connect with these families, and encourage parents to allow their children to remain in school. Currently, YWAM operates in over 180 countries around the world. What a great way to show God's love to people!

DAY 4

34.4 Review

Think about the Bible truths you have learned this year.

1. Who is one of your favorite Bible characters you studied this year?
   Answers will vary.

2. Why is this person one of your favorite Bible characters?
   Answers will vary.

3. What is an important lesson you learned from this person's life?
   Answers will vary.

4. God wants to have a relationship with you. He wants to talk to you through His Word. He wants you to talk with Him through prayer. He wants you to listen to and obey Him. He wants you to love others by serving them. Which of these do you need to work on the most?
   Answers will vary.

5. Write down a prayer of commitment to God. Share with Him your desire to grow in your relationship with Him.
   Answers will vary.

136

34.5 Review

Focus: Review and Assessment

★ PREPARATION

Make one copy of **BLM 34F Lesson 34 Test** for each student. (*Directed Instruction*)

Lesson Review

Review the Bible truths from this lesson. Cover the following concepts:

- God is the one, true God. He is omnipotent, or all-powerful. He provides for the needs of His children and offers everyone His plan of salvation.
- God showed His omnipotence when He destroyed the walls around Jericho, when He saved Daniel's friends from the fiery furnace, when Jesus healed a blind man, and when Jesus raised Lazarus from the dead.
- The Bible truth about Elijah shows that God provides, because He took care of Elijah's needs for food and water.
- God offers His plan of salvation through His Son, Jesus, who died on the cross to pay for the sins of all people. Mary and Joseph willingly accepted their role in God's plan of salvation.
- Believers can respond to God by worshipping, praising, listening to, and obeying Him. Believers should worship God for what He has done and for who He is. They are called to praise Him, even during difficult times.
- Moses and Miriam worshipped and praised God after He parted the Red Sea. David worshipped God and danced before Him as the ark of the covenant was brought into Jerusalem. Paul and Silas praised God by praying and singing while they were in prison.
- God speaks to His children today through the Bible, His Word.
- Believers should willingly obey people in authority over them.
- God's children can communicate with Him through prayer. Believers can pray and ask God to help them be bold and faithful leaders as they walk closely in relationship with Him. They will be an example for others as they boldly live a life that is pleasing to God.
- Elijah prayed for God to show His power to the prophets of Baal. Job showed true faith in God during difficult times. Daniel and his friends prayed for help and wisdom.
- When believers have a relationship with God, He will replace their fears with boldness. Esther showed boldness by going before the king to save God's people. Peter saw God's power when God sent an angel to free him from prison; Peter changed from being a fearful follower of Christ to boldly telling others about Jesus. Paul and Silas sang praises to God, prayed, and boldly shared about Jesus, even while they were in prison.
- The second greatest commandment is to love others. A follower of Jesus can love others by serving them, respecting them, encouraging them, being loyal to them, and praying for them.
- God wants everyone to know about His Son, Jesus. Believers show God they love Him when they tell others about Jesus.
- Jesus' death on the cross was the sacrificial act that saved all believers from eternal separation from God. God resurrected Jesus from the dead. Since Jesus conquered death, believers will rise again to live with Him in heaven forever.

Directed Instruction ★

Distribute a copy of **BLM 34F Lesson 34 Test** to each student. Have students complete the test. Provide answers for immediate feedback. Close this final lesson with prayer, inviting students to thank God for the things they learned this year.

340

BIBLE

Visual Aids
(VAs)

© Bible Grade 2

VA 1A Abraham Listens and Obeys God
Genesis 11:31–12:8, 21:1–3, 25:24–26, 35:22c–26; Exodus 3:13

Long ago, God spoke to a man named *Abraham* and told him to do something that wasn't very easy.

"Leave this place and go to a new land that I will show you," God commanded. And then He gave Abraham some wonderful promises. "I will give you the land and I will make you a great nation with many, many descendants. All other nations in the world will be blessed because of you."

You'll notice God didn't tell Abraham exactly what the place was called, or exactly how far away it was, or exactly how long it would take to get there. All He said was, "Follow Me and I will show you where I want you to be." To obey meant that Abraham would have to leave the place that had been his home for many years. Never again would he see the streets where he had grown up or had spent happy evenings with friends he had known all his life. He would become a wanderer until God told him to stop.

Though it was hard to do, Abraham knew that this was God's voice, and he believed that God would keep His promises. So he gathered the things he owned and set out with his family. They walked for many days and many miles, up and down the hills near the desert. The sun made them very tired and thirsty. Abraham turned his heart toward God to listen very closely for His voice.

Then one day, when Abraham and his family were traveling near a place called *Shechem*, it happened. God appeared to him and said, "This is it, Abraham. This is the land I will give to you and your descendants." So Abraham stopped and built an altar to worship God and remember the place where God spoke to him.

Abraham was so excited that he had finally found the place where God wanted him to be. He was thankful that God had guided him to a new home. But most of all, Abraham was glad he had listened to God's voice and followed His directions, because God did keep His promises. Many years later, God gave Abraham and Sarah a son named *Isaac*. Isaac became the father of *Jacob*, who had 12 sons. These sons, their sons, and many generations after them became a nation called *Israel*.

Many years later, a very special baby was born in the nation of Israel. This baby grew up and died on a cross for our sins. The Lord Jesus Christ was one of those descendants God had promised to Abraham thousands of years before. Through Jesus, the whole world has been blessed.

VA 2A Abraham Prays
Genesis 18:17–33, 19:29

Throughout his travels, Abraham prayed to God. During Abraham's journey, he settled near two towns. Most of the people who lived in these towns did not honor God. They were very wicked and sinful. There were a few people in the town who loved God. Lot, Abraham's nephew, and his family had moved to live in one of these towns.

One day, Abraham was sitting in the shade of his tent that he and Sarah lived in. Abraham looked up and saw three men standing there. Abraham was glad to have visitors. They looked like men, but really, one of the visitors was the Lord, and the other two were angels!

The Lord told Abraham that He would bring judgment to the towns because of their sin. Abraham was immediately concerned for Lot's safety. Abraham began to talk with the Lord, asking Him to spare the town that Lot lived in and to not destroy the righteous people along with the wicked. Abraham said, "Far be it for You, Lord, the righteous Judge of all the earth, to destroy the righteous along with the wicked."

Abraham asked the Lord if there were 50 righteous people within the town would the Lord destroy it. The Lord said, "No, I will spare it for their sakes if I find 50 righteous people."

Abraham then humbly asked the Lord, "What if there are 45 righteous people?" The Lord replied that if that were the case, He would not destroy it.

Abraham lowered his number to 40, and asked again. The Lord replied as before. Then, being really bold as well as scared, Abraham inquired, "What about 30?" Again the Lord replied, "No, I will not do it if I find 30 there."

Still being afraid, Abraham asked the Lord, "What if there are 20 righteous?" He was frightened that the Lord would get angry with him for asking again, but the Lord answered as before. "I will not destroy the town if there are 20 righteous."

Abraham said, "Please do not be angry with me. I am only going to speak once more. What if there are 10 righteous?" The Lord answered, "I will not destroy it for the sake of 10 righteous."

And the Lord did as He said. He remembered Abraham's face-to-face prayer for Lot and his family. The Lord allowed them to escape before the towns of Sodom and Gomorrah were destroyed.

VA 3A The Burning Bush
Exodus 2:1–4:28, Numbers 12:3

Abraham had a son named *Isaac*, and Isaac had a son named *Jacob*. Jacob's children and their descendants lived in the land of Goshen. These were the children of the nation of Israel, and they were known as *Hebrews*. Life in Goshen started out very well; however, as time went on, the kings of Egypt, who were known as *pharaohs* and who ruled over the land of Goshen, forced the Hebrews to be slaves. The Hebrews had lived in the land for around 400 years.

Toward the end of the 400 years, the pharaoh ordered that all Hebrew baby boys be killed. In an effort to save her son, one mother placed her baby in a basket. She then put the basket, which was like a boat, into the nearby river. The pharaoh's daughter had come to the river to bathe, saw the basket, and rescued the boy. She named him *Moses* and raised him as her own son.

One day, when Moses became a man, he saw an Egyptian hitting a Hebrew slave to get the man to work harder. Moses grew angry. He hit the Egyptian hard, so hard that the Egyptian died! Moses grew afraid, so he ran away from Egypt and was hiding in the land of Midian, a wilderness and desert area. Moses began working for a priest there named *Jethro*, who was a descendant of Abraham. Moses then married one of Jethro's daughters.

One day as Moses was taking care of sheep in the wilderness, something caught his eye. What he saw was very unusual. There was fire in the middle of a bush, but the bush was not burning up! Moses went closer to see this unusual thing. As he walked toward the bush, he heard a voice calling his name.

"Moses, Moses!" said the voice.

Moses answered, "Here I am!" and asked who was speaking to him. It was God! God then said, "I am the same God that Abraham, Isaac, and Jacob worshipped." God told Moses to take off his shoes and not to come any closer. This was because God was there! It was holy ground—set apart for God's use! God began describing a job that He had for Moses to do. God wanted Moses to go to Egypt to rescue the Hebrews from slavery.

Moses could not believe that God was asking him to go back to Egypt, and he pleaded with God. Moses said, "God, I am nothing compared to the pharaoh, the king of Egypt. I don't know how to tell the people who You are. They won't even believe what I tell them. Besides that, I don't speak very well and I'm scared!" God promised to be with Moses and perform mighty miracles through him so that the pharaoh would let the Hebrews leave. Moses didn't believe he could do what God wanted, so he begged God to send someone else. Even though God was angry that Moses didn't trust Him enough to do what He had asked, God had a plan. He sent Moses' brother Aaron to help Moses. Moses would hear from God and then tell Aaron what to say. So Moses set off for Egypt and met Aaron on the way. Once there, they would tell the pharaoh and the Hebrews what God had said. Moses became known as *a very humble man* because of how he obeyed God.

© *Bible* Grade 2

347

VA 4A The Red Sea Crossing

Exodus 12:31–15:21

After the last plague, which was the death of the firstborn son, Pharaoh and the Egyptians urged the Hebrews to leave Egypt, sending them away with clothing and many things made of silver and gold. The Egyptians were very scared that the Hebrews' God would end up killing all of the Egyptians if the Hebrews were not allowed to leave.

To avoid any problems with the Philistines, a warlike people, God sent the Hebrews south toward the Red Sea. He led His people in two very special ways—by day, there was a pillar of cloud, and by night, there was a pillar of fire. The cloud and fire gave the Hebrews direction and light during their journey.

After the Hebrews left, Pharaoh's heart became hardened, and he regretted asking them to leave. He wanted the Hebrews back so that they could serve him. Pharaoh gathered his Egyptian army and decided to chase after the Hebrews to capture them. Pharaoh's army had 600 chariots! When the Hebrews made it to the Red Sea, they became trapped. Rocky areas were on either side of them; the Red Sea was in front of them; and the Egyptian army was behind them. What were they going to do?

The Hebrew people were very afraid and cried out to God. Moses said to them, "Don't be afraid. Be still. The Lord will fight for you!" The pillar of cloud that was leading the Hebrews moved and went behind them.

The Hebrews and the Egyptians were separated. The cloud provided light to the Hebrews and was a curtain of darkness to the Egyptians. Neither group approached each other that night. God directed Moses to lift up his walking stick, or rod, and hold it over the Red Sea. God caused a very strong wind to blow over the sea and made a dry pathway through the sea. The Hebrews were able to walk all the way across the dry land with the sea on both sides!

In the morning, as the Egyptians chased the Hebrews into the Red Sea, God made the wheels of their chariots fall off. This made it very difficult to drive! God wanted to confuse the Egyptian army. He told Moses to stretch out his hand over the Red Sea, and the waters returned. When Moses did this, the chariots, horsemen, and Pharaoh's army were destroyed.

In response to God's power, the Hebrews trusted in God and believed in His servant Moses. When they saw that they were saved, Moses and the Hebrews sang praises to God. Miriam, Moses' sister, led the women in singing praises to God. The Hebrews praised God because He did what they could not do—He provided a way of escape from and victory over the Egyptians.

VA 5A The Ten Commandments
Exodus 31:18–34:9, 29–33

In the third month after leaving Egypt, Moses and the children of Israel camped in the desert in front of Mount Sinai. This was a familiar area to Moses—Mount Sinai was where God had spoken to Moses from the burning bush. Now God was going to speak to Moses again but in front of the children of Israel.

God told Moses to meet Him on the mountain. God's chosen people needed rules to guide them, both in the desert and when they entered the Promised Land. Why? The children of Israel had seen the Egyptians worshipping false gods and doing many sinful things. God wanted to show them the best way to live.

Moses went up the mountain and for 40 days God spoke with Moses there. God carved the rules into tablets of stone with His finger.

The people grew restless during the 40 days that Moses was gone. They said, "Who knows what's happened to Moses?" So they decided to take charge and do something that they had seen the Egyptians do. God knew what they were doing and He told Moses the people were doing wrong. Moses started

back down Mount Sinai toward the Israelite camp and, when he was almost there, he heard the people shouting. Their shouts didn't sound like those of a battle, but rather like a party. As Moses got closer, he could see what was happening in the camp. His heart was very sad. The people had used gold to make an idol shaped like a cow and they were worshipping it. Moses was so angry that he threw the stone tablets to the ground and they broke.

The people knew that the idol was not a real god. They had chosen to turn away from worshipping the one true God, and they had made their own false god. They had to suffer a terrible plague as punishment for their sin.

Moses destroyed the idol and reestablished order in the camp. He went back to the mountain, and again the Lord carved the rules for the Israelites on stone tablets. This time when Moses returned to camp, the people were not worshipping an idol. They were waiting for the rules the Lord had written for them.

The rules the Lord gave the Israelites several thousand years ago are still good for us to follow today.

© *Bible* Grade 2

VA 6A Miriam and Aaron Learn Respect

Numbers 12

During their time in the wilderness with the children of Israel, Miriam and Aaron began to complain about their brother, Moses. How sad it was for Moses' own family members to turn against him! They didn't like his choice of a wife, and they were jealous of him getting all the attention from the children of Israel. Miriam and Aaron wanted people to think that they heard from God, too!

Miriam and Aaron said, "The Lord hasn't only spoken through Moses. He has spoken through us, too!" Aaron had, after all, been used by God to help Moses speak to the children of Israel and Pharaoh, and Miriam had led the women in praises to God after God miraculously parted the Red Sea. Both Miriam and Aaron wanted to be recognized and given credit for what they had done.

Moses was a very humble man as shown by his obedience to God during the time in the wilderness. He was God's chosen leader.

When Miriam and Aaron spoke out against Moses, the Lord heard them. He immediately called Miriam, Aaron, and Moses to come out and meet Him. The Lord appeared to them as a pillar of cloud, and He spoke directly to Miriam and Aaron saying, "Listen to My words. I speak to the prophets in dreams, but I speak directly to my servant Moses. He is a faithful servant. Why weren't you afraid to speak out against him? I am angry that you have not respected Moses or his authority."

Miriam and Aaron should have been afraid to speak out against Moses, God's servant. Moses didn't lead because he wanted attention; he led because God called him to lead. Miriam and Aaron should have been content with that. Instead, they were jealous.

The Lord departed after speaking to them, and after the pillar of cloud moved away, Miriam suddenly became sick. Her skin turned white and flaky. She had a horrible disease called *leprosy*! Aaron saw this and immediately said to Moses, "Moses, please forgive us for the sin we have committed!"

Moses prayed to the Lord and asked that Miriam be healed. Miriam was restored to good health, and both she and Aaron had learned an important lesson about respecting authority—they were to follow directions of the person in charge without being jealous and without complaining.

© Bible Grade 2

353

VA 7A Joshua Leads Israel

Numbers 13:1–14:38, 27:15–23; Joshua 1:1–9; Deuteronomy 34:1–6; Hebrews 9:4

After Miriam and Aaron learned to respect the leadership of Moses, 12 Israelite men were sent to spy out the land of Canaan, the land God had promised to the children of Israel. Two of the spies were Moses' helper Joshua and Caleb. Joshua and Caleb gave a good report about what they had seen. They were confident that God would help the children of Israel possess the land. However, the adult Israelites didn't believe the good report. They didn't believe God's promise. Because of their unbelief, God would not allow the adult Israelites to cross into the Promised Land. All the Israelites would spend 40 years wandering in the desert until the last one of the unbelieving adults died. Of that whole group, only Joshua, Caleb, and the children, grandchildren, and great-grandchildren of the unbelieving Israelites would be allowed to enter the Promised Land.

At the end of the 40 years wandering in the desert, Moses was 120 years old. He was about to die. Moses asked God to choose a new leader for the Israelites, someone who could lead the people into the Promised Land. When God had made His choice, He told Moses to lay his hands on Joshua, Moses' helper, in the presence of the people and the priest Eleazar. Joshua became the new Israelite leader. Joshua was filled with God's Spirit and God's wisdom.

After Moses died, God spoke to Joshua and told him it was time to prepare the Israelites to cross the Jordan River into the land of Canaan, the land that was to become the country of Israel. God declared that everywhere Joshua

walked would become the Israelites' homeland. The Israelites would have to drive out or kill the wicked people who lived there, but God also said that He would be with Joshua the same way He had been with Moses. No enemies would be able to defeat the Israelites. Joshua was encouraged to be strong and courageous because God would be helping him lead the Israelites.

God also told Joshua and the children of Israel to be sure they obeyed the Book of the Law, laws that Moses had received from God that had been written down in a book. God's command to study and read the Book of the Law was very serious and very important. If Joshua and the Israelites obeyed the Book of the Law, they would have no reason to be afraid of their enemies because God would be with them everywhere they went. They could look forward to a safe and prosperous life in the Promised Land.

Joshua and all the people agreed. So, they crossed the Jordan River into Canaan, the Promised Land, carrying a very special gold-covered box called *the ark of the covenant*. It contained the Ten Commandments, a jar of manna, and the staff of Aaron, Moses' brother. The Israelites were now in their promised homeland.

© *Bible* Grade 2

353

VA 8A Joshua Obeys God

Joshua 6

After crossing the Jordan River and entering the Promised Land, the Israelites came to the city of Jericho. Jericho was an old, important city. Armies would sometimes try to invade Jericho. Because of this, the people of Jericho built walls around their city to protect themselves against these invaders. At least one of the walls was tall and thick. When the people of Jericho heard that the Israelites were coming to take the city, they tightly closed every gate in the tall, wide wall. They may have felt safe doing this, thinking that no one could enter.

God told Joshua that He would help the Israelites defeat the people of Jericho in battle. God's directions to Joshua were very specific and very simple. The Israelite men were to carry their weapons while marching around the city. For six days, they would march around only once each day. Then on the seventh day they were to march seven times around the city. The Israelites were not allowed to talk at all while they walked around the wall. The only time they could use their voice was on the seventh day after they heard seven priests blow seven horns, or trumpets, on the seventh trip around the walled city. They also had to wait for Joshua to give the command to shout. If they followed God's directions exactly, the city of Jericho would be theirs.

During the first six days, the Israelites marched around the city only one time each day. The priests did blow their horns, but no one made a sound with his voice. The order for marching around the city was very special, too. Some of

the armed soldiers were to march in front of the priests as the front armed guard. The ark of the covenant, a gold-covered box that the Israelites brought with them, was to be carried behind the priests with the horns. The ark held a few special things, including the Ten Commandments received by Moses at Mount Sinai. Other soldiers followed the ark of the covenant with their weapons. They were called *the rear guard.*

The people in Jericho probably thought the Israelites were crazy! Their city had withstood attacks from huge armies. Perhaps they looked out their windows and laughed at the people of God.

On the seventh day, the Israelites rose early to march around the wall seven times. After the Israelites had obeyed every command, Joshua gave the order for the people to shout as loud as they could. Wow, what a noise that must have been! At that very moment, the huge, strong wall surrounding Jericho rumbled and shook! Then the wall began to crack and crumble! Suddenly, it came falling down! The Israelites went in and captured the city. The victory belonged to the Lord!

VA 9A Joshua Follows God

Joshua 23–24

Listening to God and following Joshua's leadership helped the Israelites take over the Promised Land of Canaan. They settled there and began to build more farms and homes. Life was good! However, Joshua knew that during times of peace and comfort, the Israelites might start to forget about God. Joshua was now an old man, but he held a special meeting for all the important leaders in Israel. He held the meeting in a place called *Shechem*.

At the meeting, Joshua reminded the leaders about God's faithfulness to them as they took possession of the land. He also told them that, with God's help, they would be able to have even more of the land within their assigned borders as long as they followed God wholeheartedly. Joshua reminded the Israelites that if they chose to worship the false gods of the people who lived around them, they would be breaking their special promise to God. Then they would not be able to keep all of the land that God had given to them.

God told Joshua not to let the Israelites forget about their family's history. Joshua said, "This is what the Lord, the God of Israel, says, 'Abraham, your forefather, and his son Isaac first owned this land. Isaac's son Jacob and all the Israelites left this land to go to Egypt during a famine, a time when there was little food. Your own fathers followed Moses as he led them out of Egypt. You saw with your own eyes what I did to the Egyptians and how I have delivered you time and time again. Remember how you wandered in the desert for 40 years because you didn't trust and follow Me!'"

Joshua continued, "God has helped you to win every battle in this land. However, the only way you can stay in this land is to remain completely obedient to God and His laws. If you pay attention to the people around you, you will stop following God's laws. Make up your minds now, and decide whether or not you are going to keep worshipping the one, true God even after I die. As for me and my family, we will serve the Lord."

The Israelites answered, "We will never turn away from the Lord and serve false gods. We know that it was the Lord our God Himself who brought us out of Egypt where we were slaves. It was the Lord who protected us on our journey, and it was the Lord who helped us take over this land. We will serve the Lord because He is our God."

Joshua warned the Israelites that it would be dangerous to say they would serve the Lord and then worship and serve false gods. But, the people said again, even more clearly, that they would serve the one, true God. In doing this, the people were making a special type of promise to God. Joshua wrote down in the Book of the Law their promise and how they should obey God. He then set up a special stone under a tree there in Shechem. The stone was to be a reminder of this promise. Sometime after the people had returned to their own towns, Joshua died. He had lived for 110 years, and he had faithfully and wholeheartedly followed God all his life.

© *Bible* Grade 2

353

VA 10A Ruth Is Loyal

Ruth 1

During the time of a terrible famine, a man named *Elimelech*, his wife *Naomi*, and their two sons lived in the town of Bethlehem in Israel. Because of the famine, Elimelech's family did not have enough to eat, so Elimelech moved his family to the country of Moab. After they moved to Moab, Elimelech died.

Each of Naomi's two sons married a woman from Moab. One woman was named *Orpah* and the other was named *Ruth*. Ten years later, both of Naomi's sons died. The husbands of all three women were now dead, making Naomi, Orpah, and Ruth widows. The women were very sad.

Eventually, Naomi heard good news from her own country. The famine was over, and she could return to Bethlehem and live near her relatives. Both Ruth and Orpah prepared to go with Naomi to Bethlehem.

Naomi appreciated the kindness shown by both women, but she encouraged them to stay in their own country of Moab and live with their own mothers. Naomi hoped that they would each find a kind man to marry. Orpah and

Ruth both wanted to go with Naomi. However, Naomi encouraged them to think carefully about their decisions. If they came with her to Bethlehem, they might not be able to marry again, since they would be strangers in the land.

Orpah realized that what Naomi was saying could very well be true. So, sadly and with many tears she said good-bye to her mother-in-law. Orpah returned to her people and to their false gods. Ruth, however, was loyal and loved her mother-in-law so much that she was willing to give up any hope of marrying again. Her love and care for Naomi resulted in a very special pledge. Ruth told Naomi, "Please do not ask me to leave you, or to turn back from following you; for wherever you go, I will go; and wherever you sleep, I will sleep. Your people will be my people, and your God, my God. Where you die, I will die, and there will I be buried." Ruth then traveled with Naomi to Bethlehem.

© *Bible Grade 2*

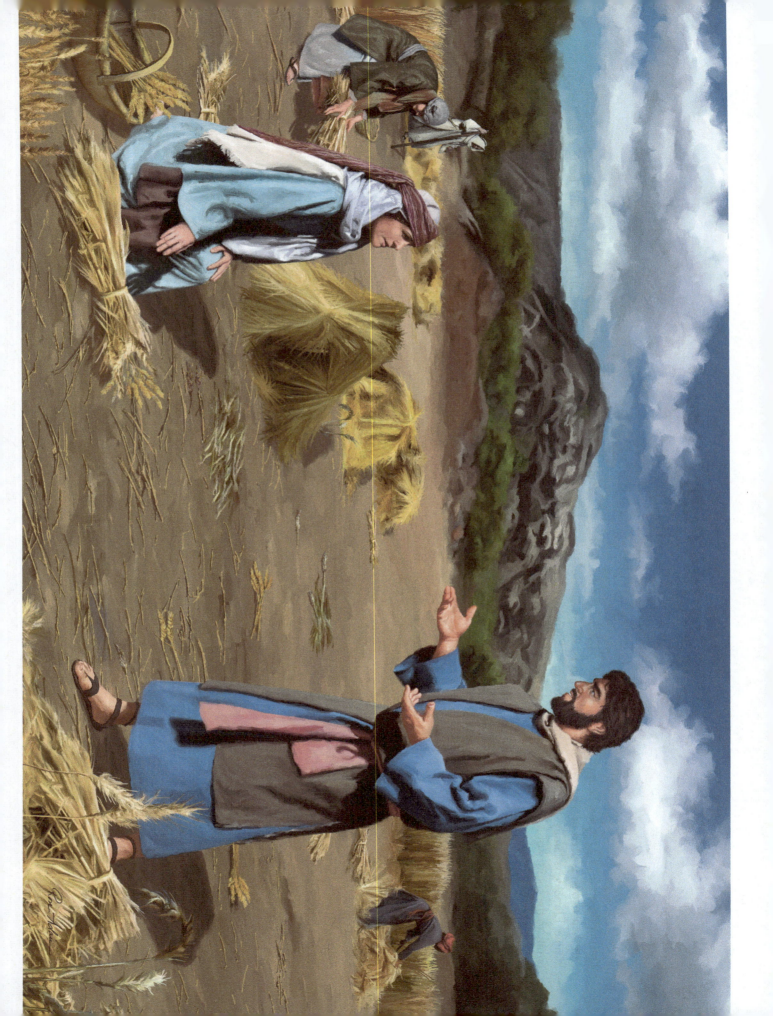

VA 11A Ruth Serves with Love

Ruth 2–4

When Naomi and Ruth arrived in Bethlehem, Naomi was recognized by some of the townspeople. They greeted her and asked about her husband and sons. Naomi answered sadly that both her husband and two sons had died in Moab, but that she had brought one of her daughters-in-law with her from that country.

Because Naomi and Ruth were widows, they had no one to care for them. God's law allowed widows to get enough to eat by gleaning. *Gleaning was picking up any leftover stalks or stems with grain left on them after the harvesters had gone through the fields cutting down the stalks of ripened grain.* Gleaning was hard work, but Ruth chose to glean to gather enough food for both herself and Naomi.

God was watching over Ruth. She went to glean in a field belonging to a man named *Boaz.* He was a relative of Naomi's late husband, Elimelech. When Boaz first saw Ruth out in the field gleaning grain, he didn't know who she was. One of the harvest workers told Boaz that Ruth was the widow of one of Naomi's sons, and that she was faithfully taking care of Naomi. Boaz was impressed that Ruth served Naomi with love. He felt responsible to help because he was a relative.

Boaz told Ruth not to go into any other farmer's fields, but to stay in his field and eat with his workers. Ruth was allowed to eat all that she wanted and even take some grain home to Naomi. Boaz also instructed his workers to leave extra grain in the fields for Ruth and not to hurt her in any way.

Naomi heard about the kind man who had befriended Ruth. Naomi recognized that Boaz was a relative of Elimelech and that Boaz could become a kinsman-redeemer. *A kinsman-redeemer was a man who was willing to marry and care for a widow of one of his family members.* Naomi told Ruth to go and see Boaz that night and ask for his protection. Ruth followed Naomi's instructions. Boaz was pleased with Ruth's respectful behavior. He told Ruth that he would marry her, unless a closer male relative wished to do so. Boaz worked out all the details needed to take Ruth as his wife. He loved her and kept her and Naomi safe for the rest of their lives.

Ruth and Boaz had a little boy named *Obed.* He grew up and became the grandfather of King David. Many, many years later, Jesus was born into the same family line.

© Bible Grade 2

383

VA 12A David Faces the Giant
1 Samuel 17

When Saul was the king of Israel, he was challenged to a battle by the Philistine army. Their fiercest warrior was named *Goliath*. Goliath was a nine-foot tall giant who was dressed in heavy metal armor. Goliath challenged the army of Israel every day for 40 days in a row. Each army set up camp on opposite hills, with only a valley to separate them. Goliath would shout across this valley to the Israelites, daring them to send someone to fight him. Goliath said that if someone were to defeat him, there would be no battle between the armies, and the Philistines would become the servants of the Israelites. But, if Goliath were to win, the Israelites would have to serve the Philistines. No one had the courage to take on Goliath!

One day, a shepherd boy named *David* was sent to the Israelite army's camp by his father, *Jesse*. Jesse asked David to take food to David's three oldest brothers who were serving in the army. David arrived, ran out to where his brothers were, and greeted them. Just then, Goliath began shouting his challenge to the Israelites. David heard Goliath and watched the Israelites shake and go back to the camp in fear.

David told King Saul that he believed he could defeat Goliath. "Why do you think you can win against Goliath?" asked King Saul. David explained, "As a boy, I fought and killed a lion and a bear as they were attacking my father's sheep. I was able to do these things because God helped me. I believe He will help me fight Goliath as well."

King Saul was impressed by what David said and had him put on the king's armor and take the king's sword to fight Goliath. The armor was heavy. David realized that he would have no time to practice fighting in armor, so he took it off. Instead, David said, "King Saul, I will take only my sling and five smooth stones to fight Goliath."

As David faced the giant, Goliath was shocked to discover that David was not a man trained for war, but just a boy. "What is this you send to fight me?" shouted Goliath to the Israelites. David spoke, "Goliath, you come against me with a sword, a spear, and a javelin, but I come against you in the name of the God of Israel, whom you have defied. I will defeat you today because this battle is the Lord's battle. He will cause Israel to win."

With those words, David ran toward Goliath. He reached into his bag for a stone to load in his sling. Taking aim, he shot at Goliath. The stone struck Goliath's forehead, and Goliath fell facedown. Quickly, David ran to Goliath and used Goliath's own sword to cut off Goliath's head. With God's help, David had defeated the Philistine giant!

When the Philistines realized that Goliath, their champion, was dead, they ran away! The Israelite army chased them and completely defeated the Philistines.

© *Bible* Grade 2

VA 13A David Leads in Thanksgiving

1 Chronicles 15:1–16:36

After the death of King Saul, David became the new king of Israel. King David loved and served the Lord with all his heart. He knew how important it was for God's people to be faithful and thankful.

King David wanted a holy place to keep the ark of the covenant, the gold-covered box that the Israelites had brought with them when they entered the Promised Land. The ark was a reminder of God's faithfulness and love for His people. So King David had a special tent made just for the ark of the covenant. Then he called upon Levites, men from the family of Aaron, Moses' brother. David gave certain Levites the task of moving the ark to the tent. They carried the ark with poles on their shoulders. This was the way that God had told Moses the ark should always be carried. The Levites who were not carrying the ark played music on stringed instruments, cymbals, and horns. Other Levites formed a choir and sang joyful songs to the Lord.

King David called the people in the country together in Jerusalem to watch the arrival of the ark. What a joyful parade it was! King David himself danced along with the music and the singing of the choirs. He and all the Levites wore special clothing in honor of the arrival of the ark of the covenant.

Once the ark was placed in its special tent, King David gave a loaf of bread, a piece of meat, and a cake of raisins to each Israelite man and woman. Then the king called for his chief musician, Asaph, to write music for the poem of thanksgiving that King David had written. This is the first part of the song:

Give thanks to the Lord, call on His name,
Let everyone know what He has done.
Sing to Him, sing praises to Him.
Tell everyone about the wonderful things that God has done.

The celebration and thanksgiving did not end that day. King David chose some of the Levites to serve at the tent where the ark was kept. These men were to continue to say prayers of praise and thanksgiving to God, blowing their trumpets regularly to remind the people of the great things that God had done.

© Bible Grade 2

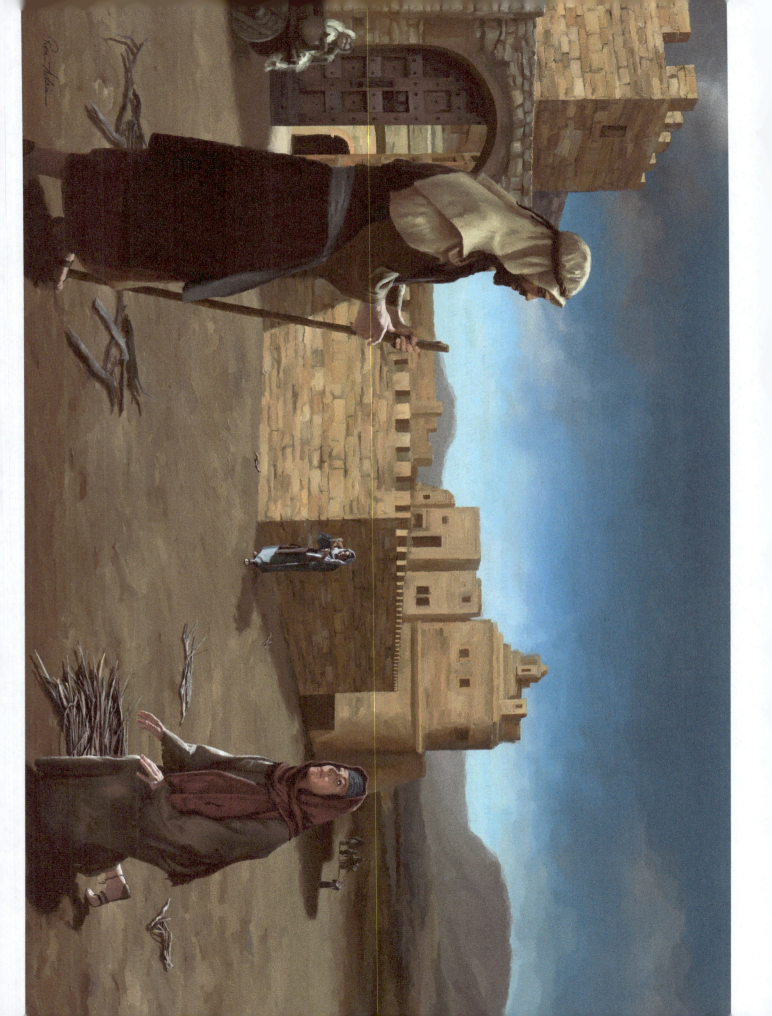

VA 14A Elijah Trusts God

1 Kings 17:1–16

Elijah was a prophet of God. A true prophet is someone who has special knowledge from God. Elijah lived during the time of the most wicked king in Israel. The king was named *Ahab*. Ahab and his wife convinced many Israelites to stop worshipping God by telling them it was all right to worship other gods, including one false god named *Baal*. Elijah knew this was wrong, and God used him to tell all of the Israelites, including King Ahab, that they needed to stop breaking God's commands and start obeying the one, true God again.

One day, Elijah told Ahab, "There will be no more rain in Israel for the next few years." This meant that Israel would experience a terrible drought, a long time period of little to no rain or dew. The rivers would dry up and no food would grow. It would be a terrible time. Elijah knew that God had warned His people many years before that He would not send rain if they followed other gods. Elijah trusted God to do just what He said.

God knew that Ahab would be angry when he heard Elijah's news. So God told Elijah to flee to a very special hiding place where Ahab would not be able to find Elijah. While Elijah was hiding in the valley near the Jordan River, God sent ravens to feed him bread and meat every morning and evening. Elijah drank from the brook Cherith. God provided what Elijah needed, and Elijah trusted Him to do so.

Eventually, the brook Cherith dried up because of the drought; so God sent Elijah to the home of a widow living in a city of Sidon. Elijah went to the city and found the widow busy gathering sticks to build a fire for cooking. Elijah asked the widow for a little drink of water and a small piece of bread to eat. The widow responded, "Sir, I only have enough flour and oil to make one last meal for myself and my son. After that, we will probably starve because there isn't any food available anywhere."

Elijah knew from his experience with the ravens that God could and would provide enough food. So Elijah said to the widow, "Please make me a little cake of bread to eat first. Then go and prepare the meal for you and your son just as you were planning to do. The Lord will not let your flour bin or your oil jar become empty until the drought has ended."

The widow did just as Elijah asked, and as the Lord promised, she and her son always had enough food. This was a miracle! There were no crops to make flour, but God kept the flour bin and oil jar full. Elijah stayed with the widow until God told him to return and talk with King Ahab.

© *Bible Grade 2*

VA 15A Elijah Is Bold
1 Kings 18:1–45

After three years of drought, God told the prophet Elijah to go speak with King Ahab. So, Elijah set off to do just as the Lord had said. When Elijah met with King Ahab, the king blamed the drought on Elijah and called Elijah a troublemaker. Elijah reminded King Ahab that Ahab was the real troublemaker in Israel because he had stopped worshipping God. King Ahab worshipped an idol named *Baal*. Not only that, King Ahab had encouraged the Israelites to worship idols, too. The disobedience of King Ahab and the people had caused the drought to occur.

As Elijah was talking to King Ahab, he told Ahab to invite the Israelites and the prophets of Baal to meet him on Mount Carmel to prove who was really God—the Lord God or Baal. When the day of the challenge arrived, Elijah and 450 prophets of Baal gathered on Mount Carmel. Elijah shouted to the people, "Make up your minds! If the Lord is God, worship Him!" Elijah boldly challenged the prophets of Baal to see if they could prove that Baal was greater than the Lord God.

Elijah told the prophets of Baal to build an altar to their god. Elijah told them to prepare it with an animal offering and wood for the fire, but not to light the fire. The prophets of Baal prepared their altar and called on the name of their god to start a fire on the altar. They jumped up and down

and danced around their altar, but no fire came. Around noon, Elijah began asking if their god was asleep. Elijah said, "Maybe Baal can't hear you because he's thinking about something else. Shout louder!" The prophets shouted louder, but nothing happened.

When evening came, Elijah gathered the people, and he built an altar to the Lord. He used twelve stones. He dug a trench around the altar, piled wood on it, and placed the animal offering on top. Finally, water from four waterpots was poured over the altar, not just one time, but three times!

Elijah prayed that God would show the Israelites that he was a true prophet of God and that they would worship the Lord God. Instantly, the Lord God answered with fire from heaven and burned up the offering, the wood, the stones, the dirt, and all of the water! The people realized immediately that the Lord was truly God, and they fell facedown, saying repeatedly, "The Lord, He is God!"

The prophets of Baal were taken to the Brook of Kishon and put to death. They no longer would lead the people of Israel away from the Lord God. Soon afterward, it started to rain. The drought was over.

© *Bible* Grade 2

371

VA 16A Nehemiah Leads
Nehemiah 1–3

Long after Elijah was taken into heaven by a whirlwind, the armies of Babylonia captured most of the Israelites from the land of Judah and took them from their homeland. Nehemiah was one of the captured Israelites. He became the cupbearer to King Artaxerxes in Persia. Nehemiah's job at the king's palace was very important because he helped keep King Artaxerxes safe by sampling everything the king drank. One day the king noticed that Nehemiah seemed very sad. Nehemiah told the king about the destruction of the city of Jerusalem in Judah. The walls were broken down and the gates were burned. There was no protection for the city. Nehemiah also shared with the king his desire to rebuild this special city.

With the king's permission and help, Nehemiah traveled to Jerusalem. King Artaxerxes sent soldiers along to protect Nehemiah. The king had given Nehemiah papers ordering the governors in the land to allow safe passage through their land so that Nehemiah could get to Jerusalem. King Artaxerxes even ordered that the keeper of the king's forest provide timber to rebuild the city.

Once Nehemiah made it to Jerusalem, he inspected the gates and the city wall at night with a few other men. Nehemiah was very sad to see how much of the city had been destroyed. None of the leaders in the area knew exactly what he was up to. Finally, after a few days, he explained to the Israelites living in and around the city that God had called him to lead in rebuilding the walls around Jerusalem. Nehemiah was glad when he saw that his people liked the idea of making Jerusalem a strong city again.

For the best defense of the city, it was necessary to repair all the gates of the city at the same time as the walls. Different teams of workers began to complete each of the gates and the sections of the wall between the gates. Everybody had a job to do.

Eliashib, the high priest, and his team of priests worked together on the Sheep Gate and the north part of the wall. The work on the west wall and the Valley Gate was completed by many workers, including some who were sons of Jerusalem district leaders. Southern district leaders and their sons worked on the sections of the south wall and its gates. The Levites, other leaders, goldsmiths, and merchants worked on the east section of the wall.

As a godly leader, Nehemiah knew that no one would be able to stop the work as long as the people continued to cooperate and trust God. However, at one point, Sanballat and Tobiah, men from neighboring areas, mocked Nehemiah because they hated him for what he was doing. They even accused Nehemiah of rebelling against the king. Nehemiah knew these men and their soldiers were trying to scare the people and delay the work. So Nehemiah continued to trust God as the project got under way, saying, "God will cause us to succeed. As God's servants, we will rebuild the walls." Nehemiah did not give up.

© Bible Grade 2

373

VA 17A Jesus Is Born

Luke 1:26–38, 2:1–20; Matthew 1:18–2:12

Thousands of years after God first promised to send the Savior, the time came for the Savior to make His entrance into the world. God sent the angel Gabriel to tell Mary, a young Israelite woman, that she had been chosen to be the mother of the promised Savior. Becoming a mother at this time seemed impossible to Mary, but Gabriel told her that God would do the impossible to bring about His plan of salvation. Mary felt honored to have been chosen by God to take part in His plan.

Then in a dream, an angel spoke to Joseph, the man chosen to be Jesus' earthly father. Joseph was instructed to name the child *Jesus* because He would bring forgiveness of sins to His people.

God planned for His Son to be born in Bethlehem, the city of David. The Roman emperor, Caesar Augustus, made a law that everyone had to return to the town where his family line began in order to be counted. Joseph was a descendant of King David, so he and Mary packed up and made the long journey to Bethlehem together. When they arrived in Bethlehem, there were no rooms available at the inn. Joseph and Mary ended up staying in a stable. That night, Jesus was born. Mary wrapped the precious baby in soft strips of cloth and made a bed for Him in a manger, a box used to hold hay for animals to eat.

Also that night, God sent an angel to announce the good news of the birth of His Son to some shepherds who were taking care of their sheep. At first, the shepherds were terrified, but the angel told them not to be afraid. He had good news for them. The Savior had come at last! The angel told the shepherds to go to Bethlehem, where they would find the baby wrapped in soft cloths and lying in a manger.

Suddenly, the whole sky was filled with angels! The angels praised God, saying:
Glory to God in the highest,
And peace on earth to all people!

After the angels left, the shepherds decided to go to Bethlehem. They found Jesus there, just as the angel had said. As the shepherds went back to their fields, they praised God and told everyone what they had heard and seen.

God also announced the birth of His Son by placing a special star in the sky. Wise men from a faraway country saw the star and traveled to Jerusalem. They knew that this star announced the birth of a king, so they asked King Herod where the child could be found. King Herod talked to his counselors and told the wise men to go to Bethlehem. King Herod asked the wise men to send word of where the child could be found, saying that he wanted to worship the young child. But, King Herod was evil and lied. He had no intention of worshipping Jesus.

The star that the wise men had seen in the east led the way to the house where Joseph, Mary, and the young child Jesus lived. The wise men gave the family gifts of gold, frankincense, and myrrh. Then God used a dream to warn the wise men not to return to evil King Herod, so they returned to their country a different way.

Jesus was born—the Messiah, the promised Savior of the world.

© *Bible* Grade 2

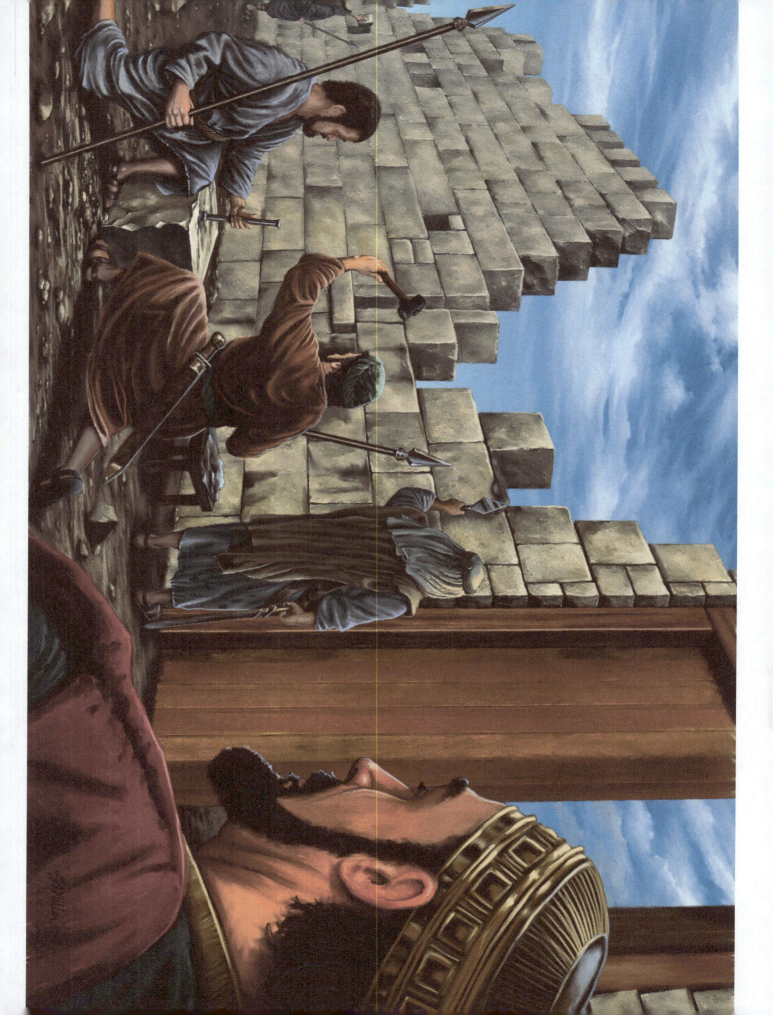

VA 18A Nehemiah Stands Firm
Nehemiah 4:1–7:5, 8:1–9:38

Nehemiah continued to direct the workers in rebuilding the wall of Jerusalem. Sanballat and Tobiah came back again to make fun of Nehemiah and the workers. When the entire wall was joined together up to half its height, Sanballat, Tobiah, and other enemy leaders became very angry. They believed that if Jerusalem were rebuilt, it would threaten the importance of their own cities. So they planned to attack Jerusalem and kill the people. Nehemiah prayed to God for strength and protection. He encouraged the Israelites by saying, "Don't be afraid of them. Remember God. He is great and awesome. Fight for your brothers, your sons, your daughters, your wives, and your houses." From then on, each person worked with one hand and held weapons—spears, shields, or bows and arrows—in the other. They slept in the city at night, taking turns guarding the city.

Not only did Nehemiah stand firm in his decision to rebuild the wall and see that it was finished, but he also dealt with unfair treatment by others. He called together the nobles and leaders of the Israelites who had been taking advantage of their own people. He directed the leaders to return the land, olive groves, and houses that they had taken from the people. And, he ordered them to repay some of the money, food, and drink. This would allow everyone to have what they needed so they could complete the work on the wall. As an example to others, Nehemiah lived simply, not building up great wealth for himself.

By this time, the wall was almost finished. Sanballat came back again with Tobiah and others to try to stop Nehemiah. Sanballat asked Nehemiah to

leave Jerusalem to meet with him. Nehemiah refused, knowing that his enemies meant to do him harm. But that didn't stop Sanballat! He kept insisting that Nehemiah come, but Nehemiah kept saying no. After the fifth time, Sanballat sent Nehemiah a letter by special delivery. Almost everything Sanballat had written in the letter was a lie about Nehemiah. During all this time, Nehemiah continued to pray and ask God to strengthen the Israelites so they could stand against their enemies.

Sanballat and Tobiah then hired a man to try to trick Nehemiah. The man told Nehemiah, "I've heard that some men are coming at night to kill you. Let's go hide in the temple." Nehemiah answered boldly, "Do you think I would run away from the enemy? No! I will not go in there!" If Nehemiah had listened to this man and hidden, Nehemiah's enemies would have called Nehemiah *a coward*. Then, they would have tried to convince the people to stop working on the wall.

The wall was quickly being built. Nehemiah was glad he had stood firm and trusted in God's protection. He was glad he had stood against Sanballat and the rest of the crowd of enemies. He gave God all the praise and thanks because God had helped the Israelites and Nehemiah to finish the task. Amazingly, after 52 days of working from morning until evening, the wall was completed! Jerusalem was once again a protected city. Even the people who lived outside the city realized that God had helped the Israelites complete the task. Nehemiah and the Israelites thanked and worshipped God. They celebrated with a special feast and made a new covenant with God.

© *Bible Grade 2*

377

VA 19A Esther Listens to Wise Advice

Esther 1–2

Many of the Jews who had been taken captive returned to Jerusalem, but others chose to stay in Babylonia. Esther, a young Jewish woman, grew up in the home of her older relative Mordecai, because her parents had died when she was a young girl. Esther respected Mordecai as she would have respected her own father. One day news came to the city of Susa in Babylonia where they both lived, that King Ahasuerus was searching for a new queen.

As the king's servants searched different cities to find a beautiful woman who might become the next queen, they immediately noticed Esther, who was beautiful. They brought her to the king's palace to wait and see if the king would choose her as the new queen. However, before she went to the palace, Mordecai told her not to tell anyone about her family background or the fact that she was a Jew. Ordinarily, this information could be known by anyone, but Mordecai's advice later proved to be very important. Esther was very careful to do everything that Mordecai told her.

About one year later, Esther was to appear before King Ahasuerus for the first time. She listened carefully to the advice of a man named *Hegai*—the king's servant—so that she would be ready to meet the king on her special day. The king was so amazed at Esther's beauty that he wasted no time in crowning her queen and holding a feast in her honor.

Later, Mordecai was sitting near the king's gate and happened to hear two guards making plans to kill King Ahasuerus. Mordecai sent a message to Queen Esther telling her to notify the king of this evil plan. She did. The plan was stopped and Mordecai was written about in the king's record book as having done a good deed to help save the king's life.

© Bible Grade 2

VA 20A Esther Risks Her Life
Esther 3–5

King Ahasuerus had many advisers helping him to manage his kingdom. The most powerful adviser was Haman. Haman was proud and selfish. He had such a powerful position that every citizen had to bow down as Haman walked by. Each time he walked near the king's gate, Haman noticed that one man never bowed down. This was Mordecai, Queen Esther's relative. Mordecai's refusal to bow down upset Haman very much because he saw it as rebellious and disrespectful.

One day, Haman discovered Mordecai was Jewish and that Jewish people bowed only to God. Growing more and more angry at Mordecai's refusal to bow to him, Haman decided that he would punish all of the Jews.

Haman did not have the power to make laws, so he went to King Ahasuerus to ask for permission to kill all of the Jews. Haman told the king that the Jewish people did not respect the king's laws. The Jewish people did respect the king, but Haman tricked the king into going along with the evil plan. King Ahasuerus gave Haman his signet ring, a special ring that had an engraved design and could be stamped into wax. With this ring, Haman could stamp the wax and make the evil plan into law. A legal paper that was stamped with the king's signet ring could never be changed. Haman quickly had the law copied and delivered to every part of the kingdom.

When Mordecai discovered what Haman was planning, he dressed in sackcloth, a rough cloth, and covered himself with ashes. This was a usual way of showing sadness at that time. Esther's servants told her what Mordecai was doing. She sent a servant to find out what was wrong. The servant told Esther that Mordecai was extremely sad because all of the Jews would be killed. The servant showed Esther a copy of the law Mordecai had sent to her.

Esther could hardly believe the news. She sent her servant back to Mordecai to tell him that she couldn't do anything to help. If she went to the king without being invited by him, and if he did not hold out his gold scepter to her, she would be killed.

The servant returned to Queen Esther with a message from Mordecai, "You will die anyway. If you remain silent, you may miss the privilege to do what God wants you to do. God has placed you where you are for such a time as this."

Esther thought about Mordecai's words. She decided to unselfishly risk her life. She asked Mordecai, all the Jews of the city, and her servants to fast with her—to not eat—for three days. After that, she would try to speak to the king, even if it meant her death.

After the third day, Esther went to the royal hall. As she stood near the entrance, the king noticed her and held out his gold scepter. Esther was relieved that the king invited her to speak with him. She invited the king and Haman to come to a special banquet. At the banquet, the king wondered if Esther had a request. Esther simply requested that he and Haman come to another banquet the following day.

After the king accepted Esther's request, Haman left the first banquet with a happy heart. He saw Mordecai at the king's gate, and Mordecai still refused to bow to Haman. Haman was very furious, and he ordered gallows to be built on which to hang Mordecai.

© Bible Grade 2

VA 21A Job Is Patient

Job 1–2, 4–25, 42

Long ago, a man named *Job* lived in a land called *Uz*. Job was a good man who loved God, prayed for his family, and did his best to stay away from sin or any type of evil. He had seven sons and three daughters, as well as large herds of sheep and camels, hundreds of oxen and donkeys, and many servants to care for all of his possessions. Everyone thought that Job was the greatest man in the land.

One day, the angels came to stand before God, and Satan came with them. God asked Satan two questions. In His first question, God asked Satan where he had been. Satan replied that he had been roaming around the earth. In the second question, God asked Satan if he had ever seen a man as loyal to God as Job. Satan replied that Job was loyal to God only because God had blessed him, but Job would turn against God if God took away all of Job's possessions. So God told Satan he could do what he wanted with any of Job's possessions, but could not take his life.

First, Satan took away all of Job's animals and his servants. Then Satan stirred up a fierce storm that killed Job's children. Finally, Satan caused Job's skin to be covered with painful sores from the top of his head to the soles of his feet. As he sat in the ashes, Job tried to relieve the pain of his sores by scraping them with a piece of broken pottery. He was utterly miserable.

But even with these tragedies, Job's loyalty to God didn't waver. Job's wife told him he should say hateful words against God, but Job would not. Three of Job's friends told him that he must have sinned and that God was punishing him, but Job still didn't speak against the Lord. Job didn't understand why he was suffering, but he patiently refused to accuse God of any wrongdoing. Job was confident that even if he were to die, God would never leave him.

Job wanted to know why these tragic events were happening. Finally, God spoke to Job and his three friends. God told them that He was all-knowing and all-powerful, and they could never completely understand the reasons behind His actions.

Even though he had to wait a long time for God to help him, Job never gave up. He kept on believing and trusting in God. God rewarded Job for his loyalty and patience and restored everything Job had lost. In fact, God gave Job twice as many possessions as he had before. Instead of 7,000 sheep, Job had 14,000! Instead of 3,000 camels, Job had 6,000. Instead of 500 oxen and 500 donkeys, Job had 1,000 of each! God also gave Job another seven sons and three daughters. And Job lived another 140 years to enjoy them all.

© Bible Grade 2

383

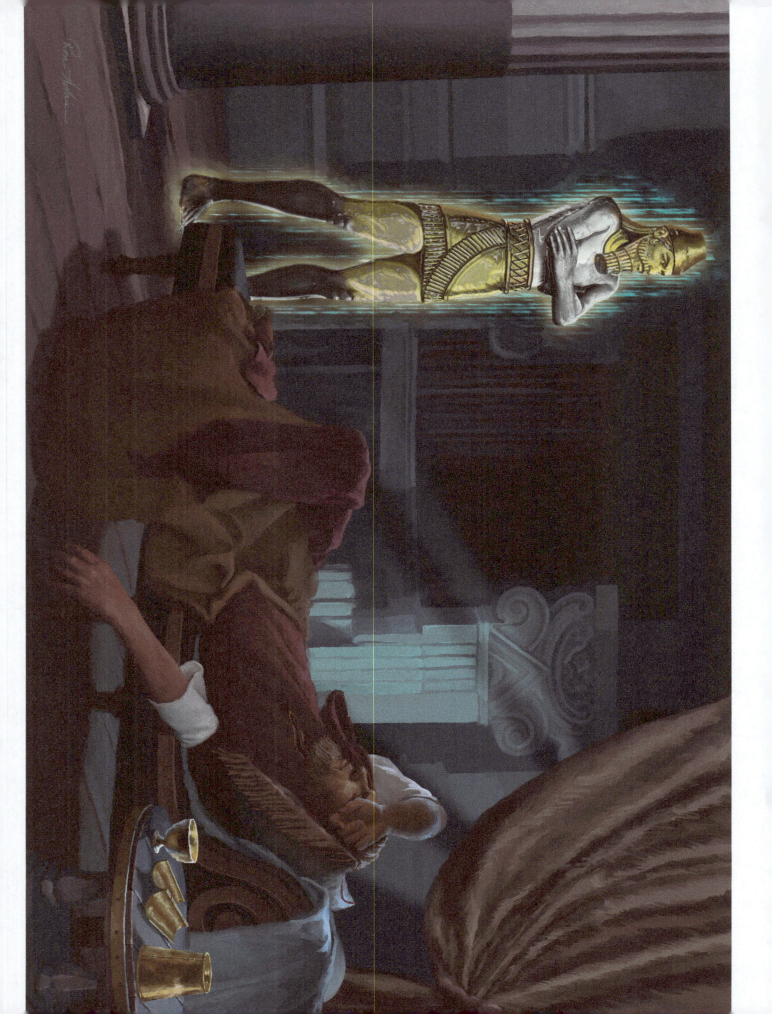

VA 22A King Nebuchadnezzar
Daniel 2

In the second year of his reign, King Nebuchadnezzar began to have trouble sleeping. One night he had a dream that really bothered him. King Nebuchadnezzar realized that this was not an ordinary dream, but one that had a meaningful message for him. He wanted to know what the dream meant.

He ordered wise men, who had been trained to reveal mysteries and solve the king's problems, to come at once. These men wanted to help the king, so they asked him what he had dreamed. Without telling them about his dream, Nebuchadnezzar insisted that they tell him what he had seen in his dream as well as what his dream meant. The men were shocked because no one had ever asked such a thing. They told the king that it was impossible for them to know what he had dreamed.

Nebuchadnezzar thought these wise men wanted to hear about his dream so that they could make up a meaning for it. Suddenly, he became very angry and ordered that every wise man in the kingdom be put to death. Because Daniel was also a wise man, he would have to be killed, even though he had never been asked to explain the king's dream.

When Daniel heard the news, he wondered why the king was so angry. The palace guard explained that the king's wise men could not tell the king what he had dreamed. Daniel boldly went before the king and asked for more

time so he could interpret the king's dream. Then Daniel went to his three friends, Shadrach, Meshach, and Abed-Nego, and asked them to pray that God would show him what the king dreamed and what it meant. Daniel and his friends were in the habit of praying. They were faithful to God. They all prayed to God for the answer to the king's demand.

That night, God responded to the faith of Daniel and his friends. God revealed both the king's dream and its meaning to Daniel. In the dream, King Nebuchadnezzar saw a large statue. The head was made of gold, its chest and arms were made of silver, its belly and thighs were made of bronze, its legs were made of iron, and its feet were part iron and part clay. King Nebuchadnezzar saw a stone that struck the statue and broke the feet into pieces. Then the entire statue of iron, clay, bronze, silver, and gold was crushed, and the wind carried the powdery pieces away so that no pieces were found. The stone that struck the image became a mountain and filled the earth. Daniel told King Nebuchadnezzar that the gold head of the statue represented King Nebuchadnezzar as ruler over the people, beasts, and birds. Other parts of the statue stood for other kingdoms that would come later, but God would set up a kingdom that would never be destroyed.

The king was amazed that God told Daniel everything the king wanted to know. King Nebuchadnezzar recognized that Daniel's God was the one, true God.

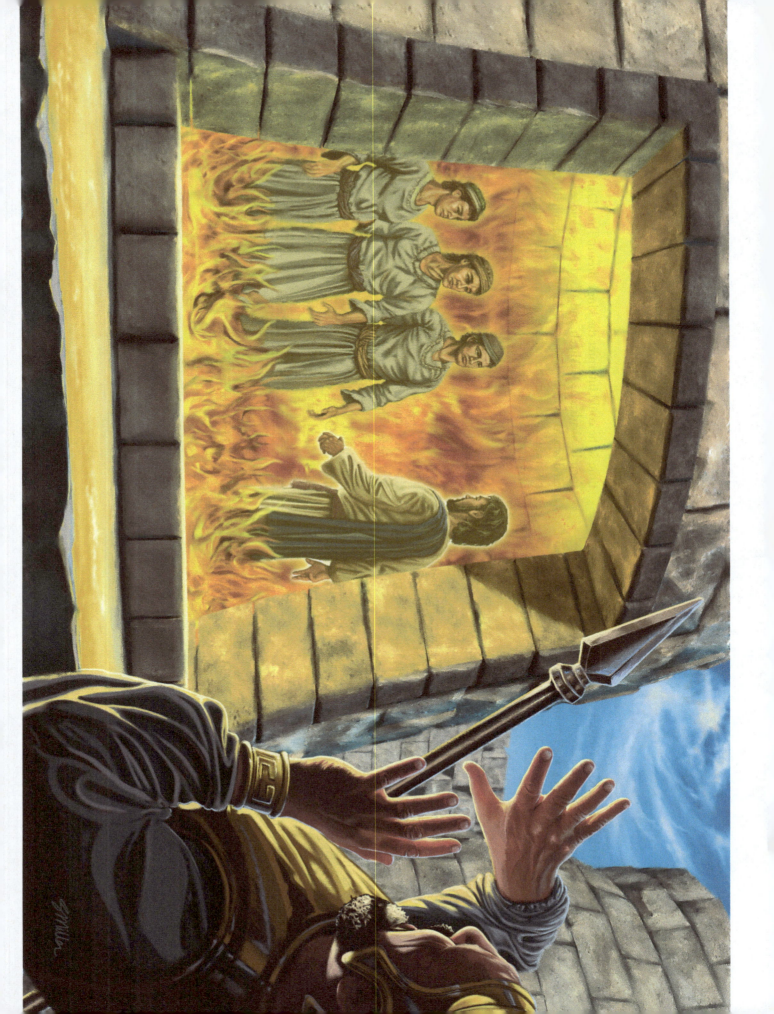

VA 23A The Fiery Furnace
Daniel 3

Shadrach, Meshach, and Abed-Nego completed their training to learn the Babylonian language. They began to serve and advise King Nebuchadnezzar. Even though they were in the foreign capital of Babylon, the three friends faithfully prayed and worshipped only the one, true God, not the false gods of the Babylonians.

One day, King Nebuchadnezzar had a huge golden statue built in his honor. He required everyone in Babylon to worship the statue whenever the king's musicians played a certain tune with the horn, flute, and stringed instruments. Because Shadrach, Meshach, and Abed-Nego worshipped God, they refused to bow down to a statue. Their refusal was noticed by others in the kingdom, and Shadrach, Meshach, and Abed-Nego were soon brought before the king. King Nebuchadnezzar was furious with them! He told the three young men that if they continued to disobey and would not bow down before the statue, they would be thrown into a blazing hot furnace. Shadrach, Meshach, and Abed-Nego refused to bow down and were confident of their faith in God's

love and power. They told the king that God would save them, even if they were thrown into the fiery furnace. Nebuchadnezzar angrily ordered that the furnace be heated seven times hotter. He had his guards grab Shadrach, Meshach, and Abed-Nego, tie them up, and throw them into the furnace! The fire was so hot that the guards who threw them into the furnace were killed by the fiery flames. It looked as if the young men would be burned alive, but God had not forgotten about them.

After a while, King Nebuchadnezzar looked into the furnace. There he saw a very strange sight. Instead of three young men in the furnace, he saw four men. All four men were alive and unharmed and walking around among the flames! The fourth man looked like the Son of God. The king was astonished and ordered that the young men come out of the furnace. Their clothes did not even smell like smoke! King Nebuchadnezzar praised the one, true God for delivering the three young men. He promoted Shadrach, Meshach, and Abed-Nego to more powerful positions in his kingdom.

© Bible Grade 2

VA 24A Daniel in the Lions' Den

Daniel 6

When King Darius was king of Babylonia, Daniel was quite an old man, but was one of the most powerful officials in the kingdom. Some of the other officials were jealous of Daniel's success. These jealous men looked for a way to get rid of Daniel, but because Daniel had done nothing wrong, the only thing these men could use against Daniel was his faithfulness in honoring God. The officials tricked King Darius into making a law that would be in place for 30 days. The law said that everyone had to pray to the king only. If anyone prayed to another person or a god, he or she would be thrown into a den filled with hungry lions!

Daniel was faithful to pray to God three times a day. He honored God by placing God first in his life. When Daniel prayed, he went to his upstairs room and opened a window that faced Jerusalem. Then he got down on his knees and prayed to God. Even though he knew about the law, Daniel did not change his habit of prayer. He boldly and confidently opened his window, thanked God, and asked for His help. The jealous officials watched Daniel praying through the window. They caught Daniel in the act of breaking

the law! They went straight to King Darius and demanded that Daniel be arrested and punished. Even though King Darius was very fond of Daniel, he could do nothing to help him because laws in those days were not able to be changed, even by the king. So King Darius was forced to carry out the punishment as stated in the law.

Daniel was thrown into the den of lions at sundown. King Darius, knowing that Daniel had confidence in God, expressed his hope that God would rescue Daniel. A stone was placed over the opening to the lions' den, shutting Daniel inside. In the morning, King Darius returned to the den and called out to Daniel to see if he was still alive. Daniel responded that God had sent an angel to shut the lions' mouths because Daniel had done nothing wrong. Daniel was lifted out of the lions' den without a scratch! King Darius then made a rule saying that everyone in his kingdom from that point on must honor Daniel's God because He is powerful and living, and His kingdom would last forever.

© Bible Grade 2

VA 25A Mary and Joseph Obey God

Matthew 1; 2:13–15, 19–23; Luke 1:26–38, 46–56, 3:23–38; 2 Samuel 7:12–17; Isaiah 7:14, 9:6–7

Many years before Jesus was born, there were prophets. These prophets said that God's promise would one day be fulfilled—a baby boy would be born to take away the sins of the world. God had a plan for this to happen.

There was a man named *Joseph* who had asked a woman named *Mary* to be his wife. Before they got married, God sent an angel to Mary. He said, "Rejoice, you are favored and blessed among women." The angel's words frightened Mary, and she wondered what they meant. The angel told her not to be afraid. He went on to say that Mary would have a baby and she should name Him *Jesus*. The angel explained that Jesus would be great. Jesus would be called the *Son of God* and He would rule over a kingdom that would never end.

Mary listened to the angel and her response was, "Let this happen to me just as you have said." Hurriedly, Mary went to a city in Judah to tell some of her family the happy news about the baby she would have. Mary believed the angel of God and she felt amazingly blessed that she would be the one to carry out God's plan for the birth of Jesus. She was so happy that she wrote a song to praise God.

Mary was now pregnant and not married. This concerned Joseph. He didn't know whether to marry her or not. An angel of the Lord came to Joseph in a dream and told him to not be afraid to take Mary as his wife. The angel said that Mary would have a baby boy and that Joseph was to name the baby *Jesus*,

because He would save people from their sins. Because of the dream, Joseph did just as the angel commanded—he married Mary.

Sometime later, Mary gave birth to baby Jesus. An angel of the Lord came to Joseph in another dream and said, "Get up, and take the young child and Mary and go to Egypt. Stay there until I tell you to leave, because Herod will kill the young child if he finds Him." Herod was the king. Joseph obeyed the angel of the Lord and took the young child and Mary to Egypt. They remained in Egypt until King Herod died.

After King Herod died, an angel of the Lord appeared to Joseph in another dream and said, "Get up and take the young child and Mary and go to Israel where it is safe for you." Joseph obeyed the angel and took the young child and Mary to Israel. He was headed toward the region of Judea in Israel, but King Herod's son was king there. This frightened Joseph. Then, God warned Joseph to head to another region of Israel called *Galilee*. Joseph obeyed and settled in a city of Galilee called *Nazareth*.

Mary and Joseph willingly obeyed God, and He used them to fulfill His promise. Jesus, the Messiah was born, and the prophecies spoken by the prophets were fulfilled. The promised Savior of the world would redeem people, providing a way for them to be restored to a right relationship with God.

© *Bible* Grade 2

VA 26A Jesus Heals a Blind Man

Luke 18:35–43

Jesus was the promised Savior of the world, the Son of God. He went throughout Israel, preaching, teaching, and healing by performing many miracles. Soon, word about Him spread and people brought Him their friends and family members who were sick, dying, or troubled, and Jesus healed them.

One day as Jesus was traveling within the country teaching people about God, He approached the city of Jericho. A large, noisy crowd gathered about Him. Suddenly, one voice was heard above the noisy crowd. It was a blind man calling out to Jesus.

"Jesus, Son of David, have mercy on me!" the blind man exclaimed.

The crowd told the blind man, "Shhh! Be quiet! You'll bother the Master."

The blind man then called out more loudly, "Jesus, Son of David, have mercy on me!" People in the crowd said, "Be quiet. We're trying to hear the Master! Go away!"

However, Jesus stopped and said, "Bring that man to Me." When the blind man stood near, Jesus asked him, "What do you want Me to do for you?"

"Lord, help me to see," responded the blind man.

Jesus answered him, saying, "Receive your sight; your faith has saved you." The blind man immediately received his sight. He then followed Jesus, calling out, "Praise God! Glorify His name! I can see! I can see!" When all the people saw that Jesus had made a blind man see, they joined in praising God too.

© Bible Grade 2

393

VA 27A Jesus Is the Good Shepherd

Matthew 9:35–38, John 10:11–16, Luke 15:1–7

Jesus traveled throughout the land of Israel. He went to the towns and villages, teaching the people. He shared with them the good news about God's kingdom and healed every disease and disability among the people.

Wherever Jesus went, large crowds gathered to hear what He had to say. Many people hoped they would be healed. As Jesus stood among the people, He was filled with compassion for them. Jesus knew they were scattered like lost sheep without a shepherd and needed someone to lead them and care for them. Jesus knew the people were in need of His help to find hope and salvation.

In those days, the people understood that the job of a shepherd was to protect and care for the sheep. Jesus said about Himself, "I am the Good Shepherd. I'm not like a shepherd who has been hired to take care of the sheep. A hired shepherd runs away when he sees a wolf coming. He doesn't care about the sheep because he doesn't own them." Jesus explained that a good shepherd will risk his life to keep his sheep safe. Jesus said that one day He would give up His own life for all people so they would be able to have everlasting life with Him in heaven.

One day, Jesus was talking to a crowd of people. The religious leaders in the crowd complained to Jesus, saying that He shouldn't talk to those they considered bad and sinful, let alone spend time with them! So Jesus began to tell a story about a lost sheep. He wanted to explain why He spent time with sinners. He asked all the people present, "Suppose you have 100 sheep, but one becomes lost. Wouldn't you leave the 99 sheep to search for the one lost sheep? Of course you would! And then when you have found the lost sheep, you'd be so happy! You'd place the sheep on your shoulders, head home, and call all your family and friends to rejoice with you." Jesus was making a point to all the people. He seeks those who are lost from Him. He explained to the religious leaders as well as the others that there is more joy in heaven over one sinner who turns to God than over 99 righteous people who need no repentance.

© Bible Grade 2

395

VA 28A Martha Grows in Faith

John 11:1–45

Lazarus and his two sisters, Martha and Mary, lived in the village of Bethany, near Jerusalem. Martha had welcomed Jesus and His disciples to her home, fixing them food and letting them spend time there. Jesus loved these sisters and their brother. They were special friends to Him.

One day when Jesus was preaching and teaching in another town, Lazarus became very sick. Martha and Mary knew Jesus had healed other people, so they sent word to Jesus to come to Bethany. When Jesus heard about Lazarus, He boldly declared to those around Him that the sickness would not end in death. However, Lazarus died before Jesus began His journey to see Martha and Mary two days later.

When Martha heard that Jesus was on His way, she met Him just outside of town. She knew that if Jesus had been there while Lazarus was alive, her brother would not have died. She said, "Jesus, I know that God will give You whatever You ask of Him. I believe that You are the Christ, the Son of God, who is come into the world." She trusted Jesus and had great faith in Him.

Martha then sent for Mary to come see Jesus. Mary and other Jews, who had gathered because of their sadness over Lazarus' death, left Martha's house.

They all met at the tomb with Jesus and were crying because they were so sad. Jesus began weeping as well.

Then Jesus gave instruction to roll away the stone that was covering the opening of the tomb, or burial cave. Martha said, "Jesus, it will stink in there because Lazarus has been dead four days." But Jesus answered, "Didn't I tell you that if you believed, you would see the glory of God?" When the stone was removed, Jesus thanked God for hearing Him days earlier when He had said that the sickness would not end in death. Jesus said this aloud so that the people nearby would believe that God had sent Him. Once He finished praying, He called out with a very loud voice, "Lazarus, come out!" And Lazarus came out! He was still wrapped in grave clothes, strips of cloth that were wound around a dead person's body. Jesus said, "Unwrap him and let him go." The sickness did not end in death after all—just as Jesus had said!

Martha trusted in Jesus as the Son of God. Now she was able to see the glory of God when Lazarus was raised from the dead, and her faith in God grew even stronger.

© Bible Grade 2

397

VA 29A Jesus' Triumphal Entry

John 12:12–19, 13:1–11

On the day after Jesus raised Lazarus from the dead, Jesus decided to go to Jerusalem to celebrate the Passover with His disciples. The disciples brought a donkey for Jesus to ride, as He had asked. The disciples didn't realize it at the time, but hundreds of years before, the prophet Zechariah had written that the Messiah King would ride into Jerusalem on a donkey. Jesus fulfilled the prophecy!

A large crowd of people who had also come to celebrate the Passover heard that Jesus was on His way to Jerusalem. They were joined by some of the people who had seen Lazarus raised from the dead. The crowd's excitement grew and grew! People decided to run out to meet Jesus as He rode into Jerusalem. Many people cut down branches from palm trees and waved them like flags. They loudly shouted praises to Jesus, saying:

Hosanna!

Blessed is He who comes in the name of the Lord!

Blessed is the King of Israel!

Jesus was greeted as the King! What a wonderful day it was!

Soon afterward, Jesus and His disciples went to an upstairs room of a Jewish home to celebrate Passover. Because most people went barefoot or wore sandals, the dusty roads made their feet very dirty. Jewish people would provide a bowl of water for family members or guests to wash their feet. Sometimes a servant would have the job of helping guests remove their sandals and wash their feet. It was a very unpleasant job!

Jesus wanted to show His disciples how to love and serve others, so He washed their feet! Peter didn't understand why Jesus, his Master, would do such a lowly job. "No, Lord," Peter said to Jesus. "I won't let You wash my feet. You are an important person, too important for such a dirty job!" Jesus stopped Peter and said, "Peter, unless you let Me wash your feet, you cannot be a part of My work on Earth." "Well, then," Peter replied, "You can wash my head and hands too!"

Jesus explained that a person who had just bathed only needed to have his feet washed and then he would be perfectly clean. However, Jesus knew that one of His disciples was clean on the outside but had a very wicked heart. That person was Judas. He would soon betray Jesus.

VA 29B Jesus' Last Supper
Matthew 26:17–30, John 17

The time had come for Jesus to eat the Passover dinner with His disciples for the last time. Sadly, Jesus told His disciples that one of them would betray Him by telling enemies where Jesus could be found. The disciples were confused, and each asked Jesus who the betrayer would be. Jesus revealed that the betrayer would be Judas, but the disciples didn't understand Jesus' words at that time.

Jesus knew that His time on the earth with the disciples was coming to an end. He wanted to give them a way to remember Him because He would soon go back to heaven. Jesus took some of the bread from the table, broke it, and blessed it. Then He gave a piece of the bread to each of the disciples to eat. Jesus explained that the bread was like His body and that He would soon die for their sins. Then Jesus took a cup of wine and shared it with the disciples, explaining that the wine was like His blood. He was going to

shed His blood for them so that they could be forgiven from all their sins. Afterward, everyone sang a hymn and went out to a hilly area known as the *Mount of Olives.*

Jesus wanted to spend some time there in prayer. He took His disciples to a quiet place and began to pray. Jesus prayed for Himself, and that the disciples would work together and not be separated by disagreements. He prayed that His disciples would have everlasting, or eternal life, that they would be kept safe from evil, and that they would know the truth. Jesus also prayed for people who would come to know Him, but did not know Him yet—even people who had not been born at that time. Jesus was praying for all believers throughout time who would choose to accept Him as Savior and trust Him as Lord!

© Bible Grade 2

401

VA 29C Jesus' Arrest, Crucifixion, and Burial
Mark 14:43–50, 14:53, 15:1–47; John 19

Jesus had done many miracles and taught the people the truth about God. He told the people that He was the Messiah, the Son of God. Many of the Jewish leaders were furious because they did not believe that Jesus was who He said He was. They were afraid that Jesus was gaining too many followers. This could mean they would lose their jobs, their popularity, their authority, and maybe even their country! Because they were afraid and angry, they looked for a way to kill Jesus.

Judas, the disciple who betrayed Jesus, had arranged for Jesus' arrest. Judas led a group of Jewish leaders and soldiers to the place where Jesus was praying with several of His disciples. The soldiers grabbed Jesus and took Him as their prisoner. One of the disciples had a sword with him. He took out his sword, struck the servant of the high priest, and cut off his ear.

Jesus saw the hearts of the Jewish leaders. "Why are you treating me like a robber?" He asked. "I was with you every day in the temple, teaching people about God, and yet you never arrested Me because people were watching. You came here at night to arrest Me so that prophecy can be fulfilled." After Jesus was led away, His disciples left Him and all of them ran off!

Then Jesus was taken to the high priest and to the Roman governor, Pontius Pilate. The Jewish leaders demanded that Jesus be sentenced to die by hanging on a cross, even though He had done nothing wrong. Pontius Pilate allowed the Jewish leaders to crucify Jesus.

The next day was Friday. Jesus was cruelly beaten and made to wear a crown of thorns and a purple robe. He was forced to carry His cross until the soldiers made another man carry it for Him to a hill called *Golgotha*, or *Calvary*. There, He was hung between two other men. When Jesus knew that His work on the earth was done, He said, "It is finished!" Then He died.

One of the soldiers guarding those who were being crucified cut Jesus' side with a spear, proving to those who were standing nearby that Jesus was truly dead. A follower of Jesus named *Joseph of Arimathea* offered to bury Jesus in a new tomb. Joseph and a man named *Nicodemus*, another follower of Jesus, brought spices and wrapped the body of Jesus in grave clothes to begin to prepare it for burial. Together, they laid Jesus in the tomb.

VA 29D Jesus Is Risen

Matthew 28:1–10, Mark 16:12–20, Luke 24:1–49, John 20:1–18, 1 Corinthians 15:3b–8

The Lord was dead, and Jesus' followers were very sad!

Tearfully, Mary Magdalene and some of her friends went to Jesus' tomb early on Sunday morning to finish wrapping Jesus' body in spices and strips of cloth, a custom for Jewish burials. Right away, the women could see that the large stone that had covered the entrance to the tomb was rolled back. They went into the tomb, but they didn't see the body of Jesus. While they were wondering what could have happened to the Lord's body, angels dressed in shining white clothing appeared to them. The women were frightened!

"Why are you looking for a living person in a tomb?" asked the angel. "He is not here, but He is risen! Remember that He told you that He had to be arrested, crucified, and on the third day rise again?" Then the women did remember. At once, they ran to tell the disciples that Jesus was alive! After hearing what the women had to say, Peter ran to the tomb. He went inside and saw the strips of linen that had covered Jesus' body in the tomb, but Jesus was not there. "Where could He be?" Peter wondered. "Could He really be alive?"

Mary Magdalene was still very upset. She met a Man standing in the garden near the empty tomb. It was Jesus, but she didn't recognize Him. The Man asked her, "Woman, why are you crying?" Mary replied, "Because someone has taken away the body of my Lord and I don't know where He is!" Then Jesus said, "Mary!" At that moment, Mary recognized Him! Jesus was alive!

Later that day, two men who were followers of Jesus were walking to a village called *Emmaus*. While they talked about all the things that had happened to Jesus, a third Man caught up to them and began to walk with them. The two followers of Jesus didn't know it, but they were walking with Jesus; they just didn't recognize Him. Jesus joined the men for supper that night. At the supper table, Jesus said a prayer and blessed the food. All at once, they recognized Jesus. He was alive!

The two men ran back to Jerusalem where they found the disciples and shared the wonderful news. As they were sharing, Jesus Himself appeared! He showed the disciples that He really was alive!

In the days that followed, Jesus appeared many times, comforting and encouraging the believers. At one of these times, over 500 people saw Jesus with their own eyes!

Jesus told the disciples to spread the good news to all people in the world. He wanted everyone to know that He had taken the punishment for their sins by dying on the cross. If they believed in Him, they would be able to live with Him in heaven forever.

© *Bible Grade 2*

VA 30A Peter Acts Boldly

Acts 12:1–17

Peter and other followers of Jesus continued to do many amazing things in the name of Jesus, and the Church continued to grow steadily.

King Herod began to persecute followers of Jesus. He had many put in prison and some were killed. King Herod had Peter arrested and kept him in prison. A Jewish festival was taking place at the time, and King Herod decided to put Peter on trial after the festival was completed. The Church began praying constantly for Peter. The night before the trial, Peter was bound with two chains between two soldiers who stood guard in the cell. Other guards were stationed outside the prison. Suddenly, an angel of the Lord stood near Peter, who had fallen asleep, and told him to get up quickly. The chains fell off Peter's hands. The angel told Peter to put on his clothes and sandals and to follow him. Peter thought he was seeing a vision—he didn't think it was

really happening. After they passed two guard stations, they came to an iron gate, which then opened all by itself! After going through the open gate and down one street, the angel left Peter. When Peter realized he wasn't seeing a vision, he understood that God had rescued him from Herod's evil plans. Immediately, he went to the house where many believers had gathered to pray for him. He knocked and told the servant who he was, but his friends did not believe her. Finally, they opened the door and were amazed to see Peter! That night, Peter left for another town where he would continue telling others about Jesus.

Peter had changed from being a fearful follower of Christ to one who boldly told others of Jesus and did as the Lord commanded.

© Bible Grade 2

VA 31A Peter and Cornelius

Acts 10

A Roman army officer named *Cornelius* lived in the coastal town of Caesarea. He loved God very much. He prayed every day and gave as much as he could to the poor. However, because he was a *Gentile*, which means *a non-Jewish person*, he was not accepted by the Jewish people. The Jewish people followed certain laws that restricted the kinds of food they could eat, especially the types of meat. Because the Gentiles didn't follow Jewish laws and ate foods that Jews were not allowed to eat, they were considered unfit to be around. Jewish people would not even go into a Gentile's home.

One day as Cornelius was praying and fasting, an angel of God came to him in a vision and called his name. "Cornelius," the angel said, "God is pleased with you!" Although he was frightened by the angel, Cornelius listened. The angel told him that he should send servants to Joppa, a town south of the coast from Caesarea, to find and bring the disciple Peter back to Cornelius' home. Peter would explain God's plan of salvation to Cornelius. Cornelius was thrilled and acted right away!

Meanwhile, Peter was staying at a friend's home in Joppa. He went up on the rooftop to pray while lunch was being prepared. As he prayed, Peter saw an unusual vision. In the vision, a large sheet filled with all kinds of animals was lowered down from heaven. A voice spoke to him, saying, "Get up, Peter. Kill and eat these animals."

This bothered Peter because all of the animals in the sheet were those that Jewish people were not allowed to eat. Peter answered the voice and said, "No! I cannot kill or eat any of those animals. The Jewish law says those are unclean. I have never eaten anything that is thought to be unclean." The voice replied, "Do not call anything dirty that God has made clean." This happened three times. Then the sheet was taken back into heaven.

Peter was confused by the strange vision. Just then, Cornelius' servants arrived at the home where Peter was staying. The servants explained who they were and that their master had seen an angel. The angel told Cornelius to send for Peter. Peter finally understood the meaning of the vision! God wanted the Gentiles to hear the message of salvation too. Peter gladly went with the servants. When they arrived in Caesarea, Cornelius fell down and began to worship Peter. Peter corrected him, letting Cornelius know that he was just a human being, and Jesus was the one he should worship. Peter explained to Cornelius and his family that God did not treat one person better than another. God loved all people, no matter what their nationality or family background. Peter told them that Jesus died on the cross for all people. Anyone who believes in Jesus receives forgiveness of sins and everlasting, or eternal, life through His name. The Holy Spirit filled the Gentile believers in Cornelius' home, and later, they were all baptized.

VA 32A Paul and Barnabas Encourage Others

Acts 4:32–36, 9:1–30

There was love and unity among the believers in Jerusalem as the Church began to grow. Believers shared what they had with one another. No one lacked anything because some of the believers who had land and houses sold them and gave the money to provide for the needs of others. One man in particular, named *Joseph*, sold his land and brought the money from the sale to the apostles to give to those who needed it. Joseph was also called *Barnabas*. He was very helpful, cheerful, and encouraging toward others.

The Church continued to grow, but not without trouble. A man named *Saul* tried to arrest believers and have them killed. One day, Saul was traveling to the town of Damascus, planning to do harm to believers there. Jesus spoke to Saul from heaven. Jesus asked why Saul was fighting against Him. Saul was amazed! He had not believed that Jesus was the Savior. Saul became a believer in Jesus that day and from that time onward became known as Paul. But the disciples were afraid of him since he had threatened and murdered believers in the past. So Barnabas took Paul to meet the apostles. Barnabas told the apostles what had happened to Paul while traveling on the road to Damascus—how Jesus had spoken to him from heaven. The apostles believed him and accepted Paul.

Barnabas helped and encouraged the Church. Barnabas befriended Paul when the disciples didn't trust Paul yet. Paul then became a missionary to many places as he shared with others about Jesus. Barnabas joined Paul on some of these journeys to spread the gospel. Paul eventually wrote letters that have since become a large part of the New Testament.

© Bible Grade 2

411

VA 33A Paul and Silas Witness

Acts 16:16–34

After Paul and Barnabas traveled as a missionary team, Paul chose a man named *Silas* to join him to continue sharing about God's plan of salvation. Paul and Silas traveled through many of the countries along the coast of the Aegean and Mediterranean Seas. They were witnessing for Jesus. This meant that they were telling people about Jesus' death and resurrection and God's plan of salvation. When they preached in the town of Philippi, they met a girl who was a slave. This girl was able to tell what would happen in the future because an evil spirit controlled her. Her owners used the girl's ability to make money for themselves. The evil spirit within the girl knew that Paul and Silas were servants of God. That spirit caused the girl to follow Paul and Silas all around the town and to shout out, "These men are servants of the Most High God, telling you the way to be saved!"

What the girl was saying was true, but the fact that the poor girl was controlled by an evil spirit was deeply troubling to Paul. So Paul turned to the girl and said to the evil spirit, "In the name of Jesus, I command you to come out of her!" At that very moment, the evil spirit left the girl! She was freed from the evil spirit, but now she could not tell the future anymore. Her owners were angry at Paul and Silas because they couldn't continue using

the girl to make money. They took Paul and Silas before the judges who had them beaten and thrown into prison. In prison, the prison keeper locked their feet in the stocks, or leg irons.

About midnight, Paul and Silas were praying and singing to God. The other prisoners were listening. Suddenly, there was a great earthquake that shook the prison. The doors flew open, and all the prisoners' chains came loose. The prison keeper woke up, saw the prison doors open, and thought that all the prisoners had escaped. He was so upset, knowing that he would be blamed for the escape, that he was about to kill himself when Paul shouted, "Don't harm yourself! We are all here!"

The prison keeper was amazed that the prisoners had not taken the opportunity to escape. He realized that Paul and Silas were servants of God and could tell him about God's plan of salvation. The prison keeper asked Paul and Silas to teach him how to be saved. They eagerly shared God's plan with him. The prison keeper brought Paul and Silas to his own home, where he and all of his family members believed in Jesus and were baptized.

© Bible Grade 2

413

Glossary
The information in parentheses refers to lesson numbers.

apostle one of the twelve men chosen by Jesus to tell others about Him (32.1)

authority the power to enforce rules or give orders, or someone who has been given the power to enforce rules (6.1)

chariot a two-wheeled vehicle, without seats, that is pulled by a horse (4.1)

commission a job or task given to someone to do (7.4)

confidence total trust or faith in someone or something (24.1)

courage doing the right thing even when afraid (12.1)

defense a means of protection (16.1)

deliverance saved or rescued from a difficult situation (23.3)

descendant a person who comes from a certain family line of parents, grandparents, and great-grandparents (1.1)

devoted showing faithfulness and commitment to someone or something (11.1)

diligence not giving up (5.3)

disciple a follower of Jesus (7.4)

faithfulness constant loyalty (22.1)

famine a time when there is little to no rain, crops do not grow, and people have a hard time finding food. (10.1)

favoritism treating a person or a group better than others (31.2)

humility thinking and caring about God and others first (3.2)

idol a person, place, or thing that is worshipped other than God (15.2)

integrity the state of being completely honest and showing respect for others (18.2)

love unselfishly accepting others (11.2)

loyalty the character trait of showing faithfulness and devotion to someone or something (10.1)

manna food miraculously provided by God for the Israelites in the desert (5.1)

mercy kindness and compassion (26.1)

miracle an act of God that is impossible by human or natural causes (4.2)

missionary someone devoted to spreading the good news of Jesus Christ (32.4)

mock to make fun of (16.3)

mourn to feel deep sadness due to someone's death or because of a loss (28.1)

Glossary

The information in parentheses refers to lesson numbers.

O

obedience following directions wholeheartedly (8.1)

opposition someone or something that is resistant to a situation (18.1)

P

Passover when the Hebrew people were passed over from harm by following God's instructions during the tenth plague (3.4)

patience waiting without complaining (20.3)

peer pressure a strong influence from people near you to do something (12.2)

persecute to treat someone in a cruel way (30.3)

plague a sudden disaster or sickness that spreads quickly and causes harm (3.3)

plan of salvation God's plan to send His Son to die on the cross to pay for the sins of all people (28.2)

prayer talking to God (2.1)

prophecy a message or instructions given directly by God to a prophet and told about something that would happen in the future (24.1)

prophet someone who has special knowledge from God (14.1)

provision a supply of something needed (14.1)

R

reconcile to restore a relationship (30.3)

redeem to buy back and restore value and worth (11.3)

repentance being sorry for sin, confessing the sin, and changing my actions (21.3)

resolve a determination to do or not do something (20.1)

respect a state of showing a proper attitude toward others, especially to those in charge (6.1)

righteous following God wholeheartedly (2.1)

S

sin anything thought, said, or done that goes against what God requires (2.1)

submission the act of accepting the authority or decision of someone else (19.1)

T

temptation a desire to do something even though it is wrong (9.4)

Trinity one God in three Persons—God the Father, God the Son, and God the Holy Spirit (25.1)

U

unselfish showing concern for others more than oneself (20.1)

W

wholeheartedly with excitement, eagerness, and full purpose of heart (9.1)

wisdom using what you know in the best way (19.2)

witness to share about the good news of Jesus with others (33.1)

DO-IT-YOURSELF
STITCH PEOPLE

2ND EDITION

THOUSANDS OF COMBINATIONS FOR
CUSTOMIZABLE CROSS-STITCH CHARACTER DESIGNS!

INCLUDES PATTERNS, STEP-BY-STEP INSTRUCTIONS,
COLOR GUIDES, ILLUSTRATIONS, EXAMPLES, & MORE.

BY ELIZABETH DABCZYNSKI-BEAN

© 2018 BEANSKI, LLC
PUBLISHED BY BEANSKI, LLC
WWW.STITCHPEOPLE.COM

ISBN: 978-0-99-882362-1

©2018 Beanski, LLC

All rights reserved. This publication may not be reproduced or transmitted in any form or by any means, electronic or mechanical, including photocopy, recording, or any information storage and retrieval system, without permission in writing from the author. Errors or omissions will be corrected in subsequent editions. This is not intended to be a full statement of Beanski LLC's rights, all of which are expressly reserved.

Beanski LLC is the exclusive copyright owner of the materials contained in its publications, including the patterns, which have been registered with the U.S. Copyright Office. As the copyright owner, Beanski LLC owns the exclusive right to create and distribute copies of the patterns and the exclusive right to create derivative works of those patterns. A derivative work is a work that is based on a pre-existing work, for example, modifications to Beanski LLC's existing patterns. See 17 U.S. Code §106. Beanski LLC intends to vigorously defend its copyrights and will not allow the trampling of its valuable assets through infringing behavior. Beanski LLC is entitled to statutory damages in an amount of up to $150,000 per pattern copied. See 17 U.S. Code §504.

Author Information: Elizabeth Dabczynski-Bean is the Founder of Stitch People

Lizzy was raised in upstate New York, has been a "Utah-n" for years, and is now a resident of sunny Southern California. A multipotentialite, or jack-of-all trades, Lizzy majored in Music Business and is currently pursuing "The Dream" of being a full-time actor. She has held jobs in technology education, interior design, theater administration, graphic design, and photography, in addition to owning and running Stitch People. Lizzy enjoys learning about fitness and nutrition, doing home improvement projects, performing musical theater, and volunteering at animal shelters when she can.

Follow Lizzy on Instagram and Twitter: @lizzydbean

Contributing Designer: Jessica Savage is a designer for Stitch People

Jess lives in South Australia, amongst the dangers of Australian wildlife and the blazing summer sun. A recovered musician and recovering research scientist, Jess has returned to her artistic roots in this next chapter of life that sees her don a fancy designer's hat. When not creating patterns, Jess enjoys being clumsy in the outdoors, writing fiction, watching Star Trek on repeat, and singing in the car. Loudly.

Follow Jess on Instagram: @cabsav

Cover Design: Myntillae Nash - www.myntifreshdesigns.com

Published by Beanski, LLC

info@stitchpeople.com | www.StitchPeople.com | @stitchpeople

This book is dedicated to Spencer Bean, Andrew Dabczynski and Diane Dabczynski.

HELLO!

I'm so excited you've decided to create a Stitch People portrait! I love Stitch People. I know you will, too.

What I love most about cross-stitch is the heritage and tradition. The summer before I released the first edition of "Do-It-Yourself Stitch People" in 2014, Spencer and I visited the Wadsworth-Longfellow home in Portland, Maine. (I highly recommend you visit if you ever get the chance!)

Hanging on the walls in the children's room in this 18th century home are cross-stitched samplers that were done by the women in the Wadsworth-Longfellow family. These samplers date back to the mid-1700's. I looked at them hanging on the wall and smiled, feeling connected to the past because here I am - and here YOU are - carrying a torch for the very same art that people have been creating for centuries.

Not only is Stitch People a way to connect to your past, it's also a way to connect to your present and future. By creating custom Stitch People portraits for yourself, family members, or friends, you can show your appreciation and love for those who are close to you. Handcrafting such a thoughtful, personal gift shows them you care, and your attention to detail will help you think about all the reasons you're grateful for them. Plus who knows - maybe over a hundred years from now, someone will be admiring your needle craft, too! These portraits are worthy of becoming family heirlooms.

I hope you find this book inspirational and helpful, and I hope you feel brave and imaginative! I invite you to let your creative juices flow and make any and all changes or additions to the designs you find in this book as you see fit to portray the likeness of the characters in your portraits. To create your very own portrait, it's as easy as mixing and matching hairstyles and clothing styles from the patterns in this book, and choosing the floss colors you'd like to use. You'll have a gorgeous family portrait in no time.

Thank you, thank you, thank you again for picking up this book. I'm so excited to work with you. Please let us know if you have any questions or comments! You may get a response from me directly, but we also have a great team of people who will take such good care of you. You can get in touch via StitchPeople.com or you can find help on the blog, in our videos, or via more that can be found on the Stitch People website.

If you're on Facebook, check out our loving and supportive "Stitch People Community" group where thousands of us hang out, share ideas, and get to know each other! We'd love to see you there. The more the merrier.

Have fun, and thanks again!
xoxo,

Lizzy

Lizzy Dabczynski-Bean
JUNE 2018

TABLE OF CONTENTS

HELLO! (WELCOME LETTER) 3

STITCH PEOPLE'S DESIGN PHILOSOPHY EXPLAINED.........6

DIY BOOK REGISTRATION 8

HOW TO USE THIS BOOK **9**

MATERIALS...12

CROSS-STITCH 101 17

CREATING YOUR PATTERN...23

    MAPPING AN EXAMPLE PATTERN...................................25

    UNDERSTANDING SPACING 29

    LAYERING CHARACTERS 30

TIPS FOR SUCCESS...34

FLOSS COMBINATIONS & UNIQUE STITCHES....................34

DESIGNING CHARACTERS...36

    WOMEN'S HAIRSTYLES 48

    WOMEN'S CLOTHING 70

    MEN'S HAIRSTYLES...83

    MEN'S CLOTHING 88

    CHILDREN & BABIES 96

CATS & DOGS & MORE 106

ACCESSORIES 123

ALPHABETS & LETTERING 130

RESOURCES 141

FLOSS COLOR RECOMMENDATIONS 142

MATERIALS CHECKLIST 145

CURLY HAIR INSTRUCTION 146

STRAIGHT HAIR INSTRUCTION 148

CLOTHING PRINT TECHNIQUES 150

LACE TECHNIQUES 152

INCLUDING DEPARTED LOVED ONES 154

STITCHING A TATTOO 156

MAKING CHARACTERS WIDER 158

EXAMPLE PATTERNS 160

FRAMING PORTRAITS 164

MORE STITCH PEOPLE PATTERNS 166

FINISHED PORTRAIT GALLERY 168

GLOSSARY 185

STITCH PEOPLE'S DESIGN PHILOSOPHY EXPLAINED

When I began designing Stitch People portraits, and writing "Do-It-Yourself Stitch People," I was faced with a conundrum: where do the customizations end, given the limitless variety of features available to the human race?

Check out this photo of me, Spencer, and my parents with Pluto at Disneyland. What is it that stands out to you about us in this photo?

To begin to illustrate the logic of why Stitch People are designed and customized the way they are, I want you to think of looking at a family photo - or any group photo for that matter. Think critically about this. What is it - really - that you notice about everyone in the photo? What makes each individual stand out?

It is this general line of thinking that I focus on when designing Stitch People portraits. I believe the greatest way to customize an individual for a cross-stitch portrait is with their hair color, hair style, clothing choices, and accessories, as well as with their placement and position within the portrait.

Think about it! Grandpa's distinct bald head, or your teenage niece's moody black hair that hangs at a steep angle across her face are distinctive traits that can be easily incorporated into a Stitch People portrait. Cousin Jenny's wild tie-dye shirts, or your son's beloved soccer jersey should absolutely help distinguish them from the other members of the family. And what better way to tell a family's story than to put Grandpa next to Grandma, little Johnny next to his favorite pal (the family dog), or Mom and Dad in the center of the portrait with their mini-me daughter and son on either side?

STITCH PEOPLE FACES

Due to the size of cross-stitched Stitch People characters - approximately 1 in. x 3 in. - the features that can fit onto a little stitch-face are few. I made the executive decision to keep things simple with Stitch People, using only eyes and a simple, smiling mouth to create the faces of our Stitch People friends. Noses can be so unique that it would be impossible to create just the right one for every person, and with such limited space, any type of nose - whether cross-stitched or back-stitched - could make the face appear cluttered, messy and overwhelmed.

STITCH PEOPLE EYES

For the eyes, I typically keep the color black, despite the fact that most people have blue, green or brown eyes. Think of it this way - when looking at a photo of a group of people, can you distinguish what color everyone's eyes are? Not usually. In the photo above, can you tell that I have hazel eyes, Dad has green eyes, Mom has brown eyes and Spencer has blue eyes? No. All we can see is that Pluto has big, black eyes - and if our eyes were as big as his, it might be worth specifying the color!

So, I personally like the look of the black eyes. I think it looks the most well-balanced. I *occasionally* use a very dark color - emerald green, chocolate brown, or navy blue - for colored eyes but I always use <u>dark</u> colors. When I've experimented with lighter colors, I find my little people look a little alien-like, and I'm going for Stitch People, not Stitch Aliens (although that's a really fun idea!) *e.g. Notice the slight difference in eye color between images 1 and 2 on the right side of page 21, where image 1 shows dark green eyes, and image 2 shows typical black eyes.*

STITCH PEOPLE BODIES

I like to keep Stitch People bodies all the same width (with respect to the various age groups). This is on purpose. Size and weight can be a very sensitive topic for people and I find it best to leave it alone, especially when a Stitch People portrait is created to be given as a gift.

When someone's personality can be captured in other ways, I think it's best to not accentuate their size (be it vertical or horizontal). Now, some folks wear their physical attributes on their sleeve, but we don't always know if it's something that is truly embraced, or simply played as being embraced to protect themselves from a truer, underlying emotion. Personally, I think it's better just to leave it alone.

Regardless, some folks still feel the desire or need to portray their Stitch People characters in a more realistic way. This often relates to body size. If you wish to design your Stitch People to be wider, you may refer to the patterns in this book to do so in a way that is still congruent with the Stitch People style on pages 158-159.

But to reiterate, I developed Stitch People to fit into a specific stylistic mold. This mold keeps each Stitch Person character at the same width, with the exception of children-sized characters. This decision was NOT made with body-shaming in mind. Rather, this was a stylistic choice to seek to portray the likeness of characters through their hairstyle, clothing style, coloring of various elements, and proximity to other characters.

To visualize this stylistic choice, think about the characters from the classic ride at Disneyland or Walt Disney World, "it's a small world." As you travel through this ride, you come across hundreds of singing and dancing statuettes that are all the same size and shape, but represent their specific nationality, race, and culture through their hairstyles, clothing styles, skin/hair/clothing coloring, and proximity to each other within the ride.

IN SUMMARY

A face is a face and a body is a body. We all have 'em, and it's not easy to change 'em. Some of us love what we got and some of us don't. Because of that, I truly believe we don't need to see every minor detail in a face or body to be able to recognize someone in a Stitch People portrait.

So yeah - we all have a face and a body. What we <u>don't</u> all have is a killer beard, or fire-engine red, curly hair, or a beloved AC-DC t-shirt, or a favorite, lime-green, vintage, A-Line skirt (that I can't fit into right now but I'm working on it!!) These are the things that become us. These are the things we choose to adorn ourselves with. These are the little, custom details we can include in our Stitch People portraits to make them truly special and truly unique.

REGISTER YOUR BOOK!

TO HAVE ACCESS TO THE EXTRA PATTERNS ONLINE AND TO BE THE FIRST TO HEAR ABOUT FREE PATTERNS, TIPS, NEW PRODUCTS AND NEWS, VISIT STITCHPEOPLE.COM/REGISTER

 **We'd love a review!** If you enjoy this book, it would really help us out if you left us a 5-star review wherever you purchased this book. If there's anything standing in the way of a 5-star review, please give us a chance to make it up to you, directly, before leaving your review. Please never hesitate to contact us directly at info@stitchpeople.com

MAKE THE MOST OF THIS BOOK & READ THIS SECTION, ENTIRELY!

HOW TO USE THIS BOOK

(OR "GETTING THE BIGGEST BANG FOR YOUR BUCK")

First, I highly recommend orienting yourself to this book before you begin. **If you have a question, chances are this book has the answer.** So please take a thorough look through this book, and familiarize yourself with the information before you begin. Second, be sure to REGISTER YOUR BOOK at <u>stitchpeople.com/register</u>. This way, you'll receive updates, extra patterns, freebies, information, and more. It's the best way to get support!

CONNECT WITH US

Facebook Community: <u>Check out our thriving community on Facebook!</u> We've built up a community of happy, helpful Stitch People fans. There is a lot of sharing and support to be had there. When you request to join, please have your order information handy, because *the Stitch People Community Facebook group is intended for owners of this book* and we want to make sure that's the case.

Before posting a question in the Facebook Stitch People Community: make sure the question isn't first answered in the book (double check the terms you're looking for in the glossary), and then use the SEARCH BAR in the Facebook group to see if someone else has already asked your same question. If not, go ahead and post!

You can also connect with us by following us on Instagram and Pinterest, or by giving us a "Like" on Facebook:

- **Facebook:** <u>Facebook.com/StitchPeople</u>
- **Instagram:** <u>@stitchpeople</u> | <u>Instagram.com/StitchPeople</u>
- **Pinterest:** <u>Pinterest.com/StitchPeople</u>

Newsletter Updates: We have had such wonderful suggestions from you, our fans, and we've created many new patterns and portrait tutorials based on your incredible ideas. Don't forget to sign up for <u>Stitch People's free newsletter at stitchpeople.com</u> (on the home page) to receive updates and free patterns straight to your inbox! There is a thriving community around this beautiful craft and I would hate for you to miss out on any of our news, updates and free patterns! To see what free patterns are currently available, visit <u>StitchPeople.com/Freebies.</u>

EXTRA PATTERNS

We often post extra digital patterns for DIY Book owners online to supplement this "DIY book." You will be able to access these patterns from **a link that will be emailed to you once you've registered your book**. We also offer FREE bonus patterns. If you're signed up for our exclusive email newsletter, you'll be notified when these are released. To see what free patterns are currently available, visit <u>StitchPeople.com/Freebies.</u>

SECTIONS OF THIS BOOK

- **Materials**: A list of what materials you'll need to complete a Stitch People portrait, along with a brief explanation of each.

- **Cross-Stitch 101**: For new and old cross-stitchers alike, this section goes over cross-stitch basics, and will get you well on your way to stitching your Stitch People portrait!

- **Creating Your Pattern**: This section will teach you, step by step, how to design and construct your Stitch People portrait.

- **Tips for Success**: A few more tips, tricks, and facts to ensure your success! You'll want to know this stuff before starting, trust me.

- **Designing Characters**: This section contains pages of graph paper design templates for you to use to keep track of your character designs, as well as pages upon pages of designs for all your Stitch People characters: women, men, children, pets, and accessories.

- **Alphabets & Lettering**: Fifteen "font" options to use in your Stitch People portraits.

- **Resources**: Other names for this section: "The Holy Grail," "El Dorado, the Lost City of Gold," "The Pot o' Gold at the End of the Rainbow," or "The Fountain of Youth's Much Cooler, Older Sister." It contains extensive resources to help make your life easier, like floss color recommendations, methods for framing, extra patterns and instructions, example patterns, and *much* more!

- **Finished Portrait Gallery**: Pages of finished portraits to give you ideas and inspiration done by me (Lizzy), and by other Stitch People Community members!

- **Glossary**: Use the glossary to look up key words, terms, or pattern elements you're looking for.

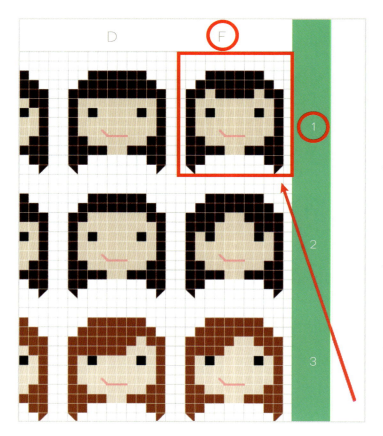

DESIGN PAGE COORDINATES

Each of the design pages in this book has a colored "tab" on the edge of the page (more about that on the next page) as well as letter and number coordinates at the top and side of the page, respectively.

As you make your pattern selections and design your characters, you can write down the approximate "coordinates" so the patterns are easy to relocate. You can do this on the character design pages (36-47). I recommend you keep the same format as you record your coordinates so they're easy to interpret:
Page # - Column Letter - Row Number.

So in the image to the left, you can identify the top, right women's hairstyle pattern by citing the page number (it's 49) and the closest column letter (E) and closest row number (1). This coordinate will read: 49-E-1.

TABS

Utilize the colored tabs along the sides of the pages. These differentiate the sections so you can easily find what you need! They also show symbols for those who may struggle with colorblindness. The tabs are as follows:

MATERIALS

The good news is all the materials you'll need for cross-stitching, or for doing a Stitch People portrait can be purchased at a local craft store, or online. You may even have a few helpful tools and materials lying around your house already.

The even better news - the back of the book contains extensive resources. It has a materials check-list on page 145 listing everything I recommend below, and has spaces to fill in what colors of embroidery floss you'll need. This way, you can easily keep track of what you need.

AIDA FABRIC: SIZE & AMOUNT

Aida fabric is traditionally used for cross-stitching. The different sizes of Aida fabric are identified by a number equal to the number of stitches that fit within an inch of space on that fabric. I believe Stitch People characters look best when stitched on **size 14 fabric.**

THIS IS AN IMAGE OF THE CROSS-STITCH STARTER KIT AVAILABLE FOR SALE AT STITCHPEOPLE.COM! IT CONTAINS ALL THE MATERIALS YOU'LL NEED TO GET STARTED WITH CROSS-STITCHING A STITCH PEOPLE PORTRAIT.

The amount of fabric you'll need will depend on the size of your portrait. Aida often comes in rolls of 15 in. x 18 in. (76.2 x 91.4 cm) which is plenty to get you started.

AIDA FABRIC: COLOR

You may work with any color of Aida fabric that appeals to you. I recommend using off-white colors, like "Oatmeal," "Light Gray," "Gray," or "Antique White" because dark floss colors pop against it, as does pure white floss.

The Aida fabric color choice is ultimately completely up to your personal preference and what you're trying to achieve. You may find yourself choosing to outline your characters, as in the example shown to the right where the woman's dress is very similar to the color of Aida fabric used. Use 1 thread of a slightly darker or slightly lighter color than that of the item you're outlining.

On the next few pages you'll see three different skin tones, three different hair colors, and three different neutral tones (black, gray, and white shirts) and how they look against different background colors that represent the wide array of Aida fabric colors that are available from various vendors.

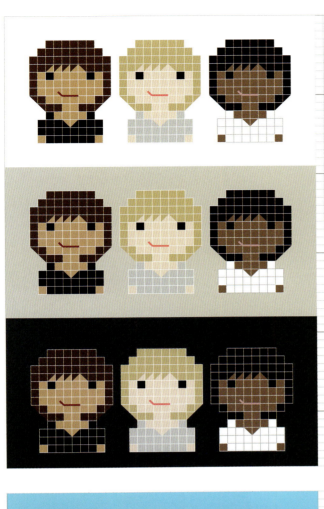

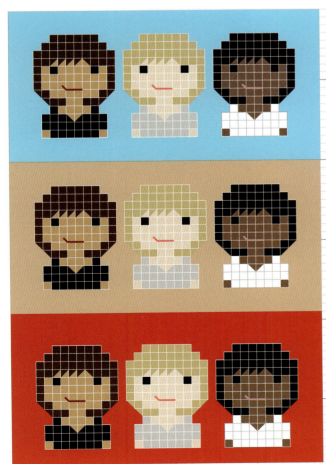

EMBROIDERY FLOSS: COLORS

I use DMC brand embroidery floss. I am not officially affiliated with DMC, I just like 'em. However, there are other popular brands of embroidery floss, and you may have your own favorite. You can find helpful color conversion charts and other similar resources online.

The colors of floss you'll need will depend entirely on the characters you choose to include in your portrait. You'll be making your own color choices. The hair colors, complexions, and personal clothing style choices of individuals you're stitching in your portrait will determine the colors you need to purchase to represent them, their clothes and accessories.

IN THE RESOURCES SECTION, PAGES 142-144 CONTAIN AN EXTENSIVE LIST OF FLOSS COLOR RECOMMENDATIONS FOR COMMON COLOR NEEDS FOR STITCH PEOPLE PORTRAITS.

Another important factor to keep in mind is whether you want to choose bold floss colors, or muted floss colors for you portrait, as a whole. My advice is to stick to one or the other, or a muted color amongst bold colors may fade away, or a single bold color against muted tones may pop too much and become distracting to the rest of the portrait. See the differences between bold and muted options to the right, and think about how it might affect the look of your portrait.

EMBROIDERY FLOSS: THREADS & STRANDS

Embroidery floss is made up of six individual threads (or strands). For Stitch People portraits, I recommend using **three** of the six threads for most of your work (skin, hair, clothing, etc.), and one to two threads for any smaller, more detailed elements of the portrait (buttons, collars, glasses, etc.). Thread recommendations will continue to be specified throughout the design pages.

EMBROIDERY HOOP

In the past, I have used a hand-held, round, 5" wooden hoop to stitch my portraits. You can get all sorts of hoops, both wooden and plastic, and you can even cross stitch without one. However, using a hoop will make your project easier to hold and work with, stabilize your work, and help keep the stitches even. I haven't noticed a difference between using wooden or plastic embroidery hoops.

PLASTIC "Q-SNAP"

During the past couple years, I have switched to using a plastic Q-Snap for my cross-stitch work. It is a square-ish plastic frame. The edges of the embroidery work are secured to the frame by smoothly rolling into the sides of the Q-Snap. I've come to prefer using this frame because it's more comfortable to hold in my hand, and the way the edges of the fabric roll into the edges of the Q-Snap leaves fewer creases on the finished work.

NEEDLE

You need at least one needle. I'd plan on having a few back-up needles, because if you're anything like me, you'll lose the first needle. I recommend a size 5 embroidery (or "crewel") needle. A smaller number will get you a larger eye, and a larger number will get you a smaller eye. I like size 5 best. I think it's comfortable to hold, easy to thread, and works great with size 14 Aida fabric and 3 strands of embroidery floss. It also has a sharp end, unlike a tapestry needle which has a blunt end. The embroidery, or crewel, needle will help you create unique stitches for your patterns that require stitching outside the holes in the Aida fabric.

SCISSORS: LARGE & SMALL

You've got to cut the Aida fabric to size, as well as cut your floss. I use plain fabric scissors for the fabric, and I use embroidery scissors to cut my embroidery floss. The smaller scissors fit great in my fingers, and they fit well in the plastic containers I use to organize my materials. (Tip: You can also use cosmetic cuticle scissors instead of embroidery scissors. They are small and easy to tote around, and can be less expensive than embroidery scissors!)

WRITING UTENSIL: PENCIL

A regular pencil will be helpful to have on hand to make marks on your patterns and even your fabric. A water-soluble pencil is best for marking on fabric, but I must admit that I just use a regular pencil. In fact, I have a box of 50 mechanical pencils at the ready! I use these frequently because, like needles, I often misplace pencils.

If you use a graphite pencil directly on the Aida fabric, be sure to draw <u>lightly</u> when mapping out your pattern on the back side of the fabric (this will be explained more, later). If you use a water-soluble pencil, you can remove your markings later with water.

Do not use pen, marker, or anything permanent with ink that may bleed through your Aida fabric.

PATTERN

You will be making your own pattern. Exciting! We'll go over how to do this on page 23. I wouldn't recommend free-handing your first portrait, but you may get to be such a whiz at Stitch People portraits that you might choose to go pattern-less sooner, rather than later.

BACKING & FRAMING (OPTIONAL)

When you're finished with your portrait, you can do a few things with it. You could frame it in the wooden embroidery hoop and hang it right up on the wall, or you can put it in a regular frame, with a glass front. Or you can get creative and make it into a pillow or do any number of other things with it!

Regardless, you must choose if you'd like to include a backing on your portrait.

For my Stitch People portraits, I use an iron-on interfacing as a backing when I'm finished. It's a way for me to polish up the finished product, so none of the messy (or neat!) back-side work can be seen. Plus, the backing sort of secures all the floss in place. You could also use a double-sided iron-on adhesive between your portrait and a pretty fabric so the backside of your portrait is even more beautiful. Iron-on adhesive backing material is available at fabric stores or online.

For reference, I usually use Pellon 420G Fashion Fuse Gray Nonwoven Fusible Interfacing. White fusible interfacing can sometimes be a little see-through, so I use gray.

DIRECTIONS FOR FRAMING YOUR PORTRAIT BOTH IN THE HOOP AND IN A REGULAR FRAME ARE IN THE RESOURCES ON PAGES 164 - 165.

CROSS-STITCH 101

Maybe you've never cross-stitched before. Maybe it's been a while since you've picked up the ol' needle and thread. Never fear! I'll go over the basics to teach you how to start on the right track, or jog your memory.

TIPS FOR SUCCESS:

If you want your cross-stitching to look beautiful, even, and consistent like it's been done by a well-seasoned pro, then these tips are for you:

- **Be consistent while creating the X shape.** Stitch all the diagonals on the bottom of the X shape such that they go the same direction (so they all look like this: ///////). Then keep the direction of the top diagonals the same, too (like this \\\\\\\).

- **Keep the tension consistent throughout all your stitches** - don't pull them too tight. Stitches should lay flat, and not distort the holes of the Aida fabric.

- To reiterate, the best way to achieve a beautiful, consistent look to your portrait is to **be sure the stitches are uniform** both in **construction** (under and over diagonal direction) and in **tension** (not too loose, not too tight).

- As you work, **keep your focus on the front side of your portrait.** Because cross stitch consists of many "ins-and-outs" (or "ups-and-downs") with the needle, it can be tempting to flip your work from front to back with each stitch you make. Resist the urge to do this. The process of cross-stitching will be much easier, and much faster if you keep your focus on the front of your portrait to allow yourself to see your portrait taking shape with each stitch.

MATERIALS

We discussed materials in the previous section, starting on page 12. For all cross-stitch projects, including your Stitch People portraits, your materials will remain the same.

THREADING THE NEEDLE & SECURING THE FLOSS

Recall that embroidery floss is made up of six threads (or strands) but you should use only 1-3 strands at a time for Stitch People portraits.

Begin by threading the needle. Ensure that all strands of embroidery floss are pulled equally through the eye of the needle. Do not tie either of the ends of the floss into a knot. This will make your work look chunky.

The cleanest, easiest option for securing the thread is to leave the cut ends of your embroidery floss loose as you begin to stitch. As you continue, secure those loose ends of the floss against the back of your fabric by using the loops you'll create naturally while stitching - tightening them around the loose ends of the floss. Until the ends are secured, you'll want to keep a finger or a thumb on the ends of the floss, against the fabric, so the ends don't pull through.

DEFINING THE CENTER POINT

When you start to stitch, you should first define the center point of the fabric and use that center point to orient the rest of the pattern to the fabric. The easiest way to find the center point is to fold the fabric in half lengthwise and width-wise, and lightly mark the center point with a pencil on the back of your fabric. (Note: it typically doesn't matter which side of the Aida fabric is the "back" as both sides are usually identical).

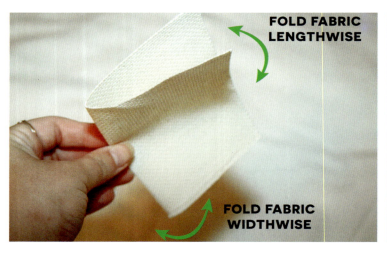
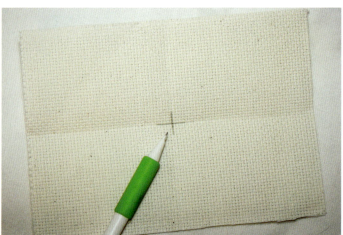

Keep in mind that the size of your pattern will vary depending on the portrait you design, so the dimensions of the Aida fabric should also vary. A good rule of thumb when cutting your Aida fabric is to include 2 in. (5 cm.) more fabric around all sides/edges than you anticipate needing to accommodate the pattern.

CREATING A CROSS STITCH

Cross-stitch embroidery art consists of creating repeating X shapes in varying colors to achieve an overall picture. Each X is created by making two diagonal stitches, one over the other, as in the diagram below.

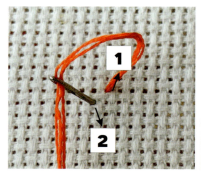
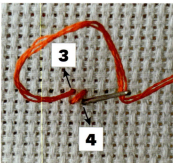

There is no wrong or right way to complete a sequence of cross-stitches. The only thing to remember is to keep the construction of your X stitches the same, but you may choose to stitch cross-stitches in whatever order you'd like. The "**Danish method**" is done by completing rows or sections, stitching the "under" diagonals all at once, and then all the "over" diagonals (for example, stitch all these: ////, then all these: \\\\). The "**English method**" is done by completing each individual X stitch one at a time (for example, stitching XXXX). You may wish to use a combination of the two methods depending on your needs.

METHOD 1 (DANISH):

COMPLETE ALL THE BOTTOM DIAGONAL STITCHES OF EACH X IN A PARTICULAR ROW, FLOSS COLOR, OR SECTION, AND THEN WORK THE SAME SECTION STITCHING THE OTHER DIRECTION, COMPLETING ALL THE TOP DIAGONAL STITCHES OF THE X.

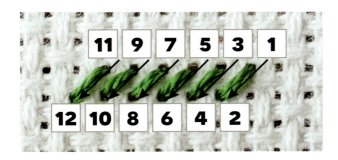

METHOD 2 (ENGLISH):

COMPLETE EACH INDIVIDUAL X SHAPE, MOVING FROM ONE FULL X TO THE NEXT.

Again - there is no right or wrong way to complete a row. Just remember the Tips for Success (p. 17): K<u>eep the directions of the diagonals of the X stitch consistent, keep the tension of your stitches consistent (not too loose, not too tight), and try not to flip your work back and forth.</u>

TYING OFF ENDS

When you're done with a specific floss color, or section of your portrait, the easiest and cleanest way to tie off the ends of your embroidery floss is to secure it to the back of your work so the floss doesn't unravel. <u>Do not create a knot</u>, because it will look chunky.

Simply tuck the needle under 3-4 loops on the back-side of your portrait, and pull the needle and remaining thread through. Clip away any excess floss with scissors.

OTHER USEFUL STITCHES

There are a number of other stitches that will be useful to you while designing and stitching your cross-stitched family portraits. Do take a minute to look through these and read the descriptions about how you might use them. They can really help to customize the look of your portraits!

HOW TO DO SPECIAL STITCHES

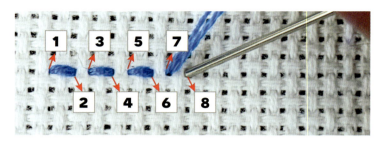

RUNNING STITCH

A SIMPLE, CONSECUTIVE "UP/DOWN" STITCH

USES: CREATING PORTRAIT BORDERS, AND TEXT UNDERLINES

This little guy is full of French knots! His cross-stitched hair has a number of French knots, loosely stitched on top of cross-stitches. These are made up of 2 strands of floss (a dark and light blonde hue). The polka dots on his jammies are French knots made up of two strands of floss (a light blue and a red).

BACK STITCH

A SIMPLE "TWO STEPS FORWARD, ONE STEP BACK" STITCH

USES: OUTLINING CHARACTERS, ADDING CHARACTER DETAILS, CREATING PORTRAIT BORDERS AND TEXT UNDERLINES

FRENCH KNOT

USES: CREATING EYES FOR BABIES, CATS, DOGS & PETS, ADDING DETAIL TO CLOTHING (BUTTONS, POLKA DOTS, ETC.), CREATING FLOWERS FOR BOUQUETS, ETC.

A FRENCH KNOT VIDEO TUTORIAL IS AVAILABLE ONLINE: HTTPS://STITCHPEOPLE.COM/FRENCHKNOT

(1) PULL THE NEEDLE AND FLOSS THROUGH THE FABRIC TO THE FRONT, AND THEN (2-3) TWIST THE FLOSS AROUND THE NEEDLE TWICE.

(4) KEEP THE FLOSS TAUT AS YOU PUSH THE NEEDLE BACK THROUGH THE FABRIC VERY CLOSE TO WHERE YOU BROUGHT IT UP IN THE FIRST PLACE.

(5-6) A KNOT WILL FORM WHILE THE NEEDLE AND REMAINING FLOSS ARE PULLED THROUGH THE LOOPED FLOSS. USE YOUR FINGERS TO KEEP THE THREAD TAUT WHILE PULLING THE NEEDLE THROUGH.

NOTE: THE SIZE OF THE FRENCH KNOT WILL VARY BASED ON THE FOLLOWING FACTORS: THE NUMBER OF **THREADS** OF FLOSS YOU USE, THE NUMBER OF TIMES THE FLOSS IS **TWISTED** AROUND THE NEEDLE, AND THE **TENSION** OF THE KNOT AS YOU PULL.

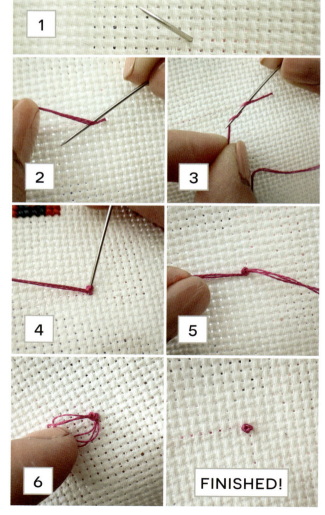

HALF STITCHES

A HALF-STITCHES VIDEO TUTORIAL IS AVAILABLE ONLINE:
HTTPS://STITCHPEOPLE.COM/HALFSTITCH

USES: CREATING DIFFERENT ANGLES, SOFTENING SQUARE EDGES, ETC.

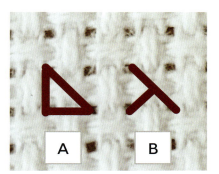

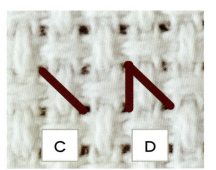

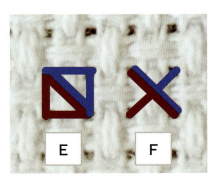

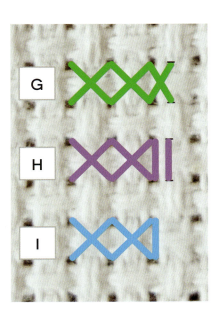

THE STITCHES TO THE LEFT SHOW DIFFERENT WAYS TO COMPLETE A **DIAGONAL HALF-STITCH**. DEPENDING ON THE CONTEXT OF WHERE THE STITCH IS PLACED, YOU MAY WISH TO COMPLETE THE HALF STITCH IN A CERTAIN WAY - BY STITCHING ALL 3 SIDES OF THE TRIANGLE **(A)(5)**, 2 SIDES OF THE TRIANGLE **(D)(3)**, OR JUST THE SINGLE DIAGONAL STITCH **(C)(4)(2)**. ALTERNATELY, YOU COULD COMPLETE THE HALF STITCH IN A TRADITIONAL WAY TO FILL IN MORE COLOR **(B)**.

IF YOU COME ACROSS A SQUARE WHERE TWO DIAGONAL HALF-STITCHES SHARE A SPACE **(5)**, YOU CAN COMPLETE THEM IN A COUPLE OF WAYS BASED ON THE CONTEXT AND YOUR PREFERENCE **(E,F)**. WHEN FINISHING THESE STITCHES, USE YOUR NEEDLE OR A FINGERNAIL TO SEPARATE THE TWO DIAGONAL STITCHES SO THEY LAY SIDE-BY-SIDE AND NOT ON TOP OF ONE ANOTHER

VERTICAL HALF-STITCHES CAN ALSO BE COMPLETED IN A NUMBER OF DIFFERENT WAYS, DEPENDING ON THE CONTEXT, YOUR NEEDS AND YOUR PREFERENCES.

FOR THE FIRST STYLE OF VERTICAL HALF-STITCH, YOU CAN CREATE A FULL CROSS-STITCH BUT SIMPLY STAB YOUR NEEDLE THROUGH THE AIDA FABRIC, BETWEEN 2 HOLES **(G)(1)** TO MAKE A MORE NARROW STITCH, COMPLETE 2, PARALLEL VERTICAL STITCHES, UTILIZING THE HOLES IN THE AIDA FABRIC FOR ONE STITCH, AND STABBING YOUR NEEDLE OUTSIDE THE HOLES FOR THE SECOND STITCH **(H)**. LASTLY, YOU COULD SIMPLY ADD A BIT OF WIDTH, EVER SO SLIGHTLY, BY COMPLETING THE STITCH AS A SINGLE, VERTICAL STITCH, USING THE HOLES OF THE AIDA FABRIC **(I)(2)**.

SEE THE DIAGRAM AT THE BOTTOM OF THE NEXT PAGE FOR A SUGGESTION AS TO HOW TO COMPLETE PARALLEL, SIDE-BY-SIDE VERTICAL HALF-STITCHES STITCHES.

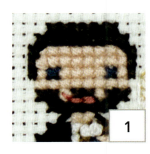

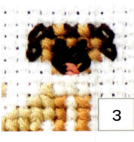

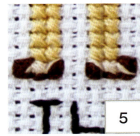

How to do special stitches

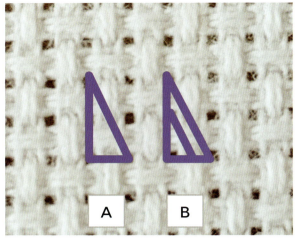
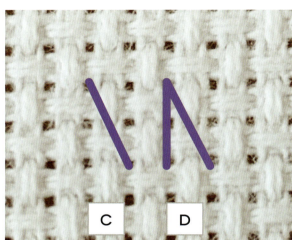
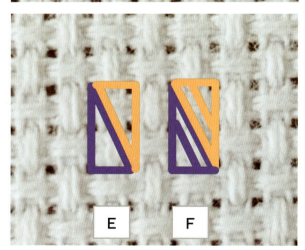

2:1 STITCHES

COMPLETING 2:1 RATIO CROSS-STITCHES CAN ADD DIFFERENT WIDTHS AND ANGLES TO YOUR PORTRAITS THAT HELP TO CAPTURE THE LIKENESS OF YOUR CHARACTERS.

A 2:1 RATIO STITCH IS ANY STITCH WHERE ONE SIDE OF THE STITCH IS 2X WIDER THAN THE OTHER SIDE OF THE STITCH.

USES: CREATING DIFFERENT ANGLES, SOFTENING SQUARE EDGES, ETC.

THESE STITCHES CAN BE COMPLETED IN A NUMBER OF DIFFERENT WAYS ACCORDING TO YOUR PREFERENCE, LIKE THE HALF-STITCHES.

ALL 3 SIDES CAN BE FINISHED **(A)**, JUST 2 SIDES CAN BE FINISHED **(D)**, OR A SINGLE, DIAGONAL LINE CAN BE COMPLETED **(C)**.

YOU CAN ALSO "FILL IN" THE TRIANGLE BY CREATING ONE MORE DIAGONAL STITCH, UTILIZING ONE HOLE OF THE AIDA FABRIC, AND PIERCING THE FABRIC AT THE OTHER END OF THE DIAGONAL BETWEEN TWO HOLES **(B)**.

IF A 2:1 STITCH EXISTS WITH TWO COLORS SHARING THE SPACE, IT CAN BE COMPLETED IN A COUPLE WAYS, DEPENDING ON CONTEXT, STYLE, AND PREFERENCE **(E)(F)**. WHEN FINISHING THESE STITCHES, USE YOUR NEEDLE OR A FINGERNAIL TO SEPARATE THE TWO DIAGONAL STITCHES SO THEY LAY SIDE-BY-SIDE AND NOT ON TOP OF ONE ANOTHER.

In the images below, see how the vertical "half" stitches are completed, as shown on the sides of the face in the pattern. Many Stitch People faces have narrow ears or sideburns. For the ears, simply complete two vertical back stitches, just outside the hole of the Aida fabric nearest to the side of the face. Then, for the sideburns, complete two vertical stitches using the Aida holes between the side of the face and the ears.

CREATING YOUR PATTERN

This is where things begin to get ever-so-slightly more complicated, but also much more fun! Because each person and Stitch People portrait is different, no single suggestion or recommendation will cover every situation. But these few general rules of thumb that I've discovered over time - and throughout hundreds of Stitch People portraits - may help.

Let's go over the steps, first, and then walk through an example.

STEP 1: DESIGN ALL CHARACTERS UP FRONT

Decide what hairstyles, clothing styles, and accessories you'd like to use for each and every character before you begin stitching. Using colored pencils, or any design method of your choice, sketch your characters out on the following character design pages (p. 36-47), or on plain graph paper. You may also use a cross-stitch design software (like MacStitch, PCStitch, or StitchSketch for iPad). When you've finalized your designs, count out the total width and height of each character.

STEP 2: CHOOSE THE SPACING OF YOUR CHARACTERS.

Once you've finalized your character designs - noting how wide and tall each character is - you will need to **decide character order and spacing.** Spacing will look different depending on the height and hairstyles (or fur-styles!) of the characters you choose to include in your portrait, so take that into account as you make your spacing decisions.

GENERAL SUGGESTIONS FOR SPACING

- <u>Between 2 adult-sized figures</u>: Include 2 - 3 squares of space
- <u>Between an adult and child or pet</u>: Include 1 - 2 squares of space
- <u>Between 2 pets, 2 children, or 1 pet and 1 child</u>: Include 1 - 2 squares of space
- Include 2 squares of space beneath the character's feet and top of the first line of text
- Include 2 squares of space between each line of text
- For every amount of space between each letter of text, double that amount of space between words

Continue reading through this section to further understand character spacing. Note the "Layering" method, at the end of this section, pages 30-33.

STEP 3: CHOOSE YOUR TEXT

If you'd like to include text at the bottom of your portrait, plan for that before beginning to stitch and include it in your pattern. **Choose what alphabet you'd like to use** (pages 130 - 140) and **count out how wide and tall your text will be.** Be mindful of the width limitations you may have regarding the size of your portrait and how you want to frame it. Choose an alphabet that will fit appropriately. Use the portrait-sizing chart on the next page to help, and then sketch your design out on the character design pages (p. 36-47, on graph paper, or with cross-stitch design software.

23

STEP 4: CUT THE AIDA FABRIC

Cut the Aida fabric to the size you'll need to complete your pattern. Remember to cut out MORE than you'll actually need - I recommend leaving an extra 2 in (5 cm) on all sides of the pattern.

Optionally, if you're worried about your fabric fraying or unraveling, you can try one of the following prevention methods:

- Fold masking tape, lengthwise, evenly around the edges of your Aida fabric.

- Cut a zig-zag pattern into all edges of your Aida fabric with scissors.

- Slightly fold each edge of your fabric over evenly, perhaps 1/4 inch, and press the folds with an iron. Use a sewing machine to secure the folded edges down by completing a tight running stitch along all edges of your Aida fabric.

- Use a liquid sealant like Fray Check or something similar along the edges of your Aida fabric.

PORTRAIT SIZING CHART*

This assumes an average character width of 11 squares, with 3 squares of space in between each character.
The actual character width & spacing will vary per portrait based on personal choices and preferences, so use this as a guideline only.

NUMBER OF CHARACTERS	STANDARD FRAME SIZE THAT WILL LIKELY WORK	FABRIC DIMENSIONS SHOULD BE EQUAL TO (OR GREATER THAN) THIS SIZE:
1 - 5	4 X 6 IN | 10.16 X 15.2 CM	6 X 8 IN | 15.2 X 20.3 CM
5 - 7	5 X 7 IN | 12.7 X 17.8 CM	7 X 9 IN | 17.8 X 22.9 CM
7 - 9	8 X 10 IN | 20.32 X 25.4 CM	10 X 12 IN | 25.4 X 30.5 CM
9 - 11	9 X 12 IN | 22.86 X 30.5 CM	11 X 14 IN | 27.9 X 35.6 CM
12+	CUSTOM FRAME / MORE THAN 14 IN / 35.6 CM WIDE	

* These are general guidelines, only. Please double-check your own portrait pattern, fabric size, and frame size to ensure a proper fit, given your customized character designs and spacing preferences.

STEP 5: MAP THE PORTRAIT ON THE FABRIC

OPTIONAL: IRON YOUR FABRIC

If the Aida fabric has been rolled up or folded, it is often helpful to run an iron over it so the fabric is easier to work with. Using a high setting meant for cotton or linen should be fine.

MAPPING STEP 1: FOLD FABRIC & DEFINE CENTER POINT

Fold your cut of Aida fabric in half both width-wise and length-wise (as shown on page 18). Choose which side of the Aida fabric will be the back side of the portrait. (Each side is typically identical, so it doesn't matter which side is front or back.) On what will be the back of your Aida fabric, mark the center point lightly with your pencil, where the length-wise and width-wise folds meet.

MAPPING STEP 2: MARKING THE OUTER EDGES

Lightly mark the outermost edges of your portrait pattern on the back of your fabric. To do this, add together the widths of each character, plus the number of squares of spacing between them. Then count the total width of your widest line of text. Whichever element is wider (total character width + character spacing, **or** width of widest line of text), is the widest measurement of your portrait. Then, count the height of your tallest character, and add to this the height of each of your lines of text, and the vertical spacing between each of these elements. This is the total height of your portrait. Divide each of these numbers (portrait's widest measurement and total height of portrait) by 2, so it's easy to split these dimensions evenly from the center point of your fabric.

Now, on the back of your portrait, work from the center point outward, defining the width and height of your portrait. Mark these outer edges lightly with a pencil.

MAPPING STEP 3: MARKING PLACEHOLDERS

I recommend drawing light outlines where each element of your portrait will be to help keep yourself oriented while you stitch and prevent mistakes along the way. Mark the edges for each character and each line of text.

Remember that the back of your portrait will be a mirror image of the front of your portrait. So as you make the placeholder marks on the back, be sure to refer frequently to the pattern you've created to double-check that everything is being placed correctly. Try to prevent mistakes by becoming very comfortable with your pattern and staying very aware while you work.

MAPPING AN EXAMPLE PATTERN

Let's walk through an example so things make a bit more sense. In this example, I'm going to stitch a simple 2-character portrait of a man and a woman side-by-side.

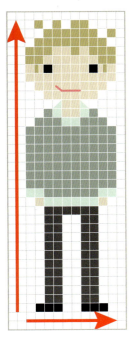

I've chosen the hair style and body for my first character, a **man**, which will be on the left of my portrait. When I put the hairstyle and body together, I can count that he is 10 stitches wide and 33 stitches tall. I've chosen the hair style and body shown to the right for the **woman**. She will be on the right of my portrait. When I put her hairstyle and body together, I count that she will be 12 stitches wide and 30 stitches tall. So the total width of these two characters combined is 22. (The man is 10 wide, and woman is 12 wide).

For this example I'm going to include four squares of space so there is some extra room on the following diagrams to make things clearer for you. The man is 10 x 33 squares, and the woman is 12 x 30 squares. With 4 squares of space between them, the total width for my characters, plus spacing, is 26. Man's width (10) + spacing (4) + woman's width (12) = 10 + 4 + 12 = 26.

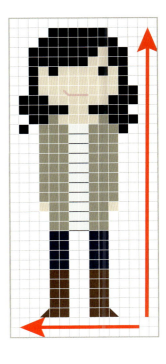

For this example, I'll choose to include two lines of text beneath my man and woman characters. I'll stitch "The Kemp Family" on the top line and "Est. 2009" on the second line, using two of the "fonts" shown on page 131. The top line will be 4 squares high, and 36 squares wide. The bottom line will be 3 squares high, and 22 squares wide. As suggested on page 23, I'll include 2 squares of space between the bottom of the characters' feet and top line of text, as well as between the two lines of text. (I'm going to let the tail of the "y" in "Family" hang in the space between the two lines of text, so I will count my spacing from the bottom of the majority of the top-line text).

Now that I know the dimensions of each element of my portrait, I'll begin by mapping out the area on my fabric. The dimensions of the outermost edges of my portrait are 44 squares high by 36 squares wide. Here's how I know:

Height: 44 is the sum of the height of the tallest character (33), plus 2 spaces beneath the character's feet, plus the height of the first line of text (4), plus 2 spaces between the lines of text, plus the second line of text (3). 33 + 2 + 4 + 2 + 3 = 44.

Width: 36 is the sum of the width of the elements of the widest piece of your portrait. In this case, it's the width of the text. "The" (8), plus 2 spaces, plus "Kemp" (11), plus 2 spaces, plus "Family" (13). 8+2+11+2+13=36

I will mark the outermost edges of my portrait, and draw outlines for each element. This is how that looks:

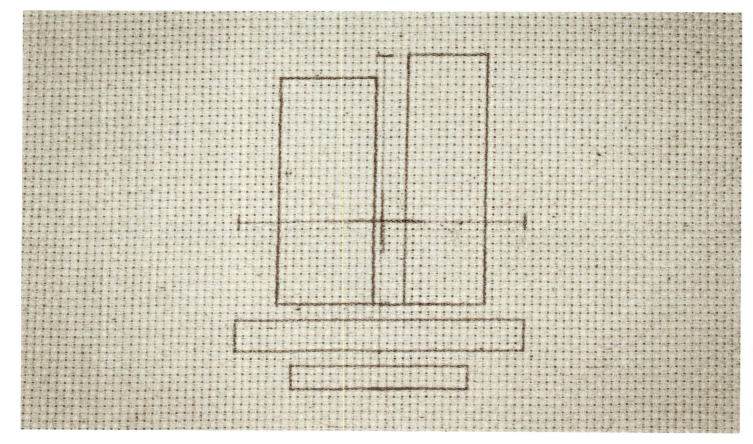

Unfortunately, many find the process of mapping out a portrait on the Aida fabric to be the most difficult step in the entire process of creating your Stitch People portrait. It can be difficult to visualize everything and count out the portrait correctly. This is why I recommend sketching everything out on the Character Design pages, first, or on graph paper. If you get frustrated, don't despair. Simply start from the beginning and work through everything slowly and carefully.

Remember, when you trace the outline of your portrait on the back of your fabric it will be the **mirror image** of what the portrait will look like on the front (see the images below). If you're using a washable, soluble pencil to make your markings you can avoid the mirror image issue by lightly marking the front of your pattern, and washing it off later, but be sure your pencil will wash off entirely before you do this.

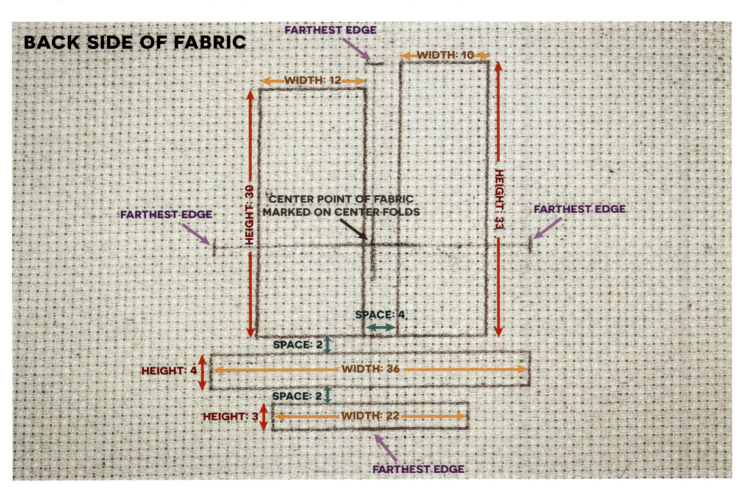

HERE IS THE SAME IMAGE FROM THE PREVIOUS PAGE. THE BACK OF THE FABRIC HAS THE PATTERN "MAPPED OUT" BUT THIS IMAGE HAS COLOR-CODED IDENTIFICATIONS TO MAKE EACH MARK EASY TO UNDERSTAND.

*Note: Do not simply place each character evenly on either side of the fabric's center point, because it may not align with the centered text due to the character designs. **Always** count the width of each element, add the widths and spacing together, divide the total by 2, and center the width measurement on either side of the center point. Think of the portrait as one cohesive design and not as individual elements.

BACK SIDE OF FABRIC

YOU DO NOT NEED TO DRAW OUT YOUR CHARACTERS OR ALPHABET COMPLETELY. I ADDED THEM HERE TO HELP YOU VISUALIZE THE MIRROR-IMAGE OF THE PATTERN ON THE BACK OF THE FABRIC, AS WELL AS THE SPACING.

FRONT SIDE OF FABRIC (MIRROR IMAGE OF BACK SIDE)

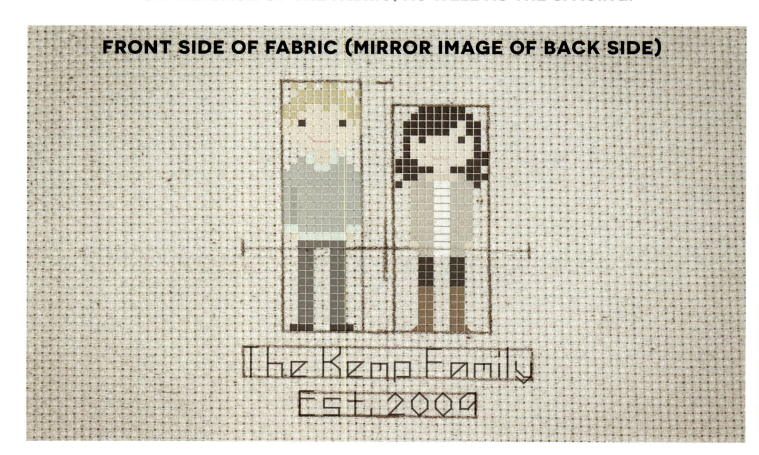

UNDERSTANDING SPACING

While spacing your characters, note the entire width of the characters, and not just the distance between their obvious elements. For example, the man in this diagram is 10 squares wide at his widest point (shoulders/arms), despite the fact that if you count at his feet, he would appear to be 8 squares wide, or counting at his head makes him seem to be 8-9 squares wide.

Similarly, the woman is 14 squares wide because her widest point is her hairstyle. She is not 8 squares wide (counting her feet or shoulders), or 10 squares wide (counting the top of her head).

You may need to adjust the spacing of your characters from what is recommended on page 23 due to the design choices of your characters.

Now, if we add a dog into this family portrait, notice what happens when we put 2 squares of space between the actual outermost edges of the dog and each human character **(A)**. Due to the actual edge of the female character (her hair), the dog looks disproportionately far from the woman and very close to the man. *(Another example of this is shown in the image at the top of page 122. There are a true 2 squares of width between each dog, but it looks disproportional due to the different directions the dogs are facing, and the widths of their ears and tails).*

If you adjust the spacing to look more natural, look closely, and you'll note that the dog's outermost edges actually "overlap" each of the human characters' outermost edges **(B)**. The dog's right ear is in the same column as the outer edge of the man's sleeve, and the dogs tail shares columns with the woman's pigtail. Despite the overlapping, the spacing certainly looks more natural than in portrait **(A)**.

If you feel your portrait is still a little empty or lopsided, consider adding an accessory, or a heart, somewhere in your portrait to fill the space **(C)**. The added heart is the only difference between portraits **(B)** and **(C)**.

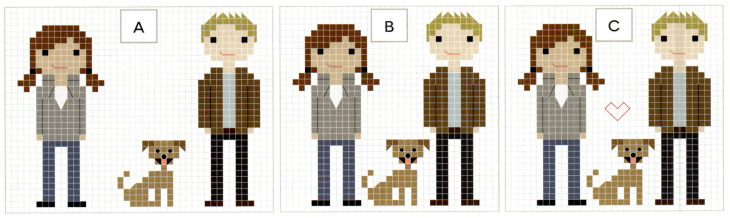

LAYERING YOUR CHARACTERS

An increasingly popular method of spacing characters in Stitch People portraits is to group them together, layering the character patterns one in front of the other.

This method of spacing serves a number of purposes, and looks best when used with a portrait of 3+ characters.

   1. It creates a "natural" look, as families usually stand for photos grouped closely together.

   2. It looks cozy! It conveys a sense of connection between characters.

   3. It's a great mechanism to use to differentiate smaller family groups within a larger family unit.

Some may find this to be a very tricky method of spacing to tackle. If you're new to Stitch People or to cross-stitching, I'd suggest completing one or two portraits using the traditional side-by-side spacing. Then, when you feel more comfortable with the process as a whole, try tackling the layering style of spacing.

HOW TO LAYER YOUR CHARACTERS

   1. Design each individual character first, down to the last detail.

   2. Count the dimensions of each character. How many squares wide and tall are they?

   3. Think about how you'd like to group the characters. Who should be standing next to whom? What pets need to sit in front of or beside certain individuals?

   4. Begin the process of determining the layering and spacing. Some find it helpful to sketch each character out as a silhouette, as shown to the right. Others can operate with even just an outline (referencing the dimensions you determined for each character in step #2).

   5. Look out for skin tone color overlap, and the covering up of vital pieces of your designs. For example, it's not recommended for the "in-front" character to cover an eye of the "in-back" character. Or, if your character's clothing has a patch or insignia on the shirt, be sure to layer characters in such a way that those design details are visible.

Look at the large family portrait on the next page to see how you might utilize this style of spacing on a larger scale.

Check out the patterns on the following pages to understand how even a square of width can make all the difference when layering characters, and you'll have to pay close attention to what spacing is right for your specific, customized character designs.

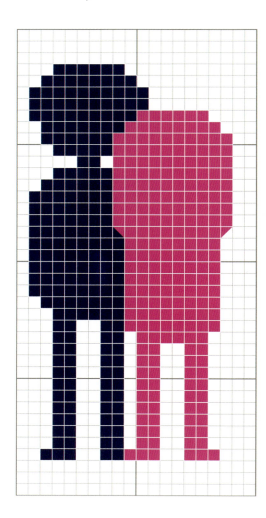

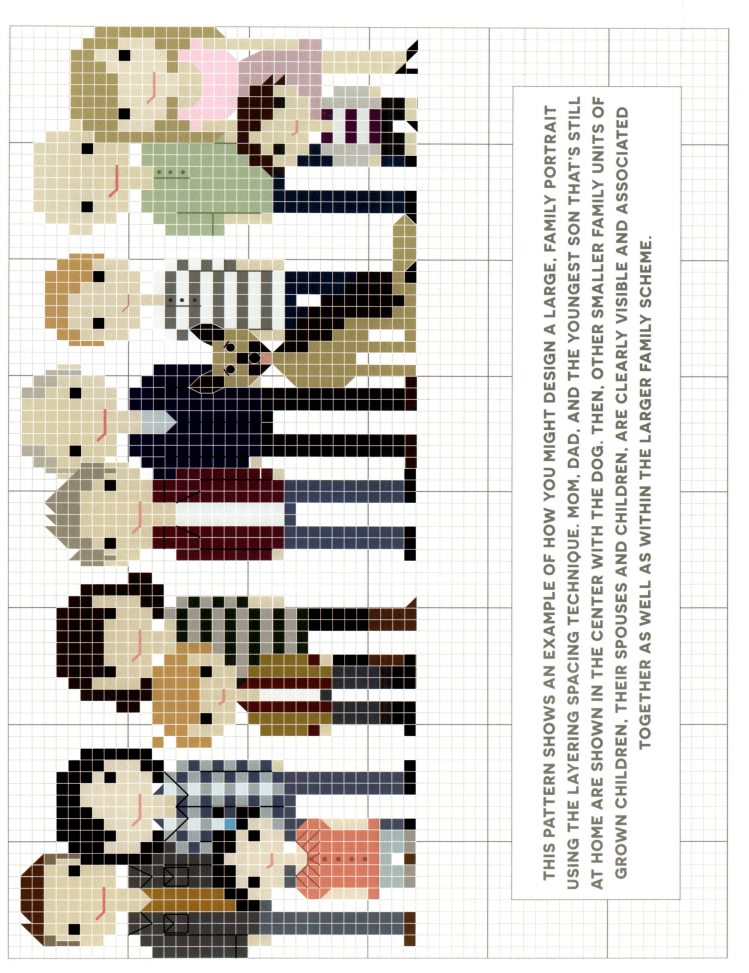

THIS PATTERN SHOWS AN EXAMPLE OF HOW YOU MIGHT DESIGN A LARGE, FAMILY PORTRAIT USING THE LAYERING SPACING TECHNIQUE. MOM, DAD, AND THE YOUNGEST SON THAT'S STILL AT HOME ARE SHOWN IN THE CENTER WITH THE DOG. THEN, OTHER SMALLER FAMILY UNITS OF GROWN CHILDREN, THEIR SPOUSES AND CHILDREN, ARE CLEARLY VISIBLE AND ASSOCIATED TOGETHER AS WELL AS WITHIN THE LARGER FAMILY SCHEME.

While Mom and Dad are a bit farther apart in portrait 1, I prefer it to portrait 2, as the closer spacing in portrait 2 creates some confusion where the daughter's hand meets the Mom's leg, and the skin tone color melts together. Portrait 3 begins to fix that problem - less of Mom's leg is visible, so it's a little more intuitive to see that the daughter's arm is atop Mom's leg. In portrait 4, we've moved Dad closer to Mom by one square's width. It doesn't change much between portraits 3 and 4 because Mom's hair doesn't cover Dad's face quite yet. Your personal preference and portrait design needs would come into play to choose between portrait 3 and 4 spacing.

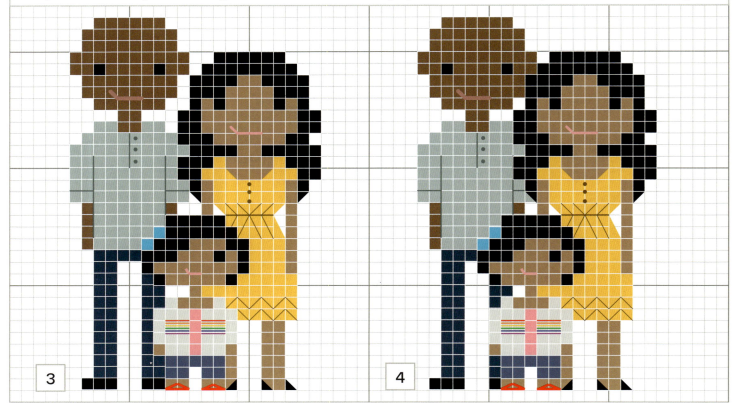

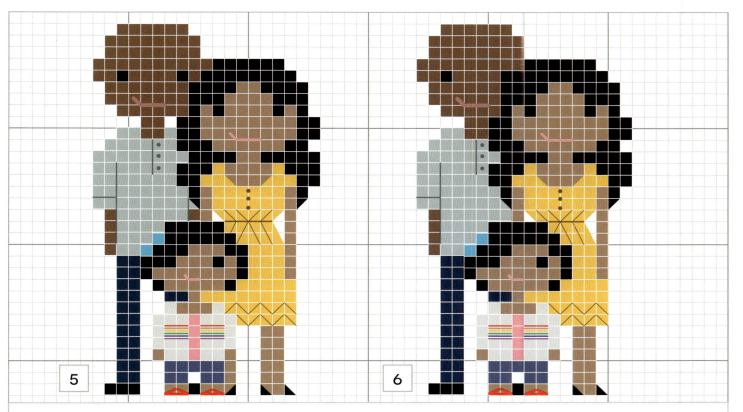

Portrait 5 moves Mom and Dad closer again by one, beginning to cover Dad's face. Portrait 6 moves Mom and Dad closer once more, and creates color confusion as Mom's arm covers Dad's arm completely, and Mom's hair begins surrounding Dad's eye - something that should be avoided. Both eyes of each character are clearly visible.

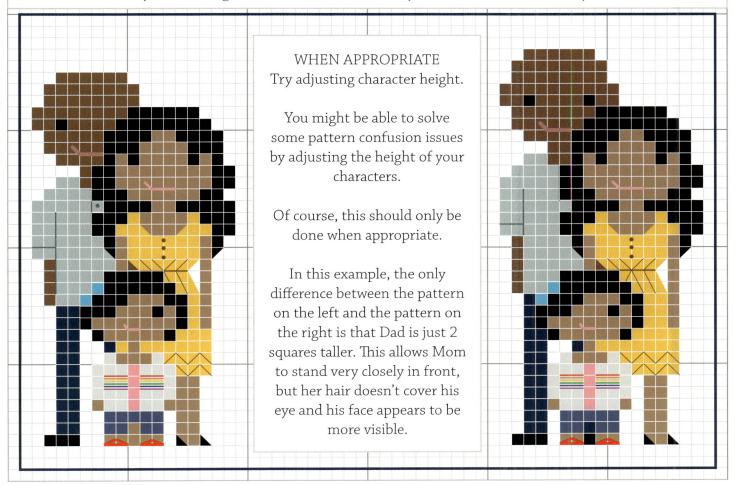

WHEN APPROPRIATE
Try adjusting character height.

You might be able to solve some pattern confusion issues by adjusting the height of your characters.

Of course, this should only be done when appropriate.

In this example, the only difference between the pattern on the left and the pattern on the right is that Dad is just 2 squares taller. This allows Mom to stand very closely in front, but her hair doesn't cover his eye and his face appears to be more visible.

TIPS FOR SUCCESS

Let's review some information and learn a few more techniques that will ensure a beautiful, custom portrait.

Consistency: The best way to achieve a beautiful, consistent look to your portrait is to be sure all stitches lay the same direction and are of the same tension.

Floss Count: Embroidery floss is made up of six individual strands, but you should only be using one to three at a time. For all elements of any character, I recommend using 3 threads unless otherwise specified in the designs on the following pages.

FLOSS COMBINATIONS & UNIQUE STITCHES

The most effective way to achieve a realistic likeness for your Stitch People characters is to **combine different colored threads** and use more than just cross-stitches to fill out your portraits, including back-stitches, French knots, half stitches, and more. Suggestions for colors and color combinations are listed on pages 142 - 144, and you can review how to complete special stitches on pages 20-22.

(1) The left man's sideburns, hair and beard are made up of cross-stitches and single-stitches that use one thread of dark brown floss on top of flesh-colored cross stitches made up of three strands of floss. His shirt pattern combines three threads of three different flosses: black, light-gray, and white. The right man's sideburns are made up of vertical back-stitches using three threads of floss. His shirt details were created by backstitching with one strand of contrasting floss.

(2) The bride's headband is back-stitched using 1 thread of DMC's "Light Effects" silver floss. Likewise, her dress is outlined via backstitching using 1 thread of gray floss. Her bouquet is a number of cream-colored, tightly stitched French knots. Her plunging V-neck utilizes 2:1 ratio stitches. A unique pattern in her skirt called for the creation of long, straight stitches on top of completed cross-stitches. The man's pocket square uses a diagonal half stitch. His boutonnière is a single French knot, and his suit detailing was created by backstitching 1 strand of floss in a color slightly lighter than the rest of his suit.

(3) The woman's dress is outlined in a single thread of light gray floss for added visibility on the light Aida fabric. Her bouquet is created from a number of different colors of floss, stitched tightly together in French knots. Her wrist has a single diagonal stitch of DMC's "light effects" silver floss as a bracelet. Her skirt was creatively back-stitched. However, the backstitching was left loose, and subsequently secured with tiny tack-style stitches, going in-and-out in the same place, catching and securing the long loose threads. The man's hair utilizes diagonal half-stitches. His bow-tie is made visible by outlining it using 1 thread of white floss (matching his shirt). His pocket square was created using a single horizontal stitch, 2 squares wide, of white floss.

(4) The woman's hair was cross-stitched using one strand of three different colors of floss combined together to create a highlighted blonde hair effect. Her red dress was stitched using three strands of red floss. The zig-zag and knot details were added using one strand of floss on top of the red cross-stitches, and the white belt was created using two strands of white floss.

(4) The man's hair displays a few diagonal half stitches, as well as single, vertical stitches for sideburns. The plaid shirt was created by using a combination of colors for each of the three colors represented in the pattern (shown on page 76 and 91). The "red" squares were created using two strands of true red, and one strand of red-orange. The "gray" squares were created using two strand of gray and one strand of red. The "white" squares were created using one strand of gray, one strand of red, and one strand of white floss.

(4) The dog was created using combinations of colors, transitioning from a combination of three different light shades of floss to a combination of light-to-medium tones, and then a combination of medium-to-dark threads around the head and face. The ears utilize different types of half-stitches, and the eyes and nose were created with French knots.

(5) The man's shirt was created by cross-stitching three strands of navy blue. Then over the top the navy, a single thread of white floss was back-stitched in horizontal lines, utilizing the holes of the Aida fabric, to add stripes. The toe and heel of the shoes were created by adding single, horizontal stitches beneath the cross stitches, using three strands of floss. The man's curly hair was created by first stitching the hair as cross-stitches, using three strands of floss. Then French knots were added randomly, using two strands of floss of the same brown color. The man's sideburns were created using single, vertical stitches that are two rows in height, and an "ear" was created on either side of the face by creating a single, vertical stitch of three strands of skin-colored floss.

The woman's hair is a combination of blonde colors, and the sunglasses atop her head, as well as her metallic-black sparkle top add personality to the portrait!

(6) Check out all of the detail in this large family portrait - French knots, single-thread cross stitches on top of three-thread cross stitches, strips, single-thread detailing, mixing of three different colors, half-stitches, and more!

MY CHARACTER DESIGNS

DESIGNING CHARACTERS

Use the next few pages to compile designs and notes about your character selections. If you need more design pages, you may make copies of the following blank pages, or download blank templates from Stitch People online:

HTTPS://STITCHPEOPLE.COM/DESIGNPAGE

For each character you choose to include in your portrait, you'll need to make the following selections:

- Skin Color
- Character Height

  (Legs and torsos can be adjusted by adding or subtracting 1 or 2 squares, vertically, based on your judgment and needs. Start with either the legs or torso, and alternate between them adding or subtracting as needed).

- Hair Style
- Hair Color(s)
- Clothing Style
- Clothing Color(s)
- Shoe Style
- Shoe Color(s)
- Accessories
- Accessory Color(s)

For your reference, each page of patterns in the following sections has both column and row coordinates to help you re-locate your selections in the future. Be sure to make a note of the *page number*, *column*, and *row* coordinates as there are hundreds of options to choose from!

EXAMPLE PATTERN:

LET'S TAKE A LOOK AT HOW YOU MIGHT FILL OUT ONE OF THE CHARACTER DESIGN PAGES.

CHARACTER NAME: Diane (Mom)

DIMENSIONS: 10 wide x 31 tall

HAIR STYLE COORDINATES:

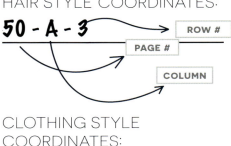

CLOTHING STYLE COORDINATES:

Top 71 - A - 2

Pants 71 - A - 2

ACCESSORIES:

Scarf 126 - D - 1,

Earrings (French knots)

COLOR CHOICES:

Dk. Blue Pants, DMC 823

Pink Shirt, DMC 224

Blue scarf, DMC 964

Skin, DMC 945

Shoe style/color? TBD

Hair Color: DMC 898

Eyes: DMC 310

Earrings: White

MY CHARACTER DESIGNS

CHARACTER NAME:

DIMENSIONS:

NOTES:

HAIR STYLE
COORDINATES:

CLOTHING STYLE
COORDINATES:

ACCESSORIES:

COLOR CHOICES:

DOWNLOAD AND PRINT MORE DESIGN PAGES FROM: HTTPS://STITCHPEOPLE.COM/DESIGNPAGE

CHARACTER NAME:

DIMENSIONS:

NOTES:

HAIR STYLE
COORDINATES:

CLOTHING STYLE
COORDINATES:

ACCESSORIES:

COLOR CHOICES:

MY CHARACTER DESIGNS

DOWNLOAD AND PRINT MORE DESIGN PAGES FROM: HTTPS://STITCHPEOPLE.COM/DESIGNPAGE

MY CHARACTER DESIGNS

CHARACTER NAME:

DIMENSIONS:

NOTES:

HAIR STYLE
COORDINATES:

CLOTHING STYLE
COORDINATES:

ACCESSORIES:

COLOR CHOICES:

DOWNLOAD AND PRINT MORE DESIGN PAGES FROM: HTTPS://STITCHPEOPLE.COM/DESIGNPAGE

CHARACTER NAME:

DIMENSIONS:

NOTES:

HAIR STYLE COORDINATES:

CLOTHING STYLE COORDINATES:

ACCESSORIES:

COLOR CHOICES:

MY CHARACTER DESIGNS

DOWNLOAD AND PRINT MORE DESIGN PAGES FROM: HTTPS://STITCHPEOPLE.COM/DESIGNPAGE

MY CHARACTER DESIGNS

CHARACTER NAME:

DIMENSIONS:

NOTES:

HAIR STYLE
COORDINATES:

CLOTHING STYLE
COORDINATES:

ACCESSORIES:

COLOR CHOICES:

DOWNLOAD AND PRINT MORE DESIGN PAGES FROM: HTTPS://STITCHPEOPLE.COM/DESIGNPAGE

CHARACTER NAME:

DIMENSIONS:

NOTES:

HAIR STYLE
COORDINATES:

CLOTHING STYLE
COORDINATES:

ACCESSORIES:

COLOR CHOICES:

MY CHARACTER DESIGNS

DOWNLOAD AND PRINT MORE DESIGN PAGES FROM: HTTPS://STITCHPEOPLE.COM/DESIGNPAGE

MY CHARACTER DESIGNS

CHARACTER NAME:

DIMENSIONS:

NOTES:

HAIR STYLE
COORDINATES:

CLOTHING STYLE
COORDINATES:

ACCESSORIES:

COLOR CHOICES:

DOWNLOAD AND PRINT MORE DESIGN PAGES FROM: HTTPS://STITCHPEOPLE.COM/DESIGNPAGE

CHARACTER NAME:

DIMENSIONS:

NOTES:

HAIR STYLE
COORDINATES:

CLOTHING STYLE
COORDINATES:

ACCESSORIES:

COLOR CHOICES:

MY CHARACTER DESIGNS

DOWNLOAD AND PRINT MORE DESIGN PAGES FROM: HTTPS://STITCHPEOPLE.COM/DESIGNPAGE

WOMEN'S HAIRSTYLES

- **Varying parts**: Center-parted hairstyles, left-parted hairstyles, and right-parted hairstyles

- **Varying lengths**; chin-length, shoulder-length, chest-length

- **Coloring**: Remember to change the skin tone and hair color based on the coloring of your characters.

  - See "Color Recommendations" on pages 142-144.

- **Neck**: Most hairstyles show the neck in addition to face and hair. I usually choose to give necks only 1 square in height but you may choose to add an additional square if you prefer the look of a longer neck. Keep that in mind when stacking a face and hair style on top of a body / outfit.

- **Shoulders**: Most hairstyles fall around and behind the shoulders, but you may choose to stitch some hair over the shoulders or torso to show a more cascading hairstyle.

- **Some styles may work for both men and women**: mix-and-match as you see fit for your specific characters.

  - The dimensions for both women's and men's faces are the same. It is only the hairstyles that vary. So in theory, men's and women's hairstyles are interchangeable.

- Note the **coordinates** around each of the design pages to help you navigate the patterns and keep track of what styles you choose for each character. These coordinates can be recorded on the **character design pages (pg. 36-47).**

  - Record the coordinates in the order of Page # - Column Letter - Row # (i.e. 50 - C - 3)

	A	B	C	D	E
1					
2					
3					
4					
5					
6					

49

	A	B	C	D	E
1					
2					
3					
4					
5					
6					

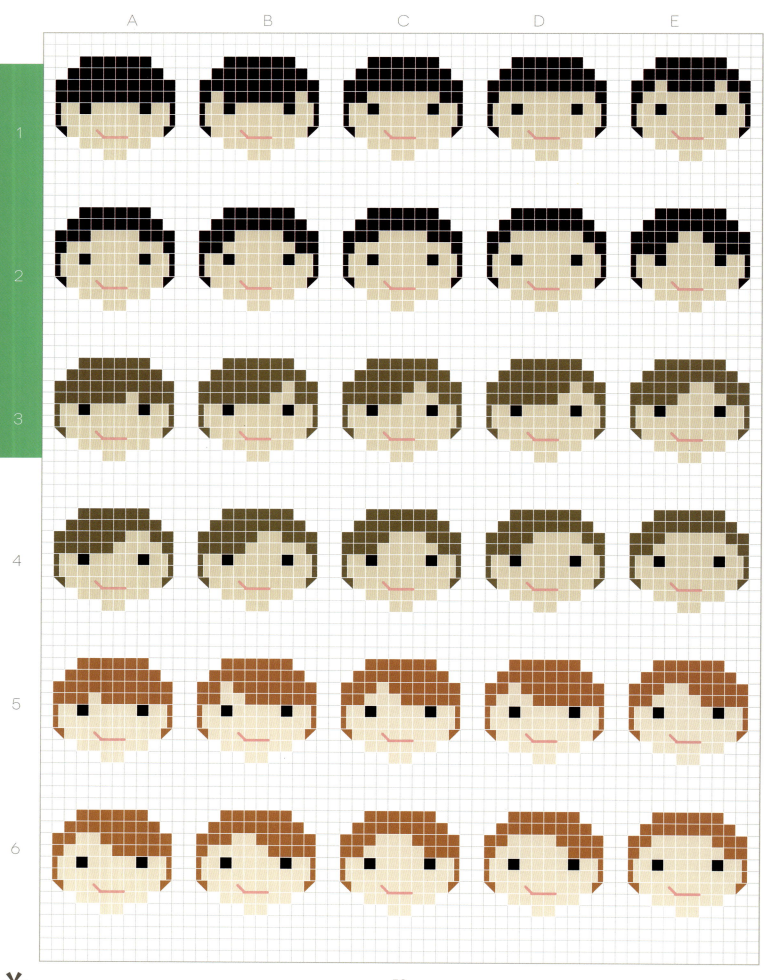

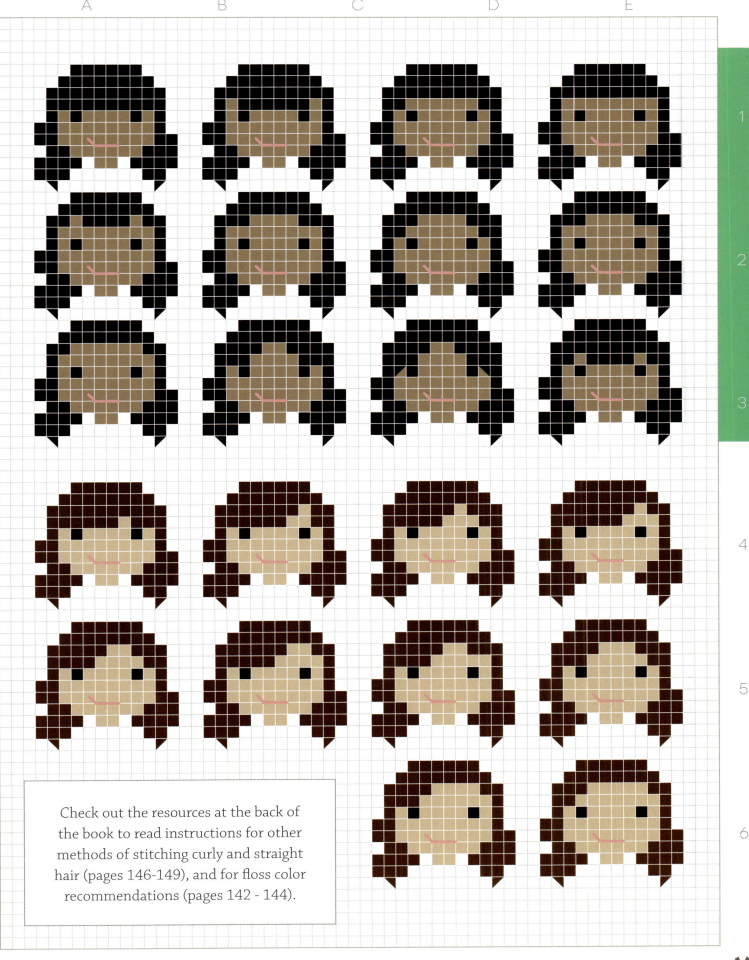

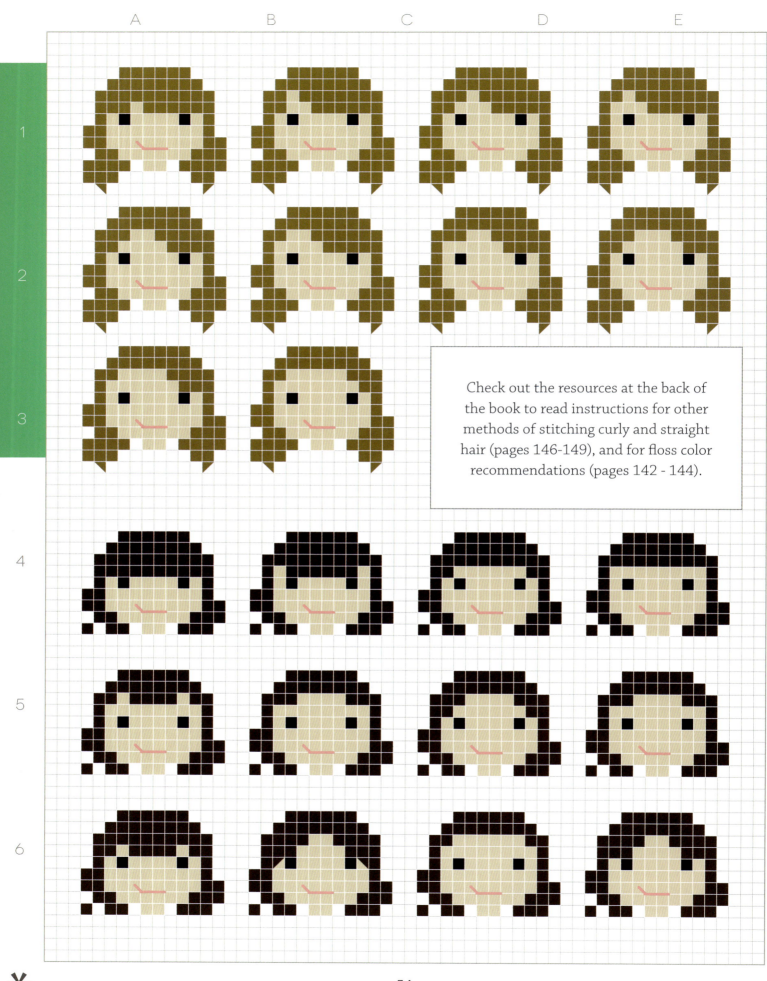

Check out the resources at the back of the book to read instructions for other methods of stitching curly and straight hair (pages 146-149), and for floss color recommendations (pages 142 - 144).

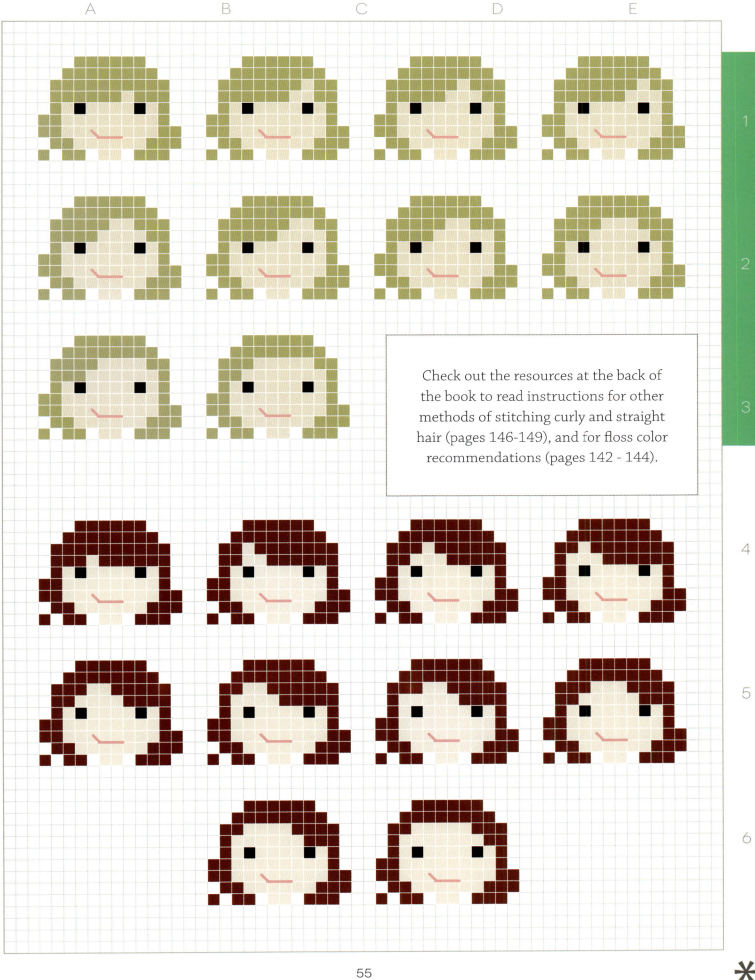

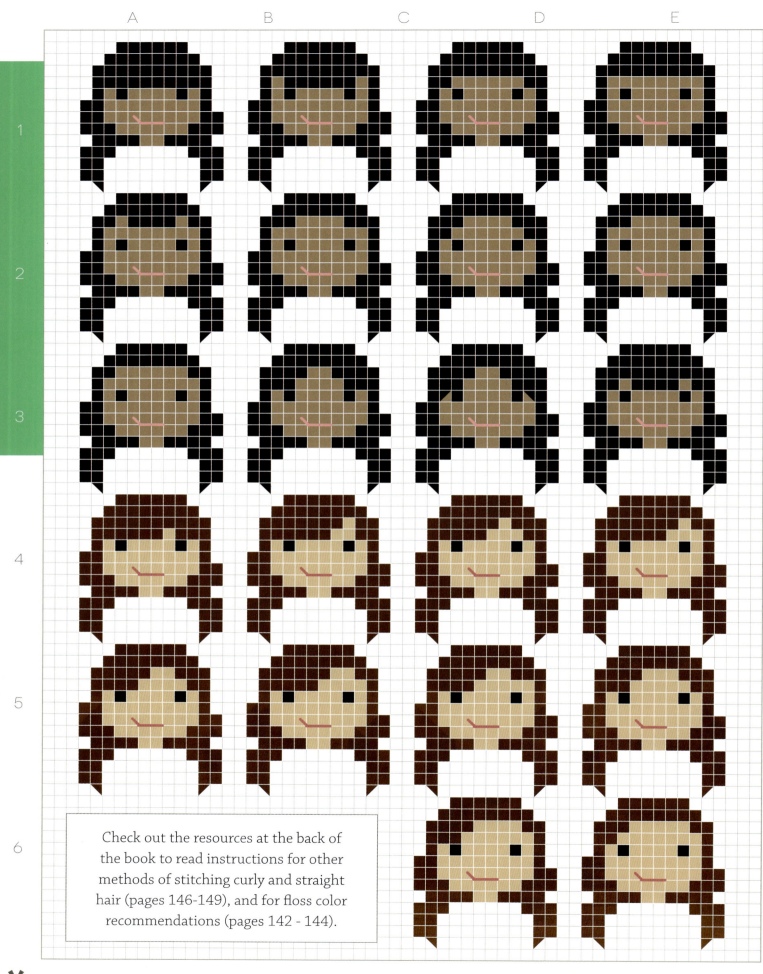

Check out the resources at the back of the book to read instructions for other methods of stitching curly and straight hair (pages 146-149), and for floss color recommendations (pages 142 - 144).

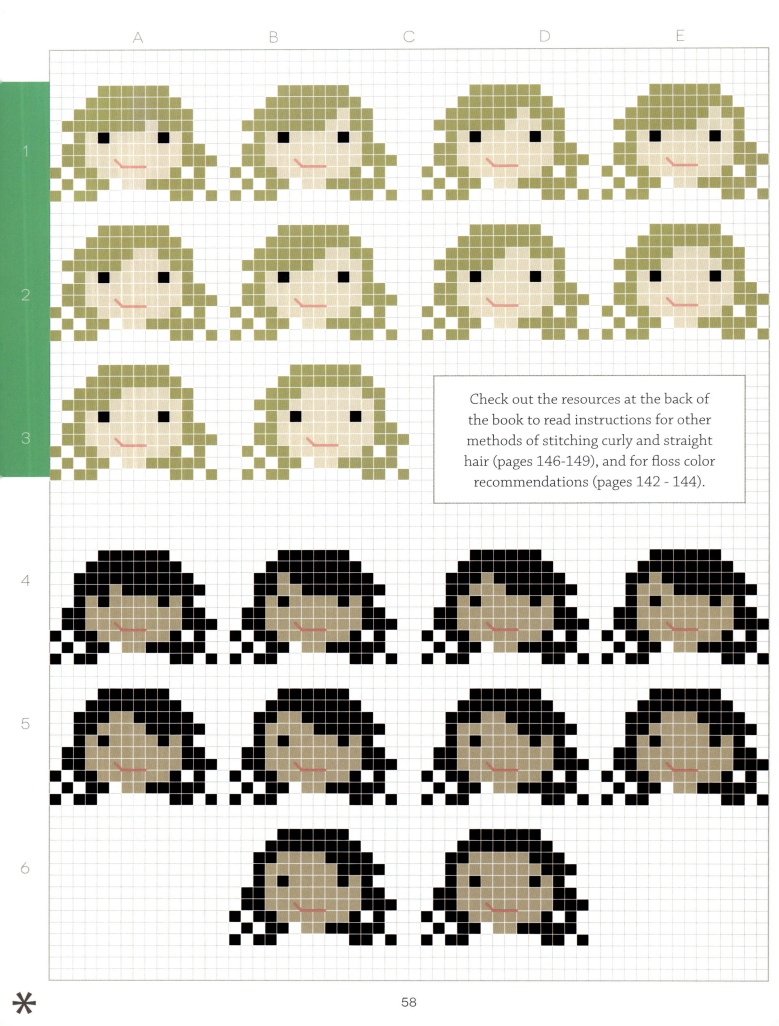

Check out the resources at the back of the book to read instructions for other methods of stitching curly and straight hair (pages 146-149), and for floss color recommendations (pages 142 - 144).

A   B   C   D   E

1

2

3

4

5

6

59

With curly hair, design it with your character in mind. Does the hair flop to one side? Does it have curls that go all over? Work within, around, and beyond the patterns here to achieve the perfect look for your curly-headed characters!

Check out the resources at the back of the book to read instructions for other methods of stitching curly and straight hair (pages 146-149), and for floss color recommendations (pages 142 - 144).

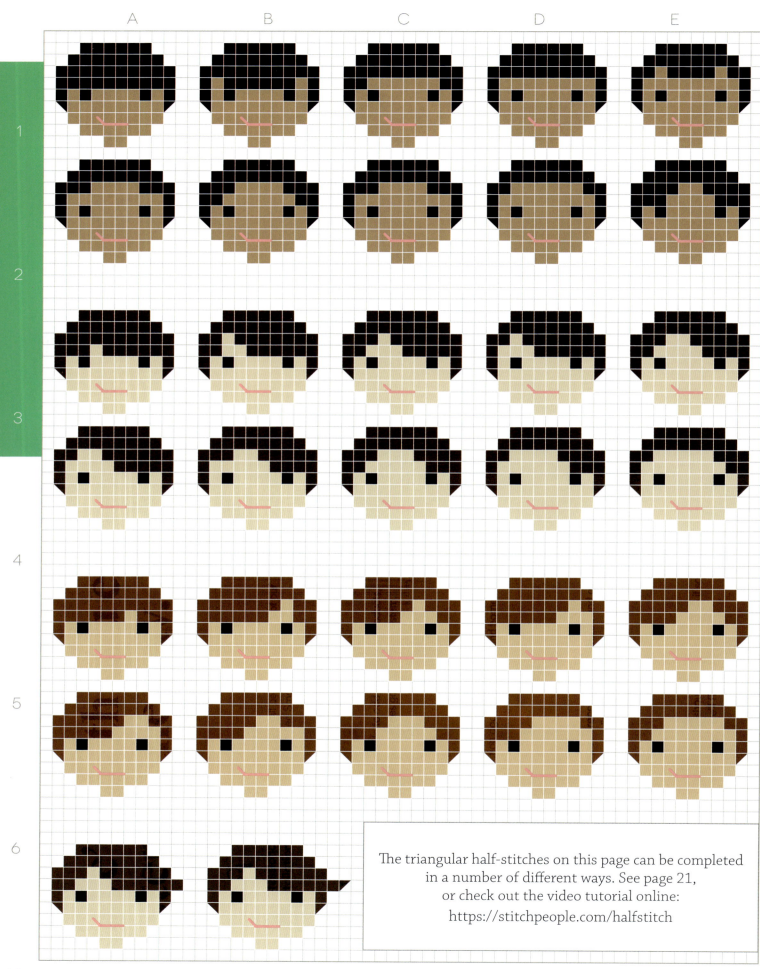

The triangular half-stitches on this page can be completed in a number of different ways. See page 21, or check out the video tutorial online: https://stitchpeople.com/halfstitch

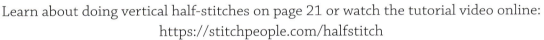

Learn about doing vertical half-stitches on page 21 or watch the tutorial video online: https://stitchpeople.com/halfstitch

If you need to make a short, curly hairstyle, try adding French knots atop your completed cross stitches to give the impression of curls. For instructions on how to do a French knot, see page 20. To see what this method looks like completed, see the image on page 20, and image 2 on page 147.

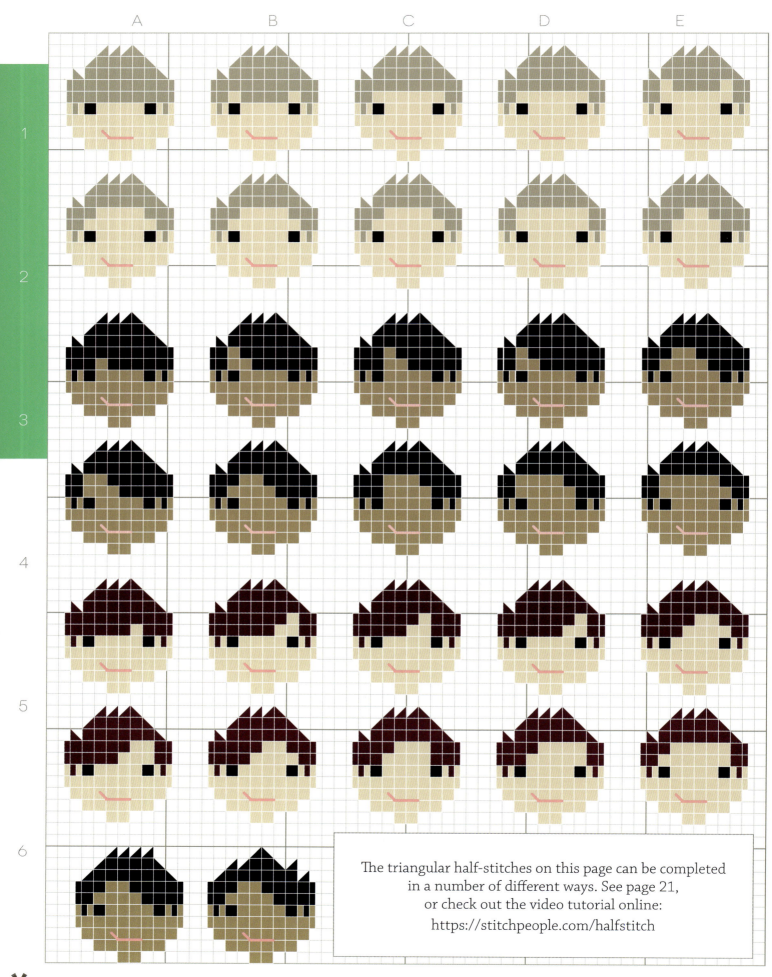

The triangular half-stitches on this page can be completed in a number of different ways. See page 21, or check out the video tutorial online: https://stitchpeople.com/halfstitch

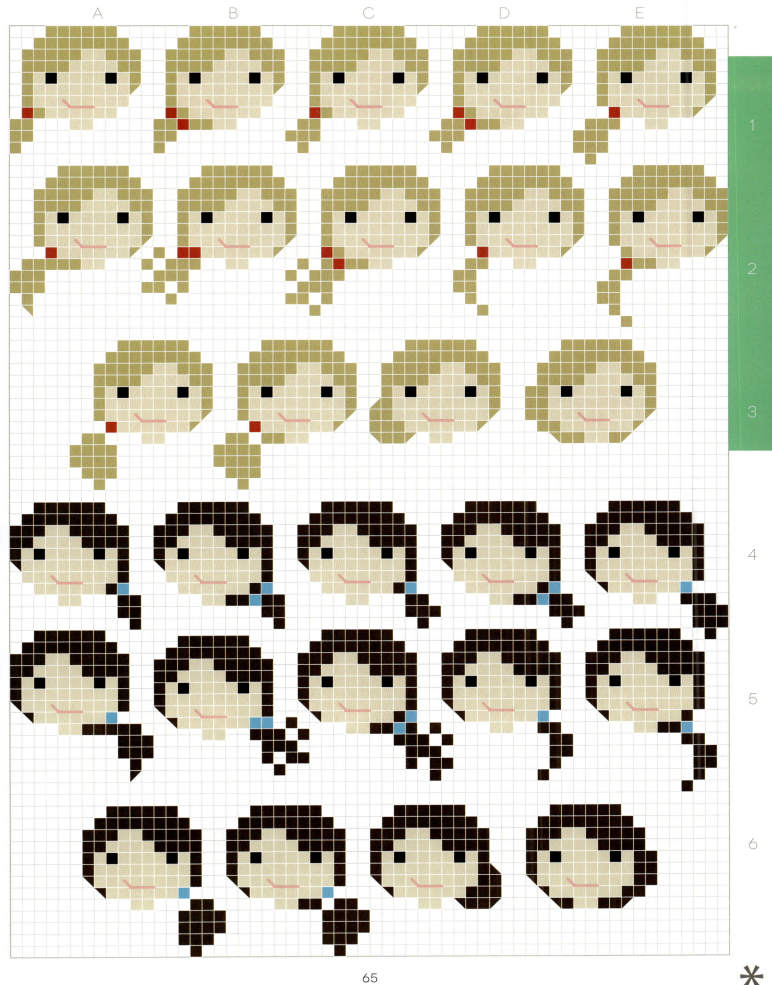

Check out pages 146–147 for instruction on how to make curly hair look more curly.

Stitch vertical and diagonal straight stitches with a single strand of hair-color floss to create a wispy effect.

Be sure to account for the width of side-buns and pigtails as you count your characters to map out your portrait! See page 29 for more info about spacing.

Don't forget, you can stitch long braids or pigtails down the front of a stitch people character's shoulders, so they're visible atop the clothing.

"Up-dos" can be tricky because most of the detail is centered at the back of the head. You can "cheat" the look of an up-do by relaxing the style to frame the face, as shown in the following examples.

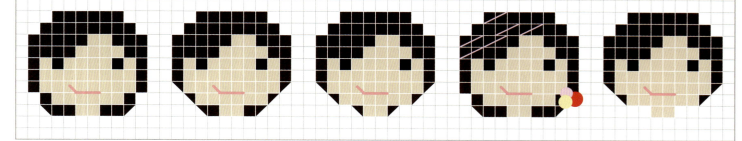

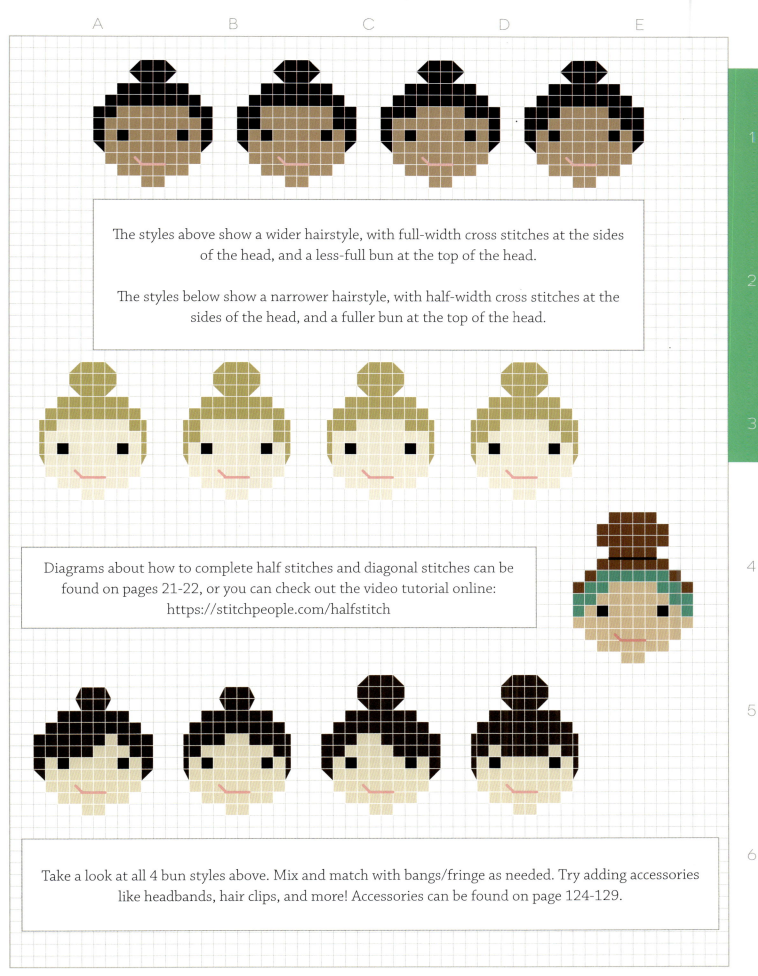

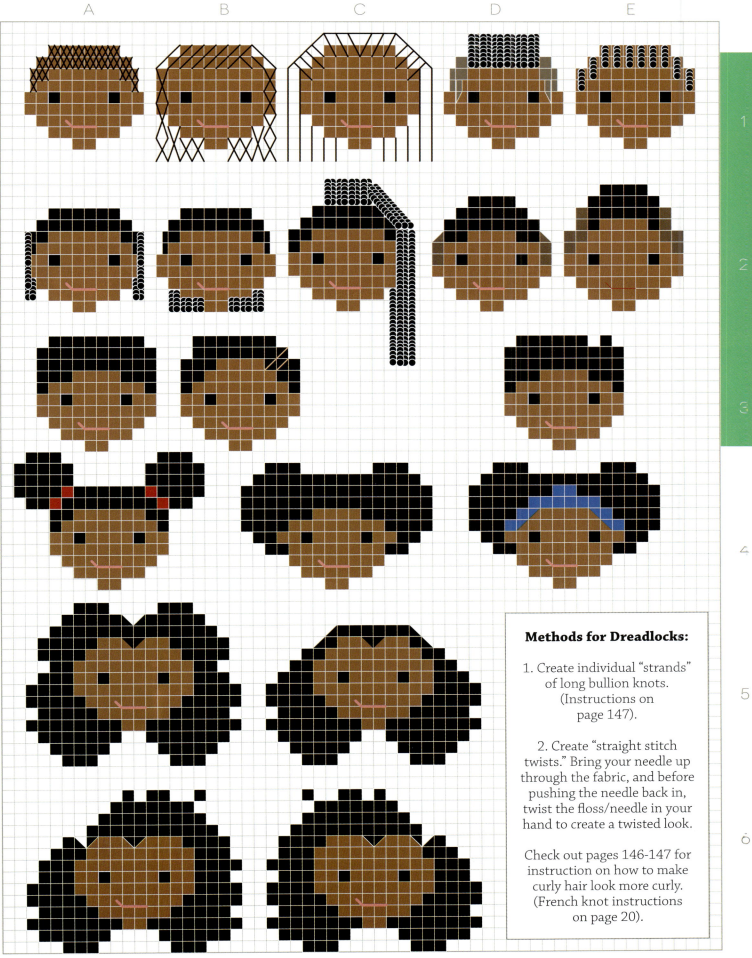

Methods for Dreadlocks:

1. Create individual "strands" of long bullion knots. (Instructions on page 147).

2. Create "straight stitch twists." Bring your needle up through the fabric, and before pushing the needle back in, twist the floss/needle in your hand to create a twisted look.

Check out pages 146-147 for instruction on how to make curly hair look more curly. (French knot instructions on page 20).

WOMEN'S CLOTHING

- **Coloring**: Remember to change the skin tone and hair color based on the coloring of your characters
  - See "Color Recommendations" on pages 142-144.

- **Mix-and-Match:** The trick with clothing is to mix and match what you need! Picking and choosing to combine various necklines, skirt widths, pant lengths, sleeve styles, (and more) can help to capture the likeness of anyone's wardrobe.

- **Character Width:** I designed Stitch People with a "template" in mind - where the likeness of a character is represented in hair style, clothing style, and coloring, and all body widths remain the same. Think of Disneyland's "it's a small world" where all the animatronic characters are the same height and width, and each country's heritage is represented through clothing, hair colors, hair styles, and skin colors.
  - Due to popular demand, I have created guidelines for creating wider Stitch People characters which can be found on page 158-159.

- **Character Height:** If you need to adjust someone's height, I recommend adding or removing height from the torso area or leg area, one square at a time, alternating between the torso and leg area if more than one square of height adjustment is needed.

- Note the **coordinates** around each of the design pages to help you navigate the patterns and keep track of what styles you choose for each character. These coordinates can be recorded on the **character design pages (pg. 36-47).**
  - Record the coordinates in the order of Page # - Column Letter - Row # (i.e. 55 - A - 2)

DESIGNING AND STITCHING CLOTHING WITH PATTERNS

Check out the resources at the back of the book to learn how to stitch clothing items that have floral, geometric, or other types of patterns! Aida fabric may be small, but patterns are totally possible!

See pages 150-153 for instructions regarding these techniques for stitching floral patterns (both large and small), lace, geometric patterns, leopard print, and more.

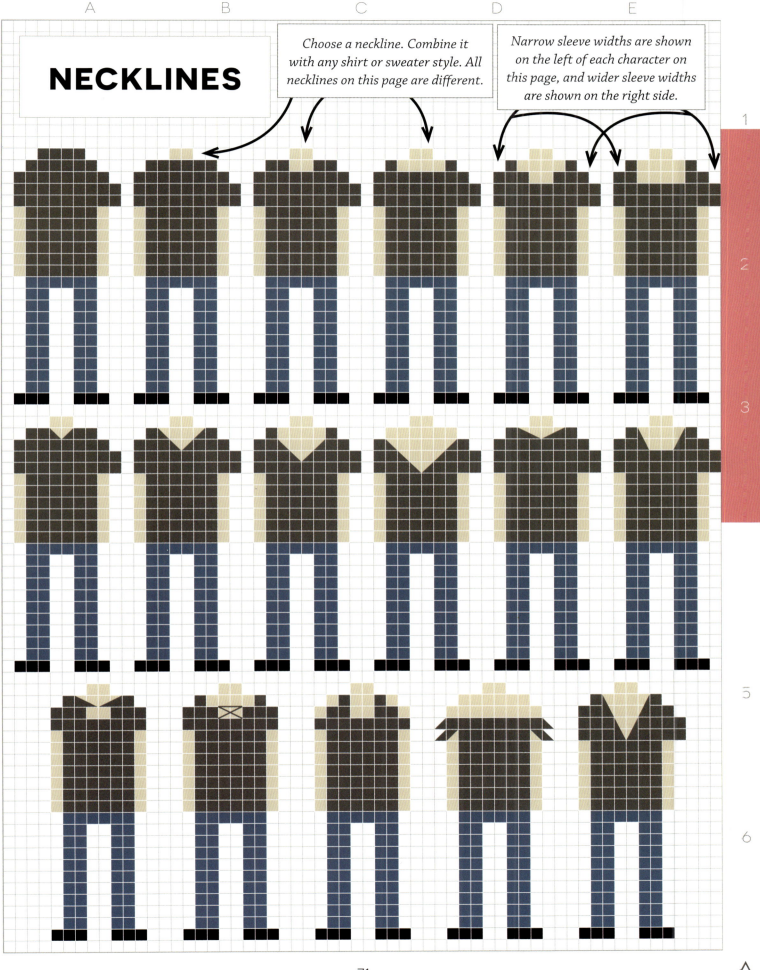

THIS PAGE SHOWS DIFFERENT SLEEVE LENGTHS. ON THE <u>LEFT</u> SIDE OF THE BODIES, THE SLEEVE IS SHOWN AS A <u>NARROW</u> SLEEVE. ON THE <u>RIGHT</u> SIDE OF THE BODIES, THE SLEEVE IS SHOWN IN THE <u>WIDE</u> SLEEVE STYLE TO HELP YOU VISUALIZE THE WIDTH DIFFERENCE, AND SELECT ACCORDING TO YOUR NEEDS FOR YOUR CHARACTERS.

STRIPED SHIRTS

(1) Cross-stitch a shirt using 3 threads of one color, and back-stitch horizontal stripes of another color atop the first color using 1 thread. (Backstitching instructions on page 20).

(2) Cross-stitch rows of different colors using three strands of floss in two different colors to achieve a striped effect.

SHOES

Combine cross-stitches and back-stitches to achieve the perfect shoe style. I recommend using 1-2 threads of floss instead of 3 for sandal details. For shoe laces, complete cross stitches with one thread atop the completed cross stitches of the shoe's color. To emphasize the bottom of the shoe, complete a straight stitch along the bottom of the completed cross stitches, using the holes in the Aida fabric to emphasize the "toe" and "heel" area of the shoe.

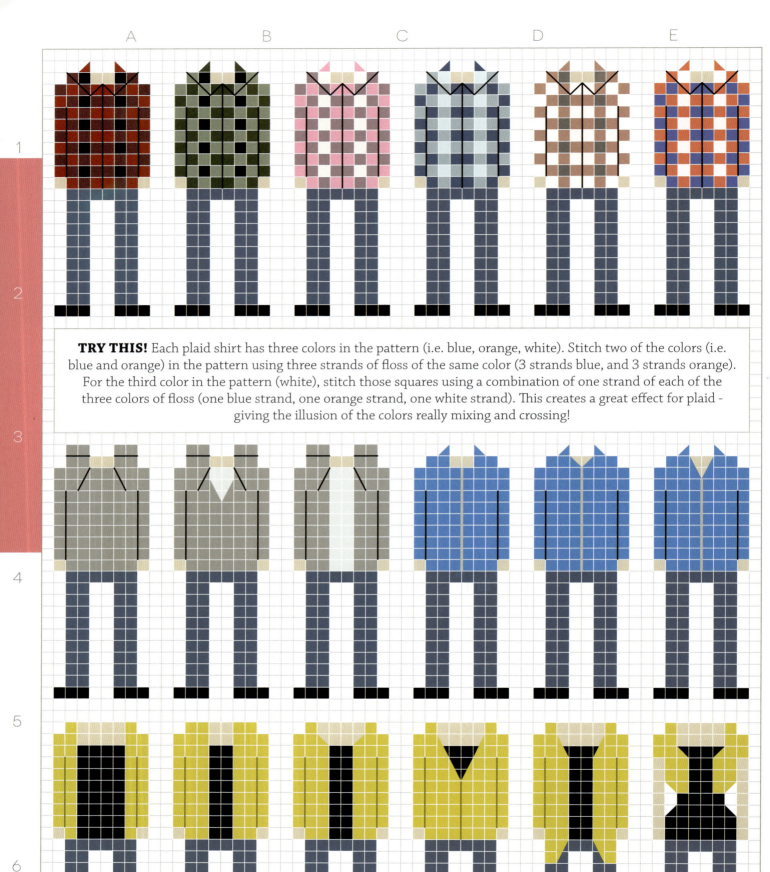

TRY THIS! Each plaid shirt has three colors in the pattern (i.e. blue, orange, white). Stitch two of the colors (i.e. blue and orange) in the pattern using three strands of floss of the same color (3 strands blue, and 3 strands orange). For the third color in the pattern (white), stitch those squares using a combination of one strand of each of the three colors of floss (one blue strand, one orange strand, one white strand). This creates a great effect for plaid - giving the illusion of the colors really mixing and crossing!

Match your favorite shoe style with your favorite outfit. Change the color of shoes as needed - natural colors, glittery shoes, or colorful sneakers can complete an outfit uniquely and perfectly!

For "graphics" on shirts, there is no need to cross-stitch the original color of the shirt beneath the colors of the graphic. Doing this may result in a chunky look to the character.

Don't forget that you can **mix and match elements from multiple patterns** to create your very own, unique, custom, personalized, 100% Y-O-U-R-S pattern like those above. Combine different necklines, waistlines, sleeve widths, shorts and skirt styles and widths, and shoe styles. Embellish with French knots, back-stitching, and half-stitches to create the perfect lines for your outfits and clothing styles. (See page 150 for more info!)

A B C D E

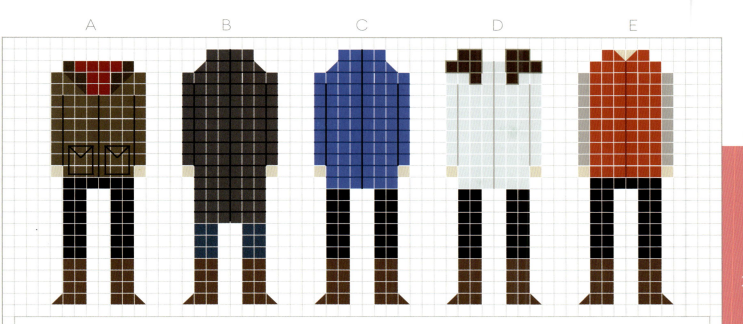

For details like buttons, pockets, and zippers, and for differentiation between torso and arms, use 1-2 threads of black, dark gray, light gray, or a darker or lighter color than the coat or other item of clothing.

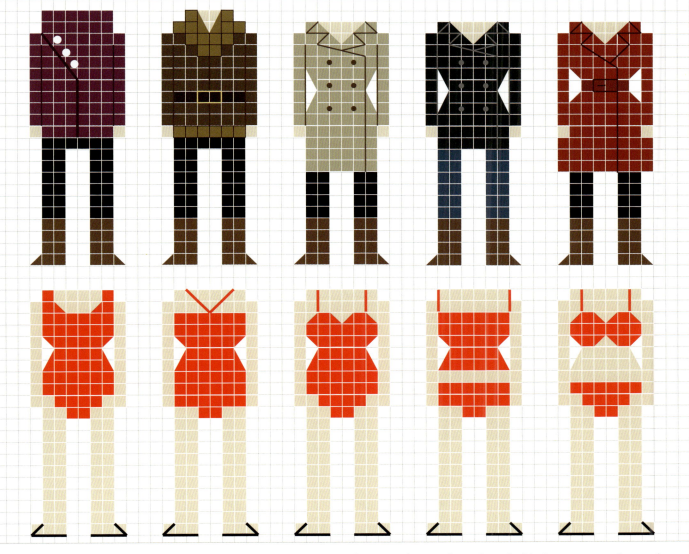

Where the swimsuit meets the legs, you may wish to complete one diagonal stitch - a half of a cross-stitch - in the color of the swim suit to "smooth" the line from the hip to the inner thigh.

White shirts on this page are shown in light gray for pattern visibility.

For collars on shirts, or other details on shirts and jackets, choose a color similar to that of the shirt or jacket, but slightly darker or lighter. Then, use 1 thread of floss to do back stitches on the jacket or shirt to achieve the differentiating lines and details of the shirt or jacket.

A	B	C	D	E

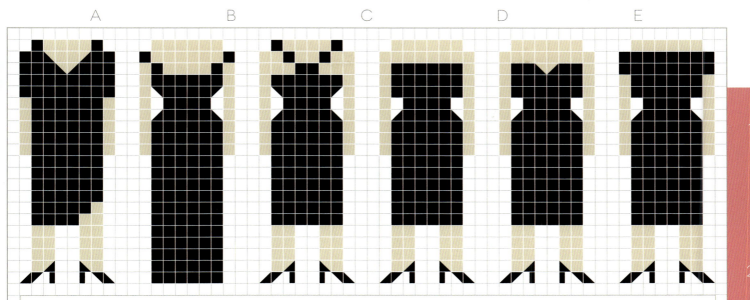

It isn't always necessary to make shoes visible. This will be up to your preference and needs.

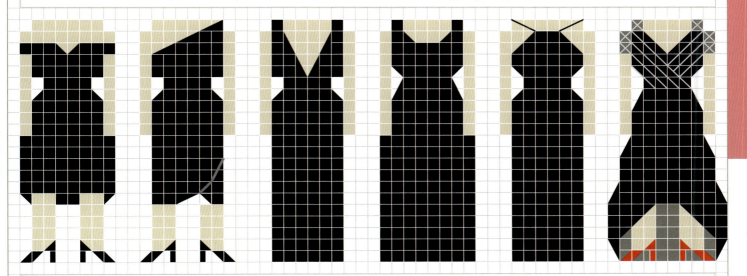

Mix and match necklines or sleeve styles from the previous pages with the various dress silhouettes on this page to portray a ball gown, wedding dress, or other elegant attire. Try mixing in 1 sparkle or metallic thread in with 2 similarly colored threads to give the dress a shiny, satin, or beaded look.

<u>Visit pages 150 - 153 to learn how to incorporate patterns or lace into your Stitch People dresses.</u>

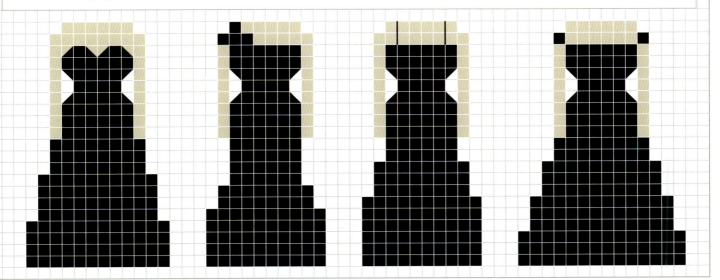

PREGNANT BELLIES

Choose your favorite hairstyles from the previous patterns and combine them with the body styles on this page to depict a pregnant character. Keep in mind most of the clothing styles on the previous pages can be adapted to accommodate a pregnant belly. These patterns are shown in plain tops and colors for clarity, but stripes, details, jackets, sweaters, and more can definitely be accommodated.

Because Stitch People portraits typically show characters in a front-facing orientation, it can be difficult to convey a three-dimensional effect like a pregnant belly. So adjusting the arm placement of the character, playing with dark-and-light dimensional contrasts, creating ruching effects with straight stitches, and adding a little width on either side of the torso are good ways to achieve the visual effect of a pregnant mama.

MEN'S HAIRSTYLES

- **Varying parts**: Center-parted hairstyles, left-parted hairstyles, and right-parted hairstyles

- **Varying lengths**; chin-length, shoulder-length, chest-length

- **Coloring**: Remember to change the skin tone and hair color based on the coloring of your characters

  - See "Color Recommendations" on pages 142-144

- **Neck**: Most hairstyles show the neck in addition to face and hair. I usually choose to give necks only 1 square in height but you may choose to add an additional square if you prefer the look of a longer neck. Keep that in mind when stacking a face and hair style on top of a body / outfit.

- **Shoulders**: Most long hairstyles fall around and behind the shoulders, but you may choose to stitch some hair over the shoulders or torso to show a more cascading hairstyle.

- Some styles may work for **both men and women**: mix-and-match as you see fit for your specific characters.

  - The dimensions for both women's and men's faces are the same. It is only the hairstyles that vary. So, in theory, men's and women's hairstyles are interchangeable.

- Note the **coordinates** around each of the design pages to help you navigate the patterns and keep track of what styles you choose for each character. These coordinates can be recorded on your **character design pages (pg. 36-47).**

  - Record the coordinates in the order of Page # - Column Letter - Row # (i.e. 87 - A - 1)

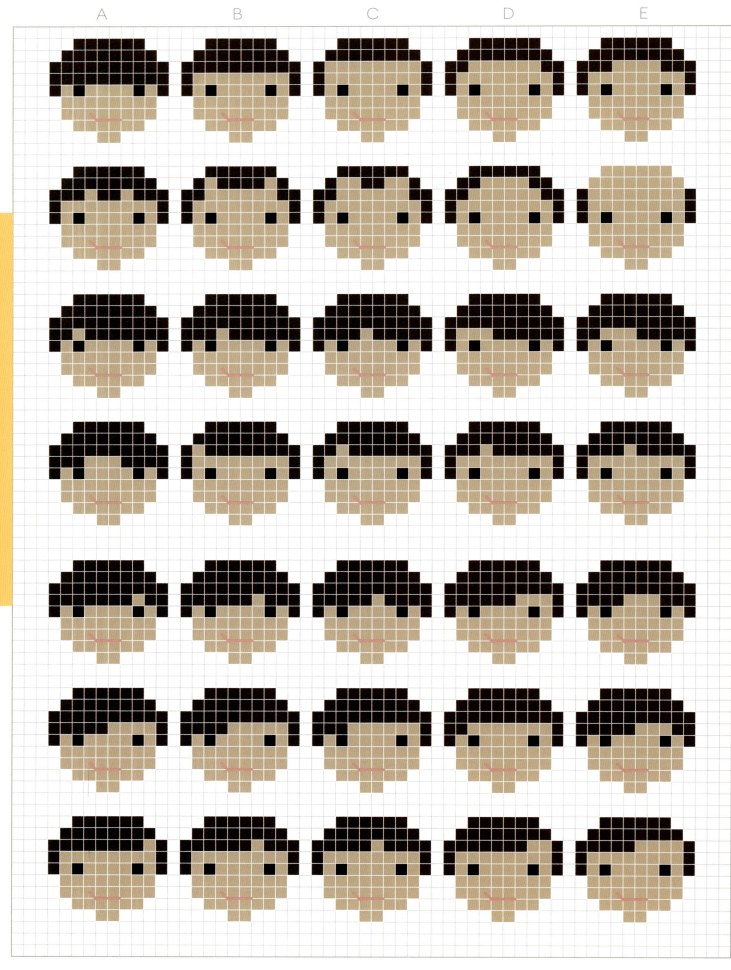

	A	B	C	D	E
1					
2					
3					
4					
5					
6					

85

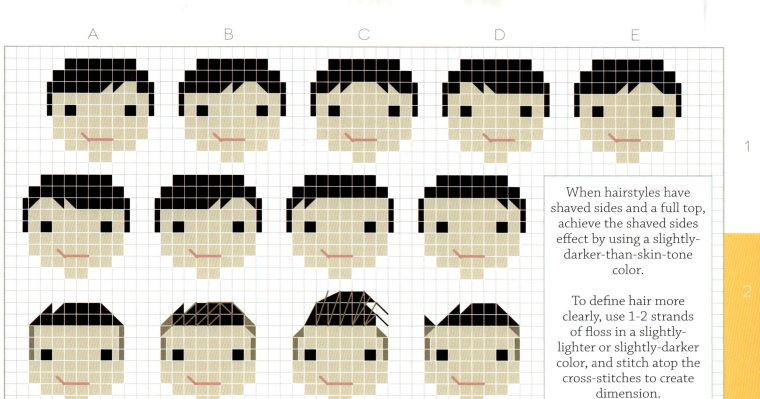

When hairstyles have shaved sides and a full top, achieve the shaved sides effect by using a slightly-darker-than-skin-tone color.

To define hair more clearly, use 1-2 strands of floss in a slightly-lighter or slightly-darker color, and stitch atop the cross-stitches to create dimension.

With **facial hair**, there are a couple options. First, you can complete the facial hair using 3 strands of floss (don't forget about combining colors if needed!) Alternately, you can stitch the whole face in the skin-tone color, and stitch facial hair on top, using 1 strand of floss in the color of the hair. This will look like stubble/scruff. Stitch **lips** atop the facial hair.

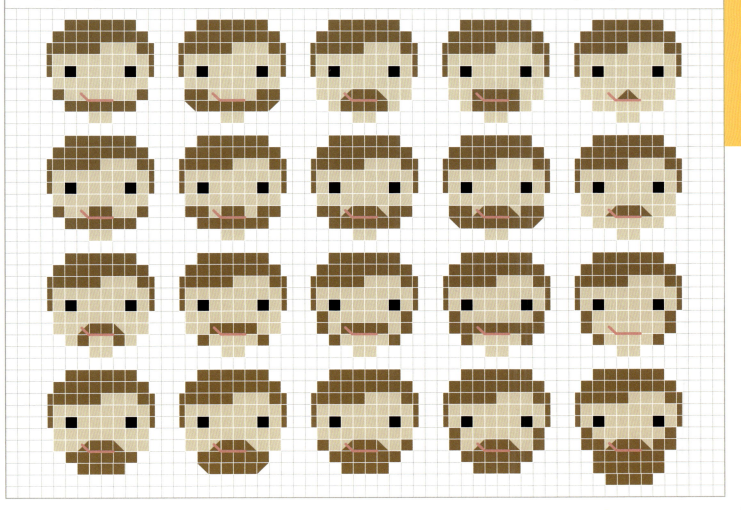

MEN'S CLOTHING

- **Coloring**: Remember to change the skin tone and hair color based on the coloring of your characters
    - See "Color Recommendations" on pages 142-144.
- **Mix-and-Match:** The trick with clothing is to mix and match what you need! Picking and choosing to combine various necklines, skirt widths, pant lengths, sleeve styles, (and more) can help to capture the likeness of anyone's wardrobe.
- **Character Width:** I designed Stitch People with a "template" in mind - where the likeness of a character is represented in hair style, clothing style, and coloring, and all body widths remain the same. Think of Disneyland's "it's a small world" where all the animatronic characters are the same height and width, and each country's heritage is represented through clothing, hair colors, hair styles, and skin colors.
    - Due to popular demand, I have created guidelines for creating wider Stitch People characters which can be found on page 158-159.
- **Character Height:** If you need to adjust someone's height, I recommend adding or removing height from the torso area or leg area, one square at a time, alternating between the torso and leg area if more than one square of height adjustment is needed.
- Note the **coordinates** around each of the design pages to help you navigate the patterns and keep track of what styles you choose for each character. These coordinates can be recorded on the **character design pages (pg. 36-47).**
    - Record the coordinates in the order of Page # - Column Letter - Row # (i.e. 55 - A - 2)

A   B   C   D   E

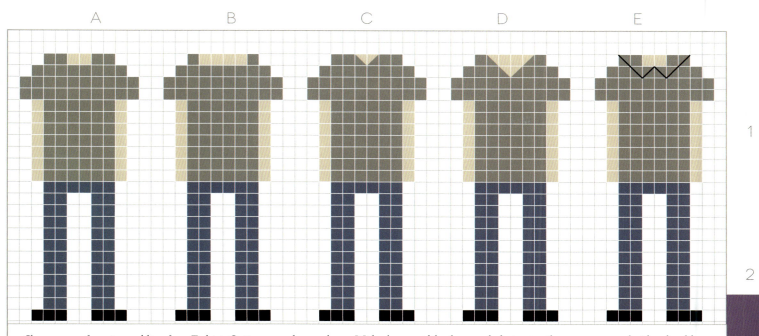

Choose your favorite neckline for a T-shirt. Options are shown above. Wide sleeve widths for men help to give the appearance of wider shoulders.

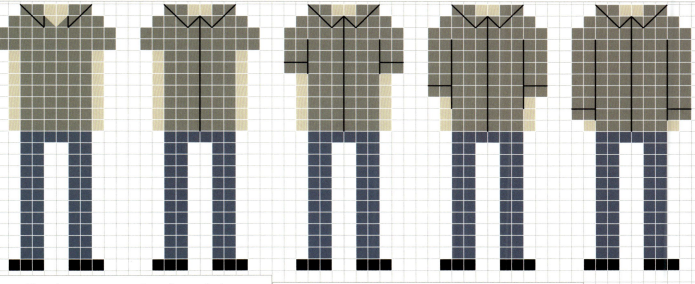

Your character may require a slimmer look.
Use narrower sleeves in this case.

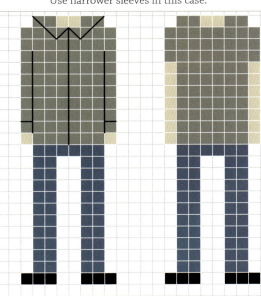

For **collars** on shirts - polo or button-down - choose a color similar to that of the shirt, but slightly darker or lighter. Use 1 thread of floss in that color, and do back stitches to illustrate the lines of the shirt, like in the picture (right).

Use 1 strand of floss in the slightly-contrasting color to create French knots for **buttons** down the front of the shirt, or on the sleeves.

To the left is an example of NARROW **sleeves** so you can see the difference in context of the wider sleeves which can create the illusion of a character having wider shoulders.

1

2

3

4

5

6

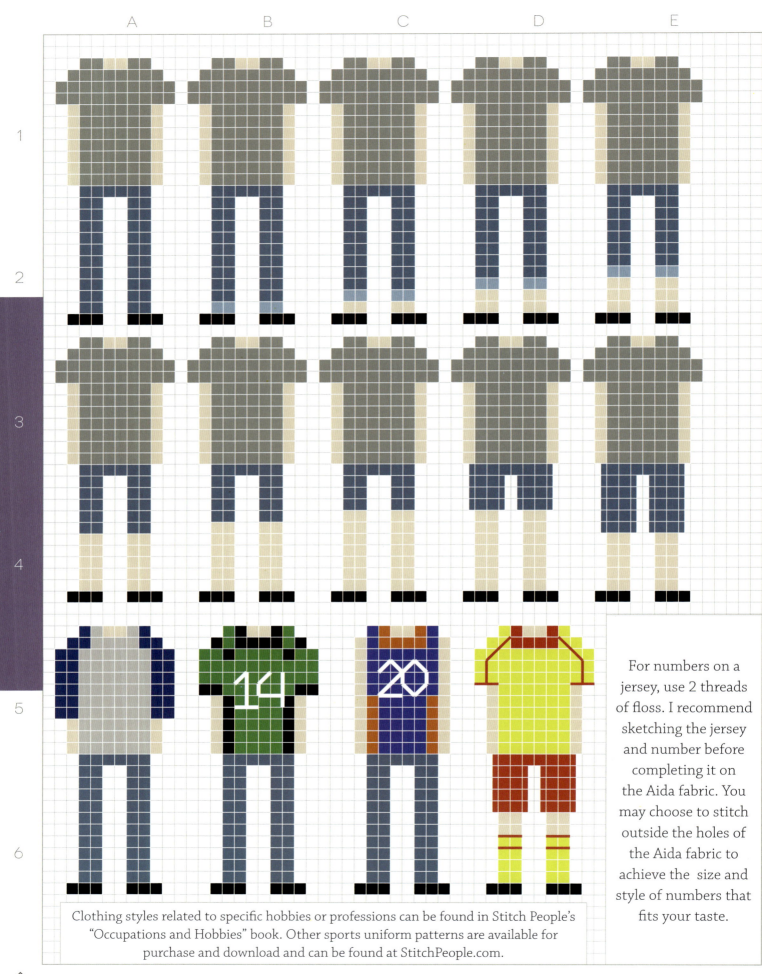

Back-stitch shirt details, and lines between the arms and body in a slightly lighter or slightly darker color than the article of clothing. Use one or two threads in a French knot for buttons. Add stripes outside predefined Aida holes, if need be, to embellish the clothing. Instructions for extra stitches are found on pages 20-22.

Mix and match complimentary colors to create stripes and argyle patterns. See pages 150-153 for more instruction about creating special fabric patterns.
For argyle, use 1 thread atop the other colors to create the crossing diagonal lines.

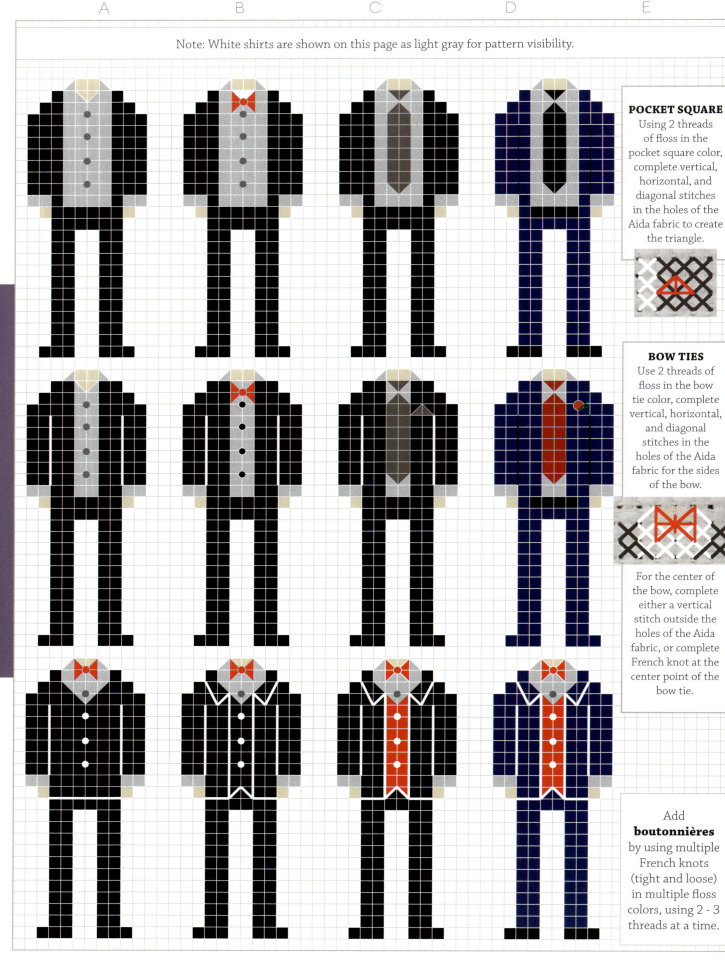

CHILDREN & BABIES

HERE'S HOW IT WORKS:

- **Babies:** Pages 104-105 show examples of very young babies: babes-in-arms, swaddled babies, babies in cradles, prams and strollers, and more.

- **Height Options:** Page 97 shows height options for children, from toddler-sized to young teen. Age suggestions listed there are *approximate*. In many circumstances, older children aren't always taller than younger children. Take a look at the designs and decide which are best for you and the characters you're stitching.

- **Head Sizes:** There are different head shapes and sizes for children on pages 98-100. These correspond with the body heights on page 97. Note the age labels and color coordination.

- **Clothing Styles:** There are endless possibilities for clothing styles. There are a few sample clothing designs for children on pages 101-103. However, you can get creative and **modify** the children's clothing styles, as well as the women's and men's clothing styles to fit the specific size of your children characters.

  Note the age labels and color coordinations to more easily match the recommended head sizes (p. 98-100) and body sizes (p. 97, 101-103) together.

- **Coloring:** Change the skin tone and colors of the clothes based on the specific individuals you choose to represent.

- **Teenagers** ages 16 - 19 typically look best when designed with adult-sized bodies. However, if the teenager is particularly thin or small, use the largest head style (page 100) and larger body sizes (yellow category).

CHOOSING A BODY SIZE FOR YOUR CHILDREN CHARACTERS

<u>In general</u>, children grow taller each year as they get older. On this page are templates for body sizes for children ages 2 - 15. See the note on the previous page regarding sizing for older teenagers.

You can use the body heights and sizes on this page as a general guideline. Be sure to make adjustments for your personal customization needs. For example, sometimes younger sisters are taller than older brothers, or a child's growth is stunted, while another child may experience a large growth spurt despite being a certain age. These body sizes are not hard and fast rules for design, merely guidelines and templates for you to use to save you from the hassle of designing them from scratch.

Use the color coding associated with the age range at the base of the character feet on this page to identify which style of head to pair the body with from the following pages. Magenta represents the 2 - 4 year old range and corresponds with page 98. Cyan represents the 5 - 11 year old range and corresponds with page 99. Yellow represents the 12 - 15 year old age range and corresponds with page 100.

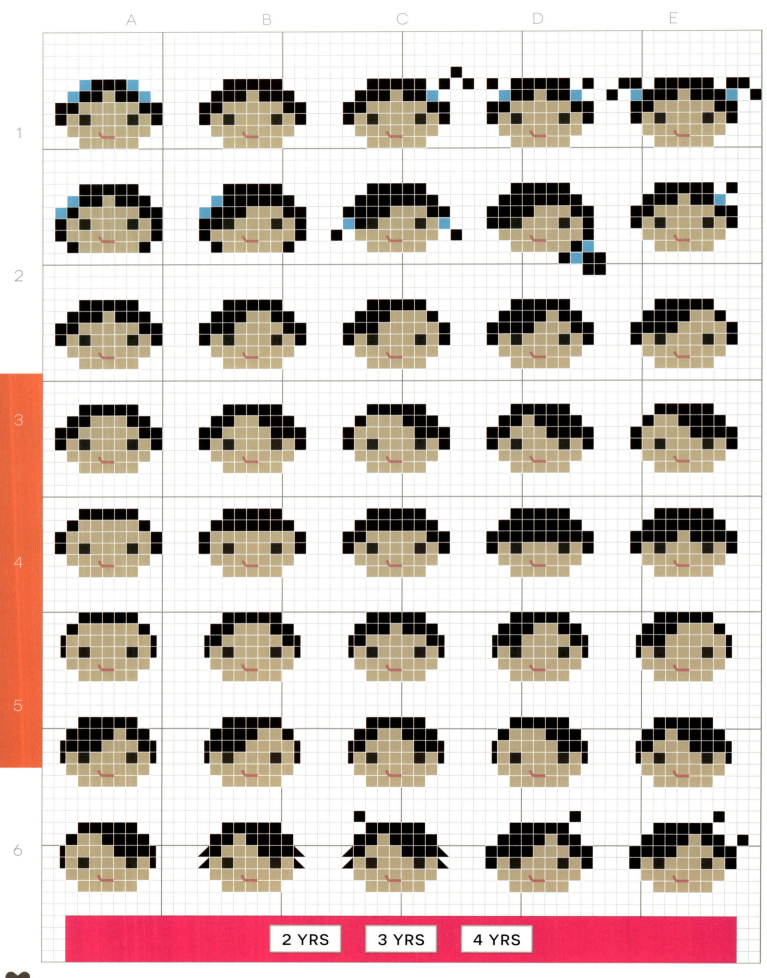

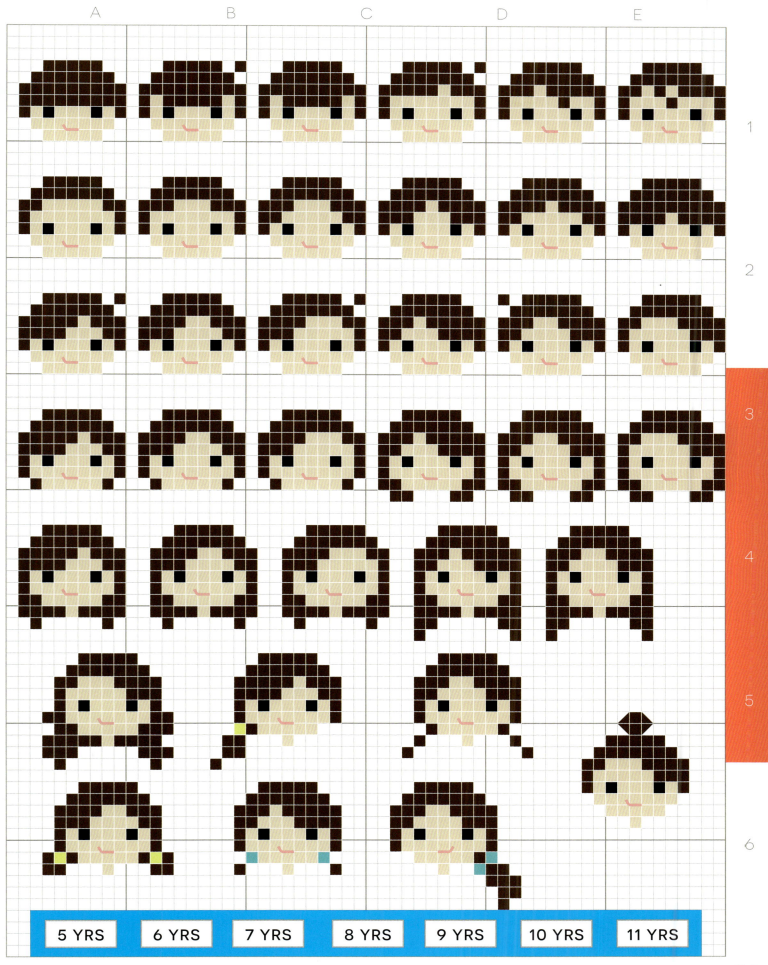

CATS & DOGS & MORE

- **Cat Breeds:** Abyssinian, American Shorthair, Bengal, Birman, British Shorthair, Burmese, Exotic Shorthair, Maine Coon, Manx, Norwegian Forest, Persian, Ragdoll, Siamese, Sphynx. Need something different or more custom? Read on!

- **Dog Breeds:** Airedale Terrier, Australian Shepherd, Beagle, Bernese Mountain Dog, Bichon Frise, Blood Hound, Border Collie, Boxer, Brittany Spaniel, Cavalier King Charles Spaniel, Chihuahua, Chow Chow, Cocker Spaniel, Collie, Corgi, Dachshund, Doberman Pinscher, English Bulldog, French Bulldog, German Shepherd, Golden Retriever, Great Dane, Greyhound, Jack Russell Terrier, Labradoodle, Labrador Retriever, Mastiff, Miniature Schnauzer, Newfoundland, Pit Bull Terrier, Pomeranian, Pug, Scottish Terrier, Sheltie, Poodle (large), Poodle (small), Rottweiler, Samoyed, Shih Tzu, Siberian Husky, Yorkshire Terrier. Need something else? Read on!

- **Fur Coloring:** Try using multiple thread colors of floss for your pet's fur. Combining hues of brown, gold, tan, red, orange, gray, black, white, and more can achieve the perfect, blended look of fur you need.

- **Fading Colors:** You can fade colors together to achieve a more natural look. For example, if a black dog has a white chest, and the fur around the chest fades from black to white, combine a thread of black, gray and white together for the stitches directly around the dog's white chest in your cross-stitch design.

- **Eyes:** Eyes can be completed with full cross-stitches or with French knots, according to what's shown in the pattern. I typically complete eyes with 2 strands of floss in a French knot.

  - **Multi-colored Eyes:** For animals with multi-colored eyes (e.g. green and black) mix 1 colored thread with 1 black thread, and then complete a French knot.

  - **Black-on-Black Eyes:** Read about this on page 110.

- **Noses:** I typically complete noses with 2-3 strands of floss in a French knot.

- **Pictures and instructions:** see pages 121-122 for pictures regarding how to complete some of the "outside-the-lines" stitches in many of the cat and dog patterns. Review how to do half-width stitches on page 20-22.

- **Don't see your dog?** Read on!

DON'T SEE YOUR DOG? HERE'S WHAT TO DO:

It is close to impossible to generate a specific pattern for every dog breed, and every color variation of every dog breed. There are close to 340 recognized dog breeds in the world, and that's just purebreds. Nowadays you can combine dog breeds and generate "designer dogs:" Peek-a-Poo, Labradoodle, etc.

Now, many dogs are the same basic shape and size. Because of that, **I can teach you to design your own dog for your Stitch People portraits, if the provided patterns don't exactly accommodate your needs.**

START WITH THE DOG'S **SHAPE**:

Many dogs have a similar shape. A Shiba Inu, Carolina dog, Koolie, Berger Picard, Hollandaise Herder, and Sulimov all originate from different continents. All of their coloring varies. And even their size varies within 10-20 lbs. But the various breed SHAPES are consistent. So, when looking at the available patterns, **ignore the listed breed**, and simply choose one that LOOKS most like your dog. Use that shape as the foundation for your dog pattern.

IF THERE IS NO MATCHING SHAPE, **MIX-AND-MATCH**:

Using the patterns from this book, you can mix-and-match dog body parts. I know how that sounds. Hear me out. Maybe use the body shape of one dog, the head of another, and the ears of another if you're not finding a pattern that's just right. If nothing else, this is a good way to get your creativity flowing. Look for specific elements and match them as needed: ear shape, face shape, chest profile, leg height, etc.

WHAT ABOUT THE DOG'S SIZE?

First, remember that Stitch People portraits are cartoon-ified versions of real people and pets. Things aren't going to be 100% true to size. If you're seeking a true size, then a chihuahua or teacup poodle, for example, should only really be 1-3 stitches in size (the hands of Stitch People are really only 1 stitch, after all, and these little guys can fit into your hand in real life!) But then it'd be impossible to really see the dog, let alone any of their detail. So **with Stitch People portraits, we exaggerate** a little bit. Cool? Cool.

With that in mind, I can confidently tell you that size variations in dogs don't matter (generally speaking). Truly. Let me put it another way: if you only have one dog in your family, all that matters is that it looks "small," "medium," or "large" in comparison to the people in the portrait. If you have two pets, all that matters is that they look "small," "medium," or "large" in comparison to the people in the portrait, and in relation to the other pet in the portrait (if there is a size difference between them)

This is why you can choose a dog based on **shape**, alone. Sheltie dogs and Collie dogs look an awful lot alike to the general population. In reality their size is quite different. Sheltie dogs are usually around 25 lbs, and Collies are usually around 75 lbs. However, if your family only has a Sheltie - who cares if you use the Collie pattern! No one will think "If they added a Stitch People Collie in there, the sizes would be ALL OFF!" No one. No one will ever, ever think that.

WHAT IF I FEEL LIKE THE PATTERN ISN'T PERFECT?

I **PROMISE YOU** the recipient of your Stitch People portrait won't be looking at your handiwork thinking "Oh darn. My Scruffy really comes up to my *knee*, and not the top of my leg like it shows in the portrait." They'll be saying "OH MY GOSH YOU PUT SCRUFFY IN THE PORTRAIT AND HE LOOKS PERFECT, LOOK AT HIS EARS AND HIS WHITE SPOTS AND HIS RED COLLAR OH MY GOSH!!!!!"

THE SHAPE IS GOOD, BUT THE SIZE IS WRONG:

Let's say you've chosen your dog shape but you still feel it's a little too big or small. Here's how to fix it:

First, ask yourself if it's *really* too big or too small.
Reference the previous page and the section entitled "What about the dog's size?"

TO ADD OR REMOVE **HEIGHT**:

I recommend adding or removing just one or two rows of height. Start with one row in the legs/feet first, and then one row in the torso area if need be. This usually gives the most natural look when increasing or decreasing the pattern size, and one or two rows can make a big difference! If you feel the dog needs more height after adding a row in the legs, and then torso area, go back to add another row of height in the legs. Try keeping your adjustments out of the head/face so as to not distort it.

For ear length, add or remove length in the middle area of the ears before altering the tops/bottoms/tips of the ears.

TO ADD OR REMOVE **WIDTH**:

I recommend adding or removing just one or two columns of width overall. First, add or remove a column of the pattern in the bum/behind area and then add/remove in the stomach area. Be careful with width. Removing more than two columns (without removing height, too) may make the pet look a bit too narrow, and adding more width (without adding height, too) may make the pet look squatty.

For ear width, start in the middle before removing the angled edges/sides of ears.

COLORING & FUR LENGTH

What will really make or break your dog design is nailing the coloring. Here are some tips and tricks you can use to get the coloring just right:

MATCH FLOSS COLORS DIRECTLY TO A PICTURE OF YOUR PET

Hold up skeins of floss to a physical photo of your pet to compare colors. (Tip: avoid holding colors directly to your computer screen. The blue-tinted back-lighting of the screen will skew what the color truly is. If comparing floss colors to a computer screen, hold the floss off to the side of your computer screen so it's not back-lit, and dim the screen a bit so the blue light is reduced).

MIX COLORS TOGETHER

A golden retriever isn't just "yellow." She'll likely be a mixture of tan, gold, ivory white, and maybe even some light, ginger browns. What about a boxer dog that has brindle brown fur - a marbled light and dark brown look? The best way to get a true, realistic look for your dog is to determine the most plentiful colors that make up your pet and use those to stitch the majority of the fur. Combine together one thread of three separate colors at a time to achieve the recommended 3 strands to stitch your X stitches. Swap out colors frequently if neeeded.

MIX COLOR SECTIONS TOGETHER

What if your golden retriever's body is primarily a mixture of tan, ivory, and ginger, but its legs are more light-tan and white, and its face is more of an all-over tan? Then stitch that!

Combine three colors for the body, (tan, ivory, ginger), combine two colors for the legs, (light-tan, white), and use only one color for the face (tan). It will be a little time consuming to swap out your floss for just one or two stitches, but it can be really worth doing if you'd like the pet to look realistic.

USE SOME EXTRA STITCHES

Using a combination of cross-stitches, back-stitches, and large, loose French knots, or small, tight French knots, your dog can have all the correct markings: spots, freckles, wrinkles, whiskers, etc. Feel free to stitch "outside the lines" to get these little details just right and put them exactly where they need to be (meaning, feel free to make stitches that don't use the specific holes of the Aida fabric.)

Examples: Spots on dalmatians can be shown using tight, small French knots. The wrinkles that define an English bulldog's face or a basset hound's jowls can be shown with back stitches using 1 thread of floss in a color that contrasts with the dog's fur.

Check out pages 20-22 for a reminder about how to complete different types of stitches.

CURLY FUR

Complete the pattern of the dog's body using cross-stitches. Then stitch varying sizes and tensions of French knots ON TOP of the existing cross stitches you've completed. This will create a curly look for the dog, that works well for curly-haired breeds like a poodle, or an Airedale terrier. See the image on page 20 and image #2 on page 147 to see how French knots on top of cross-stitching looks.

EYE & NOSE PLACEMENT

The final step to getting your dog portrait just right is to nail the eye and nose placement. Look closely at your pet's face and think about where the eyes and nose are. Are the eyes very far apart? Are they straight ahead? Are they large eyes or small eyes? Are the eyes round and open or squinty? Is the nose large? Does it sit low or high on the face?

A chihuahua and a pug both have open, round eyes that sit wide on the face. But a chihuahua's nose is larger and sits lower on the face, and a pug's nose is smaller and sits higher on the face.

A larger dog with a long snout will have a large nose (maybe requiring a full X stitch, instead of just a French knot), and it will look best to stitch that nose further down on the face to convey the depth of the snout.

A small terrier or Yorkie will have small features - little eyes and nose about the same size, in a very perfect little triangle in the center of the face.

BLACK EYES AND BLACK NOSES ON BLACK FUR

Here are a couple ideas to help black eyes and noses stand out on black fur:

- Use **black, sparkle floss**. DMC's is called "light effects." Using this, the eyes are black (as they should be) but will catch the light and pop against the non-glitter black floss.

- Combine **one or two black threads with one white thread** to stitch the eyes. It adds just enough white in there to make the eyes stand out. Be careful, though, because sometimes the eyes can look a bit wander-y.

- Use **dark gray floss**. It's just enough difference to see the eyes better on black floss/fur, but still alludes to the dark eyes the dog actually has.

- **My favorite method:** This is tricky, but worth it. Using two threads of black floss, stitch the dog's eyes as two, tight French knots. THEN switch your floss. Thread your needle with one thread of white floss. Begin a French knot in the same place you just finished one of the black French knots. Create this single-strand white French knot slowly. As you pull the white floss tight to secure the knot, guide it to loop around the existing black French knot. This will give the eye a subtle, thin white outline to help the black eyes stand out from the black fur. Don't move too quickly on this one! Patience is key, but it looks great when it's done!

IN SUMMARY

Anyone can customize any dog pattern to be the exact breed they need - pure-bread or otherwise. Start with something SIMILAR and then tweak it. Make little changes as needed, and be sure to include all the little details that make your dog YOUR dog.

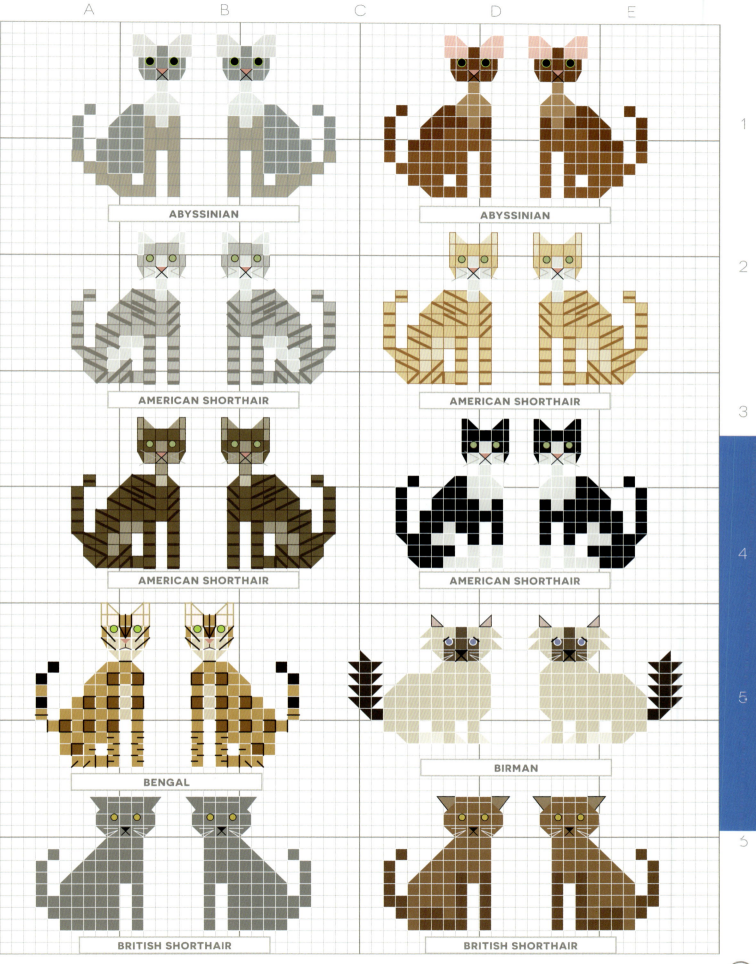

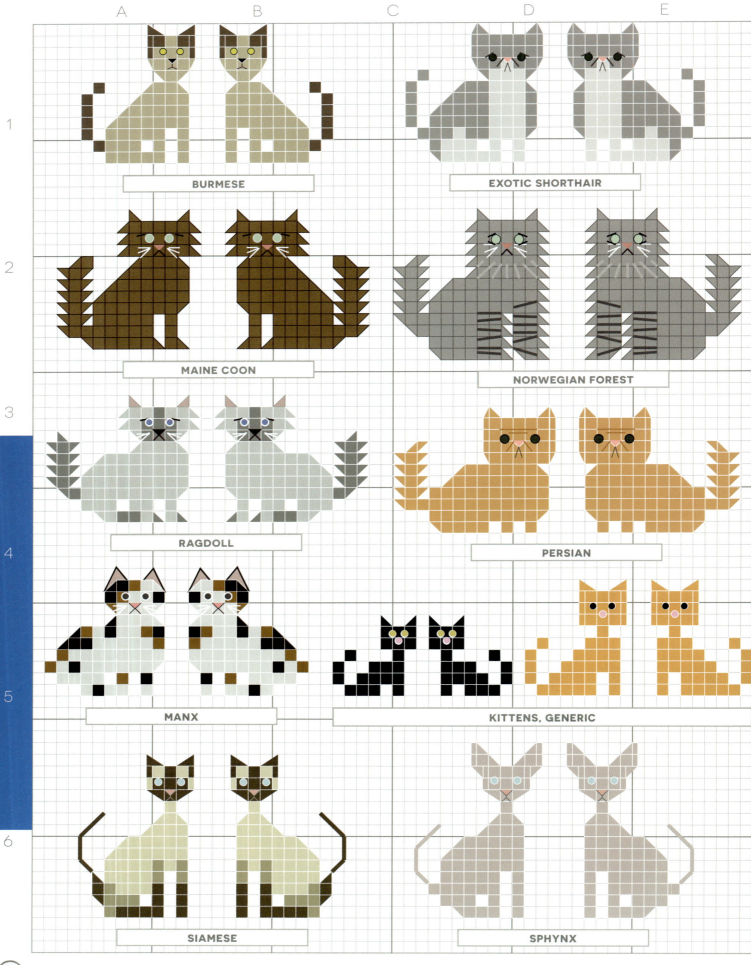

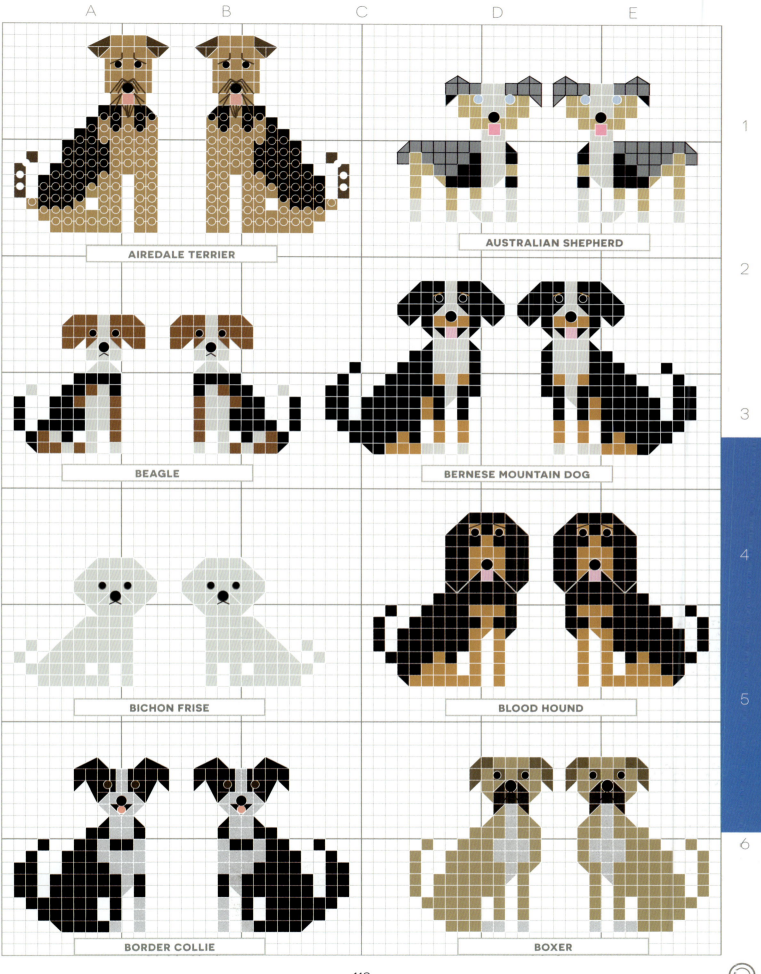

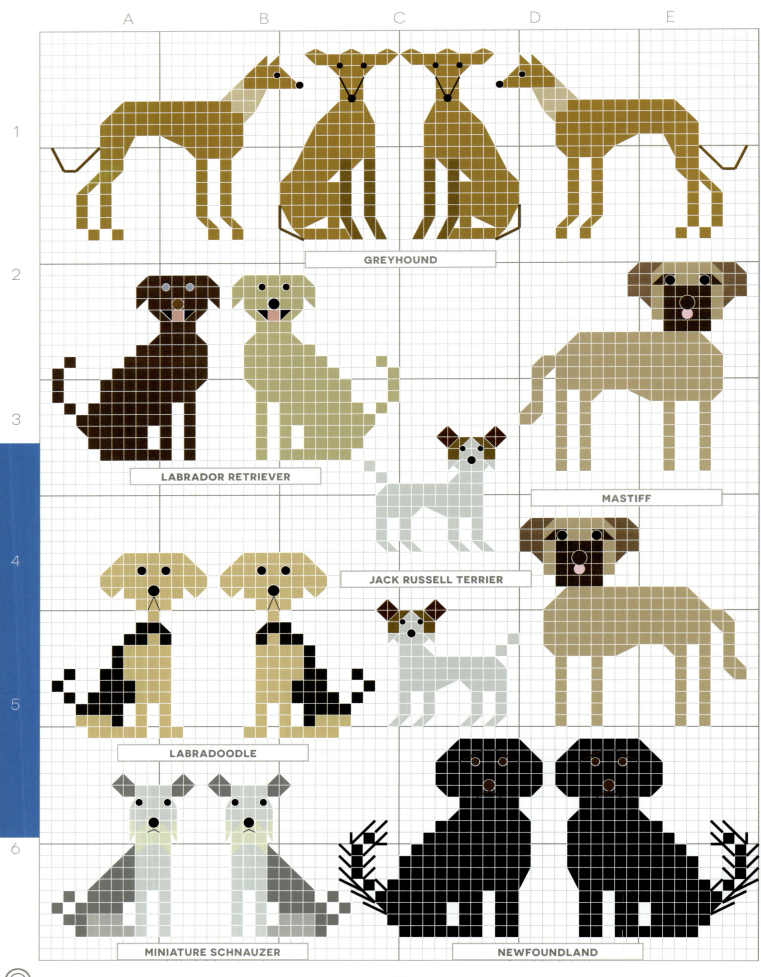

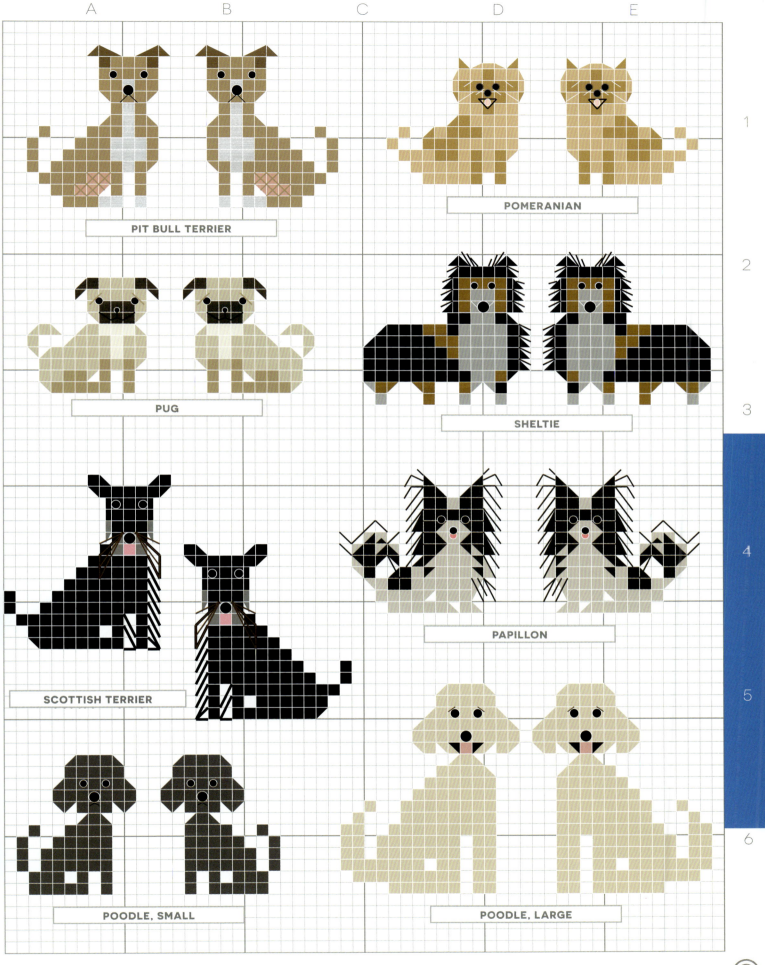

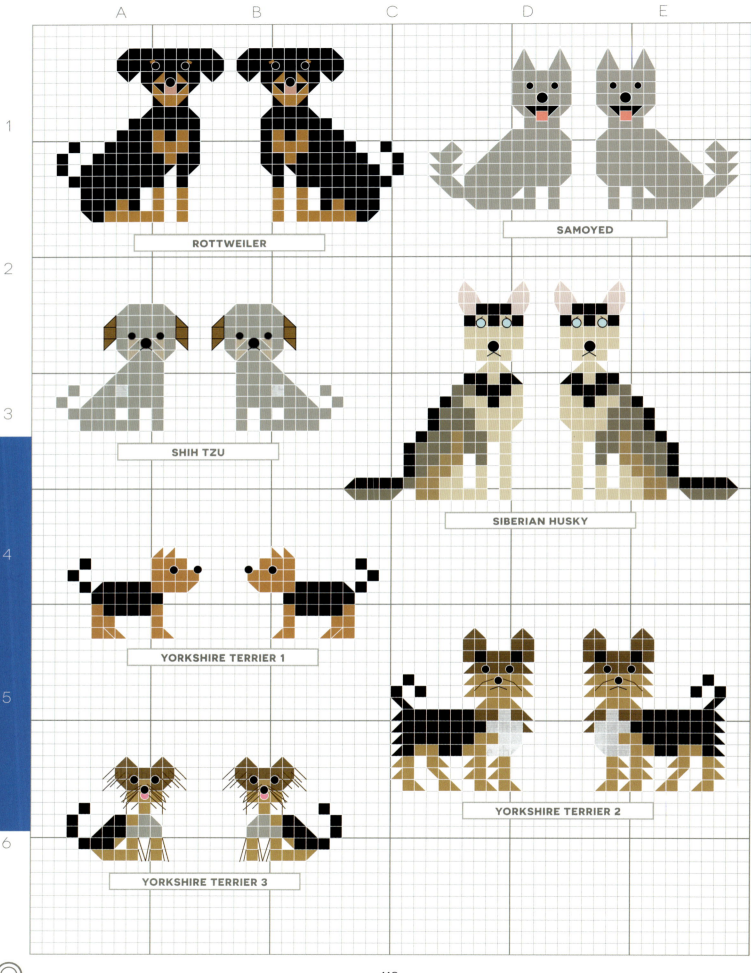

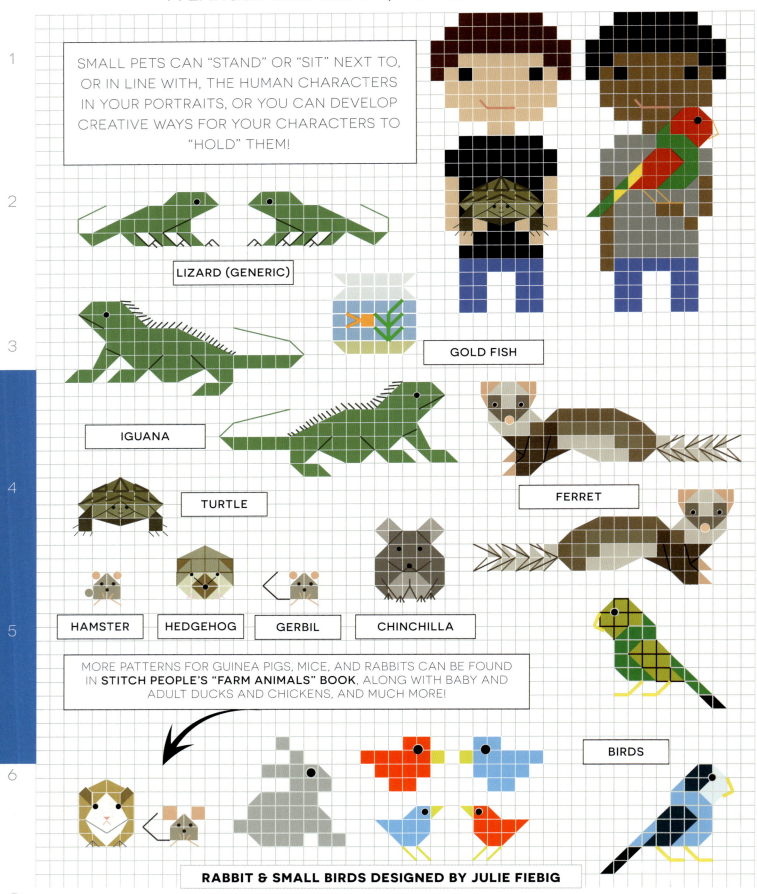

PET STITCHING TECHNIQUES

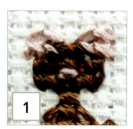

(1) The Abyssinian's **fur** was created using a few different techniques. The chest area, ears, and leg area were created with different solid colors. The back area and tail was created with a combination of colors. The **nose** and **mouth** were created with two strands of pink and black floss, respectively. Each utilize a horizontal stitch, and two small, diagonal quarter-sized stitches into the center of the square. The **eyes** are French knots (two strands of black floss), and the sides of the cat's face utilize vertical half stitches. Notice the difference in the right and left **ear** - at the point of the ears, the left ear utilizes a half stitch, and the right ear utilizes a full cross-stitch. This is to exemplify the effect tiny changes can make to customize the look of your pet.

(2) The Bengal cat's tan **fur** is a combination of various hues of tan. The **chest** and **chin** were created using three strands of light tan. Some of the body's cross stitches were created with three strands of black floss or brown floss. Randomly placed stitches of black were placed around the **body** and **legs** of the cat to create a more dynamic look. The **face** utilizes half stitches. The **eyes** were created using French knots of two strands of green floss. Around those French knots, a French knot was created with a single thread of black floss. It is tighter around the left eye and looser around the right eye to show different options.

(3) The British Shorthair cat was stitched entirely with three strands of gray floss. The **eyes** were created with French knots of two strands of black floss. Two strands of black floss were used to create the **nose**, making a single, horizontal stitch and two quarter-length diagonal stitches into the center of the square. One strand of black floss stitched in two quarter-length diagonal stitches create the **mouth**. Notice the **ears** and top of the head that stitch outside the holes of the Aida fabric. The top of the **head** utilizes half-stitches, and the ears utilize diagonal stitches free from the constraints of the Aida fabric. See the diagram for a close-up.

(4) The Persian cat was created using a combination of three strands of floss. Diagonal half stitches around the **tail** create "fluff." A single strand of darker floss was used to create detailing around the **face** and **legs**. The **eyes** were created using two strands of black floss in a French knot, and the **nose** was created using two strands of pink floss in a French knot. The **mouth** was created with two quarter-length diagonal stitches. Notice different half-stitches created around the outside of the **face** to make a fuller, rounder face.

(5) The Manx cat has a calico **fur** effect. The white color was created with two strands of white floss and one strand of light gray. The brown color was created with two strands of brown and one strand of black. The black fur was created using three strands of black floss. The **eyes** were created using French knots of two strands of gray floss. To help define the **nose** and mouth, a single strand of black floss was cross-stitched on top of a white cross stitch. The **nose** and **ears** utilize two strands of pink floss.

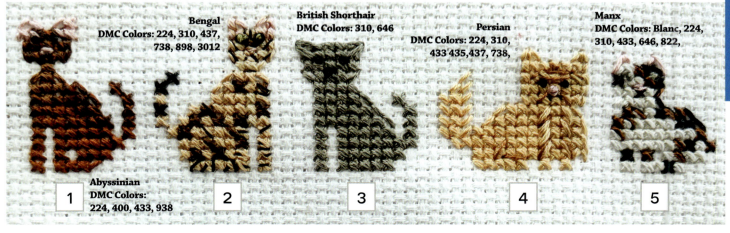

Abyssinian
DMC Colors: 224, 400, 433, 938

Bengal
DMC Colors: 224, 310, 437, 738, 898, 3012

British Shorthair
DMC Colors: 310, 646

Persian
DMC Colors: 224, 310, 433 435, 437, 738,

Manx
DMC Colors: Blanc, 224, 310, 433, 646, 822,

CATS & DOGS & MORE

Border Collie
DMC Colors: Blanc, 224, 310, 822, 838

Chow Chow
DMC Colors: 310, 434, 435, 436, 437, 738

Collie
DMC Colors: Blanc, 310, 839, 3790, 3828,

Yorkie
DMC Colors: Blanc, 224, 310, 435, 938

"Generic" Dog Pattern
DMC Colors: Blanc, 310, 436, 738, 3828

1 2 3 4 5

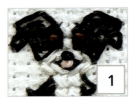

(1) The Border Collie was stitched using three strands of black floss and three strands of white floss, respectively. The **eyes** were created with two French knots and two strands of dark brown floss. The **nose** was created with a French knot of two strands of black floss. This knot was placed slightly above and on top of a French knot made of two strands of pink floss representing the **tongue**. Various styles of half knots and 2:1 ratio knots are used to soften the edges within and around the **face**. The white fur is outlined with backstitches, using one strand of light gray floss.

(2) The Chow Chow was stitched primarily using three different colors of floss mixed together, with the exception of the **tail** and **chest** which utilize three light colored strands of floss and three darker colored strands of floss, respectively. Notice the blending effect that is achieved by surrounding solid-colored areas with areas of mixed colors. The **eyebrows** are two, small diagonal stitches of one strand of black floss. The **nose** was created with a French knot placed on top of a full cross-stitch. The **mouth** was created using free-form single stitches that create slight upward-facing diagonals, and do not utilize the holes of the Aida fabric. The **fur** that cascades around the head and body of the Chow Chow was created using one strand of darker floss, creating free-form single stitches of different lengths, widths, and angles. Notice that the **face** is surrounded with vertical and horizontal half-stitches, but they blend nicely due to the free-form strands of fur that were stitched on top of those stitches.

(3) The Collie was stitched without any color blending techniques. The white floss is **outlined** with one strand of medium-gray floss. Black **detailing** was stitched on top of the cross stitching using one and three strands of black floss in various areas. Notice how the placement of the left and right ears is slightly different. The left ear sits closer to the center of the head and the right ear sits farther from the head. This was done to exemplify how even the smallest changes - one square of width difference - can create a different look for your pet. In this instance, the right ear looks more perky than the left.

(4) The Yorkie was stitched using solid dark brown on the **head**, solid black on the **back**, solid white on the **chest**, and for the middle area, a combination of two strands of lighter brown, one strand of darker brown was used. The white fur is NOT outlined. The free-flowing fur was created like the Chow Chow, using individual, long strands of a single strand of floss. Many of these strands are created outside the holes of the Aida fabric. The **tongue** was created using a French knot of two strands of pink floss. (The black **eyes** and **nose** (French knots) atop the dark brown fur are difficult to see due to photography!)

(5) The "generic" dog pattern stitched here is modeled after my dog, Pepper! The **tan color** is a combination of three different tan-toned colors (though the ears are created with three strands of the same color floss). A single strand of white floss was cross-stitched on top of the completed tan cross-stitches to create a white blending effect. The **tongue** is a cross-stitch of three strands of pink floss. The **mouth** was created with horizontal and diagonal stitches of two strands of black floss. The **eyes** and **nose** were created with French knots of two strands of black floss.

CATS & DOGS & MORE

122

ACCESSORIES

No portrait would be complete without Mom's favorite scarf, or Dad's favorite sports team cap. A wide variety of options are available when it comes to accessories, and you certainly don't have to leave anything out!

Jewelry lovers should definitely have all their favorite bling in their Stitch People portraits (p. 126), and sports fans shouldn't be left without a racket, golf club, or favorite ball (p. 124)!

You'll also notice a few different fashion scarf options (p. 126). On the character design pages (36-47), experiment with your colors of choice in creating a realistic looking scarf. Perhaps it wraps thickly around the neck, or lightly cascades down the front. Let your imagination run wild!

If you've lost a loved one, you may still want to represent their presence in your portrait with a heart, kite, or balloon floating next to or above the rest of the family - a subtle recognition of their lasting influence. Accessories can help with this portrayal. See more recommendations about this on pages 154-155.

"OKAY, BUT I'M LOOKING FOR A PATTERN FOR [INSERT YOUR SPECIFIC NEED HERE]..."

GREAT! YOU NEED SOMETHING MORE SPECIALIZED.

"Do-It-Yourself Stitch People" focuses on **general** clothing and accessory designs. These designs will apply to the majority of design needs for general Stitch People portraits. For more **specific clothing styles, career-oriented or hobby-specific accessories and attire**, check out our other book offerings:

- Stitch People Farm Animals
- Stitch People Occupations and Hobbies
- Stitch People United States Armed Forces
- Stitch People Backgrounds and Scenery
- Borders, Embellishments & Motifs (digital downoad only)
- Stitch People Holiday Patterns: Christmas, Valentine's Day, Halloween, and more! (digital downloads only)

Visit **stitchpeople.com** to see Stitch People's other product offerings.

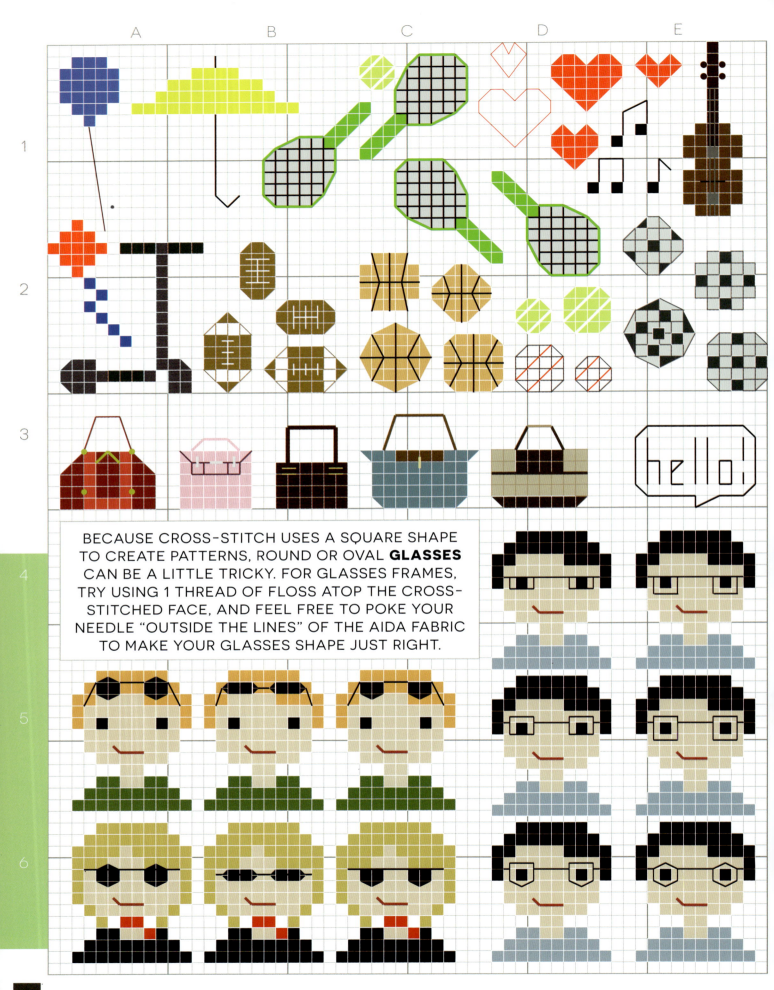

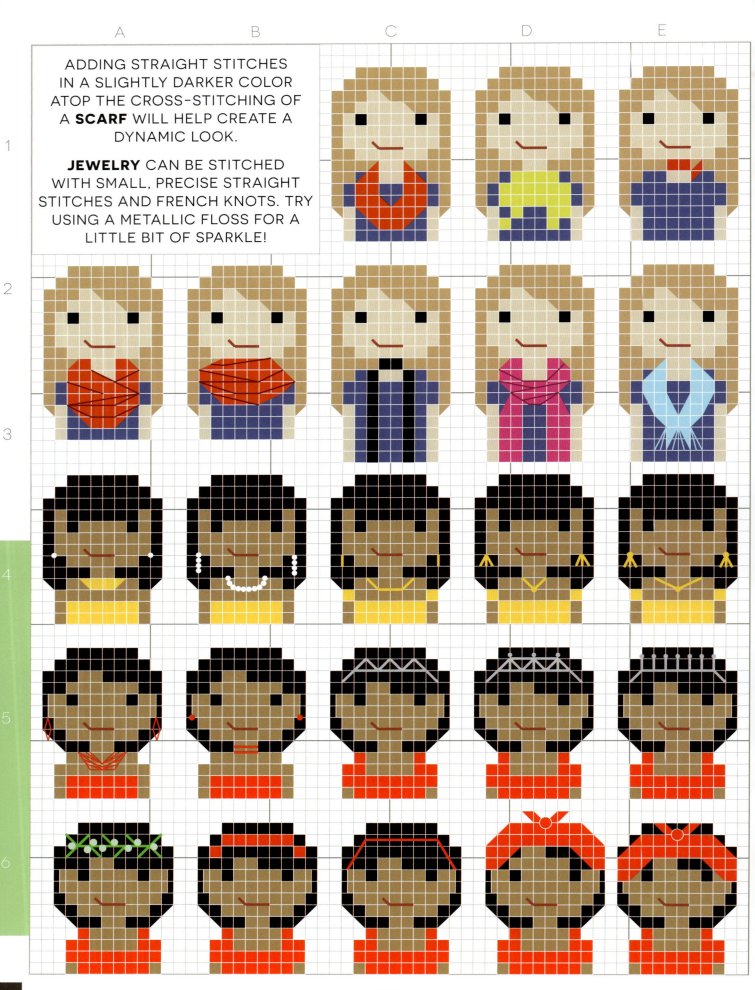

ALPHABETS & LETTERING

Most people choose to finish their portraits with a line or two of text that appears beneath the chosen characters.

Because each portrait is different, so the size of each portrait will be different, the amount of room available for text will vary. I advise that you plan out your entire portrait ahead of time, including the text you'd like to add with your portrait, either above or below the characters.

Typically, 1 - 2 lines of text will fit comfortably within a frame. If you adjust the spacing of your portrait, you may be able to accommodate 3 - 4 lines of text. Or, if you have few characters and would like more text, you may consider orienting your portrait vertically, or in a "portrait" orientation, to allow for more space beneath or above the stitched characters.

You may wish to use a different letter styling for your portrait than those provided here. There are many more fonts available for purchase and download on StitchPeople.com and there are plenty of cross-stitch alphabets available in books and online.

For a mixed family portrait, you may wish to include two names in some sort of fashion, like "The Smith and Jones Family" or "The Smiths and Joneses" or a simple "Our Family" is a popular choice.

Examples of text include:

Our Second Anniversary
September 4, 2014

CHUCK & SARAH
June 24, 2009

The Addams Family
Est. October 31, 2000

The Best Vacation Ever!
Cayman Islands, Mexico, 2010

THE WEASLEYS
"Wingardium Leviosa!"

Rory Williams and Amy Pond-Williams
Together Forever

Aa Bb Cc Dd Ee Ff Gg Hh
Ii Jj Kk Ll Mm Nn Oo Pp Qq
Rr Ss Tt Uu Vv Ww Xx Yy Zz
0123456789 . , / ! ? &

I TYPICALLY USE THE ABOVE AND BELOW FONTS FOR THE FIRST AND SECOND LINE OF TEXT IN A PORTRAIT. **YOU CAN ALSO CREATE EMPHASIS BY USING DIFFERENT FONT "WEIGHTS," CONTROLLED BY THE NUMBER OF THREADS YOU USE.** I TYPICALLY USE 2 STRANDS OF BLACK FLOSS FOR THE FIRST LINE OF TEXT, AND 1 STRAND OF BLACK FLOSS FOR THE SECOND LINE OF TEXT.

Aa Bb Cc Dd Ee Ff Gg Hh
Ii Jj Kk Ll Mm Nn Oo Pp Qq
Rr Ss Tt Uu Vv Ww Xx Yy Zz
0123456789 . , ! ? &

IF YOU NEED TO FIT MORE TEXT INTO A SMALL AMOUNT OF SPACE, TRY USING SOMETHING A LITTLE BIT SMALLER LIKE THE FONT STYLE BELOW!

Aa Bb Cc Dd Ee Ff Gg Hh Ii Jj Kk Ll
Mm Nn Oo Pp Qq Rr Ss Tt Uu Vv Ww
Xx Yy Zz 0123456789 , ! ? &

ALPHABETS & LETTERING

ALPHABETS & LETTERING

ABCDEFGHIJKL
MNOPQRSTUVW
XYZ0123456789

abcdefghijklmn
opqrstuvwxyz.,/!?&

FOR A MORE EMBELLISHED LOOK, THIS TEXT OPTION IS A LITTLE LARGER AND MORE GRAND. BE SURE TO ACCOUNT FOR ENOUGH ROOM IN YOUR PORTRAIT FOR THIS TEXT, AND ANY OTHER LARGE FONTS ON THE FOLLOWING PAGES AS YOU MAP YOUR PORTRAIT AND COUNT OUT THE WIDTH AND HEIGHT OF EACH ELEMENT. **LEAVE ENOUGH ROOM ON YOUR FABRIC AND WITHIN YOUR FRAME TO ACCOMMODATE LARGER SIZED FONTS.**

EXPLORE MORE ALPHABET CHOICES ON THE FOLLOWING PAGES AND EXPERIMENT WITH DIFFERENT CONFIGURATIONS FOR YOUR FAMILY PORTRAITS!

ABCDEFGHI
JKLMNOPQR
STUVWXYZ
1234567890
.,!?&

ALPHABETS & LETTERING

ALPHABETS & LETTERING

Aaa Bbb Ccc Ddd
Eee Fff Ggg Hhh
Ii Jjj Kkk Ll Mmm
Nnn Ooo Ppp Qqq
Rrr Sss Tt Uuu Vv
Www Xxx Yyy Zzz
1234567890.,!?&
1234567890.,!?&

ALPHABETS & LETTERING

Aa Bb Cc Dd
Ee Ff Gg Hh Ii
Jj Kk Ll
Mm Nn Oo Pp
Qq Rr Ss Tt
Uu Vv Ww Xx
Yy Zz .,!?&
1234567890

ABCDEFGHIJKL
MNOPQRSTUVW
XYZ.,!?&
0123456789

ABCDEFGHIJ
KLMNOPQRS
TUVWXYZ
0123456789
.,!?&

ALPHABETS & LETTERING

137

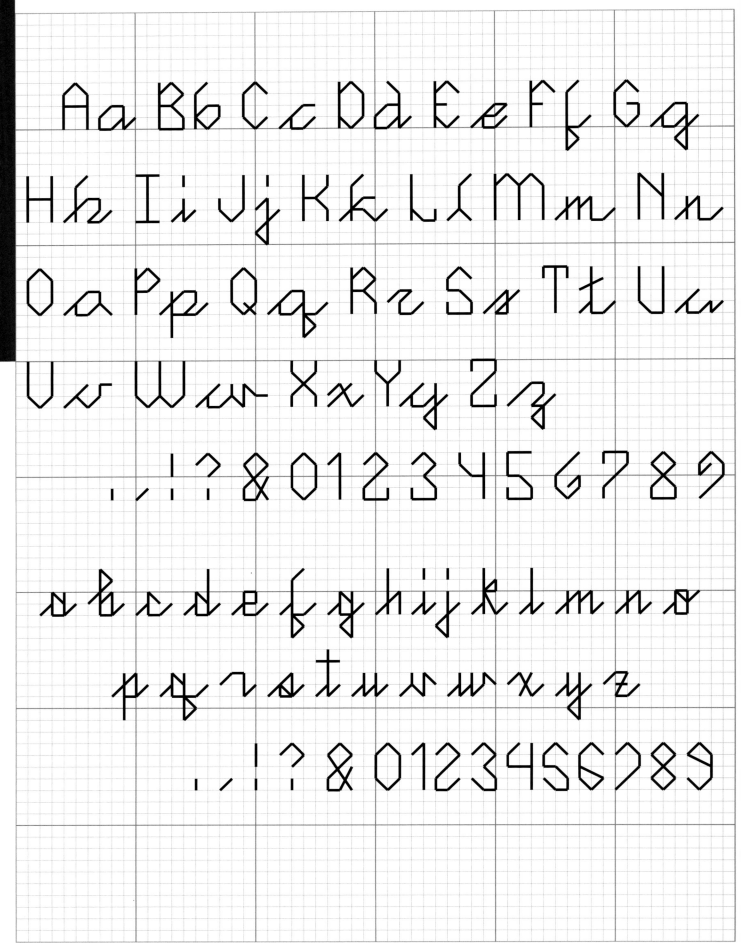

ABCDEFGHIJKLMNOPQRSTUVWXYZ
,.!?& 0123456789

ABCDEFGHIJKLMNOPQRSTUVWXYZ
,.!?& 0123456789

Aa Bb Cc Dd Ee Ff Gg
Hh Ii Jj Kk Ll Mm Nn
Oo Pp Qq Rr Ss Tt Uu
Vv Ww Xx Yy Zz
.,!?& 0123456789

ALPHABETS & LETTERING

140

RESOURCES

COLOR RECOMMENDATIONS	142-144
SKIN TONES	142
LIPS	142
EYES	142
BROWN HAIR	142
RED/AUBURN HAIR	143
BLONDE HAIR	143
BLACK HAIR	143
GRAY AND SALT & PEPPER HAIR	144
DENIM BLUE HUES	144
MATERIALS CHECKLIST	145
CURLY HAIR INSTRUCTION	146
STRAIGHT HAIR INSTRUCTION	148
MORE PATTERN TECHNIQUES	150
LACE TECHNIQUES	152
INCLUDING DEPARTED LOVED ONES	154
INCLUDING A TATTOO	156
MAKING CHARACTERS WIDER	158
EXAMPLE PATTERNS	160
FRAMING IN A FRAME	164
FRAMING IN A HOOP	165
MORE STITCH PEOPLE PATTERNS	166
FINISHED PORTRAIT GALLERY	168

RESOURCES

FLOSS COLOR RECOMMENDATIONS

These next pages contain charts of color recommendations for your Stitch People portraits. The images of floss shown here, while very close to the actual color of the floss, should **not** be used as a replacement to looking at actual, physical skeins of floss to make your choices. They are intended to be shown for reference, only.

Feel free to work outside of these suggestions, remembering that these are guidelines and not rules.

Tip: it's difficult to color match floss to digital/electronic screens because of the way devices use colored light to illuminate images and photos on the screen. I recommend printing a picture or photo to compare to floss.

Skin Tones (Light to Dark)

DMC 3770		Almost-true white, with a slight pink tint. VERY light.
DMC 3774		A slightly darker pink tint.
DMC 945		**#1 recommendation for Caucasian skin.**
DMC 738		A medium-toned skin color with yellow undertones.
DMC 437		**#1 recommendation for medium-toned skin.**
DMC 167		Similar to 3862, more yellow undertones
DMC 3862		**#1 recommendation for dark-toned skin.**
DMC 3781		Similar to 839, more cool/gray undertones.
DMC 839		Similar to 3781, more warm/red undertones.

Before diving right into your portrait, compare your skin-tone floss colors to the hair floss colors and Aida fabric to ensure the colors are clear and definable next to each other.

Lips

DMC 3712		A peachy, neutral color that looks good on the majority of skin tones.

Eyes

DMC 310		I think using black floss for eyes helps Stitch People characters look realistic (see pages 6-7). However, to show eye color, choose a dark, rich tone of eye color: navy, emerald, or chocolate brown. This will allude to color, but keep the face looking natural.

Brown Hair (Light to Dark)

DMC 3828		Light brown / dirty blonde. Yellow undertones.
DMC 3862		Light brown, red undertones.
DMC 420		Medium. Similar to 3828, darker. Gold undertones.
DMC 869		Medium-to-dark. Cool undertones.
DMC 839		Dark brown. Cooler undertones than 898.
DMC 898		Dark brown. Richer / warmer tone than 839.
DMC 3031		Darker than 839. Similar tone.
DMC 838		Darker than 3031. Similar tone.
DMC 938		Very dark brown. Rich / warm tone. Red undertones.
DMC 3371		Almost black brown.

To create dynamic or natural looking hair, in any color, **combine** up to three colors of similarly-toned floss, using no more than three strands of floss total.

Mix-and-match floss colors to achieve highlights and low-lights: for example, mix a medium brown color with a darker auburn color and a lighter strawberry blonde to achieve a red-toned, multi-dimensional brunette head of hair.

RESOURCES

142

Red / Auburn Hair (Light to Dark)

DMC 3827		Lightest auburn / strawberry blonde.	To create dynamic or natural looking hair, in any color, **combine** up to three colors of similarly-toned floss, using no more than three strands of floss total. **Mix-and-match** floss colors to achieve highlights and low-lights: for example, mix a medium brown color with a darker auburn color and a lighter strawberry blonde to achieve a red-toned, multi-dimensional brunette head of hair.
DMC 436		Medium, orange-toned light brown / blonde.	
DMC 435		Medium, red-toned light brown.	
DMC 3826		Lighter natural red hair color. Orange undertones.	
DMC 301		Darker natural red hair color. Red undertones.	
DMC 434		Cool medium auburn. Less red.	
DMC 400		Dark red/orange hue.	
DMC 433		Like 434, but darker.	
DMC 801		Like 434 and 433, but darker.	
DMC 300		Very dark red/orange color.	

Blonde Hair (Light to Dark)

DMC 712		Lightest blonde color. Creamy white.	To create dynamic or natural looking hair, in any color, **combine** up to three colors of similarly-toned floss, using no more than three strands total. **Mix-and-match** floss colors to achieve highlights and low-lights: for example, mix a medium brown color with a darker auburn color and a lighter strawberry blonde to achieve a red-toned, multi-dimensional brunette head of hair.
DMC 3823		Light blonde color. Lemon-yellow tones.	
DMC 739		Light, natural-looking blonde. Good color to MIX-IN. A full head of 739 hair blends with skin tone.	
DMC 677		Light, cool-toned blonde with gold undertones.	
DMC 738		Light-medium "dirty" blonde. Good color to MIX-IN. A full head of 738 hair blends with skin tone.	
DMC 676		Rich, medium gold-yellow tone.	
DMC 3822		Very yellow. Good medium color to MIX IN.	
DMC 437		Natural, medium blonde/light brown. Warm tone.	
DMC 422		Natural, medium blonde/light brown. Cool tone.	
DMC 3828		Similar to 422, but darker. Medium/dark blonde.	
DMC 729		Medium/dark, gold tone blonde.	
DMC 3829		Dark blonde, warm, gold undertones.	

Black Hair

DMC 310		True black.	To **tint** black hair, add 1 thread of brown or blue to 2 strands of black.
DMC 3371		Almost black, with brown tint.	
DMC 939		Almost black with blue tint.	

Continued on the next page...

Gray and Salt & Pepper Hair (Light to Dark)

DMC Blanc		True white.	It is especially important to combine colors when making a salt-and-pepper hair effect. **Combine** up to three colors of floss, using no more than three strands total, like a dark gray, medium gray, and white strand. Salt-and-pepper hair may have a **warm tone**, and not be entirely cold-tone gray. If this is the case for your character, incorporate at least one warm-tone neutral color in your floss combination. Consider "highlighting" salt-and-pepper hair with platinum blonde, or "low-lighting" salt-and-pepper hair with a medium brown, listed on the previous pages.
DMC Ecru		Off-white. Slight cream tint.	
DMC 822		Very light gray. Cool tone.	
DMC 3866		Very light gray. Warm tone.	
DMC 3033		Similar to 3866. Warmer tone.	
DMC 644		Light gray with deeper, cool gray tones.	
DMC 3024		Light gray with very slight blue tones.	
DMC 648		Similar to 3024. More blue.	
DMC 3023		Darker gray color. Cool tones.	
DMC 841		Light gray-ish taupe color. Warm, brown tone.	
DMC 3790		Medium taupe. Warm brown tone.	
DMC 840		Medium taupe. Cool brown tone.	
DMC 3787		Very dark gray. Cool tone. Slight blue tint.	
DMC 3021		Darker than 3787. Cool tone. Slight blue tint.	

Denim Blue Hues (Light to Dark)

DMC 3753		Light powder blue, not too saturated.	Compare your chosen denim floss color to the other colors in your character's outfit to be sure the undertones match and don't clash. To **create rips** on denim jeans, stitch the pants in one color of denim, using 3 strands of the same color floss. Then choose a lighter denim color, and stitch over the top the pants using 1-2 strands of the lighter floss, creating cross-stitches and/or horizontal straight stitches to create the look of ripping denim.
DMC 3752		Darker and more blue than 3753.	
DMC 932		Darker and more blue than 3752.	
DMC 169		A medium gray-blue. Cool tone.	
DMC 926		Medium gray-blue with green undertones.	
DMC 931		A true medium, denim blue. Not too blue.	
DMC 317		Dark gray with blue undertones.	
DMC 3768		Dark gray with green undertones.	
DMC 413		Dark, charcoal gray. More blue than 3799.	
DMC 3799		Dark, charcoal gray. Less saturated than 413.	
DMC 3750		A dark, denim blue.	
DMC 930		A true dark, denim blue. Darker than 931.	

MATERIALS CHECKLIST

- [ ] AIDA FABRIC
  SUGGESTED: SIZE 14

- [ ] EMBROIDERY HOOP OR QSNAP
  (SUGGESTED: 5" - 8")

- [ ] NEEDLE(S)
  (CREWEL SIZE 5, OR TAPESTRY SIZE 24)

- [ ] FABRIC SCISSORS

- [ ] EMBROIDERY SCISSORS

- [ ] WRITING UTENSIL

- [ ] PATTERN
  (MAKE YOUR OWN USING THIS BOOK!)

- [ ] BACKING & FRAME
  (OPTIONAL)

EMBROIDERY FLOSS LIST

- [ ]
- [ ]
- [ ]
- [ ]
- [ ]

- [ ]
- [ ]
- [ ]
- [ ]
- [ ]
- [ ]
- [ ]
- [ ]
- [ ]
- [ ]
- [ ]
- [ ]
- [ ]

RESOURCES

CURLY HAIR INSTRUCTION

Generally, I prefer to stitch hairstyles with cross-stitches, like the rest of the elements of Stitch People. The reason is it can be tricky to stitch hair using other stitches (not cross-stitches) without it becoming too thick and overwhelming. That can distract from the rest of the portrait. The hairstyle can become so raised with the special stitches, that the other elements have the potential to become overshadowed, or difficult for the eye to focus on beyond the thick-looking hairstyle.

That said, different types of embroidery stitches can help curly hair look a bit more natural, and it can be difficult for some people to choose what to do, so I thought I'd include a few different methods you might use to tackle stitching a curly-haired individual.

I searched for a royalty-free stock photo online for the curliest head of hair I could find. Look at this beautiful lady! Perfect!

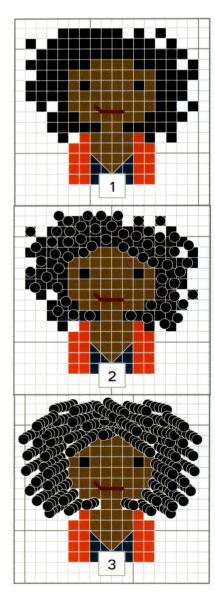

Here are a few things to note for the purposes of this example:

- In the patterns, I've represented the hair using solid black squares for visibility's sake, even though the woman's hair is not solid black.

- In the stitched examples, I've represented the hairstyle two ways: on the left side, the style is completed in solid black, as shown in the pattern, and the right side shows the style completed in a combination of floss colors, as I would do in reality for a person who's hair looks like this.

Curly hair can be represented in three ways, as described below. Choose your curly hair method based on a balance between what you think looks best, and your stitching ability and confidence: there is no one right way. I've seen receptions of Stitch People portraits by curly-haired individuals that utilize all of these styles of curly hair, and each of them has immediately understood the implied curly hair. So all of these methods DO work. See the patterns on the following page.

1. (*Top p. 146 / Left p. 147*) Cross-stitch the whole head of hair, allowing the size, shape, "stray" stitches, and occasional gaps in contour of the hair represent the curly nature of the hair.

2. (*Middle p. 146 & 147*) Cross-stitch the whole head of hair, then complete numerous, randomized French knots atop the cross-stitching to give the hair some texture and visual circular elements. This will soften the perceived square-ness or flatness of the cross-stitching alone. See page 20 for French knot instructions.

3. (*Bottom p. 146 / Right p. 147*) Stitch the head of hair using Bullion knots.

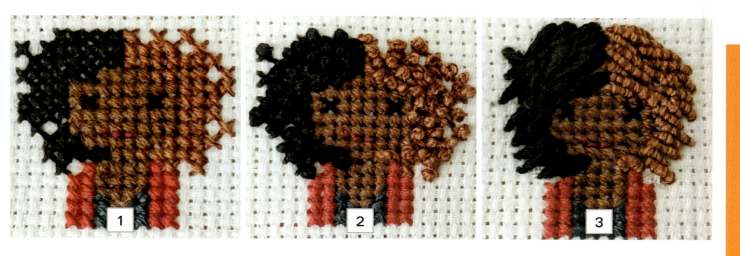

BULLION KNOT INSTRUCTIONS

1 - 3. Visualize where the "ends" of the knot will be, keeping in mind it's a bit of a longer knot in length. Bring your needle up through the fabric at one of the ends (A), and push your needle through the fabric at the other end of where the knot needs to be (B) - but do NOT pull the needle through completely. Instead, maneuver the tip of the needle up through the first point (A).

4 - 5. Wrap the excess floss around the tip of the needle counter-clockwise. Keep the floss taught, but not too tight, and wrap the floss around as many times as you need to fill in the space between (A) and (B).

6 - 8. When you've wrapped the floss enough times around the needle, lightly secure the floss with your fingers, so it doesn't unwind, and pull the needle through the spirals of floss, and slowly tighten and secure the floss into the Bullion knot. When the needle is through and the knot is tight, push the needle back through the fabric at point B.

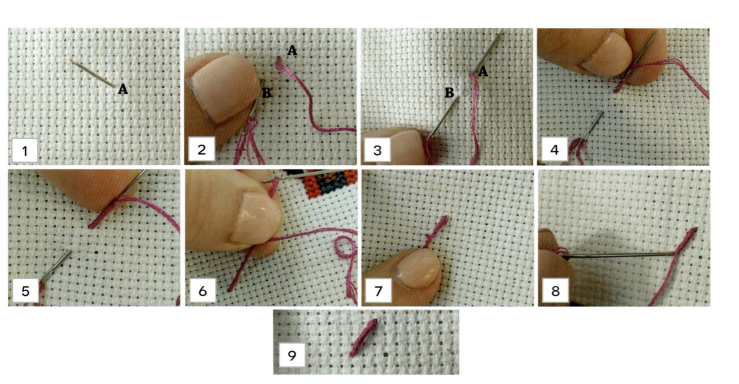

STRAIGHT HAIR INSTRUCTION

Generally, I prefer to stitch hairstyles with cross-stitches, like the rest of the elements of Stitch People. It can be tricky to stitch hair using different types of stitches without it becoming too thick and overwhelming to the face, which creates the potential for the hairstyle to distract from the rest of the portrait. The hairstyle can become so raised with the special stitches, the other elements have the potential to become overshadowed, or difficult for the eye to focus on beyond the thick-looking hairstyle.

That said, portraying straight hair in Stitch People portraits using unique stitches has become popular. You can use "couching" or "satin stitch." Couching is a method of embroidery stitch where you secure long, straight strands by stitching over them. Satin stitch involves stitching medium-length straight stitches side-by-side. My advice is to give these a try, but be careful to not get carried away with making the hair too thick.

Be patient with yourself as you try these out, as the effect can be really excellent.

COUCHING INSTRUCTIONS

1. Working from the center of the head, moving outward, make long, loose diagonal stitches. It doesn't matter exactly how many you make (but I wouldn't go overboard!) but do make an effort to keep the strands within the "boundaries" of where the hairstyle belongs - one to two columns outside the head.

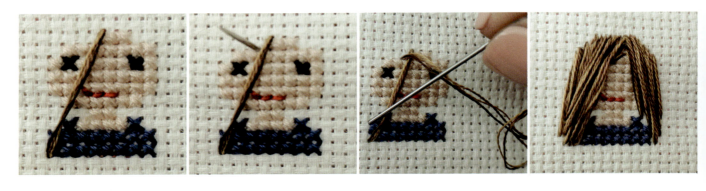

2. Once you have covered the head with long, loose stitches, you can reveal the face by "couching" down your threads. You can do this in a loose or tight way.

    A. For flow-y hair, or the look of loose bangs, bring the needle up near the inside edge of the hair, and pull the long hair stitches aside from the face by pushing the needle through the fabric on the outside of the hairstyle.

B. For a tighter hair style, bring the needle up from close to the middle of the top of the head, and feed it underneath and up through the middle of the loose stitches you've made. Catch the long, loose stitches with your needle, and push your needle through the hairstyle very close to where you brought the needle up in the first place, making a very small stitch. Repeat this a few times to secure the loose strands away from the face of the character.

(A) See the difference between these two styles. On the left of the face is the looser, flow-y style. On the right is the tighter side. (B) This picture shows what it looks like to fill in the neck area with straight stitches.

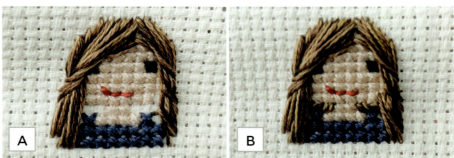

MODIFIED **SATIN STITCH** INSTRUCTIONS

Typically, the satin stitch is created by making many straight stitches of the same length, side-by-side. But using the basic idea of the of the satin stitch, and applying it to creating straight hairstyles works, too!

1. Basically, work around the head and create straight stitches of whatever lengths necessary in a side-by-side fashion to construct the hairstyle around the face. Keep in mind where hair lays naturally on a person - the bangs and front sections will typically lay over the top of the side and back sections of hair. Continue stitching where needed, filling in holes, to shape the hair around the face and working it to the appropriate length. See the pattern to the right as a reference for how stitches might lay.

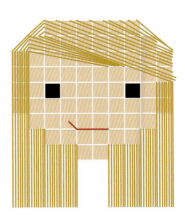

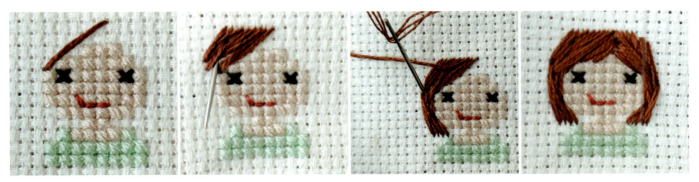

RESOURCES

CLOTHING PRINT TECHNIQUES

FLORAL PATTERNS

Floral patterns can be represented in a number of ways. How you choose to do this will be based on your personal preference, your available time, your pattern's needs, and your attention to detail.

1. Represent the various colors of the floral pattern as full, individual cross-stitches, as shown in **examples 5 and 6** on the next page.
2. Create a base layer of cross stitches in a background color (or two primary background colors), and then complete individual back-stitches, straight stitches, and cross-stitches using 1-2 threads of floss in the other colors shown in the floral pattern. **Example 2** on the next page shows this.
3. Cross-stitch the skirt entirely using the prominent background color of the floral pattern. Then stitch French knots on top of the completed cross-stitches in the other colors. In **examples 1 and 4** on the next page, you'll see there is a base of one or two colors, and a series of French knots atop the background color. Your French knots can be created of 1-3 threads, can be completed loosely or tightly, and you may choose to combine multiple floss colors to create more dynamic French knots.
4. Combine the previous two examples. Cross-stitch the skirt in one or two background color(s). Then on top, use other colors from the floral pattern. Add a combination of straight stitches, single diagonal stitches, horizontal stitches, vertical stitches, and French knots to create the illusion of a floral pattern. **Example 7** on the next page shows this.

GEOMETRIC PATTERNS

Many button-down shirts for men and women have a "checkered" or "grid" pattern. There are a few ways you can tackle this. First, you can stitch the shirt in a base color and then stitch many long back-stitches, both horizontally and vertically, using the holes of the Aida fabric to create the grid effect. **Example 8** shows this, using a base color of light gray (instead of white) for visibility. Second, you could give each "checker" color a full cross-stitch of it's own as shown in **example 9**. Third, you could complete the entire shirt using a combination of 2-3 colors (like a bright red, muted red, and white floss), as **example 10** seeks to illustrate.

LACE

Lace can be tricky to represent in Stitch People portraits, but there are many good solutions. The simplest method is to stitch the "lace" on top of the "skin." Complete the skin-tone-colored stitches as you normally would using 3 strands of floss. Then use 1 or 2 threads of the lace color (depending on how delicate the lace needs to look) and stitch full cross-stitches *on top* of the skin-colored cross-stitches. This is shown in **example 3** on the next page: a pink, lace high-low skirt. In the pattern, I used a light pink square with a dark pink outline to represent that I'd use a combination of floss colors to stitch the majority of the skirt (2 dark pink, 1 light pink). Then, using a single strand of the dark pink floss, I'd cross-stitch the "lace" on top of the legs. The high-low effect of the skirt would be shown by creating diagonal stitches at the highest point of the skirt.

See more lace techniques on the following pages!

LACE TECHNIQUES

One of the primary uses for creating a lace effect in Stitch People portraits is for wedding portraits, so the examples here show different styles of lacy wedding dresses and how you might portray them. Keep in mind, these techniques will be useful for lace effects in ANY attire - not just wedding dresses.

ABOUT LACE

When you consider creating a lace effect, take a look at the image of the lace, and ask yourself what *really* makes it look lacy. You might have to put on your abstract-thinking cap here for a minute, in a similar way you must when you're considering the eyes of your Stitch People characters, as explained on pages 6 - 7. The question there is - can you really tell what specific color the eyes are in a far-away family photo? No, not really. Generally speaking you usually only see darker areas where the eyes are, which is why I like to stitch Stitch People eyes using black floss.

The same kind of thinking applies with lace. Is it a kind of lace where you can see every single detail of a floral or geometric lace pattern? Probably not. Sometimes a larger, bolder lace pattern is more visible - and there are methods to represent that - but usually it's absolutely perfect to simply **allude** to the look of lace in your Stitch People portraits by creating non-specific texture and dimension. The building blocks we can use to create texture and dimension are manipulating color, changing stitch direction, and adding stitches.

1. MANIPULATING COLOR

There are a few ways you can manipulate color to your advantage:

- Combine threads of floss with subtly different colors to encourage a multi-dimensional look
- Create a sheer lace effect by stitching the sheer areas with a color slightly lighter than skin-tone
- Add lace detail using a slightly darker or different color of floss

2. CHANGING STITCH DIRECTION

You've read a hundred times in this book that the way to keep your cross-stitch work looking clean is to be sure all the diagonals of all the stitches are consistent. Thus, a simple way to create a bit of a textured or scattered look that can allude to the presence of lace is to alternate the direction your diagonals. With every-other cross-stitch you complete, alternate the directions of the "under" diagonal stitches, and the "over" diagonal stitches. So, you can break my A-#1 rule, as long as you're breaking it ON PURPOSE to create a lace effect!

3. ADDING STITCHES

You can utilize other types of stitches, especially simple French knots and back stitches, to add lace-like dimension on top of your uniform cross-stitching. French knots are good for alluding to a rounder, floral lace motif, and back-stitches are good for alluding to a more randomized lace pattern.

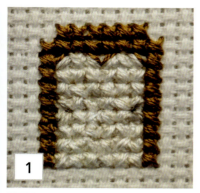

EXAMPLE 1:

TECHNIQUES USED: Manipulating Color, Changing Stitch Direction

The dress was cross-stitched using a combination of threads: two white (DMC Blanc), and one light gray (DMC 822). The cross-stitches were created by **changing the stitch direction**, alternating the "under" diagonals and the "over" diagonals of each X stitch.

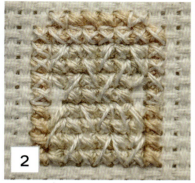

EXAMPLE 2:

TECHNIQUES USED: Manipulating Color, Changing Stitch Direction, Adding Stitches

The dress was cross-stitched uniformly (not mixed, as above) using a combination of three threads: one white (DMC Blanc), one shade of light gray (DMC 3033) and another shade of light gray (DMC 822). Diagonal back-stitches of a 2:1 ratio were randomly created atop the cross-stitching using one strand of white floss. Over-top the skin-tone cross-stitches - on the chest and arms - one strand of white floss was used to create cross-stitches to give a **sheer lace effect.**

EXAMPLE 3:

TECHNIQUES USED: Adding Stitches

The dress was cross-stitched uniformly with three strands of white floss (DMC Blanc). **French knots** of a medium tension were created on top of the cross-stitches using two strands of white floss. One strand of gray floss (DMC 648) was used to define the edges of the sleeves and dress from the white Aida fabric using back-stitches.

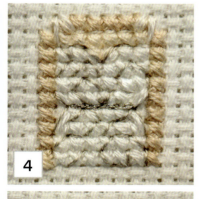

EXAMPLE 4:

TECHNIQUES USED: Adding Stitches, Manipulating Color

The dress was cross-stitched uniformly with three strands of white floss (DMC Blanc). One strand of gray floss (DMC 648) was used to **create back-stitching** atop the white cross-stitches in a randomized pattern that roughly resembled the example image. A slightly-lighter-than-skin-tone floss (DMC 3770) was used to stitch the second-to-top line of the chest area to allude to a **sheer fabric**, contrasting the skin tone color (DMC 950). One strand of white floss (DMC Blanc) was used to define the tank-top style sleeves of the dress. The belt was back-stitched using one strand of DMC Light Effects floss in silver.

EXAMPLE 5:

TECHNIQUES USED: Manipulating Color, Adding Stitches

The skirt and white areas of the dress were cross-stitched uniformly using three strands of white floss (DMC Blanc). The arms and torso of the character were cross-stitched with a slightly-lighter-than-skin-tone floss (DMC 3862) to contrast the skin tone (DMC 898) and allude to a **sheer effect**. The bolder, chunky-style lace that overlays the sheer fabric is represented using two strands of white floss, cross-stitched and half-stitched on top of the sheer-colored cross-stitches. The skirt utilizes satin stitches atop the cross stitches to create a different skirt effect. The neckline is defined with one strand of back-stitched white floss.

INCLUDING DEPARTED LOVED ONES

Here are a few ideas as to how to include departed loved ones in Stitch People portraits.

SYMBOLIC & PERSONAL ITEMS

Flowers are often a big part of funeral and memorial services. Include a single flower growing from the ground or in the hands of a living member of the family, or include a cluster of flowers, bouquet, or memorial wreath.

Something as simple as a heart can be integrated into your portrait to represent a loved one. Using a traditional red or pink color, you can't go wrong. You could also do an outline of the heart, or you could represent the heart in a color that is meaningful to the family, like yellow for a soldier, pink for breast cancer awareness, or the color(s) of a favorite sports team or alma mater.

A kite or balloon floating gracefully above a family can allude to a departed loved one. Freehand the string holding the kite or balloon down to the hands of the loved one who was closest to the departed individual.

Is there another object that was meaningful to the departed loved one? Consider including that object in addition to, or instead of, another more generic shape or item. Consider musical instruments, tools associated with a hobby, or sports paraphernalia.

HALO

You could include the deceased individual in your family portrait just like any other member of the family, but include a halo over or around their head to differentiate them, and gently remind the viewer of their passing.

DRESSED IN WHITE

Another way to include the departed individual into your portrait in a full way, is to include them as you normally would with any other character, but put them all in white clothing. You can add a halo, or not, with this choice. You could also consider positioning them behind the loved one they were closest to while living (like a spouse) as shown on the next page. (Examples are shown on the next page in light gray for pattern visibility).

BIRTH & DEATH DATE OR HEADSTONE

If your departed loved one is included in the portrait, you could subtly add the years of their birth and death beneath their feet to show that they've passed. Alternately, you could include these dates on a small headstone, as some people appreciate the symbolic representation of a headstone for their loved ones.

DEPARTED PETS

Any of the above-mentioned ideas can be used to represent a departed pet, too. Most commonly, people choose to include a pet in a portrait in full, and they will add a halo above or around the head.

STITCHING A TATTOO

With such small space to work with, it's almost impossible to precisely replicate a tattoo in a Stitch People portrait. However, you can certainly allude to a tattoo for your characters - and it's worth doing! These little details are what make Stitch People portraits so special.

COLORFUL TATTOOS & COLORFUL TATTOO SLEEVES

For colorful tattoos and colorful tattoo sleeves, look closely at the tattoo you're representing, and define the top three colors of the tattoo. Choose floss colors that match the top three colors of the tattoo, and combine one thread of floss of each of those colors to stitch the character's arm where the tattoo lays, in lieu of stitching that portion of the arm with skin-colored floss.

You can also split up the tattoo into "sections." If there are certain colors more visible at the top of the tattoo, and different colors more visible to the bottom of the tattoo, complete the tattoo's cross-stitches using appropriately different combinations of colors. See the example on the following page.

ONE-COLOR TATTOOS & BLACK AND WHITE SLEEVES

For a one-color tattoo, for example a small black tattoo on an arm, there are a couple options. Option 1) You can complete the character's full arm in the skin-tone color, except for the one (or few) squares, where the tattoo lays on the arm. Then, in those squares, combine 2 skin tone threads with 1 black thread, (or if it's a more substantial tattoo, 1 skin tone thread, 1 gray thread, and 1 black thread) and complete the arm's cross stitches. Option 2) Stitch the whole arm with 3 threads of the skin tone color, and complete an X shape or a straight stitch with a single strand of floss in the tattoo color on top of the cross-stitch of the skin tone color.

MINIMAL TATTOOS

There is a trend in tattoos for very thin, delicate, minimal tattoos. For these types of tattoos, I recommend completing the character's full arm using 3 strands of skin-tone colored floss, as usual. Then, using 1 thread of floss that matches the tattoo color, stitch over-top the skin-tone colored stitching. Because this tiny stitching is a mere representation you could complete this a number of ways: use a simple X stitch, do a single diagonal stitch, or complete a single horizontal or vertical line. Remember that whatever you choose to do doesn't have to utilize the holes of the Aida fabric and you can put your needle in-between Aida fabric holes, or into the center of the existing cross stitch, if need be.

You could also consider adding a French knot in the approximate color and location of the tattoo. I recommend using only one thread for this to keep the knot minimal, small, and succinct. See page 20 for French knot instructions.

BELOW ARE EXAMPLES OF HOW YOU MIGHT REPRESENT DIFFERENT TYPES OF TATTOOS. THE MAN ON THE LEFT SHOWS SOME MINIMAL TATTOOS. THE GIRL ON THE RIGHT SHOWS A MINIMAL VERTICAL TATTOO, AND TWO TYPES OF SLEEVE TATTOOS.

NOTE: FOR SLEEVE TATTOOS, USE ONLY THE TATTOO'S FLOSS COLORS TO COMPLETE THAT PARTICULAR SECTION OF THE ARM. (THE EXAMPLES BELOW SHOW TATTOO STITCHING OVER-TOP SKIN-TONE COLOR FOR PATTERN VISIBILITY ONLY). IF YOUR SLEEVE TATTOO USES 3 COLORS OR 3 THREADS, **DO NOT** COMPLETE THOSE STITCHES OVER-TOP EXISTING SKIN-TONE COLORED STITCHING. IT WILL LOOK CHUNKY, AS THAT SQUARE WILL HAVE 6 THREADS OF FLOSS.

HOWEVER, YOU CAN INCLUDE A THREAD OF SKIN-TONE COLORED FLOSS IN YOUR COLOR COMBINATION, IF YOU FEEL THAT THE SKIN COLOR IS PRESENT IN THE TATTOO YOU'RE REPRESENTING.

RESOURCES

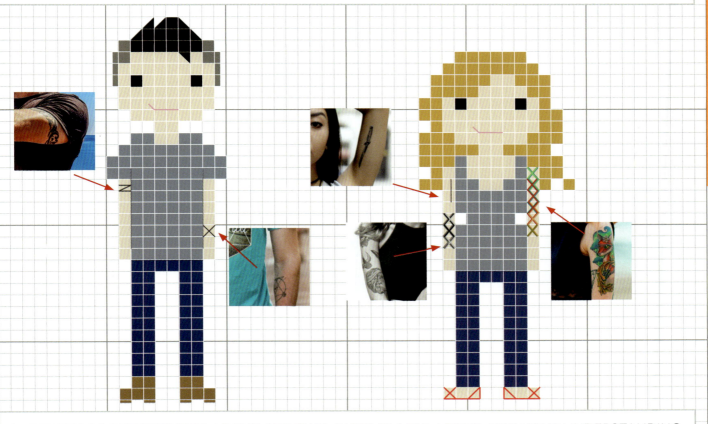

THE TATTOOS REPRESENTED ABOVE ARE SHOWN BELOW, ENLARGED, FOR YOUR UNDERSTANDING.

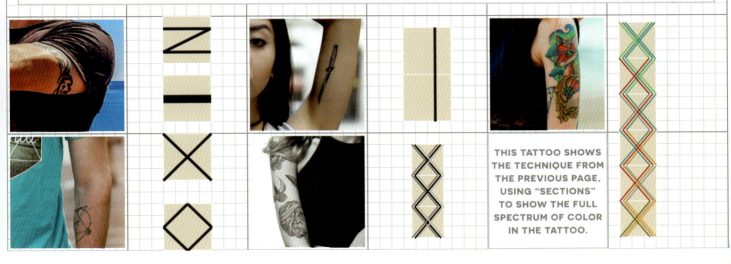

THIS TATTOO SHOWS THE TECHNIQUE FROM THE PREVIOUS PAGE, USING "SECTIONS" TO SHOW THE FULL SPECTRUM OF COLOR IN THE TATTOO.

MAKING CHARACTERS WIDER

I wish to reiterate that I developed Stitch People to fit into a specific stylistic mold. This mold keeps each Stitch People character at the same width, with the exception of children-sized characters. This decision was NOT made with body-shaming in mind. Rather, this was a stylistic choice to seek to portray the likeness of characters through their hairstyle, clothing style, coloring of various elements, and proximity to other characters.

To visualize this stylistic choice, think about the characters from the classic ride at Disneyland or Walt Disney World, "it's a small world." If you've never heard of this ride, pop it into a Google search: "Disney's it's a small world" and check out some pictures.

As you travel through this ride, you come across hundreds of singing and dancing statuettes that are all the same size and shape, but represent their specific nationality, race, and culture through their hairstyles, clothing styles, skin/hair/clothing coloring and proximity to each other within the ride. These changes are more than enough to proudly portray a country's culture, personality, and heritage.

Regardless, some folks still feel the desire or need to portray their Stitch People characters in a more realistic way. This often relates to body size. If you wish to design your Stitch People to be wider, you may refer to the patterns here to do so in a way that is still congruent with the Stitch People style.

Please do take into consideration the person(s) you are representing in your Stitch People portrait and how they may feel if portrayed stylistically or literally. When in doubt, ask them or someone close to them what their preference may be.

NOTES ABOUT CREATING WIDER CHARACTERS:

- Keep the size of the head, neck, face, and hair the same as all other patterns.
- Keep arms narrow. While in real life arms may grow thicker, it creates a very boxy look for Stitch People.
- Add width evenly to the characters - two squares wider at a time, one square's width on each side - up the legs and into the torso and shoulders. See patterns for reference.

EXAMPLE PATTERNS

The next few pages contain a few examples to help you get inspired as you start to design patterns of your own. You can use these for inspiration, or as a jumping-off point.

RESOURCES

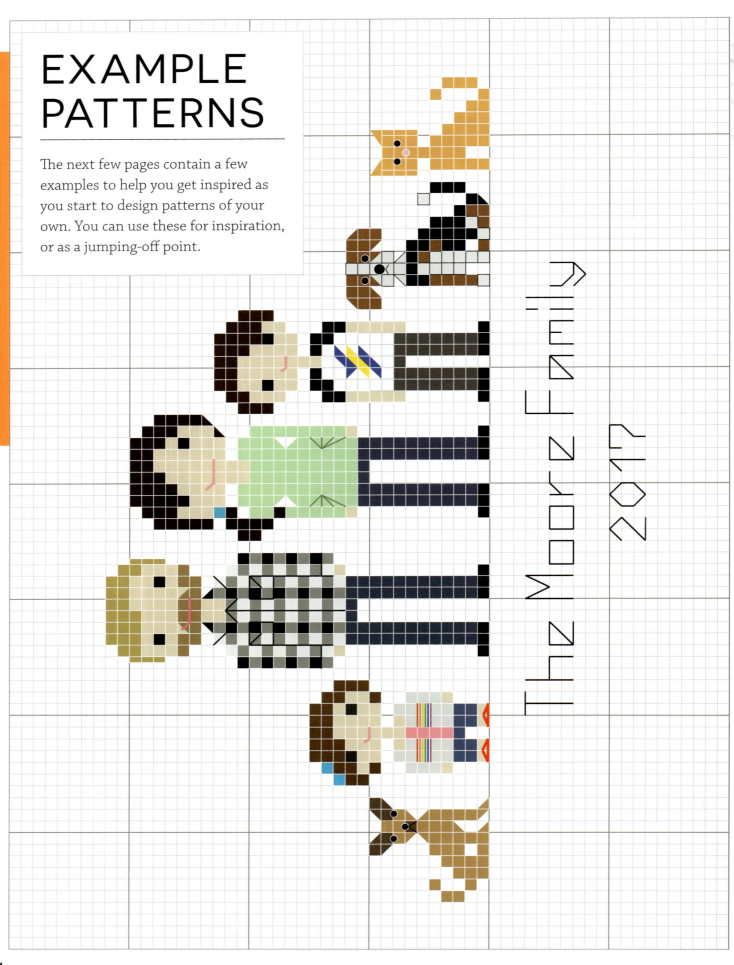

160

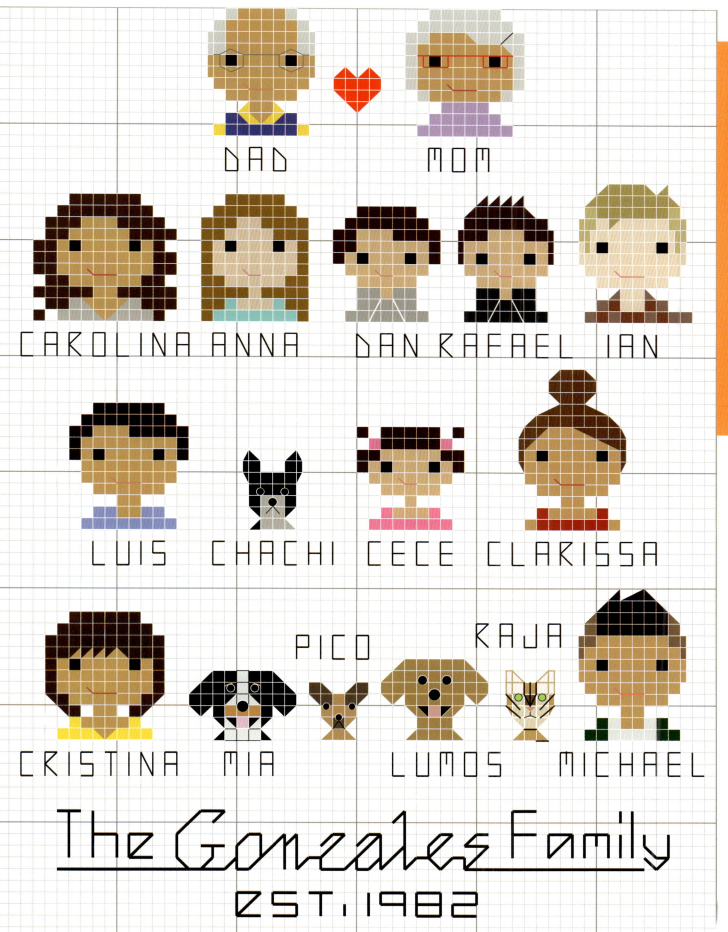

FRAMING IN A FRAME

(1) When you've completed your portrait, **(2)** remove it from the embroidery hoop. Lightly wash the finished piece if needed, using a damp cloth and mild laundry detergent. **(3-4)** Iron the edges around the finished work on the front to smooth creases. Lightly iron the back-side of the portrait (don't squish the embroidery!)

(5) If you choose to add a backing, like an iron-on interfacing, do it at this time based on provided directions. For reference, I usually use Pellon 420G Fashion Fuse Gray Nonwoven Fusible Interfacing. **(6)** If no directions are provided, a mid-to-low setting on your iron will be plenty to melt the backing onto the back side of your portrait.

(7) Cut the edges of your completed portrait to fit into your frame. This will vary depending on the size of the portrait, the mat, and frame. **(8)** Center the portrait in the mat and frame, and **(9)** secure the finished portrait lightly with either a hidden piece of tape, or by adding a thicker paper or piece of cardboard.

(10) Replace the back of the frame, and secure.

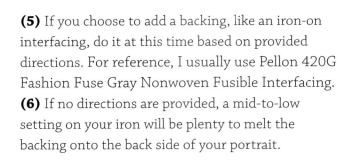
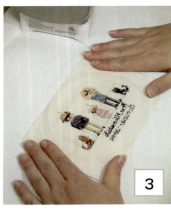

RESOURCES

FRAMING IN THE HOOP

To frame your project inside the wooden embroidery hoop, be sure your hoop is large enough to display your portrait.

(1) Remove your portrait from the embroidery hoop. Lightly wash the finished piece if needed, using a damp cloth and a mild laundry detergent. Iron the edges around the finished work on the front to smooth creases. Lightly iron the back-side of the portrait (don't squish the embroidery!) If you want to add a fusible interfacing, do it now. I usually use Pellon 420G Fashion Fuse Gray Nonwoven Fusible Interfacing.

Separate the rings of the hoop. **(2)** Trace the smooth, inner ring on the "wrong" side of the "finishing fabric" that you'll use on the back of your embroidery hoop. **(3)** Then, cut out a circle of the finishing fabric that is around 1/2 inch away from the traced embroidery hoop line.

(4) Place your completed portrait back in the embroidery hoop, making sure the design is centered, and trim the edges of the Aida fabric so there is 3/4 inch of fabric around the outer hoop.

(5) After you've finished cutting the Aida fabric, press the edges of the embroidery fabric towards the center of the embroidery hoop. **(6)** If using a wooden hoop, you might lightly iron the edge to help the edge stay down.

(7) Hold the finishing fabric to the back of the hoop, the "right side" facing out. Fold under the edges along the line you traced. **(8)(9)** Using a whip stitch, or running stitch, hand-stitch the finishing fabric to the Aida fabric, keeping it tight, and being sure to catch both the Aida fabric and backing fabric in the stitch of your choice.

RESOURCES

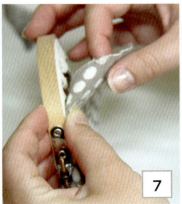
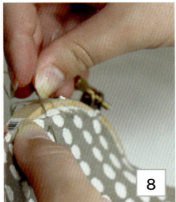

MORE FROM STITCH PEOPLE

You may find more patterns you're looking for in Stitch People's other pattern and book offerings available at StitchPeople.com. Here is a brief overview of the other books and pattern collections we have:

STITCH PEOPLE **OCCUPATIONS & HOBBIES**

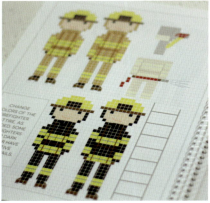

Hobby- and occupation-specific patterns, including Pilots, Captains, and Flight Attendants; Builders, Handymen, and Construction; Chauffeurs and Taxi Drivers; Clowns; Teacher and Librarians; Hairdressers; Food workers; Government workers; University & Legal robes; Medical personnel; Musicians & Instruments; Photographers; Scouts; Outdoor activities (including golf, fishing, hunting, and kayaks/canoes).

STITCH PEOPLE **UNITED STATES ARMED FORCES**

Includes combat and dress uniforms for United States Air Soldiers, Land Soldiers, Coast Soldiers, Marine Soldiers, and Water Soldiers (For trademark reasons, we can't use the actual names of the branches). Also included are flags for each branch, as well as a new alphabet!

STITCH PEOPLE **FARM ANIMALS**

Includes patterns for turkeys, roosters, chickens, geese, ducks, ducklings, chicks, guinea pigs, rabbits, mice, donkeys, buffalos, horses, sheep, cows, steers, pigs, goats, and llamas, as well as bees, bee keeper outfits, sunflowers, barns, clouds, corn stalks, wood fences, grass, bales of hay, shovels, pitchforks, red wagons, flower vases, farmer outfits, and even a new alphabet!

...AND EVEN MORE!

HOLIDAY PATTERNS, SEASONAL PATTERNS, & PORTRAIT EMBELLISHMENTS AT STITCHPEOPLE.COM

We have numbers of digital download collections of patterns that are easy to download to your computer and print from home! These include "Borders, Embellishments & Motifs", Halloween Patterns, Christmas Patterns, Summertime Patterns, Easter Patterns, Mother's Day Patterns, Valentine's Day Patterns

PLUS MORE STITCH PEOPLE FONTS

Many more fonts are available online, both individually and as a bundle.

FREEBIES VIA OUR NEWSLETTER

We offer many free patterns for various holidays throughout the year. You can have access to these free patterns by signing up for our newsletter on the homepage at StitchPeople.com. Join our tribe! We'd love to have you.

FINISHED PORTRAIT GALLERY

FINISHED PORTRAIT GALLERY

This is a "gallery" of finished portraits done by me AND other Stitch People fans to inspire you with your Stitch People portraits. Incredible customizations are possible. Notice the way the artists have chosen to combine elements, create different outfits, and even develop new clothing styles of their own! Everything is creatively unique: the Aida fabric colors, hairstyles, floss colors, text, pets - everything!

Don't forget to checkout the Stitch People Community group on Facebook where there are thousands of group members sharing their ideas.

Remember, there is no "right" or "wrong" way to create your portrait. Have fun experimenting with different configurations of families, orders of people and pets, accessories, clothing styles and colors, hair styles and colors, and even alphabet lettering styles. **Anything is possible. Have fun!**

THIS BOOK MAY NOT CONTAIN SPECIFIC PATTERNS FOR ALL THE ELEMENTS SHOWN IN THE FINISHED PORTRAITS ON THE FOLLOWING PAGES.

THE EXAMPLE PORTRAITS MAY INCORPORATE PATTERNS FROM OTHER STITCH PEOPLE PRODUCTS AVAILABLE AT STITCHPEOPLE.COM, OR THEY MAY BE THE RESULT OF THE CREATIVE IMAGINATION OF THE CROSS-STITCHERS THEMSELVES.

BY MYKAL DUNNE

FINISHED PORTRAIT GALLERY

FINISHED PORTRAIT GALLERY

The Seevers

The Chapmans
November 27, 2013

FIND PATTERNS LIKE THIS IN STITCH PEOPLE'S "UNITED STATES ARMED FORCES" BOOK

The O'Donnells
3030 Newport

The Meldal-Johnsens
2015

Randy and Max
Best Bulldogs

FIND PATTERNS LIKE THIS IN STITCH PEOPLE'S "OCCUPATIONS & HOBBIES" BOOK

Beth ♥ Clare
July 16, 2016

170

FINISHED PORTRAIT GALLERY

FINISHED PORTRAIT GALLERY

VICTORIA MARCASCIANO

KATE COLLINS

FINISHED PORTRAIT GALLERY

FINISHED PORTRAIT GALLERY

KATE COLLINS

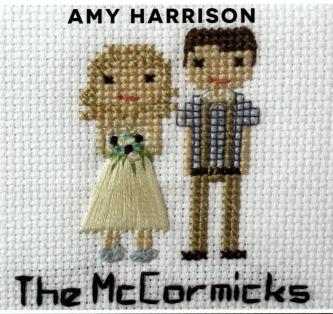

AMY HARRISON

PRISCILLA RODRIGUEZ

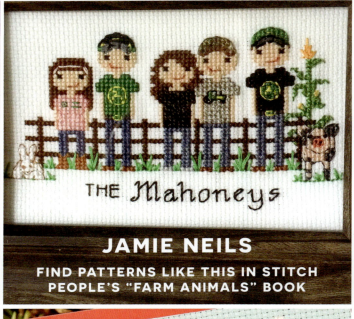

JAMIE NEILS
FIND PATTERNS LIKE THIS IN STITCH PEOPLE'S "FARM ANIMALS" BOOK

DRUMS AND OTHER INSTRUMENT PATTERNS ARE AVAILABLE IN STITCH PEOPLE'S OCCUPATIONS & HOBBIES BOOK

AMANDA SCAVONE

CHRISTMAS PATTERNS ARE AVAILABLE AT STITCHPEOPLE.COM

LINDSAY SWANTEK

MYKAL DUNNE

ALLISON LARGENT

JESSICA MCMORROW

LINDSAY SWANTEK

JEN CHAMPAGNE

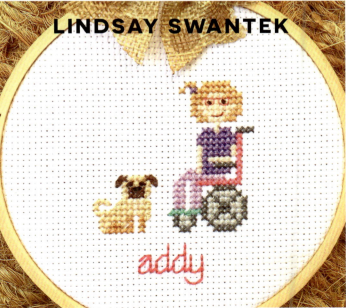
LINDSAY SWANTEK

FINISHED PORTRAIT GALLERY

FINISHED PORTRAIT GALLERY

KATIE BERNSHAUSEN

MICAH PASCHALL

KIRA RITTMAN

BIANCA MEASELS

BIANCA MEASELS

CHRISTMAS PATTERNS ARE AVAILABLE AT STITCHPEOPLE.COM

KIMBERLY MOTSINGER THOMPSON

176

ANDREA BOYLAN

BETH LEBLANC

CHARLOTTE LONG

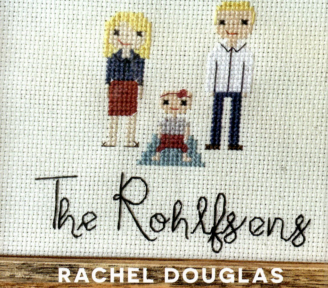

RACHEL DOUGLAS

BETSY WYNEGAR

JESSICA MCMORROW

FINISHED PORTRAIT GALLERY

FINISHED PORTRAIT GALLERY

BETSY WYNEGAR

JESSICA MCMORROW

MYKAL DUNNE

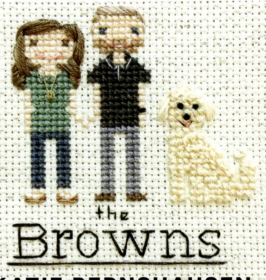
KATIE BERNSHAUSEN

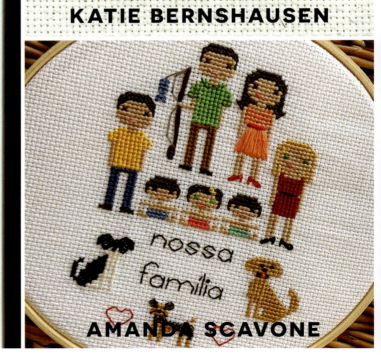
AMANDA SCAVONE

MYKAL DUNNE

PRISCILLA RODRIGUEZ

KATE COLLINS

PRISCILLA RODRIGUEZ

PRISCILLA RODRIGUEZ

LINDSAY SWANTEK

FINISHED PORTRAIT GALLERY

FINISHED PORTRAIT GALLERY

VICTORIA MARCASCIANO

KATY LLOYD

JENNIFER ROBERTS

ERIN ULKO

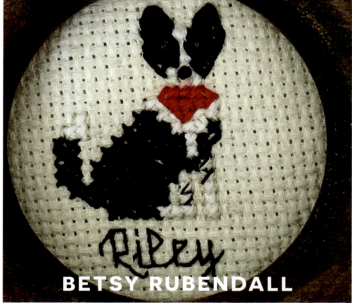
BETSY RUBENDALL

CARLENE DOUBLED THE SIZE OF THIS PORTRAIT. FOR EVERY 1 SQUARE SHOWN IN A PATTERN, SHE STITCHED AS 4 SQUARES!
CARLENE GAGNON

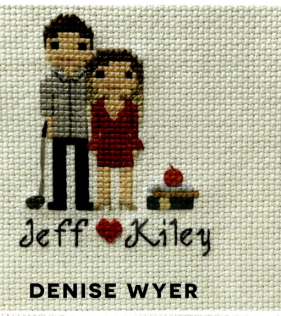

DENISE WYER

BETSY WYNEGAR

NICOLE COPPIN

MYKAL DUNNE

MICAH PASCHALL

DENISE WYER

FINISHED PORTRAIT GALLERY

FINISHED PORTRAIT GALLERY

MYKAL DUNNE

MYKAL DUNNE

TORY FERRARA

LINA HUNG

JESSICA MCMORROW

CHARLOTTE LONG

182

FINISHED PORTRAIT GALLERY

HANNAH MCCARTHY

CHARLOTTE LONG

CHARLOTTE LONG

LINA HUNG

LINA HUNG

MYKAL DUNNE

FINISHED PORTRAIT GALLERY

THIS BOOK MAY NOT CONTAIN SPECIFIC PATTERNS FOR ALL THE ELEMENTS SHOWN IN THE FINISHED PORTRAITS ON THE PREVIOUS PAGES.

THE EXAMPLE PORTRAITS MAY INCORPORATE PATTERNS FROM OTHER STITCH PEOPLE PRODUCTS AVAILABLE AT STITCHPEOPLE.COM, OR THEY MAY BE THE RESULT OF THE CREATIVE IMAGINATION OF THE CROSS-STITCHERS!

184

GLOSSARY

Abyssinian (Cat) - 111, 121

Accessories - 123-129

African - Cultural and religious patterns are available
for download at StitchPeople.com

Afro - 69, 86

Aida - 12, 18, 24-28

Air Soldiers - Available in Stitch People's
"United States Armed Forces" book

Airedale Terrier (Dog) - 113

Alphabets - 130-140, many more available for
downlaod at StitchPeople.com

American Short-hair (Cat) - 111

Arbor - Available in Stitch People's
"Backgrounds and Scenery" book

Argyle - 93

Armed Forces - Available in Stitch People's
"United States Armed Forces" book

Australian Shepherd (Dog) - 113

Baby, Babies - 96, 104-105

Backgrounds - Available in Stitch People's
"Backgrounds and Scenery" book

Backing - 16, 164-165

Back Stitch - 20, 34-35, 121-122

Bag(s) - 124

Bald, Balding - 68, 86-87

Ball(s) - 124

Balloon - 124, 155

Barns - Available in Stitch People's "Farm Animals" book

Baseball Hat - 125

Basketball - 124

Bathing Suit - 79 (women's), 95 (men's)

Beach Hat - 125

Beagle (Dog) - 113

Beanie (hat) - 125

Beard - 87

Bees, Beehive - Available in Stitch People's
"Farm Animals" book

Beekeeper - Available in Stitch People's "Farm Animals" book

Beer - 127

Bengal (Cat) - 111, 121

Bent Arms - 104

Beret (hat) - 125

Bernese Mountain Dog - 113

Bichon Frise (Dog) - 113

Bikini - 79

Bird(s) - 120

Birman (Cat) - 111

Blazer - 80 (women's), 93-94 (men's)

Blood Hound (Dog) - 113

Blouse - 71-73, 75-78, 80

Boat, Boating - Available in Stitch People's
"Backgrounds and Scenery" book

Boater (hat) - 125

Body, Bodies - 6-7 (description), 29-33 (spacing),
70-82 (women's), 88-95 (men's), 97,
101-105 (kids'), 158 (wider)

Body Height - 7, 33, 36, 70, 88, 96-97

Body Height (pets) - 108

Body Width - 6-7, 23, 26-27, 29-30, 66, 158

Body Width (pets) - 108

Bonus Patterns - See "Extra"

Book Registration - 8

Boonie (hat) - 125

Boots - 74, 77, 79, 92, 95

Borders - Patterns available for download at
StitchPeople.com

Border Collie (Dog) - 113, 122

Bouquet (flowers) - 127

Bow-tie - 34, 94

Boxer (Dog) - 113

Boy Scout - Available in Stitch People's
"Occupations & Hobbies" book

Braid(s), Braided hair - 66

British Short-hair (Cat) - 111, 121

Brittany Spaniel (Dog) - 114

Bucket Hat - 125

Buffalo(s) - Available in Stitch People's "Farm Animals" book

Builder, construction - Available in Stitch People's
"Occupations & Hobbies" book

Bullion Knot - 146-147

Bun(s) - 66-67, 69, 99-100

Bunny - 120

Burmese (Cat) - 112

Business Attire - 80 (women's), 93 (men's)

Buzz, Buzzed Hair - 68, 86-87

Cabin - Available in Stitch People's
"Backgrounds and Scenery" book

Camp, Camping, Camper - Available in Stitch People's
"Backgrounds and Scenery" book

Canada - Patterns available for download at
StitchPeople.com/Freebies

Cane - 129

Canoe - Available in Stitch People's
"Occupations & Hobbies" book

Cap & Gown - 128

Captain - Available in Stitch People's
"Occupations & Hobbies" book

Cardigan - 76-78, 80 (women's), 91 (men's),
101-103 (kids')

Cat(s) - 106, 111-112, 121

Cavalier King Charles Spaniel (Dog) - 114

Character Height - See "Body Height"

Character Width - See "Body Width"

Chauffeur - Available in Stitch People's
"Occupations & Hobbies" book

Cheerleader - 127

Chickens, Chicks - Available in Stitch People's
"Farm Animals" book

Chihuahua (Dog) - 114

Child, Children - 96-105

Chinchilla - 120

Chow Chow (Dog) - 114, 122

Christmas - Patterns available for download at
StitchPeople.com and
StitchPeople.com/Freebies

Christmas Sweater - Patterns available for download at
StitchPeople.com/Freebies

Chullo (hat) - 125

Cloche (hat) - 125

Clouds - Available in Stitch People's
"Farm Animals" book, and more in Stitch
People's "Backgrounds and Scenery" book

Clown - Available in Stitch People's
"Occupations & Hobbies" book

Coast Soldiers - Available in Stitch People's
"United States Armed Forces" book

Coat - 79 (women's), 95 (men's)

Cocker Spaniel (Dog) - 114

Cocktail Dress - 81

Coffee - 127

Collar(s) (dress shirts) - 89, 151

Collie Dog - 114, 122

Color(s) (Aida fabric) - 12-14

Color(s) (Floss) - 14, 142-144

Color Recommendations - 142-144

Combinations (Floss) - 34-35, 142-144

Community (Stitch People Facebook Group) - 3, 9, 166

Construction - Available in Stitch People's
"Occupations & Hobbies" book

"Converse" Sneakers - 77, 92

Coonskin (hat) - 125

Coordinates - 10, 36, 48, 70, 83, 88

Copyright - 2

Corgi (Dog) - 114

Corn, Corn Stalks - Available in Stitch People's
"Farm Animals" book

Cornrow(s) - 69

Couching - 148-149

Cows - Available in Stitch People's "Farm Animals" book

Cowboy Boots - 74, 92

Cowboy Hat - 125

Cradle - 105

Crib - 105

Cross Stitch(ing) - 17-19

Crown - 126

Crutches - 129

Curly Hair - 57-61, 63, 69, 86, 146-147

Dachshund (Dog) - 114

Dead / Departed - 154-155

Designing - 23-33, 36

Design Pages - 36-47

Design Philosophy (of Stitch People characters) - 6

Diagonal Stitch - 21-22, 121-122

Doberman Pinscher (Dog) - 115

Dog(s) - 106-110, 113-119, 122

Dreadlock(s) - 69

Dress(es) - 75, 77-78, 81 (women's), 101-103 (kids')

Ducks, ducklings - Available in Stitch People's
"Farm Animals" book

Earrings - 126

Earth - Pattern available for download at
StitchPeople.com/Freebies

Easter - Patterns available for download at
StitchPeople.com and
StitchPeople.com/Freebies

Embroidery Floss - 14-15, 17, 19-22, 34-35, 131, 142-
144, 147, 150-153, 156-157

Embroidery Hoop - 15, 165

English Bulldog (Dog) - 115

Example Pattern(s) - 25, 28-29, 31-33,
37, 160-163

Exotic Short-hair (Cat) - 112

Extras, Extra Patterns (Bonus Patterns) - 9

Eyes - 6, 143

Fabric - 12, 24

Face(s) - 6

Facebook Group - 3, 9, 166

Fairy Lights - See "Lights"

Farmer - Available in Stitch People's "Farm Animals" book

Father's Day - Patterns available for download at
StitchPeople.com/Freebies

Floral Vases - Available in Stitch People's
"Farm Animals" book

Fascinator (hat) - 125

Fedora (hat) - 125

Fence - Available in Stitch People's "Farm Animals" book

Ferret - 120

Fez (hat) - 125

Finished Portraits - 168-184

Fire, Fireplace, Fire Pit - Available in Stitch People's
"Backgrounds and Scenery" book

Fishing - Available in Stitch People's
"Occupations & Hobbies" book

Flats (shoes) - 74

Flight Attendant - Available in Stitch People's
"Occupations & Hobbies" book

Flip Flop - 74, 78-79, 92, 95, 102

Floral Border - Patterns available for download at
StitchPeople.com

Floral Clothing Patterns - 150-151

Floss - See "Embroidery Floss"

Floss Color Recommendations - 142-144

Flowers - 126-127, 150-151, 155

Food workers - Available in Stitch People's
"Occupations & Hobbies" book

Font - 131-140

Football - 124

Formal Attire - 81, 94

187

Fourth of July - Patterns available for download at StitchPeople.com

Framing - 16, 164-165

Freebies, Free Patterns - see "Extras"

French Bulldog (Dog) - 115

French Knot - 20, 34-35, 63, 146, 151, 153

'Fro - 69, 86

Frontiersman - See "Pioneers"

Garden, Gardening - Available in Stitch People's "Backgrounds and Scenery" book

Geese - Available in Stitch People's "Farm Animals" book

Geometric Pattern - 150-151

Gerbil - 120

German Shepherd (Dog) - 115

Girl Scout - Available in Stitch People's "Occupations & Hobbies" book

Glasses - 124

Globe - Pattern available for download at StitchPeople.com/Freebies

Goats - Available in Stitch People's "Farm Animals" book

Goatee - 86-87

Golden Retriever (Dog) - 115

Golf - 127, more available in Stitch People's "Occupations & Hobbies" book

Government workers - Available in Stitch People's "Occupations & Hobbies" book

Graduate, Graduation - 128

Grass - Available in Stitch People's "Farm Animals" book

Great Dane (Dog) - 115

Greyhound (Dog) - 116

Guinea pigs - Available in Stitch People's "Farm Animals" book

Guitar - 124

Hairdresser - Available in Stitch People's "Occupations & Hobbies" book

Half Stitch - 21-22, 121-122

Halloween - Patterns available for download at StitchPeople.com, and StitchPeople.com/Freebies

Halo - 154-155

Hammock - Available in Stitch People's "Backgrounds and Scenery" book

Hamster - 120

Handyman - Available in Stitch People's "Occupations & Hobbies" book

Hannukah - Patterns available for download at StitchPeople.com and StitchPeople.com/Freebies

Hat(s) - 125

Hay - Available in Stitch People's "Farm Animals" book

Headband(s) - 67, 126

Headstone - 154-155

Head-scarf - 68

Heart(s) - 29, 104, 124, 155

Hedgehog - 120

Heels, High Heels - 74, 77-78, 80-81

Height - See "Body Height"

Heirloom - 3

High-Chair - 105

Hijab - See "Muslim"

Hiking - Available in Stitch People's "Backgrounds and Scenery" book

Holding Hands - 104, 155

Holiday - Patterns available for download at StitchPeople.com

Hoodie - 76, 78 (women's), 92 (men's), 101-103 (kids')

Hoop - See "Embroidery Hoop"

Horse - Available in Stitch People's "Farm Animals" book

How to Cross-Stitch - 17-22

How to Use the Book - 9-11

Hunting - Available in Stitch People's "Occupations & Hobbies" book

Iguana - 120

Indian - Cultural and religious patterns are available for download at StitchPeople.com

Ink (Tattoo) - 156-157

Instagram - 2, 9

International Women's Day - Pattern available for download at StitchPeople.com/Freebies

Islam - Cultural and religious patterns are available for download at StitchPeople.com

Jacket - 76-80 (women's), 91-95 (men's)

Jack Russell Terrier (Dog) - 116

Jersey - 90

Jewelry - 126

Jewish - See "Judaism"

Judaism - Cultural and religious patterns are available for download at StitchPeople.com

Kayak - Available in Stitch People's "Occupations & Hobbies" book

Kid, Kids - 96-105

Kid's Make Believe - Available for download at StitchPeople.com

Kite - 124, 155

Kitten(s) - 112

Labradoodle (Dog) - 116

Labrador Retriever (Dog) - 116

Lace - 152-153

Layering - 30-33, 155

Legal robes - Available in Stitch People's "Occupations & Hobbies" book

Leopard Print - 151

Lettering - 130-140

Letterman Jacket - 92

Librarian - Available in Stitch People's "Occupations & Hobbies" book

Lights - Available in Stitch People's "Backgrounds and Scenery" book

Lizard - 120

Llamas - Available in Stitch People's "Farm Animals" book

Long Hair - 51, 56-57, 60-61

Maine Coon Cat - 112

Make Believe - Available for download at StitchPeople.com

Manx (Cat) - 112, 121

Map, Mapping - 23-29

Marine Soldiers - Available in Stitch People's "United States Armed Forces" book

Mastiff (Dog) - 116

Materials - 9, 12-15, 145, many materials available for purchase at stitchpeople.com

Materials Checklist - 145

May the Fourth - Pattern available for download at StitchPeople.com/Freebies

Medical Personnel - Available in Stitch People's "Occupations & Hobbies" book

Medium-Length Hair - 49, 53, 57-59

Memorial - 154-155

Military - Available in Stitch People's "United States Armed Forces" book

Miniature Schnauzer (Dog) - 116

Mormon Missionaries - Cultural and religious patterns are available for download at StitchPeople.com

Mother's Day - Patterns available for download at StitchPeople.com and StitchPeople.com/Freebies

Motorhome - Available in Stitch People's "Backgrounds and Scenery" book

Mountain(s) - Available in Stitch People's "Backgrounds and Scenery" book

Mouse - Available in Stitch People's "Farm Animals" book

Mustache - 87

Mug - 127

Music Notes - 124

Musical Instruments - Available in Stitch People's "Occupations & Hobbies" book

Muslim - Cultural and religious patterns are available for download at StitchPeople.com

National Parks - Available in Stitch People's "Backgrounds and Scenery" book

Nativity - Patterns available for download at StitchPeople.com

Naval Soldiers - Available in Stitch People's "United States Armed Forces" book

Necklace - 126

Neckline - 71 (women's), 89 (men's)

Needle(s) - 15, 17

Newfoundland (Dog) - 116

Newsboy (hat) - 125

Newsletter - 9

Norwegian Forest Cat - 112

Ombre - 68

Oxford Shirt - 80, 93

Palm Tree - See "Trees"

Panama (hat) - 125

Pant, Pants, Pant Length - 74 (women's,) 90 (men's)

Pantsuit - 80

Papillon (dog) - 117

Parrot - 120

Party Lights - See "Lights"

Passed Away - 154-155

Pattern(s) - See "Example Patterns"

Persian (Cat) - 112

Pets - 106-122

Photographer - Available in Stitch People's "Occupations & Hobbies" book

Pigs - Available in Stitch People's "Farm Animals" book

Pig-Tail(s) - 66 (women's), 98-100 (kids')

Pine Tree - See "Trees"

Pioneers - Patterns available for download at StitchPeople.com

Pit Bull Terrier (dog) - 117

Pilot - Available in Stitch People's "Occupations & Hobbies" book

Pinterest - 9

Pirate(s) - Patterns available for download at StitchPeople.com/Freebies, also see "Halloween"

Pitchfork - Available in Stitch People's "Farm Animals" book

Pixie Hair-Cut - 62-64

Plaid - 35, 76, 91

Plaited Hair - 66

Plants - See "Garden"

Pocket Square - 94

Pomeranian (Dog) - 117

Pom Poms - 127

Pony Tail(s) - 65

Poodle (Dog) - 117

Pram - 105

Pregnancy, Pregnant - 82

Pre-Teen - 96-97, 100, 103

Pork Pie (hat) - 125

Prom Dress - 81

Puffy Coat - 79 (women's), 95 (men's)

Puffy Vest - 79 (women's), 93, 95 (men's), 101, 103 (kids')

Pug (Dog) - 117

Purse - 124

Questions - 9

Rabbit - 120, more available in Stitch People's "Farm Animals" book

Racket - 124

Ragdoll (Cat) - 112

Rainbow - Available in Stitch People's "Backgrounds and Scenery" book

Red Nose Day - Patterns available for download at StitchPeople.com/Freebies

Red Wagon - Available in Stitch People's "Farm Animals" book

Register, Registration - 8

Resources - 141-167

Road, Road Signs - Available in Stitch People's "Backgrounds and Scenery" book

Roadtrip - Available in Stitch People's
        "Backgrounds and Scenery" book

Roosters - Available in Stitch People's
        "Farm Animals" book

Rottweiler (Dog) - 117

Running Stitch - 20, 34-35, 121-122

RV - Available in Stitch People's
        "Backgrounds and Scenery" book

Sailor (hat) - 125

Samoyed (Dog) - 118

San Diego - Pattern available for download from
        StitchPeople.com/Freebies

Sandals - 74, 92

Satin Stitch - 149

Scarf, Scarves - 67-68, 126

Scissors - 15

Scooter - 124

Scottish Terrier (Dog) - 117

Scout - Available in Stitch People's
        "Occupations & Hobbies" book

Settlers - See "Pioneers"

Shih Tzu (Dog) - 118

Shaved head - 68, 86-87

Sheep - Available in Stitch People's "Farm Animals" book

Shirt-dress - 77

Shoes - 74, 92

Short Hair - 50, 52, 54-55, 59, 61,

Shorts - 74 (women's), 90 (men's), 101-103 (kids')

Shovel - Available in Stitch People's "Farm Animals" book

Siamese Cat - 112

Siberian Husky (Dog) - 118

Siblings Day - Pattern available for download at
        StitchPeople.com/Freebies

Sikh - Cultural and religious patterns are available for
        download at StitchPeople.com

Size, Sizing - 23-24, 158-159

Skateboard - 128

Skiing - Available in Stitch People's
        "Backgrounds and Scenery" book

Skirt(s) - 75, 78, 80-81 (women's), 101-103 (kids')

Skirt-suit - 80

Sleeve(s), Sleeve Width - 73 (women's), 89 (men's)

Sleeve (tattoo) - 156-157

Sneakers - 74, 92

Snowboarding - Available in Stitch People's
        "Backgrounds and Scenery" book

Soccer - 124

Sombrero (hat) - 125

Spacing - 23-24, 29, 30-33

Sphynx (Cat) - 112

Sport-coat - 93

Sports - 90, 124, 127-128, many more specifics available for
        download at StitchPeople.com

St. Patrick's Day - Patterns available for download at
        StitchPeople.com/Freebies

Start / Starting - 17-18

Steers - Available in Stitch People's "Farm Animals" book

Stitch People Community - 3, 9, 166

Stopping - 19

Straight Hair - 49-52, 62-63, 84-87, 148-149

Straight Stitch - 20, 121-122, 148-149

Stripes, Striped - 73, 92-93

Stroller - 105

Suit - 80 (women's), 93-94 (men's)

Summertime - Patterns available for download at
        StitchPeople.com and
        StitchPeople.com/Freebies

Sunflowers - Available in Stitch People's
        "Farm Animals" book

Sunglasses - 124

Sunset - Available in Stitch People's
        "Backgrounds and Scenery" book

Supplies - see "Materials," many supplies available for
        purchase at stitchpeople.com

Surfboard - 127

Sweater - 76-78, 80 (women's), 91-93 (men's), 101-103 (kids')

Sweatshirt -76, 78 (women's), 92 (men's), 101-103 (kids')

Swimsuit - 79 (women's), 95 (men's)

Tabs - 11

Tattoo(s) - 156-157

Taxi Driver - Available in Stitch People's "Occupations & Hobbies" book

Teacher - Available in Stitch People's "Occupations & Hobbies" book

Teen, Teenager - 96-97, 100, 103

Tennis - 124

Text - 23, 130-140

Tiara - 126

Tie - 93-94

Tiki, Tiki Torches - Available in Stitch People's "Backgrounds and Scenery" book

Tips for Success - 17, 34-35

Toddler(s) - 97-98, 101

Top-Knot (hair) - 67 (women's), 99-100 (kid's)

Track Jacket - 76 (women's), 91 (men's), 101-103 (kids')

Trees - Available in Stitch People's "Backgrounds and Scenery" book

Trellis - Available in Stitch People's "Backgrounds and Scenery" book

Tropical - Available in Stitch People's "Backgrounds and Scenery" book

Trunks, Swim-Trunks - See "Swimsuit"

Turkey - Available in Stitch People's "Farm Animals" book

Turtle - 120

Tux, Tuxedo - 94

Tying Off - 19

Umbrella - 124

United States Armed Forces - Available in Stitch People's "United States Armed Forces" book

University Robes - Available in Stitch People's "Occupations & Hobbies" book

Up-Do (hair) - 66

Valentine's Day - Patterns available for download at StitchPeople.com and StitchPeople.com/Freebies

Varsity Jacket - 92

Vest - 79 (women's), 93-95 (men's)

Waist, Waistlines - 72

Walker - 129

Wavy Hair - 53-57

Wedding Dress - 81, 152-153

Wet-suit - 95, 127

Wheelchair - 129

Width, Wider Characters - 158-159

Wreath - 155

Yorkshire Terrier (Dog) - 118, 122

Zip-Up Sweatshirt - 76 (women's), 92 (men's), 101-103 (kids')